ROSE HANDBOOK OF BIBLE CHARTS, MAPS, AND TIMELINES

Rose Handbook of Bible Charts, Maps, and Timelines
© 2024 Rose Publishing
Published by Rose Publishing
An imprint of Tyndale House Ministries
Carol Stream, Illinois
www.hendricksonrose.com

ISBN 978-1-4964-8485-7

All rights reserved. No part of this work may be reproduced or transmitted in any form or by any means, electronic or mechanical, including photocopying, recording, or by any information storage and retrieval system, without permission in writing from the publisher.

100 Key People in the Bible and *100 Prayers in the Bible* by © Harold Wilmington; *The Dead Sea Scrolls* by © World of the Bible Ministries, Randall Price, PhD; Tabernacle cutaway, High Priest, Herod's Temple, Israel at Mt. Sinai art by Stan Stein; The Exodus, The Tabernacle (p. 85), Solomon's Temple, Herod's Temple (p. 237), Palm Sunday to Easter, Jesus' Hours on the Cross by © Hugh Claycombe; *Essential Doctrines* by © Norman L. Geisler, PhD; *The Gospels "Lost" & Found* by Timothy Paul Jones, PhD; *Christianity, Cults, and Religions* by general editor Paul Carden; *Islam and Christianity* by Rev. Bruce Green and Andras Szalai, PhD; *Worldviews Comparison* by Alex McFarland. Some stock photos used under license from Shutterstock.com. All maps by © Rose Publishing.

Most chapters previously published in *Rose Book of Bible Charts, Maps & Time Lines* (Rose Publishing, 2015), *Rose Book of Bible Charts Vol. 2* (Rose Publishing, 2008), and *Rose Book of Bible Charts Vol. 3* (Rose Publishing, 2014).

Most scripture quotations from the Holy Bible, New International Version®, NIV®. Copyright © 1973, 1978, 1984, 2011 by Biblica, Inc.™ Used by permission of Zondervan. All rights reserved worldwide. www.zondervan.com The "NIV" and "New International Version" are trademarks registered in the United States Patent and Trademark Office by Biblica, Inc.™; The (NASB®) New American Standard Bible®, Copyright © 1960, 1971, 1977, 1995, 2020 by The Lockman Foundation. Used by permission. All rights reserved. lockman.org; The Holy Bible, New Living Translation, copyright © 1996, 2004, 2015 by Tyndale House Foundation. Used by permission of Tyndale House Publishers, Carol Stream, Illinois 60188. All rights reserved.

Library of Congress Control Number: 2023034044

Printed by RR Donnelley, Hong Kong
December 2023, 1st printing

CONTENTS

Bible Overview

Bible Overview 6
Bible Timeline 18
100 Key People in the Bible 22
100 Prayers in the Bible 25
Weights, Measures, and Money 28
How We Got the Bible 30
The Dead Sea Scrolls 36
Bible Translations Comparison 43
Names of God 52
Names of Jesus 54
Names of the Holy Spirit 62

Old Testament

Noah's Ark 70
Twelve Tribes of Israel 72
The Exodus 80
Tabernacle 82
Ark of the Covenant 90
The Judges 91
Feasts of the Bible 92
Christ in the Passover 97
Kings and Prophets 105
Solomon's Temple 110
Statue in the Book of Daniel 114
Women of the Bible: Old Testament 121
Heroes of the Old Testament 129
The Ten Commandments 135
Christ in the Old Testament 142
Joseph 154
Moses 162
David 171
Esther 179
Ruth 187
Psalms 194
Psalm 23 202
Proverbs 204

New Testament

The Gospels Side by Side 212
Genealogy of Jesus 220
The Twelve Disciples 221
Parables of Jesus 227
Herod's Temple 237
Palm Sunday to Easter 240
Jesus' Hours on the Cross 242
100 Prophecies Fulfilled by Jesus 243
Evidence for the Resurrection 249
Women of the Bible: New Testament 251
The Life of the Apostle Paul 262
Armor of God 268
The Love Chapter: 1 Corinthians 13 269
Fruit of the Spirit 270
The Seven Churches of Revelation 272
Book of Revelation 274

Bible Maps

Middle East: Then and Now 286
Holy Land: Then and Now 288
Holy Land: United Kingdom 290
Holy Land: Divided Kingdom 291
Assyrian Empire 292
Babylonian and Persian Empires 294
Middle East: Fascinating Facts
 and Figures 295
Where Jesus Walked: Then and Now 296
World of the First Christians:
 Then and Now 298
Expansion of Christianity 300

Christian Living

Following Jesus	302
Who I Am in Christ	308
What the Bible Says about Forgiveness	314
What the Bible Says about Money	322
What the Bible Says about Prayer	331
Heaven	339
The Lord's Prayer	346
The Beatitudes	354
Bible Promises for Hope and Courage	361
24 Ways to Explain the Gospel	367
Spiritual Gifts	375
Spiritual Disciplines	383

Christian History and Doctrines

Essential Doctrines	395
Attributes of God	400
Creeds and Heresies	408
The Trinity	419
Baptism	424
The Lord's Supper	431
Four Views of the End Times	439
Christian History Time Line	442
Reformation Time Line	455
The Gospels: "Lost" & Found	463

Christianity, Cults, and Religions

Christianity, Cults, and Religions	473
Denominations Comparison	481
Islam and Christianity	488
Worldviews Comparison	494

Index ... 502

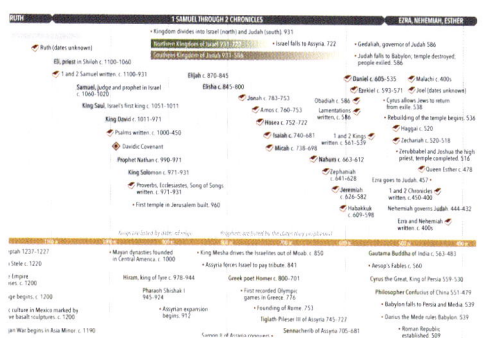

BIBLE OVERVIEW

BIBLE OVERVIEW

Old Testament - 39 books

Pentateuch - 5
GENESIS
EXODUS
LEVITICUS
NUMBERS
DEUTERONOMY

Historical Books - 12
JOSHUA
JUDGES
RUTH
1 SAMUEL
2 SAMUEL
1 KINGS
2 KINGS
1 CHRONICLES
2 CHRONICLES
EZRA
NEHEMIAH
ESTHER

Poetry & Wisdom - 5
JOB
PSALMS
PROVERBS
ECCLESIASTES
SONG OF SONGS

Major Prophets - 5
ISAIAH
JEREMIAH
LAMENTATIONS
EZEKIEL
DANIEL

Minor Prophets - 12
HOSEA
JOEL
AMOS
OBADIAH
JONAH
MICAH
NAHUM
HABAKKUK
ZEPHANIAH
HAGGAI
ZECHARIAH
MALACHI

New Testament - 27 books

Gospels & Acts - 5
MATTHEW
MARK
LUKE
JOHN
ACTS

Paul's Epistles (Letters) - 13	
ROMANS	1 THESSALONIANS
1 CORINTHIANS	2 THESSALONIANS
2 CORINTHIANS	1 TIMOTHY
GALATIANS	2 TIMOTHY
EPHESIANS	TITUS
PHILIPPIANS	PHILEMON
COLOSSIANS	

General Epistles & Revelation - 9
HEBREWS
JAMES
1 PETER
2 PETER
1 JOHN
2 JOHN
3 JOHN
JUDE
REVELATION

OLD TESTAMENT — PENTATEUCH

The Pentateuch contains stories about the creation of the world, the flood, Abraham, Isaac, Jacob, the children of Israel in Egypt, the exodus, and the time the children of Israel spent in the wilderness before entering the Promised Land. The books also record the law God gave to the people on Mt. Sinai which laid down the regulations for sacrifice, worship, and daily living. The Pentateuch is also called the Torah.

GENESIS

Who: Moses
What: The Beginnings
Where: Egypt and Canaan
When: c. 1446 BC–1406 BC
Why: To demonstrate that God is sovereign and loves his creation.

Outline (Chapter)
- Creation, Fall, and Flood (1–11)
- Abraham (12–25)
- Isaac and Jacob (26–36)
- Joseph (37–50)

Key Verse: I will establish my covenant as an everlasting covenant between me and you and your descendants after you for the generations to come, to be your God and the God of your descendants after you. (Genesis 17:7)

EXODUS

Who: Moses
What: Deliverance from Slavery
Where: Egypt and Canaan
When: c. 1446 BC–1406 BC
Why: To show God's faithfulness to the covenant and provide Israel with guidelines for holy living.

Outline (Chapter)
- Moses (1–7)
- The Plagues (8–13)
- The Exodus (14–18)
- The Law (19–24)
- Tabernacle and Worship (25–40)

Key Verse: God said to Moses, "I AM WHO I AM. This is what you are to say to the Israelites: 'I AM has sent me to you.'" (Exodus 3:14)

LEVITICUS

Who: Moses
What: Law and Sacrifice
Where: Sinai and Canaan
When: c. 1446 BC–1406 BC
Why: To instruct Israel on how to be holy and to be a blessing to others.

Outline (Chapter)
- Sacrifice (1–7)
- Priesthood (8–10)
- Clean and Unclean (11–15)
- Day of Atonement (16)
- Laws for Daily Life (17–27)

Key Verse: Consecrate yourselves and be holy, because I am the LORD your God. Keep my decrees and follow them. I am the LORD, who makes you holy. (Leviticus 20:7–8)

NUMBERS

Who: Moses
What: Census and History
Where: Borders of Canaan
When: c. 1446 BC–1406 BC
Why: A reminder of what happens when people rebel against God.

Outline (Chapter)
- Census (1–9)
- Sinai to Canaan (10–12)
- Spies and Rebellion (13–19)
- Moab (20–36)

Key Verse: The LORD bless you and keep you; the LORD make his face shine upon you and be gracious to you; the LORD turn his face toward you and give you peace. (Numbers 6:24–26)

DEUTERONOMY

Who: Moses
What: Sermons by Moses
Where: Plains of Moab
When: c. 1446 BC–1406 BC
Why: To remind the people what God expects from them.

Outline (Chapter)
- Sermon 1: Journey Review (1–4)
- Sermon 2: Laws (5–28)
- Sermon 3: Covenant (29–30)
- Final Farewells (31–34)

Key Verse: Hear, O Israel: The LORD our God, the LORD is one. Love the LORD your God with all your heart and with all your soul and with all your strength. (Deuteronomy 6:4–5)

HISTORICAL BOOKS

The 12 Historical Books continue with the story of the people of Israel and the conquest of the Promised Land in the book of Joshua, the continuous cycle of disobedience in the book of Judges, the first kings and the United Kingdom, Divided Kingdom, the Assyrian invasion, Babylonian invasion, the years in exile, and the return from exile during the Persian rule.

JOSHUA

Who: Unknown (Joshua or Samuel)
What: History of Conquest
Where: Canaan
When: c. 1300s BC
Why: To assure the people that obedience to God is rewarded.

Outline (Chapter)
- The Conquest (1–12)
- Dividing the Land (13–22)
- Joshua's Farewell (23–24)

Key Verse: Be strong and very courageous. Be careful to obey all the law my servant Moses gave you; do not turn from it to the right or to the left, that you may be successful wherever you go. (Joshua 1:7)

JUDGES

Who: Unknown (Samuel)
What: History before Kings
Where: Canaan
When: c. 1400 BC–1000 BC
Why: To stress the importance of remaining loyal to God.

Outline (Chapter)
- Reasons for Failure (1)
- The Judges: Othniel, Ehud, Shamgar, Deborah, Gideon, Tola, Jair, Jephthah, Ibzan, Elon, Abdon, and Samson (2–16)
- Days of Lawlessness (17–21)

Key Verse: In those days Israel had no king; everyone did as they saw fit. (Judges 21:25)

RUTH

Who: Unknown (Samuel)
What: Story of a Faithful Foreigner
Where: Canaan
When: c. 1350 BC–1000 BC
Why: To demonstrate the kind of faithfulness, godliness, loyalty, and love that God desires for us.

Outline (Chapter)
- Naomi and Ruth (1)
- Ruth meets Boaz (2)
- The Threshing Floor (3)
- The Marriage (4)

Key Verse: But Ruth replied, "Don't urge me to leave you or to turn back from you. Where you go I will go, and where you stay I will stay. Your people will be my people and your God my God." (Ruth 1:16)

1 SAMUEL

Who: Unknown
What: History of Events
Where: Israel and Judah
When: c. 1100 BC–931 BC
Why: To record how Israel got a king.

Outline (Chapter)
- Samuel (1–7)
- Saul (8–15)
- Saul and David (16–31)

Key Verse: But Samuel replied: "Does the LORD delight in burnt offerings and sacrifices as much as in obeying the voice of the LORD? To obey is better than sacrifice, and to heed is better than the fat of rams." (1 Samuel 15:22)

2 SAMUEL

Who: Unknown
What: History of Events
Where: Israel and Judah
When: c. 1100 BC–931 BC
Why: To demonstrate the prominence of David's line.

Outline (Chapter)
- David's Reign in Judah (1–4)
- David Unites Israel (5–10)
- David and Bathsheba (11–12)
- Family Problems (13–20)
- Conclusions (21–24)

Key Verse: I have been with you wherever you have gone, and I have cut off all your enemies from before you. Now I will make your name great, like the names of the greatest men of the earth. (2 Samuel 7:9)

1 KINGS

Who: Unknown
What: Evaluation of the Kings
Where: In Exile in Babylon
When: 561 BC–539 BC
Why: To demonstrate the value of obeying and the danger of disobeying God.

Outline (Chapter)
- King Solomon's Reign (1–4)
- Temple Construction (5–8)
- Queen of Sheba (9–10)
- Kingdom Splits (11–16)
- Prophet Elijah (17–22)

Key Verse: So give your servant a discerning heart to govern your people and to distinguish between right and wrong. (1 Kings 3:9a)

2 KINGS

Who: Unknown
What: Evaluation of the Kings
Where: In Exile in Babylon
When: 561 BC–539 BC
Why: To demonstrate the value of obeying God.

Outline (Chapter)
- The Prophet Elisha (1–8)
- Kings of Judah and Israel (9–16)
- Fall of Israel (17–21)
- King Josiah (22–23)
- Fall of Judah; Exile (24–25)

Key Verse: And Hezekiah prayed to the LORD: "LORD, God of Israel, enthroned between the cherubim, you alone are God over all the kingdoms of the earth. You have made heaven and earth." (2 Kings 19:15)

1 CHRONICLES

Who: Unknown (Ezra)
What: Review of David's Reign
Where: Judah
When: c. 450 BC–400 BC
Why: To encourage the remnant.

Key Verse: "Oh, that you would bless me and enlarge my territory! Let your hand be with me, and keep me from harm so that I will be free from pain." (1 Chronicles 4:10)

2 CHRONICLES

Who: Unknown (Ezra)
What: Highlights Kings of Judah
Where: Judah
When: c. 450 BC–400 BC
Why: To show the benefits that come from obedience.

Key Verse: As for us, the LORD is our God, and we have not forsaken him. (2 Chronicles 13:10a)

EZRA

Who: Ezra
What: History of Reconstruction
Where: Judah
When: c. 400s BC
Why: Provide a detailed account of the exiles' return and the rebuilding of the temple.

Outline (Chapter)
- The Exiles Return (1–2)
- Rebuilding the Temple (3–6)
- The Work of Ezra (7–10)

Key Verse: With praise and thanksgiving they sang to the LORD: "He is good; his love to Israel endures forever. And all the people gave a great shout of praise to the LORD, because the foundation of the house of the LORD was laid." (Ezra 3:11)

NEHEMIAH

Who: Ezra
What: History of Reconstruction
Where: Judah
When: c. 400s BC
Why: Rebuilding of the walls of Jerusalem.

Outline (Chapter)
- Nehemiah Returns (1–2)
- Rebuilding of the Walls (3)
- Threats and Persecution (4–7)
- Renewal of Covenant (8–10)
- Dedication and Laws (11–13)

Key Verse: Nehemiah said, "Go and enjoy choice food and sweet drinks, and send some to those who have nothing prepared. This day is sacred to our Lord. Do not grieve, for the joy of the LORD is your strength." (Nehemiah 8:10)

ESTHER

Who: Unknown
What: Story of Redemption
Where: Persia
When: c. 400s BC
Why: To demonstrate that, in all circumstances, God is in control.

Outline (Chapter)
- Search for a New Queen (1–2)
- Haman's Plot (3)
- Esther's Plan (4–6)
- Haman's Downfall (7)
- Esther Saves the Jews (8–10)

Key Verse: For if you remain silent at this time, relief and deliverance for the Jews will arise from another place, but you and your father's family will perish. And who knows but that you have come to royal position for such a time as this? (Esther 4:14)

POETRY & WISDOM

The five Poetry and Wisdom books include hymns, proverbs, poems, and dramas. They illustrate the creative ways the people of Israel expressed themselves to God and to each other.

JOB

Who: Unknown
What: Story of Perseverance
Where: Mesopotamia (Uz)
When: Unknown
Why: To show the sovereignty of God and to illustrate faithfulness in the midst of suffering.

Outline (Chapter)
- Job Tested (1–3)
- Job's Friends (4–31)
- Elihu's Speech (32–37)
- God's Answer (38–42)

Key Verse: I know that my Redeemer lives, and that in the end he will stand upon the earth. And after my skin has been destroyed, yet in my flesh I will see God. (Job 19:25–26)

PSALMS

Who: David, Moses, Asaph, Solomon, Ethan, Sons of Korah
What: Poetry and Song
Where: Ancient Israel
When: c. 1000 BC–450 BC
Why: To communicate with God and worship him.

Outline (Chapter)
- Book I: Psalms 1–41
- Book II: Psalms 42–72
- Book III: Psalms 73–89
- Book IV: Psalms 90–106
- Book V: Psalms 107–150

Key Verse: My mouth will speak in praise of the LORD. Let every creature praise his holy name for ever and ever. (Psalm 145:21)

PROVERBS

Who: Solomon and others
What: Wisdom
Where: Israel
When: c. 900s BC–700s BC
Why: To provide wisdom and guidance for God's children.

Outline (Chapter)
- Lessons in Wisdom (1–9)
- Proverbs of Solomon (10–22)
- Other Wise Sayings (23–24)
- Solomon's Sayings (25–29)
- Other Proverbs (30–31)

Key Verse: Trust in the LORD with all your heart and lean not on your own understanding; in all your ways acknowledge him, and he will make your paths straight. (Proverbs 3:5–6)

ECCLESIASTES

Who: Unknown (Solomon)
What: Wisdom
Where: Jerusalem
When: c. 900s BC or 500s BC
Why: A search to discover truth.

Outline (Chapter)
- The Meaning of Life (1–2)
- Life is Not Always Fair (3–6)
- Wisdom (7–8)
- No One Knows the Future (9–10)
- Obedience to God (11–12)

Key Verse: Fear God and keep his commandments, for this is the whole duty of mankind. For God will bring every deed into judgment, including every hidden thing, whether it is good or evil. (Ecclesiastes 12:13–14)

SONG OF SONGS

Who: Solomon and others
What: Love Poem
Where: Jerusalem
When: c. 900s BC or 500s BC
Why: To illustrate the joy of authentic love found in marriage.

Outline (Chapter)
- The Courtship (1–2)
- The Wedding (3–4)
- The Lasting Relationship (5–8)

Key Verse: Many waters cannot quench love; rivers cannot wash it away. If one were to give all the wealth of his house for love, it would be utterly scorned. (Song of Songs 8:7)

MAJOR PROPHETS

The five Major Prophets are not called "major" because of their message or quality, but rather because of the length of the books. The prophets brought God's word which included warning of judgment, warnings and hope for the immediate future (as well as warnings and hope for the distant future), and hope in the coming Messiah.

ISAIAH

Who: Isaiah
What: Prophecy and Judgement
Where: Judah
When: c. 701 BC–681 BC
Why: To convince the people that salvation was possible through repentance and hope in the coming Messiah.

Outline (Chapter)
- Condemnation (1–39)
- Comfort in Exile (40–55)
- Future Hope (56–66)

Key Verse: For to us a child is born, to us a son is given, and the government will be on his shoulders. And he will be called Wonderful Counselor, Mighty God, Everlasting Father, Prince of Peace. (Isaiah 9:6)

JEREMIAH

Who: Jeremiah
What: Prophecy and Judgement
Where: Judah
When: c. 626 BC–582 BC
Why: To warn Judah of their destruction, to remind them of their sin, and convince them to submit to the Babylonian invaders.

Outline (Chapter)
- Jeremiah (1–10)
- Prophetic Warnings (11–28)
- New Covenant (29–39)
- The Fall of Jerusalem (40–52)

Key Verse: "For I know the plans I have for you," declares the LORD, "plans to prosper you and not to harm you, plans to give you hope and a future." (Jeremiah 29:11)

LAMENTATIONS

Who: Unknown (Jeremiah)
What: Dirge Poem (Lament)
Where: Babylon
When: c. 586 BC
Why: To express the despair of the people of Judah over the loss of their land, city, and temple.

Outline (Chapter)
- Sorrows of Captives (1)
- Anger with Jerusalem (2)
- Hope and Mercy (3)
- Punishment (4)
- Restoration (5)

Key Verse: Because of the LORD's great love we are not consumed, for his compassions never fail. They are new every morning; great is your faithfulness. (Lamentations 3:22–23)

EZEKIEL

Who: Ezekiel
What: Prophecy and Warning
Where: Babylon
When: c. 593 BC–571 BC
Why: To confront people about their sin, give them one last chance to repent, and offer hope.

Outline (Chapter)
- Ezekiel (1–3)
- Judgment of Judah (4–24)
- Judgment on the Nations (25–32)
- The End of the Age (33–39)
- Restoration of Temple (40–48)

Key Verse: I will give you a new heart and put a new spirit in you; I will remove from you your heart of stone and give you a heart of flesh. (Ezekiel 36:26)

DANIEL

Who: Daniel
What: Prophecy and Apocalyptic
Where: Babylon
When: c. 605 BC–535 BC
Why: To convince the Jewish exiles that God is sovereign and to provide them with a vision of their future redemption.

Outline (Chapter)
- Daniel and His Friends (1–6)
- Apocalyptic Visions (7–12)

Key Verse: In the time of those kings, the God of heaven will set up a kingdom that will never be destroyed, nor will it be left to another people. It will crush all those kingdoms and bring them to an end, but it will itself endure forever. (Daniel 2:44)

MINOR PROPHETS

The 12 Minor Prophets, called "The Book of the Twelve" in the Hebrew Bible, are just as important as the Major Prophets. They are called "minor" because of the shorter length of the books.

HOSEA
Who: Hosea
What: Prophecy and Warning
Where: Israel
When: c. 752 BC–722 BC
Why: To illustrate Israel's spiritual adultery and warn of destruction.

Outline (Chapter)
- Unfaithful Wife (1–3)
- Unfaithful Nation (4–14)

Key Verse: Because you have rejected knowledge, I also reject you as my priests. (Hosea 4:6)

JOEL
Who: Joel
What: Prophecy and Judgment
Where: Judah
When: Unknown
Why: To call Judah to repentance in order to avoid judgment.

Outline (Chapter)
- Locusts (1)
- Blessings and Curses (2–3)

Key Verse: I will pour out my Spirit on all people. Your sons and daughters will prophesy. (Joel 2:28)

AMOS
Who: Amos
What: Prophecy and Judgment
Where: Israel
When: c. 760 BC–753 BC
Why: To accuse and judge Israel for injustice and lack of mercy.

Outline (Chapter)
- Neighbors Punished (1)
- Israel's Destruction (2–8)
- Future Hope (9)

Key Verse: Seek good, not evil, that you may live. Then the LORD God Almighty will be with you. (Amos 5:14)

OBADIAH
Who: Obadiah
What: Prophecy
Where: Judah
When: c. 586 BC
Why: To prophesy against Edom.

Outline (Verses)
- Judgment on Edom (1–9)
- Edom's Violations (10–14)
- Israel's Victory (15–21)

Key Verse: Because of the violence against your brother Jacob, you will be covered with shame; you will be destroyed forever. (Obadiah 10)

JONAH
Who: Jonah
What: Story of God's Mercy
Where: Nineveh
When: c. 783 BC–753 BC
Why: To show that God loves all.

Outline (Chapter)
- Jonah Flees (1)
- Jonah Prays (2)
- Jonah's Anger with God's Mercy (3–4)

Key Verse: I knew that you are a gracious and compassionate God, slow to anger and abounding in love. (Jonah 4:2)

MICAH
Who: Micah
What: Prophecy and Judgment
Where: Israel and Judah
When: c. 738 BC–698 BC
Why: To warn people of judgment and to offer hope.

Outline (Chapter)
- Judgment and Deliverance (1–5)
- Confession and Restoration (6–7)

Key Verse: To act justly and to love mercy and to walk humbly with your God. (Micah 6:8)

NAHUM
Who: Nahum
What: Prophecy and Judgment
Where: Judah and Nineveh
When: c. 663 BC–612 BC
Why: To pronounce judgment on Nineveh and the Assyrian empire.

Outline (Chapter)
- Judgment and Mercy (1)
- Nineveh's Destruction (2–3)

Key Verse: The LORD is good, a refuge in times of trouble. He cares for those who trust in him. (Nahum 1:7)

HABAKKUK
Who: Habakkuk
What: Prophecy and Judgment
Where: Judah
When: c. 609 BC–598 BC
Why: To affirm that the wicked will not prevail and to remind Judah that God is in control.

Outline (Chapter)
- Tough Questions (1–2)
- Praise to the Lord (3)

Key Verse: Yet I will rejoice in the LORD, I will be joyful in God my Savior. (Habakkuk 3:18)

ZEPHANIAH
Who: Zephaniah
What: Prophecy and Judgment
Where: Judah
When: c. 641 BC–628 BC
Why: To motivate repentance.

Outline (Chapter)
- Judgment on Judah (1)
- Judgment on the Nations (2)
- Promise of Restoration (3)

Key Verse: The great day of the LORD is near—near and coming quickly. (Zephaniah 1:14)

HAGGAI
Who: Haggai
What: Prophecy and Hope
Where: Judah
When: c. 520 BC
Why: To urge the people to complete rebuilding the temple.

Outline (Chapter)
- Rebuild the Temple (1)
- Blessings and David's Throne (2)

Key Verse: My Spirit remains among you. Do not fear. (Haggai 2:5)

ZECHARIAH
Who: Zechariah
What: Prophecy and Hope
Where: Judah
When: c. 520 BC–518 BC
Why: To give hope to the remnant.

Outline (Chapter)
- Zechariah's Visions (1–8)
- Oracles against the Nations (9–14)

Key Verse: See, your king comes to you, righteous and having salvation, gentle and riding on a donkey. (Zechariah 9:9)

MALACHI
Who: Malachi
What: Prophecy and Judgment
Where: Judah
When: c. 400s BC
Why: To examine Judah's actions and make sure God has priority.

Outline (Chapter)
- Six Prophetic Speeches (1–3)
- Day of the Lord (4)

Key Verse: The sun of righteousness will rise with healing in its wings. (Malachi 4:2)

New Testament: Gospels & Acts

The Gospels, which are the first four books of the New Testament, record the good news of God's plan for a Savior through the life, ministry, death, and resurrection of Jesus Christ. Each writer has a particular method or style to communicate the life and message of Jesus Christ.

MATTHEW

Who: Matthew (also called Levi)
What: Gospel
Where: Judea
When: c. AD 60
Why: To show Jesus as the Son of David, the Kingly Messiah who fulfills prophecy.

Outline (Chapter)
- Birth and Early Life (1–4)
- Ministry of Christ (5–20)
- Death and Resurrection (21–28)

Key Verse: Then Jesus came to them and said, "All authority in heaven and on earth has been given to me. Therefore go and make disciples of all nations, baptizing them in the name of the Father and of the Son and of the Holy Spirit." (Matthew 28:18–19)

MARK

Who: John Mark
What: Gospel
Where: Rome
When: c. AD 50s
Why: To show Jesus as the Suffering Son of Man sent to serve and not be served.

Outline (Chapter)
- Introduction (1)
- Ministry of Christ (2–10)
- Death and Resurrection (11–16)

Key Verse: Instead, whoever wants to become great among you must be your servant, and whoever wants to be first must be slave of all. For even the Son of Man did not come to be served, but to serve, and to give his life as a ransom for many. (Mark 10:43–45)

Acts is the record of the radically changed "acts" or "actions" of the followers of Jesus Christ after the resurrection. Acts opens with the out-flowing of the Holy Spirit and describes the missionary efforts of the early followers of Jesus as they spread the message of the gospel to Judea and Samaria. Acts also records the actions of the apostle Paul as he and other courageous believers continued to spread the good news of Jesus to the Jews and Gentiles of the Roman Empire.

LUKE

Who: Luke (The Physician)
What: Gospel
Where: Caesarea
When: c. AD 60–AD 62
Why: To show Jesus as the Savior of the World who has compassion for all human beings.

Outline (Chapter)
- Birth and Early Life (1–4)
- Ministry of Christ (5–19)
- Death and Resurrection (20–24)

Key Verse: Then he said to them all: "If anyone would come after me, he must deny himself and take up his cross daily and follow me. For whoever wants to save his life will lose it, but whoever loses his life for me will save it." (Luke 9:23–24)

JOHN

Who: John (The Beloved Disciple)
What: Gospel
Where: Asia Minor
When: c. AD 85–AD 95
Why: To show Jesus as the Son of God, the Word made flesh, who provides eternal life for all who believe in him.

Outline (Chapter)
- Introduction (1)
- Ministry of Christ (2–12)
- Private Ministry (13–17)
- Death and Resurrection (18–21)

Key Verse: For God so loved the world that he gave his one and only Son, that whoever believes in him shall not perish but have eternal life. (John 3:16)

ACTS

Who: Luke (The Physician)
What: History of Early Church
Where: Caesarea and Rome
When: c. AD 60–AD 62
Why: To record how the Holy Spirit acted through believers to spread the Word of God.

Outline (Chapter)
- Jerusalem (1–7)
- Judea and Samaria (8–11)
- Paul's Journeys (12–20)
- Paul Taken to Rome (21–28)

Key Verse: But you will receive power when the Holy Spirit comes on you; and you will be my witnesses in Jerusalem, and in all Judea and Samaria, and to the ends of the earth. (Acts 1:8)

PAUL'S EPISTLES (LETTERS)

The apostle Paul wrote 13 letters to young churches, pastors, and friends in order to guide, encourage, and correct them. Most of these letters served a specific purpose or addressed a specific question or problem.

ROMANS
Who: Paul
What: Letter to Roman Christians
Where: Corinth
When: c. AD 57
Why: To illustrate law, faith, salvation, and righteous living.

Outline (Chapter)
- Christian Gospel (1–8)
- Israel (9–11)
- Christian Life (12–16)

Key Verse: Therefore, I urge you, brothers, in view of God's mercy, to offer your bodies as living sacrifices, holy and pleasing to God—this is your spiritual act of worship. Do not conform any longer to the pattern of this world, but be transformed by the renewing of your mind. (Romans 12:1–2a)

1 CORINTHIANS
Who: Paul
What: Letter to Church in Corinth
Where: Ephesus
When: c. AD 55–AD 56
Why: To address division and immorality and to encourage them to love each other.

Outline (Chapter)
- Divisions (1–4)
- Morality (5–11)
- Spiritual Gifts (12–14)
- The Resurrection (15–16)

Key Verse: Love is patient, love is kind. It does not envy, it does not boast, it is not proud. It is not rude, it is not self-seeking, it is not easily angered, it keeps no record of wrongs. (1 Corinthians 13:4–5)

2 CORINTHIANS
Who: Paul
What: Letter to Church in Corinth
Where: Philippi
When: c. AD 56
Why: To defend Paul's call as an apostle, to address deceivers.

Outline (Chapter)
- Apostolic Characteristics (1–7)
- Giving (8–9)
- Paul's Defense (10–13)

Key Verse: But he said to me, "My grace is sufficient for you, for my power is made perfect in weakness." Therefore I will boast all the more gladly about my weaknesses, so that Christ's power may rest on me. (2 Cor. 12:9)

GALATIANS
Who: Paul
What: Letter to Churches in Galatia
Where: Asia Minor
When: c. AD 48–49 or AD 54–55
Why: To warn against legalism and defend justification by faith as well as Paul's apostolic authority.

Outline (Chapter)
- Paul's Defense (1–2)
- Justification by Faith (3–4)
- The Christian Life (5–6)

Key Verse: But the fruit of the Spirit is love, joy, peace, patience, kindness, goodness, faithfulness, gentleness and self-control. Against such things there is no law. (Galatians 5:22–23)

EPHESIANS
Who: Paul
What: Letter to Church in Ephesus
Where: Prison in Rome
When: c. AD 60–AD 62
Why: To show believers what it means to be a follower of Christ and encourage them in their spiritual walk.

Outline (Chapter)
- Spiritual Blessings (1–3)
- The Christian Life (4–6)

Key Verse: For it is by grace you have been saved, through faith—and this not from yourselves, it is the gift of God—not by works, so that no one can boast. (Ephesians 2:8–9)

PHILIPPIANS
Who: Paul
What: Letter to Church in Philippi
Where: Prison in Rome
When: c. AD 60–AD 62
Why: To express Paul's love and affection for the Philippians.

Outline (Chapter)
- Joy of Life (1)
- Humility of Christ (2)
- Finish the Race (3)
- Thanks and Greetings (4)

Key Verse: Do everything without complaining or arguing, so that you may become blameless and pure, children of God without fault in a crooked and depraved generation, in which you shine like stars in the universe. (Philippians 2:14–15)

COLOSSIANS
Who: Paul
What: Letter to Church in Colossae
Where: Prison in Rome
When: c. AD 60–AD 62
Why: To counteract heretical teachings and exhort believers.

Outline (Chapter)
- Thanksgiving (1)
- Work of Christ (1–2)
- Finish the Race (3–4)
- Final Greetings (4)

Key Verse: For in Christ all the fullness of the Deity lives in bodily form, and in Christ you have been brought to fullness. He is the head over every power and authority. (Colossians 2:9–10)

1 THESSALONIANS

Who: Paul
What: Letter to the Church in Thessalonica
Where: Corinth
When: c. AD 50–AD 52
Why: To emphasize Christ's return and to stress commitment.

Outline (Chapter)
- Faith and Example (1–3)
- Living for God (4)
- Christ's Return (4–5)

Key Verse: Rejoice always, pray continually, give thanks in all circumstances; for this is God's will for you in Christ Jesus. Do not quench the Spirit. Do not treat prophecies with contempt but test them all; hold on to what is good, reject every kind of evil. (1 Thessalonians 5:16–22)

2 THESSALONIANS

Who: Paul
What: Letter to the Church in Thessalonica
Where: Corinth
When: c. AD 50–AD 52
Why: To emphasize Christ's return and to encourage believers.

Outline (Chapter)
- Praise and Encouragement (1)
- Christ's Return (2)
- Pray and Work (3)

Key Verse: We have confidence in the Lord that you are doing and will continue to do the things we command. May the Lord direct your hearts into God's love and Christ's perseverance. In the name of the Lord Jesus Christ, we command you, brothers, to keep away from every brother who is idle and does not live according to the teaching you received from us. (2 Thessalonians 3:4–6)

1 TIMOTHY

Who: Paul
What: Letter to Timothy
Where: Rome
When: c. AD 62–AD 66
Why: To remove false doctrine and suggest proper leadership for the church in Ephesus.

Outline (Chapter)
- Trouble in Ephesus (1)
- Church Leadership (2–3)
- False Teachers (4)
- Discipline (5)
- Paul's Advice to Timothy (6)

Key Verse: Don't let anyone look down on you because you are young, but set an example for the believers in speech, in life, in love, in faith and in purity. Until I come, devote yourself to the public reading of Scripture, to preaching and to teaching. (1 Timothy 4:12–13)

2 TIMOTHY

Who: Paul
What: Letter to Timothy
Where: Prison in Rome
When: c. AD 66–AD 67
Why: To encourage Timothy to remain faithful in ministry even in the midst of suffering.

Outline (Chapter)
- Thanksgiving (1)
- Call to Remain Faithful (2)
- Authority of God's Word (3)
- Lead a Godly Life (3–4)

Key Verse: From infancy you have known the holy Scriptures, which are able to make you wise for salvation through faith in Christ Jesus. All Scripture is God-breathed and is useful for teaching, rebuking, correcting and training in righteousness, so that the man of God may be thoroughly equipped for every good work. (2 Timothy 3:15–17)

TITUS

Who: Paul
What: Letter to Titus
Where: Rome
When: c. AD 64–AD 66
Why: To encourage the church in Crete to do good works.

Outline (Chapter)
- Instruction for Titus (1)
- Living the Faith (2–3)
- Final Instructions (3)

Key Verse: But when the kindness and love of God our Savior appeared, he saved us, not because of righteous things we had done, but because of his mercy. He saved us through the washing of rebirth and renewal by the Holy Spirit, whom he poured out on us generously through Jesus Christ our Savior, so that, having been justified by his grace, we might become heirs having the hope of eternal life. (Titus 3:4–7)

PHILEMON

Who: Paul
What: Letter to Philemon
Where: Prison in Rome
When: c. AD 60–AD 62
Why: To appeal to Philemon to forgive and receive Onesimus, a runaway slave.

Outline (Verses)
- Salutations (1–3)
- Philemon's Love and Faith (4–7)
- Paul's Appeal (8–22)
- Final Greetings (23–25)

Key Verse: So if you consider me a partner, welcome him as you would welcome me. If he has done you any wrong or owes you anything, charge it to me. I, Paul, am writing this with my own hand. I will pay it back—not to mention that you owe me your very self. (Philemon 17–19)

GENERAL EPISTLES & REVELATION

The eight General Epistles were written by other apostles and leaders including Simon Peter, James, John, and Jude. The General Epistles were addressed to the early Christians to provide guidance, encouragement through persecution, and warnings of false teachings.

HEBREWS
Who: Unknown
What: Letter to Hebrew Believers
Where: Unknown
When: c. AD 60–AD 69
Why: To emphasize the superiority of Christ over the Old Covenant.

Outline (Chapter)
- Supremacy of Christ (1–4)
- The New Covenant (5–10)
- The Life of Faith (11–13)

Key Verse: Let us fix our eyes on Jesus, the author and perfecter of our faith, who for the joy set before him endured the cross, scorning its shame, and sat down at the right hand of the throne of God. (Hebrews 12:2)

JAMES
Who: James
What: Letter to Jewish Believers
Where: Jerusalem
When: c. AD 49
Why: Encouragement to live out one's faith within the Christian community.

Outline (Chapter)
- Living a Life of Faith (1–2)
- Faith without Works (2–3)
- Speech and Wisdom (3–4)
- Wealth and Prayer (5)

Key Verse: Everyone should be quick to listen, slow to speak and slow to become angry, because human anger does not produce the righteousness that God desires. (James 1:19–20)

1 PETER
Who: Peter
What: Letter to All Christians
Where: Rome
When: c. AD 64–AD 65
Why: To call Christians to holiness.

Outline (Chapter)
- Holiness and Submission (1–2)
- Suffering (3–4)
- Advice for Old and Young (5)

Key Verse: The end of all things is near. Therefore be clear minded and self-controlled so that you can pray. (1 Peter 4:7)

2 PETER
Who: Peter
What: Letter to All Christians
Where: Rome
When: c. AD 64–AD 65
Why: To warn against false teachers.

Outline (Chapter)
- Living Like Christ; False Teachers (1–2)
- The Return of Christ (3)

Key Verse: For prophecy never had its origin in the will of man, but men spoke from God as they were carried along by the Holy Spirit. (2 Peter 1:21)

1 JOHN
Who: John
What: Letter to All Christians
Where: Ephesus
When: c. AD 85–AD 95
Why: To emphasize love in Christ.

Outline (Chapter)
- Living in the Light (1–2)
- Living in Love (3–4)
- Living by Faith (5)

Key Verse: Whoever does not love does not know God, because God is love. (1 John 4:8)

2 JOHN
Who: John
What: Letter to the Elect Lady
Where: Ephesus
When: c. AD 85–AD 95
Why: To warn against heresy and false teachers.

Key Verse: Watch out that you do not lose what you have worked for, but that you may be rewarded fully. (2 John 8)

3 JOHN
Who: John
What: Letter to Gaius
Where: Ephesus
When: c. AD 85–AD 95
Why: To praise Gaius for his loyalty to the truth and criticize Diotrephes for his pride.

Key Verse: I have no greater joy than to hear that my children are walking in the truth. (3 John 4)

JUDE
Who: Jude
What: Letter to all Christians
Where: Unknown
When: c. AD 60s–AD 80s
Why: To warn against heresy.

Key Verse: To him who is able to keep you from falling and to present you before his glorious presence without fault and with great joy. (Jude 24)

The book of Revelation addresses seven churches in Asia Minor (Turkey today). It encourages believers who are experiencing persecution. Revelation illustrates that God is in control and that all people were created to love and worship God.

REVELATION
Who: John
What: Letter to Seven Churches
Where: Island of Patmos
When: c. AD 90–AD 96
Why: To give hope to persecuted Christians and provide a vision of Christ's return.

Outline (Chapter)
- The Seven Churches (1–4)
- Visions (5–16)
- God's Triumph (17–20)
- The New Creation (21–22)

Key Verse: Then I saw a new heaven and a new earth, for the first heaven and the first earth had passed away, and there was no longer any sea. (Revelation 21:1)

Bible Overview • 17

Bible Timeline

BIBLE HISTORY

GENESIS

- God creates the world and Adam and Eve.
- ◆ Adamic Covenant
- 🔸 Job (dates unknown)
- Noah's ark built; the flood.
- ◆ Noahic Covenant
- Tower of Babel built.

Abraham c. 2166-1991
◆ Abrahamic Covenant

Isaac c. 2066-1886

Jacob c. 2005-1859

Joseph c. 1914-1805

Hebrews (Israelites) in Egypt c. 1876-1446
- Jacob's family migrates to Egypt. c. 1876

EXODUS, LEVITICUS, NUMBERS, DEUTERONOMY

Aaron c. 1529-1407

Moses c. 1526-1406
- First Passover c. 1446
- The exodus (high date) c. 1446
- ◆ Mosaic Covenant
- Ten Commandments, other laws given. c. 1446
- Tabernacle built. c. 1446
- Israelites wander in desert. c. 1446-1406
- 🔸 Moses writes Genesis through Deuteronomy. c. 1446-1406
- Rahab saves the spies. c. 1406
- Joshua leads the Israelites into Canaan. c. 1406
- The exodus (low date) c. 1290

Some scholars date the exodus at 1290 BC (low date). The era of the Judges would then begin at around 1130 BC.

JOSHUA, JUDGES

- Era of Judges (Deborah, Gideon, Samson, and others) c. 1350-1051
- 🔸 Joshua written. c. 1300s

🔸 = Book of the Bible Written
(Dates indicate the time frame in which the book was written and/or compiled.)

◆ = Covenant

c. = Approximate Date

Dates for events before Abraham are unknown.

WORLD HISTORY

2100 BC
- Earliest forms of writing (cuneiform) in Mesopotamia. c. 3200
- Stonehenge erected in England. c. 3000
- Old kingdom pyramids built in Egypt. c. 2700-2200
- Ziggurats built in Ur. c. 2100

2000 BC
- 11th and 12th dynasties in Egypt c. 2050-1800
- City of Ur falls to Elam. c. 2000
- Hittites and Indo-European tribes form a single kingdom. c. 2000
- Beginning of Semitic alphabet. c. 2000
- Four basic elements identified in India: earth, air, fire, and water. c. 2000

1800 BC
- 13th–17th dynasties in Egypt c. 1800-1570
- Hammurabi reigns in Babylon. c. 1792-1750

1700 BC
- Hyksos rule lower Egypt. c. 1730-1570
- First Chinese dictionary, contains 40,000 characters. 1717

1600 BC
- Shang dynasty begins in China. c. 1600
- Hittites sack Babylon. 1595
- Hyksos expelled; 18th dynasty begins in Egypt. 1570

1500 BC
- Pharaoh Thutmose III c. 1504-1450
- Pharaoh Amenhotep II 1453-1426

1400 BC
- Dream Stele of Thutmose IV c. 1401
- Amarna Letters written between Canaan and Egypt. c. 1400
- Tutankhamen (King Tut) of Egypt c. 1333-1323
- Pharaoh Ramses I 1318-1317

1300 BC
- Pharaoh Seti 1317-1304
- Pharaoh Ramses II 1304-1237

Bible Timeline

JUDGES, RUTH

- Era of Judges
- Judges written. c. 1350–1000
- Ruth (dates unknown)
- Eli, priest in Shiloh c. 1100–1060

1 SAMUEL THROUGH 2 CHRONICLES

- 1 and 2 Samuel written. c. 1100–931
- Samuel, judge and prophet in Israel c. 1060–1020
- King Saul, Israel's first king c. 1051–1011
- King David c. 1011–971
- Psalms written. c. 1000–450
- Davidic Covenant
- Prophet Nathan c. 990–971
- King Solomon c. 971–931
- Proverbs, Ecclesiastes, Song of Songs written. c. 971–931
- First temple in Jerusalem built. 960
- Kingdom divides into Israel (north) and Judah (south). 931
- **Northern Kingdom of Israel 931–722**
- **Southern Kingdom of Judah 931–586**
- Elijah c. 870–845
- Elisha c. 845–800
- Jonah c. 783–753
- Amos c. 760–753
- Hosea c. 752–722
- Isaiah c. 740–681
- Micah c. 738–698
- Israel falls to Assyria. 722
- Obadiah c. 586
- Lamentations written. c. 586
- 1 and 2 Kings written. c. 561–539
- Nahum c. 663–612
- Zephaniah c. 641–628
- Jeremiah c. 626–582
- Habakkuk c. 609–598
- Daniel c. 605–535
- Ezekiel c. 593–571

EZRA, NEHEMIAH, ESTHER

- Gedaliah, governor of Judah 586
- Judah falls to Babylon; temple destroyed; people exiled. 586
- Malachi c. 400s
- Joel (dates unknown)
- Cyrus allows Jews to return from exile. 538
- Rebuilding of the temple begins. 536
- Haggai c. 520
- Zechariah c. 520–518
- Zerubbabel and Joshua the high priest; temple completed. 516
- Queen Esther c. 478
- Ezra goes to Judah. 457
- 1 and 2 Chronicles written. c. 450–400
- Nehemiah governs Judah. 444–432
- Ezra and Nehemiah written. c. 400s

Prophets are listed by the dates they prophesied.

Kings are listed by dates of reign.

1200 BC
- Pharaoh Merneptah 1237–1227
- Merneptah Stele c. 1220
- Hittite Empire collapses. c. 1200
- Iron Age begins. c. 1200
- Olmec culture in Mexico marked by massive basalt sculptures. c. 1200
- Trojan War begins in Asia Minor. c. 1190
- Egypt's power begins to decline. c. 1164
- Zhou (Chou) Dynasty begins in China. c. 1150
- Tiglath-Pileser I rules Assyria. 1114–1076
- Ramses II

1100 BC

1000 BC
- Mayan dynasties founded in Central America. c. 1000

900 BC
- Hiram, king of Tyre c. 978–944
- Pharaoh Shishak I 945–924
- Assyrian expansion begins. 912
- Ashurnasirpal II of Assyria 883–859
- Shalmaneser III of Assyria 859–824

800 BC
- King Mesha drives the Israelites out of Moab. c. 850
- Assyria forces Israel to pay tribute. 841
- Greek poet Homer c. 800–701
- First recorded Olympic games in Greece. 776
- Founding of Rome. 753
- Tiglath-Pileser III of Assyria 745–727
- Sargon II of Assyria conquers Samaria (Israel). 722

700 BC
- Sennacherib of Assyria 705–681
- Nineveh (Assyria) falls to Babylonia and Media. 612

600 BC
- King Nebuchadnezzar II of Babylon 604–562
- Gautama Buddha of India c. 563–483
- Aesop's Fables c. 560
- Cyrus the Great, King of Persia 559–530
- Philosopher Confucius of China 551–479
- Babylon falls to Persia and Media. 539
- Darius the Mede rules Babylon. 539

500 BC
- Roman Republic established. 509
- Athenian leader Pericles of Greece c. 500–429
- King Xerxes I (Ahasuerus) of Persia 485–465
- King Artaxerxes of Persia 464–424
- Peloponnesian War begins. 431

400 BC

Bible Timeline • 19

Bible Timeline

BIBLE HISTORY

🖋 = Book of the Bible written. Dates indicate the time frame in which it is believed to have been written and/or compiled.

◆ = Covenant   c. = Approximate date

BETWEEN THE OLD AND NEW TESTAMENTS

The 66 books of the Bible do not cover this 400-year period.

THE GOSPELS: MATTHEW, MARK, LUKE, JOHN

- Birth of John the Baptist. c. 5 BC
- Birth of Jesus in Bethlehem. c. 4 BC
- Jesus (age 12) amazes teachers at the temple in Jerusalem. c. AD 8
- Jesus is baptized by John the Baptist in the Jordan River. c. 26
- Jesus begins his public ministry. c. 26
- John the Baptist is arrested and killed by Herod Antipas. c. 29

WORLD HISTORY

- Plato writes *The Republic*. c. 370
- Alexander the Great conquers Egypt and Judea; Hellenization begins. 332
- Persia falls to Alexander. 330
- Alexander dies and his empire is divided. 323
- Ptolemaic Empire in Judea 323–198
- Hinduism codified in India. c. 274
- First Punic War; Romans control Italy. 264–241
- Septuagint (translation of Hebrew Scriptures into Greek) written. c. 255
- Second Punic War; Hannibal in Italy 219–201
- Great wall of China built to keep out invaders. c. 215
- Earliest of the Dead Sea Scrolls (copies of the Hebrew Scriptures) written. c. 200
- Seleucid Empire begins to rule Judea. 198
- Rosetta Stone 196
- Seleucid ruler Antiochus IV desecrates the temple in Jerusalem and tries to force Jews to abandon their law. 175–164
- Maccabean Revolt: Judas Maccabeus leads a Jewish revolt against the Seleucids. 167
- Temple in Jerusalem is rededicated (Hanukkah). c. 164
- Hasmonean dynasty 164–63
- Third Punic War; Romans control Greece. 149–146
- Ships from China reach India for the first time. 100
- Spartacus leads a slave revolt. 73–71
- Pompey conquers Jerusalem for Rome. 63
- Julius Caesar, Crassus, and Pompey form the First Triumvirate. 60
- Cleopatra VII rules Egypt. 51–31 BC
- Herod the Great rules Judea. 37–4 BC
- Caesar Augustus rules the Roman Empire. 27 BC–AD 14
- Herod begins a massive expansion of the temple complex in Jerusalem. 20 BC
- Herod Antipas rules Galilee. 4 BC–AD 39
- Caiaphas is high priest in Jerusalem. 18–36
- Emperor Tiberius of Rome 14–37
- Pontius Pilate governs Judea. 26–36
- Kuang Wu Ti founds the Later Han (Eastern Han) dynasty in China. 25

Bible Timeline

ACTS | CHRISTIAN HISTORY AFTER THE BOOK OF ACTS

AD 30
- New Covenant
- Jesus' death on the cross and resurrection in Jerusalem. c. 30
- The risen Jesus appears to his disciples and many others; ascends to heaven. c. 30
- Disciples receive the Holy Spirit during Pentecost in Jerusalem. c. 30
- Stephen martyred in Jerusalem. Christians begin to disperse throughout Judea and Samaria. c. 32
- Paul converted on the road to Damascus. 37

Caiaphas

Pontius Pilate

Herod Antipas

Emperor Tiberius

AD 40
- Emperor Caligula 37–41
- Caligula declares himself a god. 37
- Peter brings the gospel to gentiles. 40
- Emperor Claudius 41–54
- Emperor Claudius conquers Britain for Rome. 43
- Apostle James (son of Zebedee) martyred. c. 44
- Julian calendar of 365.25 days; leap year introduced. 46

AD 50
- Paul's first missionary journey c. 47–49
- James (Jesus' brother) writes the book of James c. 49
- Paul writes Galatians. c. 49
- Jerusalem Council c. 49
- Jews expelled from Rome, including Priscilla and Aquila. 49
- Paul's second missionary journey c. 49–51
- Mark writes his gospel. c. 50s
- Paul writes 1 and 2 Thessalonians. c. 50–51
- Paul's third missionary journey c. 52–57
- Paul writes 1 and 2 Corinthians. c. 55–56
- Paul writes Romans. c. 57

AD 60
- Paul's journey to Rome c. 59–60
- Paul under house arrest in Rome. c. 60–62
- Luke writes his gospel and Acts. c. 60–62
- Paul writes Ephesians, Philippians, Colossians, Philemon. c. 60–62
- Matthew writes his gospel. c. 60s
- James, the brother of Jesus, martyred. 62
- Paul writes 1 Timothy. c. 62–66
- Peter writes 1 and 2 Peter. c. 64
- Paul writes Titus. c. 64–66
- Paul writes 2 Timothy. c. 66–67
- Peter and Paul martyred in Rome during Emperor Nero's persecution of Christians. c. 66–68
- Jerusalem Christians flee rather than join the Jewish revolt against the Romans. 66
- Hebrews written. c. 60–69
- Jude written. c. 60–80s

Emperor Nero 54–68

AD 70
- Rome burns; Nero blames Christians; persecution begins. 64–68
- First Jewish Revolt against the Romans 66–73
- Qumran destroyed (the people of this settlement likely preserved the Dead Sea Scrolls). 68
- Emperor Vespasian 69–79
- Romans destroy Jerusalem and the temple. 70
- Construction begins on the Roman Colosseum. c. 71
- Masada falls to the Romans. 73

AD 80
- Mount Vesuvius erupts. 79
- Emperor Titus 79–81

AD 90
- Persecution of Christians intensifies under Emperor Domitian. 81–96
- John writes his gospel; 1, 2, and 3 John; and Revelation. c. 85–95
- Writings of early church leaders: Barnabas, Clement of Rome, Ignatius, Polycarp 85–150
- Clement I, Bishop of Rome 88
- Rise of Gnostic heresies within the church 90

AD 100
- Josephus writes *Antiquities of the Jews*, a history of the Jewish people. c. 94

Emperor Domitian (Demands the title "Lord and God.") 81–96

Emperor Nerva 96–98

Emperor Trajan 98–117

100 Key People in the Bible

Old Testament

1. **AARON** The older brother of Moses and Israel's first high priest (Num. 26:59; Ex. 28:1)
2. **ABEL** Adam and Eve's second son, killed by his brother Cain (Gen. 4:2, 8)
3. **ABRAHAM** Father of the Hebrew nation and the ultimate role model for faith (Gen. 12:1–3; 1 Chron. 1:34; 2:1; Heb. 11:8–10)
4. **ADAM** The first human being God created (Gen. 1:27; 2:7)
5. **BALAAM** A false prophet who attempted to curse Israel and prevent them from entering the Promised Land (Num. 22–24)
6. **BATHSHEBA** The wife of King David and mother of Solomon (2 Sam. 12:24)
7. **BELSHAZZAR** A Babylonian king condemned by God for his blasphemy through a written message on a wall during a drunken banquet. The message was interpreted by Daniel the prophet. (Daniel 5)
8. **BOAZ** The husband of Ruth, great-grandfather of King David and ancestor in the line leading to Jesus Christ (Ruth 4:13, 21–22; Matt. 1:5–16)
9. **CAIN** The first baby to be born on the earth and later murdered his younger brother Abel (Gen. 4:1, 8)
10. **CALEB** Joshua's faithful partner who urged Israel to enter the Promised Land at Kadesh-barnea as opposed to the 10 cowardly spies (Num. 14:6–9)
11. **CYRUS** The Persian king who issued the return decree allowing the Jews to go back and rebuild Jerusalem (2 Chron. 36:22–23)
12. **DANIEL** Prime minister in Babylon under King Nebuchadnezzar and King Darius. Interpreted the handwriting on the wall to King Belshazzar (Dan. 2:48; 6:1–3; 5:25–28)
13. **DAVID** Israel's greatest king, the father of Solomon. Author of more than one half of the Psalms (Ps. 78:70–72; 2 Sam. 12:24; 23:1–2)
14. **DEBORAH** Israelite prophetess and judge who helped Barak to defeat the Canaanites (Judg. 4:4–9)
15. **ELI** Israel's high priest who helped raise Samuel in the Tabernacle and died in great sorrow upon hearing that the Ark of the Covenant had been captured by the Philistines (1 Samuel 1:17-20; 4:12-18)
16. **ELIJAH** A fearless and rugged Israelite prophet who defeated his enemies on Mt. Carmel and was later caught up into heaven without dying (1 Kings 18:16–40; 2 Kings 2:1–18)
17. **ELISHA** Elijah's successor who parted the Jordan River, raised the Shunammite's son from the dead, and healed Namaan of his leprosy (2 Kings 2:9-14; 5:10-14)
18. **ENOCH** The first of two people taken from the earth without dying (Gen. 5:23–24; Heb. 11:5)
19. **ESAU** Jacob's brother and the father of the Edomites (Genesis 25:26; 36:43)
20. **ESTHER** The Jewish Persian Queen who saved her people from destruction (Est. 7:3–6; 8:3–8)
21. **EVE** Adam's wife and the world's first woman. She was successfully tempted by Satan (Gen. 2:22; 3:1-6; 4:1–2; 1 Tim. 2:14)
22. **EZEKIEL** Prophet and priest who became the key religious leader to the Jewish people in Babylon during the Babylonian captivity (Ezek. 1:3; 2:3–4)
23. **EZRA** A learned Jewish scribe and priest who led the second of three Jewish returns from the Babylonian captivity back to Jerusalem (Ezra 7:1–10)
24. **GIDEON** Israel's sixth military leader during the days of the Judges who defeated a vastly superior enemy army with just 300 chosen men (Judg. 6:12–14; 7:22; 8:10–12)
25. **HAGAR** Abraham's second wife and mother of Ishmael (Gen. 16:1-3, 15)
26. **HANNAH** The godly woman who cried out to God to give her a child. She gave birth to Samuel. (1 Sam. 1:20)
27. **HEZEKIAH** The thirteenth king of Judah and he was on the throne when God saved the city of Jerusalem from the Assyrian army by the death angel (2 Kings 19)
28. **HOSEA** Israelite prophet whom God commanded to marry a harlot named Gomer to illustrate Israel's spiritual adultery (Hos. 1:2)
29. **ISAAC** Abraham's promised son and father of Jacob (Gen. 17:19; 25:21–26)
30. **ISAIAH** Prophet who predicted the virgin birth of Jesus, his spirit-filled mission, his dual nature (Isa. 9:6), his death, and his millennial reign (Isa. 7:14; 11:13; 53:1–12; 2:2–4; 65:25)
31. **ISHMAEL** Abraham's first son (Gen. 16:15)
32. **JACOB** Isaac's son and the father of 12 sons from whom Israel's 12 tribes would come (1 Chron. 2:1–2)
33. **JEREMIAH** Known as Judah's weeping prophet and author of the book of Jeremiah. He later wrote a funeral song mourning the destruction of Jerusalem. (Book of Lamentations)
34. **JOB** God permitted this wealthy, righteous believer to be tormented by Satan to demonstrate God's presence and authority even in the midst of suffering. (Job 1–2, 40–42)

35. **JONAH** A prophet who was punished by God for refusing to go preach in Nineveh. He was swallowed by a fish and later preached in Nineveh which resulted in a city-wide revival. (Jonah 1–3)

36. **JONATHAN** King Saul's son and David's closest friend (1 Sam. 14:1; 18:1)

37. **JOSEPH** Jacob's favorite son, sold into slavery by his own brothers, who would later use his position in Egypt to save his brothers and father from famine (Gen. 37:3, 28; 45:7–11)

38. **JOSHUA** Moses' successor who led Israel into the Promised Land (Josh. 1:1–3; 3:1–17)

39. **JOSIAH** This sixteenth king of Judah who used the discovery of the only remaining copy of the Law of Moses to lead his people in a great revival (2 Chron. 34:1, 14–33)

40. **LEAH** Jacob's first wife who bore him six sons (including Judah and Levi) and one daughter Dinah (Gen. 30:21; 35:23)

41. **MELCHIZEDEK** The king/high priest of Salem to whom Abraham paid tithes. His priestly work later being associated with the high priestly ministry of Jesus Christ. (Gen. 14:18–20; Ps. 110:4)

42. **METHUSELAH** Died at the age of 969, the longest life span recorded (Gen. 5:27)

43. **MIRIAM** The elder sister of Moses who helped lead the Israelites through the wilderness (Ex. 15:20)

44. **MORDECAI** Queen Esther's cousin who helped her save the Jewish people from slaughter. He later became prime minister of Persia. (Est. 2:7; 4:14; 10:3)

45. **MOSES** Israel's deliverer and law giver who led his people from Egypt to the border of the Promised Land. The author of Scripture's first five books. (Ex. 14; 20; Deut. 31:9; 34:4)

46. **NAAMAN** Syrian military leader who was healed of leprosy by the prophet Elisha (2 Kings 5:14; Luke 4:27)

47. **NAOMI** Ruth's mother-in-law and the great-great-grandmother of King David (Ruth 1:3–6; 4:18–21)

48. **NEBUCHADNEZZAR** Founder and king of the Neo-Babylonian Empire who had the three godly Hebrew men thrown into a fiery furnace. Later, he promoted both them and Daniel. (Dan. 3–4)

49. **NEHEMIAH** Led the final of three return trips from Persia to Jerusalem after the Babylonian captivity. He rebuilt the walls around the city. (Neh. 7:1)

50. **NOAH** Constructed a ship at God's command and survived the great flood along with his wife, three sons, and their three wives (Gen. 6:9; 8:19)

51. **RACHEL** The beloved wife of Jacob and mother of Joseph and Benjamin (Gen. 29;18; 30:23–24; 35:16–20)

52. **RAHAB** The former harlot who saved the lives of two Israelite spies in Jericho and later was included in the genealogy of Jesus Christ (Josh. 2:6; Matt. 1:5)

53. **REBEKAH** She was the wife of Isaac and mother of Esau and Jacob (Gen. 24:67; 25:24–26)

54. **RUTH** Naomi's daughter-in-law, Boaz's wife, and King David's great-grandmother (Ruth 1:14–17; 4:21–22; Matt. 1:5, 16)

55. **SAMSON** Israel's thirteenth military leader during the time of the Judges and the strongest man who ever lived (Judg. 14:6, 19; 15:14)

56. **SAMUEL** A prophet who was raised as a Nazarite in the tabernacle and later anointed Saul and David as kings over Israel (1 Sam. 1:11, 20, 24; 9:27–10:1; 16:13)

57. **SARAH** Abraham's wife and Isaac's mother (Gen. 11:29; 21:1–7)

58. **SAUL** Israel's first king who turned away from God (1 Sam. 10:17–27; 13:13–14; 1 Chron. 10:13)

59. **SOLOMON** King David's son and the wisest man who ever lived. He was the author of Proverbs, Ecclesiastes, and Song of Songs. (2 Sam. 12:24; 1 Kings 3:11–12)

60. **ZERUBBABEL** A political leader who organized and led the first of three return trips from Babylon and Persia following the Babylonian captivity (Ezra 2:2)

New Testament

61. **ANANIAS** A devout and well respected believer living in Damascus who ministered to the blinded Saul of Tarsus following his conversion (Acts 9:10–18; 22:12–16)

62. **ANDREW** A former fisherman and one of the twelve apostles who brought his brother Peter to Christ (Mark 1:16; Matt. 10:2; John 1:40–42)

63. **APOLLOS** A gifted teacher and preacher from Alexandria who ministered in Ephesus, Greece, and Corinth (Acts 18:24–28; 1 Cor. 1:12; 3:6)

64. **BARNABAS** A godly teacher, the cousin of John Mark, who initially ministered in Antioch and later joined up with Paul during his first missionary journey (Acts 4:36; 11:22–26; 13:1–3)

65. **CAIAPHAS** The wicked high priest who plotted the death of Jesus and who later persecuted the leaders of the early church (Matt. 26:3–5, 62–65; Acts 4:6–7)

66. **CORNELIUS** A God-seeking military commander living in Caesarea who was eventually led to Christ by Simon Peter (Acts 10)

67. **ELIZABETH** The wife of Zechariah (a Jewish priest) who supernaturally gave birth to John the Baptist in her old age (Luke 1:5–7, 57–60)

68. **HEROD ANTIPAS** The ruling son of Herod the Great who beheaded John the Baptist and later ridiculed Jesus during one of the Savior's unfair trials (Matt. 14:10–11; Luke 23:10–11)

69. **HEROD THE GREAT** King of Judea and a great builder who remodeled the second Jewish temple and later attempted to kill the infant Jesus in Bethlehem (Matt. 2)

70. **JAMES THE APOSTLE** Former fisherman, the brother of John, and the first of the twelve apostles to be martyred for Christ (Matt. 4:21; 10:2; Acts 12:1–2)

71. **JAMES THE BROTHER OF JESUS** An unbeliever prior to Jesus' resurrection, pastored the Jerusalem church, and authored the book of James (John 7:3–5; 1 Cor. 15:7; Acts 15:13; 21:17–18; James 1:1)

72. **JOHN THE APOSTLE** Former fisherman, the brother of James, the beloved disciple of Jesus, and author of the gospel of John, First, Second, and Third John, and the book of Revelation (Matt. 4:18-22; Rev. 1:1)

73. **JOHN THE BAPTIST** The miracle child of elderly Elizabeth. The Nazarite evangelist who introduced Jesus, baptized him, and was martyred for his preaching (Luke 1:5–17; John 1:29; Matt. 3:13–17; 14:1–11)

74. **JOSEPH** The husband of Mary, and the godly, legal (but not physical) father of Jesus (Matt. 1:18–35)

75. **JUDAS ISCARIOT** The dishonest and demon-possessed apostle of Jesus who betrayed his master for 30 pieces of silver and then committed suicide (John 12:4–5; 6:70–71; Matt. 26:14–15; 27:5)

76. **LAZARUS** The brother of Mary and Martha whom Christ raised from the dead at Bethany (John 11)

77. **LUKE** A Gentile physician who travelled with Paul and the author of the gospel of Luke and the book of Acts (Acts 1:1; 16:8–10; Luke 1:1-4)

78. **LYDIA** A business woman and Paul's first female convert in Greece (Acts 16:14–15)

79. **MARK** The cousin of Barnabas who initially failed in the ministry. He was later restored and wrote the gospel of Mark (Acts 13:13; 2 Tim. 4:11)

80. **MARTHA** The sister of Mary who reaffirmed her faith in Jesus during the funeral of her brother Lazarus and then witnessed him being raised from the dead by the Savior (John 11)

81. **MARY, THE MOTHER OF JESUS** The virgin wife of Joseph who was chosen to give birth to the Savior of the world (Luke 1:26-38; 2:7)

82. **MARY MAGDALENE** A demon-possessed woman who was delivered by Jesus and later became the first person to see the resurrected Christ (Luke 8:2; John 20:16)

83. **MARY, SISTER OF MARTHA** She worshiped at the feet of Jesus, witnessed him raising her dead brother Lazarus, and would later anoint the body of the Savior (Luke 10:39; John 11:43; 12:1–3)

84. **MATTHEW** Former tax collector, called by Jesus to become an apostle. He would later author the book of Matthew. (Matt. 9:9; 10:3)

85. **NATHANAEL** Also known as Bartholomew. He was introduced to Christ and later was called to become one of the twelve apostles. (John 1:45–51; Mt. 10:3)

86. **NICODEMUS** A well known Pharisee and teacher. He was introduced to Christ during a midnight visit and would later help prepare Jesus' crucified body for burial. (John 3:1–15; 19:39)

87. **PAUL** A missionary, church planter, soul-winner, and theologian. He authored at least 13 of the 27 New Testament books before being martyred in Rome (Acts 13:2–3; 20:17-21; 2 Tim. 4:6–8)

88. **PETER** A fisherman who became a disciple of Jesus, denied Jesus three times, and became the spokesman at Pentecost. He authored 1 and 2 Peter. (Matt. 4:18; Luke 22:54–62; Acts 2:14–40)

89. **PHILEMON** He received a letter from the apostle Paul, urging him to forgive and restore his escaped slave Onesimus, a new convert who was returning home. (Book of Philemon)

90. **PHILIP THE APOSTLE** He led his friend Nathanael to Christ shortly after his own conversion and later was called to serve as one of the twelve apostles. (John 1:43; Matt. 10:3)

91. **PHILIP THE EVANGELIST** One of the original seven deacons in the Jerusalem church who later became a powerful evangelist (Acts 6:3–5; 8:6–8, 27–39)

92. **PILATE** The Roman governor who was pressured by the Jewish leaders to release the guilty Barabbas and to scourge and crucify the innocent Jesus (Matt. 27:2, 15–26)

93. **PRISCILLA** She and her husband, tent-makers by trade, instructed Apollos in the Scriptures and assisted the apostle Paul in his ministry (Acts 18:1–3, 24–26; Rom. 16:3–4)

94. **SILAS** Paul's faithful companion during the second missionary journey (Acts 15:40)

95. **STEPHEN** One of the original seven deacons. He ministered as an evangelist, was arrested, condemned, and stoned to death. He was the church's first martyr. (Acts 6–7)

96. **THOMAS** Known as the doubting apostle. He initially did not believe in Christ's resurrection until Jesus personally appeared to him. He had an unnamed twin brother. (John 20:19–29)

97. **TIMOTHY** One of Paul's most faithful associates. Paul addressed 1 and 2 Timothy to this godly undershepherd. (1 Tim. 1:2; 6:11; 2 Tim. 1:5)

98. **TITUS** A Greek Gentile, pastoring on the Isle of Crete. One of Paul's most trusted associates who later received a letter from Paul. (Book of Titus)

99. **ZACCHAEUS** This dishonest tax collector met Jesus while in a sycamore tree and immediately accepted Jesus as Savior. (Luke 19:1–10)

100. **ZECHARIAH** A priest who was visited by the angel Gabriel. The angel Gabriel predicted his wife would present him with a son, John the Baptist. (Luke 1:5–25, 57–80)

100 Prayers in the Bible

Genesis
1. Abraham's prayer for Lot (18:23-33)
2. Abraham's servant's prayer regarding the solution of a bride for Isaac (24:12–14)
3. Jacob's prayer before he wrestled with God at the brook of Jabbok (32:9–12)
4. Jacob's prayer in Egypt for his two favorite grandsons (48:15–16)

Exodus
5. Moses' prayer beside the burning bush as God instructs him to return to Egypt (3–4)
6. Moses' prayer at Rephidim regarding water for his people to drink (17:4–5)
7. Moses' prayer at Rephidim that God would give Joshua victory over the Amalekites (17:16)
8. Moses' prayer that God would forgive Israel for worshiping the Golden Calf (32:11–14, 31)
9. Moses' prayer to view God's glory (33:18)

Numbers
10. Moses' prayer that God's glory would continue to guide and protect Israel (10:35–36)
11. Moses' prayer for strength and help in governing Israel (11:10–15)
12. Moses' prayer that God would heal Miriam of leprosy (12:13)
13. Moses' three-fold prayer for Israel, pleading with God that he not destroy the people:
    - Following their refusal to enter the Promised Land (14)
    - Following Korah's rebellion (16)
    - Following their complaint regarding lack of bread and water (21:6–7)
14. Moses' prayer that God would bless his successor, Joshua (27:15–17)

Deuteronomy
15. Moses' unsuccessful prayer to enter the Promised Land (3:23)
16. Moses' prayer for Israel and Aaron following the Golden Calf episode (9:18–21)

Joshua
17. Joshua's prayers as he met the captain of the Lord's hosts (5:13–15)
18. Joshua's prayer following Israel's defeat at Ai (7:6–9)
19. Joshua's prayer for additional sunlight at Aijalon (10:12–15)

Judges
20. Gideon's prayer for a sign (6:17–18)
21. Manoah's prayer for his unborn son Samson (13:8)
22. Samson's prayer for supernatural strength that he might destroy his enemies (16:28)

1 Samuel
23. Hannah's prayer of petition; asking God to give her a son (1:10–11)
24. Hannah's prayer of praise; thanking God for giving her a son (2:1–10)

2 Samuel
25. David's prayer thanking God for the permanent establishment of his kingdom (7:25)
26. David's prayer asking God to permit his infant son to live (12:16)

1 Kings
27. Solomon's prayer asking God for wisdom (3:9)
28. Solomon's prayer of dedication at the completion of the temple (8:23–24)
29. Elijah's three-fold prayer:
    - That God would raise up a dead child (17:20–21)
    - That God would send fire to consume a sacrifice (18:36–38)
    - That God would take away his life (19:3–4)

2 Kings
30. Elisha's prayer that God would raise up a dead child (4:33)
31. Elisha's prayer that his servant see the angelic army that was protecting them (6:17)
32. Hezekiah's prayer that God would save Jerusalem from the Assyrian army (19:14–19)

1 Chronicles	**33.** Jabez's prayer that God would change his border (4:10)
	34. David's prayer that Jerusalem not be destroyed by a plague (21:17)
	35. David's prayer at the dedication of the building materials for the new temple (21:26)
2 Chronicles	**36.** Asa's prayer that God would deliver Jerusalem from the Ethiopian army (14:11)
	37. Manasseh's prayer for forgiveness regarding his many wicked acts (33)
Ezra	**38.** Ezra's prayer, confessing the sins of the Jewish remnant following the exile (8:21–23)
Nehemiah	**39.** Nehemiah's two-fold prayer (1:5–11): • In Persia: that God would forgive the returning Jews already in Jerusalem • To give him favor in the sight of King Artaxerxes
	40. The prayer of praise and confession by the Levites after rebuilding Jerusalem's wall (9)
Job	**41.** Job's two-fold prayer after hearing and seeing God (42:1–6): • Job's worthlessness • God's sovereignty
Psalms	**42.** The psalmist thanks God who cared for him as an earthly father and mother would (27)
	43. The psalmist thanks God for encouragement in a time of great discouragement (28)
	44. The psalmist thanks God for the permanence of the divine king and kingdom (45)
	45. David confesses his sins of adultery and murder and prays for cleansing (51)
	46. The psalmist asks God to judge all enemies of righteousness and truth (69)
	47. The psalmist contrasts the morality of man with the eternality of God (90)
	48. The psalmist offers up a prayer of praise (103)
	49. The psalmist thanks God for God's word (119:11)
	50. The psalmist thanks God for his omniscience, omnipotence, and omnipresence (139)
Isaiah	**51.** Isaiah's prayer that God would use him (6:8)
	52. Israel's prayer of praise during the millennium (12)
Jeremiah	**53.** Jeremiah's prayer of protest regarding his call to preach (1:6)
	54. Jeremiah's questions regarding God's dealing with Israel (12:1–6)
	55. Jeremiah's prayer regarding Israel's sin (14:1–10)
	56. Jeremiah's questions regarding his own ministry (15:5–21)
	57. Jeremiah's bitter complaint to God (20:7–8)
Lamentations	**58.** Jeremiah's prayer of total despair (3)
Daniel	**59.** Daniel's confessional prayer for both himself and his people (9)
Jonah	**60.** The prayer by some frightened pagan sailors (1:14)
	61. Jonah's prayer of rededication from the belly of a fish (2:2–9)
Micah	**62.** Micah's prayer of praise for God's forgiveness of his people (7)
Habakkuk	**63.** Habakkuk's prayer thanking God for his mercy, power, and salvation (3)
Matthew, Mark, Luke, John	**Prayers prayed by Jesus:** **64.** Before choosing his twelve disciples, for wisdom in their selection (Luke 6:12–13) **65.** Thanking the Father for revealing great truths to the 70 disciples (Matt. 11:25–30) **66.** Asking that Lazarus be raised to prove the Father had sent the Son (John 11:41–42)

Matthew, Mark, Luke, John

67. Asking the father to comfort his troubled soul and glorify the Father's name (John 12:27–28)

68. He prays for himself, his disciples, and all believers (John 17)

69. Asking that his Father's will be done three times in the Garden of Gethsemane (Mark 14:35–41)

70. His three-fold prayer on the cross:
- First prayer: "Father, forgive them" (Luke 23:24)
- Second prayer: "My God, my God, why have you forsaken me?" (Mark 15:34)
- Third prayer: "Father, into your hands I commit my spirit" (Luke 23:46)

Luke

71. Zechariah's prayer for a son (1:11–20)

72. Simeon's prayers at the dedication of the infant Jesus (2:29–30)

73. The publican's prayer for forgiveness (18:13)

Acts

74. The prayer session of the 120 in the Upper Room just prior to Pentecost (1:14)

75. The apostles' prayer of thanking God for the privilege of suffering for him (4:23–30)

76. The apostles' prayer for the newly selected deacons (6:6)

77. The prayer of the dying Stephen asking God to forgive those who were stoning him (7:59–60)

78. The prayer of Peter and John that the Samaritans would receive the Holy Spirit (8:15)

79. Paul's prayer of submission upon seeing the resurrected Christ en route to Damascus (9:5)

80. Peter's prayer that God would raise up Dorcas from the dead (9:40)

81. Cornelius's prayer that he might be saved (10:2)

82. The prayer of the Jerusalem church that Peter might be released from prison (12:5)

83. The prayer of the Antioch church for the missionary efforts of Paul and Barnabas (13:1–3)

84. The midnight prayer of the imprisoned Paul and Silas at Philippi (16:25)

85. Paul's prayer for the Ephesian elders who had met him in Miletus (20:32)

86. Paul's prayer for some disciples at Tyre (21:5)

87. Paul's prayer for the healing of Publius's sick father on the Isle of Malta (28:8)

Romans, 2 Corinthians

88. Paul's prayer for Israel's salvation (10:1)

89. Paul's prayer that God would remove his thorn in the flesh (12:8)

Ephesians

90. Paul's first prayer for the Ephesian church (1:17–23)

91. Paul's second prayer for the Ephesian church (3:14–19)

Colossians, Philemon, Hebrews, Revelation

92. Paul's prayer for the church at Colosse (1:9–14)

93. Paul's prayer for Philemon (4–7)

94. The author of Hebrews' prayer for believers (13:20–21)

95. Heaven's two-fold prayer of praise to God:
- Thanking him for his great work in creation (4:11)
- Thanking him for his great work in redemption (5:9–14)

96. The prayer of the martyred souls in heaven (6:10)

97. The prayer of the saved multitude during the great tribulation (7:10–12)

98. The prayer of the heavenly saints thanking God for Christ's millennial reign (11:15)

99. The heavenly saints thanking God for the marriage of Christ and his bride the church (19:6–8)

100. The prayer of John that Christ would soon appear (22:20)

TABLE OF WEIGHTS AND MEASURES

WEIGHT

BIBLE	US/IMPERIAL	METRIC
Old Testament		
talent (60 minas)	75 pounds	34 kilograms
mina (50 shekels)	1.25 pounds	0.6 kilogram
shekel (2 bekas)	0.4 ounce	11.3 grams
pim (0.66 shekel)	0.33 ounce	9.4 grams
beka (10 gerahs)	0.2 ounce	5.7 grams
gerah	0.02 ounce	0.6 gram
New Testament		
pound (Roman litra)	12 ounces	340.2 grams

LENGTH

BIBLE	US/IMPERIAL	METRIC
Old Testament		
cubit (2 spans)	18 inches	46 centimeters
span (3 handbreadths)	9 inches	23 centimeters
handbreadth (4 fingers)	3 inches	7.6 centimeters
finger	0.75 inch	1.9 centimeters
New Testament		
mile (8 stadions)	4858 feet	1.5 kilometers
stadion (100 fathoms)	200 yards	183 meters
reed (3 paces)	9 feet	2.7 meters
fathom (2 paces)	6 feet	1.8 meters
pace	3 feet	0.91 meters

LIQUID MEASURES

BIBLE	US/IMPERIAL	METRIC
Old Testament		
cor or homer (10 baths)	58 gallons	220 liters
bath (6 hins)	5.8 gallon	22 liters
hin (12 logs)	1 gallon	3.8 liters
kab or cab	1.3 quarts	1.23 liters
log	0.7 pint	0.3 liter
New Testament		
firkin	10 gallons	39.9 liters

TABLE OF WEIGHTS AND MEASURES

DRY MEASURE

BIBLE	US/IMPERIAL	METRIC
Old Testament		
cor or homer (10 ephahs)	6 bushels	218 liters
lethek (5 ephahs)	3 bushels	109 liters
ephah (10 omers)	23 quarts	18.9 liters
seah	7.7 quarts	7.3 liters
omer	2.3 quarts	2.2 liters
kab or cab	1.3 quarts	1.2 liters
New Testament		
bushel	7.7 quarts	7.3 liters
measure	1.2 quarts	1.1 liters
pots	1.2 pints	0.6 liter

MONEY IN THE BIBLE

MONETARY VALUES

NAME (EQUIVALENT)	VALUE
Old Testament	
shekel	$0.32 – $9.60*
mina (50 shekels)	$16.00 – $480.00
talent (60 minas)	$960.00 – $28,000.00
New Testament	
mite or lepton	$0.0012
farthing or quadran (2 mites)	$0.0024
penny (1 Roman denarius)	$0.16 (daily wage of a laborer)
mina or pound (100 Roman denarii)	$16.00
talent (240 Roman aurei)	$960.00

*value depends on weight of currency (light or heavy) and type of currency (silver or gold)

How We Got the Bible

TEN KEY POINTS

1. The Bible is inspired by God (2 Timothy 3:16-17; 2 Peter 1:20-21).

2. The Bible is made up of 66 different books that were written over 1,600 years (from approximately 1500 BC to AD 100) by more than 40 kings, prophets, leaders, and followers of Jesus. The Old Testament has 39 books (written approximately 1500-400 BC). The New Testament has 27 books (written approximately AD 45-100). The Hebrew Bible has the same text as the English Bible's Old Testament, but divides and arranges it differently.

3. The Old Testament was written mainly in Hebrew, with some Aramaic. The New Testament was written in Greek.

4. The books of the Bible were collected and arranged and recognized as inspired sacred authority by councils of rabbis and councils of church leaders based on careful guidelines.

5. Before the printing press was invented, the Bible was copied by hand. The Bible was copied very accurately, in many cases by special scribes who developed intricate methods of counting words and letters to ensure that no errors had been made.

6. The Bible was the first book ever printed on the printing press with moveable type (Gutenberg Press, 1455, Latin Bible).

7. There is much evidence that the Bible we have today is remarkably true to the original writings. Of the thousands of copies made by hand before 1500, nearly 5,900 Greek manuscripts from the New Testament alone still exist today. The text of the Bible is better preserved than the writings of Plato or Aristotle.

8. The discovery of the Dead Sea Scrolls confirmed the astonishing reliability of some of the copies of the Old Testament made over the years. Although some spelling variations exist, no variation affects basic Bible doctrines.

9. As the Bible was carried to other countries, it was translated into the common language of the people by scholars who wanted others to know God's Word. Today there are still 2,000 groups with no Bible in their own language.

10. By AD 200, the Bible was translated into seven languages; by 500, 13 languages; by 900, 17 languages; by 1400, 28 languages; by 1800, 57 languages; by 1900, 537 languages; by 1980, 1,100 languages; by 2014, 2,883 languages had some portions of Scripture.
(Source: The Wycliffe Global Alliance)

Old Testament Written
(approx. 1500-400 BC)

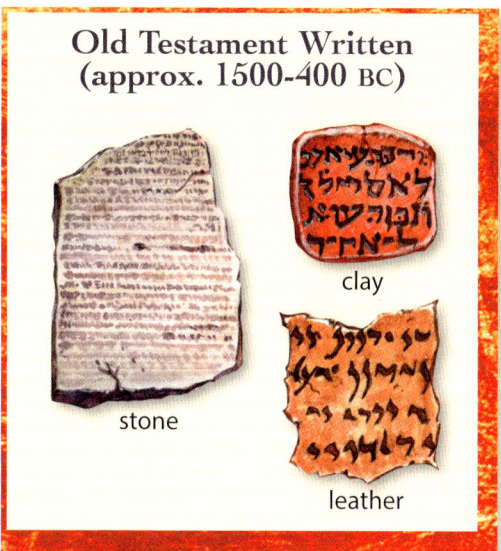

stone
clay
leather

New Testament Written
(approx. AD 45-100)

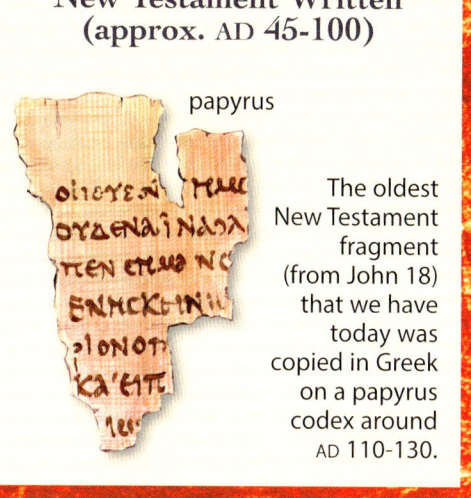

papyrus

The oldest New Testament fragment (from John 18) that we have today was copied in Greek on a papyrus codex around AD 110-130.

Bible Copied on Papyrus

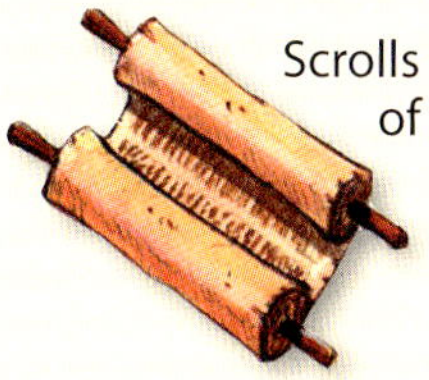

Scrolls of leather, and later of papyrus, were used to make copies of the Scriptures.

A papyrus codex is a bound volume made from sheets folded and sewn together, sometimes with a cover. They were used more than scrolls after AD 1-100.

Bible Copied on Fine Animal Skins

Fine quality animal skins from calves or antelope (vellum) and sheep or goats (parchment) were used for over 1,000 years to make copies of the Bible approximately AD 300-1400. Two of the oldest vellum copies (AD 325-350) that exist today are the Vatican Codex and the Sinaitic Codex.

Bible Printed by Printing Press after 1455

Wycliffe Bibles were inscribed by hand on vellum in the 1300s-1400s. Some copies took ten months to two years to produce and cost a year's wage.

The Bible was the first book to be printed with Gutenberg's printing press in 1455.

The Bible, God's Word to the World

The Bible is now printed on paper in many languages. It is also available in many digital formats.

32 • How We Got the Bible

2000 BC

Old Testament events are written down in Hebrew (portions in Aramaic) over centuries. In Exodus, the Lord tells Moses to write in a book. Other Old Testament writers, inspired by God, include leaders, kings and prophets. Together, these writings on leather scrolls and other materials are called the Hebrew Scriptures or Old Testament.

500 BC

Ezra, a priest and scribe, collects and arranges some of the books of the Hebrew Bible—the Old Testament—about 450 BC, according to Jewish tradition.

The Septuagint is the Greek translation of the Hebrew Bible (the Old Testament). It is translated in 250-100 BC by Jewish scholars in Alexandria, Egypt. (The word *Septuagint* means seventy, referring to the tradition that 70 or 72 men translated it. It is often abbreviated LXX, the Roman numeral for seventy.)

200 BC

The books are arranged by subject: historical, poetic, and prophetic. It includes the Apocrypha (meaning "hidden"), referring to seven books that were included in the Hebrew Bible until AD 90 when they were removed by Jewish elders.

A Scribe

Papyrus, a plant, is cut into strips and pressed into sheets of writing material and can be made into a scroll or a codex. The New Testament books were probably first written on papyrus scrolls. Later Christians begin to copy them on sheets of papyrus which are bound and placed between two pieces of wood for covers. This form of early book is known as a codex.

Papyrus

AD 1

Time of Jesus
4 BC–AD 33?

Jesus quotes the Old Testament (Scriptures) often. He says that he did not come to destroy the Scriptures, but to fulfill them. He says to his disciples, "This is what I told you while I was still with you: Everything must be fulfilled that is written about me in the Law of Moses, the Prophets and the Psalms." Then he opened their minds so they could understand the Scriptures. (Luke 24:44-45)

AD 100

Followers of Jesus
Matthew, Mark, Luke, John, Paul, James, Peter, and Jude write the Gospels, history, letters to other Christians, and the Revelation between AD 45 and 100. The writers quote from all but eight of the Old Testament books. These writings in Greek are copied and circulated so that by about 150 there is wide enough use of them to speak of the "New Testament" ("New Covenant"). The new covenant God made with people was promised in Jer. 31:31-34 and referred to by Jesus (Lk. 22:20) and Paul (1 Cor. 11:25) and in the letter to the Hebrews.

AD 200

Early Coptic Translation

Old Testament Apocrypha
Evidence derived from first century AD writers Philo and Josephus indicates that the Hebrew canon did not include the Apocrypha.

Earliest Translations
200-300 Latin, Coptic (Egypt), and Syriac (Syria).

Church Fathers accept the writings of the Gospels and Paul's letters as *canonical* (from a Greek word referring to the *rule* of faith and truth). Origen lists 21 approved New Testament books. Eusebius lists 22 accepted books.

AD 300

The New Testament books are collected and circulated throughout the Mediterranean about the time of Constantine, the Roman emperor who legalizes Christianity in 313. By 400 the standard of 27 New Testament books is accepted in the East and West as confirmed by Athanasius, Jerome, Augustine and three church councils. The 27 books of the New Testament were formally confirmed as canonical by the Synod of Carthage in 397, thus recognizing three centuries of use by followers of Christ.

*Saint Matthew
Lindisfarne Gospels
Approximately 900*

Jerome starts translating the Scriptures into Latin in 382 and finishes 23 years later. This translation, called the Latin Vulgate, remains the basic Bible for many centuries.

Jerome

How We Got the Bible • 33

AD 500

Roman Empire declines. Germanic migrations (378-600) cause new languages to emerge.

The Masoretes are special Jewish scribes entrusted with the sacred task of making copies of the Hebrew Scriptures (Old Testament) approximately 500-900. They develop a meticulous system of counting the number of words in each book of the Bible to make sure they have copied it accurately. Any scroll found to have an error is buried according to Jewish law.

AD 600

Christianity reaches Britain before 300, but Anglo-Saxon pagans drive Christian Britons into Wales (450-600). In 596, Augustine of Canterbury begins evangelization again.

Caedmon, an illiterate monk, retells portions of Scripture in Anglo-Saxon (Old English) poetry and song (676).

Aldhelm of Sherborne, 709, is said to have translated the Psalms.

Bede

Bede, a monk and scholar, makes an Old English (Anglo-Saxon) translation of portions of Scripture. On his deathbed in 735, he finishes translating the Book of John.

Alfred The Great, King of Wessex (871-901) translates portions of Exodus, Psalms, and Acts.

Aldred, Bishop of Durham, inserts a translation in the Northumbrian dialect between the lines of the Lindisfarne Gospels (950).

Aelfric (955-1020) translates portions of the Old Testament.

AD 1300

Normans conquer England (1066) and make French the official language. No English translation work produced until the 1300s.

Middle English emerges, popularized by works such as the *Canterbury Tales* and Richard Rolle's *Psalter* (1340).

John Wycliffe

First English Bible is translated from Latin in 1382 and is called the Wycliffe Bible in honor of priest and Oxford scholar John Wycliffe. During his lifetime, Wycliffe had wanted common people to have the Bible. He also criticized a number of church practices and policies. His followers, derisively called Lollards (meaning "mumblers"), included his criticisms in the preface to the Wycliffe Bible. This Bible is banned and burned. Forty years after Wycliffe's death, his bones are exhumed and burned for heresy.

In 1408, in England, it becomes illegal to translate or read the Bible in common English without permission of a bishop.

World's first printing press with moveable metal type is invented in 1455 in Germany by Johann Gutenberg. This invention is perhaps the single most important event to influence the spread of the Bible.

The Gutenberg Bible is the first book ever printed. This Latin Vulgate version is often illuminated by artists who hand paint letters and ornaments on each page.

Gutenberg Bible Page

AD 1500

Erasmus, a priest and Greek scholar, publishes a new Greek edition and a more accurate Latin translation of the New Testament in 1516. His goal is that everyone be able to read the Bible, from the farmer in the field to the weaver at the loom. Erasmus' Greek text forms the basis of the *"textus receptus"* and is used later by Martin Luther, William Tyndale, and the King James translators.

Erasmus

Martin Luther translates the New Testament into German in 1522.

William Tyndale, priest and Oxford scholar, translates the New Testament from Greek (1525), but cannot get approval to publish it in England. He moves to Germany and prints Bibles, smuggling them into England in sacks of corn and flour. In 1535 he publishes part of the Old Testament translated from Hebrew. In 1536, Tyndale is strangled and burned at the stake. His final words are "Lord, open the King of England's eyes."

Tyndale is called the "Father of the English Bible" because his translation forms the basis of the King James Version. Much of the style and vocabulary we know as "biblical English" is traceable to his work.

William Tyndale

34 • How We Got the Bible

AD 1500

The Coverdale Bible is translated by Miles Coverdale (1535) and dedicated to Anne Boleyn, one of King Henry VIII's wives. This is the first complete Bible to be printed in English.

Tyndale's Initials printed in the Matthew's Bible

The Matthew's Bible, translated by John Rogers under the pen name "Thomas Matthew," is the first Bible published with the king's permission (1537). Printed just one year after Tyndale's death, its New Testament relies heavily on Tyndale's version, and even has a tribute to him on the last page of the Old Testament. Tyndale's initials are printed in 2 ½-inch block letters. Later Thomas Cromwell, advisor to King Henry VIII, entrusts Coverdale to revise Matthew's Bible to make the Great Bible.

The Great Bible (1539) is placed in every church by order of Thomas Cranmer, archbishop under King Henry VIII. This Bible is chained to the church pillars to discourage theft.

The "Chained Bible"

AD 1555

England's Queen Mary bans Protestant translations of the English Bible. John Rogers and Thomas Cranmer are burned at the stake. Later some 300 men, women and children are also burned.

The Geneva Bible Exiles from England flee to Geneva, Switzerland, and in 1560 print the Geneva Bible, a complete revision of the Great Bible with the Old Testament translated from Hebrew. The Geneva Bible contains theological notes from Protestant scholars John Calvin, Beza, Knox, and Whittingham. It is the first Bible to use Roman type instead of black letter. This is the Bible of Shakespeare and the one carried to America by the Pilgrims in 1620. The 1640 edition is the first English Bible to omit the Apocrypha.

AD 1600

Bishops Bible A new translation begins under Queen Elizabeth in 1568. It is translated by several bishops of the Church of England in answer to the Geneva Bible.

Rheims-Douai Bible was translated into English from the Latin Vulgate by Catholic scholar Gregory Martin, while in exile in France (New Testament in 1582/Old Testament in 1609). It becomes the standard translation for the Catholic church.

King James Bible Page from 1611 version

King James Version or Authorized Version King James I of England commissions 54 scholars to undertake a new Bible translation. Over the next six years, six teams of scholars using the Bishops Bible and Tyndale's Bible, as well as available Greek and Hebrew manuscripts, complete the new version in 1611. The King James Version (also called the "Authorized Version," even though King James never gave the finished version his royal approval) is revised several times. The edition used today was revised in 1769.

The King James Version remained the most popular Bible for more than 300 years.

King James

AD 1800

Older Manuscripts Discovered! Between 1629 and 1947, several of the earliest known copies of the Bible are found.

Codex Alexandrinus, a copy of the New Testament from approximately 400, perhaps the best copy of the book of Revelation, is made available to western scholars in 1629.

Codex Sinaiticus (earliest complete copy of the New Testament, copied in approximately 350) is found in St. Catherine's Monastery near Mt. Sinai.

The Revised Version (1885) In 1870, scholars in England decide to revise the King James Version to reflect the findings from the manuscripts discovered during the two previous centuries. Their goal is to use better Hebrew and Greek texts and to retranslate words based on new linguistic information about ancient Hebrew.

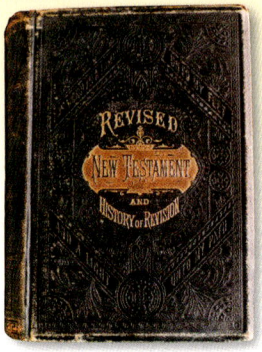
The Revised Version

Codex Vaticanus (earliest and probably best copy known of the New Testament from approximately 350) is released to scholars in 1889 by the Vatican Library.

How We Got the Bible • 35

AD 1900

The Dead Sea Scrolls, found in a cave in 1947 by a shepherd, contain the oldest known copies of portions of the Old Testament. These copies were made between 100 BC and AD 100.

A Qumran Cave near the Dead Sea

A Scroll of Isaiah that is part of the Dead Sea Scrolls is the oldest complete manuscript of any book of the Bible (copied around 100). The copies of Isaiah discovered in the Qumran caves prove to be remarkably close to the standard Hebrew Bible, varying slightly in the spelling of some names. They give overwhelming confirmation of the reliability of the Masoretic copies.

During the 1900s more than a hundred New Testament manuscripts are found in Egypt.

A Ugaritic Grammar is published in the 1960s. Ugaritic is an ancient language similar to Hebrew and helps scholars understand Hebrew vocabulary and poetry.

Scroll of Isaiah

AD 1900

Modern Translations
The knowledge from newly discovered manuscripts has led to hundreds of new translations.

1885
The English Revised Version
A British revision of the King James Version.

1901
American Standard Version (ASV)
Revision of the King James Version in American English.

1926
Moffatt Bible
A very popular modern-language version.

1931
Smith-Goodspeed, An American Translation
Modern American English.

1952
The Revised Standard Version (RSV)
A revision of the ASV. New Testament revised 1971.

1958
J.B. Phillips' New Testament in Modern English
A paraphrase, originally made for youth.

1965
The Amplified Bible
Uses word-for-word ASV with added words to communicate insights on original texts.

1966
Jerusalem Bible
Translation by Catholic scholars in Jerusalem. The New Jerusalem Bible, 1985.

1970
New English Bible
"Timeless" modern English. Revised in 1989.

1970
New American Bible (NAB)
Official version of the Catholic Church. Revised New Testament in 1986.

1971
New American Standard Bible (NASB)
Literal word-for-word translation. Updated in 1995.

1971
The Living Bible
Popular paraphrase.

1976
The Good News Bible (Today's English Version) (TEV)
Vernacular English translation.

1978
New International Version (NIV)
Dignified, readable.

1982
New King James Version (NKJV)
Modernization of the King James Version using the same manuscripts.

AD 2000

1987
New Century Version (NCV)
Puts biblical concepts into natural terms.

1989
Jewish New Testament
English translation using traditional Jewish expressions.

1989
New Revised Standard Version
"Gender neutral" revision of the RSV.

1991
Contemporary English Version
"Natural, uncomplicated" English.

1995
God's Word
Contemporary English.

1996
New Living Translation (NLT)
A revision of The Living Bible to make it a translation.

1996
New International Reader's Version (NIrV)
A simplified version of the NIV with a 3rd- or 4th-grade reading level.

2001
English Standard Version (ESV)
Literal update of the RSV.

2002
The Message (MSG)
A paraphrase from the original languages.

2004
Holman Christian Standard Bible (HCSB)
Balance between word-for-word and thought-for-thought.

2005
Today's New International Version (TNIV)
Modernization of the New International Version.

2005
New English Translation (NET)
Available only on the Internet, with extensive translator's notes.

THE DEAD SEA SCROLLS

WHAT ARE THE DEAD SEA SCROLLS?

The Dead Sea Scrolls are a collection of 931 documents discovered over a half century ago in a region of the Judean desert in what is today called the West Bank. The scrolls date from different periods—as early as 300 BC to AD 40—and were hidden in caves along the edge of the Dead Sea. The discovery of the Dead Sea Scrolls is the greatest literary and archaeological discovery of our time. The scrolls are not the original documents that make up the Hebrew Bible (the Old Testament), but they are the oldest copies of those documents that we have today. The Dead Sea Scrolls have shed new light on the practice of the Jewish religion during the periods when the books of the Bible were composed. They have given us a snapshot of the world Jesus ministered in with his twelve disciples. And they have helped us better understand the society in which the early church first started.

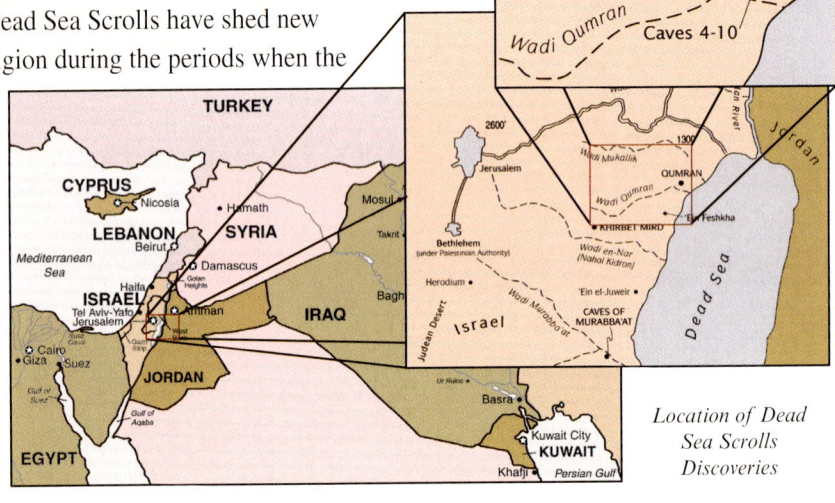

Location of Dead Sea Scrolls Discoveries

The scrolls are believed to be from the "library" of a group of first-century Jews who separated themselves from the rest of society by living out in the desert at a site known as Qumran. The scrolls contain a variety of writings: portions of every book of the Old Testament except the Book of Esther, commentaries on the books of the Bible, rules for religious rituals and community life, texts designed to prepare the Qumran sect for a war at the End of Time, marriage contracts, deeds of sale, calendars, horoscopes, and writings that claimed to foretell the future.

The texts are composed in three languages—Hebrew, Aramaic, and Greek. They are written on leather parchment (made from goat or sheep skins) and papyrus (a form of early paper). One scroll is inscribed on pure copper and is known as the Copper Scroll. It appears to be a treasure map, detailing directions to 66 places throughout the Judean desert where immense amounts of gold, silver, and other precious items were hidden. Due to the secretive and mysterious way the texts were written and the loss of identifying physical features in the region today, all attempts to locate the treasure have thus far proven unsuccessful.

Canonical Division (According to the Hebrew Bible)	Old Testament Book	Number of Qumran and other Manuscripts (?=possible fragment)
Pentateuch (Torah)	Genesis	24
	Exodus	18
	Leviticus	18
	Numbers	11
	Deuteronomy	33
Prophets (Nevi'im) Former Prophets	Joshua	2
	Judges	3
	1-2 Samuel	4
	1-2 Kings	3
Latter Prophets	Isaiah	22
	Jeremiah	6
	Ezekiel	6
	Twelve (Minor) Prophets	10
Writings (Ketubim)	Psalms	39
	Proverbs	2
	Job	6
The Five Scrolls	Song of Songs	4
	Ruth	4
	Lamentation	4
	Ecclesiates	3
	Esther	0*
	Daniel	8
	Ezra-Nehemiah	1
	1-2 Chronicles	1
	Total	231
	Adjusted	223*

*The total has been adjusted to read 8 less, since 6 scrolls from Qumran contain portions of two books (counted 2X), and 1 scroll from Wadi Murabba'at contains portions of 3 books (counted 3x).

Qumran Manuscripts, which are copies of Books of the Old Testament

HOW WERE THE SCROLLS DISCOVERED?

In 1946, shepherds of the Ta'amireh Bedouin tribe settled in a desert area between Bethlehem and the Dead Sea, where they tended their flocks and herds. According to local hearsay, a teenager by the name of Muhammed edh-Dhib ("Muhammed the Wolf") went in search of a stray goat. Believing it to have wandered into one of the caves that honeycombed the limestone cliffs, he threw a rock into the cave to scare it out. Instead of hearing the bleat of a goat, he heard the sound of breaking pottery.

Inside Cave 1

He climbed up into what is today called Cave 1 and found ancient clay storage jars filled with seven scrolls. Four of these scrolls were sold in Bethlehem to an antiquities dealer known as Kando. He in turn sold them for $97.20 to the archbishop of the Monastery of St. Mark's in Jerusalem, the Metropolitan (a high office in the priesthood of the Syrian Orthodox Church) Mar Athanasius Yeshue Samuel. The other three were sold to Feidi Salahi, another antiquities dealer in Bethlehem, who in turn sold them to Hebrew University Professor Eleazar Sukenik in Jerusalem.

The Bedouin shepherds searched more caves, bringing most of their finds to Kando. Meanwhile, the Metropolitan permitted John Trever of the American Schools of Oriental Research to publish news and photographs of the find to the world in April 1948. Soon after, British archaeologists conducted a careful survey of the region and discovered several other caves with scrolls, including those along a terrace at Qumran. Of these, Cave 4 yielded approximately 15,000 fragments representing some 600 manuscripts. These were not found in storage jars but beneath the cave floor, indicating a rapid burial because of impending danger—perhaps the Roman invasion of Jewish territory in AD 68 that led two years later to the complete destruction of Jerusalem. Cave 7 was also unique in that it contained the fragments of 19 texts in Greek—the same language used to write the New Testament.

Cave 4

Shrine of the Book

When the Arab-Israeli war broke out in 1948, the Metropolitan took his four scrolls to the United States and offered them for sale in an ad in the Wall Street Journal. Yigael Yadin, an archaeologist and the son of Professor Sukenik, anonymously purchased the scrolls for the State of Israel for $250,000. Later these four scrolls and three others were put on public display at the Shrine of the Book, a museum built in Jerusalem especially for scrolls. The State of Israel also houses other scrolls in a climate-controlled basement of the Rockefeller Museum in Jerusalem. Some scrolls are located in other countries, such as the Copper Scroll in the Citadel Museum in Amman, Jordan.

WHAT DO WE KNOW ABOUT THE SITE OF THE SCROLLS?

Many of the scrolls were found in Caves 4-10 along the terrace known as Qumran, where archaeologists were quick to notice ancient ruins of buildings. Because the caves would have only been accessible via the Qumran plateau, archaeologists began to investigate a connection between the scrolls and the site.

Archaeologist Roland de Vaux supported the connection with his discovery of pottery kilns that were used to fire the scroll jars and with his excavation of a two-story building that contained the remains of writing benches and ink wells. Roland de Vaux (in the 1950s), Yitzhak Magen (in the 1990s), and Randall Price (as recently as 2005) have uncovered deposits of animal bones overlaid with sherds (broken pottery). The Dead Sea Scrolls speak of ritual meals, and several scholars contend that the animal bone deposits that were found buried in a ritual manner are the remains of these ritual meals.

Qumran Site

Some scholars believe that the site of Qumran may have been originally the biblical "City of Salt" mentioned in a list of cities in this region in Joshua 15:61-62. Scholars have suggested the following time line for the historical development of the Qumran site.

There appears to have been two main phases, one beginning in the time of the Jewish king Alexander Jannaeus (134-104 BC) and continuing until a destruction of buildings in the settlement in 31 BC, and a final phase in the late Second Temple period (4-1 BC) until the destruction of the site in AD 68 by the Roman army's response to the First Jewish Revolt of AD 66-73. Thereafter for a short time the site was turned into a Roman garrison.

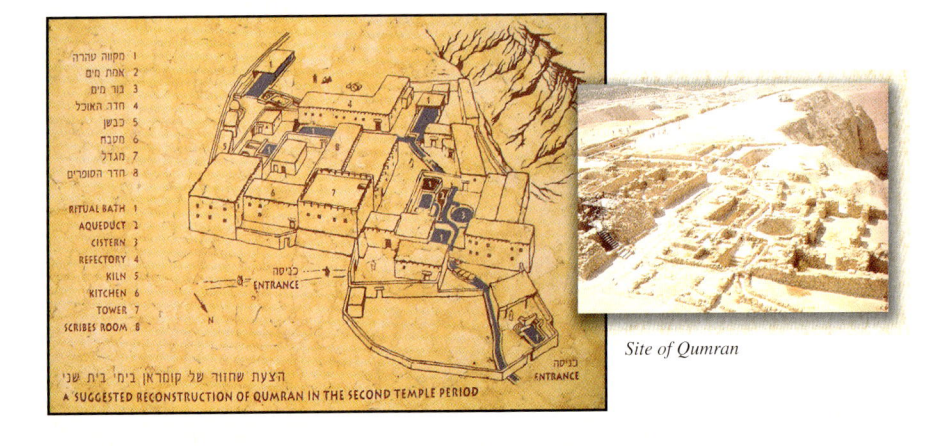

The Dead Sea as seen from Qumran

Site of Qumran

WHAT DO THE SCROLLS TELL US ABOUT THE OLD TESTAMENT?

The ancient keepers of the scrolls purposely hid their treasures, trusting that the God of whom they spoke in those documents would guard those documents until the proper time. That time, it turns out, would be our time, some 2,000 years later. Perhaps the most significant single contribution of the scrolls has been their witness to the earliest known text of the Hebrew Bible.

Portion of a Scroll

Before the discovery of the scrolls, the oldest known complete Hebrew manuscript of the Old Testament was a Masoretic text (made by Jewish scribes called Masoretes), which is known as the Ben Asher Codex located today in the Public Library of Leningrad, Russia. It dates to about AD 1008. Although this Masoretic version of the Bible is ancient, it was still penned 1,000 years after the last book of the Old Testament was written (around 325 BC). But because it was the oldest existing Hebrew manuscript, the Ben Asher Codex served as the basis for the scholarly standard edition of the Hebrew Bible, Kittel's *Biblia Hebraica*, as well as Christian translations of the Old Testament such as the King James Version.

The Dead Sea Scrolls confirm the accuracy of Bible translation over the years, despite skeptics' accusations that these translations were flawed. As copies of copies of copies of the Old Testament books were made over the centuries, many scholars concluded that mistakes may have been introduced into the Masoretic texts. Comparisons with other ancient versions of the Old Testament, such as the Greek Septuagint, Latin Vulgate, and Samaritan Pentateuch, seemed to confirm this "transmission" problem and called into question the integrity and reliability of the traditional Hebrew text.

These doubts were settled with the discovery in Cave 1 of a copy of the entire Book of Isaiah dated to 125 BC. This is 1,000 years earlier than the Masoretic Ben Asher Codex. When compared to the Ben Asher Codex, this scroll proved to be identical to the later version of Isaiah in more than 95 percent of the text. The 5 percent variation consisted primarily of obvious slips of the pen and spelling alterations, many of which are no more significant than the difference in meaning between the word "over" being used in place of the word "above."

This accuracy also proved to be the case for all the other biblical scrolls among the Dead Sea Scrolls. Although interesting differences and additions do appear and are of great value in understanding the history of the transmission of the biblical text, on the whole the witness of the scrolls is to the exceptional preservation of the biblical text through the centuries.

Abbreviations For the Dead Sea Scrolls
Example: 4Q521 2:6
4 = number of the cave in which the document was found
Q = Qumran
521 = designated number for the scroll
2 = column number (abbreviated Col.)
6 = line numbers
This scroll is a reference to Text 521, from Cave 4 at Qumran, column 2, line 6

WHAT DO THE SCROLLS REVEAL ABOUT JEWISH HISTORY?

One thing the scrolls demonstrate is that a number of Jewish groups who separated themselves from society by living in "separatist" communities flourished during what is called the Second Temple Period. The Second Temple Period is the period from 520 BC to AD 70. It is called the "Second Temple" because in 520 BC, the Jews were allowed to rebuild Solomon's temple, which had been destroyed by King Nebuchadnezzar. This second temple stood until it was destroyed by the Romans in AD 70. The separatist Jewish groups included the Pharisees, Sadducees, the Zealots—all of whom we read about in the Gospel stories—as well as the Essenes, and the Siccari. So far as we know, none of these groups left behind documents concerning their sects. The exception would be the authors and collectors of the Dead Sea Scrolls. Some believe the Essenes produced and collected the scrolls. Whether or not scrolls belonged to the Essenes, the texts provide historians with original writings on the beliefs and practices of other sects of this period with which the Qumran Jews interacted.

The discovery of the scrolls shows us that Second Temple Judaism, although similar to the older biblical Judaism we read about in the Old Testament, was not identical to it. Neither was Second Temple Judaism identical to what is called Rabbinic Judaism, which began to emerge after the destruction of the Second Temple in AD 70. As a result, the scrolls give us a snapshot of a moment of great disagreement and change in the Jewish practices and beliefs of the day. For example, in many of the writings, the Qumran Jews condemn what they viewed as the ritual abuses of the priests of the day who ran the temple (the same group of Pharisees that Jesus often criticized). Below is a portion of the War Rule. The War Rule is a scroll that contains a prophecy that God would soon destroy these corrupt Temple Jews, as well as a prophecy about the defeat of the Gentile powers oppressing Israel in an end-of-time battle.

> **The War Rule (Scroll abbreviation: 1QM 1:5-8)**
> Col. 1^5[Then the]re* shall be a time of salvation for the People of God, and a time of dominion for all men of His forces, and the eternal annihilation for all the forces of Belial. ^{6}There shall be g[reat] panic [among] the sons of Japheth, Assyria shall fall with no one to come to his aid, and the supremacy of the Kittim shall cease, that wickedness be overcome without a remnant. ^{7}There shall be no survivors of [all the Sons of] Darkness.
> ^{8}Then [the Sons of Rig]hteousness shall shine to all ends of the world, continuing to shine forth until [the] end of the appointed seasons of darkness.
>
> * [ ] brackets indicate proposed translation or difficult or missing letters or words.

WHAT DO THE SCROLLS REVEAL ABOUT EARLY CHRISTIANITY?

The scrolls opened a window into the time surrounding the climactic events leading up to the birth of the early church, a period that witnessed the development of an end-times movement in Judaism, the birth and ministry of Jesus, the destruction of Jewish independence, the rise of Christianity, and the formation of Rabbinic Judaism.

More particularly, the messianic emphasis (that the long-awaited Messiah of Israel would soon come with power) and prophetic orientation found in many of the scrolls provide insight into the religious viewpoint expressed in the New Testament and early Christianity. When considering the history and religious controversy depicted in the scrolls, it reaffirms the Jewishness of Jesus, the Gospels, and Christianity. In addition the scrolls help us better understand the Apostle Paul's vocabulary and his discussion of customs.

The scrolls also provide help in resolving questions related to Christian interpretation of the Old Testament. For example, Christian tradition has accepted the reading of the Greek Septuagint version of Psalm 22:16, which reads: "They have pierced my hands and feet." This reading appeared to justify a messianic interpretation, where this statement was a prophecy of Christ's crucifixion. At odds with this reading was the Hebrew-language Masoretic Text, which reads "like a lion are my hands and my feet." Because of this it was thought those who made the Septuagint translation (followed here by the New Testament) had mistakenly read the Hebrew word as a verb (= "pierced") rather than a noun (= "lion"). However, the Greek Septuagint, and Christian copyists, were proven to be correct when the Psalms Scroll clearly indicated a verb instead of a noun and reads "they pierced" rather than "like a lion."

WHAT DO THE SCROLLS REVEAL ABOUT THE NEW TESTAMENT?

Since the scrolls generally come to us from a time before the formation of Christianity, they offer a context for understanding the expected nature and role of the Messiah in Judaism. Many of the scrolls from Cave 4 demonstrate a high view of the coming Messiah as being a divine agent with supernatural qualities and powers. These words from a Cave 4 scroll illustrate this understanding:

The Messianic Apocalypse (Scroll abbreviation: 4Q521 2:6-13)

Col. 2 [6]His spirit will hover over the humble, and He renews the faithful in His strength. [7]For He will glorify the pious with the th[ro]ne of His eternal kingdom, [8]free the captives, open the eyes of the blind, raise up those op[pressed]. [9]And for[ev]er I shall hold fast [to] the [ho]peful and pious […] [10][…] holy [Messiah] will be delayed […] [11]and the Lord shall do glorious things which have not been done, just as He said. Lord.

[12]For He shall heal the critically wounded, He shall resurrect the dead, He shall proclaim good news to the poor, [13]He shall […], He shall lead the [ho]ly ones, and the hungry He shall enrich…

The scrolls also explained the sense of prophetic purpose of the Qumran sect in the Judean desert in terms of Isaiah's statement, "A voice is crying, Prepare a way for the Lord in the wilderness" (Isaiah 40:3), the same expression of purpose given by John the Baptist in the Gospels. The scrolls also contain "beatitudes" (4Q525) similar to those of Jesus' Sermon on the Mount (Matthew 5:3-12) and on the Plain (Luke 6:20-23), use vocabulary unique to the New Testament ("sons of light," "works of righteousness," "Belial"), and have similar political and social views on such subjects as predestination, the Temple, divorce, and prophetic events climaxing in a messianic age. With respect to motive for the Sanhedrin's condemnation of Jesus and approval for the Roman punishment of crucifixion, the Temple Scroll shows that the condemnation was based on an interpretation of Deuteronomy 21:22-23 in which the punishment of hanging a man on a tree is mentioned. The Temple Scroll states that this was the prescribed punishment for sedition (betraying the Jewish nation), and this agrees with the statement of the high priest Caiaphas in John 11:49 that Jesus was guilty of this crime.

The discovery of the Dead Sea Scrolls was heard around the world, because the scrolls prove the accuracy of the Bible we have today, shed light on the culture in which Jesus lived, and provide fresh and new insight into the context of early Christianity.

THE HISTORY OF QUMRAN

Period	Date	Main Development of Building Projects
Israelite Period	7th-8th centuries BC	Enclosure wall, round cistern
Period Ia	c. 134-104 BC	Two rectangular cisterns, inlet channel
Period Ib	c. 103-31 BC	Tower, more cisterns, western block, use of south plateau
Interruption in Occupation (31-4 BC) — Buildings destroyed by fire, allegedly as the result of an earthquake (reported to have occurred in 31 BC by Joseph Flavius, War 1:270-72; Antiquities 15:121-22).		
Period II	c. 4 BC-AD 68	Repairs to Ib structures, two reservoirs, use of south plateau
Destruction of Jewish Settlement (AD 68 by Roman Army)		
Period III	after AD 68	Use of part of main block, southeast cistern, water-channel

Author: J. Randall Price, Ph.D, author of *Secrets of the Dead Sea Scrolls* and *The Stones Cry Out: What Archaeology Reveals about the Truth of the Bible*, is the Director of Excavations at the Qumran Plateau and is president of World of the Bible Ministries, Inc.

People and Events in Israel

700 BC — 600 BC — 500 BC — 400 BC — 300 BC — 200 BC

- Simon II anointed high priest
- Esther becomes queen
- Beginning of return of exiles to Jerusalem
- Second Temple is built and dedicated
- Joshua serves as Zadokite high priest (Haggai 1:1)
- Nehemiah completes walls of Jerusalem
- Alexander the Great conquers Israel
- Ptolemy IV attempts to enter temple
- Qumran sect in Damascus?

25 years between lines

Events at Qumran

150 BC — 125 BC — 100 BC — 75 BC — 50 BC — 25 BC — AD 1 — AD 50 — AD 100

- Antiochus IV desecrates the temple; the Maccabean Revolt begins
- Death of Judas Maccabeus (leader of the revolt)
- Simon anointed high priest. Jews rule themselves for 79 years
- Jerusalem besieged by Antiochus VII Sidetes of Syria
- John Hyrcanus destroys Samaritan temple on Mt. Gerizim; forces the Judaization of Idumea
- Alexander Jannaeus in civil war with Pharisees, who are aided by Demetrius III Eucaerus
- Period Ia founding of settlement; time of John Hyrcanus (?) (late date)
- Founding of Qumran Settlement near the Dead Sea (early date)
- Period Ib begins, marked by building at time of Alexander Jannaeus, leader of Judea
- Forces of Aristobulus II besieged by the Roman general Pompey on Temple Mount. Jewish rule falls to Rome on Yom Kippur.
- King Herod, aided by Roman general Sosius, takes Jerusalem from Antigonus
- Period of Herod the Great's building
- Period Ib ends either with Parthian invasion (40 BC) or earthquake (31 BC)
- Birth of Jesus of Nazareth
- Period II begins, at the time of Herod the Great's death
- Ministry of John the Baptist
- Crucifixion of Jesus of Nazareth
- Conversion of Paul
- Jewish historian Josephus in Galilee
- Civil war in Jerusalem, leading to destruction of site of Qumran
- Antonius Felix, procurator
- Period II ends, destruction at hands of Roman forces during First Jewish Revolt
- Period III, Roman military occupation of Qumran

Bible Translations

For more than 2,000 years, scholars have been translating the Bible. The Old Testament was written over a 1,500-year period before the birth of Christ. It was written primarily in Hebrew, with a few portions in Aramaic. The New Testament was written within 70 years of Christ's death and resurrection (AD 50–100). The writers of the New Testament wrote in *Koine* Greek ("common" Greek). The original manuscripts have not survived, but God's Word has been preserved through meticulous copying.

Three primary methods of translation (and a fourth approach) have evolved over the centuries:

Word-for-Word — Scholars translate each word based upon the word usage at the time of the writing. No translation is actually "word for word," but the intent is to come as close as possible. This method is also called *formal equivalence*.

Balance — Scholars attempt to mediate between a word-for-word approach and a thought-for-thought approach. This method is sometimes called *optimal equivalence*.

Thought-for-Thought — Scholars translate the meaning of each thought. This is how most non-biblical translation for modern books is done. This method is also called *functional* (or *dynamic*) *equivalence*.

Paraphrase — This is a restatement of a translation in modern terms and vocabulary, often expanded for clarity. This approach is sometimes called *free translation*.

Why Do New Translations Continue to Appear?

Words change. Modern language changes constantly, and the Bible must use understandable words for everyday life.

Our understanding of ancient languages changes. The Bible was written using hundreds of words that are no longer understood. Scholars continue to discover the meanings of words and phrases, and either update or create new translations.

Translators' purposes vary. When an ancient word may be translated correctly in several different ways, the translators' purpose affects which words are chosen.

COLOR KEY
- Word-for-Word
- Balance
- Thought-for-Thought
- Paraphrase

	King James Version (KJV)
BIBLE TRANSLATION In order by date of release	
TRANSLATION METHOD & READING GRADE LEVEL	Word-for-Word Reading Grade Level: 12
YEAR Year the complete Bible was released and later revisions	1611, current edition 1769
TRANSLATORS Number of scholars and linguists involved in translating	54 translators divided into six panels
SPONSORS Organizations and people who sponsored the translation	King James I of England
TEXTUAL BASIS English Bibles and Greek and Hebrew manuscripts used	**English Bibles:** Bishop's Bible (1568), Tyndale's Bible (1535) **Old Testament:** Masoretic Texts: Complutensian Polyglot, Antwerp Polyglot **New Testament:** Textus Receptus
PURPOSE The reason for and goal of the translation	In response to Protestant concerns of inaccuracies in earlier English versions (Tyndale's, Geneva, Bishop's).
NOTABLE Interesting facts	The most widely printed and distributed version of the Bible. Used for devotional reading and Bible study by adults who prefer the English found in older versions.
SAMPLE VERSES Matthew 4:19 and John 3:16–17 as they are found in the most recent edition	And he saith unto them, Follow me, and I will make you fishers of men. —Matthew 4:19 For God so loved the world, that he gave his only begotten Son, that whosoever believeth in him should not perish, but have everlasting life. For God sent not his Son into the world to condemn the world; but that the world through him might be saved. —John 3:16–17

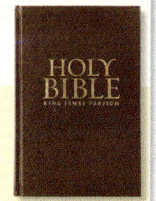

Bible Translations Comparison

	American Standard Version (ASV)	Revised Standard Version (RSV)	Amplified Bible (AMP)
METHOD	Word-for-Word Reading Grade Level: 12	Word-for-Word Reading Grade Level: 10	Word-for-Word, plus amplification of meaning Reading Grade Level: 11
YEAR	1901	1952, NT updated in 1971	1965, revised in 2015
TRANSLATORS	30 American scholars who were part of the English Revised Version project in 1885	32 translators	Frances E. Siewert and 12 other translators
SPONSORS	British scholars from a variety of denominations	International Council of Religious Education	The Lockman Foundation and Zondervan Publishing House
TEXTUAL BASIS	**English Bibles:** English Revised Version, King James Version **Old Testament:** Masoretic Text, Septuagint **New Testament:** Westcott-Hort Greek New Testament	**English Bible:** American Standard Version **Old Testament:** Masoretic Text, Dead Sea Scrolls, Septuagint **New Testament:** Nestle-Aland Novum Testamentum Graece	**English Bible:** American Standard Version **Old Testament:** Rudolf Kittel's Biblia Hebraica, Dead Sea Scrolls, Septuagint **New Testament:** Westcott-Hort Greek New Testament, Nestle-Aland Novum Testamentum Graece
PURPOSE	To address about 300 suggestions from American translators to change the English Revised Version to acceptable American word usage.	Revision of the ASV. To preserve the best of the Tyndale-King James Bible heritage; to put the Bible's message in simple, enduring words.	To allow the reader to better understand the meaning of words as they were used in their original context.
NOTABLE	This version has earned a reputation as being very true to the Greek and Hebrew texts. Formal and used for serious Bible study.	Received some criticism because translators followed the Hebrew (Masoretic) Text and used the concrete term *young woman* instead of *virgin* (Isa. 7:14).	Unique system of punctuation, typefaces, and synonyms to more fully explain words. The 2015 edition improved the text to read smoothly with or without amplifications.
SAMPLE VERSES	And he saith unto them, Come ye after me, and I will make you fishers of men. —Matthew 4:19 For God so loved the world, that he gave his only begotten Son, that whosoever believeth on him should not perish, but have eternal life. For God sent not the Son into the world to judge the world; but that the world should be saved through him. —John 3:16–17	And he said to them, "Follow me, and I will make you fishers of men." —Matthew 4:19 For God so loved the world that he gave his only Son, that whoever believes in him should not perish but have eternal life. For God sent the Son into the world, not to condemn the world, but that the world might be saved through him. —John 3:16–17	And He said to them, "Follow Me [as My disciples, accepting Me as your Master and Teacher and walking the same path of life that I walk], and I will make you fishers of men." —Matthew 4:19 For God so [greatly] loved *and* dearly prized the world, that He [even] gave His [One and] only begotten Son, so that whoever believes *and* trusts in Him [as Savior] shall not perish, but have eternal life. For God did not send the Son into the world to judge *and* condemn the world [that is, to initiate the final judgment of the world], but that the world might be saved through Him. —John 3:16–17

Bible Translations Comparison • 45

	Revised New Jerusalem Bible (RNJB)	New American Bible, Revised Edition (NABRE)	New American Standard Bible (NASB)
METHOD	Word-for-Word Reading Grade Level: 9	Word-for-Word Reading Grade Level: 6.6	Word-for-Word Reading Grade Level: 11
YEAR	1966, updated in 1985 and 2019	1970, NT updated in 1986 and OT in 2011	1971, revised in 1995 and 2020
TRANSLATORS	36 translators	55 translators	54 translators
SPONSORS	Roman Catholic Church	Catholic Biblical Association of America	The Lockman Foundation
TEXTUAL BASIS	**Bible:** Bible de Jérusalem (French translation, 1961) **Old Testament:** Masoretic Text, Septuagint **New Testament:** Eclectic Greek texts	**Old Testament:** Masoretic Text, Septuagint, Vulgate, Dead Sea Scrolls, Hebrew text behind the Liber Psalmorum **New Testament:** Nestle-Aland Novum Testamentum Graece, United Bible Societies' Greek New Testament	**Old Testament:** Biblia Hebraica Stuttgartensia, Biblia Hebraica Quinta, Septuagint, Dead Sea Scrolls, Targums **New Testament:** Nestle-Aland Novum Testamentum Graece, Editio Critica Maior
PURPOSE	A response to Pope Pius XII's request for a more clear, skilled translation by Dominicans and others at École Biblique in Jerusalem.	A response to Pope Pius XII's request for a more clear, skilled translation by the Catholic Biblical Association of America.	To closely follow the word and sentence patterns of the biblical authors.
NOTABLE	First published as the Jerusalem Bible (1966), then as the New Jerusalem Bible (1985). The RNJB is a wholesale revision of the Jerusalem Bible text. Includes the Apocrypha.	Widely used by Roman Catholics of all ages. Includes the Apocrypha. The 1986 version, New American Bible (NAB), is the official translation used in U.S. Catholic Church Mass.	If the literal definition for an expression was determined to be unclear for contemporary readers, an equivalent modern expression was used. The more literal expression is described more fully in the footnotes. Used by adults for serious Bible study.
SAMPLE VERSES	And he said to them, 'Come after me and I will make you fishers of people.' —Matthew 4:19 For God loved the world so much that he gave his only-begotten Son, so that everyone who believes in him may not perish but may have eternal life. For God sent his Son into the world not to judge the world, but so that the world might be saved through him. —John 3:16–17	He said to them, "Come after me, and I will make you fishers of men." —Matthew 4:19 For God so loved the world that he gave his only Son, so that everyone who believes in him might not perish but might have eternal life. For God did not send his Son into the world to condemn the world, but that the world might be saved through him. —John 3:16–17	And He said to them, "Follow Me, and I will make you fishers of people." —Matthew 4:19 For God so loved the world, that He gave His only Son, so that everyone who believes in Him will not perish, but have eternal life. For God did not send the Son into the world to judge the world, but so that the world might be saved through Him. —John 3:16–17

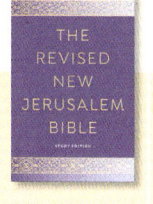

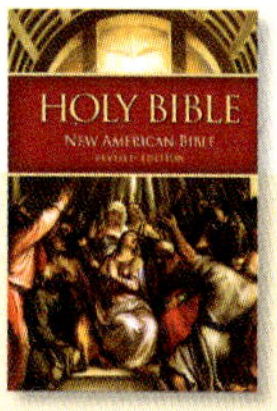

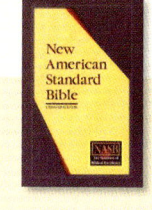

Bible Translations Comparison

	Good News Translation (GNT)	New International Version (NIV)	New King James Version (NKJV)
METHOD	Thought-for-Thought Reading Grade Level: 6	Balance Reading Grade Level: 7	Word-for-Word Reading Grade Level: 9
YEAR	1976, revised in 1992	1978, revised in 1984 and 2011	1982
TRANSLATORS	R. Bratcher (New Testament) plus six others (Old Testament)	115 translators	119 translators
SPONSORS	American Bible Society	New York Bible Society (now known as Biblica)	Conceived by Arthur Farstad; commissioned by Thomas Nelson Publishers
TEXTUAL BASIS	**Old Testament:** Biblia Hebraica **New Testament:** United Bible Societies' Greek New Testament	**Old Testament:** Biblia Hebraica, Dead Sea Scrolls, Septuagint, Aquila, Symmachus and Theodotian, Vulgate, other ancient manuscripts **New Testament:** Eclectic text	**English Bible:** King James Version **Old Testament:** Masoretic Text **New Testament:** Textus Receptus **Footnotes:** Nestle-Aland Novum Testamentum Graece
PURPOSE	To provide a Bible for non-native English speakers.	To provide a modern translation acceptable to many denominations. The 2011 revision brought the translation into line with contemporary biblical scholarship and shifts in English usage.	To produce a modern language translation that would maintain the structure and beauty of the King James Version.
NOTABLE	Endorsed by many evangelistic and denominational groups. Used by children and believers for whom English is not their first language. This is the translation used in the popular *JESUS* film.	Currently the best-selling Bible version. The 2011 revision uses more inclusive language. Five percent of the text affected by word changes in the 2011 revision.	Indicates where other Greek and Hebrew manuscripts differ. Used for devotional reading and Bible study by adults who prefer the English found in older versions.
SAMPLE VERSES	Jesus said to them, "Come with me, and I will teach you to catch people." —Matthew 4:19 For God loved the world so much that he gave his only Son, so that everyone who believes in him may not die but have eternal life. For God did not send his Son into the world to be its judge, but to be its savior. —John 3:16–17	"Come, follow me," Jesus said, "and I will send you out to fish for people." —Matthew 4:19 For God so loved the world that he gave his one and only Son, that whoever believes in him shall not perish but have eternal life. For God did not send his Son into the world to condemn the world, but to save the world through him. —John 3:16–17	Then He said to them, "Follow Me, and I will make you fishers of men." —Matthew 4:19 For God so loved the world that He gave His only begotten Son, that whoever believes in Him should not perish but have everlasting life. For God did not send His Son into the world to condemn the world, but that the world through Him might be saved. —John 3:16–17

Bible Translations Comparison

	New Century Version (NCV)	New Revised Standard Version Updated Edition (NRSVue)	Contemporary English Version (CEV)
METHOD	Thought-for-Thought Reading Grade Level: 5.6	Word-for-Word Reading Grade Level: 8	Thought-for-Thought Reading Grade Level: 5.4
YEAR	1987, revised in 1991 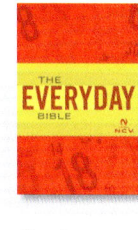	1989, updated edition 2021 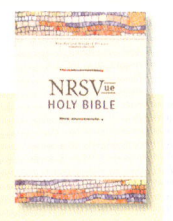	1995 
TRANSLATORS	More than 50 translators	56 translators	More than 100 translators (including reviewers)
SPONSORS	World Bible Translation Center, a subsidiary of Bible League International	Society of Biblical Literature and National Council of Churches	American Bible Society
TEXTUAL BASIS	**Old Testament:** Biblia Hebraica, Septuagint **New Testament:** United Bible Societies' Greek New Testament	**English Bible:** New Revised Standard Version **Old Testament:** Biblia Hebraica Stuttgartensia, Biblia Hebraica Quinta, Dead Sea Scrolls, Septuagint, Vulgate, Syriac Peshitta, Aramaic Targums **New Testament:** United Bible Societies' Greek New Testament, Editio Critica Maior, Society of Biblical Literature's Greek New Testament	**Old Testament:** Biblia Hebraica Stuttgartensia, Septuagint **New Testament:** United Bible Societies' Greek New Testament
PURPOSE	To make a readable version that uses modern terms such as measurements and geographic names.	To update and refine the New Revised Standard Version (1989) and reflect the latest scholarship in textual criticism and linguistics.	To translate the Bible into the speech patterns found in modern communication.
NOTABLE	Use of footnotes to clarify ancient customs and other concepts requiring special explanation. Figures of speech and idioms are translated according to their meaning. Widely used by children and teenagers for personal devotional reading.	The NRSVue is historically ecumenical in its reception, being accepted by Episcopal, Presbyterian, and US Catholic Bishops.	Recommended for children and people who do not speak English as a first language. The drafting, reviewing, editing, revising, and refining of the CEV extended over ten years.
SAMPLE VERSES	Jesus said, "Come follow me, and I will make you fish for people." —Matthew 4:19 God loved the world so much that he gave his one and only Son so that whoever believes in him may not be lost, but have eternal life. God did not send his Son into the world to judge the world guilty, but to save the world through him. —John 3:16–17	And he said to them, "Follow me, and I will make you fishers of people." —Matthew 4:19 For God so loved the world that he gave his only Son, so that everyone who believes in him may not perish but may have eternal life. Indeed, God did not send the Son into the world to condemn the world, but in order that the world might be saved through him. —John 3:16–17	Jesus said to them, "Come with me! I will teach you how to bring in people instead of fish." —Matthew 4:19 God loved the people of this world so much that he gave his only Son, so that everyone who has faith in him will have eternal life and never really die. God did not send his Son into the world to condemn its people. He sent him to save them! —John 3:16–17

Bible Translations Comparison

	God's Word Translation (GW)	New International Reader's Version (NIrV)	New Living Translation (NLT)
METHOD	Balance Reading Grade Level: 5.1	Thought-for-Thought Reading Grade Level: 2.9	Thought-for-Thought Reading Grade Level: 6.3
YEAR	1995	1996, revised in 1998 and 2014	1996, revised in 2004 and 2015
TRANSLATORS	84 translators	40 scholars, including some of the original New International Version translators	90 translators
SPONSORS	God's Word to the Nations Bible Society	Biblica (formerly International Bible Society) and Zondervan Publishing House	Tyndale House Publishers
TEXTUAL BASIS	**Old Testament:** Biblia Hebraica Stuttgartensia **New Testament:** Nestle-Aland Novum Testamentum Graece	**English Bible:** New International Version	**English Bible:** The Living Bible (1971) **Old Testament:** Biblia Hebraica Stuttgartensia, Dead Sea Scrolls, Septuagint, Vulgate, Syriac Peshitta, Samaritan Pentateuch **New Testament:** United Bible Societies' Greek New Testament, Nestle-Aland Novum Testamentum Graece
PURPOSE	To accurately translate the meaning of the original texts into clear, everyday language.	To provide a translation with simple words and short sentences to appeal to a lower reading level.	To provide an easy-to-read modern version.
NOTABLE	This version was translated by a committee of biblical scholars and English reviewers to ensure accurate, natural English. Used by teenagers and adults for personal devotions, worship, and Bible study.	This translation has the lowest reading level of any English translation on the market. Used by children and developing English readers for devotion and worship.	A translation in the style of the Living Bible. Removes theological terms, such as *justification*, using the definition instead for clarity. Used by teenagers and adults for personal devotions, worship, and Bible study.
SAMPLE VERSES	Jesus said to them, "Come, follow me! I will teach you how to catch people instead of fish." —Matthew 4:19 God loved the world this way: He gave his only Son so that everyone who believes in him will not die but will have eternal life. God sent his Son into the world, not to condemn the world, but to save the world. —John 3:16–17	"Come and follow me," Jesus said. "I will send you out to fish for people." —Matthew 4:19 God so loved the world that he gave his one and only Son. Anyone who believes in him will not die but will have eternal life. God did not send his Son into the world to judge the world. He sent his Son to save the world through him. —John 3:16–17	Jesus called out to them, "Come, follow me and I will show you how to fish for people!" —Matthew 4:19 For this is how God loved the world: He gave his one and only Son, so that everyone who believes in him will not perish but have eternal life. God sent his Son into the world not to judge the world, but to save the world through him. —John 3:16–17

Bible Translations Comparison

	English Standard Version (ESV)	The Message (MSG)	Christian Standard Bible (CSB)
METHOD	Word-for-Word Reading Grade Level: 8	Paraphrase Reading Grade Level: 6	Balance Reading Grade Level: 7
YEAR	2001 	2002 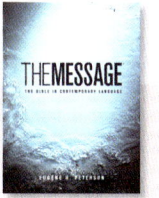	2004, revised in 2017 
TRANSLATORS	More than 100 translators	Eugene Peterson	More than 100 translators
SPONSORS	Good News/Crossway Board of Directors	NavPress	Holman Bible Publishers, a division of LifeWay Christian Resources
TEXTUAL BASIS	**English Bible:** Revised Standard Version (1971 edition) **Old Testament:** Biblia Hebraica Stuttgartensia, Dead Sea Scrolls, Septuagint, Samaritan Pentateuch, Syriac Peshitta, Vulgate **New Testament:** United Bible Societies' Greek New Testament, Nestle-Aland Novum Testamentum Graece	**Old Testament:** Biblia Hebraica **New Testament:** Greek New Testament	**Old Testament:** Biblia Hebraica Stuttgartensia **New Testament:** Nestle-Aland Novum Testamentum Graece, United Bible Societies' Greek New Testament
PURPOSE	To produce a modern, readable, and accurate translation in the tradition of the Tyndale Version (1535) and King James Version (1611).	To re-create the common language in which the Bible was written into today's common language.	To make the most readable text possible while maintaining the integrity of the translation.
NOTABLE	Theologically conservative. Inclusive language was typically avoided. An "essentially literal" translation that seeks to capture the precise wording of the original text and personal style of each Bible writer.	Intended to be used as an aid to understanding traditional Bible translations. Used for devotional reading.	First published in 2004 as Holman Christian Standard Bible (HCSB). Revised in 2017 as Christian Standard Bible (CSB) to improve readability and clarity. Whereas HCSB rendered *YHWH* as *Yahweh*, CSB renders this name as LORD. CSB does not capitalize pronouns referring to God (he, his, etc.) as HCSB did. Used by teenagers and adults for devotions and Bible study.
SAMPLE VERSES	And he said to them, "Follow me, and I will make you fishers of men." —Matthew 4:19 For God so loved the world, that he gave his only Son, that whoever believes in him should not perish but have eternal life. For God did not send his Son into the world to condemn the world, but in order that the world might be saved through him. —John 3:16–17	Jesus said to them, "Come with me. I'll make a new kind of fisherman out of you. I'll show you how to catch men and women instead of perch and bass." —Matthew 4:19 This is how much God loved the world: He gave his Son, his one and only Son. And this is why: so that no one need be destroyed; by believing in him, anyone can have a whole and lasting life. God didn't go to all the trouble of sending his Son merely to point an accusing finger, telling the world how bad it was. He came to help, to put the world right again. —John 3:16–17	"Follow me," he told them, "and I will make you fish for people." —Matthew 4:19 For God loved the world in this way: He gave his one and only Son, so that everyone who believes in him will not perish but have eternal life. For God did not send his Son into the world to condemn the world, but to save the world through him. —John 3:16–17

Common English Bible (CEB)

METHOD: Balance
Reading Grade Level: 7

YEAR: 2011

TRANSLATORS: 117 translators

SPONSORS: Church Resources Development Corp., a co-op of publishers representing Presbyterian Church U.S.A., Episcopal & United Methodist Churches, and others.

TEXTUAL BASIS:
Old Testament: Biblia Hebraica Stuttgartensia, Biblia Hebraica Quinta, Gottingen Septuagint, Ralf's Septuagint
New Testament: Nestle-Aland Novum Testamentum Graece

PURPOSE: To make the Bible accessible to a broad range of people and to give readers a smooth and natural reading experience.

NOTABLE: Diverse team of translators from twenty-two faith traditions in American, African, Asian, European, and Latino communities. Used by teenagers and adults for church worship and personal Bible study.

SAMPLE VERSES:
"Come, follow me," he said, "and I'll show you how to fish for people." —Matthew 4:19

For God so loved the world that he gave his only Son, so that everyone who believes in him won't perish but will have eternal life. God didn't send his Son into the world to judge the world, but that the world might be saved through him.
—John 3:16–17

Important Words to Know

APOCRYPHA – Several books and additions included in early Greek and Latin translations of the Old Testament. Since the Hebrew canon does not include the Apocrypha, it began to be removed from English Bibles as early as the Geneva Bible in 1640. By 1827, it was omitted from most Protestant Bibles.

BIBLIA HEBRAICA – Latin for "Hebrew Bible." Refers to modern editions of the Masoretic Text that contain a set of text-critical notes showing variants based on early translations (such as the Septuagint) and manuscript discoveries.

DEAD SEA SCROLLS – Some of the oldest known copies of portions of Old Testament, unearthed in the 1940s near the Dead Sea, with some scrolls dating to as early as 300 BC.

ECLECTIC TEXT – Translators examined every ancient Greek manuscript available and then selected the variant that seemed best. Eclecticism practices textual criticism in order to determine which variant is most accurate to the original writing. In theory, eclecticism shows no favoritism for one text-type over another. However, the oldest manuscripts (Alexandrian text-type) are typically favored.

GREEK MANUSCRIPTS – The New Testament is the most well-documented written material from the first century. Several thousand manuscript copies of New Testament books exist. Because these were copied by hand, there are slight differences (variants) between manuscripts. (Study Bibles usually list the differences. Most variants are in spelling and place names, and none affect Christian doctrine.) Scholars have put these manuscripts into groups, called text-types:

- **Western Text-Type** (also called Popular text) – These manuscripts were grouped together because they were hand copied before AD 400 and were not copied in Alexandria, Egypt.

- **Byzantine Text-Type** (also called Constantinopolitan, Syrian, Ecclesiastical, or Majority) – The largest number of surviving manuscripts fit into this group for any of three possible reasons: (1) They were considered superior to Alexandrian manuscripts; (2) they were more readily available and widely circulated when Christianity became legal under Emperor Constantine; or (3) Byzantine churches were the only churches in the Roman Empire that continued to copy manuscripts in Greek after the fourth century.

- **Alexandrian Text-Type** (also called Neutral or Egyptian) – The oldest manuscripts available today are in this group. They survived due to the dry climate of Egypt that preserved the writing material. They include Codex Vaticanus, Codex Sinaiticus, Codex Alexandrinus, and the more recently discovered Oxyrhynchus, Chester Beatty, and Bodmer Papyri (dated before AD 300).

GREEK NEW TESTAMENT – A general reference to any of the editions of the New Testament in *Koine* Greek, the kind of Greek spoken in the time of Jesus.

INCLUSIVE LANGUAGE – Language that neither refers to male or female (gender neutral) nor adult or child (age neutral) if the terms do not specify a gender or age. Translators who strive for inclusive language emphasize the gender neutrality of some Greek and Hebrew terms that have been traditionally translated with a masculine orientation.

MASORETIC TEXT – The texts of the Hebrew Bible carefully copied by generations of Jewish scholars using a strict set of proofreading guidelines. It is named for the medieval Masoretes, scribes who added vowel points, text-critical notes, and other important elements.

SEPTUAGINT – A translation of the Old Testament into Greek, completed before the birth of Jesus. Also called the LXX, the Latin numeral for seventy, referring to the tradition that seventy translators worked on it.

TEXTUS RECEPTUS – Latin for "received text." The Greek New Testament assembled by Erasmus and others in the 1500s.

VULGATE – From *vulgo,* meaning "to make common." A fifth-century translation of the Bible into Latin. It was the most popular version of the Bible in the Western church for over 1,000 years.

Bible Translations Comparison • 51

The Three Most Popular Greek Texts

When translating the Bible, scholars examine one or more Greek texts of the New Testament. Each text varies slightly. It is important that scholars show the texts they are using and how they deal with the differences. Here are the three most popular texts used.

	RECEIVED TEXT (TEXTUS RECEPTUS)	**WESTCOTT-HORT**	**NESTLE-ALAND AND UNITED BIBLE SOCIETIES**
Groupings	Based on Byzantine text-type	Based on Alexandrian text-type	Also known as Novum Testamentum Graece, Greek New Testament, and Critical Text
Date	**1516:** Several Greek New Testaments published by various scholars (Erasmus, Stephanus, Beza, Elzevirs)	**1881:** Westcott-Hort was the standard Greek text until 1945.	Latest editions: **2012:** Nestle-Aland, 28th Ed. **2014:** United Bible Societies, 5th Rev. Ed.
Foundation for	• KJV • NKJV	• ERV • ASV	• RSV • AMP • RNJB • NABRE • NASB • GNT • NIV • NCV • NRSVue • CEV • GW • NLT • ESV • CSB • CEB
Based on	A few **Byzantine text-type** manuscripts (12th–14th centuries). Some of the book of Revelation was translated back into Greek from the Latin Vulgate because there were no Greek manuscripts of Revelation available to the translators at that time.	**Alexandrian text-type** manuscripts: Codex Vaticanus (4th century) which was housed in the Vatican library since at least 1478, but not available to most scholars until the late 19th century. Codex Sinaiticus (4th century) which was found in 1859. Codex Alexandrinus (5th century) which had been stored away in Alexandria until it was made available to western scholars in 1629.	**Eclectic text** based on Byzantine and Alexandrian text-type manuscripts. Text reliability was assessed by examining external evidence (date, source, amount, relationship to other manuscripts) and internal evidence (the text itself). Recently discovered manuscripts: Oxyrhynchus Papyri (1898); Chester Beatty Papyri (1930); Bodmer Papyri (1955).
Supporters say	Based on Byzantine text-type, the only manuscripts available prior to 1516. Appears to agree with early copies of the New Testament dating before AD 200. A large number of Byzantine text-type manuscripts exists, however, only a few are before AD 600.	Based on the earliest manuscripts available by 1881. Alexandrian text-type manuscripts were a result of scribes using reliable texts and careful copying. The manuscripts are older than Byzantine text-type, but only a few have been discovered.	Scholars believe they have used the most reliable portions from all of the manuscripts (Byzantine, Alexandrian, and Western), including the most recently discovered papyri.
Critics say	Erasmus did not have the Greek manuscripts discovered after 1516 and consulted no more than six Greek manuscripts. Erasmus had to use portions of the Vulgate, making it a translation of a translation. Byzantine text-type went through substantive editing to create a harmonious and smooth text.	The translators did not consider the Byzantine text-type manuscripts. They were not able to use manuscripts discovered after 1881 such as Oxyrhynchus, Chester Beatty and Bodmer Papyri. These papyri are dated earlier than previous manuscripts and some scholars consider them to be the most reliable manuscripts available today.	A few scholars argue that Alexandrian text-type manuscripts have been influenced by Egyptian pagan and Gnostic teachings. However, the majority of scholars disagree and prefer this Greek text.

Names of God

NAME OF GOD	MEANING	APPLICATION
ADONAI	The Lord My Great Lord	God is the Master and majestic Lord. God is our total authority.
EL	The Strong One	He is more powerful than any false god. God will overcome all obstacles. We can depend on God.
EL ELOHE YISRAEL	God, the God of Israel	The God of Israel is distinct and separate from all false gods of the world.
EL ELYON	The God Most High	He is the Sovereign God in whom we can put our trust. El Elyon has supremacy over all false gods.
ELOHIM	The All-Powerful One Creator	God is the all-powerful creator of the universe. God knows all, creates all, and is everywhere at all times. The plural of "El".
EL OLAM	The Eternal God The Everlasting God	He is the Beginning and the End, the One who works his purposes throughout the ages. He gives strength to the weary.
EL ROI	The God Who Sees Me	There are no circumstances in our lives that escape his fatherly awareness and care. God knows us and our troubles.
EL SHADDAI	The All Sufficient One, The God of the Mountains, God Almighty	God is the all-sufficient source of all of our blessings. God is all-powerful. Our problems are not too big for God to handle.
IMMANUEL	God With Us "I AM"	Jesus is God in our midst. In him all the fullness of Deity dwells in bodily form.
JEHOVAH	"I AM," The One Who Is The Self-Existent One	God never changes. His promises never fail. When we are faithless, he is faithful. We need to obey him.
JEHOVAH-JIREH	The Lord Will Provide	Just as God provided a ram as a substitute for Isaac, He provided His son Jesus as the ultimate sacrifice. God will meet all our needs.
JEHOVAH-MEKADDISHKEM	The Lord Who Sanctifies	God sets us apart as a chosen people, a royal priesthood, holy unto God, a people of his own. He cleanses our sin and helps us mature.
JEHOVAH-NISSI	The Lord Is My Banner	God gives us victory against the flesh, the world, and the devil. Our battles are His battles of light against darkness and good against evil.
JEHOVAH-RAPHA	The Lord Who Heals	God has provided the final cure for spiritual, physical, and emotional sickness in Jesus Christ. God can heal us.
JEHOVAH-ROHI	The Lord Is My Shepherd	The Lord protects, provides, directs, leads, and cares for his people. God tenderly takes care of us as a strong and patient shepherd.
JEHOVAH-SABAOTH	The Lord of Hosts The Lord of Armies	The Lord of the hosts of heaven will always fulfill his purposes, even when the hosts of his earthly people fail.
JEHOVAH-SHALOM	The Lord Is Peace	God defeats our enemies to bring us peace. Jesus is our Prince of Peace. God brings inner peace and harmony.
JEHOVAH-SHAMMAH	The Lord Is There The Lord My Companion	God's presence is not limited or contained in the tabernacle or temple, but is accessible to all who love and obey him.
JEHOVAH-TSIDKENU	The Lord Our Righteousness	Jesus is the King who would come from David's line, and is the one who imparts his righteousness to us.
YAH, OR JAH	"I AM," The One Who Is The Self-Existent One	God never changes. His promises never fail. When we are faithless, he is faithful. God promises his continuing presence.
YHWH	"I AM," The One Who Is The Self-Existent One	God never changes. His promises never fail. When we are faithless, He is faithful.

Names of God • 53

REFERENCE	COMMENTS
Ps. 8; Isa. 40:3–5; Ezek. 16:8; Hab. 3:19	**Pronounced: ah-doe-NI** *Adonai* (plural) is derived from the singular *Adon* (Lord). This term was pronounced in substitution of *YHWH* (considered too sacred to be uttered).
Ex. 15:2; Num. 23:22; Deut. 7:9; (Mark 15:34)	**Pronounced: el** Occurs more than 200 times in the Old Testament (including compounds). Generic Semitic name for God, used by other cultures to refer to their gods. *El* is used in compound proper names such as Isra-*el* (wrestles with God), Beth-*el* (House of God), and *El*-isha (God is salvation).
Gen. 33:20; Ex. 5:1; Ps. 68:8; 106:48	**Pronounced: el el-o-HAY yis-raw-ALE** The name of the altar that Jacob (Israel) erected after his encounter with God and God's blessing upon him (Gen. 32:24–30; 33:19–20).
Gen. 14:17–22; Ps. 78:35; Dan. 4:34; (Acts 16:17)	**Pronounced: el EL-yuhn** Melchizedek, the king of Salem (Jeru "Salem") and the priest of God Most High, referred to God as "El Elyon" three times when he blessed Abram.
Gen. 1:1–3; Deut. 10:17; Ps. 68; (Mark 13:19)	**Pronounced: el-o-HEEM** Plural form of *El*. This name is usually associated with God in relation to his creation. Some people use the plural word "Elohim" as proof for the Trinity (Genesis 1:26). *Elohim* is also used to refer to false gods and even human judges (Ps. 82:6–7; John 10:34).
Gen. 21:33; Ps. 90:1–2; Isa. 40:28; (Rom. 1:20)	**Pronounced: el o-LAHM** Jesus Christ possesses eternal attributes. He is the same yesterday and today and forever (Heb. 13:8). He obtained eternal redemption for us (Heb. 9:12).
Gen. 16:11–14; Ps. 139:7–12	**Pronounced: el ROY** Hagar called the Lord by this name beside a fountain of water in the wilderness. God knows all of our thoughts and feelings. Jesus knew the thoughts of those around him, demonstrating that he is *El Roi* (Matt. 22:18; 26:21, 34; Luke 5:21–24).
Gen. 17:1–3; 48:3; 49:25; 35:11; Ps. 90:2	**Pronounced: el-shaw-DIE** Some scholars suggest that *Shaddai* refers to God's power evident in his judgment. Others suggest that *El Shaddai* means "God of the Mountains." God refers to himself as "El Shaddai" when he confirms his covenant with Abraham.
Isa. 7:14; 8:8–10; (Matt. 1:23)	**Pronounced: ih-MAN-u-el** This name indicates that Jesus is more than man. He is also God. Isaiah said that the child born to the virgin would be called "Immanuel." (Isaiah 7:14; 9:6) He is the radiance of God's glory and the exact representation of His nature (Hebrews 1:3).
Ex. 3:14; 6:2–4; 34:5–7; Ps. 102	**Pronounced: juh-HO-vah** A 16th-century German translator wrote the name *YHVH* (*YHWH*) using the vowels of *Adonai*, because the ancient Jewish texts from which he was translating had the vowels of *Adonai* under the consonants of *YHVH*. By doing this, he incorrectly came up with the name Jehovah (*YaHoVaH*).
Gen. 22:13–14; Ps. 23; (Mark 10:45; Rom. 8:2)	**Pronounced: juh-HO-vah JI-rah** Also known as YHWH-Jireh. Abraham called the place "The Lord will provide" where God provided a ram to be sacrificed instead of his son Isaac. Jesus said that he was the bread of life and anyone who comes to him will be provided for (John 6:35).
Ex. 31:12–13; (1 Peter 1:15–16; Heb. 13:12; 1 Thess. 5:23–24)	**Pronounced: juh-HO-vah mek-KAH-dish-KIM** Also known as YHWH-Mekaddishkem. We have been set apart, made holy, and redeemed by the blood of Jesus Christ, our *Jehovah-Mekaddishkem*. Therefore, we are to continue to live our lives holy and pleasing to God (1 Peter 1:13–25).
Ex. 17:15–16; Deut. 20:3–4; Isa. 11:10–12; (Eph. 6:10–18)	**Pronounced: juh-HO-vah NEE-see** Also known as YHWH-Nissi. Name of the altar built by Moses after defeating the Amalekites at Rephidim. Isaiah prophesies that the "Root of Jesse" (Jesus) will stand as a banner for the peoples (Isa. 11:10).
Ex. 15:25–27; Ps. 103:3; Ps. 147:3; (1 Peter 2:24)	**Pronounced: juh-HO-vah RAH-fah** Also known as YHWH-Rapha. Jesus demonstrated that he was *Jehovah-Rapha* in his healing of the sick, blind, lame, and casting out demons. Jesus also heals his people from sin and unrighteousness (Luke 5:31–32).
Ps. 23:1–3; Isa. 53:6; (John 10:14–18; Heb. 13:20; Rev. 7:17)	**Pronounced: juh-HO-vah RO-hee** Also known as YHWH-Ra'ah (RAH-ah). Jesus is the good shepherd who lay down his life for all people.
1 Sam. 1:3; 17:45; Ps. 46:7; Mal. 1:10–14; (Rom. 9:29)	**Pronounced: juh-HO-vah sah-bah-OATH** Also known as YHWH-Sabaoth. Many English versions of the Bible translate *Sabaoth* as Almighty. "Jehovah-Sabaoth" is often translated as *The Lord Almighty*. *Sabaoth* is also translated as *Heavenly Hosts* or *Armies*.
Num. 6:22–27; Judg. 6:22–24; Isa. 9:6; (Heb. 13:20)	**Pronounced: juh-HO-vah shah-LOME** Also known as YHWH-Shalom. Name of the altar built by Gideon at Ophrah to memorialize God's message "Peace be unto thee." Isaiah tells us that the Messiah will also be known as the "Prince of Peace," our *Jehovah-Shalom* (Isaiah 9:6).
Ezek. 48:35; Ps. 46; (Matt. 28:20; Rev. 21)	**Pronounced: juh-HO-vah SHAHM-mah** Also known as YHWH-Shammah. God revealed to Ezekiel that the name of the New Jerusalem shall be "The Lord is there." Through Jesus Christ, the Spirit of God dwells in us (1 Cor. 3:16).
Jer. 23:5, 6; 33:16; Ezek. 36:26–27; (2 Cor. 5:21)	**Pronounced: juh-HO-vah tsid-KAY-noo** Also known as YHWH-Tsidkenu. All people sin and fall short of God's glory, but God freely makes us righteous through faith in Jesus Christ (Rom. 3:22–23). God promised to send a King who will reign wisely and do what is just and right. The people will live in safety (Jer. 23:5–6).
Ex. 3:14; 15:2; Ps. 46:1; 68:4; Isa. 26:4	**Pronounced: Yah** Shorter form of *Yahweh*. It is often used when combined with other names or phrases. *Hallelujah* means "Praise Yah (the Lord)," *Elijah* means "God is Yah (the Lord)," and *Joshua* means "Yah (the Lord) is my salvation."
Ex. 3:14; Mal. 3:6	**Pronounced: YAH-way** God's personal name given to Moses. Also called the tetragrammaton ("four letters"). Occurs about 6,800 times. Translated "LORD" in English versions of the Bible, because it became common practice for Jews to say "Lord" (Adonai) instead of saying the name *YHWH*.

NAMES OF JESUS

Name	References	Meaning	Insights	Related Titles (by root word and/or theme)
ALMIGHTY	Revelation 1:8	Jesus is all-powerful.	Christ is the All-Powerful Lord. Nothing is beyond His reach or impossible for Him.	Mighty God, Mighty in Battle, Potentate, Power of God (Isaiah 9:6; Psalm 24:8; 1 Timothy 6:15; 1 Corinthians 1:24)
AUTHOR AND FINISHER	Hebrews 12:2	Jesus is our start and finish.	Jesus was at the beginning of creation and will be there to the end. He is both the author of all that is and the one who sees His creation through to the end.	Alpha and Omega, Beginning and End, First and Last (Revelation 1:8; 21:6; 22:13)
BELOVED	Ephesians 1:6	Jesus is at the center of God's love.	Christ is the Beloved Son of the Father, and as such, the desire of all people who love God. All who love God will be drawn to Jesus.	Desire of all nations (Haggai 2:7) Associate of God (Zechariah 13:7)
BRANCH	Isaiah 11:1; Jeremiah 23:5; Zechariah 3:8; 6:12	Jesus is the shoot from David's line.	Jesus is the offshoot of the line of David and paradoxically also the root. He is the vine on which we depend for life and nourishment.	Nazarene (Netzer = Branch in Hebrew; Matthew 2:23; Isaiah 11:1) Root of David, Shoot, Vine (Revelation 5:5; Isaiah 11:10; 53:2; John 15:1)
BREAD OF LIFE	John 6:32-35	Jesus is our sustenance.	Jesus was born in Bethlehem, which means "the house of bread." He is our spiritual nourishment and the sustenance of the world. All things are kept alive by Him.	Living Bread (John 6:51) Living Water (John 7:37, 38)
BRIDEGROOM	Matthew 9:15; John 3:29; Rev. 21:9	Jesus leads and cares for us.	Jesus is the bridegroom and His church is the bride. He is the head of the church and cares for her.	Head of the Church (Ephesians 5:23) Head of the Body (Ephesians 4:15, 16)
BRIGHT MORNING STAR	Revelation 22:16	Jesus lights our way.	Jesus is the brightest star in the heavens and the Light of the World. We shall not lose our way in His light.	Day Star (2 Peter 1:19) Star (Numbers 24:17) Sunrise (Luke 1:78) Sun of Righteousness (Malachi 4:2)
CARPENTER	Mark 6:3	Jesus is one of us.	Jesus, the creator of wood, became a worker of wood, and died on a cross of wood (Galatians 3:13) for us.	Carpenter's Son (Matthew 13:55)

Names of Jesus • 55

Name	References	Meaning	Insights	Related Titles (by root word and/or theme)
CHOSEN ONE	Luke 23:35	Jesus is God's Chosen One.	Jesus is God's Chosen One, chosen for glory and great sacrifice. We, in Him, are God's chosen people.	Elect One (Isaiah 42:1)
CHIEF CORNERSTONE	Isaiah 28:16; Psalm 118:22; Ephesians 2:20; 1 Peter 2:6	Jesus is our rock of safety.	Jesus is the cornerstone which the religious leaders rejected, but which God chose from eternity to build His house, a temple of living stone! We can rely on Him as our solid foundation.	Foundation, Living Stone, Precious Stone, Rock, Rock of Offense, Stone (1 Corinthians 3:11; 1 Peter 2:4; Isaiah 28:16; 1 Corinthians 10:4; 1 Peter 2:8; Psalm 118:22)
DOOR	John 10:9	Jesus is our gateway.	Jesus is our opening to God. He is the only way to heaven.	Door of the Sheepfold (John 10:7) See *Way*.
EMMANUEL/ IMMANUEL	Isaiah 7:14–8:8; Matthew 1:23	Jesus is God with us.	Jesus was born on earth as a real human being. He entered space and time to become one of us so we might be with God forever.	Only Begotten God (John 1:18)
ETERNAL FATHER	Isaiah 9:6; 1 John 1:1-3	Jesus is forever.	Christ had no beginning and has no end. He is the source of time, space and all creation.	Head of the Creation of God (Revelation 3:14)
FAITHFUL AND TRUE WITNESS	Revelation 1:5; 3:14	Jesus is faithful.	Christ is Truth in the flesh. His witness is always faithful. We can trust His word.	Amen (Revelation 3:14) Faithful and True (Revelation 19:11) Truth (John 14:6)
FIRSTBORN	Hebrews 12:23; Revelation 5	Jesus is our elder brother.	Christ is the firstborn of the dead, the first-fruits of a new humanity, resurrected in new form. As our eldest brother (Hebrews 2:11), He is heir of all things. (The importance of the firstborn is also connected to Passover. At the Exodus, the firstborn child of the Hebrews was "passed over." He was saved from death by the sacrifice of a lamb.)	First-fruits (1 Corinthians 15:20) Firstborn from the Dead (Colossians 1:18)
GOD	John 1:1,14-18; Romans 9:5; Titus 2:13; Heb. 1:8	Jesus is God.	Christ is in His very nature God and all the fullness of that essence is in Him. He is worthy of our worship.	Fullness of God (Colossians 2:9) See *Son of God* and *Yahweh*.

Name	References	Meaning	Insights	Related Titles (by root word and/or theme)
HEAD OF THE CHURCH	Ephesians 5:23	Jesus leads the church.	Jesus is the leader and Lord of the church. True believers will follow Him as He cares for them and directs their way.	Head of the Body (Ephesians 4:15, 16) See *Bridegroom*.
HIGH PRIEST, APOSTLE	Hebrews 3:1, 2	Jesus is our prophet and priest.	An apostle is someone who has directly communicated with God and is authorized to speak for him. A high priest is God's appointed person to represent the people to himself. Jesus is both God's spokesman and our representative to God.	Bishop of Souls, Minister of the Sanctuary, the Prophet (1 Peter 2:25; Hebrews 8:1-2; Deuteronomy 18:15, 18; John 6:14)
HOLY ONE	Mark 1:24; Acts 2:27; 3:14; Psalm 16:10	Jesus is perfect.	Christ is without sin and evil. Because of this, He became the only perfect man to walk upon the earth. Therefore, He is the only one who could die to save us.	Holy Child, Lord Our Righteousness, Righteous One, Sanctification (Acts 4:30, Jeremiah 23:5, 6; 1 John 2:1; 1 Corinthians 1:30)
HOPE	1 Timothy 1:1	Jesus is our confidence.	Jesus is our only source of hope in the world. His conquest of death gives us confidence now and for the future.	Hope of Glory (Colossians 1:27) Hope of Israel (Jeremiah 17:13)
IMAGE OF THE INVISIBLE GOD	2 Corinthians 4:4; Colossians 1:15	Jesus is the perfect picture of God.	Because Christ and the Father are one in nature, Jesus perfectly reflects God. When we look at Him, we see what God looks like as a man.	Exact Representation of His Nature (Hebrews 1:3)
JESUS	Matthew 1:21	Jesus saves.	Jesus is the Greek form of the Hebrew *Yeshua* (Joshua). The name means "Yahweh (Jehovah) is salvation."	Yeshua (Joshua)
JUDGE/RULER	John 5:22, 23; Micah 4:3; Acts 10:42	Jesus is our judge as well as our advocate and lawyer.	Jesus, the very one who is our Advocate before the bar of God's justice, has been made the Judge of all. (Romans 8:33, 34)	See *Wonderful Counselor*.

Names of Jesus

Name	References	Meaning	Insights	Related Titles (by root word and/or theme)
KING OF KINGS	Revelation 17:14	Jesus is king over all.	Christ is the king over all kings and rulers. As subjects in His kingdom, we owe Him our complete allegiance.	King, King of Israel, King of the Jews, Lord of Lords, Master, Prince, Ruler Sovereign (Matt. 21:5; Jn. 1:49; Matt. 2:2; Rev. 19:16; Lk. 8:24; Dan. 9:25; 1 Tim. 6:15)
LAMB OF GOD	John 1:29, 36; 1 Peter 1:19; Rev. 5:6-12; 7:17	Jesus is our sacrifice.	Jesus is the fulfillment of the whole sacrificial system (Hebrews 7:26-29), especially as our Passover Lamb. As the Lamb of God, Jesus' sacrifice pays for our sins past, present, and future.	Offering (Hebrews 10:10) Passover (1 Corinthians 5:7) Propitiation (1 John 2:2) Sacrifice (Ephesians 5:2)
LAST ADAM	1 Corinthians 15:45	Jesus is the Father of a new human nature.	The first Adam brought sin and death. Jesus is the Last Adam, bringing life. From Him flows eternal life.	Man, Second Man, Son of Man (Daniel 7:13-14; Mark 9:31; John 19:5; 1 Corinthians 15:47; 1 Timothy 2:5)
LIGHT OF THE WORLD	John 8:12	Jesus is the light.	Jesus' radiance reveals God. Knowing Jesus is to know and see what God is like. Those who follow Him will not walk in darkness (John 8:12).	Light, Radiance of God's Glory (John 1:4, 5; Hebrews 1:3) See *Bright Morning Star.*
LION OF THE TRIBE OF JUDAH	Genesis 49:9, 10; Revelation 5:5	Jesus is David's son.	Jesus fulfills the Old Testament prophecies, being from the tribe of Judah and the lineage of David.	Son of David (Matthew 12:23) See *King of Kings.*
LIVING WATER	John 4:10; 7:38	Jesus is our spiritual drink.	Christ is the fountainhead of the life that wells up inside every believer like an unending spring.	Fountain Life-Giving Spirit (Jeremiah 2:13; Zechariah 13:1; 1 Cor. 15:45)
LORD OF LORDS	Revelation 19:16; 1 Timothy 6:15	Jesus is Lord.	Jesus is Lord over all! He has this title by right as the Son of God and Creator of the Cosmos. It is also a title He has earned by His humble work of becoming human in order to redeem us through His death.	Lord (Philippians 2:11) See *King of Kings.*

Name	References	Meaning	Insights	Related Titles (by root word and/or theme)
MAN OF SORROWS	Isaiah 53:3	Jesus bore our sorrows.	Jesus did not come to enjoy a life of happy kingship over the world. He came to carry the world's sins and sorrows, that we might have eternal joy with Him and God the Father.	Servant, Slave (Isaiah 42:1, 2; 49:7; 52:13–53:12; Matthew 12:18-20)
MASTER	Matthew 8:19	Jesus is our teacher.	*Master* means "teacher" or "rabbi." Jesus is the final source of truth concerning God. He is the only teacher who can show us the way to go.	Rabbi, Rabboni, Teacher, Truth (John 20:16; John 14:6, 7)
MESSENGER OF THE COVENANT	Malachi 3:1	Jesus is God's final messenger.	*Messenger* and *angel* are the same word in both the Old and New Testaments. Christ is God's ultimate messenger of the New Covenant of God's grace and head of God's angelic armies.	Angel of the Lord, Captain of the Lord's Host (Exodus 3:2; Judges 13:15-18; Joshua 5:14)
MESSIAH	Daniel 9:25; John 1:41; 4:25	Jesus is Messiah.	*Messiah* is the Hebrew word, translated into Greek, as *Christ*. Both words mean "Anointed One" (one especially appointed by God for His plan and purpose).	Christ, Anointed One (Matthew 1:16; Psalm 2:1, 2)
PRINCE OF PEACE	Isaiah 9:6	Jesus is our peace.	Christ is our peace. He has ended the conflict between God and man by His death on the cross. He has also given us internal peace by the love that is planted in our hearts by His Spirit.	Peace (Ephesians 2:14) King of Salem (Hebrews 7:1, 2)
PROPHET	John 6:14; 7:40; Deut. 18:15-22; Luke 7:16; Matthew 21:11	Jesus is the prophet foretold.	Long before Jesus was born, Moses and others prophesied that a prophet like him would come speaking God's words. Jesus is that Prophet, the ultimate and final spokesman for God.	See *High Priest*.

Names of Jesus

Name	References	Meaning	Insights	Related Titles (by root word and/or theme)
REDEEMER	Job 19:25	Jesus is our redemption.	Christ's death is the payment that redeems us from the debt we owe to God's law, ransoming our lives and guaranteeing us a place in His family.	Kinsman, Ransom, Redemption, Guarantee (Ruth 2:14; Matthew 20:28; 1 Timothy 2:6; 1 Corinthians 1:30; Hebrews 7:22)
RESURRECTION AND THE LIFE	John 11:25	Jesus is life.	Christ is Life itself. Death could not hold Him, nor can it hold any who are in Him.	Living One (Revelation 1:18) See *Firstborn*.
SAVIOR	Luke 1:47-2:11; John 4:42; 1 John 4:14	Jesus is our salvation.	Christ is the Savior of the world, come to deliver us from the power of death. He is the one who seeks and saves the lost.	Captain of Salvation, Deliverer, Horn of Salvation, Salvation (Hebrews 2:10; Romans 11:26; Luke 1:69; 2:30)
SHEPHERD	1 Peter 2:25	Jesus is the good shepherd.	Jesus came to care for and to lead lost sheep, lost men and women. His sheep know His voice and no one can take them from His hands.	Door of the Sheepfold, Good Shepherd (John 10:7, 14) See *Door*.
SHILOH	Genesis 49:10	Jesus is our promised peace.	*Shiloh* may be translated as "to whom the scepter belongs," or as a name derived from the Hebrew word for peace. Jesus fulfills the prophecy by being the King to whom the scepter belongs and our Prince of Peace.	See *Messiah* and *Prince of Peace*.
SON OF GOD	Luke 1:35; Hebrews 4:14	Jesus is the Son of God by nature.	Christ is the only "natural" Son of God, which means He partakes in the Divine nature fully. We become God's children by adoption and inherit all creation in, and with, Christ.	Only Begotten, Son of the Most High, Heir (John 1:14, 18; Luke 1:32; Hebrews 1:2) See *God*.
TRUE VINE	John 15:1	Jesus is our evergreen source of life.	Jesus is our connection to the source of life. As God He has life in Himself. Having become a man He extends that life to all who believe.	See *Branch*.

Names of Jesus

Name	References	Meaning	Insights	Related Titles (by root word and/or theme)
THE WAY, THE TRUTH, AND THE LIFE	John 14:6; Acts 9:2	Jesus is our path to God.	Jesus is the Way to God. He is the path to truth and life. No mere human teacher, He is the map, the road, the destination and the one who has gone ahead of us.	Forerunner, Jacob's Ladder (Hebrews 6:20; Genesis 28:12; John 1:51)
WISDOM OF GOD	1 Corinthians 1:24, 30	Jesus is our wisdom from God.	Though the reference in Proverbs is not a strict prophetic word about Christ, the concept of wisdom as a person and associate of God is fulfilled in Jesus. To know Jesus is to be connected to the wisdom of the ages.	*Compare personified wisdom* (Proverbs 8:22-31; Luke 11:49)
WONDERFUL COUNSELOR	Isaiah 9:6	Jesus is our defense attorney.	Christ is our Wonderful Counselor before God. He comforts, consoles and counsels us as our Mediator and Intercessor. As our Advocate before God, He defends us like a lawyer before the bar of God's justice, offering Himself as a payment for our crimes.	Advocate, Comforter, Consolation of Israel, Daysman, Intercessor, Mediator, Paraclete (1 John 2:1; John 14:16; Luke 2:25; Job 9:33; 1 Timothy 2:5) See *Judge*.
WORD	John 1:1, 14.	Jesus is God's Word.	Jesus is the speech uttered by God the Father, impelled by the breath of God's Spirit. He is not merely information, but the effective, powerful Word that calls creation out of nothing and life out of death.	Word of God, Word of Life (1 John 1:1)
YAHWEH (JEHOVAH*)	Isaiah 40:3-5; Matthew 3:3; 28:19; Philippians 2:6-11; Exodus 3:14	Jesus has God's name.	The holy name *Yahweh* means "He who is." It expresses the idea that only God has self-existent being. The name was so holy that the Jews would not utter it out loud. Christ possesses this name.	I AM; Who was, Who is and Who is to come (Mark 6:50; Luke 21:8; John 8:24, 28, 58; Revelation 4:8)

*Using the vowels of *Adonai* (Lord) and the consonants of *YHVH* (God), a 16th-century German translator incorrectly translated *YHVH* as *YaHoVah*, resulting in the name *Jehovah*. Yahweh is the more accepted spelling for God's name.

Names of God	Meaning	References	Parallel Verses Referring to Jesus
YAHWEH-YIREH	God Will Provide	Genesis 22:13, 14	"I am the bread of life." (John 6:35)
YAHWEH-MEKADDISHKEM	The Lord Who Sanctifies	Exodus 31:12, 13	We have been made holy by the blood of Jesus. (Hebrews 13:12)
YAHWEH-NISSI	The Lord is My Banner	Exodus 17:15, 16	Jesus, the root of Jesse, is our banner. (Isaiah 11:10)
YAHWEH-RAPHA	The Lord Who Heals	Exodus 15:25-27	By His stripes we are healed. (1 Peter 2:24)
YAHWEH-ROHI	The Lord is My Shepherd	Psalm 23:1-3	"I am the good Shepherd." (John 10:11)
YAHWEH-SABAOTH	The Lord of Hosts	1 Samuel 1:3	Jesus will come as King of Kings. (Revelation 1:8)
YAHWEH-SHALOM	The Lord is Peace	Numbers 6:22-27	Jesus is the Prince of Peace. (Isaiah 9:6)
YAHWEH-SHAMMAH	The Lord is There	Ezekiel 48:35	Jesus said that He will be present in our hearts. (Matthew 28:20)
YAHWEH-TSIDKANU	The Lord Our Righteousness	Jeremiah 23:5, 6; 33:16	Because of Jesus, we are righteous before God. (2 Corinthians 5:21)

NAMES OF THE HOLY SPIRIT

THE HOLY SPIRIT

Much controversy and confusion exists in understanding who the Holy Spirit is and what he does.

- Many consider the Spirit to be impersonal, rather like a force—the energy or power of God. The Scriptures confirm the powerful nature of the Holy Spirit. He is named the Power of God and Spirit of Might, and yet the Bible tells us much more about him. Unlike a mere force, he can be lied to (Acts 5:3–4), he can be grieved (Ephesians 4:30), he has a name (Matthew 28:19).

- Other people see the Spirit as the common bond of love among God's people. The Scriptures call him the Spirit of grace, of mercy and of comfort; but he is also called the Spirit of truth and judgment (discernment), indicating that he is more than simply a warm fuzzy feeling we get when we are together.

- Some understand the Holy Spirit as the mind, the intellect, behind creation. To be sure, he is the Spirit of wisdom and understanding, but more than a cosmic computer. He is in fact God, the third Person of the Trinity.

Studying the names of the Spirit found in the Bible will help us get a fuller, well-rounded idea of who he is and how he operates and so allow us to worship and serve God in a fuller and richer capacity.

Study Tip

In addition to Paul's list of gifts, the apostle Peter also mentions gifts, dividing them into speaking and serving categories (1 Peter 4:10–11). Compare Paul's list to see how it also divides roughly into half speaking and half serving gifts. The book of Acts is also another great place to see the gifts in action. As you read through the book make a note whenever you encounter the use of one of the gifts.

GIFTS OF THE HOLY SPIRIT

The Bible clearly teaches that the Spirit distributes gifts to everyone who believes in Christ. The following is a list of gifts and the chapters where they are found.

The Holy Spirit gives gifts with particular spiritual functions for the benefit of the entire church. Paul's teaching in 1 Corinthians 12 speaks about the organic unity of Christ's body, the Church. The gifts complement each other and work together for the common good, much as the parts of the body are designed to do. Because this is true, the gifts are given to the church as a whole. It is only within the context of the believing community that the gifts are made to work and only within that community that they can be discovered in the first place.

fting depends on how we view the Holy Spirit. He is God's gift to us as individuals and as a body (see Acts 2:38 and 10:45). Individuals who have come into this life, the life of Christ, are automatically part of a larger whole. These gifts operate as parts of a whole. Gifting, reception of the Spirit, and membership in the Body of Christ are all connected in the life of the believer and for the good of the whole church.

	Rom 12	1 Cor 12	Eph 4
Apostleship		X	X
Prophecy	X	X	X
Evangelism			X
Pastoring			X
Teaching	X	X	X
Exhortation	X		
Knowledge		X	
Wisdom		X	
Discerning of Spirits		X	
Leadership	X		
Administration		X	
Service/Helps	X	X	
Acts of Mercy	X		
Giving	X		
Healing		X	
Faith		X	
Miracles		X	
Speaking & Interpreting Tongues		X	
Miscellaneous: Perhaps Celibacy Hospitality	(Matthew 19:12) (Romans 12:13)		

Names of the Holy Spirit

Name	References	Meaning	Application	Comments
BREATH OF THE ALMIGHTY	Job 33:4	The Holy Spirit is the life-giving breath of God.	The Holy Spirit is the source of life from God. He is the one, through Christ, who connects us to God.	The words in both Hebrew and Greek for "wind," "breath," and "spirit" all have similar origins. The idea of flowing life-giving air (see *Spirit of Life*) is what is meant.
COUNSELOR COMFORTER	John 14:16, 26; 15:26; Romans 8:26	The Holy Spirit comforts, counsels and gives strength.	The Holy Spirit is our strength and comfort. We are to turn to him when we are in trouble and when we are weak, being assured that he intercedes with and for us.	*Paraclete* is the Greek word behind this name. It refers to an advocate, someone called alongside to strengthen and fight on behalf of another (see *Spirit of Counsel*).
SPIRIT OF COUNSEL	Isaiah 11:2	The Holy Spirit counsels and teaches us as we grow in Christ.	We need to make use of God's guidance by letting the Holy Spirit lead us and teach us.	Jesus is called the Wonderful Counselor (Isaiah 9:6). Just as the Holy Spirit led Jesus to the wilderness (Luke 4:1), he leads us to truth as our Counselor (John 14:26).
ETERNAL SPIRIT	Hebrews 9:14	The Holy Spirit is eternal God.	The Spirit is no mere created force. He is the timeless Creator who loves us eternally.	The Holy Spirit is co-eternal with God the Father and God the Son.
FREE SPIRIT	Psalm 51:12	The Holy Spirit is God's generous and willing spirit.	God gives us his willing Spirit to change our hard hearts and give us freedom.	Without God's Spirit who makes us willing to receive him, we would never be free from the prison of sin.
GOD	Acts 5:3–4	The Holy Spirit is the Third Person of the Trinity. He is God.	The Holy Spirit is not a thing, a force, nor mere power. He is personal, and we are to worship and obey him as God.	We are to understand that God is one in his essence, but three in Person.
GOOD SPIRIT	Nehemiah 9:20; Psalm 143:10	God's Good Spirit will teach and lead us in all that is good.	The Holy Spirit is God's good gift to us for help in the present.	We are not alone in the world. Christ's very own Spirit is with us to work all things for our good.

Names of the Holy Spirit

Name	References	Meaning	Application	Comments
HOLY SPIRIT	Psalm 51:11; Luke 11:13; Ephesians 1:13; 4:30	God is Spirit and that Spirit is holy. He is the Spirit of holiness.	The same Holy Spirit given to us for life is given to make us holy as well.	The term *Holy Ghost* is sometimes used in place of *Holy Spirit*. *Ghost* today has a negative idea attached to it. The use of the qualifier "holy" is to distinguish God's Spirit from evil spirits.
LORD	2 Cor. 3:16–17	Like Jesus and the Father, the Holy Spirit is also addressed and worshiped as Lord.	The Holy Spirit is God present with us. He is our Lord.	The lordship of the Spirit means we are to obey him and not grieve him.
POWER OF THE HIGHEST	Luke 1:35	The Spirit is God's power, the greatest power there is.	God's power, the Holy Spirit can accomplish things through us that we cannot do ourselves.	The same Greek word for *power* is the word from which we derive *dynamite*.
SPIRIT OF MIGHT	Isaiah 11:2	The Holy Spirit is the Spirit of Strength.	Jesus' Spirit is God's strength given to us.	Jesus told us he would give us the Power of the Spirit (Acts 1:8).
SPIRIT OF ADOPTION	Romans 8:15	He is the Spirit by which we are made God's children.	God's love toward us as his children comes through the Holy Spirit. As the Spirit persuades us, we become part of God's family.	We may actually refer to God as "Daddy" (*Abba* in Aramaic) or "Father" because we have Jesus' Spirit in us.
SPIRIT OF BURNING	Isaiah 4:4	The Spirit is God's fire of purification.	God's Spirit cleanses and purifies from evil.	The Spirit of God often appears as fire (Matthew 3:11; Acts 2:3).
SPIRIT OF JUDGMENT	Isaiah 4:4; 28:6	The Spirit of God brings conviction and judgment.	God's Spirit discerns and divides good from evil.	Jesus said the Holy Spirit would convict and judge the world (John 16:8).

Names of the Holy Spirit

Name	References	Meaning	Application	Comments
SPIRIT OF CHRIST (JESUS CHRIST)	Romans 8:9; 1 Peter 1:11	The Holy Spirit is Jesus' own spirit of love shared with the Father.	Jesus has shared the Spirit of love with those who believe him.	The very same Spirit of love that the Father shares with the Son is now given to us (1 John 1:3).
SPIRIT OF GLORY	1 Peter 4:14	The Spirit always gives glory to Christ.	Christ's life is what the Spirit focuses us on.	The Holy Spirit is shaping our lives into the glorious pattern of Christ.
SPIRIT OF GOD	Genesis 1:2; 1 Cor. 2:11; Job 33:4	The Holy Spirit is the Spirit of the Triune God.	God is Spirit and truth (John 4:24).	The Holy Spirit is the essence and core of the relationship between the Father and the Son.
SPIRIT OF YAHWEH / SPIRIT OF THE LORD YAHWEH	Isaiah 11:2; Isaiah 61:1	The Spirit has the sacred name of God—Yahweh.	The Spirit can be called by the sacred name because he is God.	Jesus told his disciples to baptize in the name (singular) of the Father, Son and Holy Spirit (Matthew 28:19).
SPIRIT OF GRACE	Zech. 12:10; Hebrews 10:29	God's Spirit is a merciful spirit.	We come to know God's grace only when the Spirit opens our hearts.	Jesus accomplished the work of grace for us on the cross, but it is the Spirit who applies that grace to us by giving us faith.
SPIRIT OF KNOWLEDGE	Isaiah 11:2	The Spirit is the Spirit of clarity of mind.	The Spirit does not lead to confusion but to true knowledge (1 Corinthians 14:33).	Jesus is the shoot from Jesse's stem—in other words, the Messiah—that Isaiah prophesied; Jesus had the fullness of the Spirit of knowledge (Isaiah 11:1–2).
SPIRIT OF TRUTH	John 14:17; 15:26	The Holy Spirit is about truth, not falsehood.	The Spirit leads us to truth, not error.	Jesus said he is truth. We receive his Spirit of truth.
SPIRIT OF UNDERSTANDING	Isaiah 11:2	The Spirit is understanding itself.	Not merely technical knowledge, the Spirit comprehends and understands our needs.	Jesus said the Spirit would help us understand (John 16:12–15).

Name	References	Meaning	Application	Comments
SPIRIT OF WISDOM	Isaiah 11:2; Ephesians 1:17	The Holy Spirit is wise.	The Spirit is not merely intellectual, but personal as well: He is wise in the way he leads us.	Wisdom is highly valued by God (see Proverbs). The Spirit is the source of all true wisdom.
SPIRIT OF LIFE	Romans 8:2	The Holy Spirit is life-giving (John 6:63).	Just as our biological life requires breath and breathing, we need God's Spirit, his breath to truly live.	Jesus said he is life (John 14:6). His Spirit is the giver of that life.
SPIRIT OF THE LIVING GOD	2 Cor. 3:3	The Holy Spirit is the Spirit of the God of life.	The Spirit of God is living and the giver of life to us.	God is called the Living God because he is life and the source of life through his Spirit to the world.
SPIRIT OF PROPHECY	Revelation 19:10	It is the Holy Spirit who inspires true prophecy.	Because the Spirit is the source of prophecy, he helps us understand God's word.	All Scripture is inspired (God-breathed). The Spirit is the breath of inspiration (2 Timothy 3:16).
SPIRIT OF REVELATION	Ephesians 1:17	God's spirit reveals his truth.	It is the work of the Spirit to reveal God and his truth to us. (See *Spirit of Prophecy* and *Spirit of Truth*.)	Revelation comes from the Father through Jesus by the Spirit who is the voice of God in us.
SPIRIT OF THE FATHER	Matthew 10:20	The Holy Spirit is the Spirit of the Father shared with Jesus.	The Spirit of the Father and of Jesus has been sent to us by them.	The Spirit shared between the Father and Son, the Spirit of love, is now given to us. (See *Spirit of Christ* and *Spirit of the Son*.)
SPIRIT OF THE FEAR OF THE LORD	Isaiah 11:2	The Spirit is the Spirit of reverence toward the Lord.	The Holy Spirit will always lead us to revere God.	God is to be given awe and reverence. It is the Holy Spirit who inspires this attitude in us.
SPIRIT OF THE LORD (GOD)	Acts 5:9	The Spirit is the presence of the Lord.	We are to worship and obey the Spirit as Lord.	The name indicates the identity of the Spirit as our Lord.

Name	References	Meaning	Application	Comments
SPIRIT OF THE SON	Galatians 4:6	The Spirit is the Spirit of Jesus, the Son, whom he shares with the Father.	The loving Spirit of the Son of God is now given to us.	The Spirit draws us into the love and fellowship that is between the Father and the Son.
SPIRIT	Matthew 4:1; John 3:6; 1 Timothy 4:1	The Holy Spirit is sometimes simply called "Spirit."	The Spirit is the integral essence of life, love, and truth.	The Spirit is truly the source of all life; everything that exists does so only because of him.

The Trinity

In the simplest of terms, Christians believe that there is only one God, and this one God exists as one essence in three Persons—the Father, the Son, and the Holy Spirit.

Why do Christians Believe in the Trinity?
- The Bible clearly teaches that there is only one God, yet it calls all three Persons God.
- There is only one God (Deuteronomy 6:4; Isaiah 44:6, 8; 45:5a).
- The Father is God (1 Corinthians 8:6; Ephesians 4:4–6).
- The Son is God (John 1:1–5, 14; John 10:30–33; John 20:28; Hebrews 1:6–8; Philippians 2:9–11; see these passages about Jesus' deity: Isaiah 7:14; Isaiah 9:6; John 1:1; John 1:18; John 8:58, 59; John 10:30; Acts 20:28; Romans 9:5; 10:9–13; Colossians 1:15, 16; Colossians 2:9; Titus 2:13; Hebrews 1:3, 8; 2 Peter 1:1; 1 John 5:20).
- The Holy Spirit is God (Acts 5:3, 4; 2 Corinthians 3:17; Exodus 34:34; 2 Corinthians 3:16).

Fruit of the Spirit

In Galatians 5:16–25, the Apostle Paul contrasts two different motivations for life: one that allows the sinful nature to lead it, and another that follows the promptings and guidance of the Spirit. The sinful nature produces attitudes and actions that oppose God's will (Galatians 5:19–21). The Spirit naturally leads one to attitudes and actions that are in step with the will of God. Paul calls these attitudes and actions *fruit of the Spirit*. Fruits are the way plants reproduce—they carry the seeds. They are aromatic, colorful and tasty so that they can please and attract carriers of their seed, who spread them and allow the plant to reproduce. The life of a person whom the Spirit leads produces fruit: attitudes and behavior that are pleasing to God and other people. These *fruit of the Spirit* are: **love, joy, peace, patience, kindness, goodness, faithfulness, gentleness and self-control** (Galatians 5:22–23).

Spirit and Prayer

The Spirit of God is the Spirit of prayer. We can only approach God through Christ with the help of the Spirit. Jesus is humanity's only access to God (John 14:6). Since his ascension, Christ has not been physically present on earth; the only way to lay our requests and worship before him, and so before God, is by means of the Holy Spirit.

Jesus promised the gift of the Spirit in the life of his disciples (John 14:16–17) and the Bible tells us that one of the crucial tasks of the Spirit is to inspire and guide our prayers. When our weaknesses prevent us from relating to God correctly, the Spirit intercedes for us—that is, he pleads our case before God (Romans 8:26–27)—so we can rest assured that the Spirit is praying alongside us, making our prayers what they ought to be.

If we understand prayer as communication with God, then we will be able to see it more fully as a dialogue, rather than a monologue on our part. Prayer is a two-way conversation; the other half of our worship before God is God's guidance and clarity of his will to us. Just as we may only reach God in the Spirit through the truth of Christ (John 4:24), so also God's guidance and teaching comes to us only through Christ by means of the Spirit (John 14:26; 15:26; 16:12–14).

Blasphemy Against the Holy Spirit

Jesus said, *"People will be forgiven for their sins and whatever blasphemies they utter, but whoever blasphemes against the Holy Spirit can never have forgiveness"* (Mark 3:28).

The issue of blasphemy against the Spirit has bothered many Bible readers.

What is blasphemy against the Holy Spirit?
Blasphemy involves an utterance or action that purposefully defames God. Blasphemies against God are prohibited by the third commandment (Exodus 20:7), yet people regularly misuse God's name and are forgiven. Jesus' name is a target of abuse, yet Christ himself teaches that these offenses may be forgiven (Luke 12:10). What makes blasphemy of the Holy Spirit different?

Jesus seems to be speaking about something bigger than mere words or actions directed against God's Spirit. The context (Mark 3:30) helps us to see that what Jesus' accusers were involved in was insisting that Jesus' Spirit (the Holy Spirit) was at the core demonic, satanic, evil! The point seems to be not that the name calling itself could not be forgiven, but that the ramifications of their words would cause the speakers to reject God's only offer of salvation.

Why?
Because the Holy Spirit is God's final witness to Christ and his salvation! Whatever one may say of Christ, if the whisper of the Spirit in the ear or the shout of his voice in creation and history is ignored fully and finally, there
can be no forgiveness, because there will be no regeneration, no conversion, no repentance.

Blasphemy of the Holy Spirit is thus tied to one of the Spirit's most important works—revelation. In the end, it is the Spirit of Truth, the Spirit of Revelation who must turn the minds and hearts of the human race. If we do not listen to him, we shall never receive Christ, and if we never receive Christ, God will never forgive us.

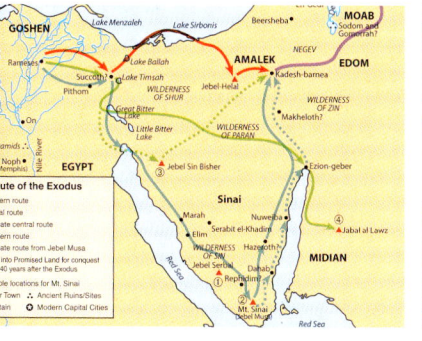

OLD TESTAMENT

NOAH'S ARK

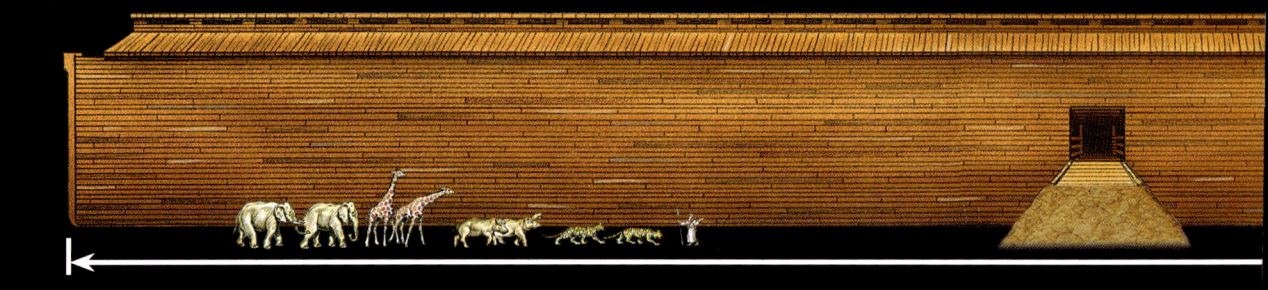

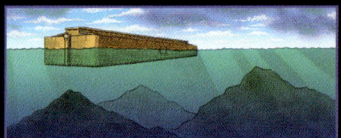

About 100 to 120 Years
God Grieves Over Corrupt Earth; Tells Noah to Build an Ark

God is sorrowful about the great wickedness and violence in all the people on the earth, and sees their evil thoughts. He tells Noah, who is righteous and "walked with God," that He will destroy the people and the earth with a flood. God gives Noah plans to build an ark and be saved. Noah does everything God tells him to do. Building the ark took about 100 years when Noah was about the ages of 500 to 600. Gen. 6:3-22; 5:32; 7:6

7 Days
God Shuts Door of Ark

God tells Noah and the animals to go into the ark. After seven days, God shuts them in. Genesis 7:7, 10, 16

40 Days
The Flood Begins

Underground waters burst forth and rain falls 40 days and nights, covering the ground. Noah, his three sons, and their wives are safe in the ark along with every kind of animal and bird. Genesis 7:11

110 Days
Water Covers All The Earth

After the rain ends, the water covers all the land and mountains. The ark floats safely high above the ground. Even the highest mountains are under more than 20 feet (nearly 7 meters) of flood waters. Nothing is left alive anywhere on earth, except for Noah and those in the ark. The water covers the earth for 150 days. God sends a wind across the waters and the waters recede. Genesis 7:17–8:1

Noah's Ark • 71

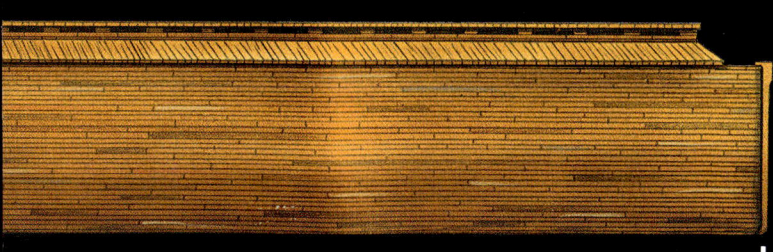

450 feet (138 meters)

45 ft. (13.5 m)

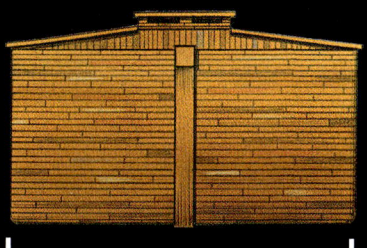

75 feet (23 meters)

74 Days
The Water Goes Down and The Ark Rests
God does not forget Noah, his family, and the animals in the ark. He makes the water go down. On the 17th day of the seventh month of the year, the ark rests in the Ararat mountains, five months from the start of the flood. Genesis 8:1-4

40 Days
Mountain Tops Are Seen
The water lowers. The mountain tops can be seen on the first day of the 10th month, two and a half months later. After 40 days, Noah checks the water. Genesis 8:5, 6

28 Days
Noah Sends Out Birds
Noah sends a raven out of a window. Then he sends a dove every seven days. At last it brings an olive leaf; and finally it doesn't return. Genesis 8:6-12

22 Days
601 Years Old
Noah was 600 years old when the rain began. Now he is age 601 on the first day of the year. Noah wonders if the land is dry. Genesis 7:11; 8:13

57 Days
Noah Opens the Roof
Noah opens the ark roof and sees that the earth is almost dry. By the 27th day of the second month, the earth is completely dry. God tells Noah that they can leave the ark and the animals can go, reproduce, and live all over the earth. Genesis 8:13-19

A New Start
Noah builds an altar and offers animal and bird sacrifices pleasing to the Lord. The rainbow is a sign of God's promise to never again destroy all creatures with a flood. Genesis 8:20-9:17

Twelve Tribes of Israel

Reuben
"See, a son!"
Water

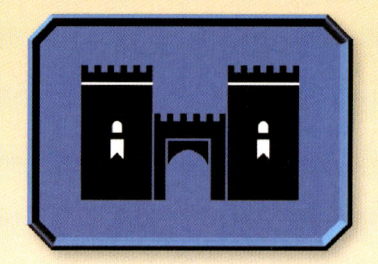

Simeon
"Hearing"
Gate

Levi
"Attached"
Breastplate of the high priest

Judah
"Praise"
Lion

Dan
"Judge"
Snake

Naphtali
"My struggle"
Deer

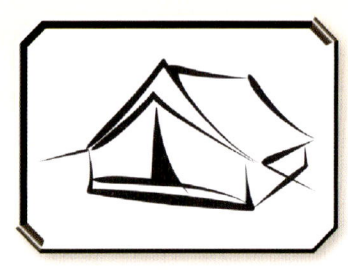

Gad
"Good fortune" / "warrior"
Tents

Asher
"Happy"
Tree

Issachar
"There is a reward"
Donkey

Zebulun
"Dwelling"
Ship

Joseph
"He will increase"
Sheaf of grain

Benjamin
"Son of the right hand"
Wolf

Twelve Tribes of Israel

THE 12 TRIBES OF ISRAEL were the family groups descended from the biblical patriarch Jacob. The tribes are important because God worked through the tribes to fulfill his purposes—especially his purpose of bringing from the tribe of Judah Jesus the Savior, the Lion of Judah.

- In the book of Genesis, we see God blessing and working through a family: Jacob and his 12 sons. (God renames Jacob as "Israel.")
- Then God works through a nation: Israel—the descendants of Jacob's sons arranged into 12 tribes. God brings them out of Egypt and into the Promised Land.
- In the New Testament, we notice God working through a different group of 12: Jesus' 12 disciples. They spread the good news of salvation.
- In the book of Revelation, we are reminded of a remnant of 144,000 people sealed by God—12,000 from each of the 12 tribes of Israel.

BREASTPLATE OF THE HIGH PRIEST

In the Old Testament, the high priest wore a breastplate made of linen and gold with 12 inlaid, precious stones inscribed with the names of the tribes.

- Exodus 28:15–30 lists the stones right to left, as Hebrew is read right to left. The tribal names inscribed on the stones may have followed the order of how the tribes marched in the wilderness (Num. 2–3).
- Instead of Levi and Joseph, the tribes of Joseph's sons—Manasseh and Ephraim—were represented on the breastplate.
- The exact identity and color of some of the stones remain uncertain.

Zebulun	Issachar	Judah
Gad	Simeon	Reuben
Benjamin	Manasseh	Ephraim
Naphtali	Asher	Dan

TIME LINE *Dates are approximate*

Abraham is called by God to go to Canaan; God makes a covenant with Abraham that Abraham's descendants will be "a great nation" (Gen. 12:1–7).

2080 BC

1928-1908 — **Jacob** (Abraham's grandson) marries Leah and Rachel; they and their handmaidens bear 12 sons (Gen. 29–30).

1897-1884

1876 — **Famine** prompts Jacob's family to migrate to Egypt where they are reunited with Joseph (Gen. 42–46).

Joseph is sold into slavery by his brothers. In Egypt, he rises to prominence (Gen. 37–41).

Jacob blesses his sons on his deathbed (Gen. 49).

1859 — **In Egypt:** Jacob's descendants remain there 430 years, part of that time in slavery.

The Exodus: Moses leads the Israelites (Jacob's descendants) out of Egypt (Ex. 3–14).*
First census of Israelite tribes at Sinai (Num. 1–3).

1446 — **Wilderness Wanderings:** Israelites live in the wilderness for 40 years.
Tabernacle built at Sinai (Ex. 26). Tribes camp around tabernacle under their family banners (Num. 2).

Second census in Moab (Num. 26). Moses blesses tribes before his death (Deut. 33).

1406-1405 — **Joshua** leads the tribes into Canaan and divides the land among the tribes (Josh. 1).

Era of Judges begins*

1350 — *Some scholars date the exodus at c. 1290. For this "low date," the dates for wilderness wanderings and beginning of the era of judges would slide to the right 156 years, compressing the era of judges.

King David conquers Jerusalem (2 Sam. 5).

1051 — **King Saul** unites the tribes into one kingdom (1 Sam. 9–11).

1011

Kingdom splits: Southern tribes become Kingdom of Judah; Northern tribes become Kingdom of Israel (1 Kings 12).

Babylonia conquers Kingdom of Judah, destroys temple, exiles people to Babylon (2 Kings 25). In exile, distinctions between the tribes become less important. The people become known as Jews.

960 **931** **722** — **Assyria** conquers Kingdom of Israel (2 Kings 17). **586** **538-516 BC** — **Persia** conquers Babylonia and allows the Jews to return to the land and rebuild the temple in Jerusalem (2 Chron. 36:23).

King Solomon builds the temple in Jerusalem (1 Kings 6).

Tribe symbols are based on tradition and most reflect Jacob's blessings in Genesis 49. Bible scholars differ about the dates, meanings of names, and specific tribe locations. We have tried to ensure that the material presented here is consistent with widely held interpretations among Bible scholars.

The Families of Abraham, Isaac, and Jacob (Israel)

ABRAM and SARAI
To Canaan (Genesis 12)
The Land Promised (Genesis 15)

— Hagar (Egyptian Handmaiden) —

Renamed **ABRAHAM** **and SARAH** **ISHMAEL**

Cast out (Gen. 21)

ISAAC

— Mount Moriah (Gen. 22)

Father of Arabs (Gen. 25)

— Married Rebekah —

ESAU

JACOB

— Fled to Haran

Father of Edomites (Gen. 36)

— Married Leah —

— Married Rachel —
Bilhah (Handmaiden) —
— Zilpah (Handmaiden)

1-REUBEN
2-SIMEON
3-LEVI
4-JUDAH

5-DAN
6-NAPHTALI

7-GAD
8-ASHER

9-ISSACHAR
10-ZEBULUN

11-JOSEPH

— Married Asenath

Jacob renamed ISRAEL

MANASSEH
EPHRAIM

12-BENJAMIN

Joseph sold into slavery in Egypt

Pharaoh gave Joseph power over Egypt

— Moved to Egypt —

The Children of ISRAEL in Egypt 430 years, part of that time in slavery

Twelve Tribes of Israel • 75

Reuben

Meaning: "See, a son!"

Symbol: Water (or mandrake plant; Gen. 30:14)

Stone/Color: Turquoise (or emerald) / Greenish-blue

Family: First son of Jacob, born to Leah

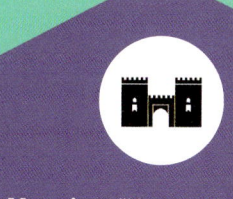

Size: First Census: 46,500. Second Census: 43,730.

Location: The tribe settled outside the Promised Land, east of the Jordan River in rich pasture lands suitable for their large herds and flocks (Num. 32:1). Included Mt. Nebo from which Moses viewed the Promised Land.

Jacob's Blessing: Jacob called his firstborn "my might, the first sign of my strength, excelling in honor, excelling in power." But Reuben had relations with Bilhah, Rachel's handmaiden (Gen. 35:22), so Jacob rebuked him saying that he is "unstable as water" and he will "no longer excel" (Gen. 49:3–4 NKJV).

Moses' Blessing: "Let Reuben live and not die, nor his people be few" (Deut. 33:6).

Notable: Reuben intervened on behalf of Joseph to save him from being killed by his brothers. Nevertheless, when Reuben returned, he discovered that his brothers had sold Joseph to slave traders (Gen. 37).

The tribe of Reuben kept their word by helping the other tribes conquer the Promised Land, though they themselves settled outside the land (Num. 32; Josh. 1:12–18). Yet at other times, they seemed indecisive and failed to assist in battle (Judg. 5:15–17).

Simeon

Meaning: "Hearing"—God has heard

Symbol: Gate, like the gate of Shechem (or a sword)

Stone/Color: Lapis lazuli (or sapphire) / Blue

Family: Second son of Jacob, born to Leah

Size: First Census: 59,300. Second Census: 22,200. Between the two censuses—a span of 40 years—the size of the tribe significantly decreased. Though it's not clear why, it's possible that they suffered more severely than the other tribes from the plagues recorded in the book of Numbers (See Num. 25).

Location: Enclave of land in Judah, likely with scattered settlements in Judah. Included Beersheba.

Jacob's Blessing: Along with his brother Levi, Simeon attacked the people of the city of Shechem to avenge the assault on his sister Dinah (Gen. 34:24–31). Jacob rebuked Levi and Simeon saying, "their swords are weapons of violence. Let me not enter their council ... for they have killed men in their anger.... I will scatter them in Jacob and disperse them in Israel" (Gen. 49:5–7).

Moses' Blessing: Moses does not mention the tribe of Simeon.

Notable: When Jacob's sons went to Egypt to buy food during a famine, Joseph imprisoned Simeon as a guarantee that Benjamin, their youngest brother, would be brought to Joseph (Gen. 42–43).

The tribe was known for being shepherds, often migrating in search of pasturelands for their flocks, possibly a fulfillment of Jacob's prophecy that Simeon will be scattered and dispersed (1 Chron. 4:24–43).

LEVI

Meaning: "Attached" Leah believed that having given birth to another son, Jacob would become attached to her.

Symbol: Breastplate of the high priest

Stone/Color: Not represented on the breastplate / Often associated with the tabernacle colors: gold, purple, blue, and red.

Family: Third son of Jacob, born to Leah

Size: First Census: Not counted with the other tribes because they were caretakers of the tabernacle, not fighting men. They were counted separately and numbered 22,000. Second Census: 23,000.

Location: Joshua gave them 48 towns throughout the Promised Land in which to live and serve as ministers of the law among the tribes.

Jacob's Blessing: Along with his brother Simeon, Levi attacked the people of the city of Shechem to avenge the assault on his sister Dinah (Gen. 34:24–31). Jacob rebuked them for the attack (Gen. 49:5–7).

Moses' Blessing: "Bless all his skills, Lord, and be pleased with the work of his hands" (Deut. 33:11).

Notable: The priests were chosen from the tribe of Levi. Levites who were not chosen to be priests, however, still participated in caretaking of the tabernacle (Num. 3:5–10). Once a year, on the Day of Atonement, the high priest wore the breastplate with the precious stones and entered the Most Holy Place of the tabernacle. He sprinkled a sacrificed animal's blood on the mercy seat of the ark of the covenant to atone for the people's sins (Lev. 16). The Levites sided with the Southern Kingdom of Judah and migrated to Jerusalem after the Northern Kingdom engaged in idol worship and rejected the Levites as priests (2 Chron. 11:13–17). When the Jews returned to the land after exile, Ezra had to send a special delegation to persuade some of the Levites to return (Ezra 8:15–36). Moses, Aaron (the first high priest), Miriam, Ezra, Ezekiel, John the Baptist, and Barnabas were from the tribe of Levi.

JUDAH

Meaning: "Praise"

Symbol: Lion

Stone/Color: Carnelian (or ruby) / Red

Family: Fourth son of Jacob, born to Leah

The genealogy in the Gospel of Matthew shows how Jesus was a descendant of Judah through the royal lineage of King David (Matt 1; Ps. 89:3-4; Isa 9:6; Heb. 7:14; Rev. 5:5). Christ was born in Bethlehem as Micah prophesied (Mic. 5:2).

Size: First Census: 74,600. Second Census: 76,500. Largest of the tribes.

Location: Very large allotment of land. Included Jerusalem, Bethlehem, Hebron, and Gaza.

Jacob's Blessing: "You are a lion's cub, Judah; you return from the prey, my son. Like a lion he crouches and lies down, like a lioness—who dares to rouse him? The scepter will not depart from Judah, nor the ruler's staff from between his feet, until he to whom it belongs shall come and the obedience of the nations shall be his" (Gen. 49:9–10).

Moses' Blessing: "Hear, Lord, the cry of Judah; bring him to his people. With his own hands he defends his cause. Oh, be his help against his foes!" (Deut. 33:7).

Notable: Judah convinced his brothers to spare Joseph's life and sell him to slave traders for a profit instead of kill him (Gen. 37). Later, Judah unknowingly had relations with his daughter-in-law Tamar. When it was revealed, he confessed his wrongdoing (Gen. 38). The tribe of Judah led the other tribes on their march toward the Promised Land. The tribe camped on the east side of the tabernacle—the only side with an entrance (Num. 2). Leaders like Caleb, David, and Zerubbabel were from the tribe of Judah, as were prophets like Amos, Micah, Isaiah, and Zephaniah.

Twelve Tribes of Israel • 77

DAN

Meaning: "Judge"
Symbol: Snake (or scales of justice)
Stone/Color: Topaz (or beryl) / Color unknown, possibly light green
Family: Fifth son of Jacob, born to Rachel's handmaiden Bilhah

Size: First Census: 62,700. Second Census: 64,400.

Location: Small portion of land that included Joppa (Tel Aviv today). The tribe, however, failed to conquer the Philistines in the land and migrated to the northernmost part of Canaan (Judg. 18).

Jacob's Blessing: "Dan will provide justice for his people.... Dan will be a snake by the roadside" (Gen. 49:16–17).

Moses' Blessing: "Dan is a lion's cub, springing out of Bashan" (Deut. 33:22).

Notable: The tribe of Dan is reprimanded in the Song of Deborah for not joining in battle (Judg. 5:17). Samson was from this tribe (Judg. 13:2, 24). King Jeroboam built a pagan temple in Dan (1 Kings 12:29). Amos includes Dan in his list of idolaters (Amos 8:14).

NAPHTALI

Meaning: "My struggle"
Symbol: Deer (doe)
Stone/Color: Jasper / Reddish-brown
Family: Sixth son of Jacob, born to Rachel's handmaiden Bilhah

Size: First Census: 53,400. Second Census: 45,400.

Location: Hill country of Galilee.

Jacob's Blessing: "Naphtali is a doe let loose; He bears beautiful fawns" (or "gives beautiful words" Gen. 49:21).

Moses' Blessing: Naphtali is "full of blessing" (Deut. 33:23).

Notable: In the Song of Deborah, the tribe is praised for its courage (Judg. 5:18). Barak was from Naphtali (Judg. 4:6). The tribe assisted Gideon in battle (Judg. 7:23). They volunteered fighting men to support David against King Saul (1 Chron. 12). Jesus began his ministry in Galilee, fulfilling Isaiah's prophecy (Matt. 4:13–22; Isa. 9:1–2).

GAD

Meaning: "Good fortune" (or "warrior")
Symbol: Tents, like a battlefield camp
Stone/Color: Emerald (or diamond) / Possibly a stone with little color
Family: Seventh son of Jacob, born to Leah's handmaiden Zilpah

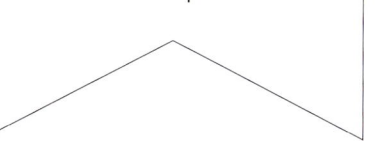

Size: First Census: 45,650. Second Census: 40,500.

Location: Fertile land outside the Promised Land, along the Jordan River (Num. 32).

Jacob's Blessing: "Gad will be attacked by a band of raiders, but he will attack them at their heels" (Gen. 49:19).

Moses' Blessing: Gad is commended for carrying "out the LORD's righteous will, and his judgments concerning Israel" (Deut. 33:21).

Notable: Gadites who supported David in his conquest of Jerusalem were described as "brave warriors, ready for battle and able to handle the shield and spear" (1 Chron. 12:8).

Meaning: "Happy"
Symbol: Tree (or food)
Stone/Color: Onyx / Black
Family: Eighth son of Jacob, born to Leah's handmaiden Zilpah

Asher

Size: First Census: 41,500. Second Census: 53,400. The tribe significantly increased.

Location: Northern coastal region along the Mediterranean Sea.

Jacob's Blessing: "Asher's food will be rich; he will provide delicacies fit for a king" (Gen. 49:20).

Moses' Blessing: "Let [Asher] be favored by his brothers, and let him bathe his feet in oil" (Deut. 33:24).

Notable: Asher is not included in King David's list of chief rulers, possibly indicating that by the time of David the tribe had lost its significance (1 Chron. 27:16–22). The prophetess Anna, who recognized the infant Jesus as the Messiah, was from the tribe of Asher (Luke 2:36–38).

Meaning: "There is a reward"
Symbol: Donkey (or sun and moon)
Stone/Color: Chrysolite (or topaz) / Yellowish-green
Family: Ninth son of Jacob, born to Leah

Issachar

Size: First Census: 54,400. Second Census: 64,300.

Location: Fertile Jezreel Valley. Included Nazareth.

Jacob's Blessing: "Issachar is a sturdy donkey.... When he sees how good the countryside is and how pleasant the land, he will bend his shoulder to the load and submit himself to hard labor" (Gen. 49:14–15 NLT).

Moses' Blessing: Mentioned along with Zebulun as tribes who will "feast on the abundance of the seas, and on the treasures hidden in the sand" (Deut. 33:18–19).

Notable: Deborah commended the tribe of Issachar for standing with the Israelites in battle (Judg. 5:15). During the time of David, the tribe was known for its wisdom: "men who understood the times and knew what Israel should do" (1 Chron. 12:32).

Meaning: "Dwelling"
Symbol: Ship
Stone/Color: Beryl (emerald) / Possibly green
Family: Tenth son of Jacob, born to Leah

Zebulun

Size: First Census: 57,400. Second Census: 60,500.

Location: Small portion of southern Galilee.

Jacob's Blessing: "Zebulun will live by the seashore and become a haven for ships" (Gen. 49:13).

Moses' Blessing: Zebulun and Issachar will "feast on the abundance of the seas, and on the treasures hidden in the sand" (Deut. 33:18–19).

Notable: Deborah commended this tribe for risking their lives (Judg. 5:18). They supported David with "undivided loyalty" (1 Chron. 12:33). When Hezekiah called for spiritual renewal, people from Asher, Manasseh, and Zebulun humbled themselves and traveled to Jerusalem (2 Chron. 30:10). Jesus began his ministry in Galilee—the land of Zebulun and Naphtali—fulfilling Isaiah's prophecy (Matt. 4:13–22; Isa. 9:1–2).

Twelve Tribes of Israel • 79

JOSEPH

Meaning: Joseph: "He will increase."

Manasseh: "One who forgets." God made Joseph forget all his hardships (Gen. 41:51).

Ephraim: "Double fruitfulness." God made Joseph fruitful in the land of his suffering (Gen. 41:52).

Symbol: Sheaf of grain (or grapevine)

Stone/Color:
Manasseh: Agate / Yellowish-brown

Ephraim: Jacinth / Orangish-red

Family: Eleventh son of Jacob, born to Rachel. Joseph's sons are Manasseh and Ephraim.

Size: Manasseh: First Census: 32,300. Second Census: 52,700. Population greatly increased.

Ephraim: First Census: 40,500. Second Census: 32,500. Population decreased.

Location: The descendants of Joseph's two sons became recognized as two tribes and were given territory when they entered the Promised Land.

Manasseh: Two large portions of land east and west of the Jordan River. The eastern section (Golan Heights and part of Syria today) was outside the Promised Land. Those in the eastern section are referred to in the Bible as the half-tribe of Manasseh.

Ephraim: Small portion of land (part of the West Bank today). Included Bethel where Abraham built an altar (Gen. 12:8) and where God confirmed the Abrahamic covenant with Jacob (Gen. 28).

Jacob's Blessing: Joseph is "a fruitful vine" (Gen. 49:22). Jacob blessed Joseph's sons saying that Ephraim would be greater than Manasseh the firstborn (Gen. 48).

Moses' Blessing: "May the LORD bless [Joseph's] land ... with the best gifts of the earth and its fullness" (Deut. 33:13–17).

Notable: Though Joseph was sold into slavery by his jealous brothers, God raised Joseph to a place of prominence in Egypt. Joseph stored up grain for a coming famine. When his brothers traveled to Egypt to purchase grain during the famine, Joseph was reconciled to them. He said, "You intended to harm me, but God intended it for good to accomplish what is now being done, the saving of many lives" (Gen. 50:20). Jeroboam (who led the secession of northern tribes), Joshua, Deborah, and Samuel were from the tribe of Ephraim (Judg. 4; 1 Sam. 1; 1 Kings 12; 1 Chron. 7).

BENJAMIN

Meaning: "Son of the right hand"

Symbol: Wolf

Stone/Color: Amethyst / Purple

Family: Twelfth son of Jacob, born to Rachel. Rachel named him Ben-Oni, "son of my sorrows," as she was dying in childbirth, but Jacob renamed him Benjamin, "son of the right hand" which indicates a favored son (Gen. 35:18).

Size: First Census: 35,400. Second Census: 45,600.

Location: Small portion of land just north of Jerusalem, a strategic position in ancient Israel.

Jacob's Blessing: "Benjamin is a ravenous wolf; in the morning he devours the prey, in the evening he divides the plunder" (Gen. 49:27).

Moses' Blessing: "Let the beloved of the LORD rest secure in him, for he shields him all day long" (Deut. 33:12).

Notable: In Egypt, Joseph tested his brothers by saying that he would keep Benjamin as his slave. When Judah pleaded with Joseph not to deprive his father of Benjamin, Joseph was moved to reveal his true identity and be reconciled with his brothers (Gen. 44–45). In the era of the judges, a civil war nearly obliterated the tribe of Benjamin (Judg. 20). King Saul was from the tribe of Benjamin (1 Sam. 9:1–2). After Saul's death, the tribe fought against David for control of the kingdom, but eventually sided with David (2 Sam. 2). Jeremiah, Mordecai, and the apostle Paul were from the tribe of Benjamin (Jer. 1:1; Est. 2:5–6; Phil. 3:5).

The Exodus

The EXODUS Journeys of the Children of Israel from Egypt to Canaan
EXODUS 12 to JOSHUA 7

The Great Sea (Mediterranean)

1. Passover. Sprinkling blood on the doorframes. *Exodus 12:22*
2. Bones of Joseph brought out. *Exodus 13:19*
3. Crossing the Red Sea. *Exodus 14:22*
4. Pharaoh pursues. *Exodus 14:23*
5. Bitter water made sweet (MARAH). *Exodus 15:23-25*
6. Wells of water (ELIM). *Exodus 15:27*
7. Manna and quail given (ELIM). *Exodus 16:13-18*
8. Water from rock (REPHIDIM). *Exodus 17:6*
9. Hands of Moses supported (REPHIDIM). *Exodus 17:11-13*
10. Ten Commandments given (MT. SINAI). *Exodus 19-20*
11. Golden Calf. The Lord angered. Moses breaks tablets. *Exodus 32:2-20*
12. The Tabernacle set up. *Exodus 40:17*
13. More quail. *Numbers 11:31-33*
14. Miriam smitten. *Numbers 12:1-10*
15. Returning spies. *Numbers 13:23-25*
16. Presumptuous Israelites defeated. *Numbers 14:40-45*
17. Earth swallows Korah, Dathan, and Abiram. *Numbers 16:31-33*
18. Moses strikes the rock. *Numbers 20:10, 11*
19. Death of Aaron. *Numbers 20:27, 28*
20. Bronze snake. *Numbers 21:4-9*
21. Battle fought. *Numbers 21:21-26*
22. Moses views promised land from Mt. Nebo. *Deuteronomy 34:1-5*
23. Crossing the Jordan. *Joshua 3:12-17*
24. The fall of Jericho. *Joshua 6:20*

Places: RAMESES, PITHOM, SUCCOTH, EGYPT, SINAI, MARAH, ELIM, REPHIDIM, Mt. Sinai, Wilderness of Paran, KADESH-BARNEA, HAZOROTH, EZION-GEBER, ELATH, Gulf of Ezion Geber, The Red Sea (Western Arm), MIDIAN, Red Sea, CANAAN, ARAD, JERICHO, Jordan River, Dead Sea, Mt. Nebo, AMMON, MOAB, OBOTH, IYE ABARIM, EDOM

Lines show sequence and general direction of journey only.
- EGYPT TO KADESH BARNEA
- KADESH BARNEA TO ELATH
- ELATH TO JERICHO

The Israelite tribes fled past the Egyptian system of border posts, through the Red Sea and into the desert, where they avoided the main military and trade routes leading across northern Sinai. The less frequently traveled "Way of the Sea" led to the remote turquoise and copper mining region northwest of Mt. Sinai.

Inset map: Way of the Land of the Philistines, Desert of Shur, Way to Shur Trade Route, Way of the Sea, Desert of Zin, River Nile, EGYPT, SINAI, Mt. Sinai

Miles: 0, 20, 40, 60, 80, 100
Kilometers: 0, 50, 100, 150

Art as seen in the Thompson Chain Reference® Bible.

Time Line of the Exodus
c. 1897 BC–1404 BC (Low Date: c. 1741 BC–1248 BC)

Joseph
c. 1897 BC–1884 BC (c. 1741 BC–1728 BC)
Joseph is sold into slavery in Egypt by his brothers. He later becomes an official "over all the land of Egypt."

Moses' Birth
c. 1525 BC (c. 1369 BC)
Moses is born to a Hebrew slave. He's placed in a basket to avoid being killed by Pharaoh, the king of Egypt, when he is rescued by royalty and raised as a prince of Egypt.

The Red Sea
c. 1446 BC (c. 1290 BC)
The people of Israel pass safely through the Red Sea. Pharaoh, the Egyptian army, and 600 chariots are covered by the sea as they pursue the Israelites.

Mt. Sinai
c. 1446 BC–1445 BC (c. 1290 BC–1289 BC)
After providing food for the Israelites, God gives Moses and the people his law as well as instructions for the tabernacle on Mt. Sinai. When returning from the top of the mountain, Moses is angered that people are worshiping a golden calf.

Moses' Death
c. 1405 BC (c. 1249 BC)
Moses climbs to the top of Mt. Nebo where God shows him the Promised Land. He may not enter because he disregarded God's instructions and struck the rock at Meribah. Moses dies on Mt. Nebo at the age of 120.

Timeline: 1850 BC (1694 BC) — 1650 BC (1494 BC) — 1450 BC (1294 BC) — 1440 BC (1284 BC) — 1430 BC (1274 BC) — 1420 BC (1264 BC) — 1410 BC (1254 BC) — 1400 BC (1244 BC)

Israel in Egypt
c. 1876 BC (1720 BC)
Jacob, who is also called Israel, moves his entire family to Egypt to be with Joseph. After some time, Israel's descendants (the Israelites) become slaves in Egypt.

Ten Plagues
c. 1446 BC (1290 BC)
God sends ten plagues on Egypt leading to Israel's release by Pharaoh and the beginning of the Exodus. The tenth plague is the death of every "first born" in Egypt. The Passover feast celebrates Israel's deliverance from death when the Lord "passes over" their homes because door posts have the blood of a perfect lamb on them.

Joseph's Bones
c. 1446 BC (1290 BC)
Joseph's bones are carried out of Egypt. An oath had been made to Joseph, that when God comes to lead Israel to the Promised Land, they need to carry Joseph's bones out with them.

Spies Report
c. 1444 BC (1288 BC)
Spies return from scouting the Promised Land. The people doubt God's promise and fear the people of Canaan. Only two spies give an encouraging report. Israel is punished with 40 years of wandering in the wilderness before they can enter the Promised Land.

The Promised Land
c. 1404 BC (1248 BC)
Israel enters the Promised Land under the leadership of Joshua, son of Nun. The people cross through the Jordan River on dry ground with the ark of the covenant before them. Once across, the children of Israel begin their conquest of the Promised Land by destroying Jericho.

Some scholars date the exodus around 1290 BC (low date) and others date it about 156 years earlier 1446 BC (high date).

Key People

Moses
Moses led the children of Israel out of Egypt and through the wilderness. Moses was the key figure during the exodus. He received the law from God on Mt. Sinai, and is known as the author of the Torah, the first five books of the Old Testament.

Aaron
Aaron was Moses' older brother and spokesperson. Aaron was the first high priest and all high priests after him had to be a descendant of Aaron. Aaron died on Mt. Hor at age 123.

Pharaoh
Pharaoh was a king of Egypt and was considered to be a god to the Egyptians. God hardened Pharaoh's heart so he could prove to Pharaoh, Egypt, and the Israelites that he is the true God.

Miriam
Miriam was Moses' older sister. She was the first woman called a prophetess in Scripture. Miriam was an important leader during the exodus. Like Aaron, she was successful when she supported Moses, but failed when she went against him. She died at Kadesh, just before entering the Promised Land.

Joshua, son of Nun
Joshua was the leader of the military during the exodus and was one of the two spies to give an encouraging report from Canaan. He lead the Israelites into the Promised Land after Moses died. Joshua died and was buried at Timnath Serah in the hill country of Ephraim after conquering the lands of Canaan for Israel.

THE TABERNACLE

Tribe of **Reuben** (South)
Tribe of **Simeon** (South)
Tribe of **Gad** (South)

The families of **Kohath** (Numbers 3)

The families of **Moses Aaron Nadab Eleazar Ithamar**

Tribe of **Issachar** (East)
Tribe of **Judah** (East)
Tribe of **Zebulun** (East)

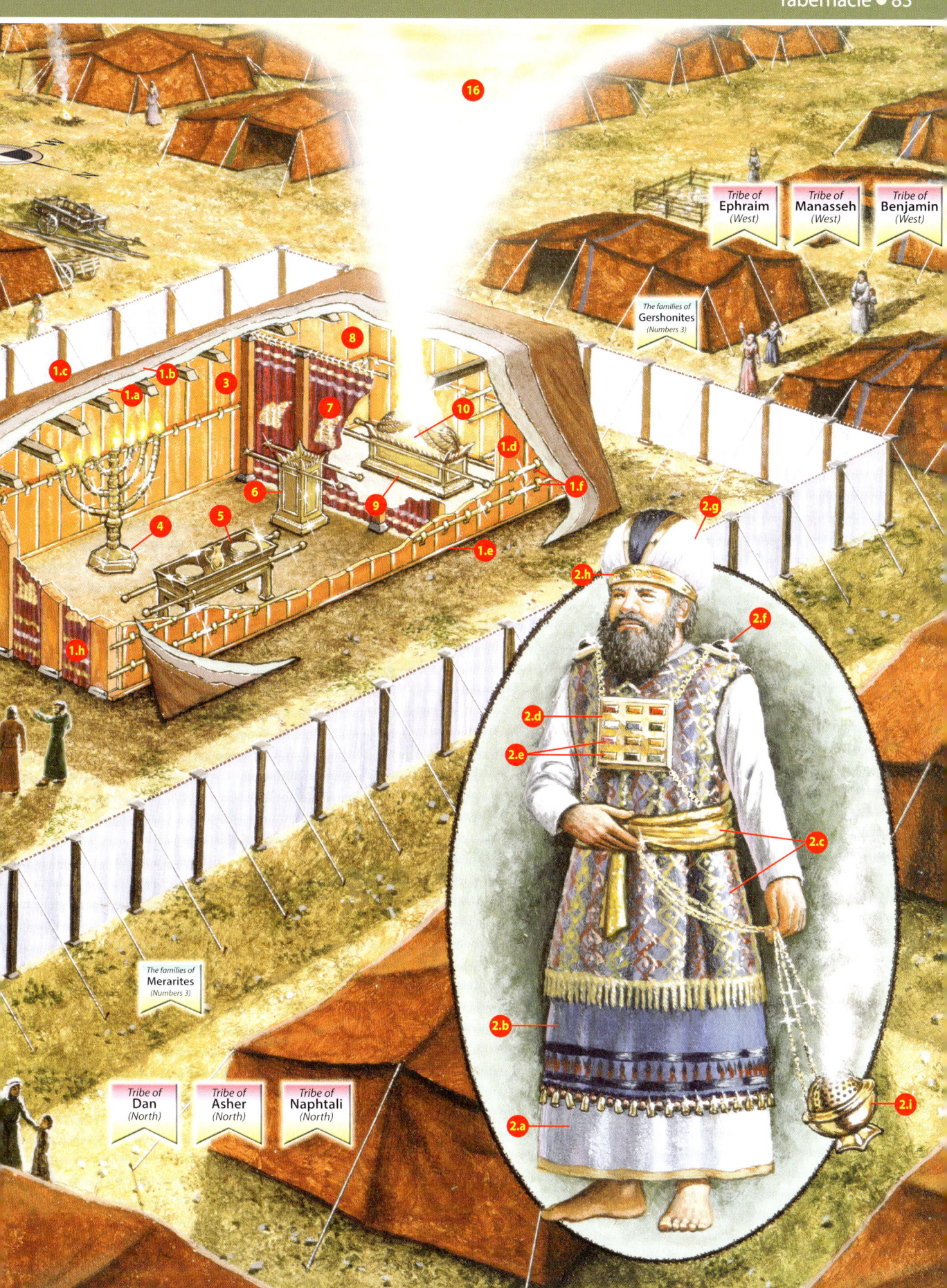

Tabernacle • 83

Tribe of **Ephraim** (West)
Tribe of **Manasseh** (West)
Tribe of **Benjamin** (West)

The families of **Gershonites** (Numbers 3)

The families of **Merarites** (Numbers 3)

Tribe of **Dan** (North)
Tribe of **Asher** (North)
Tribe of **Naphtali** (North)

Key to the Tabernacle

1. The Tabernacle (Enlarged to show detail)
(Ex. 26:1–37) (The new holy temple; Eph. 2:19–22)
30 cubits long x 10 cubits wide x 10 cubits high
(45 ft x 15 ft x 15 ft or 13.8 m x 4.6 m x 4.6 m)
The general appearance of the tabernacle was that of a rectangular box. It was divided into two sections—the Holy Place and the Most Holy Place (Holy of Holies).
a. Goats' hair covering with linen beneath (Ex. 25:4; 26:7)
b. Ram skin covering dyed red (Ex. 25:5; 26:14)
c. Badger, porpoise, or sea cow skin covering (Ex. 25:5)
d. Boards (48 boards, Ex. 26:15-25)
e. Sockets (100 total, 96 silver sockets for the boards, four under the pillars of the veil)
f. Bars (Ex. 26:26–29)
g. Pillars, hooks (Ex. 26:32–37; 36:36–38)
h. Curtains at the entrance (Ex. 26:1–6)

2. The High Priest and His Holy Garments
(Ex. 28:1–43; 39:1–31) (A great high priest; Heb. 4:14–15)
a. Embroidered coat (Ex. 28:4; Ps. 132:9)
b. Robe with golden bells and pomegranates (Ex. 28:34)
c. Ephod and girdle (Ex. 28:4)
d. Breastplate and the Urim and Thummim (Ex. 28:30)
e. Stones in the breastplate (12 tribes of Israel) (Ex. 28:17–21)
f. Shoulder stones of onyx (Ex. 28:9–12; 39:6–7)
g. Mitre (Ex. 28:4, 39)
h. Turban or Holy Plate or crown (diadem) of gold inscribed, "Holy to the Lord" (Ex. 28:36; 29:6)
i. The Censer of burning coals (Lev. 16:12–13; Heb. 9:4)

3. The Holy Place
(Ex. 26:33, Heb. 9:2, 6)
10 cubits wide x 20 cubits long (15 ft x 30 ft or 4.6 m x 9.2 m)
The priests entered into the Holy Place daily to minister to the Lord. The table of showbread (bread of the presence) stood on the right. The seven-branched golden lampstand stood on the left. The altar of incense stood in the Holy Place right in front of the veiled Most Holy Place.

4. The Golden Lampstand (Candlestick)
(Ex. 25:31–40)
The lampstand was made of pure, hammered gold, one solid piece. It had a central shaft with six branches, three on each side, making it a seven-branched lampstand. Each branch had knobs, flowers, and an almond-shaped bowl to hold pure olive oil. It was part of the priests' ministry to keep the lamp burning perpetually.

5. The Table of Showbread (Bread of the Presence)
(Ex. 25:23–30; Heb. 9:2)
2 cubits long x 1 cubit wide x 1½ cubits high
(36 in x 18 in x 27 in or 92 cm x 46 cm x 69 cm)
The table of showbread was made of shittim (acacia) wood. It was overlaid with gold and had a crown or frame of gold around it that was as wide as a man's hand. A ring of gold was put on each of the four legs, to put the carrying poles through. The carrying poles were made of shittim wood overlaid with gold. Also made of pure gold were the dishes, pans, pitchers and bowls. Twelve loaves of bread were placed on the table, six in a row. Fresh bread was placed there every Sabbath.

6. The Altar of Incense
(Ex. 30:1–10; Heb. 9:2)
1 cubit long x 1 cubit wide x 2 cubits high
(1½ ft x 1½ ft x 3 ft or 46 cm x 46 cm x 92 cm)
The altar of incense was made from shittim (acacia) wood. Its four corners each had a horn made from one piece. Its top, sides, and horns were overlaid with gold, with a crown or molding all around the top. Aaron, the high priest, burned incense upon it every morning and evening. Once a year, on the Day of Atonement, the horns of the altar were sprinkled with the blood of the sin offering.

7. The Veil
(Ex. 26:31–33; Heb. 10:19–20)
A woven veil of blue, purple, and scarlet thread, with designs of cherubim embroidered on it, was hung on four pillars of acacia wood overlaid with gold. Four gold hooks were put in four sockets of silver. The veil was hung from these, and was a divider between the Holy Place and the Most Holy Place.

8. The Most Holy Place (Holy of Holies)
(Ex. 26:3–34, Heb. 9:3)
10 cubits long x 10 cubits wide (15 ft x 15 ft or 4.6 m x 4.6 m)
Also called the Holy of Holies, here resided the ark of the covenant. It was exactly one-half the length of the Holy Place. The shekinah glory of God rested upon the lid of the ark (mercy seat). The high priest entered the Most Holy Place once a year, on the Day of Atonement, to sprinkle blood on the mercy seat to atone for his sins and the people's sins.

9. The Ark of the Covenant
(Ex. 25:10–16; Heb. 9:4)
2½ cubits long x 1½ cubits wide x 1½ cubits high
(45 in x 27 in x 27 in or 115 cm x 69 cm x 69 cm)
The ark was made of acacia wood. It was overlaid with gold, inside and out. A gold crown or molding was set around the edge of the top. Four gold rings, one in each leg were placed for the carrying poles. The poles were acacia wood overlaid with gold. The mercy seat was set on top of the ark.

10. The Mercy Seat
(Ex. 25:17–22; Heb. 9:5)
2½ cubits long x 1½ cubits wide (45 in x 27 in or 115 cm x 69 cm)
The mercy seat was made of pure gold. It had a winged cherub on each side, facing each other with wings outstretched above them, toward each other. The mercy seat was beaten or hammered from one solid piece of gold. It was placed above the ark.

11. The Gate of the Court
(Ex. 27:16; 38:18–19; John 10:9)
20 cubits wide x 5 cubits high (30 ft x 7½ ft or 9.2 m x 2.3 m)
The entrance to the court was made with:
a. Hanging curtains (blue, purple, scarlet, white) (Ex. 27:16; 38:18)
b. Four pillars of brass (Ex. 27:14–16; 38:14–15)
c. Sockets of bronze (brass) (Ex. 27:14–15)
d. Hooks and fillets (clasps) of silver (tops of pillars) (Ex. 27:10–11)

12. The Offerings
(Heb. 8:3; 9:11–14, 18–22; 10:1–4)
- Burnt offering (bull, sheep, goats or birds) (Lev. 1:1–17)
- Grain offering (Lev. 2:1–16)
- Peace offering (goat or lamb) (Lev. 3:1–17)
- Sin offering (bull or lamb) (Lev. 4:1–35)
- Trespass offering (female of the flock, lamb, goat kid, or bird or grain) (Lev. 5–6)

13. The Court Fence (Not shown to scale)
(Ex. 27:9–18; 38:9–17; 40:33)
100 cubits long x 50 cubits wide x 5 cubits high
(150 ft x 75 ft x 7½ ft or 46 m x 23 m x 2.3 m)
The court fence was the outer border of the tabernacle site. It consisted of the following:
a. Linen curtains (white) (Ex. 27:9–16; Rev. 19:8)
b. Pillars, sockets, hooks, and fillets (tops and rods) (Ex. 27:11, 17)
c. Pins of bronze (brass) (Ex. 27:19; 38:20)

14. The Bronze Altar (Brazen Altar)
(Ex. 27:1–8, 40:6, 10, 29)
5 cubits long x 5 cubits wide x 3 cubits high
(7½ ft x 7½ ft x 4½ ft or 23 m x 23 m x 1.38 m)
The bronze altar was made of shittim (acacia) wood. It was square and covered with bronze (brass). The four corners had horns overlaid with bronze. Also there were pans to receive ashes, shovels, basins, fleshhooks (forks), and fire pans, all of bronze. A bronze grate with a bronze ring in each corner was put under the brazen altar. Staves (carrying poles) were made of shittim wood covered with bronze to carry the altar.

15. The Bronze Laver (Basin)
(Ex. 30:17–21; 40:7, 30–32; Eph. 5:26; Heb. 10:22)
A large laver (basin) of bronze, in which the Aaron and his sons washed their hands and feet, was placed between the bronze altar and the tabernacle. The Lord said if they did not wash when they came near the altar to minister, they would die.

16. The Cloud and the Pillar of Fire
(Ex. 25:8, 22; 29:43; 40:34–38)
The Lord manifested his presence with a cloud by day and a pillar of fire by night. It would rest above the tabernacle, directly above the mercy seat. When the cloud or pillar of fire moved, the children of Israel followed it. Wherever it stopped, they camped there until it moved again.

The Tabernacle

The new religious observances taught by Moses in the desert centered on rituals connected with the tabernacle, and amplified Israel's sense of separateness, purity, and oneness under the Lordship of Yahweh.

A few desert shrines have been found in Sinai, notably at Serabit el-Khadem and at Timnah in the Negev, and show marked Egyptian influence.

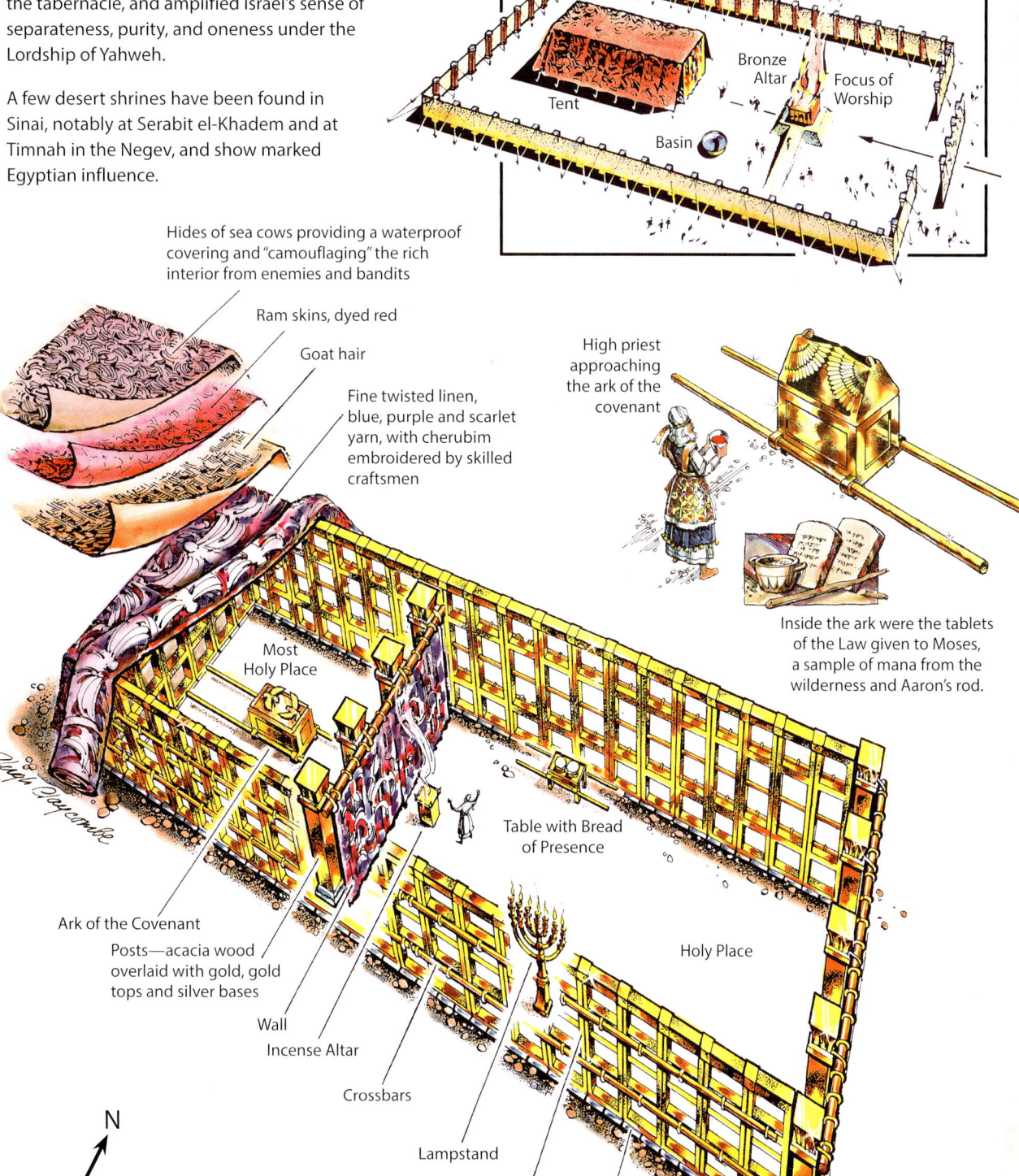

- Bronze Altar
- Focus of Worship
- Tent
- Basin

- Hides of sea cows providing a waterproof covering and "camouflaging" the rich interior from enemies and bandits
- Ram skins, dyed red
- Goat hair
- Fine twisted linen, blue, purple and scarlet yarn, with cherubim embroidered by skilled craftsmen

High priest approaching the ark of the covenant

Inside the ark were the tablets of the Law given to Moses, a sample of mana from the wilderness and Aaron's rod.

- Most Holy Place
- Ark of the Covenant
- Posts—acacia wood overlaid with gold, gold tops and silver bases
- Wall
- Incense Altar
- Crossbars
- Lampstand
- Table with Bread of Presence
- Holy Place
- Upright frames—acacia wood overlaid with gold
- Silver bases

N

The Tabernacle: Pattern of Worship

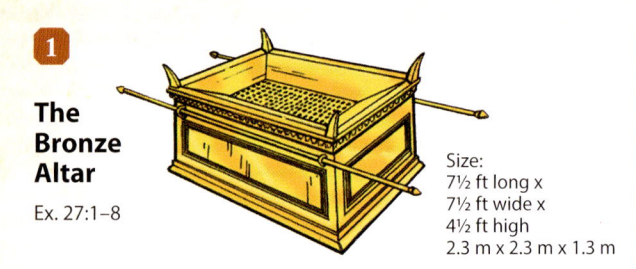

1. The Bronze Altar
Ex. 27:1–8

Size:
7½ ft long x
7½ ft wide x
4½ ft high
2.3 m x 2.3 m x 1.3 m

God wanted to dwell among his people. How does a holy God dwell among sinful people? First God required the people to sacrifice a perfect animal for their sins (Lev. 17:11). The blood of the animal was important to justify the people before God. Only the finest animal—a perfect one—was good enough. Sacrifices needed to be offered on a regular basis (Heb. 9:25).

The person bringing the offering would put his hand on the head of the lamb while it was killed. This symbolically put the person's sins onto the animal, and the animal died in his place.

To think about:
- Jesus is our perfect sacrifice and shed his blood for our sins. (John 1:29; Rev. 13:8; Heb. 10:10; Rom. 4:25.) Jesus was not only the perfect sacrifice, but his sacrifice covered all sin—past and future. No more sacrifices are required.
- In Romans 12:1, we are told to present our bodies as a living sacrifice. What does this mean to you?

2. The Bronze Laver
Ex. 30:18; 38:8

Size: None indicated

The next step was for the priests only. In fact, the rest of the work was performed by the priests on behalf of the people.

After making the sacrifice, the priest washed himself at the bronze laver. This washing purified the priest and prepared him to enter the tabernacle. In Exodus 30:20, God says they must wash so that they do not die when they enter the tabernacle.

The bronze laver was made from brass mirrors donated by the women. The Bible does not describe the laver completely, but perhaps it had a shiny mirrored surface which would help the priest wash thoroughly and to remind him that the Lord sees past the outward appearance, straight into the heart.

To think about:
- Even though we Christians have accepted Jesus' sacrificial death on our behalf, we too need to be cleansed.
- Read 1 John 1:8–9. How would Jesus' disciples understand this verse?

3. The Golden Lampstand
Ex. 25:31–40; 26:35

Size: Dimensions are unknown

From the laver, the priest passed through a veil into the Holy Place. The room he entered had three objects: a golden lampstand on the south, a table on the north, and an altar of incense to the west just before the veil to the Most Holy Place (Holy of Holies).

The unique lampstand was beaten from a single piece of gold. It was not pieced together. Scripture tells us it was fueled by oil, not wax. It had lamps at the top of each branch, not candles.

Its purpose was to provide light in this otherwise dark room. Trimming the lamp wicks to keep them burning brightly was an important job for the priest.

To think about:
- Jesus called himself the light of the world in many places in the Bible (John 12:46).
- Christians are called to be lights. See Acts 13:47. How are we lights?

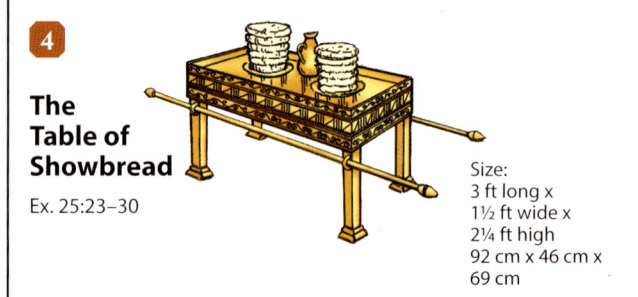

4. The Table of Showbread
Ex. 25:23–30

Size:
3 ft long x
1½ ft wide x
2¼ ft high
92 cm x 46 cm x 69 cm

On the table of showbread, Aaron and his sons placed twelve loaves of bread (bread of the presence) made from fine flour. These twelve loaves represented the twelve tribes of Israel. The table with the loaves was a continual reminder of the everlasting promises, the covenant between God and the children of Israel, and a memorial of God's provision of food. The bread was eaten by Aaron and his sons and was replaced every week on the Sabbath.

To think about:
- Jesus called himself the Bread of Life (John 6:35, 51). He said that those who came to him would never hunger again. Physical bread—even the special bread of the tabernacle—is consumed. But the spiritual Bread of Life, Jesus, gives eternal life.
- Hebrews 8:6–7 and 10:16 tell of a better covenant through Jesus, one superior to the Old Testament covenant to Israel. The law would be written on people's hearts, not on tablets of stone.

5. The Altar of Incense
Ex. 30:1–10

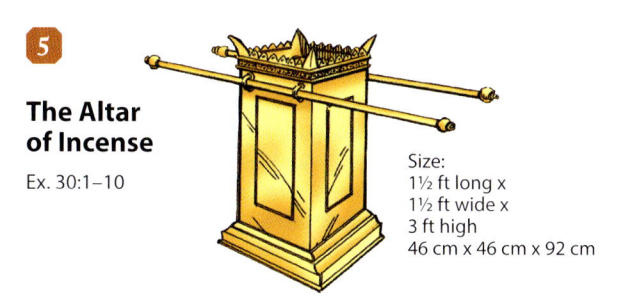

Size:
1½ ft long x
1½ ft wide x
3 ft high
46 cm x 46 cm x 92 cm

The Lord required that special incense be burned constantly on the altar of incense. It was a special sweet incense, a mixture of spices to be used only for the tabernacle (Ex. 30:35–37). God specifically required this recipe. None other was to be burned on the altar. It was a matter of life and death, as Leviticus 10:1–2 clearly shows us, when two of Aaron's sons offered a "strange fire" before the Lord and were struck dead. In the New Testament, the priest Zechariah was in the Holy Place when an angel appeared near the altar of incense (Luke 1:5–13). The angel announced that God had heard his prayers and he and his wife would have a son (John the Baptist).

To think about:
- Incense represents the prayers of the faithful. There are several references to this in the book of Revelation (5:8; 8:3–4).
- Are our prayers a sweet incense toward God?

6. The Veil
Ex. 26:33; 30:10

Size:
At least 15 ft wide 4.6 m

The veil separated the holy place from the most holy place where the ark of the covenant was kept. It was a barrier between God and humans. Once a year, Aaron would enter the Most Holy Place (Holy of Holies) through this veil. The veil was a heavy woven cloth stretching for ten cubits (15 ft or 4.6 m). There was no separation in the middle. The high priest had to go around the side to enter the most holy place. Later when the temple was constructed, it followed a similar design. The veil of the temple was torn from top to bottom when Jesus died. This symbolizes the ability of every believer, not just a high priest, to approach God through the death of Jesus.

To think about:
- For hundreds of years, the Israelites needed a human high priest to represent them before God (1 Tim. 2:5; Heb. 8:1; 9:11; 10:11–12). Name a few ways in which Jesus is a better high priest than Aaron.

7. The Ark of the Covenant and the Mercy Seat
Ex. 25:10, 14–16; 25:22; Heb. 9

Size:
3¾ ft long x 2¼ ft wide x 2¼ ft high
1.15 m x 69 cm x 69 cm

The central focus of the entire tabernacle was the Most Holy Place (Holy of Holies) where God spoke to the high priest above the mercy seat—the area where the winged cherubim face each other. Annually, the high priest would sprinkle blood on the mercy seat to atone for the sins of all the people.

God's purpose and desire is to dwell among his people and to commune with them. The layout of the tabernacle, along with the steps of sacrifice, cleansing, and remembering God's promises, is designed to bring sinful mankind to a loving and holy God.

To think about:
- Christianity is not a religion in which humans reach to know God. It is God who approaches his creatures and makes it possible for them to know him (John 6:44; Eph. 2:8–9).
- Our efforts to be "good people" are not enough to approach God. Jesus alone is the Way to God (John 14:6; Heb. 10:19–23).

Israelites Communed with God through the Tabernacle	Christians Commune with God through Jesus
1. Bronze altar for sacrifices	Christ's sacrifice
2. Bronze laver for washing	Cleansing through confession
3. Lampstand	Enlightened by the Holy Spirit
4. Table of showbread	Fed by the Living Word
5. Altar of incense	Prayer, communication, intercession
6-7. Through the veil into the Most Holy Place	Entering God's presence boldly through Christ
8. Priests and the garments	Service to God and others

Why is the tabernacle important today?
1. Today, we are God's dwelling place. (1 Cor. 6:19)
2. God's holy presence is among us. (Ex. 40:34–38)
3. As believers, we are part of a priesthood. (1 Peter 2:5–9; Rev. 5:10; 20:6; Heb. 4:16)
4. The tabernacle shows a pattern of worship prescribed by God. (Heb. 10:19–25)

The Garments of the High Priest

- The priest dressed first in a tunic and mitre (a turban) of fine linen.
- The mitre had a gold plate (or crown) inscribed with the words "HOLINESS TO THE LORD" just over the priest's forehead. The Hebrew words can also be translated "Set Apart as Holy to the Lord." This was worn in the Lord's presence so that the people's sacrifices would always be acceptable to God.
- The priest wore a blue robe with the ephod (a vest or waist coat) with stones on each shoulder bearing the names of the sons of Israel.
- Over the ephod, the priest wore a gold breastplate that was set with twelve precious stones carved with the names of the twelve tribes of Israel. This was worn over his heart and was to continually remind the Lord of his people.
- The Urim and Thummim were kept in the priest's pocket over his heart as objects used to determine the Lord's will for his people.

To think about:

Our service to God is to be holy and set apart. As we pray for others and bring their names and burdens to God, we remember that God loves his children with deep affection. (Read Jer. 31:3.)

Christ is our example as high priest: he is righteous and merciful. He was willing to sacrifice his life for us and now lives to intercede for us (Matt. 20:25–28; Heb. 7:25).

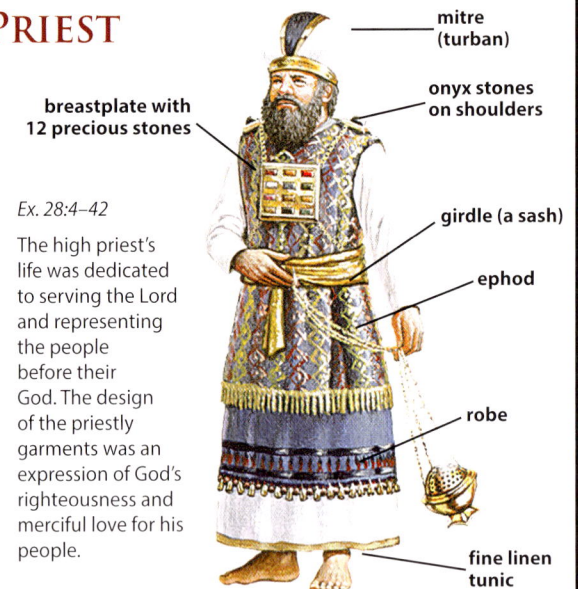

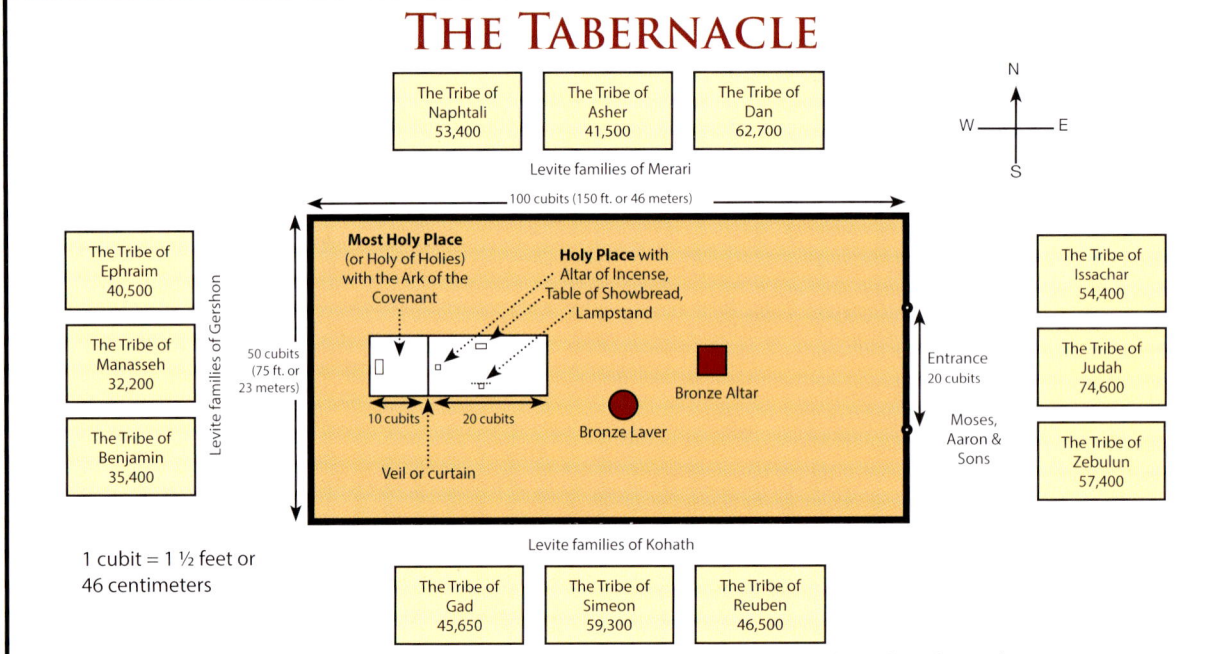

Labels on illustration: mitre (turban), onyx stones on shoulders, breastplate with 12 precious stones, girdle (a sash), ephod, robe, fine linen tunic

Ex. 28:4–42

The high priest's life was dedicated to serving the Lord and representing the people before their God. The design of the priestly garments was an expression of God's righteousness and merciful love for his people.

The Tabernacle

Tribes around the tabernacle:

North (Levite families of Merari): The Tribe of Naphtali 53,400; The Tribe of Asher 41,500; The Tribe of Dan 62,700

West (Levite families of Gershon): The Tribe of Ephraim 40,500; The Tribe of Manasseh 32,200; The Tribe of Benjamin 35,400

East (Moses, Aaron & Sons — Entrance): The Tribe of Issachar 54,400; The Tribe of Judah 74,600; The Tribe of Zebulun 57,400

South (Levite families of Kohath): The Tribe of Gad 45,650; The Tribe of Simeon 59,300; The Tribe of Reuben 46,500

Tabernacle diagram: 100 cubits (150 ft. or 46 meters) by 50 cubits (75 ft. or 23 meters). Most Holy Place (or Holy of Holies) with the Ark of the Covenant (10 cubits). Holy Place with Altar of Incense, Table of Showbread, Lampstand (20 cubits). Veil or curtain. Bronze Laver. Bronze Altar. Entrance 20 cubits.

1 cubit = 1 ½ feet or 46 centimeters

What is the Tabernacle?

The tabernacle was a moveable "tent of meeting" that God commanded Moses to build (Ex. 25:1–2; 25:8–9). God wanted to dwell among his people, the Israelites. He wanted to have fellowship with them and be able to communicate with them (Ex. 25:22).

The tabernacle and its courtyard were constructed according to a pattern set by God, not by Moses. We study the tabernacle to understand the steps that the Lord laid out for a sinful people to approach a holy God. The tabernacle became the place that God dwelt with his people for 400 years: from the exodus until the time of King Solomon when the temple was built.

The tabernacle was in the center of the Israelite camp. The 12 tribes of Israel were encamped around it. The figures in the boxes refer to the number of males age 20 or over in each tribe (Num. 1–3). The total would be 603,550.

Fascinating Facts about the Tabernacle:

- There are 50 chapters in the Bible that discuss the tabernacle.
- The tabernacle would have fit in half of a football or soccer field.
- The tabernacle of the Old Testament was a "shadow" of things in heaven. Hebrews 8:1–5 tells us that the real tabernacle is in heaven. This is where Jesus himself is our high priest.
- The tabernacle was built using many expensive materials: gold, silver, bronze, precious woods, and rare cloth. In modern terms the cost would exceed $1 million. Offerings from the Israelites paid for the materials (Ex. 35:22–36:3).
- The Israelites were so generous they gave more than was needed. Moses had to command them to stop giving (Ex. 36:6).

Sacrifices in the Tabernacle

SACRIFICE	MEANING TODAY
Sin Offering and Guilt Offering *(Lev. 4–6; Num. 15:1–12)* Sin offerings and guilt offerings focused on paying for sin. The sin offerings atoned for sins against God. The guilt offerings addressed sins against others, and included paying damages with interest. Various animals were offered, depending on the person's position and income. Priests and leaders, as examples to others, had to offer larger sacrifices for sin, while the poor offered what they could afford. Blood was sprinkled on the altar, the parts of the animals were burned, often with wine poured on them (drink offering). Other parts were roasted for the priests. Since the priests were full-time tabernacle workers, sacrificed animals were their main source of food. 	**Christ's Offering** Isa. 53:10; Matt. 20:28; 2 Cor. 5:21 **Paying for Damages** Matt. 5:23–24; Luke 19:1–10 **Poor** Luke 2:2–24; 21:1–4 **Leaders as Examples** 1 Tim. 3:1–7; 5:19–20 **Providing for Christian Workers** Phil. 4:18; 1 Cor. 9:13–14; 1 Tim. 5:17–18
Burnt Offering *(Lev. 1)* This sacrifice represented complete dedication and surrender to God. The animal, usually an unblemished male, bears the worshiper's sins, and dies in his/her place. After the blood was sprinkled on the altar, the animal was completely burned up. None of it was roasted for eating. 	**Surrender** Ps. 51:16–17; Matt. 26:39; Rom. 12:1 **Dedication** Phil. 2:17; 2 Tim. 4:6–7
Grain (Meal) Offering *(Lev. 2)* This offering was given to God in thankfulness. The people brought fine flour, unleavened cakes, or roasted grain to the priests. The priests burned a symbolic handful at the altar, and could partake of the rest. There was very little ceremony involved. 	**Giving** Matt. 26:6–10; 2 Cor. 9:7–11 **Praise** Ps. 100; Heb. 13:15–16 **Thankfulness** Ps. 147; Phil. 4:6
Fellowship (Peace) Offering *(Lev. 2; 7:11–21)* This offering symbolized fellowship and peace with God through shed blood. After some meat was ceremonially waved and given to the priests, worshipers and their guests could share in the feast as a meal with God. 	**God's Peace** Col. 1:20; Acts 10:36 **God's Feast** Luke 14:15–24; 1 Cor. 11:17–26; Jude 1:12; Rev. 3:20

The Journey of the Ark of the Covenant from Mt. Sinai

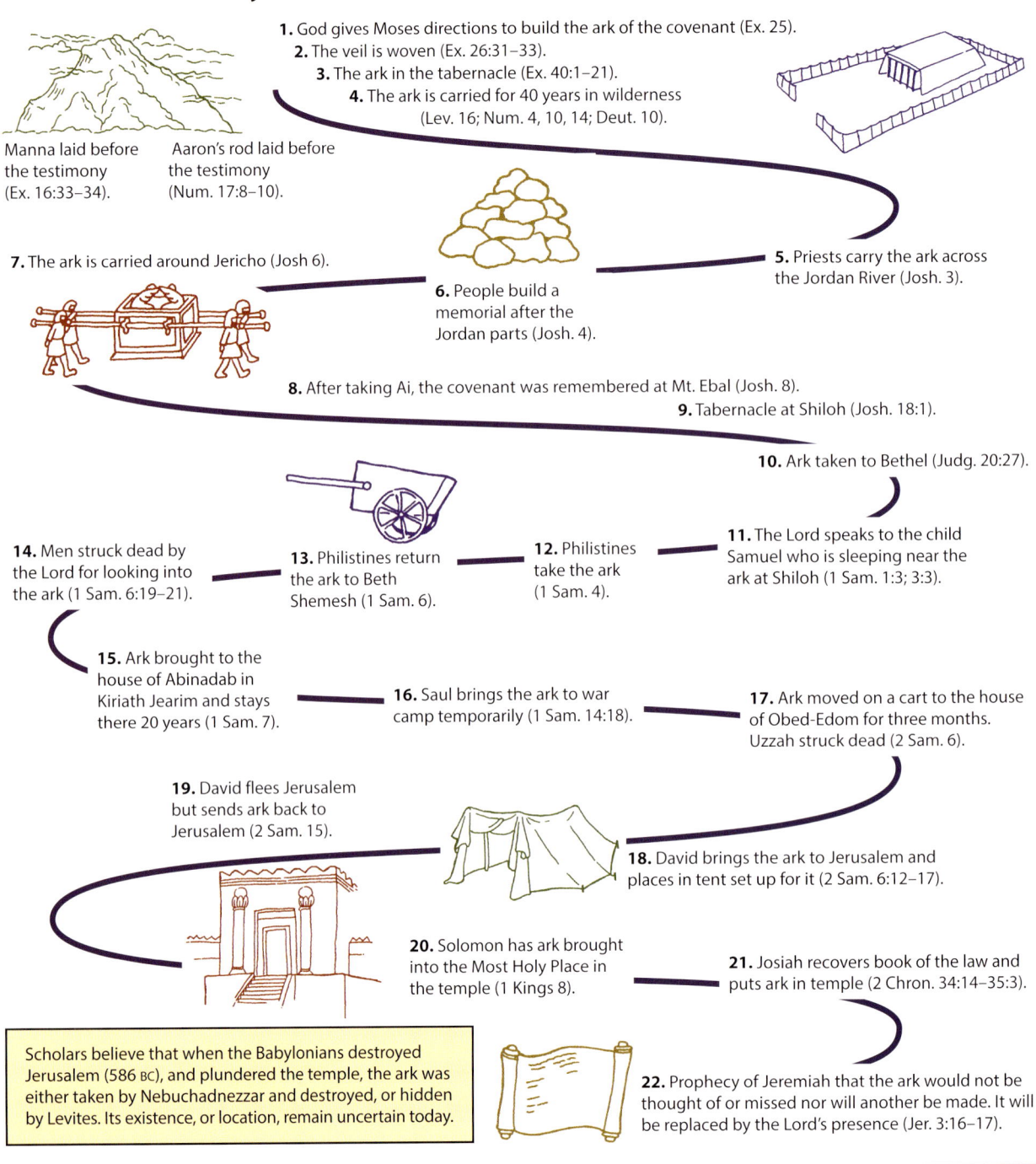

Manna laid before the testimony (Ex. 16:33–34).

Aaron's rod laid before the testimony (Num. 17:8–10).

1. God gives Moses directions to build the ark of the covenant (Ex. 25).
2. The veil is woven (Ex. 26:31–33).
3. The ark in the tabernacle (Ex. 40:1–21).
4. The ark is carried for 40 years in wilderness (Lev. 16; Num. 4, 10, 14; Deut. 10).
5. Priests carry the ark across the Jordan River (Josh. 3).
6. People build a memorial after the Jordan parts (Josh. 4).
7. The ark is carried around Jericho (Josh 6).
8. After taking Ai, the covenant was remembered at Mt. Ebal (Josh. 8).
9. Tabernacle at Shiloh (Josh. 18:1).
10. Ark taken to Bethel (Judg. 20:27).
11. The Lord speaks to the child Samuel who is sleeping near the ark at Shiloh (1 Sam. 1:3; 3:3).
12. Philistines take the ark (1 Sam. 4).
13. Philistines return the ark to Beth Shemesh (1 Sam. 6).
14. Men struck dead by the Lord for looking into the ark (1 Sam. 6:19–21).
15. Ark brought to the house of Abinadab in Kiriath Jearim and stays there 20 years (1 Sam. 7).
16. Saul brings the ark to war camp temporarily (1 Sam. 14:18).
17. Ark moved on a cart to the house of Obed-Edom for three months. Uzzah struck dead (2 Sam. 6).
18. David brings the ark to Jerusalem and places in tent set up for it (2 Sam. 6:12–17).
19. David flees Jerusalem but sends ark back to Jerusalem (2 Sam. 15).
20. Solomon has ark brought into the Most Holy Place in the temple (1 Kings 8).
21. Josiah recovers book of the law and puts ark in temple (2 Chron. 34:14–35:3).
22. Prophecy of Jeremiah that the ark would not be thought of or missed nor will another be made. It will be replaced by the Lord's presence (Jer. 3:16–17).

Scholars believe that when the Babylonians destroyed Jerusalem (586 BC), and plundered the temple, the ark was either taken by Nebuchadnezzar and destroyed, or hidden by Levites. Its existence, or location, remain uncertain today.

"But only the high priest entered the inner room, and that only once a year, and never without blood, which he offered [by sprinkling on the ark] for himself and for the sins the people had committed in ignorance. ... When Christ came as high priest of the good things that are already here, he went through the greater and more perfect tabernacle that is not man-made, that is to say, not a part of this creation. He did not enter by means of the blood of goats and calves; but he entered the Most Holy Place once for all by his own blood, having obtained eternal redemption."
— Hebrews 9:7, 11–12

"Then God's temple in heaven was opened, and within his temple was seen the ark of his covenant. And there came flashes of lightning, rumblings, peals of thunder, an earthquake and a great hailstorm."
—Revelation 11:19

The Judges

Israel Disobeys → **Israel is Oppressed** → **Israel Cries Out** → **God Raises up a Deliverer** → **Israel is Delivered** → **Israel is at Peace** → (cycle repeats)

Judge	Description	Years Judged
OTHNIEL	After 8 years of oppression from King Cushan of Aram, Othniel went to war and delivered Israel.	40 years
EHUD	After 18 years of oppression from King Eglon of Moab, Ehud killed Eglon, went to war against Moab, and was victorious.	80 years
SHAMGAR	Shamgar killed 600 of the Philistines with a poking device used to move animals along.	unknown
DEBORAH	After 20 years of oppression from King Jabin of Canaan, Deborah convinced Barak to attack. Barak was victorious.	40 years
GIDEON	After 7 years of Midianite oppression, Gideon defeated the Midianites with only 300 men, using trumpets and jars.	40 years
TOLA	The son of Puah son of Dodo from the tribe of Issachar. He lived in Ephraim.	23 years
JAIR	A man from Gilead who had 30 sons who rode 30 donkeys, and they had 30 towns in Gilead.	22 years
JEPHTHAH	After 18 years of Ammonite oppression, Jephthah delivered Israel after making a vow with the Lord.	6 years
IBZAN	Ibzan was from Bethlehem. He had 30 sons and 30 daughters.	7 years
ELON	Elon was from the tribe of Zebulun.	10 years
ABDON	Abdon, son of Hillel, had 40 sons and 30 grandsons who rode on 70 donkeys.	8 years
SAMSON	A Nazarite with superhuman strength. He killed 1,000 Philistines with a jawbone; destroyed a Philistine temple.	20 years

Feasts of the Bible

Holiday	Date Observed	Scripture Basis	General Information
PASSOVER (Pesach) פֶּסַח	14 NISAN (March or April)	Leviticus 23:4–5 Exodus 12:1–4	**Commemorates God's Deliverance of Israel Out of Egypt** Pesach (PAY-sahk) means to "pass over." The Passover meal, seder (SAY-der), commemorates the Israelites' deliverance from slavery in Egypt. The Lord sent Moses to lead the children of Israel from Egypt to the Promised Land. When first confronted by Moses, Pharaoh refused to let the people go. After sending nine plagues, the Lord said the firstborn males of every house would die unless the doorframe of that house was covered with the blood of a perfect lamb. That night, the Lord "passed over" the homes with blood on the doorframes. The tenth plague brought death to the firstborn sons of Egypt, even taking the life of Pharaoh's own son. Finally, Pharaoh let the children of Israel go. Passover was to be a lasting ordinance for generations to come.
UNLEAVENED BREAD (Hag HaMatzot) חַג הַמַּצוֹת	15-21 NISAN (March or April)	Leviticus 23:6–8 Exodus 12:15–20	**In Leviticus 23, Hag HaMatzot (Hawg Hah-MAHT-zot) or Hag HaMatzah, also known as the "Feast of Unleavened Bread,"** is mentioned as a separate feast on the fifteenth day of the same month as Passover. Today, however, the feasts of Pesach, Unleavened Bread, and Firstfruits have all been incorporated into the celebration of Passover, and reference to Passover means all three feasts. Passover is celebrated for eight days, 14–21 Nisan. The Lord said that for seven days the children of Israel must eat unleavened bread. This bread, made in a hurry without yeast, represents how the Lord brought the Israelites out of Egypt in haste. In Scripture, leaven also represents sin. Today, cleansing the house before Passover is often a symbolic search to remove any hypocrisy or wickedness. Unleavened Bread is one of the three pilgrimage feasts when all Jewish males were required to go to Jerusalem to "appear before the Lord" (Deut. 16:16).
FIRSTFRUITS (Reishit) רֵאשִׁית	16 NISAN (March or April)	Leviticus 23:9–14	**Offerings are Given for the Spring Barley Harvest** On Reishit (Re-SHEET) people offered the first ripe sheaf (firstfruits) of barley to the Lord as an act of dedicating the harvest to him. On Passover, a marked sheaf of grain was bundled and left standing in the field. On the next day, the first day of Unleavened Bread, the sheaf was cut and prepared for the offering on the third day. On this third day, Reishit, the priest waved the sheaf before the Lord. Counting the days (omer) then begins and continues until the day after the seventh Sabbath, the 50th day, which is called Shavuot or Pentecost (the next feast on the calendar). Jewish people rarely celebrate Reishit today, but it has great significance for followers of Jesus as the most important day of the year, the day of Jesus' resurrection.
FEAST of WEEKS or PENTECOST (Shavuot) שָׁבֻעוֹת	6 SIVAN (May or June)	Leviticus 23:15–22	**Offerings are Given and Commemorates the Giving of the Law** Fifty days after Passover, Shavuot (Sha-voo-OTE) is celebrated. Also known as Pentecost, Feast of Weeks, the Feast of Harvest, and the Latter Firstfruits, it is the time to present an offering of new grain of the summer wheat harvest to the Lord. It shows joy and thankfulness for the Lord's blessing of harvest. Often called Matan Torah (giving of the Law), it is tied to the Ten Commandments because it is believed God gave Moses the Ten Commandments at this time. The book of Ruth is often read to celebrate the holiday. Shavuot is one of the three pilgrimage feasts when all Jewish males were required to go to Jerusalem to "appear before the Lord" (Deut. 16:16).

Feasts of the Bible • 93

Yeshua (Jesus) | Fascinating Facts

PASSOVER

Yeshua (Jesus): Jesus ate the Passover with his disciples, saying that he had eagerly desired to eat this Passover with them before he suffered and that he would not eat it again until the kingdom of God comes (Luke 22:7–16). After the Passover meal, they sang a hymn and went to the Mount of Olives (Matt. 26:30). The hymn sung during Passover is the Hallel, which includes Psalm 118:22: "The stone the builders rejected has become the cornerstone." Jesus is the cornerstone that the builders rejected (Matt. 21:42; 1 Peter 2:7). Jesus was crucified as the "Lamb of God who takes away the sin of the world" (John 1:29). The Lord's Supper is a remembrance of his sacrifice as the perfect Passover Lamb and the fulfillment of the new covenant between God and man (Luke 22:20; 1 Cor. 5:7; Eph. 2:11–13). Prophecy of this sacrifice is found in Psalm 22. The Hebrew prophet Isaiah also spoke of the sufferings and sacrifice of the Messiah (Isa. 53).

Fascinating Facts:
- Jesus' parents traveled to Jerusalem yearly to celebrate Passover. At age 12, Jesus went with them (Luke 2:41–50).
- The Passover lamb must be a perfect male with no blemish (Ex. 12:5).
- The cup of the Lord's Supper is the third cup of the Passover Seder, the Cup of Redemption. The bread of the Lord's Supper is the Afikomen. It is the matzah that is broken, hidden, found, bought for a price, and then eaten to end the meal. *Afikomen* means "I came" in Greek.

Scriptures: Ex. 12; Num. 9; 28:16–25; 2 Chron. 35:1–19; Ezra 6:19; Ezek. 45:21; Matt. 26; Mark 14; Luke 22; John 6:4; 11; 13; 19; 1 Cor. 5:7

UNLEAVENED BREAD

Yeshua (Jesus): Unleavened bread (matzah) is a symbol of Passover. Leaven represents sin (Luke 12:1; 1 Cor. 5:7–8). Matzah stands for "without sin" and is a picture of Jesus, the only human without sin. Jesus said that the "bread of God is he who comes down from heaven and gives life to the world" and that he (Jesus) is the "bread of life," the "bread that came down from heaven," "the living bread" which a person may eat and not die (John 6:32, 35, 41, 48). While leaven is a symbol of sin, the Messiah is "unleavened" or sinless. He conquers the grave with his resurrection because he is not a sinner under the curse of death. Jesus was scourged and pierced at his crucifixion. As the prophet Isaiah proclaims, "By his stripes we are healed" (Isa. 53:5 KJV). All of the festivals instituted by God, including Passover and Unleavened Bread, are "shadows of things to come" (Col. 2:17).

Fascinating Facts:
- The only type of bread eaten during the eight days of Passover/Unleavened Bread is matzah. It is made with flour and water only, not any leaven. It is striped and pierced during baking. Matzot is plural for matzah.
- The utensils used must never touch leaven. Bakery goods are made with matzah meal.
- On the night before Passover, the father does a final search for any remaining leaven in the house. Traditionally, by candlelight, he sweeps any remaining bread crumbs onto a wooden spoon with a goose feather. When finished, the bread crumbs, the feather, and the spoon are placed in a bag and burned the next morning.

Scriptures: Ex. 23:15; 34:18; 2 Chron. 30; Ezra 6:22; Acts 12:3; 20:6

FIRSTFRUITS

Yeshua (Jesus): Firstfruits is a picture of Jesus' resurrection. Jesus rose on the third day of Passover season, 16 Nisan, the day of Firstfruits. That event gave new meaning to this agricultural holiday. The apostle Paul, a Jewish believer and rabbi, wrote, "But Christ has indeed been raised from the dead, the firstfruits of those who have fallen asleep. For since death came through a man, the resurrection of the dead comes also through a man. For as in Adam all die, so in Christ all will be made alive. But each in turn: Christ, the firstfruits; then, when he comes, those who belong to him" (1 Cor. 15:20–23). Jesus' resurrection is the promise of the future resurrection of believers (John 5:28–29). Although most believers in Jesus have never heard of Reishit, they celebrate it as Resurrection Day, or Easter.

Fascinating Facts: Biblical events that happened on this day:
- The manna, which God provided from heaven as food for the Israelites while they wandered in the wilderness, stopped after they crossed the Jordan River into the Promised Land (Josh. 5:10–12).
- Queen Esther risked her life to save the Jewish people from annihilation (Est. 3:12–5:7).
- Jesus rose from the dead on the third day (Luke 24:44–47).

PENTECOST

Yeshua (Jesus): Jesus told his disciples to wait in Jerusalem following his crucifixion, resurrection, and ascension. They were all together in the upper room for Shavuot on the 50th day after the Sabbath of Passover week, thus, the first day of the week. The Holy Spirit filled the house with a sound like a mighty wind and what appeared to be tongues of fire, and filled the disciples (Acts 2). The apostle Peter referred to the prophet Joel who said that God would "pour out his Spirit on all flesh" (Joel 2:28–32). Peter also said that the risen and exalted Jesus had poured out the Holy Spirit (Acts 2:32–33). The people responded to Peter's message with repentance, and about 3,000 were baptized (Acts 2:41). The new covenant between God and Israel (Jer. 31:31; Heb. 9:14–15) was initiated on Shavuot, 50 days after the death of Christ.

Fascinating Facts:
- Shavuot is celebrated 50 days after Passover, so it became known as Pentecost, which means "50" in Greek. The days from Passover to Shavuot are counted at weekly Sabbath services.
- Special foods for this holiday are dairy foods, such as cheesecake and cheese blintzes, because the Law is compared to milk and honey.
- Homes and synagogues are decorated with flowers and greenery, which represent the harvest and the Torah as a "tree of life." Observant Jews often spend the night reading and studying the Torah.

Scriptures: Ex. 34:22; Deut. 16:9–10; 2 Chron. 8:13; Ezek. 1 (Traditional reading); Acts 2:1–41; 20:16; 1 Cor. 16:8; James 1:18

Feasts of the Bible

Holiday	Date Observed	Scripture Basis	General Information
FEAST of TRUMPETS or NEW YEAR (Yom HaTeruah, Rosh HaShanah) רֹאשׁ הַשָּׁנָה	1 TISHRI (September or October)	Leviticus 23:23–25	**The Beginning of the Civil New Year** The Ten Days of Repentance with Rosh HaShanah (Rosh Ha-SHA-nah) on the first day and Yom Kippur on the last day make up the High Holy Days. Jewish tradition says that God writes every person's words, deeds, and thoughts in the Book of Life, which he opens and examines on this day. If good deeds outnumber sinful ones for the year, that person's name will be inscribed in the book for another year on Yom Kippur. During the Rosh HaShanah synagogue services, the shofar (ram's horn) is blown 100 times.
DAY of ATONEMENT (Yom Kippur) יוֹם כִּפֻּר	10 TISHRI (September or October)	Leviticus 23:26–32	**The Day the High Priest Makes Atonement for Sin** Yom Kippur (Yome Ki-POOR), also known as Day of Atonement, is the most solemn holy day of the Jewish people. *Yom* means "day" and *Kippur* means "atonement" or "covering." *Atonement* means the reconciliation of God and humankind. The ten days which include Rosh HaShanah and Yom Kippur are known as the "days of repentance." Yom Kippur is the final day of judgment when God judges the people. The shofar (ram's horn) is blown at the end of the evening prayer service for the first time since Rosh HaShanah. In Bible times, the high priest sacrificed an animal to pay for his sins and the sins of the people. When the high priest was finished with the atonement sacrifice, a scapegoat was released into the wilderness to carry Israel's sins away (Lev. 16:8–10, 20–22, 29–34).
FEAST of BOOTHS or TABERNACLES (Sukkot) חַג הַסֻּכּוֹת	15–22 TISHRI (September or October)	Leviticus 23:33–43	**Commemorates the Forty-Year Wilderness Journey** Sukkot (Soo-KOTE or SOO-kote), also known as "Feast of Tabernacles," is a week-long celebration of the fall harvest and a time to build booths (temporary shelters of branches) to remember how the Hebrew people lived under God's care during their forty years in the wilderness (Neh. 8:14–17). The celebration is a reminder of God's faithfulness and protection. Jewish people continue to celebrate Sukkot by building and dwelling in temporary booths for eight days. The four special plants used to cover the booths are citron, myrtle, palm, and willow (Lev. 23:39–40).
FEAST of DEDICATION (Hanukkah / Chanukah) חֲנֻכָּה	25 KISLEV- 2 TEVET (November or December)	John 10:22 Also Book of Maccabees (Apocrypha)	**Commemorates the Purification of the Temple** Hanukkah (KHA-noo-kah), the Feast of Dedication, celebrates the Maccabees' victory over the Greeks and the rededication of the temple in 165 BC after Seleucid king Antiochus Epiphanes defiled it by sacrificing a pig on the altar. The Maccabees' victory is recorded in the books of Maccabees in the Apocrypha. Hanukkah is also known as the Feast of Lights because of a legendary miraculous provision of oil in the temple. After cleansing the temple, the supply of oil to relight the eternal flame (the symbol of God's presence) was only enough for one day. But God performed a great miracle, and the flame burned for the eight days necessary to purify new oil.
FEAST of LOTS (Purim) פּוּרִים	14 or 15 ADAR (February or March)	Book of Esther	**Commemorates the Preservation of the Jewish People** Purim (POOR-im) marks the deliverance of the Jews through Jewish Queen Esther in Shushan, Persia (Susa, Iran). The annual celebration of Purim is a joyous feast remembering the foiled plot of Haman to kill all the Jews living within King Xerxes's (Ahasuerus's) kingdom. Esther's cousin Mordecai uncovered the plot and warned Esther, who then told the king. The king had Haman executed, and 14 and 15 Adar became days of joy and feasting (Est. 9:18–32). Purim is celebrated on 14 Adar in most cities except those cities surrounded by walls since the time of Joshua. Walled cities celebrate Purim on 15 Adar (Shushan Purim).

Yeshua (Jesus)	Fascinating Facts	
Rosh HaShanah is sometimes referred to as the Day of Judgment. Jesus said he has the authority to judge people (John 5:24–27) and the apostle Paul referred to him as the judge of "the living and the dead" (2 Tim. 4:1). God does have a book of life; Revelation 21:27 calls it the "Lamb's book of life." The only way to have one's name inscribed in it is through faith in Jesus as Savior from sin, and then it is permanent (John 10:27–30). Those whose names are not in the book will be judged and sentenced to hell: "Anyone whose name was not found written in the book of life was thrown into the lake of fire" (Rev. 20:15).	• A common custom is sending cards to relatives and friends to wish them a happy, healthy, and prosperous new year. The message includes the greeting, *L'shanah tovah tikatevoo*, which means "May you be inscribed [in the Book of Life] for a good year." • It is traditional to eat apple slices dipped in honey. The apples represent provision, and the honey represents sweetness for the coming year. Scriptures: Num. 29:1–6	FEAST of TRUMPETS
The Holy of Holies, in the temple, was separated from the congregation by a veil from floor to ceiling. It was entered once a year on Yom Kippur, when the high priest offered the blood sacrifice of atonement on behalf of the people. When Jesus died on the cross, the thick veil was ripped from top to bottom (Luke 23:44–46). Christ came as high priest and entered the Holy of Holies (heaven itself) once for all, not by the blood of goats and calves but by his own blood, having obtained eternal redemption (Heb. 9:11–28). Believers in Jesus accept his sacrifice on the cross as the final atonement for sin, "being justified freely by his grace through the redemption that is in Christ Jesus" (Rom. 3:21–25). When Messiah returns, Israel will look on him, whom they pierced, and repent (Zech. 12:10). On this day of repentance, Israel will be forgiven and permanently restored (Isa. 66:7–14; Rom. 11:26).	• After the temple was destroyed in AD 70, Jewish people could no longer offer the prescribed sacrifices for atonement of sins. They have substituted prayer, good works, and charitable donations hoping to take away the penalty for their sins. • Yom Kippur is a day of fasting. No work is done on this day, including at home. Many Jewish people spend the day at synagogue, praying for forgiveness of their sins. Immediately after the evening service, they have a "break fast" meal. • The book of Jonah is read during the afternoon service. Scriptures: Lev. 25:9; Num. 29:7–11; Ezek. 45:20; Zech. 12:10–13:9; Acts 27:9	DAY of ATONEMENT
Two ceremonies were part of the last day of Sukkot: (1) Giant golden lampstands were lit in the temple courtyard, and people carrying torches marched around the temple, then set these lights around the walls of the temple, indicating that Messiah would be a light to the Gentiles (Isa. 49:6). (2) A priest carried water from the pool of Siloam to the temple, symbolizing that when Messiah comes the whole earth will know God "as the waters cover the sea" (Isa. 11:9). When Jesus attended the Feast of Tabernacles, on the last day of the feast, he said, "If anyone is thirsty, let him come to me and drink (John 7:37). The next morning while the torches were still burning, he said, "I am the light of the world" (John 8:12). Sukkot represents the final harvest when all nations will share in the joy and blessings of God's kingdom (Zech. 14:16–19).	• The sukkah, or booth, is a temporary structure built of wood or wood and canvas. The roof is made of branches and leaves, with enough open spaces to see the stars. It is decorated with fall flowers, leaves, fruits, and vegetables. Many Jewish people erect booths on their lawns or balconies and eat at least one meal a day in them. • A lulav, made up of willow, palm, and myrtle branches, is waved in all four directions (north, south, east, and west) and up and down to symbolize that God's presence is everywhere. Scriptures: Num. 29:12–40; Deut. 16:13–15; Ezra 3:4; John 7	FEAST of BOOTHS
Although the history behind Hanukkah is recorded in books that were written in the time between the Hebrew Scriptures and the New Testament, the book of John tells us that it was celebrated in Jesus' day (John 10:22–23). The Feast of Dedication is a reminder of those who courageously remain faithful to God in the face of persecution. One of the major themes throughout the New Testament is remaining faithful to Christ, especially during persecution (Matt. 5:10–12; 1 Cor. 4:12; 2 Cor. 4:9). The book of Revelation speaks specifically to the persecution believers will face before the return of Christ (Rev. 2:10; 13:10).	• Hanukkah is primarily a family celebration that centers around the lighting of a nine-candle menorah, or candlestick, called a hanukkiyah. Each night another candle is lit with the center candle called a shammash, or servant candle, until all nine are lit. • Holiday foods include latkes (potato pancakes) and donuts fried in oil. The oil is a reminder of the miracle of the oil. • Perhaps because Hanukkah falls close to Christmas, it is now traditional to give presents, often one per night. • Children play dreydel games with a top that reminds them of the great miracle of God's deliverance from the Greeks.	FEAST of DEDICATION
Purim is a celebration of God's faithful protection of his people. The Jews of Esther's day were delivered from an irrevocable decree of the Persian king Ahasuerus. God also has an irrevocable decree that all people are sinners and deserve death (Gen. 2:17; Rom. 3:23). However, the Messiah delivers all who believe in him from that irrevocable decree as well (Isa. 53; Rom. 6:23). Many have and may continue to persecute believers in Messiah, but Isaiah's prophecy says that they will not prevail because "God is with us," or literally because of *Immanuel* (Isa. 8:10). God's name is not mentioned in the book of Esther, but his providence and provision are obvious.	• The word *purim* means "lots" and refers to the lot Haman cast to decide the day for the destruction of the Jewish people (Est. 3:7). • Purim is a happy and noisy holiday. To celebrate, the megillah (scroll of the book of Esther) is read in the synagogue. Whenever Haman is mentioned, everyone boos, stamps their feet, and shakes noisemakers (called groggers). Whenever Mordecai is mentioned, everyone cheers. • Hamantashen are three-cornered cookies which represent Haman's hat. Other customs include parades, dressing up as characters and reenacting the story of Esther, parties, carnivals, and giving gifts to the poor (Est. 9:22).	FEAST of LOTS

Feasts and Holidays Calendar

The Gregorian calendar, used by most western nations today, was established by Pope Gregory VIII in 1582. It is a solar calendar. The Jewish calendar uses both lunar and solar movements. The months are determined by the moon, and the year is determined by the sun. The Jewish day begins at sunset.

There are 12 months in the Jewish calendar, each with 29 or 30 days. Approximately every third year is a leap year containing an extra month. This adjustment is necessary to ensure that the major festivals stay in their appointed seasons.

To determine the Jewish calendar year, simply add 3761 to the western calendar year. For example, the Jewish year 5785 begins on October 3 of the Gregorian year 2024.

Gregorian Year	2024	2025	2026	2027	2028	2029	2030	2031
Holiday	\multicolumn{8}{c}{(Starts at Sundown the previous day)}								
Pesach (Passover)	April 23	April 13	April 2	April 22	April 11	March 31	April 18	April 8
Hag HaMatzot (Unleavened Bread)	April 24	April 14	April 3	April 23	April 12	April 1	April 19	April 9
Reishit (Firstfruits)	April 25	April 15	April 4	April 24	April 13	April 2	April 20	April 10
Shavuot (Pentecost)	June 12	June 2	May 22	June 11	May 31	May 20	June 7	May 28
Jewish Year	5785	5786	5787	5788	5789	5790	5791	5792
Rosh HaShanah (New Year; Trumpets)	Oct. 3	Sept. 23	Sept. 12	Oct. 2	Sept. 21	Sept. 10	Sept. 28	Sept. 18
Yom Kippur (Day of Atonement)	Oct. 12	Oct. 2	Sept. 21	Oct. 11	Sept. 30	Sept. 19	Oct. 7	Sept. 27
Sukkot (Tabernacles or Booths)	Oct. 17	Oct. 7	Sept. 26	Oct. 16	Oct. 5	Sept. 24	Oct. 12	Oct. 2
Hanukkah (Feast of Dedication)	Dec. 26	Dec. 15	Dec. 5	Dec. 25	Dec. 13	Dec. 2	Dec. 21	Dec. 10
Purim (Feast of Lots)	March 24 2024	March 14 2025	March 3 2026	March 23 2027	March 12 2028	March 1 2029	March 19 2030	March 9 2031

CHRIST IN THE PASSOVER

"For Christ, our Passover lamb, has been sacrificed. Therefore, let us keep the Festival."
—1 Corinthians 5:7-8

OLD TESTAMENT ORIGIN OF THE PASSOVER

THE PASSOVER is the Old Testament feast that celebrates and remembers God's liberation of Israel from Egypt. After Joseph saved Egypt from starvation (Genesis 41), the Israelites lived in Egypt as guests. Eventually, the Egyptians forgot about Joseph and enslaved the Israelites for hundreds of years (Exodus 1:6–14). Overburdened with work and mistreatment, the Israelites suffered a great deal and called out to the Lord. God responded to their cry and raised a great leader, Moses, who challenged the Pharaoh and Egypt's power.

The book of Exodus explains how God freed his people from Egypt. Because of the hardness of Pharaoh's heart, God punished Egypt with ten plagues (Exodus 7–11). However, instead of recognizing the true God of heaven and earth, Pharaoh grew angrier and oppressed the Israelites even more. One way Pharaoh increased the Israelites' suffering was by refusing to give them straw, one of the key materials to produce bricks.

However, God would not be denied. As the plagues continued, the suffering shifted from the Israelites to the Egyptians. The nation paid dearly for Pharaoh's stubbornness. During the last plague, God killed all the first-borns—humans and animals—in the land of Egypt.

> THE YEAR AD 70 marks a defining moment in the history of Judaism. The Roman armies destroyed the temple. The temple played a crucial role in the Jewish faith. Until then, the main component of the Passover was the sacrifice of the lamb in the temple. When the temple disappeared, the Haggadah, the "telling" of God's acts of deliverance, became the central part of the Passover. Today a roasted lamb shank bone symbolizes the lamb that would have been sacrificed in the temple.

God gave his people a way to escape the destruction: the blood of a perfect lamb could take the place of the first-born in the family. God gave Moses specific instructions to follow the night that God's punishment passed over the Israelite homes (Exodus 12). They were to sacrifice a perfect lamb (and mark their door frames), make unleavened bread, and gather bitter herbs. The Israelites ate this meal standing up, ready to leave Egypt at any moment. This celebration is now called the Passover because God "passed over" the homes marked with the lamb's blood. The Passover feast was to be repeated throughout the generations as a memorial forever.

The Passover Celebration and Its Symbolism

First Cup and Kiddush ("Sanctification")

Seder Before the *Seder* began, traditionally a woman lit special candles to mark the commencement of this sacred time. Immediately after this, the head of the table raised the first cup of wine—the cup of sanctification—and blessed it.

Lord's Supper According to Luke 22:17–18, "After taking the cup, he gave thanks and said, 'Take this and divide it among you. For I tell you I will not drink again of the fruit of the vine until the kingdom of God comes.'"

The First Washing of the Hands and the Bitter Herbs

Seder As everyone got ready to partake of the Passover meal, the leader of the Passover washed his hands. Then a plate with salted water was passed around into which everyone dipped a piece of lettuce or parsley (*karpas*). The salt was a reminder of the tears the Israelites shed during their bondage in Egypt. The green herb was a reminder of a new beginning.

Lord's Supper Jesus went further than the traditional hand washing and taught his disciples humility by washing their feet (John 13:1–17). During the remembrance of the Israelites' tears, Judas' betrayal was likely also a bitter experience for Jesus (Mark 14:20).

The Afikomen

Seder The leader took three *matzo* breads and placed them in a special bag with three compartments. The middle *matzah* was broken and one piece placed back in the *matzo* bag. The other piece was hidden under a pillow and was called *Afikomen*.

Lord's Supper Although the practice of the *Afikomen* goes back to antiquity, it is quite possible that it originated after the Romans destroyed the Second Temple in AD 70. In other words, it probably was not practiced in Jesus' time.

The Second Cup and the Haggadah

Seder The leader took the second cup of wine (the cup of plagues) and blessed it. No one drank from it until the *Haggadah* ("the telling") was finished. At this point a child asked the four questions and the leader of the ceremony would tell the story of God's redemption in the Exodus. Traditionally, the answer had to cover at least three elements of the Passover celebration: (1) The Passover sacrifice, (2) the bitter herbs, and (3) the unleavened bread (*matzo*). The four questions can be found in the box to the right.

Lord's Supper In the Gospel account of the Lord's Supper, the words, "This is my body…" are Jesus' re-interpretation of the Passover. It is here that the sacrificed lamb and the unleavened bread receive greater meaning: Jesus is the Lamb of God (John 1:29) sacrificed in our place (1 Peter 1:17–21) and he is the Bread of Life that comes down from heaven (John 6:33–35).

The Haggadah includes four questions. Today, the *Haggadah* is the central part of the Passover *Seder*.

1. On all nights we may eat either leavened or unleavened bread, but on this night, only unleavened bread. Why is this night different from all other nights?

2. On all other nights, we eat all kinds of herbs, but on this night, we eat bitter herbs. Why is this night different from all other nights?

3. On all other nights, we do not dip our vegetables even one time, but on this night we dip them twice, in salt water and *charoset*. Why is this night different from all other nights?

4. On all other nights, we eat either sitting or reclining, but on this night, we eat only reclining. Why is this night different from all other nights?

BASED ON EXODUS 6:6—7. Jewish tradition has incorporated four cups of wine into the Passover celebration. "Therefore, say to the Israelites: 'I am the LORD, and I will bring you out from under the yoke of the Egyptians. I will free you from being slaves to them, and I will redeem you with an outstretched arm and with mighty acts of judgment. I will take you as my own people…'"

The Cup of SANCTIFICATION	"… I will *bring* you…"
The Cup of PLAGUES	"… I will *free* you…"
The Cup of REDEMPTION	"… I will *redeem* you…"
The Cup of PRAISE (also called Cup of Acceptance)	"… I will *take* you…"

FIRST PART OF THE HALLEL AND THE SECOND CUP

SEDER At the end of the *Haggadah*, the leader raised the second cup of wine and invited all to sing the first part of the *Hallel*, which is the recitation of Psalms 113 and 114. Then everyone drank the second cup, the cup of plagues.

LORD'S SUPPER The New Testament does not give a detailed account of Jesus' last actions, but rather focuses on the New Covenant (1 Cor. 11:25) and Jesus' sacrifice about to occur. Although they might have recited the first part of the *Hallel* and taken the second cup, it is not registered in the Scriptures.

SECOND HAND WASHING AND PASSOVER MEAL

SEDER All washed their hands once again. Then the leader took the *matzo* breads and broke them into pieces. The leader dipped the bread into a mixture of bitter herbs and distributed them to the participants. The meal was then taken.

LORD'S SUPPER As was traditional in the celebration of the Passover, Jesus dipped a piece of bread; however, he used this moment to indicate who his betrayer would be (John 13:26).

THE GRACE AFTER MEALS AND THE THIRD CUP

SEDER When the meal was finished, no one ate any other food. Instead, the leader of the celebration poured a third cup of wine. Everyone offered another blessing on the third cup of wine, called the cup of redemption, and drank from this cup.

LORD'S SUPPER After the meal, Jesus got up, took a *matzah* bread, and said, "This is my body given for you; do this in remembrance of me" (Luke 22:19). Then he continued with the third cup. He blessed it and said, "This is the cup of the new covenant in my blood; do this, whenever you drink it, in remembrance of me" (1 Corinthians 11:25).

THE SECOND PART OF THE HALLEL AND THE FOURTH CUP

SEDER Once everyone drank the third cup, they recited the second part of the *Hallel* (praise), which consists of Psalms 115–118. No one drank wine between the third cup and the end of the second part of the *Hallel*. At the end of the singing, they drank the fourth cup of wine, called the cup of praise. Then the *Seder* ended.

LORD'S SUPPER Jesus and the disciples finished the Lord's Supper, and Matthew tells us, "When they had sung a hymn, they went out to the Mount of Olives" (Matthew 26:30). The hymn was probably the *Hallel*. The fourth cup was not drunk! "I tell you, I will not drink of this fruit of the vine from now on until that day when I drink it anew with you in my Father's kingdom" (Matthew 26:29). The last cup of the Passover will be drunk at the wedding feast of the Lamb (Revelation 19:9).

THE OLD TESTAMENT PASSOVER

The Passover was a celebration, remembrance, thanksgiving and participation in God's mighty acts of salvation for his people. The New Testament equivalent of the Passover, the Lord's Supper, functions in similar ways for Christians today.

1. The Lord's Supper is a time of remembrance and thanksgiving (Luke 22:19; 1 Corinthians 11:24–25).

2. The Lord's Supper is a time for refreshing and communion (Romans 5:10; 1 Corinthians 10:16).

3. The Lord's Supper is a time for anticipation and recommitment (1 Corinthians 11:26, 28–29).

A Seder for Christians

This is a shortened description of the *Seder*. Celebrating this *Seder* would take about as long as celebrating the Lord's Supper. A more complete *Seder*, which would take significantly longer, can be found in the reference books mentioned at the end.

Introduction

Candle Lighting

A WOMAN *or older girl lights the candles, then she reads this blessing:* Blessed are you, O Lord our God, ruler of the universe, who has set us apart by his word, and in whose name we light the festival lights.

First Cup, the Cup of Sanctification

LEADER *holds the glass of wine or juice and explains that this is the first of four cups, the cup of sanctification.*

EVERYONE *lifts his or her cup and reads the blessing:* Blessed are you, O Lord our God, ruler of the universe, who creates the fruit of the vine. *All drink a little.*

Parsley

LEADER *holds up parsley and says:* This parsley represents life, which God gives us.

Then he holds up the bowl of salt water and says: This salt water represents the tears of the Israelites because of the suffering they endured as slaves in Egypt. Blessed are you, O Lord our God, ruler of the universe, who creates the fruit of the earth.

EVERYONE *takes a piece of parsley, dips it in salt water, and eats it.*

Haggadah, the Four Questions

LEADER *says:* We celebrate the Passover to remember how God brought the Israelites out of Egypt, and we review the story by asking and answering four questions.

A CHILD *reads the following:* On all other nights we eat bread or *matzah*. On this night, why do we eat only *matzah*? On all other nights, we eat all kinds of vegetables. On this night, why do we eat only bitter herbs? On all other nights, we do not dip our vegetables. On this night, why do we dip them twice? On all other nights, we eat sitting or reclining. On this night, why do we eat only reclining?

LEADER *says:* On Passover we eat only *matzah*, flat bread without yeast, because the Israelites did not have time for their bread dough to rise when they left Egypt. Leaven, or yeast, is a metaphor for the bad influence of sin in our lives. It is a way to represent physically that we are now a new creation in Christ (2 Corinthians 5:17). We get rid of the leaven, which is the old life of sin.

THE LEADER *holds up the plate with three matzo, takes out the middle piece, breaks it into two, wraps half in a napkin, and says:* This bread of affliction reminds us that Jesus suffered for our sins.

Read Isaiah 53:5 and Zechariah 12:10 aloud.

LEADER *says:* I am going to hide this broken piece of *matzah*, called the *Afikomen*, which means "that which comes last." Later the children will look for it. The one who finds it gets a prize. *Children close their eyes while someone hides the Afikomen. Then the leader takes a piece of the other half of broken matzah and passes the rest around for everyone to take a piece. All eat.*

LEADER *says:* On Passover we eat bitter herbs to remember the Israelites' terrible life of slavery in Egypt.

EVERYONE *takes a piece of matzah, scoops horseradish onto it, and eats it.*

LEADER *says:* On Passover we dip vegetables twice. We have already dipped parsley in salt water to remind us of the Israelites' tears. But we also dip our vegetables in sweet *charoset* [chah-**roh**-set]. This reminds us that even in slavery, the Israelites had hope in God.

Christ in the Passover • 101

EVERYONE *takes another piece of matzah, scoops charoset onto it, and eats it.*

LEADER *says:* On Passover we recline, or sit comfortably, as free people. In contrast, the Israelites ate the first Passover meal standing, ready to leave any minute.

THE PASSOVER STORY

LEADER *summarizes the story of Passover from Exodus 1–7. Rabbi Gamaliel, teacher of Rabbi Saul (Paul the Apostle), said that in telling the Passover story one must remember these three things:*

1. The matzah (unleavened bread)
2. The maror (bitter herbs)
3. The Pesach (Passover lamb)

THE SECOND CUP, THE CUP OF PLAGUES

LEADER *says:* Pharaoh refused to let the Israelites go, so God sent ten plagues to change his mind. Now we have the second cup, the cup of plagues. Instead of drinking it, we are going to name the plagues, dip our fingers in our cups, and drop wine or juice on our plates each time a plague is named.

EVERYONE *does so, reading each plague three times:* blood, frogs, lice, flies, cattle disease, boils, hail, locusts, darkness, death of the firstborn.

PASSOVER LAMB

LEADER *holds up the bone and says:* This bone reminds us of the Passover lamb that was killed. *He briefly summarizes Exodus 11–12.*

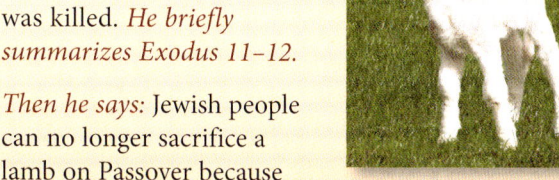

Then he says: Jewish people can no longer sacrifice a lamb on Passover because the temple was destroyed. But no one needs to make a sacrifice because Jesus died as the Passover lamb to take the punishment for our sin.

LEADER *holds up the betzah (the boiled and roasted egg) and says:* The egg symbolizes mourning and reminds us that the temple was destroyed, a sad event for the Jewish people.

FIRST PART OF THE HALLEL

LEADER *says:* At this point in the *Seder*, we recite together the words of Psalms 113 and 114.

EVERYONE *drinks some of the second cup, the cup of plagues.*

PASSOVER MEAL

EAT THE DINNER: *(possibly roasted lamb or glazed chicken, gefilte fish, matzo ball soup, stuffing, potatoes, vegetables, fruit, and sponge cake).*

AFIKOMEN

CHILDREN *look for the matzah that was hidden earlier, and the leader gives the one who finds it a little money.*

LEADER *says:* When Jesus celebrated the last Passover before his death, he took the *Afikomen*, broke it, and blessed it.

ALL READ: Blessed are you, O Lord our God, ruler of the universe, who brings forth bread from the earth.

LEADER *says:* Then Jesus gave some of the *matzo* to his disciples and said, "This is my body given for you; do this in remembrance of me" (Luke 22:19).

He breaks off a piece of the Afikomen and passes it around for everyone to take a piece. All eat.

Third Cup, the Cup of Redemption

LEADER *says:* Then Jesus took the third cup, the cup of redemption, and said the blessing.

ALL READ: Blessed are you, O Lord our God, ruler of the universe, who creates the fruit of the vine.

LEADER *says:* Then Jesus said, "This cup is the new covenant in my blood, which is poured out for you" (Luke 22:20).

EVERYONE DRINKS.

Cup of Elijah

LEADER *holds up the cup from the place at the table that has been saved for Elijah and says:* This cup is for Elijah the prophet, who will come before the Messiah returns. *Read Malachi 4:5.*

LEADER *says:* Jewish people look for Elijah's return on Passover, so they set a place for him at the table and open the door to welcome him. Christians acknowledge that Elijah has come again in the presence of John the Baptist (Matthew 11:14), and also that the Messiah has come. We open the door in expectation of the second coming of the Messiah: Maranatha! (Revelation 22:20).

VOLUNTEER *opens the door.*

The Second Part of the Hallel and the Fourth Cup, the Cup of Praise

LEADER *says:* After Jesus and his disciples ate the *Afikomen* and drank the third cup, Matthew 26:30 says they sang a hymn.

READ *Psalm 118 together.*

LEADER *lifts his cup and says:* The last cup is the cup of praise. Let us read the blessing together: Blessed are you, O Lord our God, ruler of the universe, who creates the fruit of the vine.

ALL DRINK.

LEADER *says:* The *Seder* ends with a traditional wish for celebrating the next Passover: Next year in Jerusalem!

The End

The Afikomen

✡ A practice in the contemporary celebration of the Passover—possibly also an ancient practice—is to take three *matzo* breads and place them in a special bag with three compartments.

✡ At one point in the celebration, the middle bread is taken out and broken into two pieces. One of the pieces is returned to the middle bag and the other one is hidden under a pillow. Traditionally, children look for it.

✡ When a child finds the piece of *matzah*, the leader of the celebration must "rescue" it by paying some money to the child.

✡ At the end of the meal, when the Passover Seder is complete, the *Afikomen* is revealed.

Messianic Symbolism

✡ We come as children to the Lord and we are rewarded when we find him.

✡ Jewish Christians who continue celebrating the Passover in the traditional way understand this practice to symbolize important Christian beliefs.

✡ The three matzo breads placed in the one bag point to God's very nature: Three persons in one.

✡ The breaking of the second bread and hiding it under a pillow symbolize Jesus' sacrifice on the cross and his resurrection from the tomb.

✡ The hiding of the *Afikomen* for the duration of the Seder represents Christ being hidden from our view for three days in the tomb.

✡ Today the *matzo* breads are pierced and striped because of the way the bread is made. In the past, *matzah* looked like pita bread.

✡ Today many Jewish Christians understand the piercing and the stripes to symbolize the piercing of Jesus on the cross (Jn. 19:34) and his flogging by the Roman soldiers (Jn. 19:1).

Leaven

✡ Leaven is something added to bread to make it rise (for example, yeast). Leaven requires time to expand.

✡ In Exodus 12:14–20 God commanded the Israelites to prepare unleavened bread as a way to remind them of the haste with which they had to leave Egypt.

✡ In those times, a leftover piece of fermented dough was used to make a new batch of dough rise. Today we use yeast to leaven the dough.

✡ Leaven is prohibited only at the Passover and in foods dedicated to the Lord by fire (Leviticus 2:11).

✡ In the Passover, removing leaven may represent a complete break from the previous life of slavery in Egypt and the coming into a new life under the Lord.

✡ However, for the peace offering (Leviticus 7:13) and the bread offered during Pentecost (Leviticus 23:17), leavened breads are required.

✡ This requirement suggests that in the Bible leaven does not always represent sin.

Leaven in the New Testament

IN THE NEW TESTAMENT LEAVEN MAY BE USED AS A SYMBOL OF EITHER GOOD OR BAD INFLUENCE:

✡ In Matthew 13:33 Jesus uses the image of leaven to explain the kingdom of heaven. Like leaven, the kingdom of heaven works unseen, powerfully, and relentlessly.

✡ In Luke 12:1, Jesus warns the disciples to beware of the Pharisees' teachings because, like leaven, they corrupt everything they touch.

✡ The Apostle Paul uses leaven imagery in 1 Corinthians 5:6–8 to emphasize the effect of bad influence: it spreads quickly and quietly. In other words, "malice and wickedness" corrupt everything just as leaven spreads and transforms the whole lump of bread.

✡ For Jews today, cleaning the house of yeast symbolizes getting rid of any sins in their lives. When a Jewish family prepares the home for the Passover celebration, they are required to search and remove any leaven from their house.

✡ This parallels the searching of the heart and repentance that Christians do when coming to the communion table.

The Passover in the Bible

In Exodus 12, God gives Moses the instructions and requirements for the Passover.

EXODUS 12	CHRIST
12:1–2—The feast marked a new year, a new beginning for the Israelites.	In Christ, every believer is a new creation (2 Corinthians 5:17). Old things and the old life are past.
12:5—A male lamb in its first year was taken into the home on the tenth of Nisan (the first month of the Jewish calendar). While in the home, it was closely inspected to see if there were any blemishes or disfigurements. If it was without defect, it was then sacrificed on the fourteenth of Nisan.	Christ was closely inspected by: • Pilate (Matthew 27:11–26; Luke 23:1–6; 13–25; John 18:28–19:16) • Herod (Luke 23:8–12) • Annas (John 18:12–13; 19–24) • Caiaphas (Matthew 26:57). They could find no fault in him. Christ is the "lamb without blemish or defect" (1 Peter 1:19).
12:6—The "whole community" of God's people was required to participate in the sacrifice.	Accepting Christ's sacrifice is required for all who want to be part of God's community (Romans 3:21–26).
12:7, 12, 22—The blood of the sacrificed lamb was applied to the doorframe—the lintel and side posts. Because of the covering of blood, the house was spared from God's plague.	Christ shed his blood to rescue his people. We need to be covered or justified by the blood of the Lamb to be rescued from condemnation (Romans 3:25; 5:9). Christ is the Lamb that takes away the sins of the world (John 1:29).
12:14—The Passover was to be kept as a remembrance forever.	During the Last Supper, Jesus refers to the bread as "my body given for you; do this in remembrance of me" (Luke 22:19).
12:46—God commanded Israel not to break any bones of the sacrificed lamb.	To speed up Jesus' death, the Roman soldiers were going to break his legs. However, Jesus was already dead, so his bones remained unbroken (John 19:32–33).

"John saw Jesus coming toward him and said,
'Behold, the Lamb of God,
who takes away the sin of the world!"
—John 1:29

PROPHETS

Biblical prophets were God's servants especially called to be his witnesses. God sent prophets to his people during times of crisis. Old Testament prophets were intermediaries between God and his people. They brought the word of God to people. As Scripture says, *"Surely the Sovereign LORD does nothing without revealing his plan to his servants the prophets"* (Amos 3:7).

PROPHET	PROPHESIED	DATE (BC)*	HOME/LOCATION
Samuel	To Israel	1060–1020	Ramah
Elijah	To Israel	870–845	Tishbe
Elisha	To Israel	845–800	Abel Meholah
Jonah	To Nineveh	781	Gath-hepher
Amos	To Israel	765–754	Tekoa
Isaiah	To Judah	760–673	Jerusalem
Hosea	To Israel	758–725	Israel
Micah	To Judah	738–698	Moresheth-gath
Nahum	Concerning Nineveh	658–615	Elkosh
Jeremiah	To Judah	650–582	Anathoth
Zephaniah	To Judah	640–626	Unknown
Ezekiel	To Exiles in Babylonia	620–570	Babylon
Daniel	In Babylon	620–540	Babylon
Habakkuk	To Judah	608–598	Unknown
Obadiah	Concerning Edom	590	Judah
Zechariah	To Judah	522–509	Jerusalem
Haggai	To Judah	520	Jerusalem
Malachi	To Judah	465	Unknown
Joel	To Judah	450	Jerusalem

* Dates are approximate

Kings of the United & Divided Kingdoms

United Kingdom

NAME	EVALUATION	REIGN (BC)	END OF LIFE	REFERENCE
Saul	Good to Bad	1051–1011	Died in Battle	1 Sam. 9–31; 1 Chron. 8–10
David	Good	1011–971	Natural Causes	1 Sam. 16—1 Kings 2 1 Chron. 11–29
Solomon	Mostly Good	971–931	Natural Causes	1 Kings 1–11; 2 Chron. 1–9

Divided Kingdom — Kings of Israel (Northern Kingdom)

NAME	EVALUATION	REIGN (BC)	END OF LIFE	REFERENCE
Jeroboam	Bad	931–910	Struck down by God	1 Kings 11:26–14:20 2 Chron. 9:29–13:20
Nadab	Bad	910–909	Killed by Baasha	1 Kings 15:25–31
Baasha	Bad	909–886	Natural causes	1 Kings 15:16–16:7 2 Chron. 16:1–6
Elah	Bad	886–885	Killed by Zimri	1 Kings 16:6–14
Zimri	Bad	885 (7 days)	Suicide	1 Kings 16:9–20
Omri*	Bad	885–874	Natural causes	1 Kings 16:15–28
Ahab	Bad	874–853	Wounded in battle	1 Kings 16:28–22:40 2 Chron. 18:1–34
Ahaziah	Bad	853–852	Fatally injured in a fall	1 Kings 22:40—2 Kings 1:18 2 Chron. 20:35–37
Joram (Jehoram)	Bad	852–841	Killed by Jehu	2 Kings 3:1–27; 9:14–26 2 Chron. 22:5–7
Jehu	Bad	841–814	Natural causes	2 Kings 9:1–10:36 2 Chron. 22:7–9
Jehoahaz	Bad	814–798	Natural causes	2 Kings 13:1–9
Jehoash	Bad	798–782	Natural causes	2 Kings 13:9–14:16 2 Chron. 25:17–25
Jeroboam II	Bad	793–753	Natural causes	2 Kings 14:23–29
Zechariah	Bad	753	Killed by Shallum	2 Kings 14:29; 15:8–12
Shallum	Bad	752 (1 month)	Killed by Menahem	2 Kings 15:10–15
Menahem	Bad	752–742	Natural causes	2 Kings 15:14–22
Pekahiah	Bad	742–740	Killed by Pekah	2 Kings 15:22–26
Pekah	Bad	752–732	Killed by Hoshea	2 Kings 15:25–31 2 Chron. 28:5–8
Hoshea	Bad	732–722	Removed by Assyria	2 Kings 15:30; 17:1–6

*Tibni unsuccessfully contended for the throne against Omri (885–880 BC). 1 Kings 16:21–22

DIVIDED KINGDOM — Kings of Judah (Southern Kingdom)

NAME	EVALUATION	REIGN (BC)	END OF LIFE	REFERENCE
Rehoboam	Bad	931–913	Natural causes	1 Kings 11:43–12:24; 14:21–31 2 Chron. 9:31–12:16
Abijah	Bad	913–911	Natural causes	1 Kings 14:31–15:8 2 Chron. 12:16–14:1
Asa	Good	911–870	Severe foot disease	1 Kings 15:8–24 2 Chron. 14:1–16:14
Jehoshaphat	Good	873–848	Natural causes	1 Kings 22:1–50 2 Chron. 17:1–21:1
Jehoram (Joram)	Bad	853–841	A painful disease	2 Kings 8:16–24 2 Chron. 21:1–20
Ahaziah	Bad	841	Killed by Jehu	2 Kings 8:24–29; 9:14–29 2 Chron. 22:1–9
Queen Athaliah	Bad	841–835	Killed by her army	2 Kings 11:1–20 2 Chron. 22:10–23:21
Joash	Good	835–796	Killed by his officials	2 Kings 11:1–12:21 2 Chron. 22:10–24:27
Amaziah	Good	796–767	Killed by his officials	2 Kings 12:21; 14:1–20 2 Chron. 24:27–25:28
Uzziah (Azariah)	Good	792–740	Skin disease	2 Kings 14:21–22; 15:1–7 2 Chron. 26:1–23
Jotham	Good	750–732	Natural causes	2 Kings 15:32–38 2 Chron. 26:23–27:9
Ahaz (Jehoahaz)	Bad	735–716	Natural causes	2 Kings 16:1–20 2 Chron. 27:9–28:27
Hezekiah	Good	716–687	Natural causes	2 Kings 18:1–20:21 2 Chron. 28:27–32:33
Manasseh	Bad	697–643	Natural causes	2 Kings 21:1–18 2 Chron. 32:33–33:20
Amon	Bad	643–641	Killed by his officials	2 Kings 21:18–26 2 Chron. 33:20–25
Josiah	Good	641–609	Wounded in battle	2 Kings 21:26–23:30 2 Chron. 33:25–35:27
Jehoahaz (Shallum)	Bad	609 (3 months)	Died in Egypt	2 Kings 23:30–34 2 Chron. 36:1–4
Jehoiakim (Eliakim)	Bad	609–598	Died in Babylon	2 Kings 23:34–24:6 2 Chron. 36:4–8
Jehoiachin (Jeconiah)	Bad	597 (3 months)	Died in Babylon	2 Kings 24:6–16; 25:27–30 2 Chron. 36:8–10
Zedekiah (Mattaniah)	Bad	597–586	Died in Babylon	2 Kings 24:17–25:7 2 Chron. 36:10–13

Kings & Prophets

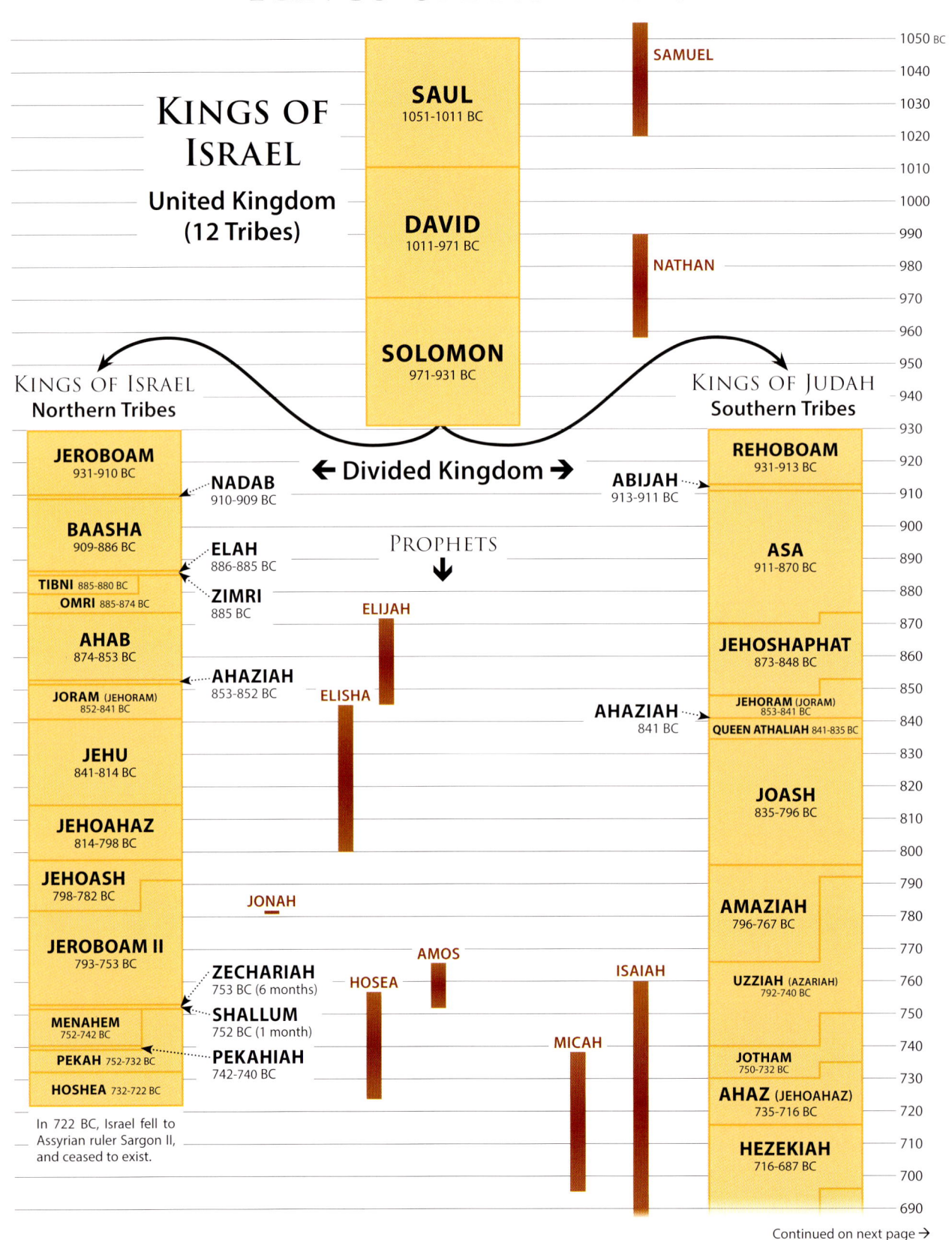

Kings of Israel — United Kingdom (12 Tribes)

King	Reign
SAUL	1051–1011 BC
DAVID	1011–971 BC
SOLOMON	971–931 BC

Prophets (United Kingdom): SAMUEL (c. 1050 BC), NATHAN (c. 980 BC)

Divided Kingdom

Kings of Israel — Northern Tribes

King	Reign
JEROBOAM	931–910 BC
NADAB	910–909 BC
BAASHA	909–886 BC
ELAH	886–885 BC
ZIMRI	885 BC
TIBNI	885–880 BC
OMRI	885–874 BC
AHAB	874–853 BC
AHAZIAH	853–852 BC
JORAM (JEHORAM)	852–841 BC
JEHU	841–814 BC
JEHOAHAZ	814–798 BC
JEHOASH	798–782 BC
JEROBOAM II	793–753 BC
ZECHARIAH	753 BC (6 months)
SHALLUM	752 BC (1 month)
MENAHEM	752–742 BC
PEKAHIAH	742–740 BC
PEKAH	752–732 BC
HOSHEA	732–722 BC

In 722 BC, Israel fell to Assyrian ruler Sargon II, and ceased to exist.

Kings of Judah — Southern Tribes

REHOBOAM	931–913 BC
ABIJAH	913–911 BC
ASA	911–870 BC
JEHOSHAPHAT	873–848 BC
JEHORAM (JORAM)	853–841 BC
AHAZIAH	841 BC
QUEEN ATHALIAH	841–835 BC
JOASH	835–796 BC
AMAZIAH	796–767 BC
UZZIAH (AZARIAH)	792–740 BC
JOTHAM	750–732 BC
AHAZ (JEHOAHAZ)	735–716 BC
HEZEKIAH	716–687 BC

Prophets (Divided Kingdom)

- ELIJAH
- ELISHA
- JONAH
- AMOS
- HOSEA
- ISAIAH
- MICAH

Continued on next page →

Kings and Prophets

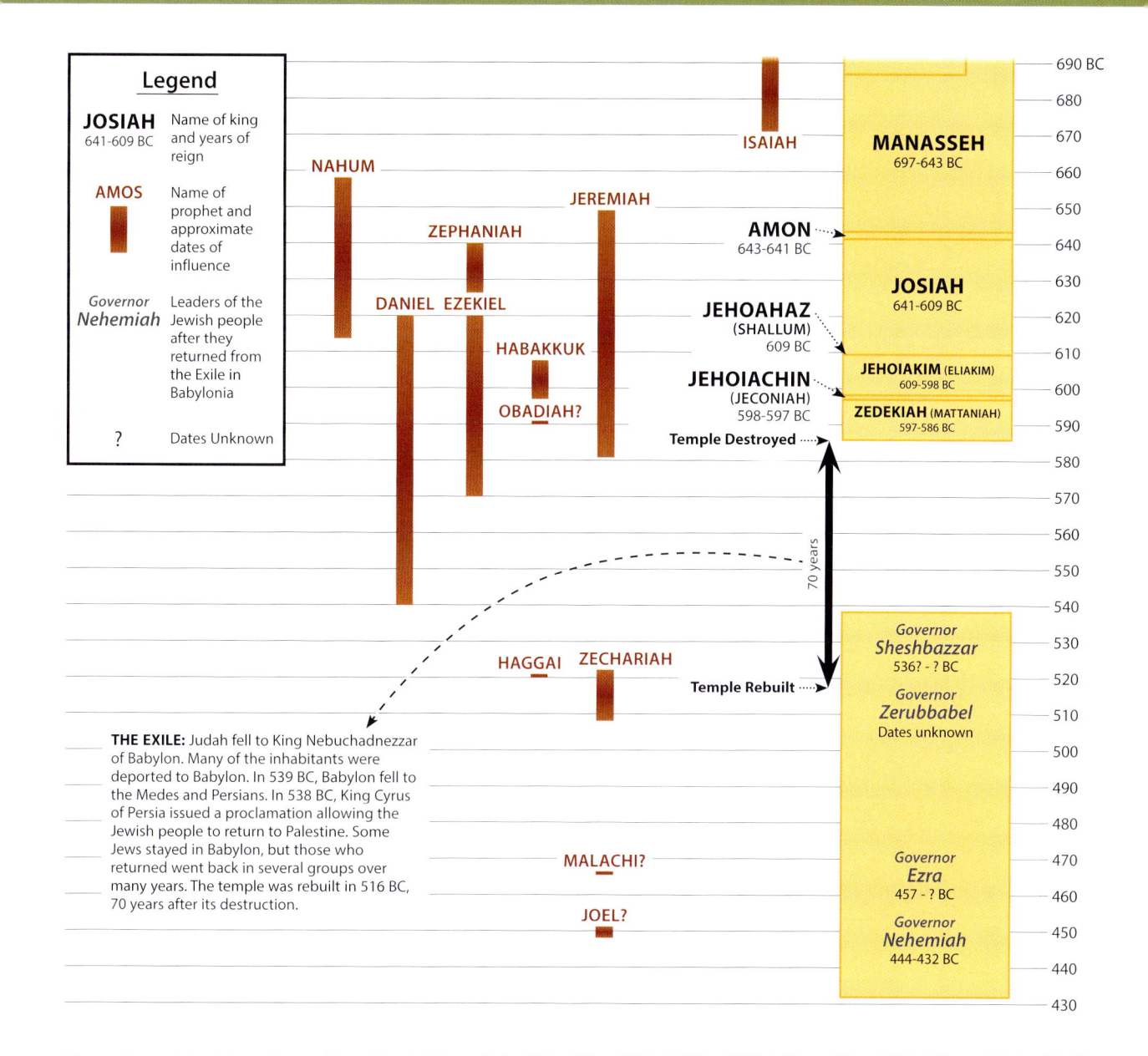

Legend

JOSIAH 641-609 BC — Name of king and years of reign

AMOS — Name of prophet and approximate dates of influence

Governor **Nehemiah** — Leaders of the Jewish people after they returned from the Exile in Babylonia

? — Dates Unknown

Timeline

Prophets:
- NAHUM
- ZEPHANIAH
- JEREMIAH
- DANIEL
- EZEKIEL
- HABAKKUK
- OBADIAH?
- ISAIAH
- HAGGAI
- ZECHARIAH
- MALACHI?
- JOEL?

Kings of Judah:
- **MANASSEH** 697-643 BC
- **AMON** 643-641 BC
- **JOSIAH** 641-609 BC
- **JEHOAHAZ (SHALLUM)** 609 BC
- **JEHOIAKIM (ELIAKIM)** 609-598 BC
- **JEHOIACHIN (JECONIAH)** 598-597 BC
- **ZEDEKIAH (MATTANIAH)** 597-586 BC

Temple Destroyed → 70 years → Temple Rebuilt

Governors after the Exile:
- *Governor* **Sheshbazzar** 536? - ? BC
- *Governor* **Zerubbabel** Dates unknown
- *Governor* **Ezra** 457 - ? BC
- *Governor* **Nehemiah** 444-432 BC

THE EXILE: Judah fell to King Nebuchadnezzar of Babylon. Many of the inhabitants were deported to Babylon. In 539 BC, Babylon fell to the Medes and Persians. In 538 BC, King Cyrus of Persia issued a proclamation allowing the Jewish people to return to Palestine. Some Jews stayed in Babylon, but those who returned went back in several groups over many years. The temple was rebuilt in 516 BC, 70 years after its destruction.

Fascinating Facts

DOMINANT POWERS IN THE MIDDLE EAST:
900-612 BC - Assyria   612-539 BC - Babylonia   539-332 BC - Medo-Persia

What made a king "good" or "bad"?

The biblical writers were not as interested in a king's abilities as an administrator as they were in the king's desire to follow God's commands. Kings that followed God's law and those who outlawed the altars to foreign gods, the high places, and idol worship were designated as good. Those who did not, were evil. The Bible uses the phrase "He did evil in the eyes (or *sight*) of the Lord," to evaluate the king's reign. In secular history, one of the important kings was Omri of Israel, who conquered the Moabites; but in the Bible this evil king's victories go unmentioned.

Dates of the kings adapted from Edward R. Thiele's *Chronology of the Hebrew Kings*. Used by permission of Zondervan.
Dates of the prophets from Alfred J. Hoerth's *Archaeology and the Old Testament*. Used by permission of Baker Book House.
Special thanks to Alfred J. Hoerth, Director of Archaeology, Emeritus, Wheaton College.

SOLOMON'S TEMPLE

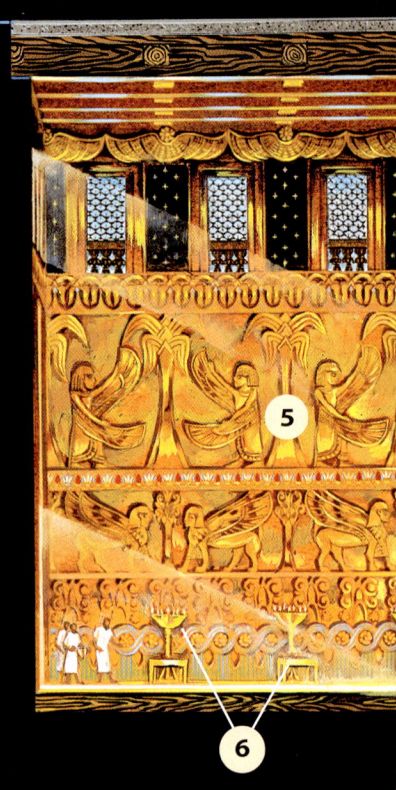

The Temple is shown here with the north wall removed. East is at the left; west is to the right.

BRONZE ALTAR
Fires transformed sacrifice to ash.

"THE SEA" held 17,500 gallons (66 kiloliters) for ceremonial washing (1 Kings 7:23).

BRONZE PILLARS
"Jakin" and "Boaz" supported the roof of the **PORTICO**.

HOLY PLACE

LAMPSTANDS, TABLES for bread of the presence.

BIBLICAL SOURCES
1 Kings 6–8; 1 Chron. 28–29; 2 Chron. 2–5. Interior dimensions (in Royal Cubits) Length: 102.5 ft (31.5 m) Width: 34.2 ft (10.5 m) Height: 5 stories (15.75 m) (In common cubits)—90 ft (27 m) by 30 ft (9 m); 4½ stories high (13.5 m)

ARK OF THE COVENANT—Beneath wings of guarding cherubim was this gold-covered chest carried from the wilderness of Sinai. Its lid was regarded as the very throne of God; upon it the high priest placed life (blood) and from here God poured forth his mercy.

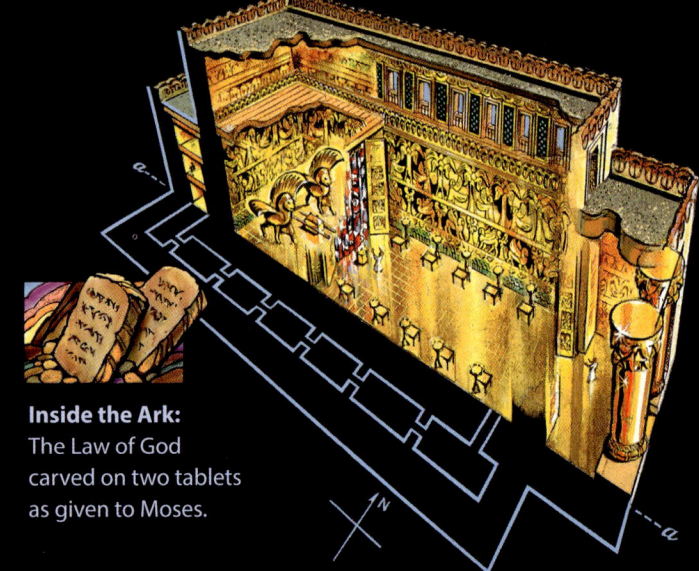

Inside the Ark: The Law of God carved on two tablets as given to Moses.

Solomon's Temple • 111

Notice the shaft of morning sunlight, as it hits the solid gold floor and walls, reflecting throughout.

INCENSE ALTAR for time of prayer.

BARRIER TAPESTRY "veil" or "curtain" with blue, purple, crimson design on linen.

CHERUBIM—Massive sculptures touched each other wingtip to wingtip and wall to wall.

BEDROCK upon which the temple rested was once a threshing floor honorably purchased by Solomon's father, David. (2 Sam. 24:24)

ART FORMS—"On the walls … he (Solomon) carved cherubim, palm trees," "so he overlaid the whole interior with gold" (1 Kings 6). These were not objects of worship but only for God. Cherubim were winged spiritual beings guarding sacred objects. Scripture says the temple was decorated with various colors, turquoise, and marble, inlaid and painted possibly similar to other ancient temples

STORE ROOMS or "Treasuries" three stories high surrounded temple on sides and rear, and contained the king's wealth.

Living creatures being led to the temple for sacrifice. Their blood would bear away the sin of a repenting and praying people temporarily.

SACRIFICE—Creature killed and its blood (life) drained away into vessels, placed on horns and base of altar then (daily) before Barrier Tapestry. Other portions were eaten or burned.

THE TEMPLE CONSTRUCTION began in 966 BC, took seven years to build, and was destroyed by the Babylonians in 586 BC. Solomon relied on the architects of King Hiram of Tyre. Therefore, his temple was an expression of the Syrian "long room plan" of that region and period of history

THE TEMPLE TOUR

The temple in the Bible was built in 960 BC by King Solomon. To understand the temple's purpose, it is important to know that God made the world and established the rules. God told Adam that the result of sin was death, Adam disobeyed, and sin, death, and disease entered the world. In spite of this, God loved his people and had mercy.

Before Jesus' death and resurrection, God provided a way to atone for sin so that people could be in his holy presence. God allowed the blood of a perfect animal to temporarily take the place of the sinner's life. This blood sacrifice took away sin and made the sinner right with God temporarily. God loved the world so much that he sent his son Jesus to atone, or take away, a believer's sin once and for all. The blood of Jesus Christ was the final sacrifice needed (Gen. 2:17; 4:3–7; Lev. 1; 16:1–2; Isa. 59:2; Rom. 3:23; Heb. 10:26–31).

Here are steps to peace with God during the time of the temple ("Then") and today ("Now").

❶ BRONZE ALTAR
Then: God required the people to regularly sacrifice a perfect animal (lambs, goats, doves, bulls) for their sins. The blood of the animal justified the people before God and restored their relationship with him.
Now: Jesus is our perfect sacrifice. He led a sinless life and willingly died for our sins to make us right with God for all time. No more sacrifices are required (Lev. 17:11; Heb. 9:25; John 1:29; Rev. 13:8; Heb. 10:10; Rom. 4:25).

❷ SACRIFICE
Then: The person bringing the offering put his hand on the head of the animal while it was killed, symbolically putting his sins onto the animal. The animal died in his place.
Now: Jesus is the Lamb of God, just as bulls or lambs were sacrificed. We are told to present our bodies as a living sacrifice acceptable to God, holy, not conformed to the world, and with a renewed mind (John 1:29; Rom. 12:1–2).
  We are to offer God another kind of sacrifice: praising his name, doing good, and sharing with others (Heb. 13:15–16).

❸ "THE SEA" (Bronze Basin)
Then: Priests washed themselves at the basin, purifying themselves before entering the temple. It was about 15 feet (4.6 m) across and held more than 10,000 gallons (38,000 liters) of water. It stood on 12 bronze oxen.
Now: Believers in Christ are saved and cleansed by the blood of Jesus. Even though we have accepted Jesus' sacrificial death on our behalf, we too need to be cleansed, spiritually. If we confess our sins, God will forgive and cleanse us (Ex. 30:18; 38:8; 1 Kings 7:23–26; 1 John 1:7–10).

❹ BRASS PILLARS (Bronze Pillars)
Then: The pillars, called "Jakin" on the right and "Boaz" on the left, supported the roof of the portico. They were 27 feet (9 m) high.
Now: Those who are faithful to Jesus through trials will be made "a pillar" in the temple of God (Rev. 3:12).

❺ HOLY PLACE
Then: Only priests were allowed to enter the Holy Place. They did this daily.
Now: Believers in Jesus have been made holy through Jesus' sacrifice and can go directly to God (Ex. 29–30; Heb. 9–10).

❻ GOLDEN LAMPSTANDS AND TABLES OF SHOWBREAD
Then: Ten gold lampstands and ten tables for bread were made for the temple (1 Kings 7:49; 2 Chron. 4:7–8, 19–20).
Now: Christ is the light of the world and the bread of life (John 9:5; 6:48–51).

❼ GOLDEN INCENSE ALTAR
Then: Prayers were offered at the gold altar of incense where special sweet incense required by God was burned.
Now: The prayers of God's people are a sweet incense to God (1 Kings 6:22; 2 Chron. 4:19; Ex. 30:35–37; Rev. 5:8).

❽ THE VEIL
(Curtain, doors of olive wood)
Then: The veil separated the Holy Place from the Most Holy Place where the ark of the covenant rested, separating a holy God from sinful people. Once a year only the high priest entered here.
Now: Believers in Jesus may enter God's presence through prayer because they are made acceptable to God by the blood of Jesus, the great high priest. When Jesus died, the temple veil tore in two from top to bottom (2 Chron. 3:14; 1 Kings 6:31–35; Ex. 25–26; Matt. 27:51; Heb. 10:19–22).

❾ MOST HOLY PLACE
Then: The Most Holy Place (Holy of Holies) was God's throne room where he would meet and give his commands, between the two cherubim, on the mercy seat over the ark of the covenant. The high priest sprinkled blood on the mercy seat on the Day of Atonement to atone for the sins of the people for that year.
Now: Believers can come boldly before God's throne of grace (Heb. 4:16).

❿ CHERUBIM
Then: Massive olive-wood sculptures of cherubim, winged creatures, represented the guardians of God's divine presence. These cherubim were overlaid with gold and they touched each other, wingtip to wingtip and wall to wall. When God banished man from the garden of Eden, he placed cherubim and a flaming sword to guard the way to the tree of life (1 Kings 6:19–29; Gen. 3:24).
Now: Believers can have eternal life in God's presence through faith in Jesus Christ (John 3:16–17).

⓫ ARK OF THE COVENANT
Then: The ark was a carved wooden box overlaid with gold. Inside was the Law of God (the Ten Commandments) inscribed on two tablets of stone. Its lid, the mercy seat, represented the meeting place between God and humans (Ex. 25:10–22).
Now: God wants to commune with us today. He made it possible to know him through Jesus (John 14:6; Heb. 9:4; 10:22).

⓬ STOREROOMS (Treasuries)
Then: Three-story rooms contained the treasures of God's temple and the dedicated gifts. These treasures were plundered several times.
Now: We are commanded by Jesus to not lay up treasures for ourselves on earth, but to lay up treasures in heaven (1 Chron. 28:11–12; Matt. 6:19–21).

JESUS AND THE TEMPLE

Birth

About forty days after his birth Jesus' parents brought him into the temple to be presented to the Lord, as required in the Law. They would have offered a sacrifice of a pair of doves or two young pigeons. (Luke 2:22–24; Lev. 12:3–8)

The Holy Spirit revealed to Simeon, a righteous and devout man, that he would see the Lord's Christ before he died. Moved by the Spirit, he came into the temple and took the baby Jesus in his arms and praised God, saying, "My eyes have seen your salvation . . . a light for revelation to the Gentiles and for glory to your people Israel." (Luke 2:25–33)

An elderly prophetess named Anna, who was worshiping, fasting and praying in the temple night and day, gave thanks to God and spoke about the child to all who were looking forward to the redemption of Jerusalem. (Luke 2:36-38)

Twelve Years Old

When Jesus was twelve years old, his family went to the Passover feast in Jerusalem. Three days after it ended, his parents found him in the temple courts, sitting among the teachers, listening and answering questions. All who heard him were astonished at his understanding and answers. He said he had to be doing his Father's business. (Luke 2:41–50)

From Thirty Years Old

Jesus was about thirty years old when he began his ministry. After he was baptized, he was tempted by the devil for forty days. The Devil led him to the highest point of the temple and dared him to throw himself down since he was the Son of God. Jesus said, "It is written, you must not put the Lord your God to the test." The Devil left for a while. (Matt. 3:16–17; 4:1–7; Luke 4:1–13; Deut. 6:16)

Jesus taught in the temple often. (Matt. 12; 21; 24; 26:55; Mark 11–15; Luke 18–21; 22:53; John 2–10; 18:20)

Jesus drove out all those buying and selling in the temple. He said that his house was a house of prayer, but they had made it a den of thieves. (Matt. 21:12–13; Mark 11:15–17; Luke 19:45–46; John 2:14–15)

Jesus healed blind and sick people in the temple. (Matt. 21:14)

Jesus told parables in the temple. (Matt. 21:23–46; 22:1–14; Mark 12:1–11)

Jesus watched people give money in the temple. He commented on the widow who gave all she had. (Mark 12:41; Luke 21)

Jesus said that he was greater than the temple. (Matt. 12:6)

He said, "Destroy this temple, and I will raise it again in three days," referring to his death and resurrection. (John 2:19–22; 22:21)

© Hugh Claycombe

Statue in the Book of Daniel
Daniel 2:26–45

Head of Fine Gold
Babylonia (626–539 BC)

Chest and Arms of Silver
Medo-Persia (539–332 BC)

Belly and Thighs of Bronze
Greece (332–63 BC)

Legs of Iron and Feet of Iron and Clay
A Divided Kingdom/Rome

The Stone
The Everlasting Kingdom of God

"There before you stood a large statue—an enormous, dazzling statue, awesome in appearance."
—Daniel 2:31

The illustration of the statue is based on a carving of King Nebuchadnezzar's grandson, Nabonidus. It is the most accurate representation of the Babylonian style of art.

Head of Fine Gold—Babylonia (626-539 BC)

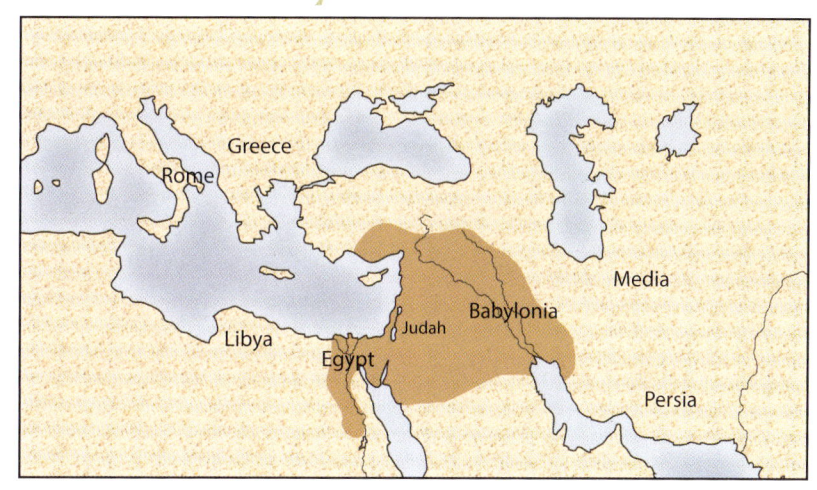

Historical and Bible Background

- About 600 years before Jesus was born, Babylonia (Iraq today) was the most powerful and wealthy kingdom in the Middle East.
- King Nebuchadnezzar of Babylon besieged Jerusalem and took Daniel and others captive to Babylon to serve in his court. Nebuchadnezzar also took some of the sacred objects and vessels from the temple of God back to Babylon.
- One night, Nebuchadnezzar had a dream. The king threatened to kill his advisors if they could not both tell him the dream and interpret it (Dan. 2:5–11).
- Daniel asked the king for some time to interpret the dream. After Daniel prayed, God revealed the dream and its meaning to him (Dan. 2:12–23).
- The dream showed a statue with four sections. The head was gold. The chest was silver. The belly and thighs were bronze. The legs were made of iron and the feet were iron mixed with clay. A large rock struck and destroyed the statue and became a huge mountain and filled the whole earth (Dan. 2:31–35).
- Daniel told King Nebuchadnezzar the dream and interpreted it (Dan. 2:36–45). The king made Daniel ruler over Babylon.

Head of the Statue (Daniel 2)

The head of the statue, made from fine gold, represented the kingdom of Babylonia, which the Lord gave King Nebuchadnezzar to rule. The gold symbolized the superior power of Babylonia. Eventually Babylonia would be destroyed by an inferior kingdom. When King Nebuchadnezzar heard Daniel's interpretation, he said, "Surely your God is the God of gods and the Lord of kings and a revealer of mysteries, for you were able to reveal this mystery."

Vision of Beasts – Lion (Daniel 7)

More than 50 years after King Nebuchadnezzar's dream, Daniel had a vision about four great beasts (that were like a lion with eagle's wings, a bear, a leopard, and a terrifying powerful beast). The four beasts are four kingdoms. Nebuchadnezzar of the Babylonian kingdom is compared to a lion in Jeremiah 4:7; 50:44, and to an eagle in Ezekiel 17:3, 11–12. Images of lions with eagle's wings were popular in Babylonia, and can be found on ancient Babylonian architecture and currency. (Daniel 7:4)

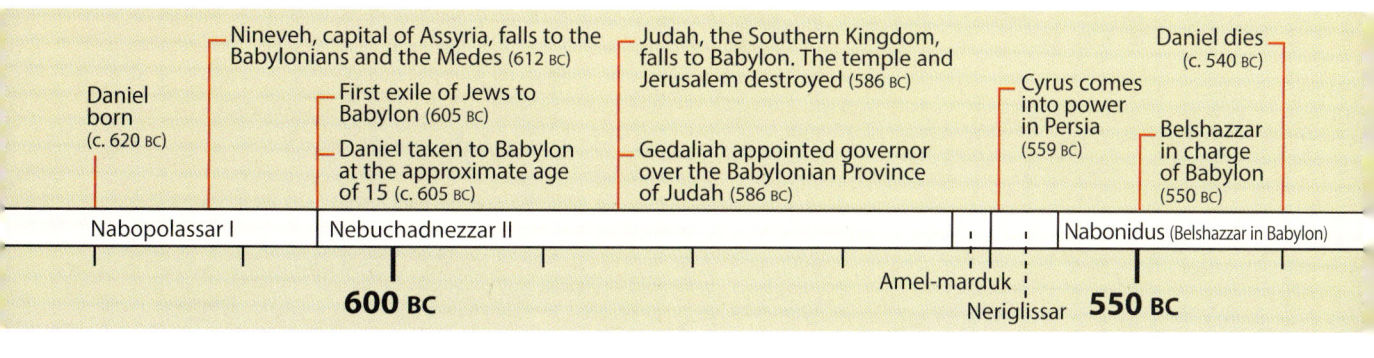

Timeline

- Daniel born (c. 620 BC)
- Nineveh, capital of Assyria, falls to the Babylonians and the Medes (612 BC)
- First exile of Jews to Babylon (605 BC)
- Daniel taken to Babylon at the approximate age of 15 (c. 605 BC)
- Judah, the Southern Kingdom, falls to Babylon. The temple and Jerusalem destroyed (586 BC)
- Gedaliah appointed governor over the Babylonian Province of Judah (586 BC)
- Cyrus comes into power in Persia (559 BC)
- Belshazzar in charge of Babylon (550 BC)
- Daniel dies (c. 540 BC)

Nabopolassar I | Nebuchadnezzar II | Amel-marduk | Neriglissar | Nabonidus (Belshazzar in Babylon)

600 BC — 550 BC

Chest and Arms of Silver—Medo-Persia (539-332 BC)

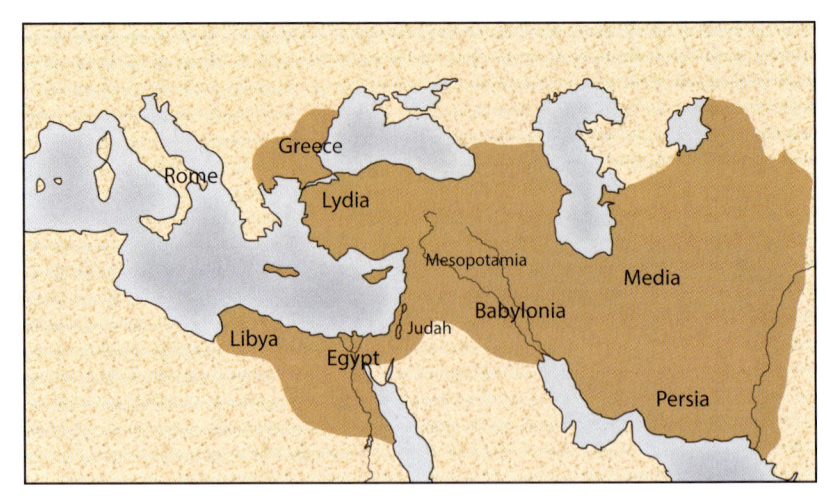

Historical and Bible Background

- In 539 BC, Darius the Mede (from Media) took Babylon without a fight.
- By 538 BC, Mesopotamia and Judah were under Persian rule. Later the Persians gained control of Egypt and Libya.
- King Cyrus and the other kings of the Persian empire developed a policy that allowed all people the freedom to worship their own gods, and live their own ways.
- In 538 BC, Cyrus issued a decree ordering the restoration of the Jewish community. Jews were allowed to return to Jerusalem and rebuild the temple (Ezra 1:2–4).
- The Persians paid to rebuild the temple in Jerusalem (Ezra 6:8).
- The vessels taken by King Nebuchadnezzar of Babylon were returned to their rightful place in Jerusalem (Ezra 1:7–11).
- In 457 BC, King Artaxerxes of Persia sent Ezra to Judah for religious reform and spiritual guidance (Ezra 7:1–6).
- Nehemiah governed Judah from 444-430 BC. While in Judah, Nehemiah rebuilt the walls of Jerusalem.

Chest and Arms of Statue (Daniel 2)

The chest and arms made of silver represented the kingdom of Medo-Persia, which is the second power that would rise after Babylonia. Silver, which is of lesser value than gold, symbolized the inferior status of Medo-Persia to Babylonia. Eventually Persia would be conquered by another kingdom.

Vision of Beasts – Bear (Daniel 7)

Daniel's vision of the beasts had shown a beast that looked like a bear. The bear was raised on one side, which may illustrate the dominance of Persia over Media. It had three ribs in its mouth, which may have illustrated the three major empires Persia conquered (Babylon, Egypt, and Lydia). The bear was commanded to devour much flesh, which may have been a reference to Persia's military expansion throughout the ancient world.

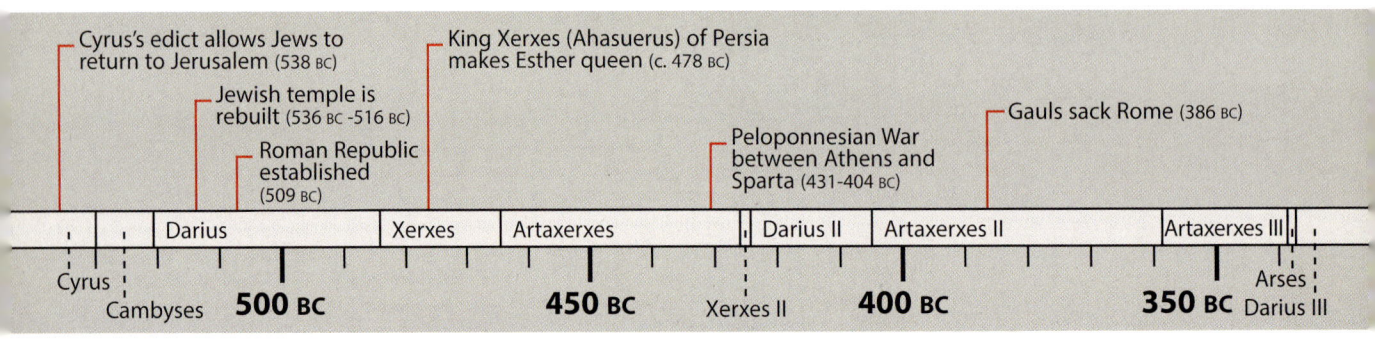

Timeline

- Cyrus's edict allows Jews to return to Jerusalem (538 BC)
- Jewish temple is rebuilt (536 BC -516 BC)
- Roman Republic established (509 BC)
- King Xerxes (Ahasuerus) of Persia makes Esther queen (c. 478 BC)
- Peloponnesian War between Athens and Sparta (431-404 BC)
- Gauls sack Rome (386 BC)

Rulers: Cyrus, Cambyses, Darius, Xerxes, Artaxerxes, Xerxes II, Darius II, Artaxerxes II, Artaxerxes III, Arses, Darius III

500 BC — 450 BC — 400 BC — 350 BC

Belly and Thighs of Bronze—Greece (332-63 BC)

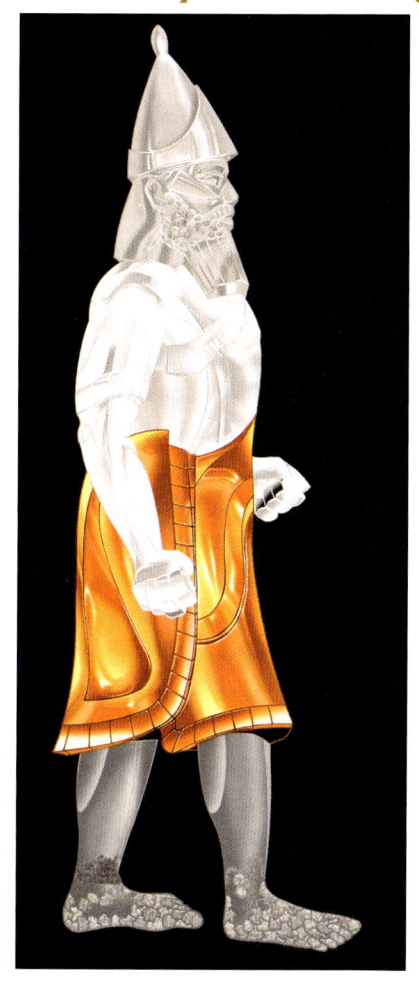

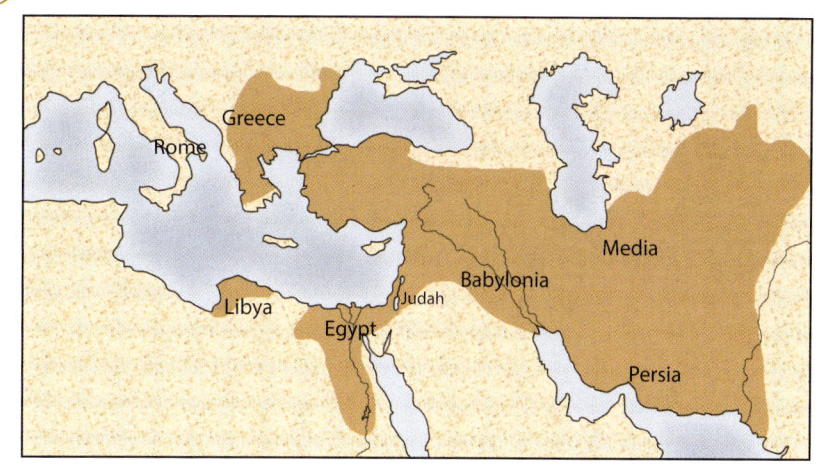

Historical and Bible Background

- In 332 BC, Alexander the Great of Greece conquered the kingdom of Persia, and expanded his kingdom as far east as the Indus river.
- Alexander the Great brought with him rapid Hellenization, the spread of Greek culture, language, and religion into the entire civilized world.
- After Alexander's death in 323 BC, his generals fought over the conquered land.
- After more than 40 years of struggles and warfare (323–280 BC), four major divisions emerged: Egypt (Ptolemies), Syria (Seleucids), Macedonia (Antigonids), and Pergamum (Attalids).
- For over 150 years, the Jews were either under the control of the Ptolemies or the Seleucids.
- From 175–163 BC, the Seleucid ruler Antiochus IV Epiphanes tried to force the Jews to abandon their law and adopt Greek culture. In 167 BC, he desecrated the Jewish temple by sacrificing a pig on an altar to the Greek god Zeus.
- In response to the desecration of the temple, a Jewish priest named Judas Maccabeus led a revolt.
- Maccabeus won, and in 164 BC, the temple was cleansed and rededicated. This rededication is celebrated every year as Hanukkah.

Belly and Thighs of Statue (Daniel 2)

The belly and thighs made of bronze represent the kingdom of Greece. This third kingdom would extend throughout the known world. Bronze, which is of lesser value than silver, symbolized the inferior status of Greece to that of Persia. Eventually Greece would be conquered by another kingdom.

Vision of Beasts – Leopard (Daniel 7)

Daniel's vision of the leopard with four heads and four wings may represent the kingdom of Greece. The four wings may illustrate the speed of Alexander the Great's conquest. The four heads may represent the division of Alexander's kingdom into four provinces after Alexander's death: Egypt under the Ptolemies, Syria under the Seleucids, Macedonia under the Antigonids, and Pergamum under the Attalids.

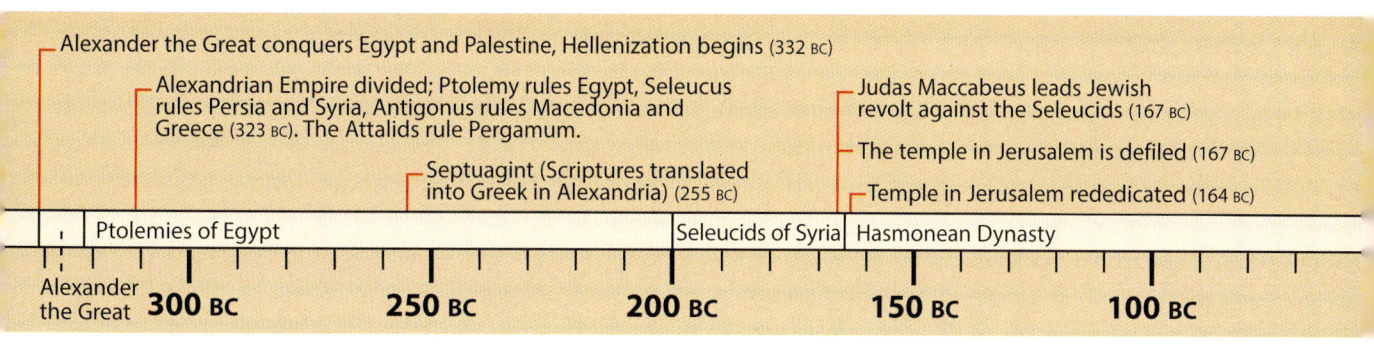

- Alexander the Great conquers Egypt and Palestine, Hellenization begins (332 BC)
- Alexandrian Empire divided; Ptolemy rules Egypt, Seleucus rules Persia and Syria, Antigonus rules Macedonia and Greece (323 BC). The Attalids rule Pergamum.
- Septuagint (Scriptures translated into Greek in Alexandria) (255 BC)
- Judas Maccabeus leads Jewish revolt against the Seleucids (167 BC)
- The temple in Jerusalem is defiled (167 BC)
- Temple in Jerusalem rededicated (164 BC)

| Ptolemies of Egypt | Seleucids of Syria | Hasmonean Dynasty |

Alexander the Great | 300 BC | 250 BC | 200 BC | 150 BC | 100 BC

Legs of Iron and Feet of Iron and Clay—Rome

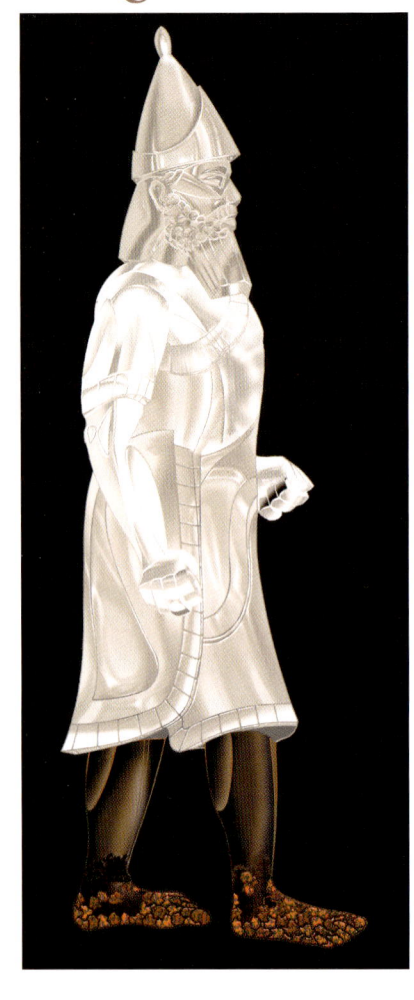

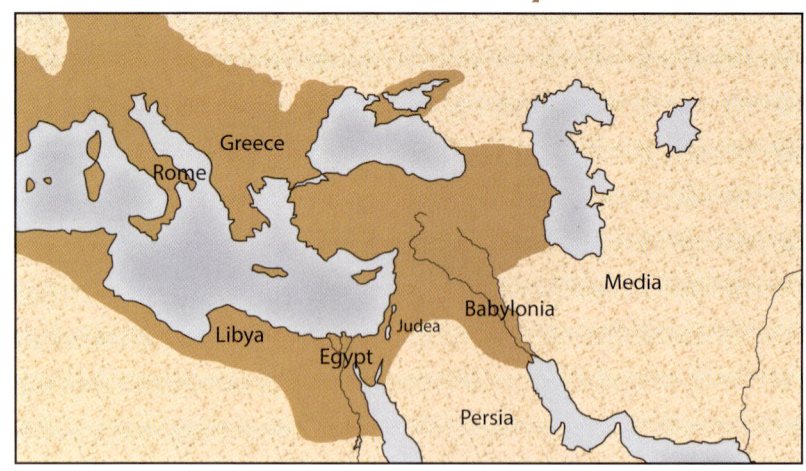

Historical and Bible Background

- Scholars suggest that the fourth kingdom is the Roman empire; however, the Bible does not specifically identify this kingdom as Rome.
- In 63 BC, Roman General Pompey conquered Jerusalem.
- On March 15, 44 BC, Julius Caesar was assassinated by Brutus and Cassius, who fled to the East. Two years later, Octavian and Mark Antony defeated Brutus and Cassius at the Battle of Philippi.
- In 37 BC, Herod the Great was appointed king of Judea by Octavian and Mark Antony.
- In 27 BC, Caesar Augustus (Octavian) became the first Roman Emperor.
- During his reign, Herod the Great began to refurbish the temple in Jerusalem.
- Jesus was born in Bethlehem, c. 6–4 BC.
- In AD 6, Judea became a Roman province ruled by a governor.
- Jesus Christ was crucified by the governor of Judea, Pontius Pilate. Three days after his death, Jesus rose from the dead and was seen by more than 500 people (c. AD 30).
- In AD 70, the Romans destroyed the Jewish temple and Jerusalem.
- Over time, the Roman Empire weakened due to conflict within its borders and invaders attacking from outside.
- The Roman Empire fell in AD 476.

Legs and Feet of Statue (Daniel 2)

The legs were made of iron and the feet were a mixture of both iron and clay. The legs of iron suggest that this kingdom would be strong as iron and would break, smash and crush things. This kingdom would be a divided kingdom, different from the others, both strong and weak, like iron is strong and clay is brittle. This kingdom would have a mixture of people who would not be united (Dan. 2:41–43; 7:23).

Vision of Beasts – Terrifying Beast (Daniel 7)

Daniel had a vision of a terrifying beast with ten horns and iron teeth. The beast's ten horns are ten kings that would rise from this kingdom. After them, another man (the "little horn" with eyes and a mouth that boasts) would speak against God and persecute God's people. Three of the first horns (kings) would be uprooted. Eventually the terrifying beast would be thrown into the blazing fire.

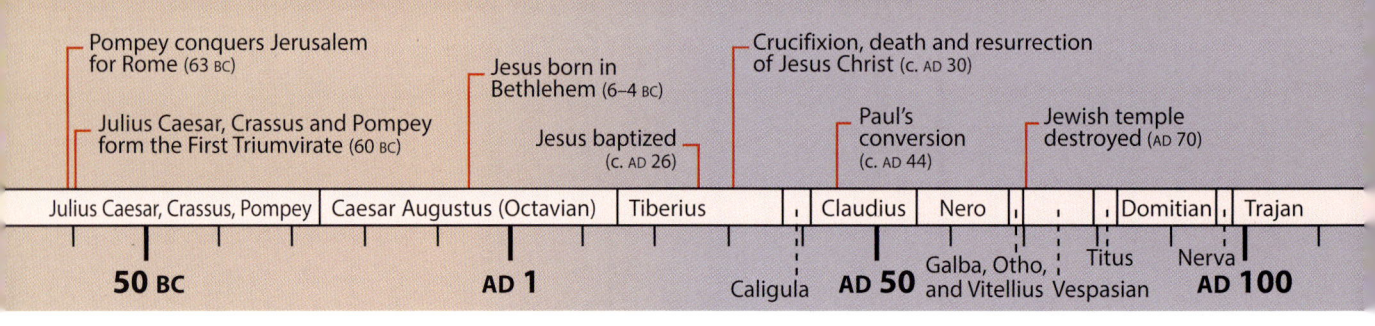

Timeline:

- Pompey conquers Jerusalem for Rome (63 BC)
- Julius Caesar, Crassus and Pompey form the First Triumvirate (60 BC)
- Jesus born in Bethlehem (6–4 BC)
- Jesus baptized (c. AD 26)
- Crucifixion, death and resurrection of Jesus Christ (c. AD 30)
- Paul's conversion (c. AD 44)
- Jewish temple destroyed (AD 70)

Rulers: Julius Caesar, Crassus, Pompey | Caesar Augustus (Octavian) | Tiberius | Caligula | Claudius | Nero | Galba, Otho, and Vitellius | Vespasian | Titus | Domitian | Nerva | Trajan

50 BC — AD 1 — AD 50 — AD 100

Stone Cut Out—Everlasting Kingdom

Bible References & Spiritual Application

- The stone represents God's eternal kingdom that is more powerful than any other kingdom.
- At the time of Daniel, the temple in Jerusalem was in shambles and the people of Israel were placed in captivity. The defeated captives may have feared that their God was weak and unfaithful.
- Daniel's writing demonstrates that in the midst of despair, God is still present, powerful, and in control. Kingdoms and rulers come and go, but God is ultimately in charge (Dan. 2:20–21; 7:9–14, 27).
- Despite Babylonia's wealth and power, Daniel emphasized that God's kingdom is eternal and more powerful than any earthly kingdom (Dan. 2:44).
- The book of Daniel shows that God did not forget his promises. God's promises have been fulfilled in the Son of Man (Dan. 7:13–14), who established an everlasting kingdom on earth (Dan. 2:44; 7:27).

The Rock (Daniel 2)

A stone was cut out, not by human hands, and it struck the statue on its feet of iron and clay and broke them in pieces. Then the rest of the statue broke into pieces and what remained was carried away in the wind. Then the stone that struck the statue became a great mountain that filled the whole earth. Daniel told the king that God will set up a kingdom that will crush all earthly kingdoms and bring them to an end. God's kingdom will never be destroyed and will endure forever.

Vision of Beasts
The Son of Man (Daniel 7)

After seeing the four beasts in a vision, Daniel saw one like a son of man, coming with the clouds of heaven. The son of man (Jesus) approached the Ancient of Days (God, the Father) and was led into his presence. The son of man was given authority, glory and sovereign power. All peoples, nations and people of every language worshiped him. His dominion is an everlasting dominion that will not pass away, and his kingdom will never be destroyed.

The Son of Man – The Alpha and Omega, the beginning and the end, the first and the last. Revelation 22:13

The Statue and the Vision of Beasts

NEBUCHADNEZZAR'S DREAM (Daniel 2)	DANIEL'S VISION (Daniel 7)	THE KINGDOMS (Dates kingdom occupied Judah)
HEAD (FINE GOLD)	LION with eagle's wings	BABYLONIA King Nebuchadnezzar to Belshazzar (605 BC – 539 BC)
CHEST AND ARMS (SILVER)	BEAR raised on one side; three ribs in its mouth	MEDO-PERSIA King Cyrus to Darius III (539 BC – 332 BC)
BELLY AND THIGHS (BRONZE)	LEOPARD with four wings and four heads	GREECE Alexander the Great and the Four Divisions (332 BC – 63 BC)
LEGS (IRON) & FEET (IRON AND CLAY)	BEAST iron teeth, ten horns; small horn with eyes and mouth	A DIVIDED KINGDOM Many scholars believe this kingdom to be Rome (63 BC through the time of Jesus)
STONE (CUT OUT, NOT BY HUMAN HANDS)	SON OF MAN (Jesus Christ)	THE EVERLASTING KINGDOM OF GOD

Women of the Bible: Old Testament

The Bible is full of women who became unexpected heroines and surprising instruments in God's story. Women played many crucial roles in Scripture, though it is easy to miss their significance. Following are brief, illustrated word portraits of eleven women from the Old Testament. Each sketch includes hidden meanings such as names, ironies in the stories, and the culture of the times. What the Bible does not say about someone or something is often as important as what the Bible actually says.

Women in the Ancient World

When reading such ancient texts, it is easy to forget how different things were in Old Testament times. In some ways, the role of a woman depended on her social status: Married women with children were more highly regarded than single or childless ones. In some ways, women were treated as property, to be used as necessary according to the situation. In other ways, they had a powerful influence on those around them. Notable women in the Old Testament navigated life using faith, discernment, and good judgment as their main tools. They were, like we all are, a mixture of strength and weakness, of sin and goodness. Their circumstances, struggles, hopes, and dreams have much to teach about living a life of faith with God.

Sarah and Hagar

	Sarai, later known as Sarah	Hagar
Biblical References	Genesis 12, 16, 17, 18, 21, 23	Genesis 16 and 21
Location and Dates	Canaan, around 2100 BC	Canaan, around 2100 BC
Meaning of Name	Both forms of the name mean "princess"	Hagar probably means "stranger"
Key Events	• Barren wife of Abraham • Abraham passed her off as his sister in exchange for safety—twice • Offered her slave, Hagar, to Abraham as concubine • Laughed at God's promise of a son • Bore a son named Isaac (meaning "laughter") at age 90	• Sarah's Egyptian slave • Given to Abraham as surrogate wife • Bore Ishmael (meaning "God hears") • Visited by the Angel of the Lord • Abraham expelled her from the household • Received promises from God
How God Used Her	Sarah's life showed that God is faithful to his promises. Although her life was in danger and her barrenness made it look impossible for God to fulfill his word, Isaac, the son of the promise, was born.	Although Hagar was considered a piece of property and used for her child-bearing abilities, God blessed her and her child. The birth of Ishmael, "God hears," is an encouragement to all who suffer.

Key Story

In her culture, Sarai's barrenness was what defined her. Sarai's lot in life was to be used as a piece of property, subjected to the whims and fears of her husband. While traveling through foreign lands, Abraham gave away his wife to guarantee his own survival and, as it turns out, enrichment. However, if Abraham was quick to give her up, God was not. He protected her and, eventually, restored her back to her husband.

God promised a son, but the years passed by and Abraham and Sarah were still childless. So Sarah decided to follow custom and gave her slave to her husband to have children through her. We can only imagine Sarai's suffering and longing leading to her decision to move aside. Sarah gave Abraham her own slave, Hagar, so he could have children. Hagar was also used as property; her existence was confined to the needs of her master and mistress. She became a surrogate for Sarah. Hagar gave birth to a son, Ishmael, and her new child and new social standing gave her boldness. Much as Sarah had used her social condition of owner before, Hagar used her new concubine position and her child-bearing ability against her mistress. Sarah severely punished Hagar (Genesis 16:9). Although we do not find out what happened to Hagar after she fled with her son, we do know that God promised to bless her and Ishmael in a special way.

In a miraculous intervention, God fulfilled his promise to Sarah by giving her a son, a future, a new reality. Many years later, Sarah was the first person to be buried in the Promised Land.

Life Application

🡆 A reminder that even in moments of doubt, suffering, and when facing what seems impossible, there is nothing impossible for God.

🡆 God keeps his promises in his own time.

🡆 God protects the weak.

Tamar

Biblical References	Genesis 38; Matthew 1:3
Location and Dates	Palestine, northern border of Judah, around 1880 BC
Meaning of Name	Probably "palm tree"
Key Events	• Married Judah's first son, Er • Married Judah's second son, Onan, after Er died • Judah sent her away after Onan died • Had twins with Judah • Perez, one of the twins, was an ancestor of King David • She is mentioned in Jesus' genealogy in Matthew 1:3
How God Used Her	God used Tamar to confront Judah with his sinful ways and convict him to change. Such a change was important for the leadership role that Judah was to have in his family and in the future of God's people (see Genesis 43–45).

KEY STORY

After marrying Tamar, Judah's eldest son, Er, passed away, leaving Tamar widowed and childless. Following biblical law, Onan, Judah's second son, married her but died soon thereafter. Instead of continuing the same practice and giving her to his third child, Judah blamed Tamar for the deaths and sent her away to her family. Tamar went away dejected and robbed of her future. She was a widow, childless, tied to Judah's family and unable to marry again. Although Judah promised to give her to his third child, he had no intention of keeping his promise, "for he feared that he would die like his brothers…" (Genesis 38:11). What is a person with almost no value, power, or influence to do in this unjust situation? Tamar still had her desire for justice. She used it to deal with her deceitful father-in-law.

We know more about Judah than Tamar. We know that he was impulsive, like his brothers, and scheming (Genesis 37:26-27). Moreover, he was a man for whom God seemed to play a secondary role, his own interests being in the place of honor. Tamar knew all of this and kept tabs on Judah's whereabouts and doings (Genesis 38:13). She made a plan that God used to straighten what Judah had twisted. It was a desperate, dangerous plan with little possibility of success, except for the fact that God was still in charge.

Her plan was deceivingly simple. She disguised herself as a prostitute and sat by the road at the entrance of Enaim. The Hebrew *petah enaim* means "eye-opener," giving the reader a clue for what is about to happen. It turned out to be an eye-opener for both Judah and the reader! As the story continues, Judah realized he had been trapped. His initial reaction of indignation evaporated when he saw his own seal, cord, and staff. Judah justified Tamar and her actions with the words, "She is more righteous than I…." Judah's words were not only his recognition of his own failing, but they also imply God's declaration that Tamar acted more in the spirit of the law than did Judah. The text continues narrating the birth of yet another set of twins, in which the second, Perez, was to be highly favored. Perez turned out to be David's ancestor and Jesus' own ancestor (Matthew 1:3).

LIFE APPLICATION

↪ God blesses people who seek righteousness.

↪ God can take what began as evil and turn it into good.

Miriam

Biblical References	Exodus 2:1-10, 15; Numbers 12, 20
Location and Dates	Egypt and Sinai Desert, around 1400 BC
Meaning of Name	Either "bitterness" or "rebellion"
Key Events	• Moses' sister, who tended Moses in the basket and cleverly reunited the baby with their mother • Led Israelites in song and dance after crossing the Red Sea, celebrating God's victory over Pharaoh • Called a "prophetess" (Exodus 15:20) • Rebelled against Moses; God severely punished her (Numbers 12) • Died before entering the Promised Land (Numbers 20:1)
How God Used Her	Miriam is a good example of humanity: She combined good and bad characteristics. She displayed great leadership qualities for the people, but she also rebelled against God's authority—just as the Israelites would in the desert and during the rest of their history. Yet, God chose her to rescue Moses, to lead the people, and to speak for him as a prophetess.

Key Story

When Pharaoh grew afraid of the Israelite slaves—for they were many—and decided to kill the male babies to control the Israelite population, Moses' mother hid him to save him. She put him in a basket and into the river Nile, hoping he would escape alive. Pharaoh's daughter found the baby. We are first introduced to Moses' daring sister as she takes him from Pharaoh's daughter to his own mother to be his nanny (Exodus 2:1-10). Although the Bible does not name her, most scholars assume that the girl is Miriam herself. With great courage and cunning, the girl understood the significance of what she witnessed and constructed a plan that was divinely blessed. The child Moses was returned to his mother and raised as a Hebrew.

Many years later, after the Israelites' traumatic chase through the desert with Pharaoh's armies at their heels and the wondrous crossing of the Red Sea, an awe-stricken, exhausted and still terrified people broke into a song. Miriam led the women in dancing and singing. She was called "the prophetess, the sister of Aaron" (Exodus 15:20). The song celebrated the liberating act of God on behalf of his people, Israel. It also marked the beginning of a long and tortuous journey through the wilderness into the Promised Land. Miriam, the prophetess, became a symbol or a microcosm of what was to be of Israel: from such a glorious moment by the Red Sea to anger, rebellion, disease and death in the wilderness.

First, Miriam challenged Moses' decision to marry a Cushite woman (Numbers 12). No reason is given for her anger—whether there was some traditional animosity against Cushites, with whom Israel probably shared its life of slavery in Egypt—or whether the Cushite was only an excuse for Miriam and Aaron's rebelliousness. Then Miriam questioned whether Moses was the only one to whom God spoke. Miriam had already been called a prophetess, so why did she question it? Regardless, God was displeased with Miriam and Aaron. God reaffirmed his commitment to Moses and Moses' status as a unique prophet. God's wrath punished Miriam by striking her with a skin disease. God punished only Miriam; Aaron was left unpunished. But through Moses' prayer for his sister, God only banished Miriam from the camp for seven days. The Israelites did not move during that time. They waited for Miriam during her punishment; afterwards, they welcomed her back into the community.

We do not read much more about Miriam until we are briefly informed of her death (Numbers 20:1). She, like the rest of Israel, did not get to see the Promised Land. Israel lived in the wilderness, with hope and rebellion, with courage and indecision. Miriam reflected all too well Israel's own ambivalence. Miriam was a woman of courage and determination, shrewd judgment, and impulsiveness. Despite her rebelliousness, God chose her as a leader and prophetess for his people in the desert. She was the first female prophetess in the history of God's people.

Life Application

☙ God loves us even when we are as ambivalent—trusting one moment, skeptical the next, faithful now, rebellious later—as Miriam.

☙ God forgives our rebellions even as he forgave Miriam.

☙ God is loving and merciful, yet he will punish disobedience and rebellion.

☙ God also uses imperfect individuals to lead his own people.

Rahab

Biblical References	Joshua 2, 6; Matthew 1:5; Hebrews 11:31; James 2:25
Location and Dates	Jericho, around 1400 BC
Meaning of Name	Rahab probably means "broad, extended"
Key Events	• Lived in the city of Jericho • Was a prostitute • Gave refuge to the spies that Joshua sent to the city • Believed that God had delivered the city into the hands of the Israelites • Became a member of God's people • Is mentioned in Jesus' genealogy in Matthew 1:5
How God Used Her	God used Rahab to save the Israelite spies, who brought encouraging words to Joshua and all the Israelites. Rahab also became God's messenger to bring strength and courage to the Israelites. Eventually, she played another important role in God's plan, as she was an unexpected ancestor of Jesus.

Key Story

After the Exodus from Egypt and wilderness wanderings, a whole generation of Israelites had died, including Moses. The first generation of freed slaves had sent spies into the Promised Land, but they failed to trust that God would make them victorious against their enemies. Because of their rebellion against God, the original generation of freed slaves died in the wilderness. Now a new generation was ready to enter the Promised Land. The new generation had a new leader, Joshua. Again Joshua sent new spies into the mighty city of Jericho, the first great city in the Promised Land. This time, the spies found refuge in the house of a prostitute, Rahab. Even though the Israelites were threatening her city and her very life, Rahab recognized that God was with the Israelites, so she decided to help them and hid the spies.

Throughout chapter one, Joshua had been encouraging the people to carry on God's plans. It seemed as if they had not seen enough of God's power to be sure that, as he had promised, "The LORD your God is with you wherever you go" (Joshua 1:9).

Rahab believed without having seen God in action, and she anticipated God's promises without being part of God's own people. She was able to confess, "I know that the LORD has given you the land" (Joshua 2:9). Rahab became the messenger of the Lord to Israel to infuse strength and courage. Rahab was three times vulnerable: she was a woman, she was Canaanite, and she was a prostitute. She had taken a great risk, and she had demonstrated surprising faith and courage. Joshua received her and her family as members of God's people. But that is not all. We must wait until the New Testament, Matthew 1:5, to learn another fact about Rahab: She is also named in Jesus' genealogy. Jesus, the savior of the world, is descended from this brave Canaanite woman.

Life Application

- God uses unexpected means to encourage his people.
- Rahab understood who God was and was willing to abandon all to become a member of God's people.
- God can use any person for his own purposes.

Jesus' Genealogy
Most genealogies from the time of Jesus did not even mention women. But Jesus' family tree is unique. It includes:

Tamar	Widowed twice, humiliated, and sent away; yet the Lord gave her children and honor
Rahab	A prostitute who was not an Israelite, but from Jericho, a city at war with Israel
Ruth	A foreigner from Moab, a country that often warred with Israel
Bathsheba	Became pregnant by King David; her husband was murdered
Mary	Mother of Jesus, from a poor area of Israel, probably a teenager

Notably, several of the women were non-Israelites, whose efforts for a future and whose courage and wisdom God blessed and prospered. Even the list of Jesus' ancestors reminds that Jesus is the Savior for all people: Jews and Gentiles, male and female.

Deborah and Jael

	Deborah	Jael
Biblical References	Judges 4 and 5	
Location and Dates	Palestine, around 1350 BC	
Meaning of Name	Deborah means "bee"	Jael means "mountain goat"
Key Events	• Judge and prophetess in Israel • Delivered God's word to Barak, who was in charge of the Israelite armies • Prophesied that the glory of the battle belonged to a woman instead of Barak	• Wife of Heber the Kenite (distant relatives of Israelites) • Gave refuge to Sisera, general of the enemy • Killed Sisera by driving a tent peg through his temple
How God Used Her	She brought God's word to Barak. Despite Barak's hesitance to obey, Deborah went with him.	Jael became God's instrument of deliverance for the Israelites.

Key Story

The people of Israel were in the Promised Land, but they had failed to take full possession of it. In their struggle for survival and for identity, the tribes of Israel were caught in a cycle of sin and violence. Joshua had died. Without a leader, the Israelites had entered a cycle of disobedience, punishment and liberation. So God raised judges to fight for his people and liberate them from suffering. After the death of Joshua, it had become an evil time: "Everyone did what was right in his own eyes" (Judges 21:25). Although the focus could be on Israel's sin and human evil in general, the stories are really about God—about God's patience, love, grace and redemptive power.

Once again the Israelites were oppressed and they cried out to the Lord for deliverance. Israel went to Deborah, which means *bee*, to enjoy the sweetness of God's word, since Deborah was also a prophetess. Deborah summoned Barak, which means *lightning*, and she communicated to him God's orders to gather an army and go to Mount Tabor to fight Sisera, the commander of the enemy armies. Israel was overmatched and outnumbered. It is said that when the Lord sends lightning, it obeys (Job 38:35), but surprisingly, *lightning* (Barak) refused to go unless Deborah came along. Deborah took on roles that seem exclusive to men: those of prophet and judge. Ironically, she offered both judgment and prophecy against Barak. Deborah's words were decisive: "The road on which you are going will not lead to your glory, for the Lord will sell Sisera into the hand of a woman" (Judges 4:9). Instead of enjoying the sweetness of the honey, Barak suffered the sting of a judgment announcement. As readers, we expect that woman to be Deborah, but we are in for a surprise.

When the battle took place, it was God who fought for his people; in a flashback to the Israelites' crossing of the Red Sea and the destruction of Pharaoh's army, Sisera's powerful chariots were swept away in a flood. Sisera escaped alive and ran for a safe place. Sisera fled to the camp of Heber the Kenite. Instead of the ally Heber, whose name means *companion*, Sisera found Jael, Heber's wife. Sisera, the powerful general now unexpectedly humbled by defeat, expected to find comfort and safety in this place. What danger could come from a humble *goat*, which is what *Jael* means? Jael gave Sisera milk instead of water. Her readiness to serve, the extra kindness to offer milk instead of water, and her covering him for comfort, all reassured Sisera of his safety. He ordered Jael to stand at the entrance of the tent, where she should be waiting for her husband, and turn away any pursuers. But Sisera was not to wake up. Jael, the humble *goat*, took on the role of *lightning*, and killed the powerful and confident Sisera.

Deborah's prophecy came true with Jael: the glory of the day belongs to her. Jael became God's instrument of deliverance. Jael's actions are sanctioned positively in verse 23: "So on that day God subdued Jabin…."

Life Application

☞ God has chosen to use the humble and the meek to carry on his plans.

☞ Even if people refuse to follow God's orders, like Barak did, God's plans cannot be thwarted.

☞ Becoming God's instrument requires courage and initiative.

BATHSHEBA

Biblical References	2 Samuel 11, 12; 1 Kings 1, 2; Matthew 1:6
Location and Dates	Jerusalem, around 970 BC
Meaning of Name	Bathsheba means "daughter of seven" or "daughter of oath"
Key Events	• Wife of Uriah, the Hittite, a commander of King David's armies • David took Bathsheba as his wife • Their first child died as punishment for David's sin • Mother of King Solomon
How God Used Her	God allowed her relative innocence to contrast with David's guilt. Although she suffered much by being used by David, losing her husband and losing her baby, God restored Bathsheba by giving her another baby, Solomon, who became king and through whom God preserved the Messianic lineage.

KEY STORY

King David is the central figure of the book of Samuel. This episode represents the turning point in his life—David's disobedience is the dividing line between a life of victory and one of decline. During this crucial moment in the life of God's people, Bathsheba takes a heartbreaking role.

Not much is said about her in the texts, but much is implied. It is necessary to "read the silences" to understand what the biblical text has to say about this complex person. Bathsheba's introduction is very brief: she was bathing, she was beautiful, she was married, David desired her, they had intercourse and she became pregnant. In all of this, Bathsheba uttered only the words: "I am pregnant." We do not know how she felt about the news; we are not granted a view into her heart, just the cold, matter-of-fact statement. Yet, those words require much courage. The words came as a warning, as a plea, as an accusation, which David took very seriously. He devised an evil plan to kill Uriah. David's plan resulted in greater evil: he moved from coveting, adultery, abuse of power, to murder.

Bathsheba lamented her husband's death and, in time, became David's wife. Note that she is not named again for some time; we are simply told that, "When the wife of Uriah heard that Uriah her husband was dead, she lamented over her husband" (2 Samuel 11:26). This shift is significant. During David's sinful actions, Bathsheba is called "Uriah's wife" instead of "Bathsheba" so that her condition of wife and the name of her murdered husband are brought to the reader's attention. And, again, when God's punishment reaches David and allows the child to die, we read "And the LORD afflicted the child that Uriah's wife bore to David" (12:15). These omissions are reminders that David is on trial here, not Bathsheba.

When the first part of the punishment was completed, Bathsheba was restored again by having her name and her future back: "Then David comforted his wife, Bathsheba, and went in to her and lay with her, and she bore a son, and he called his name Solomon" (12:24).

Bathsheba disappears from the biblical account again, although she comes back at a defining moment in the history of Israel when David's successor to the throne is in question. Prodded by the prophet Nathan, Bathsheba intercedes with King David on behalf of Solomon, her son. This quiet woman does the Lord's will and takes a powerful step. She wins the king's favor and Solomon is named the successor.

LIFE APPLICATION

- God does not tolerate sin.
- However, he forgives and restores as well.
- God can turn around evil things into hopeful and good situations.

O LORD, do not rebuke me in your anger or discipline me in your wrath. Be merciful to me, LORD, for I am faint; O LORD, heal me, for my bones are in agony. My soul is in anguish. How long, O LORD, how long? Turn, O LORD, and deliver me; save me because of your unfailing love.

Psalm 6:1-4

Naomi and Ruth

	Naomi	Ruth
Biblical References	Ruth; Matthew 1:5	
Location and Dates	Bethlehem and Moab, around 1350 BC	
Meaning of Name	Naomi means "pleasant"	Ruth means "friend, companion"
Key Events	• Wife and widow of Elimelech • Mother of Mahlon and Kilion, who died soon after their father • Changed her name to Mara, which means "bitterness" • Returned to Bethlehem with Ruth • Restored through Ruth	• Moabitess who married Mahlon • Became a widow • Refused to abandon Naomi and returned with her to Bethlehem • Met Boaz, a relative of her late father-in-law Elimelech • Confronted him with his kin redeemer responsibility • Married Boaz and bore Obed, grandfather of King David
How God Used Her	God turned Naomi's lament into joy; he proved once again to be a faithful provider and loving God. Despite the pain of the losses, God restored Naomi through the blessing of Ruth.	God allowed Ruth to be an example of what it means to be a daughter of the promise. She became adopted into God's family. God rewarded her faithfulness by granting her a son who was grandfather of King David. Ruth is also mentioned in Jesus' genealogy in Matthew 1:5.

Key Story

The story of these two extraordinary women is filled with sadness, joy, ironies, laughs, faith, bravery, and hope. The first irony appears in verse 1: There was a famine in Bethlehem, which means "House of Bread." The second irony follows: a man of Judah had to travel as an immigrant to the land of his most bitter enemies: Moab. Elimelech, "My God is King," and his wife Naomi, "Pleasant," traveled with their two sons, Mahlon and Kilion (or what could be translated as "Sickly and Weakly"). Their names are a clue that things were to go wrong very soon. All three men died. Naomi's life was fraught with grief and suffering. Her life, as she herself recognized later on, was better captured by the name she took, Mara, "Bitterness." When she had lost everything and saw no hope at all, Naomi advised her daughters-in-law to return to their homes and hope for another marriage there. Naomi had nothing else left to offer to them. Orpah returned home, but Ruth refused to follow her example.

The text says, "Ruth clung to her" (1:14). Ruth, the Moabite, renounced her land, her heritage and gods for Naomi's: "For where you go I will go, and where you lodge I will lodge. Your people shall be my people, and your God my God. Where you die I will die, and there will I be buried" (1:16-17). Like Naomi who had lost everything and changed her identity to start all over again, Ruth chose to lose everything and seek a new identity, a new future, a new life.

In this new life, Ruth had to learn to survive as a widow in a strange land. She went out to find food. Although Naomi claimed the Lord had abandoned her, Ruth found a relative of Naomi, Boaz, who was wealthy, generous and single. Following her mother-in-law's good judgment and plan, Ruth acted decisively for a future for her and Naomi. She confronted Boaz and called him to responsibility. The foreign woman reminded the Israelite what God had commanded concerning care for relations. Boaz, however, was a gentle, upright person, who treated Ruth kindly from the beginning. In fact, Boaz was not the first in line to redeem Ruth, since she had a closer relative. Yet Boaz's love for Ruth and obedience of God's will led him to become Ruth's redeemer.

Eventually, Boaz married Ruth, who bore a child, thus restoring both Ruth and Naomi. Ruth's son, Obed, was David's grandfather.

Life Application

➥ Ruth's willingness to abandon everything to follow God's ways is an example for all.

➥ God's call to obedience and to being his own is for all.

➥ Boaz's love and willingness to obey God resulted in great blessing from God.

Esther

Biblical References	Esther
Location and Dates	Persia, around 480 BC
Meaning of Name	Esther is a Persian name, probably meaning "star." Hadassah, her Hebrew name, means "myrtle."
Key Events	• Jewish young woman living in Persia • Chosen to become King Xerxes' wife • Made Queen of Persia • Interceded for the Jews when Haman plotted to destroy them • God used her to save his people • Established the beginning of the Feast of Purim
How God Used Her	Through Esther's action, God saved the Jews from destruction and brought them peace and security.

Key Story

Esther's story is one of survival, faith, audacity, and God's protecting hand. It is a dramatic story of a beautiful orphaned girl who found herself thrown into the world of royal life, court intrigue, murderous plots, pride and hatred. Unlike modern-day fairy tales of a prince and a happily ever after, Esther's life became a nightmare. She had to worry not only about her own survival but also that of her people. The survival of a people was on the shoulders of a beautiful, terrified, young girl.

Esther's life was not in her hands. She depended on her uncle Mordecai, on the eunuch in charge of the king's harem, and, mostly, on the whims and tantrums of an unpredictable ruler, Ahasuerus—also known as Xerxes. God did not seem to pay any attention! How was she to make a difference? It was not with strength, influence, wealth, or even wisdom; rather, it was by using characteristics common to many biblical heroines: shrewdness, courage and trust that God was acting behind the scenes.

Upon discovering a plot to destroy all the Jews in the Persian Empire, Mordecai persuaded Esther that only she was in a position to help, "And who knows but that you have come to royal position for such a time as this?" Esther planned to use her position, and whatever power that may imply, to defend and save her people. Being a queen did not immunize her from danger, for the king was truly unpredictable—she would be risking her life to go to him uninvited. With great courage and faith, she accepted this danger, saying, "If I die, I die" (Esther 4:16).

Esther invited the king and Haman, his trusted advisor, who happened to be the person plotting the killing of all the Jews, to two banquets. During the second banquet, Esther revealed her Jewish identity and the plot to destroy her and her people. The enraged king sent Haman to the very gallows he built for the Jews. Through Esther's courageous action, God saved the Jews from destruction and brought them peace and security.

I will extol the LORD at all times;
his praise will always be on my lips.
My soul will boast in the LORD;
let the afflicted hear and rejoice.
Glorify the LORD with me;
let us exalt his name together.

Psalm 34:1-3

Life Application

➣ God can use any person to carry on his will.

➣ God protects his people from danger.

➣ Even when God appears to be absent, he is present and active in our lives.

HEROES OF THE OLD TESTAMENT

Hero	Date	Bible Reference
Noah	Before 2500 BC	Genesis 5:29 to Genesis 9:29
Abraham	2166 BC to 1991 BC	Genesis 11:26 to Genesis 25:10
Jacob	2005 BC to 1859 BC	Genesis 25:19 to Genesis 50:14
Joseph	1914 BC to 1805 BC	Genesis 30:24 to Genesis 50:26
Moses	1526 BC to 1406 BC	Exodus 2:1 to Deuteronomy 34:7
Joshua	1491 BC to 1381 BC	Exodus 17:9 to Joshua 24:29
Gideon	Between 1300 BC and 1100 BC	Judges 6:11 to Judges 8:35
David	1041 BC to 971 BC	1 Samuel 16:1 to 1 Kings 1:53
Elijah	870 BC to 845 BC	1 Kings 17:1 to 2 Kings 2:11
Daniel	620 BC to 540 BC	Daniel 1:1 to Daniel 12:13

NOAH | ABRAHAM "ABRAM"

SUMMARY

Noah: The people in Noah's day were so wicked that God was filled with grief. God decided to destroy the world with a flood. He instructed Noah, a righteous person, to build an ark so he and his family could survive the flood.

Following God's instructions, Noah built an ark with three decks, a door, a roof, and a window. It took Noah at least 100 years to build the ark. God sent two of every living creature to Noah, and seven of every "clean" animal and bird.

When Noah was 600 years old God shut him, his family, and the animals in the ark. It rained for 40 days and nights and the waters flooded the earth for 150 days. The waters receded, and after being in the ark for over a year, they finally exited the ark on Mt. Ararat.

Noah made a sacrifice to God and God made a covenant with Noah promising to never destroy the world with a flood. God put the rainbow in the clouds as a sign of that covenant. (Genesis 5:32-9:17)

Abraham: Abraham, originally Abram, was born in Mesopotamia. God promised Abram that he would be the father of a great nation and that Sarai would give birth to a son. God also commanded Abram to leave his home and move to a place God would show him. Abram obeyed. Once in Canaan, God promised the land to Abram's offspring. Later, a famine caused Abram to move to Egypt. Abram feared that the Egyptians would kill him to take his wife, so he told them that Sarai was his sister.

When Abram was 85 years old, and Sarai was 75 years old, they still had no children, so Sarai offered Abram her slave girl Hagar. Not trusting God's promise, Abram married Hagar and she had a son named Ishmael. Years later, God gave Abram the sign of circumcision and changed his name to "Abraham," and Sarai's name to "Sarah."

Sarah gave birth to Isaac. When Isaac had grown, God tested Abraham by telling him to sacrifice Isaac. As Abraham prepared to obey, God stopped him and provided a replacement sacrifice. (Genesis 11-12; 16-19; 21:1-7; 22:1-19)

VERSE

Noah was a righteous man, blameless among the people of his time, and he walked with God. —Genesis 6:9

Abram believed the LORD, and he credited it to him as righteousness. —Genesis 15:6

CHARACTER

Noah:
- Righteous and blameless (Genesis 6:9; Hebrews 11:7)
- Obedient (Genesis 6:22)
- Faithful and trusting (Hebrews 11:7)

Abraham:
- Righteous (Genesis 15:6; Romans 4:3)
- Cowardly (Genesis 12:11-13; 20:2)
- God fearing (Genesis 22:12)
- Faithful (Hebrews 11:8-11, 17)

SYMBOLISM

Noah:
- Jesus compared the end times to the days of Noah. (Matthew 24:35-39; Luke 17:26-30)
- Peter compared the floodwaters to baptism. At the time of Noah eight people were saved through water. Water baptism celebrates Christ's resurrection, which saves believers from sin. (1 Peter 3:20)

Abraham:
- Abraham's willingness to sacrifice his son can be compared to Christ's sacrificial death on the cross. (Genesis 22:1-19; Luke 22:39-53)
- Abraham's willingness to sacrifice his son showed that he believed that God could raise someone from the dead. (Hebrews 11:17-19)

CHALLENGES

Noah:
- Witnessing the destruction of all living things. (Genesis 6:7)
- Following God's commands to build an ark. (Genesis 6:22)
- Seeing friends and neighbors reject God. (1 Peter 3:20; 2 Peter 2:1-5)
- Being on board the ark for over a year. (Genesis 7:6-10)
- Being responsible for the lives of his family and all living things. (Genesis 7:6-10)

Abraham:
- Leaving his family behind and moving to a strange unknown land. (Genesis 12:1-5)
- Not having the courage to protect his wife. (Genesis 12:11-13; 20:2)
- Not believing that God could give him a son in his old age. (Genesis 16:1-4; 17:17, 18)
- Witnessing the destruction of his sinful neighbors. (Genesis 18:20-33)
- Willing to give up his most important possession (Isaac) to obey God. (Genesis 22:1-19)

LESSONS

Noah:
- God is patient with sinners and urges all people to repent of their sins while warning of upcoming judgment. (1 Peter 3:20; 2 Peter 2:1-5; 3:1-13)
- God offers people the way of salvation. (Genesis 6:18; 1 Peter 3:20; 2 Peter 2:1-5)
- Judgement comes unexpectedly. (Matthew 24:35-39; Luke 17:26-30)

Abraham:
- God keeps his promises, even if it takes longer than we expect.
- Those who believe in God and his promises are considered righteous. (Genesis 15:6)
- All people who believe in Jesus Christ receive the blessing of Abraham, which is to be God's chosen and beloved children. (Romans 4:12-18; Galatians 3:6-16)
- The evidence of true faith is found in our actions. (James 2:20-22)

Heroes of the Old Testament • 131

JACOB
"ISRAEL"

JOSEPH
"ZAPHENATH-PANEAH"

	JACOB	JOSEPH
SUMMARY	Jacob was the youngest of twins. When they were older, Jacob tricked his brother out of his birthright and his blessing. Escaping his brother Esau's anger, Jacob fled more than 400 miles away, to the city of Haran. On the way, in Bethel, Jacob had a dream of angels ascending and descending a staircase into heaven. In the dream, God promised to be with Jacob. In Haran, Jacob met a girl named Rachel and offered her father Laban seven years of service for her hand in marriage. After seven years, Laban gave him his daughter Leah instead. Jacob agreed to work another seven years for Rachel's hand. After 20 years, and having 11 sons and one daughter, Jacob returned to Canaan. The night before making amends with his brother Esau, Jacob wrestled with "a man" at Penuel and Jacob was renamed "Israel," which means "the one who strives with God." Traveling through Canaan, Rachel died giving birth to Benjamin, Jacob's twelfth son. Finally, Jacob reunited with his father and settled in Hebron. (Genesis 25:34; 27:1–30:24; 31:1–33:17)	Joseph was the favorite son of Jacob. Jacob gave him a special coat. Joseph had two dreams that suggested his family would bow down to him. Jealous of Joseph and angry about his dreams, his brothers sold him as a slave to some traders on their way to Egypt. In Egypt, Joseph was sold to Potiphar, an officer who was captain of the guard. The LORD gave Joseph success, and he was put in charge of the household. Potiphar's wife tried to seduce Joseph. When Joseph resisted her, she falsely accused him, and he was imprisoned. While in prison, Joseph worked hard, took on more responsibility, and remained faithful to God. The LORD gave Joseph the ability to interpret dreams. Joseph interpreted two dreams for Pharaoh predicting seven years of plenty and then seven years of famine. Pleased with Joseph, Pharaoh made him second-in-command of Egypt. During the famine, Joseph's brothers came to Egypt to buy food. After testing their loyalty, Joseph revealed who he was, forgave his brothers, and had his entire family—known as the Israelites—move to Egypt. (Genesis 37:1-28; 39:1–46:33)
VERSE	"Your name will no longer be Jacob, but Israel, because you have struggled with God and with men and have overcome." —Genesis 32:28	"You intended to harm me [Joseph], but God intended it for good to accomplish what is now being done, the saving of many lives." —Genesis 50:20
CHARACTER	• Sly and deceitful (Genesis 25:29-34; 27:1-29; 30:25-43) • Resourceful and assertive (Genesis 30:37-43; 32:22-30) • Apprehensive (Genesis 32:3-21; 34:30-31; 43:6) • Faithful (Hebrews 11:21)	• Spoiled and arrogant as a young man (Genesis 37:2-14) • Humble and matured (Genesis 39-40) • Wise and discerning (Genesis 50:19-21; Acts 7:9, 10) • Faithful (Hebrews 11:22)
SYMBOLISM	• Jacob had a dream of a staircase bridging the gap between heaven and earth. (Genesis 28:10-17) • Jesus bridges the gap that sin creates between God and people. (Genesis 28:12; John 1:51)	• Joseph was betrayed, imprisoned, suffered, and sat at the right hand of the Pharaoh. Joseph suffered in order to save his people. (Genesis 37-50) • Jesus was betrayed, suffered, was crucified, died, rose, and now sits at God's right hand. Jesus died to save the world from sin. (Hebrews 12:2, 3)
CHALLENGES	• Having trouble being honest. (Genesis 27:5-29; 30:37-43) • Fear of facing his brother Esau who wanted to kill him. (Genesis 32:3-21) • Having difficulty trusting God to provide for him and his family without taking things into his own hands. (Genesis 32:3-21; 33:1-3) • Having problems maintaining control and order in his family. (Genesis 34:1-31; 35:22; 37-38)	• Dealing with the favoritism of his father, Jacob. (Genesis 37:2-14) • Being sold into slavery by his brothers. (Genesis 37:18-36) • Being pursued by the wife of his master, Potiphar, and imprisoned. (Genesis 39:1-18) • Suffering unjustly in prison. (Genesis 39:19–40:23) • Handling the responsibility of leading a nation through a terrible famine. (Genesis 47:13-26)
LESSONS	• God's plans and promises will prevail, even in the midst of human weakness. (Genesis 28:13-15; 35:9-12) • We often reap what we sow. Our sin will find us out. (Genesis 29:15-30; 30:25-36; Numbers 32:23) • Great transformation can occur under the power of God. (Genesis 32:22-32)	• Being God's servant might mean having to stay strong through adversity and false accusation, as well as resisting sexual temptation, greed, and vengeance. (Genesis 37:18-36; 39-45) • Repay evil with good and forgive those who wrong you. (Genesis 45:4-15) • God can take what was intended for evil and use it for good. (Genesis 50:20)

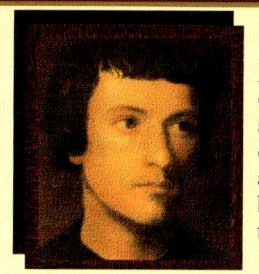

MOSES

JOSHUA
"Hoshea"

SUMMARY

Moses: Moses was born to a Hebrew slave family in Egypt. The Pharaoh issued a decree to kill all Hebrew boys. Moses' mother put him in a basket and placed it in the Nile. He was rescued by an Egyptian princess, and was raised in the palace.

When Moses was 40, he went out to his people. He murdered an Egyptian who was beating a Hebrew slave. Fearing Pharaoh, Moses escaped to Midian.

When Moses was 80, God called to him from a burning bush and commanded him to lead the Israelites out of Egypt. Moses felt inadequate, so God revealed to Moses His divine name and provided him with the ability to perform several miracles to prove his authority. Moses reluctantly obeyed, and after calling down ten plagues on Egypt, he lead the people from Egypt to Canaan for 40 years.

Important events: Parting of the Red Sea, receiving the 10 Commandments, selecting judges, building the Tabernacle. He died on Mt. Nebo, within sight of the Promised Land. (Exodus 1– Deuteronomy 34)

Joshua: Joshua was a military leader during the journey to the Promised Land, often serving as Moses' second-in-command. Joshua was the only one allowed to go up Mt. Sinai with Moses, and was not in the camp when the people formed and worshiped the golden calf.

Joshua was one of the twelve spies sent to "spy out the land of Canaan." He and Caleb were the only two spies to encourage the people to invade Canaan as God had commanded. They urged the people to trust God, but the other spies were afraid and convinced the people to retreat back to Egypt. As a result, Joshua and Caleb were the only two Israelites over the age of twenty who were allowed to enter the Promised Land.

Before Moses died, Joshua was commissioned by Moses and ordained by God as the leader of the Israelites. After Moses died, Joshua lead the Israelites in the conquest of the Promised Land. Joshua encouraged the Israelites to only serve God. (Exodus 17:13; 24:13; Numbers 13:1–14:38; Deuteronomy 31:1-8; Joshua 1–11, 23–24)

VERSE

Moses: "So now, go. I am sending you [Moses] to Pharaoh to bring my people the Israelites out of Egypt." —Exodus 3:10

Joshua: "But as for me [Joshua] and my household, we will serve the LORD" —Joshua 24:15

CHARACTER

Moses:
- Reluctant and complaining (Exodus 3:6-13; 4:10-17; Numbers 11:15)
- Courageous yet humble (Exodus 2:15-17; 5:1-3; 33:12-23; Numbers 12:3)
- Moral and upright (Exodus 32; Numbers 12:6-8)
- Trustworthy and faithful (Hebrews 3:5; 11:24-29)

Joshua:
- Servant minded and loyal (Exodus 24:13; 32:17; Numbers 14:6-10)
- Obedient (Joshua 6:1-21)
- Committed and influential (Joshua 24:14-27)
- Filled with the Spirit of wisdom (Deuteronomy 34:9)
- Faithful (Hebrews 11:30)

SYMBOLISM

Moses:
- The tenth plague was the death of the oldest son. The Israelites put the blood of a perfect lamb on their doorframes, so the angel of the LORD would "pass over" their homes. (Exodus 12:1-13)
- Jesus is the perfect "Lamb of God" and God "passes over" our sins, because of His blood. (John 1:29)

Joshua:
- Joshua, which means "Yahweh is salvation," delivered the people of Israel from the wilderness into the Promised Land. (Deuteronomy 31:7, 8)
- Jesus, the Greek name for Joshua, delivers all believers from the wilderness of sin. (Matthew 1:21)

CHALLENGES

Moses:
- Choosing his people over the benefits of Egyptian life (Exodus 2:11-13)
- Escaping the wrath of the king after murdering the Egyptian (Exodus 2:15)
- Speaking poorly (Exodus 4:10)
- Leading the Israelites from Egypt, through the desert, to the Promised Land. (Exodus 1 - Deuteronomy 34)
- Being the "middle man" between a complaining people and a just God. (Exodus 11:4-20)

Joshua:
- Remaining loyal to Moses and obedient to God when others were worshiping idols and complaining. (Exodus 32:17; Numbers 14:6-10)
- Leading the Israelites through the flooded Jordan river and preparing them to attack a fortified city. (Joshua 3:1–6:27)
- Dividing the land fairly and preparing the Israelites to continue to serve and obey God while in the Promised Land. (Joshua 13:8–24:28)

LESSONS

Moses:
- God may call someone who feels inadequate in order to accomplish a task. (Exodus 3-4)
- God is faithful and just. He faithfully remembers His people and justly deals with their disobedience. (Exodus 3:7-10; Numbers 14:20-24)
- One cannot effectively do ministry alone. It is necessary to delegate responsibilities to other leaders. (Exodus 18:13-26)

Joshua:
- When people dedicate their lives to God through faithful and humble service, God will use them for a greater purpose. God has a plan for everyone, even if it means standing in someone else's shadow. (Joshua 1:1-9)
- God calls people to trust Him, even in the midst of opposition and persecution. (Numbers 14:6-10; Joshua 6:1-27)

Heroes of the Old Testament • 133

GIDEON
"JERUBBAAL"

DAVID

SUMMARY

Gideon was a farmer who was summoned by an angel to save the Israelites from the invading Midianites. Gideon pointed out that he was the least of his clan, and his clan was the weakest in tribe of Manasseh.

The angel commanded Gideon to destroy an altar to Baal, so Gideon took ten of his servants and destroyed the altar that night. The next day, the people tried to kill Gideon. Gideon's father said if Baal was god, he could defend himself, so Gideon was renamed "Jerubbaal," which means "Let Baal contend against him." Then God called Gideon to gather an army to attack the large Midianite army.

Gideon sought reassurance by asking for dew to appear on a fleece, but not on the floor, for one night and then dew on the floor, but not on the fleece, the next night. God gave Gideon this sign to reassure him of success. When the troops arrived, God narrowed them down from 32,000 to 300 men. Gideon and these 300 men defeated the Midianites armed only with jars and torches.

The people tried to make him king, but Gideon refused. At the end of his life, Gideon disobeyed God by building an idol. (Judges 6–8)

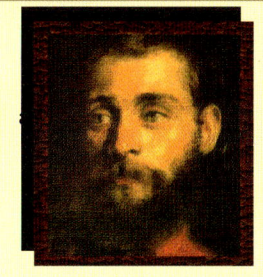

David was the youngest son of Jesse from the tribe of Judah. Before he became king of Israel, David was shepherd for his father's flocks in Bethlehem. Early on, David was anointed by the prophet Samuel.

A talented musician, David was called to play in King Saul's court. Later, a Philistine giant named Goliath challenged anyone in Israel to one-on-one combat. David accepted the challenge and defeated him with a stone from a sling.

Following his victory over Goliath, David was placed in charge of a thousand troops. He became a loyal friend to Saul's son, Jonathan and married Saul's daughter, Michal. David's success aroused a jealous rage in Saul. David had to flee, and he became a hunted outlaw.

After Saul died, David became king and united Israel. He made Jerusalem the capital city and brought the Ark of the Covenant to Jerusalem. David committed adultery with Bathsheba and murdered her husband. He was punished with the death of their infant son, but God forgave him. David was the father of Solomon and God gave him the plans for the Temple. (1 Samuel 16:1–1 Kings 1:53; 1 Chronicles 11:1–29:30)

VERSE

"But Lord," Gideon asked, "how can I save Israel? My clan is the weakest in Manasseh, and I am the least in my family." —Judges 6:15

"The LORD has sought out a man after his own heart and appointed him [David] leader of his people." —1 Samuel 13:14

CHARACTER

- Doubtful and reluctant (Judges 6:13-17, 27, 36-40; 7:9-15)
- Mighty and brave (Judges 6:12; 7:16–8:21)
- Humble (Judges 8:22, 23)
- Irresponsible (Judges 8:24-27)
- Faithful (Hebrews 11:32)

- Faithful, loyal, and brave (1 Samuel 17:1–18:8; 20:1-42; 24:1-22; Hebrews 11:32-34)
- Passionate and worshipful. Wrote many of the Psalms (2 Samuel 5:1–7:29; Psalm 27:4; 101)
- Lustful yet remorseful (2 Samuel 11:1–12:15; Psalm 51)
- A man after God's own heart (1 Samuel 13:14; Acts 13:22)

SYMBOLISM

- Gideon's purpose was to save Israel from the invading Midianites. When asked to be king, Gideon refused and told them that the LORD will rule over them. (Judges 8:23)
- Jesus refused earthly kingship and reminded people that his kingdom was not of this earth. (John 6:15; 18:36)

- David wrote that the Messiah would sit at the right hand of God, and rule forever. He would be the people's priest (go-between) with God. (Psalm 110)
- Jesus is the Messiah, who sits at God's right hand, and is the priest (middle man) for all who believe in him. (Acts 2:34; Hebrews 5:5-10)

CHALLENGES

- Trusting God without fear of death and without demanding a sign. (Judges 6:25-40; 7:10-15)
- Taking on the enormous army of the Midianites with only 300 men. (Judges 7:1-22)
- Standing firm and resisting the temptation to become the first king of Israel. (Judges 8:22, 23)
- Acting responsibly as a leader and judge of Israel. (Judges 8:24-27)

- Challenging the Philistine giant Goliath at a young age. (1 Samuel 17:1-58)
- Remaining loyal to king Saul even while Saul was trying to kill him. (1 Samuel 24:1-22; 26:1-25)
- Committing adultery with Bathsheba and murdering her husband, Uriah, one of his loyal warriors, to cover it up. (2 Samuel 11:1-26)
- Managing his dysfunctional family. (2 Samuel 13:1–19:8)

LESSONS

- God can do great things with a willing person, even if that person doubts and is afraid. (Judges 6:12–7:22)
- It is not by the strength of men that God accomplishes His purpose but by the power of the Spirit. (Judges 7:2-7)
- Leaders are responsible for the spiritual welfare of their people. (Judges 8:24-27)

- Strength comes from faith in God who desires justice and ultimately peace. (1 Samuel 17:1-58)
- God created all people with the desire to worship Him with all of their heart. (Psalm 18; 19; 27; 103; 122; 138)
- God forgives sin and can redeem any situation. (2 Samuel 11:1-26; Psalm 51)

ELIJAH

DANIEL
"BELTESHAZZAR"

SUMMARY

Elijah was a prophet who brought his message of the LORD to Israel primarily during the reign of evil King Ahab and Queen Jezebel.

Jezebel was a foreign princess from the Phoenician city of Sidon. She worshiped Baal and Asherah and supported their prophets. When Jezebel oppressed and executed the true prophets of God, Elijah pronounced a drought on Israel and went into hiding for three years.

Elijah returned to challenge the prophets of Baal to a contest on Mt. Carmel. Two altars were constructed, and Elijah urged Baal's prophets to pray saying, "the God who answers by fire, he is God." The prophets of Baal prayed, but Baal did not answer. Then Elijah drenched water on his sacrifice three times, prayed, and fire from heaven consumed the sacrifice, the water, and altar. After the contest, the drought ended, and Elijah escaped to Mt. Horeb (Mt. Sinai). At Mt. Horeb, Elijah was depressed and felt alone, but the LORD comforted him.

Elijah returned to choose his successor Elisha, before he was taken to heaven by a whirlwind. (1 Kings 17:1-19:21; 2 Kings 2:11)

Daniel was a young noble from Judah, who was taken captive by King Nebuchadnezzar II of Babylonia in 597 BC. The Babylonians forced Daniel into exile nearly 800 miles from his home. In Babylon, Daniel was chosen to serve in the royal court.

When Daniel was offered the food and drink of the king's court, he requested to have only vegetables and water. He remained loyal to God and the traditions of his people and refused the food. Daniel was rewarded by God for his loyalty and devotion.

Daniel became known as an interpreter of dreams and one who received visions. He foresaw the rise and fall of empires and the coming of the Kingdom of God. Eventually, Daniel was promoted and placed over all the wise men and over the entire province of Babylon.

When Darius the Mede was king, he wanted to place Daniel over the entire kingdom. Jealous of Daniel, the other rulers convinced the king to prohibit prayer to anyone but the king. Daniel prayed to God, and the rulers forced the King to throw him into a lion's den. God shut the mouths of the lions and delivered Daniel. (Daniel 1-2; 4-12)

VERSE

"Answer me, so these people will know that you, O LORD, are God, and that you are turning their hearts back again." —1 Kings 18:37

Now Daniel so distinguished himself among the administrators and the satraps by his exceptional qualities. —Daniel 6:3

CHARACTER

- Courageous (1 Kings 18:13-38; 21:17-24; 2 Kings 1:1-16)
- Zealous and loyal to God (1 Kings 19:10)
- Compassionate (1 Kings 17:8-24)
- Influential (Malachi 4:6)
- Prayerful (James 5:17)

- Disciplined and trustworthy (Daniel 1:8; Daniel 6:4-10)
- Wise and discerning (Daniel 1:20; 2:14; 5:12; 7-8; 9:20-12:13)
- Prayerful and obedient (Daniel 6:10-11; 9:1-19)
- Blameless (Daniel 6:22)
- Faithful (Hebrews 11:33)

SYMBOLISM

- The prophet Malachi said that God will send Elijah to prepare peoples' hearts for the Messiah. Jesus said that the spirit of Elijah was present in the ministry of John the Baptist, who prepared the way for the Him [Jesus the Messiah]. (Malachi 4:5, 6; Matthew 17:12, 13)

- Daniel foresaw several future events including: The rise and fall of four empires. He foresaw Christ's sacrifice, final victory, glorified appearance, and Christ's ultimate judgment of the world. (Daniel 2:1-45; 7:8-28; 8:10-12; 9:24-26; 10:5, 6; Hebrews 7:25-28; 10:11-18; Revelation 1:13-16; 20:7-15)

CHALLENGES

- Pronouncing judgment on the religious establishment of a nation and confronting powerful leaders and officials who want to kill him. (1 Kings 17:1; 18:1-17; 20:35-43; 21:17-26; 2 Kings 1:1-16)
- Trusting God to take care of him, in a foreign land, by a foreign woman. (1 Kings 17:8-24)
- Challenging the king and queen of Israel along with 850 Canaanite prophets to a showdown. (1 Kings 18:17-40)

- Remaining obedient to the laws and statues of God, even in the presence of harsh persecution and the threat of death. (Daniel 1:8; 6:10)
- Resisting the temptation to conform to the culture of Babylon. (Daniel 1:8; 6:10)
- Having to deliver difficult and condemning messages to powerful kings. (Daniel 2:27-45; 4:19-27; 5:13-30)

LESSONS

- God's hears the prayers of the faithful and provides for them. (1 Kings 17:1-24; 8:42-45)
- God's word and authority is confirmed with action. (1 Kings 17:1-7, 14-16; 18:20-40)
- The power of God is found in His "still small voice." (1 Kings 19:11-13)
- One may feel hopeless, depressed, and alone. God is with us and will never desert us. (1 Kings 19:4-18)

- People who obey God are supposed to live in and be a part of the world, but they are to stand firm to their beliefs when the world tries to steal their devotion away from God. (Daniel 1:8; 6:10; Matthew 5:13)
- When faced with persecution and fear, pray and lay your concerns on God. God will help you. (Daniel 6:10-11; 9:1-19; Philippians 4:6; James 1:5; 1 Peter 5:9)

The Ten Commandments

THEN AND NOW

The set of rules, the Ten Commandments, are the code of law given by God directly to Moses on Mount Sinai. After the exodus, when God delivered the Israelites from slavery in Egypt, his chosen people almost immediately lost sight of God's power and goodness to them. They resented their hardships and began to complain. They became quarrelsome and difficult to govern. Moses sought God's help on Mount Sinai (Ex. 15–18).

The Old Testament

God himself engraved his will for the people on two tablets of stone. The first group of commandments laid out the rules to protect the harmony between God and people. The second group was designed to maintain respect between people. It was vital to the stability of the forming tribal nation that everyone act in a trustworthy manner. Selfishness risked the community's survival. When a person broke a commandment, he had to pay a penalty, repay the person he had injured, and make a sacrifice to restore peace with God.

The law must be viewed as a great, gracious gift from the God of Israel to his people. Unlike all the other ancient near eastern gods, the Lord God revealed his will and made it very clear how to please him and how to properly conduct one's life in order to get along in society. Despite the gift of these divine commands for governing relationships, the people set up idols and worshiped them, they lied, and stole from one another. Many of their leaders were corrupt, and they refused to honor God. Over the next 1,400 years, the law was often forgotten and the worship of the true God was abandoned. God called to the people. Sometimes they would return to God and be restored. Other times, they would ignore him and suffer devastating hardships.

The Lord said that someday he would send a Savior and would have a new covenant with his people. The law would be written on their hearts, not just on stone tablets. They would do the right thing because they loved God (Jer. 31:31–33).

The New Testament (New Covenant)

God sent a Savior, Jesus Christ, to live a perfect life and take the penalty for sin through his death on the cross. Through his sacrifice, he made forgiveness and friendship with God possible, and made us perfect in God's eyes through faith (Rom. 3:20; Gal. 2:16; 3:9–14). Jesus came to fulfill the law, and taught that the spirit of the law was as important as the letter of the law (Matt. 23:23).

WHICH IS THE MOST IMPORTANT COMMANDMENT?

When the Pharisees asked Jesus which commandment in the law was the greatest, Jesus said, "'Love the Lord your God with all your heart and with all your soul and with all your mind.' This is the first and greatest commandment. And the second is like it: 'Love your neighbor as yourself.' All the Law and the Prophets hang on these two commandments" (Matt. 22:37–40).

Every law is based on a principle. In Jesus' day, many people were obeying the law, but they weren't upholding God's principles. Jesus told the parable of the Good Samaritan to illustrate this concept (Luke 10:25–37). In this parable, a man is attacked on a road and left for dead. As time passes, a priest and a Levite (someone who knows the law well) pass by the man and do not help him. Later, a Samaritan (considered to be a lower-class person) comes across the injured man and helps him; he even pays for his medical treatment. The law did not allow anyone to touch a dead body. Even though this man was not dead, he may have appeared to be dead to those passing by. The Samaritan risked disobeying the law in order to show mercy to an injured man. The priest and the Levite passed by the man for fear of breaking this law.

For Jesus, showing mercy to others and truly loving your neighbor is far more important than obeying a ceremonial purity law. Jesus encouraged people to live by the spirit of the law rather than the letter of the law. He wanted people to make sure they understood *why* we obey a commandment. Paul wrote that with Christ the law is no longer written on tablets of stone, but it is written on our hearts (2 Cor. 3:1–17). The reason we break a commandment stems from what is in our hearts. In the same way, the reason we obey a commandment is because our hearts have been transformed in Christ.

"By this we know that we love the children of God, when we love God and observe His commandments. For this is the love of God, that we keep His commandments; and His commandments are not burdensome."

—1 John 5:2–3 NASB

EXODUS 20:1-17

And God spoke all these words: "I am the Lord your God, who brought you out of Egypt, out of the land of slavery.

You shall have no other gods before me.

You shall not make for yourself an idol in the form of anything in heaven above or on the earth beneath or in the waters below. You shall not bow down to them or worship them; for I, the Lord your God, am a jealous God, punishing the children for the sin of the fathers to the third and fourth generation of those who hate me, but showing love to thousands who love me and keep my commandments.

You shall not misuse the name of the Lord your God, for the Lord will not hold anyone guiltless who misuses his name.

Remember the Sabbath day by keeping it holy. Six days you shall labor and do all your work, but the seventh day is a Sabbath to the Lord your God. On it you shall not do any work, neither you, nor your son or daughter, nor your manservant or maidservant, nor your animals, nor the alien within your gates. For in six days the Lord made the heavens and the earth, the sea, and all that is in them, but he rested on the seventh day. Therefore the Lord blessed the Sabbath day and made it holy.

Honor your father and your mother, so that you may live long in the land the Lord your God is giving you.

You shall not murder.

You shall not commit adultery.

You shall not steal.

You shall not give false testimony against your neighbor.

You shall not covet your neighbor's house. You shall not covet your neighbor's wife, or his manservant or maidservant, his ox or donkey, or anything that belongs to your neighbor."

The Ten Commandments

1. NO OTHER GOD
THOU SHALT HAVE NO OTHER GODS BEFORE ME.

PRINCIPLE: God is the creator and Lord of the universe. He deserves our first loyalty.

MEANING: Put God first and give him our devotion. God should always be our highest priority, over everyone and everything. A god is anything a person allows to rule his or her life. Other gods could include: deities of other religions, superstitions, horoscopes, money, possessions, career, personal comfort, family, friends, addictions, fame, power, security, romance, sex, church, extreme patriotism—anything that comes before God.

BIBLE EXAMPLES:
- Abraham proved that God was his first priority by being willing to give up his own son (Gen. 22:1–14).
- The people of Israel were worshiping other gods, so the prophet Elijah challenged the prophets of those gods to a contest. Elijah prayed that God would answer him so all would know that the Lord is God. The Lord answered and proved his superiority (1 Kings 18:20–40).
- God commanded the prophet Hosea to marry a prostitute who was unfaithful to him, so that Hosea might understand how God feels when his people turn to other gods (Hos. 1–3).
- Daniel and his three friends, Shadrach, Meshach, and Abednego, risked their lives because they remained devoted to the Lord as their only God (Dan. 1; 3; 6).

JESUS' TEACHINGS:
- When asked, "Which is the greatest commandment in the Law?" Jesus replied, "Love the Lord your God with all your heart and with all your soul and with all your mind. This is the first and greatest commandment" (Matt. 22:26–38).
- In the Sermon on the Mount, Jesus said, "No one can serve two masters. Either he will hate the one and love the other, or he will be devoted to the one and despise the other. You cannot serve both God and Money" (Matt. 6:24).
- Jesus said, "Worship the Lord your God, and serve him only" (Luke 4:8).

EXPLANATIONS:
- Jesus said that all the commandments and rules in the Bible hang on two basic principles: (1) loving God with all of your heart, mind, soul, and strength (first four commandments) and (2) loving your neighbor as yourself (next six commandments).
- In the Old Testament, people were offering sacrifices to God because the law commanded them to do so. God wanted sacrifices and burnt offerings as an outward sign of a right heart attitude. God wants to be acknowledged, and he wants people to show mercy to others (Hos. 6:6). He wants us to obey the laws and rules he gives us because we treasure him and we want to serve him.

2. NO IDOLS
THOU SHALT NOT MAKE UNTO THEE ANY GRAVEN IMAGE.

PRINCIPLE: God is spirit and is bigger and more powerful than any representation.

MEANING: Put faith in God only. Idol worship is worshiping or serving anything in the place of God. Idolatry can also include the worship of the true God *through* an idol. God does not forbid or condemn all representations of people and animals. God commanded that ornamental artwork be made in order to make things beautiful. When we worship something we can see, touch, or control, we miss the power and grandeur of God.

BIBLE EXAMPLES:
- The prophet Habakkuk wrote that idolatry is when man trusts his own creation more than God (Hab. 2:18–19).
- While Moses was receiving the Ten Commandments, the Israelites created a golden calf, bowed down, and sacrificed offerings to it. God became very angry with them (Ex. 32:1–24).
- Gideon made an idol, which became a snare for his family, because Israel worshiped the idol instead of God (Judg. 8:26–27).
- The prophet Isaiah spoke of idol worship, saying a man will burn a tree for warmth or cooking while using the same tree to fashion an idol for worship (Isa. 44:9–20).
- The apostle Paul associated idolatry with impurity, lust, evil desires, and greed (Col. 3:5).

JESUS' TEACHINGS:
- Jesus said, "Do not store up for yourselves treasures on earth, where moth and rust destroy, and where thieves break in and steal" (Matt. 6:19).
- Jesus said, "For everyone who exalts himself will be humbled, and he who humbles himself will be exalted" (Matt. 23:12).
- When the Samaritan woman asked Jesus whether to worship God in Jerusalem or Samaria, he said, "True worshipers will worship the Father in spirit and truth, for they are the kind of worshipers the Father seeks. God is spirit, and his worshipers must worship in spirit and in truth" (John 4:23–24).

EXPLANATIONS:
- God instructed Moses to build a tabernacle that contained furniture overlaid with bronze or gold, a solid gold lampstand, and the ark of the covenant overlaid with gold (Ex. 25:1–27:21). Solomon had Hiram the Bronzeworker mold a bronze sea (basin) and had it placed upon twelve bronze oxen statues (1 Kings 7:23–26).
- God gives many people the gift of craftsmanship and the abilities to make beautiful images. To sculpt, paint, or design something can bring glory to God. Yet, God is spirit and cannot be represented by any image crafted by human hands. To do so would be an insult to the very nature of God. He also desires that we worship him in spirit, and not through something we ourselves created (John 4:23–24).

3 — DO NOT MISUSE GOD'S NAME
THOU SHALT NOT TAKE THE NAME OF THE LORD THY GOD IN VAIN.

PRINCIPLE: God's name is holy, powerful, and glorious.

MEANING:
God's name is holy and should be treated with respect. There is power in the Lord's name and it shouldn't be used lightly. Because God is spirit, we know him through what he says about himself. To take his name in vain violates God's nature. As God's creation, everything a person says and does should be done in order to praise and glorify God (1 Cor. 10:31).

BIBLE EXAMPLES:
- When a man named Shelomith blasphemed the name of God with a curse, the Lord commanded that he be taken outside the camp and stoned to death (Lev. 24:10–16).
- Jesus was accused of blasphemy because he claimed to be God (John 10:33).
- The high priest claimed that Jesus broke the third commandment by claiming to be God, and he condemned Jesus to death for this blasphemy (Matt. 26:62–66).
- James warned believers to watch what they say because the tongue is capable of evil and poison and can easily corrupt a person (James 3:5–9).

JESUS' TEACHINGS:
- Jesus said, "Every sin and blasphemy will be forgiven men, but the blasphemy against the Spirit will not be forgiven.… Men will have to give account on the day of judgment for every careless word they have spoken. For by your words you will be acquitted, and by your words you will be condemned" (Matt. 12:31, 36–37).
- Jesus said to begin praying with, "Our Father in heaven, hallowed be your name" (Matt. 6:9).
- In the Sermon on the Mount, Jesus said, "Do not swear at all: either by heaven, for it is God's throne; or by the earth, for it is his footstool.… Simply let your 'Yes' be 'Yes,' and your 'No,' 'No'" (Matt. 5:33–35, 37).

EXPLANATIONS:
- Jews and Jewish scribes would go to great measures in order to avoid saying or writing the Lord's name for fear of blasphemy. The Bible says we are to pray, heal, and baptize in Jesus' name (Matt. 28:19; Mark 16:17; John 14:13; 16:23; Acts 3:6).
- What we say is very important and it is a glimpse into who we are (James 3:9–12). God loves us and wants us to love and worship him in whatever we are doing and at all times. God wants us to use his name; it is holy and powerful. If we can show respect for the names of our fathers, mothers, teachers, and doctors, then how much more should we respect the name of our sovereign God.

4 — REST ON THE SABBATH
REMEMBER THE SABBATH DAY, TO KEEP IT HOLY.

PRINCIPLE: God values rest, spiritual refreshment, and time for his people to worship him.

MEANING:
As a gift, God gives all people a day to rest after six days of labor. God knew how to preserve his creation, and rest was a necessary component to that preservation. Without rest, valuable topsoil is used up and the land becomes useless. In the same way, without rest, human beings become unproductive. Without spiritual refreshment, we can have rested bodies inhabited by unrested minds. The very center of rest is the worship of God. It is where we find our fulfillment because worship is what we were made for.

BIBLE EXAMPLES:
- The Sabbath was ordained in creation and ordered by God even before the commandments were given on Mount Sinai (Gen. 2:2–3; Ex. 16:23–29).
- Death was the prescribed punishment for working on the Sabbath (Ex. 35:2–4).
- The prophet Isaiah wrote that God detested meaningless sacrifices and empty obedience to religious festivals, to new moon celebrations, and to the Sabbath day (Isa. 1:11–13).
- God instituted seven holidays as sacred assemblies and special Sabbath days (Lev. 23).
- Every fiftieth year was to be a sabbath year, the Year of Jubilee, in which the land would not be tilled, slaves were freed, and alienated property restored (Lev. 25:8–33).

JESUS' TEACHINGS:
- One day, Jesus started healing people on the Sabbath and many people came to him to be healed. The synagogue ruler told the people to come back and be healed on any day but the Sabbath. The ruler thought healing on the Sabbath was a violation of the fourth commandment. Jesus rebuked him and told the people that it is acceptable to have mercy on someone on the Sabbath, even if it may appear to violate the law (Luke 13:10–17).
- Jesus said, "The Sabbath was made for man, not man for the Sabbath. So the Son of Man is Lord even of the Sabbath" (Mark 2:27–28). In this way, Jesus declared that a person may do good on the Sabbath.

EXPLANATIONS:
- In the Old Testament, the Sabbath was observed on Saturday, the seventh day of the week, because God rested on the seventh day after creating the universe. Jesus rose from the dead on Sunday morning, the first day of the week. Through Christ's death and resurrection, he instituted a new creation (Gal. 6:14–16). Since Christ's resurrection, most believers have been recognizing Sunday as "the Lord's day" (Acts 20:7; 1 Cor. 16:1–2; Rev. 1:10).
- Some suggest that followers of Jesus should still observe the Sabbath on Saturday rather than on Sunday. Others suggest that the Sabbath can happen on any day of the week. The Sabbath is to be a holy day, to rest, refocus, and praise God for creating us anew in Christ.

The Ten Commandments

5 Honor Your Parents
HONOUR THY FATHER AND THY MOTHER: THAT THY DAYS MAY BE LONG UPON THE LAND WHICH THE LORD THY GOD GIVETH THEE.

6 Do Not Murder
THOU SHALT NOT KILL.

PRINCIPLE

God wants all people to respect and honor those he's placed in authority.

God created human life and holds it sacred.

MEANING

Treat parents with respect, no matter what the situation may be. Most parents made great sacrifices to bring up their children. No one is a perfect parent, and in some cases, fathers and mothers are dishonorable and have caused pain and grief. Even in these cases, when parents may not deserve it, God expects us to honor them for his sake. God promises long life to those who honor their parents. Scripture also makes it clear that sometimes we must follow God instead of obeying parents.

Murder is the unlawful killing of another human being, usually premeditated. The Hebrew word *ratsach*, always translated as "murder," is used for this commandment to contrast this prohibition with other forms of killing such as accidental death, war, self-defense, capital punishment, and the killing of animals. God created human beings in his own image. To take someone's life into one's own hands is to destroy the image of God.

BIBLE EXAMPLES

- The book of Proverbs says that wisdom comes from obeying one's parents (Prov. 23:22–25).
- Jesus was obedient to his earthly parents as he grew up in Nazareth (Luke 2:51).
- The apostle Paul commanded children to obey their parents in everything, and he reminded them that the fifth commandment contained a promise. If children honor their parents, they will enjoy long life (Eph. 6:1–3; Col. 3:20).
- After the flood, Noah became intoxicated. Seeing Noah in this condition, his son Ham made fun of him to his brothers, Shem and Japheth. Even though Noah was irresponsible, Ham received a curse for dishonoring his father. Shem and Japheth were blessed because they honored their father (Gen. 9:20–27).

- After the flood, God instructed Noah and the generations to follow that death is the prescribed punishment for murder (Gen. 9:6).
- Cain, Simeon, Levi, Moses, Joab, David, Absalom, and Paul were all guilty of murder (Gen. 4:8; 49:5–7; Ex. 2:11–12; 2 Sam. 3:27; 11:14–15; 13:28; Acts 9:1).
- The Bible says that God hates and detests hands that shed innocent blood (Prov. 6:16–17).
- Paul encouraged the believers in Rome to live at peace with everyone. He said that personal revenge belongs to God only (Rom. 12:18–19).
- John wrote that anyone who hates his brother is a murderer, but that true love is evident in those who lay down their lives for others (1 John 3:15–16).

JESUS' TEACHINGS

- Jesus rebuked the Jewish authorities of his day for not taking care of their aging parents. He said that they made up excuses in order to avoid having to honor their parents (Matt. 15:4–6).
- Jesus taught that he must be a priority even above one's family. He said, "Anyone who loves his father or mother more than me is not worthy of me; anyone who loves his son or daughter more than me is not worthy of me" (Matt. 10:37).
- Jesus honored and respected his parents by obeying them while he grew up and by providing for his mother's care once he was gone (Luke 2:51; John 19:26–27).

- Jesus said, "You have heard that it was said to the people long ago, 'Do not murder, and anyone who murders will be subject to judgment.' But I tell you that anyone who is angry with his brother will be subject to judgment" (Matt. 5:21–22).
- Jesus said that instead of an eye for an eye, "If someone strikes you on the right cheek, turn to him the other also" (Matt. 5:38–39).
- Hearing the leaders threatening to stone a woman to death, Jesus said, "If any one of you is without sin, let him be the first to throw a stone at her" (John 8:7).

EXPLANATIONS

- The Hebrew word *kabed* means to make honorable or to glorify. This verb has a wide range of connotations that far exceeds simple obedience. It is important to obey parents, but children must also show their parents respect. The Bible strictly warns children against cursing and abusing their parents (Ex. 21:15, 17).
- On the other hand, Jesus clearly pointed out that God must be the priority. God's will is more important than the will of one's parents (Matt. 10:37). When parents command or model something that is against God's will or clearly goes against loving God and neighbor, they can still be honored without being obeyed.

- God values life and wants his people to preserve the lives of others and love their neighbors as themselves. This is an important factor of which to be mindful whenever the taking of the life of another human being is considered, such as in war, self-defense, or capital punishment.
- Jesus makes it clear that hatred for one's neighbor is the core cause for murder (Matt. 5:21–22). It is this same hatred that is forbidden by this commandment. As with the breaking of all other commandments, murder comes from the heart.

7. NO ADULTERY
THOU SHALT NOT COMMIT ADULTERY.

8. DO NOT STEAL
THOU SHALT NOT STEAL.

PRINCIPLE

God values faithfulness and sexual purity.

God values productivity, integrity, and generosity.

MEANING

Be faithful to one's husband or wife. Marriage vows made before God should be kept in spite of difficulties. Sex is a gift from God and is reserved for marriage only. Any sexually immoral act that betrays those vows, including premarital sex, is considered adultery. When we break the seventh commandment, we are sinning against God, our spouse, and against our own bodies (1 Cor. 6:18).

Respect other people's possessions. Stealing includes taking items that don't belong to us, defaulting on loans, not paying bills, cheating on tests, goofing off at work, cheating on income taxes, taking sick time when you or your dependents are not sick, stealing cable services, illegally downloading or copying software, music, movies, or printed material, and not giving to God.

BIBLE EXAMPLES

- The Bible says that anyone who commits adultery should be put to death (Lev. 20:10).
- God equates unfaithfulness to him with adultery (Jer. 3:6–9).
- After King David committed adultery with Bathsheba, the prophet Nathan confronted him. David repented and wrote Psalm 51, a psalm of repentance. David wrote, "Create in me a pure heart, O God, and renew a steadfast spirit within me. Do not cast me from your presence or take your Holy Spirit from me" (Ps. 51:10–11).
- Jesus forgave a woman who had been caught in adultery. He told her that no one condemned her and to go and sin no more (John 8:10–11).

- The apostle Paul wrote to the Ephesians telling them to stop stealing and to start working for their money, so that they could share with the needy (Eph. 4:28).
- The Bible says that all people are to pay their taxes and repay their debts. The Scriptures warn against defaulting on loans and neglecting bills (Rom.13:6–8; Prov. 22:26–27).
- The prophet Malachi wrote that when people don't bring their full tithe and offering to God, they are stealing directly from God. God promises to bless those who bring him their full tithe and offering (Mal. 3:8–12).

JESUS' TEACHINGS

- Jesus said, "You have heard that it was said, 'Do not commit adultery.' But I tell you that anyone who looks at a woman lustfully has already committed adultery with her in his heart" (Matt. 5:27–28).
- Jesus also said, "I tell you that anyone who divorces his wife, except for marital unfaithfulness, and marries another woman commits adultery" (Matt. 19:9).
- Jesus said, "Anyone who divorces his wife, except for marital unfaithfulness, causes her to become an adulteress, and anyone who marries the divorced woman commits adultery" (Matt. 5:31–32).

- Jesus said, "Therefore I tell you, do not worry about your life, what you will eat or drink; or about your body, what you will wear. Is not life more important than food, and the body more important than clothes? Look at the birds of the air; they do not sow or reap or store away in barns, and yet your heavenly Father feeds them. Are you not much more valuable than they?" (Matt. 6:25–26).
- Jesus said, "And if someone wants to sue you and take your tunic, let him have your cloak as well…. Give to the one who asks you, and do not turn away from the one who wants to borrow from you" (Matt. 5:40–42).

EXPLANATIONS

- Jewish law allowed a man to divorce his wife for any reason. Jesus' teachings shocked the disciples. They responded with, "If this is the situation between a husband and wife, it is better not to marry" (Matt. 19:10).
- Paul taught that abandonment by an unbelieving spouse was also grounds for divorce (1 Cor. 7:15).
- Jesus said that the condition of the heart that leads to adultery is lust. Paul wrote, "Whatever is true, whatever is noble, whatever is right, whatever is pure, whatever is lovely, whatever is admirable—if anything is excellent or praiseworthy—think about such things" (Phil. 4:8).

- The Bible warns against taking out loans. The Bible also encourages those who do take out loans to repay their debt. Jesus encouraged those who loan money to forgive the debts of others. Jesus also encouraged people to give freely and allow others to borrow things from you without asking anything in return.
- Jesus is presenting a picture of a caring kingdom, a kingdom where people give to others freely out of love. In Christ's kingdom, there would be no need for stealing out of lack of food, clothing, or shelter. In addition, there would be no need for loans or debt because peoples' needs are cared for by one another. In fact, the early church expressed these principles in how they cared for each other (Acts 4:32–37).

The Ten Commandments • 141

9 DO NOT LIE
THOU SHALT NOT BEAR FALSE WITNESS AGAINST THY NEIGHBOUR.

10 DO NOT COVET
THOU SHALT NOT COVET THY NEIGHBOUR'S HOUSE…NOR ANY THING THAT IS THY NEIGHBOUR'S.

PRINCIPLE

God is truth and he values honesty.	God values humility, contentment, and peace.

MEANING

Be trustworthy and maintain integrity by being honest. Lying can take the form of gossip, false accusations, blame, and self-deceit. It is important to keep promises and be responsible to the commitments we make. Liars cannot be trusted, and even when a liar tells the truth, he or she may not be believed. The Bible forbids attempting to deceive God.

Be content with what we have. Don't long for things that belong to others. Avoid the pursuit of happiness and joy through the accumulation of material wealth, possessions, someone else's spouse, and other's friends. Don't allow earthly things to fill a void that only God can fill. Ask God to provide what we need. God promises that he will take care of our needs if we seek him first and not money, popularity, or possessions.

BIBLE EXAMPLES

- The Bible says that the wise keep all falsehoods and lies far from them (Prov. 30:8).
- God hates a lying tongue, and delights in those who tell the truth (Prov.12:22).
- Those who speak the truth are valued by kings (Prov. 16:13).
- Ananias and Sapphira sold some property and claimed to donate the entire amount to the church. Instead, they kept some of the money for themselves. The apostle Peter said they were free to keep some of the money, but since they claimed to bring the entire amount, they lied to the Holy Spirit. Their lie resulted in immediate death by the hand of God (Acts 5:1–11).

- King Saul was jealous of David's success and coveted the respect and praise David received (1 Sam. 18:6–9).
- King David coveted his neighbor Uriah's wife Bathsheba and he committed adultery with her. David then murdered Uriah to cover up his treachery (2 Sam. 11:1–27).
- The apostle Paul encouraged the early church to be content with what they had and warned them about loving money and possessions. Paul said that the love of money is a root of all kinds of evil; it causes greed, envy, and pride (Phil. 4:11–12; 1 Tim. 6:6–10).
- The apostle John warned believers about loving the world and the things of the world. He said that anyone who loves the world does not have the love of God in him (1 John 2:15).

JESUS' TEACHINGS

- Jesus said, "The good man brings good things out of the good stored up in him, and the evil man brings evil things out of the evil stored up in him. But I tell you that men will have to give account on the day of judgment for every careless word they have spoken. For by your words you will be acquitted, and by your words you will be condemned" (Matthew 12:35–37).
- Jesus said, "I am the way and the truth and the life. No one comes to the Father except through me" (John 14:6).

- Jesus said, "So do not worry, saying, 'What shall we eat?' or 'What shall we drink?' or 'What shall we wear?' For the pagans run after all these things, and your heavenly Father knows that you need them. But seek first his kingdom and his righteousness, and all these things will be given to you as well" (Matt. 6:31–33).
- Jesus said, "A man's life does not consist in the abundance of his possessions" (Luke 12:15).
- A rich young man with a lifelong commitment to keeping all the commandments came to Jesus and asked what more he needed to do. Jesus' response went right to the heart of the tenth commandment: "One thing you lack," he said. "Go, sell everything you have and give to the poor, and you will have treasure in heaven. Then come, follow me" (Mark 10:17–23).

EXPLANATIONS

- Before Joshua led the Israelites into the promised land, he sent spies into Jericho. Rahab housed the spies and helped them escape. When the authorities asked about the spies, Rahab deceived them and thereby saved the spies. Later, Rahab was saved because she honored God by protecting the spies. Her decision to mislead and deceive her leaders as to the whereabouts of the Israelite spies was honored by God (Josh. 2:1–6; 6:17–25).
- Truth-telling makes for a functional and just society. People who tell the truth can be trusted. Sensitive application of honesty and truth nurtures relationships and fosters community.

- Advertising and marketing often feeds on customers' discontent by appealing to a person's selfish nature. These advertisers promise people fulfillment if they buy their product. Their ads seem to suggest that when you purchase a particular item, you will be surrounded by friends, a beautiful spouse, and a really great, enjoyable life. These advertisers know that people covet and that people have the tendency to be dissatisfied with what they have.
- God wants us to be content with what we have and to keep our eyes focused on him; not on things of this world (Phil. 4:11–12).

CHRIST IN THE OLD TESTAMENT

FORESHADOWING CHRIST

There are different ways to study how the Old Testament anticipates, reveals, promises, or foreshadows Christ. In the following pages Christ's presence in the Old Testament is discerned by using typology. Typology was a very common way to interpret the Old Testament in the early history of the church. When carefully done, typology opens windows into the history of God's activity in the world that otherwise can be easily missed.

By looking for parallels or similarities between biblical people, events (for example, the Exodus anticipates how Christ frees us from the slavery of sin), and things (for example, the tabernacle, which John 1:14 connects with Jesus), we can see God setting up history for the coming of Christ and doing it not simply by speaking a prophetic word, but by arranging the affairs of human beings. When we understand this great truth, we can hope to believe our own lives too point to Christ, and rejoice in the Lord of history who makes such wonderful stories of us!

> THE NEW TESTAMENT IS IN THE OLD CONCEALED;
> THE OLD TESTAMENT IS IN THE NEW REVEALED.
> —Augustine

CHRIST is the key to what God had been pointing to in all the history of God's people. One way to see this is to examine parallels between Old Testament people, events, and things, and the life of Jesus in the New Testament.

We find some of these parallels in Romans 5. Paul writes that sin entered into the world through one man, Adam, and sin led to death for all men, for all have sinned. He also writes that Adam was a figure of someone who was to come (Romans 5:12).

Paul said that if the sin of one person, Adam, would cause many to die, how much more could the gift of God's grace, by one person—Jesus Christ, cause many to be righteous and have eternal life!

The Bible is full of these parallels or "types." In the example above, this method (typology) calls Adam the type and Christ the antitype (opposite).

Adam

ADAM (Genesis 2–3)

Adam was the first human God created. He was responsible to care for the Garden of Eden. His disobedience of God's commandment introduced sin and death, so humanity and all of creation became corrupted by sin.

ADAM	CHRIST
Adam was the first person in this creation.	In his resurrection, Jesus is the first person in this New Creation (1 Corinthians 15:23).
Adam was called the son of God (Luke 3:38).	Christ is the Son of God (John 1:14).
Adam was God's administrator or ruler (Genesis 1:28).	Christ is God's Anointed to be King (Matthew 1:16).
Adam was the head of the race (Genesis 3:20).	Christ Jesus is the Head of the New Creation (Romans 5:12–24).
His actions brought consequences to his children causing them to inherit sin and death (Genesis 3:16–19).	His actions brought consequences to God's children causing them to inherit righteousness and life (Romans 5:12–19; 1 Corinthians 15:20–22, 45–49).
Adam joined Eve and rebelled against God (Genesis 3:6).	Christ redeemed his bride (the church) by obeying God (Revelation 19:7–9).
Adam's shame required the death of an animal to cover it (Genesis 3:21).	Christ was shamed, stripped and slain to cover our shame (Matthew 27:27–35).
Instead of closeness with God, we experience isolation and loneliness. Instead of love and care for each other, we experience violence and hatred.	Through Christ's redemptive action, we can experience true life, a close relationship with God and his love, and care for others.

QUESTIONS

Because of Adam's sin, the good world God made became corrupt. How does Christ "fix" what Adam "broke?" (Romans 5:15–19)

ADAM is a good first example of a *type*. It shows very clearly that typology focuses on specific events or character traits rather than on the person as a whole. There are big differences between Adam and Christ; in fact, they are opposites of one another. So it is not that Adam was *like* Christ; rather, some features of his story *parallel* Christ's life and ministry. Some are positive and others are negative.

Noah

NOAH (Genesis 6–9)

When God had decided to destroy the world with a flood as a punishment for humanity's sin, God chose Noah and his family to save them from the flood. Noah built an ark to save the animals.

NOAH	CHRIST
Noah was a kind of "second Adam" since all living human beings come from him (Genesis 8:15–9:17).	Christ is called "the second man" (Adam) since eternal life can only be found in him (1 Corinthians 15:47).
Noah's ark provided refuge for all kinds of animals (Genesis 6:19–7:5).	Christ's body (the church) provides salvation for all, both Jew and Gentile (Romans 11:11; Galatians 3:28–29).
Human evil had reached an unacceptable high. So God decided to undo his creation with a flood (Genesis 6:6–7).	When the time is right for God, he will undo his creation by fire (2 Peter 3:12–13) to re-create it (Revelation 21:1).
Noah's ark was delivered from the flood waters (Genesis 7:7).	Christ's body (the church) was delivered from death through the water of baptism (1 Peter 3:21).
Noah offered a sacrifice of blood (Genesis 8:20–9:6).	Christ offered himself as a sacrifice (1 Peter 1:18–19).
Noah's ark came to rest on Mount Ararat on the Jewish month of Nisan 17 (Genesis 8:4).	Christ's resurrection took place on Nisan 17 (which corresponds to the month of March or April).
Although Noah was not perfect, he is described as a "righteous man, blameless among the people of his time, and he walked with God" (Genesis 6:9).	Jesus was the perfect, blameless man (Hebrews 4:15).

QUESTIONS

Each of us is a bit like Noah. See 2 Peter 3:12–14. We too know this world will end. How should we live today?

What made Noah a "righteous man" even though his life was far from perfect?

Abraham

ABRAHAM (Genesis 12–25)

God chose Abraham and commanded him to leave his home and travel to an unknown place. God promised Abraham that he would be the father of a great nation and that Sarah, his wife, would give him a son. Through this son, God would bless all the nations. When they were elderly, Abraham and Sarah had Isaac, the son of the promise.

ABRAHAM	CHRIST
Abraham is called the "Father of the Faith" (Genesis 15; Romans 4:16–18).	Christ is the author and perfecter of faith (Hebrews 12:2).
Abraham was willing to sacrifice his only son (Genesis 22:2), and Isaac was ready to do what his father said (Genesis 22:9).	God the Father was willing to sacrifice his only Son (John 3:16) and Jesus was ready to do what his Father said (John 10:17–18).
Abraham's faith allowed him to trust that God would keep his word, even if that meant raising Isaac from the dead.	As Abraham's faith allowed him to look forward to Jesus' own resurrection with hope, we now look backwards to that same resurrection that gives us hope (1 Corinthians 15:54–58).
Abraham's sacrifice took place on Mount Moriah (Jerusalem; Genesis 22:2; 2 Chronicles 3:1) and a ram was substituted for Isaac (Genesis 22:8, 13–14).	Christ was sacrificed on the outskirts of Jerusalem (John 19:17–18) and he is the Lamb of God (John 1:29–31).
Abraham's son (Isaac) was the child of the promise. The book of Hebrews connected Isaac to the idea of resurrection (Hebrews 11:17–19).	God's Son Jesus is the child of promise (Isaiah 9:6) who is resurrected (1 Corinthians 15:1–11).
In Isaac's birth, all nations were to be blessed (Genesis 12:3).	In Jesus Christ all nations are blessed (Acts 28:28; Matthew 28:18–20).

QUESTIONS

Throughout the Bible, there is a theme of sacrificing lives, wishes, and desires. How could Abraham's story help you in your faith journey?

Melchizedek

MELCHIZEDEK (Genesis 14:18-20)

After Abraham came back from fighting enemy armies to free Lot, his nephew, Melchizedek, king of Salem, met him on the road with a gift of bread and wine. Abraham recognized him as a fellow believer and priest of the true God by giving to him one tenth of his earnings, which was the king's share (see 1 Samuel 8:15, 17).

MELCHIZEDEK	CHRIST
Melchizedek's name means "king of righteousness."	Christ is the Righteous One (Acts 3:14; Jeremiah 23:5–6).
Melchizedek was king of Salem (Jerusalem). The word "salem" means peace (Genesis 14:18; Hebrews 7:2). He was king before David.	He is the Prince of Peace (Isaiah 9:6) and the rightful king of Jerusalem for all time.
Melchizedek was a priest of God Most High (Genesis 14:18) before Aaron and the Levitical priesthood. (Aaron and his sons were ordained as the priestly family for Israel in Leviticus 8.)	Christ's High priesthood precedes and is superior to any other priesthood—that is, the priesthood of Aaron in Leviticus 8 and of Melchizedek in Genesis 14 (see Hebrews 7:4–10).
Old Testament priests offered blessings for God's people (see Numbers 6:22–27).	As High Priest (Hebrews 7:4–10), Christ blesses God's people with every spiritual blessing (Ephesians 1:3).
Melchizedek blesses Abraham on God's behalf (Genesis 14:19–20).	Christ blesses us, Abraham's spiritual children (Galatians 3:29).

QUESTIONS

Read Hebrews 8. What does it mean that Christ is high priest?

Ephesians 1:3 says that believers are blessed with every spiritual blessing. List some "spiritual blessings" that you have seen in your life in the past week.

Joseph

JOSEPH (Genesis 37–50)

Joseph was a son of Jacob and Rachel (Genesis 35:24). After Joseph's jealous brothers threw him into a pit, he was taken to Egypt and sold as a slave. In Egypt, God blessed Joseph, who became second only to the king of Egypt. God used Joseph to bless the nations by wisely storing grain in times of abundance so they were ready for the famine to come.

JOSEPH	CHRIST
Joseph was rejected by his own brothers (Genesis 37:19–20), stripped of his robe, and thrown into a pit (Genesis 37:22–24). Sold into slavery, he eventually landed in a dungeon in Egypt (Genesis 37:28; 39:20).	Christ was rejected by his own (John 1:11). He was stripped of his robe, condemned to death and descended to hell (Matthew 27:27-31; John 19:23–24; 1 Peter 3:18–20).
Joseph was an exemplary servant (Genesis 39:1–6). Though he was tempted he did not give in to temptation (Genesis 39:7–12).	Christ came as a servant (Philippians 2:7). He was tempted, but did not sin (Hebrews 4:15).
Joseph was unjustly accused and condemned (Genesis 39:13–20). In prison Joseph interpreted a dream of life to one of his fellow prisoners and death to another (Genesis 40:6–23). He was raised out of the dungeon to sit at Pharaoh's right hand (Genesis 41:14–45).	Christ was unjustly accused and condemned (Matthew 26:57–68; 27:11–25). While on the cross, Jesus' words promise life to one of the thieves condemned with him (Luke 23:39–43). Jesus was raised from the prison of death to sit at the right hand of God the Father (Acts 2:33; 5:31).
Joseph had a meal with his brothers before he revealed himself to them (Genesis 43:16). When he did reveal himself, Joseph saved his brothers' lives (Genesis 45:3–15). Joseph's actions also saved Egypt and many others (Genesis 50:20).	Jesus had a last supper with his disciples (Matthew 26:17–30). After his death and resurrection he revealed himself to them alive, which brought about salvation for them and the world (Luke 24; 1 Corinthians 15:1–11).
In Joseph, God partially fulfilled his promise to Abraham to bless all the nations of the world (Genesis 12:1–3), since Joseph's actions helped the nations of the world survive the terrible famine (Genesis 41:57).	In Christ, God completely fulfilled his promise to Abraham (Genesis 12:1–3), since Christ died for the sins of the world, and Jesus commanded: "go and make disciples of all nations...." (Matthew 28:19).

QUESTIONS

Joseph was abused, betrayed, and mistreated, yet he (like Christ) was a blessing even to those who hurt him. How does this apply to your life?

Moses

MOSES (Exodus–Deuteronomy)

God called Moses to lead the Israelites out of Egypt. Moses became Israel's leader, prophet, and judge. He went with Israel from Egypt to the Promised Land in Canaan and during the wanderings in the desert. God gave his Law to Israel through Moses.

MOSES	CHRIST
Surrounding the birth of Moses, innocent children were killed by Pharaoh (Exodus 1:22).	Surrounding the birth of Jesus, King Herod killed innocent children in Bethlehem (Matthew 2:16).
Moses had to flee his natural land because of Pharaoh's persecution (Exodus 2:15).	Jesus and his family had to flee their native land because of Herod's persecution (Matthew 2:14).
Pharaoh died and Moses returned after he is told: "All the men are dead that sought your life" (Exodus 4:19).	Herod died and Jesus returned after "…those who sought the child's life are dead" (Matthew 2:20–21).
Moses' prayer healed Miriam of leprosy (Numbers 12:10–13).	Jesus cleansed the leper (Matthew 8:2–3).
Moses chose 12 messengers, one from each tribe. Hoshea, who becomes Moses' close associate, is renamed Joshua (Numbers 13:2–16).	Jesus chose 12 apostles who will judge Israel's 12 tribes. Simon, one of those closest to Jesus, was renamed Peter (Matt. 16:17–19; Mark 3:16–17).
Moses prayed over the miracle of the manna and quails (Exodus 16:1; Numbers 11:31).	Jesus performed the miracle of the loaves and fish twice (Matthew 14:13–21; 15:32–39).
The dividing of the Red Sea took place under Moses' command (Exodus 14:15–22).	Jesus walked on the sea and calmed the storm (Matthew 14:22–36).
Moses was on a mountain for the blessing of the commandments (Ex. 19:20; Deut. 6:5–25).	Jesus was on a mount when he gave the Beatitudes and his commandments (Matthew 5:1–12).
A cloud overshadowed Moses, Aaron and Miriam and the voice of God was heard (Numbers 12:5–8).	A cloud overshadowed Peter, James, and John with Jesus, and the voice of God was heard (Matthew 17:1–5).
God promised to raise up a prophet like Moses (Deuteronomy 18:15).	Christ is the prophet that God promised, but he is greater than Moses (Hebrews 3:1–6).
Although Moses brought Israel to the border of the Promised Land, as a punishment for his own rebellion, he could not enter it (Numbers 20:1–13).	Because of his obedience, Jesus brings people into Paradise (Luke 23:43).

QUESTIONS *Examine the story of Moses and the rock (Numbers 20:1–13). Why did God punish Moses so harshly? Even Moses, the giver of the Law, was not able to perfectly obey the Law. Jesus perfectly obeyed the Law. What does Jesus' perfect obedience mean for us today? (Philippians 2:8).*

Joshua

JOSHUA (Numbers 27:12–23; Deuteronomy 31:1–8; Book of Joshua)

Joshua, whose earlier name was Hoshea, was one of the twelve spies that Moses sent to "explore the land of Canaan." Only he and Caleb encouraged the people to trust God and take possession of the land of Canaan, which God had promised to Abraham. When Moses died, Joshua became the leader who brought Israel into the land of Canaan.

JOSHUA	CHRIST
Joshua's name is actually the same name as Jesus: "Yehoshua," or "Yeshua" for short, means "The LORD saves."	Jesus' name is the Greek form of the name Yeshua. Like Joshua, Jesus led his people into salvation, yet in a greater sense of eternal life.
Joshua was God's prophetic leader who stepped into Moses' shoes (Joshua 1:1–9).	Jesus fulfilled Moses' prophecy: "The Lord your God will raise up for you a prophet like me from among you…." (Deuteronomy 18:15; see also, Acts 3:22–23).
Joshua parted the Jordan river so that Israel could cross over (Joshua 3:7–17).	Jesus walked on water and called others to come over to him (Matthew 14:25–29).
Joshua led God's people into the Promised Land, the inheritance God promised to Abraham (Joshua 1:2–3).	Jesus leads God's people into the Promised Land, his inheritance (Matthew 25:34; Ephesians 1:13–14).
Joshua's army pulled down earthly strongholds (Joshua 6).	Jesus' army pulls down spiritual strongholds (2 Corinthians 10:3–5).
Joshua's army was arrayed in earthly armor (Joshua 6:9).	Jesus' army is arrayed in spiritual armor (Ephesians 6:10–17).
Joshua described himself as God's servant (Joshua 24:15).	Jesus described himself as a servant (Luke 22:27; John 13:1–17; Philippians 2:7).
Joshua led God's people to rest in the Promised Land (Joshua 21:44).	Jesus' followers are led into rest in this new creation (Hebrews 4:1).

Questions

Joshua's army was armed for physical battle, but Jesus' followers are armed for spiritual battle. Discuss the spiritual armor that God has given us in Ephesians 6:10–17.

Samuel

SAMUEL (1 and 2 Samuel)

Samuel was a prophet of God at the end of the days of the Judges. Samuel guided the people of Israel when there was still no king. When God allowed the existence of a king in Israel, Samuel anointed Saul to be king. When God rejected Saul and chose David as the new king, Samuel also anointed David.

SAMUEL	CHRIST
Samuel's mother, Hannah, was blessed by the High Priest Eli before the birth of Samuel (1 Samuel 1:17).	Mary, the mother of Jesus, was blessed by an angel before the birth of Jesus (Luke 1:30).
Samuel's mother, Hannah, uttered a prayer praising God for goodness to her. This took place in the presence of the priest Eli (1 Samuel 2:1–11).	Jesus' mother, Mary, spoke a lengthy prayer in the priestly house of Zechariah and Elizabeth. This prayer is remarkably similar to Hannah's prayer (Luke 1:46–56).
After nursing Samuel, Hannah brought him to the tabernacle with a sacrifice to dedicate him to God (1 Samuel 1:24–28). Eli received the child (1 Samuel 1:23).	After a period of purification, Mary and Joseph brought Jesus to the temple with an offering (Luke 2:22–24). Simeon received the child (Luke 2:25–28).
The parents went up every year to the tabernacle (1 Samuel 2:19).	The parents went up every year to the temple (Luke 2:41).
The child, Samuel, sat and served in the tabernacle (1 Samuel 2:18; 3:21).	The child, Jesus, sat and served in the temple (Luke 2:46–50).
"And the child, Samuel, grew and increased in favor, both with the Lord, and also with men" (1 Samuel 2:26).	"And Jesus grew in wisdom and stature, and in favor with God and man" (Luke 2:52).
Samuel was given to Israel after a long silence from God (1 Samuel 3:1).	Jesus was given to Israel after a long silence from God.
Samuel partially fulfilled God's promise of raising a prophet like Moses (Deut. 18:15; 1 Samuel 3:19–21).	Christ is the ultimate fulfillment of God's promise to raise a prophet like Moses. However, Jesus is greater than Moses (Hebrews 3:1–6).
Samuel established the position of kingship in Israel (1 Samuel 10:24–25).	Jesus established the true kingship of Israel and the world (Luke 1:32–33).

QUESTIONS

Being in favor with God means to please God. Read 1 Thessalonians 4:1–12 and discuss different ways to please God.

David

DAVID (1 and 2 Samuel)

David was a shepherd who bravely faced and killed Goliath, a Philistine enemy of Israel. Eventually, God chose David to become king of Israel after Saul. King David settled Israel in the conquered land of Canaan and expanded the kingdom. Despite David's sins, God called David "a man after my own heart" (1 Samuel 13:14 and Acts 13:22).

DAVID	CHRIST
God gave David victory against Goliath (1 Samuel 17:45–47).	God gave Christ victory over death (1 Corinthians 6:14).
David was pursued by Saul, the rejected king of Israel (1 Samuel 19).	Jesus was pursued by Herod, the illegitimate king of Judah (Matthew 2:13–18).
David's enemies came after him, but were overpowered by the Holy Spirit (1 Samuel 19:18–24).	Jesus' enemies came to arrest him and were overpowered by the Holy Spirit at Jesus' word (John 18:1–11).
David had a friend and advocate in Jonathan who spoke up for David at the risk of his own life (1 Samuel 20).	Jesus had a friend and advocate in John the Baptist who spoke up for Jesus at the risk of his own life (John 3:22–30).
David's hungry men ate the bread of the Presence (1 Samuel 21:1–6).	Jesus' hungry disciples ate grain on the Sabbath (Matthew 12:1–8).
David was tempted and fell (2 Samuel 11).	Jesus was tempted and did not fall (Hebrews 4:15).
Even with David's imperfections, God loved David and made a covenant with him (2 Samuel 7:11–16).	Christ, in his love for humanity, made a new covenant (Matthew 26:28; Hebrews 12:24).
David's son, Solomon, whose name means "Peace," inherited David's throne (1 Kings 1:29–30).	David's offspring, Jesus, is called the Prince of Peace and he holds David's throne forever (Isaiah 9:6; Luke 1:31–33).
David's experiences are reflected in the Psalms: Psalm 22, Psalm 31, Psalm 32, Psalm 35, Psalm 40, Psalm 41, Psalm 45, Psalm 68, Psalm 69, Psalm 109, Psalm 110.	Jesus' experiences are fulfillments of these Psalms: Psalm 22, Psalm 31, Psalm 32, Psalm 35, Psalm 40, Psalm 41, Psalm 45, Psalm 68, Psalm 69, Psalm 109, Psalm 110.

QUESTIONS

In Psalm 22 David expressed the feeling that God abandoned him and lamented for it. Jesus repeated it while he was hanging on the cross. Have you ever felt as if God has abandoned you? In the previous Psalms, which feelings or experiences can you identify with?

Elijah & Elisha

ELIJAH AND ELISHA (1 Kings 17—2 Kings 9)

Elijah was a prophet who confronted the king and queen with their sin. He also called all of Israel to repent and obey the Lord. God showed his power through Elijah's ministry. Elijah chose Elisha as his successor as a prophet in Israel. As with Elijah, God demonstrated his power through Elisha's ministry.

ELIJAH & ELISHA	CHRIST
Elijah's call to repentance on behalf of God came at a time of great unfaithfulness (1 Kings 19:14–18).	Christ's announcement of the kingdom of God came at precisely the time God had prepared (Mark 1:15).
While in the desert, ravens took care of Elijah (1 Kings 17:6). At another time in the wilderness traveling on a 40-day journey, an angel fed him (1 Kings 19:3–8).	Jesus was tempted in the desert after a 40-day fast. Angels took care of him (Matthew 4:2, 11; Mark 1:13; Luke 4:2).
Elijah called his disciple, Elisha, who left his oxen and home to follow Elijah (1 Kings 19:19–21).	Jesus called his disciples and they immediately left their homes and fishing (Matthew 4:18–22).
Elijah raised a widow's son from the dead and gave him back to his mother (1 Kings 17:17–24).	Jesus raised a widow's son in the town of Nain and gave him back to his mother (Luke 7:11–17).
Elijah called down fire from heaven on his enemies (2 Kings 1:12).	Jesus refused to let his disciples call fire from heaven on his enemies (Luke 9:52–56).
Elisha cleansed the leper Naaman (2 Kings 5:1–19).	Jesus cleansed the leper (Matthew 8:1–3; Mark 1:40–42; Luke 5:12–13).
Elisha raised a prominent woman's son from the dead (2 Kings 4:8–37).	Jesus raised a prominent man's daughter from the dead (Matthew 9:23–25; Mark 5:35–42; Luke 8:41–55).
Elisha multiplied food on two separate occasions (2 Kings 4:1–7, 42–44).	Jesus multiplied food on two separate occasions (Matthew 14:13–21; 15:29–39).
A person was resurrected when he was thrown into Elisha's tomb and touched his bones (2 Kings 13:21).	A woman was healed when she touched Jesus' garments (Matthew 9:18–22).

QUESTIONS *At one point when Elijah felt alone and defeated, God showed him that God had preserved his faithful people. God let Elijah know he was not alone. When have you felt alone, misunderstood, ready to give up, like Elijah did? How does Elijah's story in 1 Kings 19:3–18 help you deal with these moments? Elisha's response to Elijah's calling was to drop everything and follow him. Jesus' disciples had a similar response to his call. What does it mean for the church today? How is God calling us to serve him?*

Zerubbabel & Joshua

ZERUBBABEL AND JOSHUA (Ezra 3–6; Zechariah 3–6)

As a punishment for Israel's rebellion, God allowed the Babylonian Empire to destroy Jerusalem, the temple, and take the Jews captive to Babylon. After 70 years, God allowed the Jews to return to Jerusalem. One of the tasks the Jews had was to rebuild the temple. Zerubbabel (a descendant of David) and Joshua (a high priest) were the leaders that God chose to accomplish this task.

ZERUBBABEL & JOSHUA	CHRIST
Zerubbabel was the son of David, heir to the throne and leader of Israel in his day (Ezra 2:1–2; see Matthew 1:13 and Luke 3:27).	Jesus is the son of David and King of Israel. He is the leader of all God's people (Luke 1:32–33).
Zerubbabel helped lay the foundation and completed the second temple (Zechariah 4:9; Ezra 3:11; 6:14–15).	Jesus' body, which was raised from the ground, is the new temple and his people are called a "body," which is that "temple" on earth (John 2:19–22; Romans 12:5; 1 Cor. 12:27; 1 Cor. 3:10; Ephesians 2:21).
Zerubbabel laid the capstone of the rebuilt temple to shouts of "Grace, grace to it" (Zechariah 4:7).	Jesus is called the cornerstone (Acts 4:11; Ephesians 2:20; 1 Peter 2:7). He is the foundation and source of God's grace (John 1:17).
Joshua was the high priest in Israel at the time the temple was about to be rebuilt (Zechariah 3:1).	Jesus' name is the New Testament Greek form of the Old Testament Hebrew name Joshua. He is the true and ultimate High Priest (Hebrews 7).
God clothed Joshua with clean garments so he could stand in the presence of the Holy God (Zechariah 3:3–5).	Christ clothes us with his righteousness (Galatians 3:27). He is standing in the heavenly temple in the robes of the Great High Priest (Revelation 1:12–18).
Satan tried to accuse him, but God himself defended Joshua (Zechariah 3:1–5).	Satan tried to destroy Jesus, but Jesus defeated Satan (Hebrews 2:14)
Both Joshua and Zerubbabel were spoken of as anointed ones who stand before the Lord (Zechariah 4:14).	"Christ" is the New Testament Greek for the Old Testament Hebrew word "Messiah." "Messiah" means "anointed one."

QUESTIONS *God is building his new temple (Romans 12:5). Paul explains the church by comparing it with a "body" (1 Corinthians 12:12–31). God builds this temple by giving gifts to every believer (1 Corinthians 12:7). Some of the gifts the Apostle Paul lists are gifts of wisdom, knowledge, faith, healing, prophecy, tongues, teaching, administration, serving, encouraging, leadership, mercy, and love. Where do you see these gifts in use today?*

JOSEPH

🔲 GOD IN THE LIFE OF JOSEPH

The story of Joseph (Genesis 37–50) teaches about faith and trust, and God's power in times of suffering. It's also a thrilling story of a 17-year-old boy who was …
- Favored by his father
- Resented by his ten older brothers
- Thrown into a pit in the wilderness
- Sold into slavery and never returned home

Later — just when it appeared his life was improving — he was:
- Stalked by someone powerful and vengeful
- Falsely accused and imprisoned
- Abandoned in jail without friends or supporters to defend him
- Forgotten by people who owed him a favor

But throughout the misery, God was there with Joseph.

Joseph's story gives hope on four levels:

1. Personal: God has a purpose in our suffering. God grew Joseph from immaturity to strength and mercy.
2. Family: God used bad circumstances to save Joseph's family and change attitudes.
3. Nationally: God used Joseph's misfortunes to save many lives and set up the rest of the biblical story that leads to the saving of the world through Christ.
4. Beyond: God used this event to bring blessing to the world long past biblical days. We, too, are part of God's larger plan that calls for patience and trust during times of suffering. Just as God blessed Joseph's faithfulness, God will bless our faithfulness.

🔲 BEGINNING OF THE PROMISE (Read Gen. 12:1–3)

This story begins long before Joseph's birth. It begins with his great-grandfather, Abraham, a nomadic sheep and goat herder who lived in the dry, hot region of the Middle East known then as Canaan and today as Israel.

Although Joseph is the main character, the story is really about God's promise to Abraham's descendants.

> *God appeared to Abraham and made two promises:*
> - *I will make you a great nation.*
> - *All the nations of the earth will be blessed by you. (Gen. 12:1–2)*

God's promise to Abraham changed the direction of humanity. Human disobedience and rebellion turned God's creation upside down. Instead of being a good and blessed creation, human rebellion resulted in a cursed creation and a cursed history (see Gen. 1–3).

God promised Abraham to start a new history of blessing with him and his family.

God's promise lies with a family; it is not an ideal family—it resembles many families today, with struggles, deep problems, sadness, and grief.

Question: God gave Abraham some specific promises. What are some promises in the Bible that God gives to everyone who believes in him?

🔲 A DYSFUNCTIONAL FAMILY

The story of Joseph begins in Gen. 37:1, with his father Jacob "in the land of Canaan." This simple statement is a reminder that God is implementing his promise to Abraham. Then the biblical story introduces Joseph and his brothers. It is immediately clear that their relationships are broken and that the potential for conflict is great.

◘ PLAYING FAVORITES (Read Gen. 37:1–4)

Joseph is Jacob's youngest and favorite son. This favoritism is evident in a few short lines in the story.

Two main clues of this favoritism:

1. The "coat of many colors," or "richly ornamented robe," was a gift from Jacob to Joseph. Whatever the robe was, it was a special and precious garment indicating that Joseph was not meant for a life of fieldwork like the other sons.
2. The other telling comment is of "a bad report" (see box) Joseph brings about his brothers. Jacob foolishly sends the favored son to check on his brothers. By this time, Joseph's actions and attitudes have hurt his relationship and angered his brothers.

> The Bible describes a similar robe in only one other place, 2 Sam. 13:18. There Tamar, King David's daughter, wears a similar robe and we read, "for this was the kind of garment the virgin daughters of the king wore" (2 Sam. 13:18).

◘ JOSEPH'S DREAM (Read Gen. 37:5–11)

Joseph's ten older brothers resent their father's favoritism as much as Joseph's attitude. Young Joseph fails to understand the depth of his brothers' loathing toward him. With little tact and wisdom, Joseph shares his dreams with his family. One night, Joseph dreams that his brothers and parents bow before him. The Bible does not say that Joseph's dreams come from God. In fact, we do not know that is the case until the end of the story, when the dreams become reality. It is also the straw that breaks the camel's back for his brothers.

> The expression ***"bad report"*** is also used in Ps. 31:13, Jer. 20:10, and Ezek. 36:3, where it is used for the whispering of hostile people.

The Wages of Deceit

Jacob's relationship with his sons reflects a lifetime of deceit. Jacob deceived Isaac, his father, for his blessing—cheating his brother Esau out of a blessing that was rightfully Esau's. Jacob fled his brother's anger and traveled to Haran to live with his uncle Laban (Gen. 27). There, Jacob fell in love with Laban's youngest daughter, Rachel. However, Laban tricked Jacob into working seven years for his daughter, but he gave his oldest daughter, Leah, to Jacob in marriage. Jacob had to work another seven years for Rachel.

Jacob's love for Rachel was always greater than his love for Leah. However, God granted Leah many sons from Jacob, whereas Rachel was not able to give birth. Rachel finally bore a son to Jacob, Joseph (Gen. 29:31–30:24). Jacob's love for Joseph became an extension of his love for Rachel.

◘ DECEIVING THE DECEIVER (Read Gen. 37:12–36)

The strained relationships among family members anticipate a potentially tragic ending. Jacob sends Joseph to check on his brothers who are herding sheep far away—an unwise decision considering the previous "bad report" from Joseph and the already weak relationships among his children. Joseph's brothers find a perfect opportunity to be rid of their youngest brother. The brothers throw Joseph in a pit and want to kill him. Reuben hopes to rescue Joseph, but Judah, one of two eldest brothers, argues that it is better to make some money from the deal. Instead of killing him, they sell Joseph to a trading caravan going to Egypt. Joseph, although alive, ends up as a slave in Egypt. Jacob is cruelly deceived by his sons, who return with a bloodied coat/robe and a terrible lie: Joseph is dead.

Question: Perhaps Joseph's brothers felt they had gotten away with a clever deception. But the Bible tells us that God is the Lord of Justice. Can you think of another story from the Bible that illustrates God's eventual triumph over wicked actions?

The Promise in Danger

Can God's promise to Abraham (or any other promise) ever be in danger? Absolutely not. God is always faithful to his promises. However, in times of trouble, it is difficult to remember this truth and easy to assume the worst. No, the promise is not in danger; though Joseph might find it difficult to believe while being dragged away from his family and into slavery. As readers, we can do nothing but weep along with Jacob: weep for Jacob's pain, for Joseph's fate, and for the brothers' hardness.

🔲 A STORY WITHIN A STORY (Read Gen. 38)

Right in the middle of the story of Joseph, the Bible pauses and tells a separate story.

Joseph's brother Judah, now a grown man with three sons, tries to deceive his daughter-in-law, Tamar, by promising to follow the biblical laws that will protect her but actually refusing to carry them out. As time goes by, Tamar realizes she has been denied her proper rights; she turns around and deceives Judah.

In a family with a history of lying and violence, betrayal and hatred, how did God change Judah's heart? Judah had to admit that his actions had been wrong—far worse than his daughter-in-law's. He admitted that Tamar was more righteous than he was. Judah, a man unable to regret his mistreatment of his brother Joseph and his father, who lies and does injustice to his daughter-in-law, is a changed man. He is finally able to confess his error and make things right for Tamar.

While Joseph is in Egypt, God starts the change in Joseph's brothers.

Question: Joseph probably had no idea that God was working in the lives of his family members, but God knew what he was doing. What is an example from your own experience in which God was working in a way that was hidden from you at the time?

Judah and Tamar by Horace Vernet

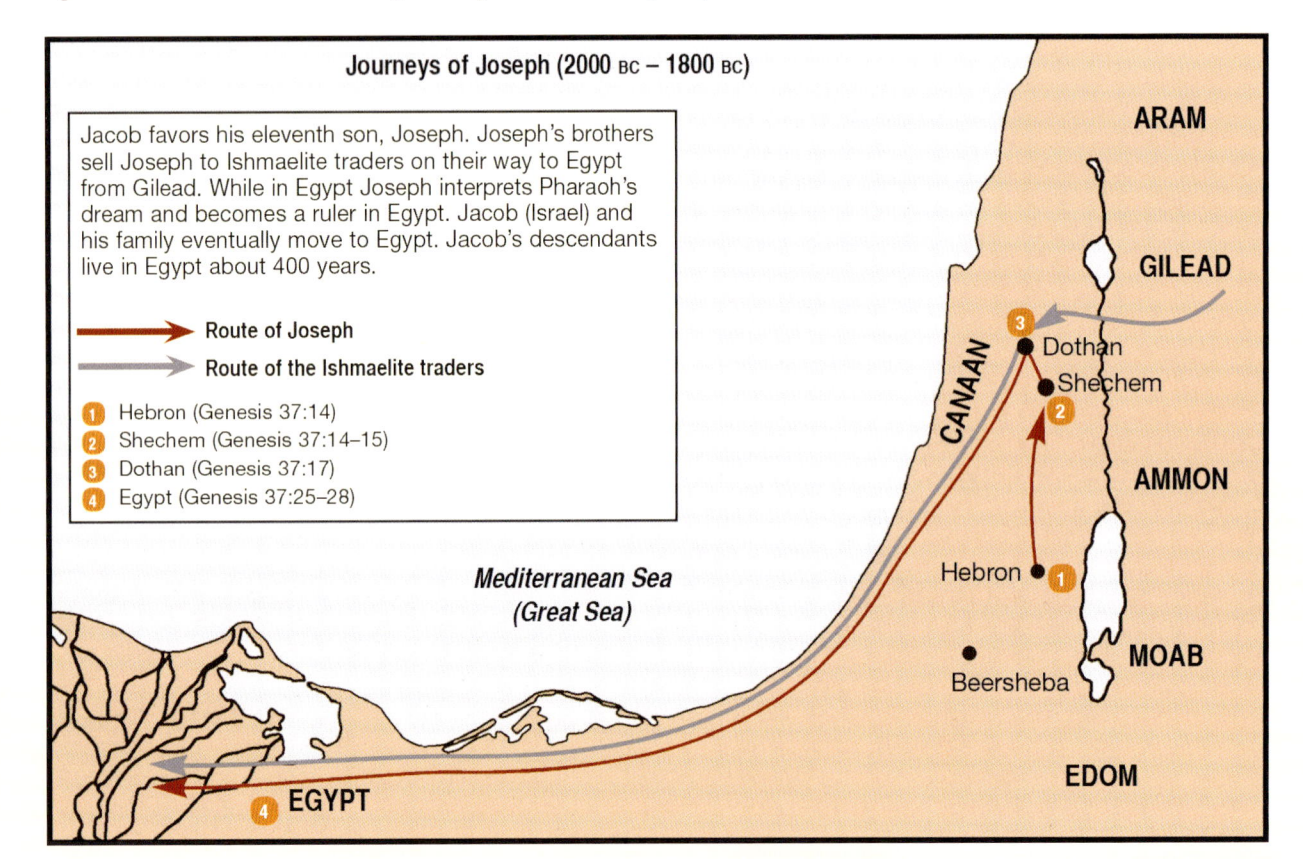

Journeys of Joseph (2000 BC – 1800 BC)

Jacob favors his eleventh son, Joseph. Joseph's brothers sell Joseph to Ishmaelite traders on their way to Egypt from Gilead. While in Egypt Joseph interprets Pharaoh's dream and becomes a ruler in Egypt. Jacob (Israel) and his family eventually move to Egypt. Jacob's descendants live in Egypt about 400 years.

→ Route of Joseph
→ Route of the Ishmaelite traders

1. Hebron (Genesis 37:14)
2. Shechem (Genesis 37:14–15)
3. Dothan (Genesis 37:17)
4. Egypt (Genesis 37:25–28)

🔲 FROM POWERLESS TO POTIPHAR'S (Read Gen. 39:1–6)

Joseph goes from being the beloved son to being sold as a powerless slave in a powerful Egyptian officer's home. Potiphar is the captain of Pharaoh's bodyguard. In spite of this terrible reversal of fortunes, Scripture tells us, "The Lord was with Joseph." We do not know if Joseph, the shepherd boy, knew the language. It is unlikely that he was educated at the level of Egyptian upper class, but the Bible is clear that Joseph does not give up. He works hard and contributes to Potiphar's household. Every small responsibility he handles is successful. Over time, Potiphar realizes that the Lord is with this slave, and Potiphar puts Joseph in charge of everything he owns.

REJECTION AND REVENGE (Read Gen. 39:7–19)

Potiphar's wife wants Joseph to sleep with her, but Joseph refuses, calling her proposed actions
- a breach of his responsibilities
- a betrayal of Potiphar who has trusted him
- a sin against God

She will not take no for an answer, so she stalks him. Day after day she talks with him, trying to seduce him. But one day, they are in the house alone and she grabs his clothing. Her grip must have been strong, because to get away he had to shed that garment and run outside. This final rejection leads her to revenge. She calls out to the men in the household and claims she has been attacked. When Potiphar hears, he is angry and throws Joseph in jail.

Question: Even when Joseph did what was right, he still received punishment as though he were guilty! Jesus said, "Blessed are those who are persecuted for righteousness sake for theirs is the kingdom of heaven" (Matt. 5:10). How do you understand Joseph's story in light of these words? How do you understand your own story?

FROM POTIPHAR'S TO PRISON (Read Gen. 39:20–23)

Joseph is not given a trial; he is unfairly thrown into a jail for the king's prisoners. Scripture says he was there for many years. It was another reversal of fortunes. A good man treated wrongly, framed, betrayed by his employer's wife despite his flawless performance.

No one would blame Joseph for becoming angry and bitter, but he didn't. However, "the Lord was with Joseph" (Gen. 39:2). Joseph used his administrative skills to help, and over time was put in charge of all the prisoners and the prison organization. He found favor with the chief jailer, whose confidence in Joseph was so high that he didn't even supervise Joseph.

Question: What are some common reactions and emotions people have when they suffer injustice? How is it possible to avoid becoming bitter when treated unfairly?

MORE HOPES DASHED (Read Gen. 40)

Two new prisoners from Pharaoh's household were placed in the jail for offending their master. Joseph was put in charge of them and took care of them for a long time. One night both men had troubling dreams, and in the morning Joseph noticed they were sad because there was no one to explain the dreams to them. Joseph told them that interpretations of dreams belonged to God and if they told him, he would explain it.

THE CUPBEARER AND BAKER'S DREAM

	Dream	**Interpretation from God**
Cupbearer	A vine with three branches producing grapes. Grapes were squeezed and the juice given to Pharaoh.	In three days Pharaoh will give you back your job.
Baker	Carrying three baskets of bread for Pharaoh on his head. Birds came and ate them.	In three days Pharaoh will have you executed.

Interesting points:
- Joseph noticed that the men were troubled in the morning and asked about it. He who had been insensitive to his brothers' feelings now cared about others.
- Joseph gave credit to God rather than to himself, despite having a reputation as a clever man.
- Joseph asked the cupbearer to remember him and asked for help to get him out of jail.

Within three days both predictions come true. The cupbearer is restored to his place of privilege and the baker is executed. But the cupbearer forgets about Joseph, and Joseph continues to live in a dungeon several more years.

Questions: Even in prison, Joseph used his gifts to bless others. What are some difficult circumstances in your life in which you can use your gifts to bless others?

▢ PHARAOH'S DREAM (Read Gen. 41:1–36)

One night Pharaoh has two dreams that none of his magicians and wise men can interpret.

Dream 1	Seven cows come out of the Nile River. They are sleek and fat and grazing. Seven more cows come out of the Nile. These are ugly and gaunt. They eat the sleek fat cows.
Dream 2	Seven ears of plump good grain appear on one single stalk. Then seven thin and scorched ears sprout up and swallow the plump ears.

Suddenly the cupbearer remembers Joseph and tells about the Hebrew slave who interpreted his own dream two years before. Pharaoh calls for Joseph. Joseph has to shave and change clothes from his prison garb. Pharaoh says, "I have heard it said about you, that when you hear a dream you can interpret it." Joseph replied, "It is not in me; God will give Pharaoh a favorable answer."

When Joseph hears the dreams, he calls them parallels having the same message.

Interpretation

After seven years of abundance in the land of Egypt, seven years of famine will ravage the land. The double dream means that God will surely do this and do it soon.

Recommendation

Pharaoh should find a wise supervisor to put in charge. Then appoint overseers who will collect and store one fifth of the annual food harvests in Egypt for the seven good years. This reserve will keep the people of Egypt from perishing.

Questions: It is easy to become overly confident and start taking credit for the good that happens in our lives. In what ways can a person give credit to God?

▢ WHAT A DIFFERENCE A DAY MAKES
(Read Gen. 41:37–57)

Pharaoh sets Joseph over all Egypt, gives him his signet ring of authority, clothes him in fine linen and emblems of power, and puts him in a chariot and makes him his second-in-command.

For 13 years, Joseph has been a slave in Egypt and now he is second in command, and given every honor of status and fame and a notable marriage. At age 30, he is given the responsibility to travel through Egypt and supervise the storage of grain in locations owned by Pharaoh. He is so successful and the abundance is so great that even he can no longer keep track of the massive amounts of harvest.

▢ JOSEPH'S BROTHERS IN EGYPT (Read Gen. 42:1–44:34)

Just then, Joseph's brothers arrive in Egypt on a mission to save their family from starvation. This surprise encounter sparks a series of events that transforms Joseph and his brothers' lives forever.

As his brothers arrive and bow down to the Egyptian lord, Joseph recognizes his brothers, but they do not recognize him. The statement reminds the readers of the brothers asking their father to *recognize* (the Hebrew word means *recognize*, "examine" in the NIV) Joseph's bloodied garment (Gen. 37:32). This recognition brings Joseph's memories back like a flood. As his son Manasseh's name reminds us, Joseph had been able to forget his difficult past (see Gen. 41:51; Manasseh probably means "to forget"). Now, the memories, the pain, the anger, and the doubts arise with renewed impetus.

Of Dreams and Gods

Dreams were important in the ancient world, especially in Egypt. The Egyptians had texts that priests would use to interpret dreams. Dreams were windows into the world of the gods. For this reason, priests were the people who could best interpret them.

When Pharaoh asks Joseph to interpret his dreams, Joseph replies, "I cannot do it, but God will give Pharaoh the answer he desires" (Gen. 41:16). Joseph claims that his God, the God of the Bible, can do something Pharaoh's gods have failed to do. Joseph is confident because, as he said before, "Do not interpretations belong to God?" (Gen. 40:8). It is an astonishing claim. Although the Egyptians were quite open to other people's gods, they were confident their own gods were superior. Joseph's claim suggests that the interpretation of dreams belongs to God because revelation through dreams comes from God! Joseph is proclaiming God's superiority over the Egyptians gods.

> Part of God's promise to Abraham finds fulfillment through Joseph here. However, another important part of God's promise was that Abraham's descendants would make a great nation. This part of the promise implies a people and a land. The story is not over, the promise is still incomplete.

Joseph Accuses His Brothers

Joseph speaks harshly to the brothers and accuses them of being spies. This is not a light issue; the brothers understand immediately that they are in mortal peril. The Egyptian lord does not have to offer proofs for his accusation and could execute them at any moment with a simple command. Sheer terror makes them tell the truth about themselves: "We are all the sons of one man. Your servants are honest men, not spies." Their claim is another way to say they have clan responsibilities.

Joseph tests their claim of being honest men and accuses them again of being spies. The brothers insist, "Your servants were twelve brothers, the sons of one man, who lives in the land of Canaan. The youngest is now with our father, and one is no more" (Gen. 42:13). Joseph learns more about his family—his father is still alive and his youngest brother, Benjamin, is with him.

In this brief episode we can imagine a divided Joseph: a man full of anger and overwhelmed with memories but also full of wisdom and responsibility. Joseph is a changed man. However, if Joseph is changed, have his brothers changed at all? Are they still the same foolish men, willing to destroy a person's life to quench their anger?

Question: Joseph had the opportunity and the means either to take revenge or to hope for reconciliation. Whether a person chooses to get even or seek peace will make all the difference. How have you seen these different choices play out in real life situations?

Joseph Tests His Brothers

Joseph tests his brothers more than once, first by hiding his true identity, then by making them leave Simeon as a guarantee that they would return with their youngest brother. The brothers fail to persuade their father to let them bring Benjamin with them to Egypt. Jacob, a broken man, bitterly reminds them of Joseph—Jacob refuses to trust them with Benjamin's life for he fears the ending will be as tragic as that of Joseph's. Reuben makes a proposal: the lives of his two children for the life of Benjamin. Jacob has already lost two children (Joseph and Simeon). Why would he risk losing Benjamin and two grandchildren? Reuben's proposal is reckless. Jacob decides not to send Benjamin with them.

Since the famine is so severe, Jacob's sons need to return to Egypt. Judah steps forward and makes a wise suggestion. If something happens to Benjamin, Judah accepts the guilt and responsibility himself. It is a wise and mature proposal. In the ancient world, a verbal promise was not a thing lightly taken. Verbal commitments were a guarantee of action. Because of Judah's promise, Jacob reluctantly accepts; the brothers are on their way back to Egypt.

Joseph continues the charade. He knows his brothers will return for his brother Simeon; but would they do the same for Benjamin?

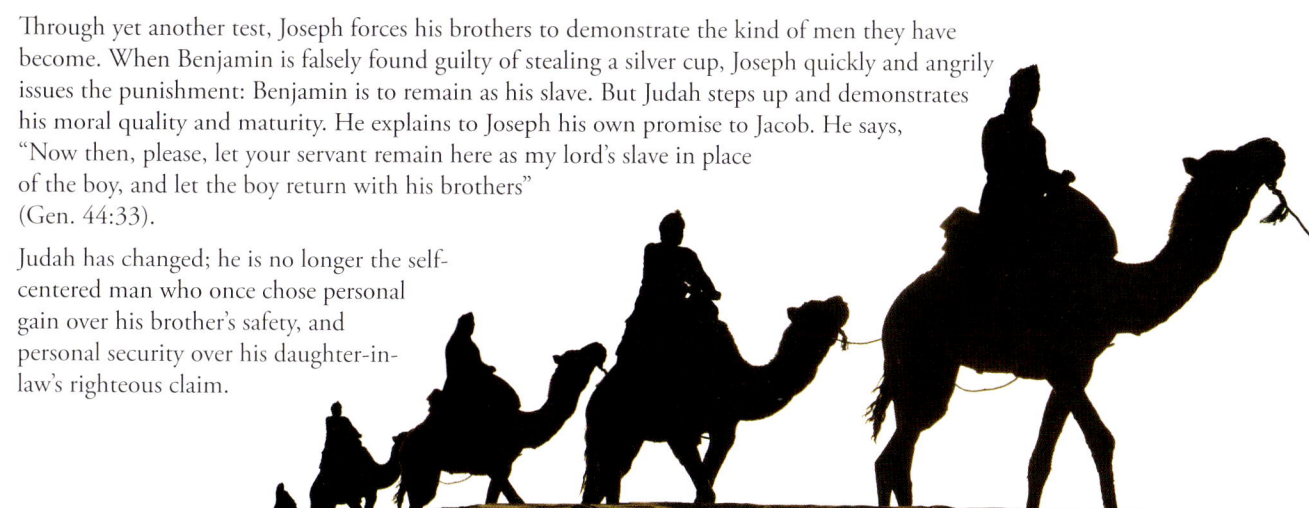

Through yet another test, Joseph forces his brothers to demonstrate the kind of men they have become. When Benjamin is falsely found guilty of stealing a silver cup, Joseph quickly and angrily issues the punishment: Benjamin is to remain as his slave. But Judah steps up and demonstrates his moral quality and maturity. He explains to Joseph his own promise to Jacob. He says, "Now then, please, let your servant remain here as my lord's slave in place of the boy, and let the boy return with his brothers" (Gen. 44:33).

Judah has changed; he is no longer the self-centered man who once chose personal gain over his brother's safety, and personal security over his daughter-in-law's righteous claim.

RECONCILIATION IN EGYPT (Read Gen. 45:1–50:26)

Joseph cannot control himself and reveals his identity. While Joseph is moved to tears, his brothers are terrified when they finally recognize him. Joseph makes the wise and powerful statement: "But God sent me ahead of you to preserve for you a remnant on earth and to save your lives by a great deliverance. So then, it was not you who sent me here, but God" (Gen. 45:7–8). Joseph and Pharaoh invite Jacob and everyone in his family to come to Egypt.

Before leaving Canaan, the land God had promised to Abraham, Jacob has a dream. In the dream, God tells him, "I am God, the God of your father…. Do not be afraid to go down to Egypt, for I will make you into a great nation there. I will go down to Egypt with you, and I will surely bring you back again" (Gen. 46:3–4). God is renewing his promise to Abraham. God will make Abraham's descendants into a great nation *in* Egypt. Then, God will give this new nation a land where God will dwell with them.

Years later, after Jacob's death, Joseph's brothers still wonder if now Joseph will take revenge against them. Instead, Joseph says, "Don't be afraid. Am I in the place of God? You intended to harm me, but God intended it for good to accomplish what is now being done, the saving of many lives" (Gen. 50:19–20).

Question: Why is forgiveness often so difficult? What are the benefits of forgiving someone who has hurt you?

THE GOD WHO WAS THERE

Joseph	• Joseph moved from Canaan to Egypt. • He moved from being a spoiled, foolish young man to being a wise man. • He moved from anger and forgetfulness to forgiveness and restoration. • He is redeemed from his sufferings in Egypt. • He is redeemed from being the victim of violence and injustice from his brothers. • He is redeemed from his own anger and memories. • He is redeemed by learning wisdom and trusting in God.
Jacob	• Jacob moved from being the deceiver to being deceived. • He moved from the joy of his favorite son to the tragedy of his supposed death. • He moved from being a man defeated to being a man with a future. • He is redeemed by receiving God's renewed promise. • Though he had become a broken man, God's gracious acts through Joseph allow Jacob to have a renewed sense of hope for the future. • This hope includes the promises that God made to Abraham.
Joseph's Brothers	• They moved from their wicked deeds to willingness to accept their responsibility. • They are redeemed from their early, evil ways.
Judah	• Judah moved from being a man merely concerned with his own well-being to one willing to accept the consequences of his actions. • Later, when Jacob blesses his children, Judah receives this blessing: "The scepter will not depart from Judah, nor the ruler's staff from between his feet" (Gen. 49:10). • From Judah, King David would be born, and later, Jesus, the promised Messiah, the one who fulfilled God's promises. • Judah is redeemed from his previous egotism. • He becomes the leader of the children of Israel. • Through him, the Messiah is born.

Through Joseph's life, we can learn how God moves in the lives of his people. Throughout the story, we find God at crucial moments. He is not always acting directly, but his presence is constant, causing or enabling all possible movement: geographic, moral, from foolishness to wisdom. Through the movement in Joseph's story, God redeems a broken family.

Although this story does not explain every case of suffering and grief, it instructs us on how to acquire the necessary wisdom that will allow us to face such experiences. The Bible recognizes that doctrinal statements are not enough to deal with suffering and grief. Wisdom allows us to see life from God's perspective. When we can see life through wisdom, we can trust that God will allow "neither death nor life, neither angels nor demons, neither the present nor the future, nor any powers, neither height nor depth, nor anything else in all creation, will be able to separate us from the love of God that is in Christ Jesus our Lord" (Rom. 8:38–39) and that "all things God works for the good of those who love him…" (Rom. 8:28).

Question: Everyone has experienced some sort of trouble in life. What has happened to you that has later turned into a benefit?

Joseph's Family Tree

The story of Joseph is part of the larger story of how God fulfilled his promise to Joseph's great-grandfather, Abraham. Just like his father had done, Jacob blessed his children before dying (the brief sentence below summarizes Jacob's blessings to each of his children in Gen. 49:1–27). The traditional list of Israel's twelve tribes includes Joseph's sons, Ephraim and Manasseh, but not Joseph. Jacob adopted Joseph's sons as his own children (Gen. 48:5–20). By doing this, Jacob exalted Joseph to his own level as a patriarch of the Tribes of Israel, and granted his children a sharing in the promises God made to Abraham. (Because Levi's descendants became the priestly tribe, they did not partake in the distribution of the promised land. Thus, they are not counted in the twelve tribes of Israel.)

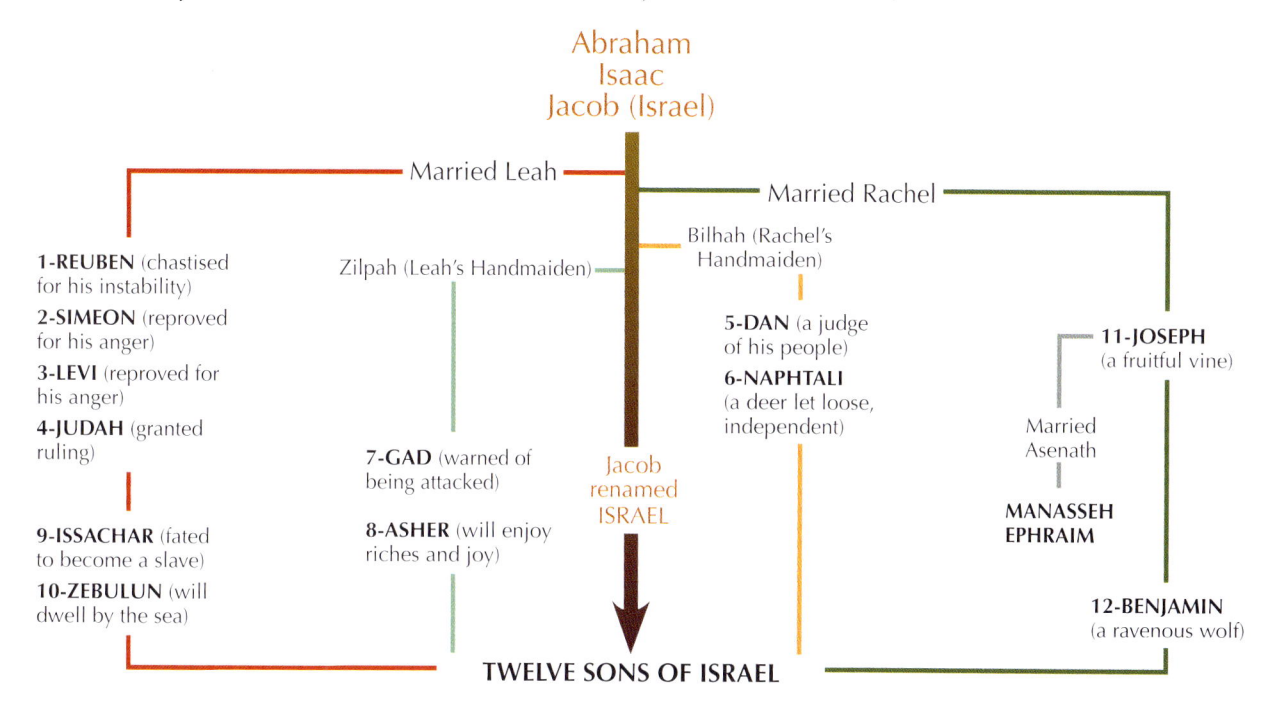

Abraham
Isaac
Jacob (Israel)

Married Leah — Married Rachel

Zilpah (Leah's Handmaiden)
Bilhah (Rachel's Handmaiden)

1-REUBEN (chastised for his instability)
2-SIMEON (reproved for his anger)
3-LEVI (reproved for his anger)
4-JUDAH (granted ruling)
5-DAN (a judge of his people)
6-NAPHTALI (a deer let loose, independent)
11-JOSEPH (a fruitful vine)

Married Asenath

MANASSEH
EPHRAIM

7-GAD (warned of being attacked)
8-ASHER (will enjoy riches and joy)
9-ISSACHAR (fated to become a slave)
10-ZEBULUN (will dwell by the sea)
12-BENJAMIN (a ravenous wolf)

Jacob renamed ISRAEL

TWELVE SONS OF ISRAEL

Life of Joseph Time Line

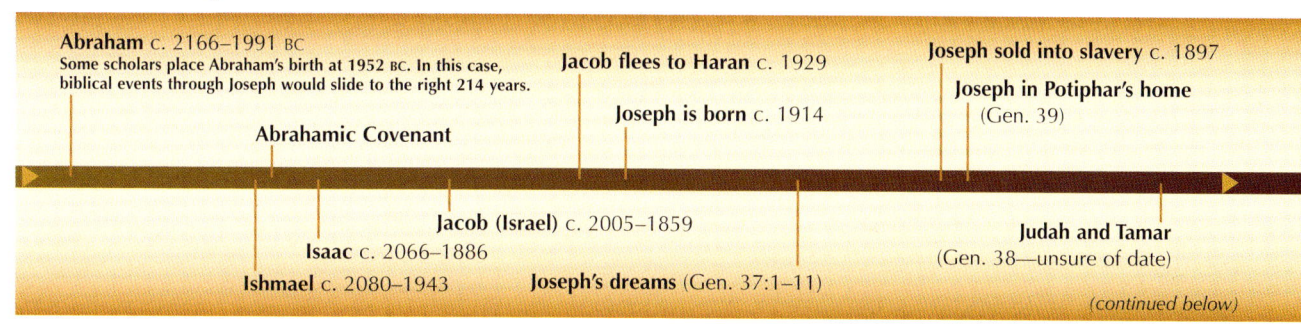

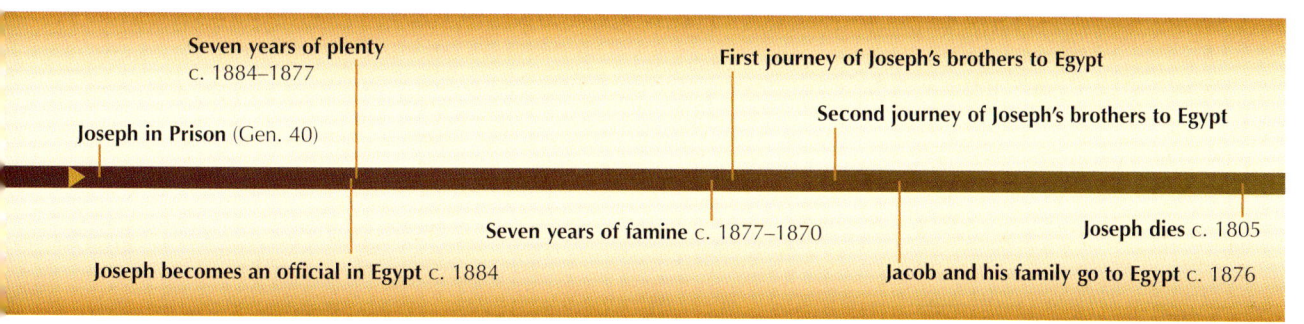

Abraham c. 2166–1991 BC
Some scholars place Abraham's birth at 1952 BC. In this case, biblical events through Joseph would slide to the right 214 years.

Abrahamic Covenant

Isaac c. 2066–1886
Ishmael c. 2080–1943
Jacob (Israel) c. 2005–1859

Jacob flees to Haran c. 1929
Joseph is born c. 1914
Joseph's dreams (Gen. 37:1–11)

Joseph sold into slavery c. 1897
Joseph in Potiphar's home (Gen. 39)
Judah and Tamar (Gen. 38—unsure of date)

(continued below)

Seven years of plenty c. 1884–1877
First journey of Joseph's brothers to Egypt
Second journey of Joseph's brothers to Egypt

Joseph in Prison (Gen. 40)

Joseph becomes an official in Egypt c. 1884
Seven years of famine c. 1877–1870
Jacob and his family go to Egypt c. 1876
Joseph dies c. 1805

Moses

*Since then, no prophet has risen in Israel like Moses, whom the LORD knew face to face, who did all those miraculous signs and wonders the LORD sent him to do in Egypt, to Pharaoh and to all his officials and to his whole land. **For no one has ever shown the mighty power or performed the awesome deeds that Moses did in the sight of all Israel.*** —Deuteronomy 34:10–12

- A baby in danger became a liberator.
- A man who disliked the limelight became a leader.
- An 80-year-old shepherd faced a mighty Pharaoh.
- A man slow of speech became a prophet.
- A husband and father became a priest.
- A simple, humble man became God's servant.
- The life of this man changed the life of a nation-to-be.

Moses was perhaps the most important person in the Old Testament. His life was bound to the life of God's people, the children of Israel, and to God himself. In a special way, Moses represented Israel to God and God to Israel. Thus, learning about Moses means learning about God's people and about God himself.

The Hebrew People

Moses was born in Egypt to a Hebrew slave family.

- The Hebrew people had originally come to Egypt about 400 years before, after a time of famine. Jacob (also known as Israel) and his sons moved to Egypt, where Jacob's son Joseph had become the second most important ruler after Pharaoh.
- After Joseph died, the Israelites were thriving. God was fulfilling his promise to Abraham to give him many descendants and bless them (Gen. 17:4–7): "The Israelites were fruitful and multiplied greatly and became exceedingly numerous, so that the land was filled with them" (Ex. 1:7).
- However, eventually Egypt's pharaohs forgot Joseph and worried about the great strength of the Hebrew people. Besides enslaving the children of Israel, the Pharaoh, moved by fear, began a murderous policy to control the Israelite population growth. By the Pharaoh's decree, all male newborns were to be thrown into the Nile River.
- It seemed as though Pharaoh had the upper hand. However, God planned to make Abraham's descendants fruitful and a great nation. Pharaoh opposed God's will and plan. God was behind the scenes, engineering a great deliverance for his people.

The Birth of Hope

In that time of grief, suffering, and danger, Moses was born. Although Pharaoh had intended to destroy Israel and frustrate God's plans to bless them, God worked through the most unexpected people to save the child. The baby's mother put the baby in a basket in the Nile to save him. The baby's sister Miriam wisely talked Pharaoh's daughter into giving the baby back to his mother to raise him. In contrast to the Pharaoh's evil intentions, his own daughter's tender and compassionate heart became a tool for the baby's salvation.

Thus the child Moses was born to a slave family, rescued by a noble person, nurtured by his own slave mother, and educated as a member of the Egyptian nobility. As we read the story of Moses' birth and rescue, we understand that God was working behind the scenes. What we might miss is that Moses' own story anticipated what was about to happen to Israel.

Moses	Israel
Moses came out of the Nile River miraculously "reborn."	Israel miraculously came out of the Red Sea as a people with a new identity.
Moses became aware of the injustice and acted to save his people (Ex. 2:11–12).	God heard and was concerned with the fate of his people; he acted decisively to save his people.
Moses had to flee the anger of Pharaoh into the wilderness (Ex. 2:15).	Israel had to flee Egypt into the wilderness (Ex. 14:8–9).
Moses met God at the burning bush on Mt. Sinai (Ex. 3:1).	Israel met God while camping around the base of Mt. Sinai (Ex. 19:1–2).
Moses, an Egyptian (Ex. 2:19), became the deliverer of some troubled shepherds.	God chose Moses, the shepherd, to deliver his people from Egypt.

Moses' Name

- The Hebrew name *Moses* sounds like the Hebrew verb for "to draw out."
- Pharaoh's daughter named the child Moses because "I drew him out of the water" (Ex. 2:10).
- But the name *Moses* has an Egyptian meaning as well and is found in many Egyptian names: Ra-messes, Thut-mose, Ah-mose.
- The first part of each name is related to an Egyptian deity (Ra, Thut, Ah). The second part of each name (*messes/mose*) means "boy" or "son." Moses can be an Egyptian name meaning *boy*, *son*, or *child*.

DIVINE APPOINTMENT

In a fit of anger, Moses killed an Egyptian who was mistreating an Israelite. His life changed radically. After being a noble, Moses became a fugitive. Fleeing into the wilderness, he began a new life: a new home, a new clan, a wife and children, a new profession as shepherd. He remained with Reuel, the Medianite high priest, and married his daughter, Zippora. In time, Gershon, his son, was born (Ex. 2:22).

Meanwhile, back in Egypt, the cruel pharaoh died—but another equally ruthless pharaoh took his place, and the Hebrew people cried out to God under their burdens. Exodus notes that God entered the scene directly: he listened, remembered, and acted in favor of his people (Ex. 2:23–25).

God called out to Moses from a burning bush on Mt. Sinai (Ex. 3:4).

- God identified himself as the God of Moses' forefathers. With reverence, Moses removed his sandals because God's presence made the ground holy (Ex. 3:5).
- God announced that he had seen his people's misery and was sending Moses to bring them out of Egypt. Moses protested that he was not the right person for the job. God offered signs that he would be with him:
  - Israel would worship God on the same mountain (3:12).
  - God revealed his own name to Moses (3:14).
  - God would perform great wonders (3:20).
  - Israel would not leave Egypt empty-handed (3:21).
  - God showed his power by changing Moses' staff into a snake (4:2–4).
  - God made Moses' hand leprous and restored it back to health (4:6–7).

Insight

Moses' encounter with God at the burning bush revealed much about God, Moses, and the children of Israel.

- God is faithful to his promises—he had not forgotten his covenant with Abraham.
- God chose and equipped Moses to be his special representative to Egypt to free his people.
- Moses' role became defined as that of an intermediary between God and Israel. From this moment on, Moses spoke to God on behalf of the children of Israel and to Israel on behalf of God.

CLASH OF THE GODS

When Moses went to see the Pharaoh, he confronted a person who the Egyptians considered a divinity. In the eyes of the Egyptians, it would seem that a foreign god was challenging their own god, Pharaoh. A clash of the gods was the natural result. Having grown up in the Egyptian court, Moses' fear and hesitancy make sense: he was an 80-year-old humble shepherd, how could he confront a "divine being"? On the surface, Moses and Aaron were facing the Pharaoh and his magicians; yet, at another level of reality, the God of Moses, the Lord, the Creator of heaven and earth, was facing the false gods of the Egyptians.

Pharaoh stubbornly refused to allow his Hebrew slaves to leave the country. The Scriptures tell us that God was also behind Pharaoh's hardened heart. Pharaoh's obstinacy happened so that Moses, and the children of Israel, would know that the Lord, the God of Abraham, Isaac, and Jacob, is the real and only God (Ex. 4:5; 9:16). As God had foreseen, Pharaoh opposed Moses and worsened the life conditions of the Israelites by denying them straw to make their bricks, making it much more difficult to meet their quotas.

As God challenged and defeated the gods of Egypt with each plague, Moses and the people of Israel witnessed God's power over creation, the gods of Egypt, and Egypt itself. For example, God defeated Ra, the sun-god, one of Egypt's main gods, in the ninth plague: Darkness.

> **Insight**
>
> Through the exodus experience, God created a people for himself. In time, he started a relationship with this people that would define the rest of God's involvement with humanity.
>
> Christ's work on the cross is the miracle that brings us salvation and defines believers as a new people. "This salvation, which was first announced by the Lord, was confirmed to us by those who heard him. God also testified to it by signs, wonders and various miracles, and gifts of the Holy Spirit distributed according to his will" (Heb. 2:3–4).

> **Aaron**
>
> Aaron was Moses' and Miriam's brother and the first High Priest of Israel. God assigned Aaron to be Moses' assistant (4:14–17). As Moses' assistant (4:14–17), Aaron served throughout the Exodus and the journey through the wilderness. As the High Priest, Aaron was in charge of the Tabernacle and all the activities around it. Despite his closeness to God and Moses, Aaron committed a terrible sin when he agreed to build an idol—the Golden Calf—for Israel (Ex. 32:1–10).
>
> Aaron died in the wilderness, and the community mourned him for 30 days (Num. 20:22-29). The New Testament contrasts Aaron's imperfect priesthood with Jesus' perfect priesthood (Heb. 5:2–5; 7:11–12).

AGENT OF DELIVERANCE

In the last, decisive plague, God killed the firstborns in all the land of Egypt, including Pharaoh's own son. Pharaoh, a broken man, allowed Israel to leave Egypt. As God had promised, the Israelites left Egypt with Egyptian silver, gold, and clothing (Ex. 3:21–22; 12:35–36).

However, Pharaoh changed his mind and chased the Israelites to kill them (Ex. 14:5).

With a column of fire separating them, Pharaoh's troops trapped Israel against the Red Sea. Moses took charge in the midst of the Israelites' doubts and fears. God promised to fight for the Israelites. As they crossed the Red Sea in a mighty miracle of deliverance, a new people was born: God's people, a nation in formation. Just as baptism symbolizes a new beginning in the life of the Christian, the crossing of the Red Sea was a new beginning for Israel as a people (1 Cor. 10:1–2). Pharaoh's army disappeared as the waters closed in on them. God's deliverance was complete.

DIVINE PRESENCE

As the Israelites moved away from the sea toward Sinai, they rejoiced for their liberation (Ex. 15:1–21), grumbled and complained against Moses and Aaron (16:3; 17:3), and disobeyed God's instructions (16:20, 27). The Israelites asked for the basics for life: food and water. God provided in a miraculous way. For food, God gave them manna and quail. As for the water, God instructed Moses to strike a rock to give water to the Israelites (17:6).

Even after seeing God's providence over and over, the Israelites ask the question that highlights a central issue in the book of Exodus, the whole Bible, and the life of Moses: "Is the Lord among us or not?" (17:7). One of the central themes of the book of Exodus is God's presence among his people.

God's Presence with Moses

God's double revelation to Moses on Mount Sinai (Ex. 3 and 19) established that God's presence was with Moses.

The battle against the Amelekites in Exodus 17 shows that God's presence with Moses represented God's presence with the Israelites. When Moses held his staff above his head, the Israelites defeated the Amelekites. When Moses lowered his arms to rest them, the fate of the battle turned against Israel. This event illustrates Moses' intercession in favor of Israel, and God's presence with Moses.

When the Israelites arrived at the foot of Mount Sinai, God made it clear that his demonstration of power—the thunder, lightning, and the thick cloud—had a specific purpose: "so that the people will hear me speaking with you and will always put their trust in you" (19:9).

Moses represented God to the people of Israel. God's presence with Moses was a sign for the Israelites to know that God was with them as well. Moses' authority and guidance represented God's own authority and guidance.

God's presence with Moses remained the visual sign of God's presence with Israel until the Israelites built the Tabernacle. The Tabernacle, then, became the visual representation of God's presence in the midst of his people (Ex. 25:8). In a late Jewish tradition, the term *shekinah* became associated with God's presence. *Shekinah* is derived from a Hebrew word meaning "dwelling." God's presence, the *shekinah*, was represented by a cloud during the day and the column of fire during the night.

The Covenant at Sinai

The Tabernacle, God's visible presence with Israel, also symbolized God's willingness to travel with his people through their wilderness journey. The wilderness, itself a symbol of the chaos and lifeless forces that oppose God, was a training ground for Israel to learn what it meant to be God's people. God had promised to be with them and live with them. However, God is holy, whereas the Israelites lived with many impurities and sin. How could they live in the presence of a holy God?

For the purpose of teaching Israel how to live as God's people in his presence and in the Promised Land, God gave Moses the Ten Commandments. The covenant at Sinai became the basis for God's relationship with Israel.

Moses was a kind of mediator of this covenant. When he climbed the mountain, he was representing the Israelites before God. When he descended the mountain, Moses was representing God to the people. The essence of the covenant remains, though the basis for it has changed. That is, in the old covenant, God inscribed the words of the covenant on stone; Israel would treasure them and keep them close to their hearts and minds forever. Their entire life should have been determined by these words.

But humans are forgetful and rebellious. The Israelites broke the terms of the agreement on repeated occasions. For that reason, God had promised to instead inscribe his Law in people's hearts (Deut. 30:6) and send a perfect mediator of a new covenant, the Messiah, Jesus (Heb. 9:15).

The Ten Commandments

The Ten Commandments are a summary of the agreement (covenant) that God made with Israel at Sinai. Israel agreed to keep (obey) the terms of their agreement (stipulations of the covenant) and God agreed to be their God and King (bless, protect, and provide for them).

Insight

In Christ, we can enjoy a relationship with God like the one Moses enjoyed. God revealed himself in a special way through Christ. Because of the presence of the Holy Spirit in us, we have direct access to God!

> ### Jesus as Mediator
>
> Sin separates humans from God. We can only relate to him indirectly, through covenants, sacrifices, and human intercessors (priests and prophets). As the perfect priest and prophet, Jesus is the only mediator we need. As a prophet, he communicated God's will through his teachings and ministry (Heb. 1:1–2). As a priest, he offered the only perfect sacrifice that could bring us back to God (Heb. 10:10–14). The letter to the Hebrews makes it clear that Jesus is a mediator like Moses but superior to him.
>
> - **1 Timothy 2:5:** *For there is one God and one mediator between God and men, the man Christ Jesus.*
> - **Hebrews 9:15:** *For this reason Christ is the mediator of a new covenant, that those who are called may receive the promised eternal inheritance—now that he has died as a ransom to set them free from the sins committed under the first covenant.*

Leading through the Wilderness

The Israelites spent 26 months camped at the feet of Mt. Sinai (Num. 10:11). They learned what it meant to be God's people and how to live with God's presence in their midst (most of the instructions in the book of Leviticus).

Organized as an army, Israel traveled from Sinai to the Promised Land. God, as Israel's King, led the march through the wilderness and dwelt in the middle of the Israelite camp. At different times during the journey, both Israel and Moses rebelled and expressed their discontent.

The Twelve Spies

As the Israelites approached the Promised Land, God instructed Moses to send twelve men to explore the land. Their report confirmed all that God had promised: a land flowing with milk and honey! However, they also brought bad news: the people in the land were too strong. Filled with fear despite the assurances from Moses, Joshua, and Caleb, the Israelites rebelled and refused to follow God's instructions to conquer the land. God's punishment was terrible: that whole generation would die in the wilderness, except for Joshua and Caleb. The Israelites wandered in the wilderness for 40 years. Joshua and Caleb, the two faithful spies who trusted God, were the only two from that generation who entered the Promised Land.

Korah's Rebellion

Korah, a Levite, incited a rebellion against Aaron and Moses' leadership. Korah said to Moses and Aaron, "You have gone too far! The whole community is holy, every one of them, and the Lord is with them. Why then do you set yourselves above the Lord's assembly?" Moses turned to God to find out his will, and God again communicated very clearly: As the rebel group gathered around the tents of Korah, Dathan, and Abiram, "the earth opened its mouth and swallowed them and their households, and all those associated with Korah" (Num. 16:32).

The complaints of Israel and Moses are different: while Israel rebelled against God's authority, Moses' complaining came from a secure relationship of friendship. Because God treated Moses as a friend, Moses could appeal to God's own promises and honor (see Ex. 32:11–13; and Num. 14:13–19). These remarkable examples force us to wonder why God punished Moses and Aaron so severely in Numbers 20:12: "But the Lord said to Moses and Aaron, 'Because you did not trust in me enough to honor me as holy in the sight of the Israelites, you will not bring this community into the land I give them.'"

Water from the Rock

The Scriptures make it clear that Moses did something that offended God; something so serious that God severely punished him. What was his sin? These are some possible answers:

1. It is possible that Moses' speech to the Israelites (Num. 20:10) was the offense. God commanded Moses to speak to the rock—not the people (Num. 20:8).
2. It is possible that Moses was claiming for himself the miracle he was about to perform: "... must we bring you water out of this rock?" (Num. 20:10).
3. It is possible that Moses was supposed to speak to the rock, not strike it.
4. It is possible that Moses' sin was a combination of the last three options—or that the Scriptures tell us only that God punished Moses and Aaron and the reason behind the punishment, but not the precise offense.

How exactly did Moses' action show lack of trust and failure to give honor to God? Let us remember that God performed a similar miracle before in Exodus 17:1–7. There, at the rocky wilderness of Sinai, the people quarreled with Moses and asked for water. God ordered Moses to use his staff to strike the rock. Before the elders of the Israelites, Moses struck the rock and water came gushing out. In Numbers 20, the need for water arose once again. This time, however, God ordered Moses to speak to the rock.

Moses' sin might be a question of expectations. The people expected God to deliver them from their thirst in the same way he had done it before. Yet, the Bible is clear that we cannot put God in a box; that God is and does far more than we can imagine.

Perhaps giving the Israelites water by speaking to the rock was a miracle they were not expecting; such a miracle could have had a stronger effect on their faith. By repeating the way the miracle was done previously, Moses "robbed" glory from God's miraculous provision. Preventing God from acting in new and sometimes surprising ways may reflect a lack of faith and trust in God's goodness and wisdom.

Moses Strikes the Rock by James Tissot, c. 1896-1902

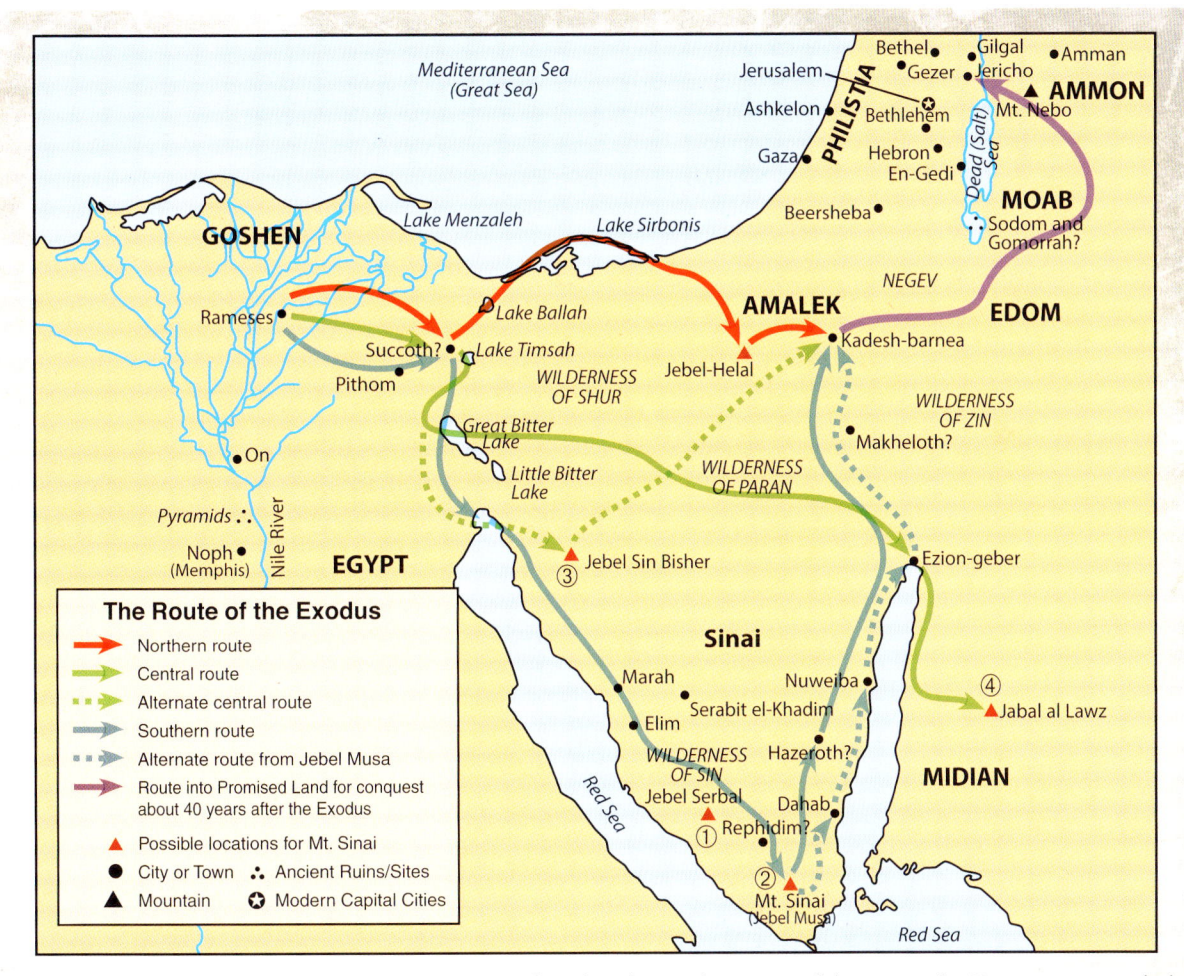

The Route of the Exodus

- → Northern route
- → Central route
- ⇢ Alternate central route
- → Southern route
- ⇢ Alternate route from Jebel Musa
- → Route into Promised Land for conquest about 40 years after the Exodus
- ▲ Possible locations for Mt. Sinai
- ● City or Town ∴ Ancient Ruins/Sites
- ▲ Mountain ✪ Modern Capital Cities

Traditionally, many people believe that Mount Sinai is found in the southern part of the peninsula. However, some scholars believe that the mountain might be found in the northern part of the peninsula or, even, outside of the peninsula in what was one location for ancient Midian. These are the four most common suggestions for the location of Mount Sinai.

① In the south, *Jebel* (Mount) *Serbal*
② In the south, *Jebel Musa*
③ In the north, *Jebel Sin Bisher*
④ Outside of the Sinai Peninsula, in Midian, *Jabal al Lawz*

Last Wishes and Death

At the end of 40 years' journey, Moses and a new generation of the children of Israel arrived at the eastern border of the Promised Land.

This new generation did not witness firsthand God's mighty acts of salvation in Egypt nor his revelation at Sinai. They also needed to be instructed in what it meant to be God's people. Their identity, based on God's Law, would protect them as they entered the Promised Land and would guide them as they became a nation. Joshua, the faithful spy, was chosen to succeed Moses as leader.

At the edge of the Promised Land, at the end of the wilderness wanderings and of Moses' life, Moses instructed Israel.

Moses' instructions to the Israelites in the book of Deuteronomy can be summarized as follows:

> **Insight**
>
> Moses stood at the edge of the Promised Land; he could see it but could not enter it. Yet, Moses died full of hope for what he could witness. It is similar for Christians. We stand at the edge of the Promised Land, but cannot enter it quite yet. Until we do, we continue to wander in this life, knowing that although we are not of this world, the Lord has sent us into this world to serve him while we await for his return (John 17:13–19).

About God	God is one.	4:1–40; 6:4
	God is faithful and merciful.	1:8, 19–46; 7:1–26; 8:1–20; 9:1–10:11
	God is powerful.	2:1–3:11; 4:1–40; 7:1–26
About Israel	God chose Israel.	4:5–9; 10:14–15; 14:1–2, 21
	The land God promised to Israel is good.	1:25; 6:10–11; 8:7–13; 11:8–15
	Israel must love, serve, fear, and obey God.	6:5; 10:12–13; 13:4
	Israel must not have other gods (idolatry); rather, Israel must serve and worship God properly.	4:9–31; 5:6–10; 7:1–5; 8:19–20; 12:1–32; 13:1–18
	God's Law is meant for all areas of life in the Land.	12:1–27:26

After instructing Israel, Moses climbed Mount Nebo, where God allowed him to see the Promised Land. Moses did not enter the land, but died there. God buried him in the valley, east of the Jordan. Moses did not die of old age, nor of sickness; rather, "Moses was 120 years old when he died. His eye was undimmed, and his vigor unabated" (Deut. 34:7).

Jews across the Red sea by Wilhelm Kotarbinski, 1890

MOSES AND CHRIST JESUS

Because Moses is so significant, the writer of the letter to the Hebrews uses him to highlight Jesus' ministry. It's almost as if the writer were making the argument: if Moses, being this important, falls short before Jesus, and you believe Moses, shouldn't you believe Jesus even more?

Moses' life illustrates the human need for a mediator. Moreover, his life points to the life of that Mediator we need: Jesus Christ.

Moses' life shows a God full of grace and mercy, compassion and love, yet also holy and just. His life shows us the possibilities for a full relationship with God, a relationship in which we are no longer servants but friends (John 15:14–15).

Finally, Moses' life points to Christ in some other important ways:

Moses	Christ
Surrounding the birth of Moses, Pharaoh killed innocent children in Egypt—Ex. 1:22.	Surrounding the birth of Jesus, King Herod killed innocent children in Bethlehem—Matt. 2:16.
Moses had to flee his native land because of Pharaoh's persecution—Ex. 2:15.	Jesus had to flee his native land because of Herod's persecution—Matt. 2:14.
Pharaoh died and Moses returned after he was told: "All the men are dead that sought your life"—Ex. 4:19.	Herod died and Jesus returned after "…those who sought the child's life are dead"—Matt. 2:20–21.
Moses fasted 40 days before he delivered God's words to the people—Ex. 34:28.	Jesus fasted 40 days before he began to preach—Matt. 4:2, 17.
Moses was on a mountain for the blessing of the commandments—Ex. 19:20.	Jesus was on a mount when he gave his Beatitudes and commandments—Matt. 5:1–12.
Moses' own people question his authority—Ex. 2:14.	Jesus' own people question his authority—Matt. 13:54–55.
The dividing of the Red Sea took place under Moses' command—Ex. 14:15–22.	Jesus walked on the sea and calmed the storm—Matt. 14:22–32.
A cloud overshadowed Moses, Aaron and Miriam and the voice of God was heard—Num. 12:5–8.	A cloud overshadowed Peter, James and John with Jesus, and the voice of God was heard—Matt. 17:1–5.
Moses' face shown with God's glory—Ex. 34:30.	Jesus face shown with God's glory—Matt. 17:2.
God promised to raise up a prophet like Moses—Deut. 18:15.	Jesus Christ is the prophet that God promised; yet, he is even greater than Moses—Heb. 3:1–6.
Moses brought God's people to the border of the Promised Land—Num. 33:1–56; Deut. 1:5.	Jesus brings God's people into Paradise—Luke 23:43.

Time Line of Moses' Life

Dating the Exodus event is very difficult. Scholars have proposed two different possible dates for the Exodus: A "high" and a "low" date. In this time line, we follow the traditional "high" date.

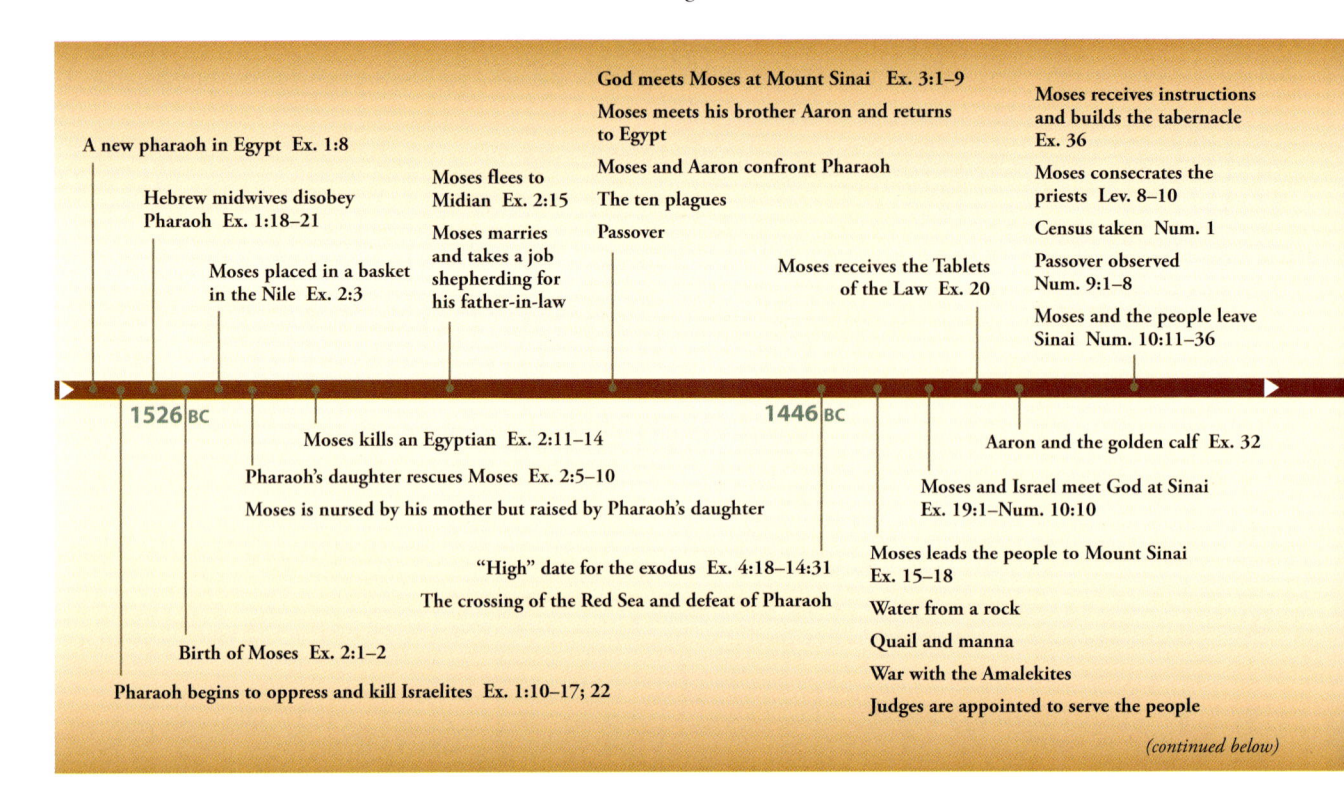

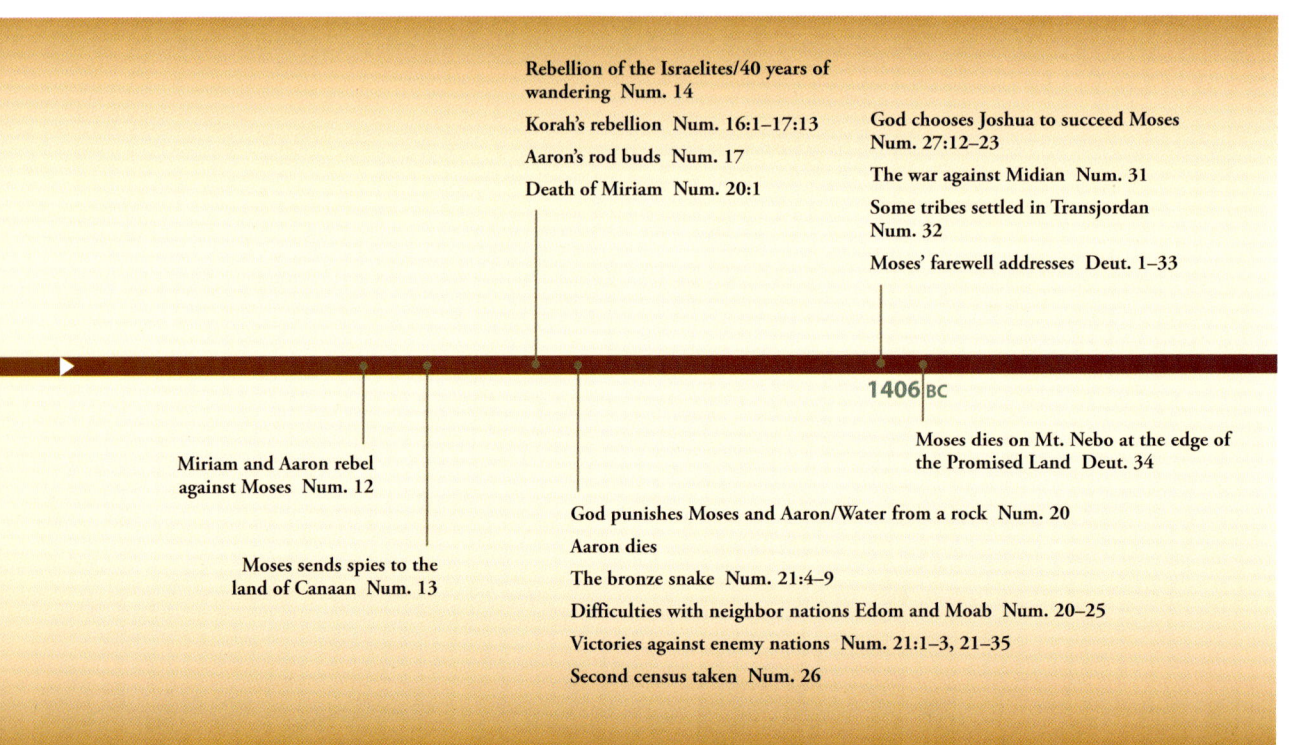

- A new pharaoh in Egypt Ex. 1:8
- Hebrew midwives disobey Pharaoh Ex. 1:18–21
- Moses placed in a basket in the Nile Ex. 2:3
- Moses flees to Midian Ex. 2:15
- Moses marries and takes a job shepherding for his father-in-law
- God meets Moses at Mount Sinai Ex. 3:1–9
- Moses meets his brother Aaron and returns to Egypt
- Moses and Aaron confront Pharaoh
- The ten plagues
- Passover
- Moses receives the Tablets of the Law Ex. 20
- Moses receives instructions and builds the tabernacle Ex. 36
- Moses consecrates the priests Lev. 8–10
- Census taken Num. 1
- Passover observed Num. 9:1–8
- Moses and the people leave Sinai Num. 10:11–36

1526 BC

1446 BC

- Moses kills an Egyptian Ex. 2:11–14
- Pharaoh's daughter rescues Moses Ex. 2:5–10
- Moses is nursed by his mother but raised by Pharaoh's daughter
- "High" date for the exodus Ex. 4:18–14:31
- The crossing of the Red Sea and defeat of Pharaoh
- Aaron and the golden calf Ex. 32
- Moses and Israel meet God at Sinai Ex. 19:1–Num. 10:10
- Moses leads the people to Mount Sinai Ex. 15–18
- Water from a rock
- Quail and manna
- War with the Amalekites
- Judges are appointed to serve the people
- Birth of Moses Ex. 2:1–2
- Pharaoh begins to oppress and kill Israelites Ex. 1:10–17; 22

(continued below)

- Rebellion of the Israelites/40 years of wandering Num. 14
- Korah's rebellion Num. 16:1–17:13
- Aaron's rod buds Num. 17
- Death of Miriam Num. 20:1
- God chooses Joshua to succeed Moses Num. 27:12–23
- The war against Midian Num. 31
- Some tribes settled in Transjordan Num. 32
- Moses' farewell addresses Deut. 1–33

1406 BC

- Miriam and Aaron rebel against Moses Num. 12
- Moses sends spies to the land of Canaan Num. 13
- God punishes Moses and Aaron/Water from a rock Num. 20
- Aaron dies
- The bronze snake Num. 21:4–9
- Difficulties with neighbor nations Edom and Moab Num. 20–25
- Victories against enemy nations Num. 21:1–3, 21–35
- Second census taken Num. 26
- Moses dies on Mt. Nebo at the edge of the Promised Land Deut. 34

David

A Man After God's Own Heart

King David's humanity is clear and compelling to any reader. Modern readers, centuries after his time, can still relate to his story. The Bible presents a realistic picture of a man who loved God, became a great instrument in God's plans, and was deeply flawed. David is a person we can easily relate to.

Although David's victories are exciting and stir our imaginations, David's failures and humility are what make him a powerful character and his life so meaningful. David's life shows that human weakness is the perfect opportunity for God's grace, power, strength, forgiveness, justice and holiness to shine incomparably.

Samuel—Last of the Judges

In order to understand David's role in the story of Israel, we must see him in contrast to Israel's previous leaders.

- Forty years before David, Samuel was the last of the judges who brought order and unity as God's priest and prophet.
- Samuel symbolized God's own willingness to hear his people—*Samuel* means "God has heard."
- The people asked him to give them a king, an act that seemed to show disrespect for the Lord.
- He was hesitant, but God directed him to grant their request.
- He anointed Israel's first king, Saul—the name *Saul* means, "The one who was requested."
- Later he brought God's judgment against Saul when Saul rebelled against the Lord.
- He anointed David to be king instead of Saul.

> **The Judges**
> When God brought Israel out of Egypt, Israel was not a nation yet. It was, rather, a group of tribes. When they arrived in the Promised Land, the land was distributed among the Israelites. At that point, each tribe governed itself separately. When a crisis arose, God would choose special leaders to fight in favor of God's people. They received a special calling; often God's Spirit empowered them in special ways to carry on a special task.

The Prophet Samuel fresco painting.

> "We want a king over us. Then we will be like all the other nations, with a king to lead us and to go out before us and fight our battles." When Samuel heard all that the people said, he repeated it before the Lord. The Lord answered, "Listen to them and give them a king." —1 Sam. 8:19–22

Saul, First (and Failed) King of Israel

- Saul was "without equal among the Israelites..." (1 Samuel 9:2).
- Under his leadership, the Philistine threat was weakened but not eliminated.
- Saul was reluctant to become king. After Samuel anointed him, Saul returned to his regular activities (1 Sam. 11:5).
- Saul led Israel's armies to battle to save the city of Jabesh (1 Sam. 11).
- After an impressive victory, the people of Israel accepted Saul as their king.
- Saul made bad decisions that threatened his own kingship.

Why was Asking for a King a Bad Idea?

- The Tribes of Israel were without a king because God himself was their King. He governed them through the Law (Torah, the first five books of the Bible) and through the leadership of chosen people: judges, priests, prophets at crucial times.
- Israel was a chosen nation. God chose Israel to be his own treasured possession (Ex. 19:5). Israel should not have been like the nations around them (this is the theme of the whole book of Deuteronomy; see, for example, chapters 7 and 8).
- One of the purposes of the Law (Torah) was to help Israel be different from the peoples who lived around them (Deut. 7).

Call of David—The Singing Shepherd

- God rejected Saul because of his rebelliousness.
- God sent Samuel to anoint the new chosen king of Israel.
- When Samuel visited David's father Jesse, Samuel expected the new king to be like Saul: impressive and imposing. Yet, God led the prophet to the last son: a small, young shepherd boy.
- After Samuel anointed him, David went back to his sheep.
- Although God had rejected Saul and anointed David as the new king, Saul continued to be king for sometime—perhaps for another 15 years or so.
- During that time, David came to be part of the royal court as a musician.
- David's music helped Saul find relief from his anguish.

It is good to know that God looks deep in our innermost being, that he knows our secrets, both the great goodness and great evil we are capable of doing. Still, Jesus came to die for each of us so we can become like David: people after God's own heart!

The Battle Is the Lord's

- Just as Saul was tested, David needed to be tested as well.
- Saul's life was filled with fear and depression.
- When the Philistines challenged Israel, the king of Israel had to lead God's armies to victory.
- However, when the mighty Philistine hero, Goliath, challenged the Israelites to fight him, all cowered in terror (1 Sam. 17:11).
- Saul failed again to lead Israel's armies.
- During this battle, Jesse, David's father, sent David to check on his older brothers at the field of battle (1 Sam. 17:17–19).
- As he arrived and heard the commotion in the camp, David was surprised with the Philistine's defiance of God's army.
- With great courage and faith, David accepted the challenge and stepped forward to fight the Philistine.

Contrasting Warriors

The Bible's description of Goliath is important. It stands in contrast to David.

Opponent	Goliath	David
Description	Terrifying, giant warrior	Shepherd boy
Height	Nearly nine feet tall	Unknown and unimpressive
Weapons	Sword, spear, and javelin of bronze and iron; armor weighing about 125 pounds	Shepherd's staff and sling, five pebbles; a heart of faith and complete trust in the Lord

"Who is this uncircumcised Philistine that he should defy the armies of the living God?" (17:26).

David's answer showed his utter confidence in his God: "You come against me with sword and spear and javelin, but I come against you in the name of the Lord Almighty, the God of the armies of Israel, whom you have defied" (17:45). The battle ended before it had even started. Like many other parts of the Bible show, no one and nothing can stand against the Lord of creation (see Ex. 15:1–18).

Israel's Singer of Songs

David was called "Israel's singer of songs." David was gifted artistically as well as with weaponry. Among the many Psalms that are attributed to him are some that form key prophetic texts in the New Testament. Psalm 16:10 is quoted by both Peter and Paul as prophetically fulfilled in Christ's resurrection (Acts 2:27, 13:35). Psalm 110:1 is the most quoted Old Testament verse in the New Testament, and 110:4 figures heavily in the book of Hebrews as pointing to the superior priesthood Christ exercised on our behalf. Jesus himself uses Psalm 110:2 to baffle his critics concerning the question of the Messiah's identity (Matt. 22:41–46).

Ancient armies often allowed a fight between champions to decide the fate of the battle. However, behind the military practice was the understanding that it was not only champions fighting. Rather, the gods themselves fought on behalf of each army. At stake was more than just a battle: the name (or fame) of the Lord himself was on the line.

FRIENDS TO THE END

Among the many events that make David's life unique, his friendship with Jonathan, King Saul's son, stands out:

- The two became friends after David's triumph over Goliath.
- The Scripture says, "Jonathan became one in spirit with David, and he loved him as himself" (1 Sam. 18:1).
- The friendship was costly to Jonathan. At his own risk, Jonathan protected David on more than one occasion. Although King Saul was out to kill David, Jonathan remained true to his bond. Jonathan protected David by giving him advanced knowledge of Saul's plans.
- Before fleeing from Saul's court, David promised to be kind to Jonathan's descendants. They parted as friends with many tears.
- Jonathan died in battle against the Philistines along with his father. David expressed his deep sorrow and love for Jonathan in a poem called "The Lament of the Bow" (2 Sam. 1:17–27). The words, "Your love for me was wonderful, more wonderful than that of women," reflect this deep friendship of precious and rare value.

Jonathan's Token to David by Leighton

ATTITUDES OF THE HEART

Saul's Attitude Toward David		David's Attitude Toward Saul	
Saul was jealous	1 Sam. 18:9	David remained respectful	1 Sam. 18:18
Saul attempted to make David fail	1 Sam. 18:11	David obeyed Saul's command	1 Sam. 18:5
Saul tried to kill David	1 Sam. 19:1–24	David refused to kill Saul	1 Sam. 24:6; 26:9–12
"I have treated you badly"	1 Sam. 24:17	"You have treated me well"	1 Sam. 24:17

HOW THE MIGHTY HAVE FALLEN

David's life took an unpredictable turn. David became an outlaw, escaping Saul's many attempts to kill him (1 Sam. 22:1–2). The Bible describes a difficult, if exciting, time in exile from his land. David's life went from being an independent fighter, to being in the midst of the Philistines—acting like a madman to avoid being killed (1 Sam. 27)—to serve as a mercenary for the Philistine king Achish (1 Sam. 29).

While Saul remained acting king of Israel, especially in the Northern Tribes. David increased his influence and power, especially in the Southern Tribes. After Saul's death, David strengthened his position in the Southern Tribes and became king of Judah. In the North, Saul's son Ishbosheth became king over Israel (2 Sam. 2:8–9). During two years (2 Sam. 2:10), the two kingdoms warred with each other, but "David grew stronger and stronger, while the house of Saul grew weaker and weaker" (2 Sam. 3:1).

David Contemplating the Head of Goliath by Orazio Gentileschi

> ### Of Fools and Fair Women
> During David's outlaw years, as he struggled to survive the elements and a hostile, insane king, he must have had a difficult time maintaining the compassion and civility necessary for kingly service. The story of David and Abigail shows David's sensitivity to his own failings and serves as another reminder of what made him "a man after God's own heart": "May you be blessed for your good judgment and for keeping me from bloodshed this day and from avenging myself with my own hands."
> (See 1 Sam. 25.)

SAUL'S DECLINE AND DAVID'S RISE TO POWER

Saul	David
Saul hunted down David to kill him. The king neglected his task of protecting the land against its enemies, especially the Philistines.	David fled Saul fearing for his life. The young warrior continued to fight and defeat the Philistines.
Saul's relationships with his family suffered from the king's increasing rage.	David reaffirmed and strengthened his relationship with Jonathan, Saul's eldest.
Saul consulted a medium to conjure Samuel because the Lord did not answer him.	David constantly inquired the Lord for his next decision (1 Sam. 23:2, 4; 30:8).
Saul took his own life to avoid falling into the hands of the Philistines	David lamented the death of Saul and Jonathan. He became the king of Israel.
Saul's heir Ishbosheth was assassinated.	David executed the murderers of Ishbosheth.

DAVID'S VICTORIES

Because of his focus on the Northern territories and his obsession to capture David, King Saul never conquered Jerusalem. Since the times of Joshua, the Israelites had been unable to conquer the city (see Josh. 15:63). The city belonged to a Jebusite tribe (2 Sam. 5:6–15). The leaders of Jerusalem were very confident in the strength of the city. They bragged that even blind people could repel David's attack (2 Sam. 5:6). However, with a brilliant military move, David conquered the city and made it his own.

Conquering Jerusalem was David's first action as king of Israel. Jerusalem was important because:

1. Jerusalem was important for David as the new king of all Israel. Hebron was a traditional seat of power for the Southern Tribes. David had to unify the North and the South.
2. Jerusalem became a symbol of the unity of the kingdom of Israel. Eventually, Jerusalem, David's city (2 Sam. 5:7), became God's city as well (2 Chron. 6:6).

David's victory against the Philistines was David's second action as king of Israel. Throughout this time, David continued to inquire of the Lord for guidance (2 Sam. 5:19). God continued to give David victory after victory. Another important victory was for David to bring the ark of the covenant to Jerusalem. Although the actual transport of the ark to Jerusalem proved tragic with the death of Uzzah, eventually David brought it to Jerusalem with great celebration and joy (2 Sam. 6). Bringing the ark to Jerusalem showed David's commitment to God. The ark represented God's presence. David recognized that God himself was the King of Israel. He recognized that all authority and blessings proceeded directly from God's presence.

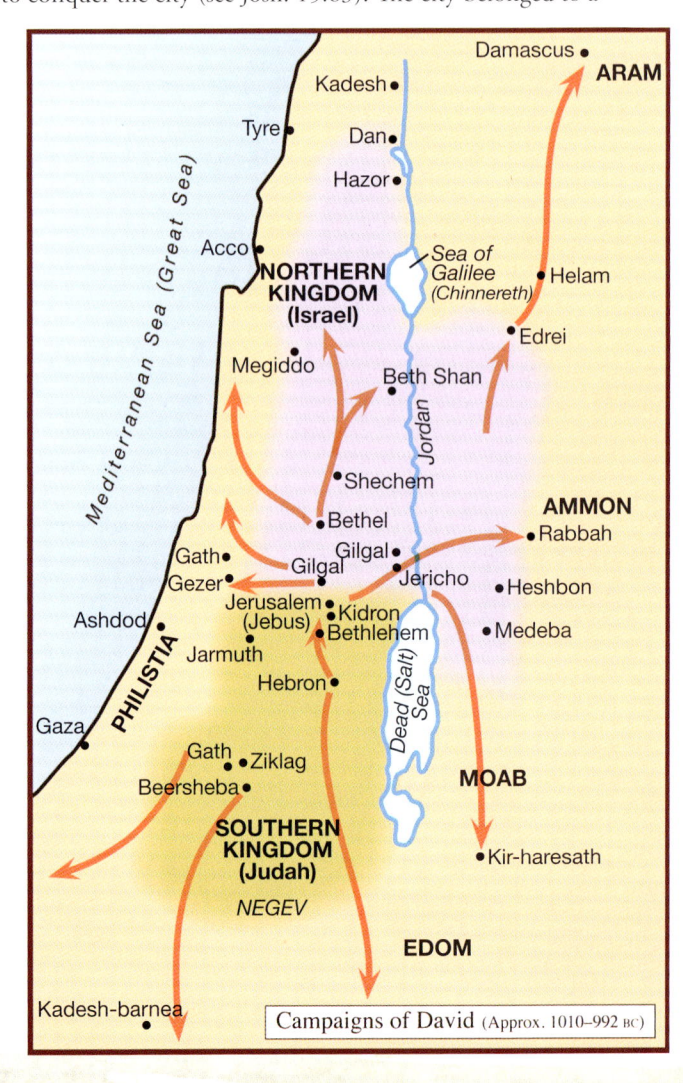

Campaigns of David (Approx. 1010–992 BC)

God's Covenant with David

The high point of David's life came in a moment when David experienced some peace. "The Lord had given him rest from all his enemies around him" (2 Sam. 7:1; see Deut. 3:20; 12:10; 25:19). During moments of respite, David wondered about a house for the Lord. The prophet Nathan first agreed that David should build a temple. God, however, directed the prophet to bring a different message to the king. David would not build the house of God. Rather, God would build a house for David! It was a reversal of what David expected. This reversal plays on two meanings of the expression building a house: (1) Building an actual temple ("the house of God"); (2) building a dynasty ("the house of David").

God's dwelling place

The Bible makes it clear that God chose Jerusalem, Zion, to be his dwelling place on earth. Just like he had chosen to live in the midst of his people in the wilderness after the Exodus, God chose to continue living in their midst. However, David was not to build it. First Chronicles 22:8 states the reason: David was a man of war with much blood on his hands. Instead, Solomon, David's son, would build the temple (1 Chronicles 22:9).

David's house

Another characteristic of ancient kings was that they established dynasties, or houses. The principle that the Israelite king would not be like the kings of the other nations still applied. God's promise did not intend to be merely for David. The establishment of David's house had enormous implications for God's own plans. God made a covenant with David to use his family line to bring about a change unlike any other in history. Through David's lineage, the Messiah, God's own Son, would be born to redeem the world. This promise was also God's confirmation of David as Israel's king.

A King-Sized Sin

As David rejoiced in his victories and blessings, he stayed home while his troops went out to fight against the Amelakites. During an idle stroll, David saw a beautiful woman bathing and lusted after her. The woman was Bathsheba, daughter of one and wife of another of David's most trusted men (known as "The Thirty," 2 Sam. 23:34, 39). What the king desired, the king got. When Bathsheba became pregnant, David tried to hide his sin by making Uriah, Bathsheba's husband, sleep with her. When Uriah refused to do so because of his military responsibilities, David stepped up his plans. He plotted to kill Uriah in the field of battle. After Uriah died as a soldier and Bathsheba mourned him, she became David's wife. "But the thing David had done displeased the Lord" (2 Sam. 11:27). God sent the prophet Nathan to confront David. Although David thought he had gotten away with his crimes, Nathan's clever story caused David to discover and recognize his sin (2 Sam. 12:1–12).

> **Family Ties**
> Bathsheba also happened to be the granddaughter of Ahithophel, David's counselor who later betrayed David by siding with Absalom in his rebellion.

David's sin was terrible: coveting, adultery, abuse of his authority, and finally murder. In the ancient world, kings had absolute authority. If they desired to take a plot of land (or someone's wife or house), they just did it (see 1 Kings 21). Saul attempted to act like any other king by ignoring Samuel's instructions: he acted as a law unto himself. David, on the other hand, knew he had committed a terrible sin and tried to hide it. He knew he was below God's law and accountable to it. Despite David's foolishness, God's will mattered to him. David showed his repentance by confessing his sin (2 Sam. 12:13), fasting and praying (2 Sam. 12:16–23).

Both David and Saul did great evil before God. However, the effects on Saul and David's role in God's plans were very different. Saul's rebelliousness cut him out of his role as king. David's sins brought about a terrible punishment but did not affect his role in God's plans to bring the Messiah through his lineage.

A man after God's own heart

God punished David's sin. The punishment was as terrible as the sin. The prophet Nathan, who had brought great words of assurance and affirmation to David (2 Sam. 7), brought the dire news to the king. Because of his violent acts, "the sword will never depart from your house" (2 Sam. 12:10). In addition, the baby that was still to be born would also die (12:14). David's agony is reflected in Psalm 51. Despite the severe punishment, God forgave David! (2 Sam. 12:13). God's amazing grace accepted David's repentance, faith, and regret.

David is one of us: people who have sinned, sought, and found God's forgiveness.

Bathsheba Goes to King David by Cecchino del Salviati

David's Family Tree

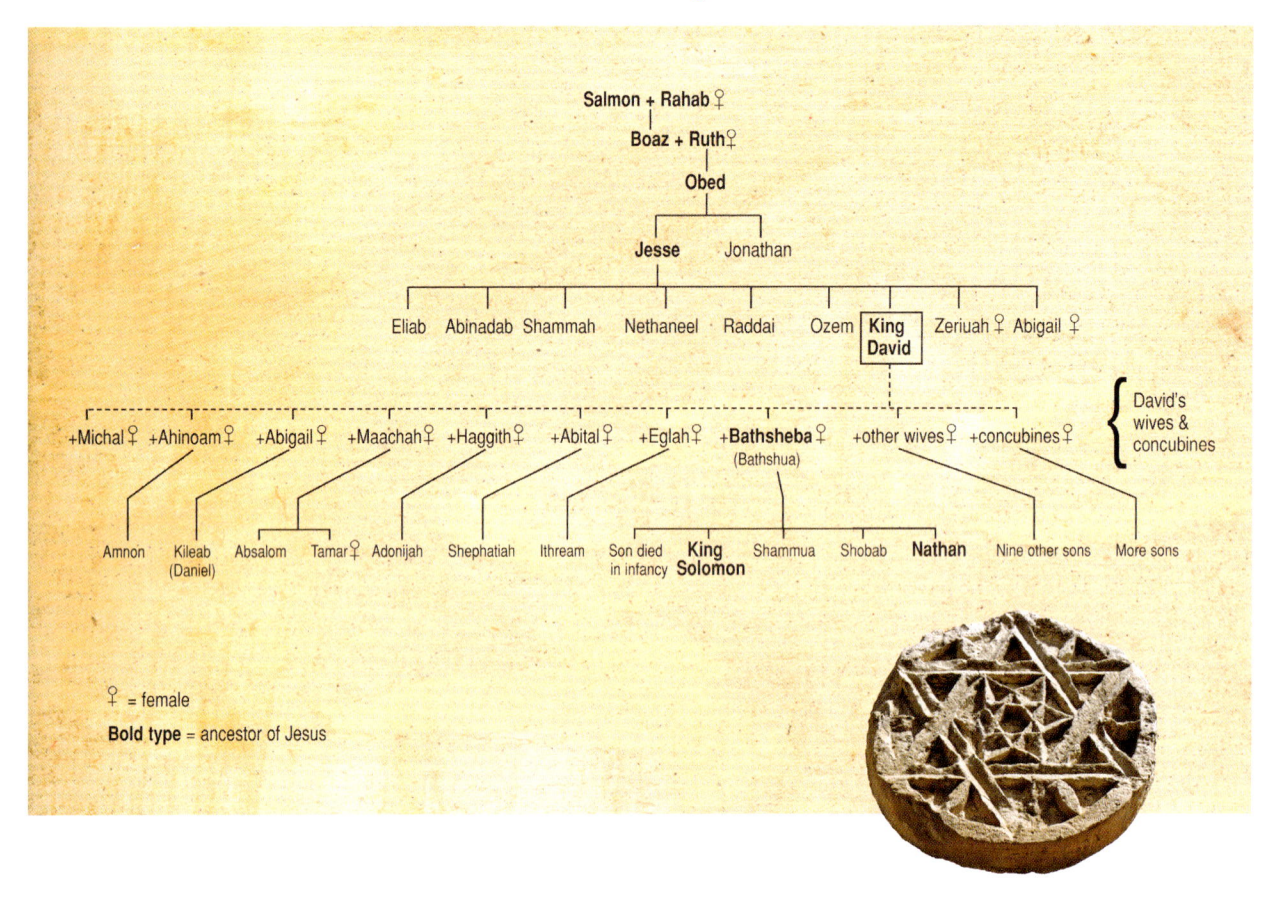

```
                    Salmon + Rahab ♀
                        │
                    Boaz + Ruth ♀
                        │
                      Obed
                        │
            ┌───────────┴───────────┐
           Jesse                  Jonathan
             │
  ┌──────┬──────┬──────┬──────┬──────┬──────┬──────┬──────┐
 Eliab Abinadab Shammah Nethaneel Raddai Ozem King  Zeruiah♀ Abigail♀
                                          David
```

David's wives & concubines:
+Michal♀ +Ahinoam♀ +Abigail♀ +Maachah♀ +Haggith♀ +Abital♀ +Eglah♀ +Bathsheba♀ (Bathshua) +other wives♀ +concubines♀

Children:
Amnon | Kileab (Daniel) | Absalom, Tamar♀ | Adonijah | Shephatiah | Ithream | Son died in infancy, King Solomon | Shammua, Shobab, Nathan | Nine other sons | More sons

♀ = female
Bold type = ancestor of Jesus

The Sword Will Never Depart

The Bible provides sorrowful examples of God's punishment happening in David's family throughout the generations.

Reference	Event	Result
2 Sam. 13	Amnon raped Tamar.	Absalom killed Amnon.
2 Sam. 14–18	Absalom rebelled against David and tried to take over the kingdom.	David had to escape Jerusalem. Absalom took over the kingdom and made David's concubines his. Absalom dies later escaping David's armies.
1 Kings 1	Before David died, Adonijah declares himself as the new king of Israel.	God chose Solomon as the new king. However, the kingdom would eventually be divided into two kingdoms (1 Kings 12–14).

An Inglorious Ending

After much struggle and grief, David arrived at the end of his life. Through the book of Samuel, David had been a strong man of war and authority. However, in 1 Kings 1:1–4, King David is an old man, incapable of staying warm, and out of touch with what is happening in his kingdom.

David's last kingly act was choosing the next king of Israel. Instead of choosing Adonijah, the oldest son alive (and who was already acting as though he was the next king), David chose Solomon. Although the book of Kings is not clear why David made this choice, the book of Chronicles states that God himself had chosen Solomon (1 Chron. 22:6–10).

A Glorious Foreshadowing

Through David's life, we can see God setting up history for the coming of Christ. Many events in David's life point to the life of Jesus Christ, the Messiah.

David	Christ
David was pursued by Saul, the rejected king of Israel (1 Sam. 19).	Jesus was pursued by Herod, the illegitimate king of Judah (Matt. 2:13–18).
David's enemies came after him, but were overpowered by the Holy Spirit (1 Sam. 19:18–24).	Jesus' enemies came to arrest him and were overpowered by the Holy Spirit at Jesus' word (John 18:1–11).
David had a friend and advocate in Jonathan who spoke up for David at the risk of his own life (1 Sam. 20).	Jesus had an advocate in John the Baptist who spoke up for Jesus at the risk of his own life (John 3:22–30).
David was tempted and fell (2 Sam. 11).	Jesus was tempted and did not fall (Heb. 4:15).
Even with David's imperfections, God loved David and made a covenant with him (2 Sam. 7:11–16).	Christ, in his love for humanity, made a new covenant (Matt. 26:28; Heb. 12:24).
David's son, Solomon, whose name means "Peace," inherited David's throne (1 Kings 1:29–30).	David's offspring, Jesus, is called the Prince of Peace and he holds David's throne forever (Isaiah 9:6; Luke 1:31–33).

When we see David's life in the light of this great truth, we can have hope to believe that our own lives, too, point to Christ, and joy in the Lord of history who makes wonderful stories out of us.

Anointed Ones

David, the great king of Israel, is one of the most important characters in the Bible. David was a powerful warrior, an insightful musician, and a hero of the faith. He is also important for his connection to Christ.

God promised to build a house for David (2 Sam. 7:8–16). God meant that David's lineage would endure forever. God fulfilled his promise with the birth of Solomon. However, the greatest fulfillment of this promise is the birth of Jesus Christ.

The words *Messiah* and *Christ* mean *anointed*. That is, when God chose a person for some task, that person would have been anointed with oil. Anointment symbolized God's choice, empowerment, and favor on the person anointed. People were anointed for specific tasks. Over time, it became clear that God's plans included a special Messiah. God anointed Jesus to be King and Savior of humanity.

All human rulers were flawed and sinful; but Christ, although fully human, was flawless: "...one who has been tempted in every way, just as we—yet was without sin" (Hebrews 4:15). Through Christ's obedience, death, and resurrection, God would forgive and make a people for himself. In Christ, all of God's promises and plans come to pass.

Time Line of David's Life

Events in approximate order. Exact dates unknown.

- David is born (1041 BC)
- Saul becomes jealous of David's popularity and success
- Saul's son Jonathan declares lifelong friendship with David
- David commands some of King Saul's troops
- David marries King Saul's daughter, Michal
- Saul tries to kill David; David lives in exile
- Saul takes Michal and marries her to another man
- David gathers a band of soldiers; they fight Israel's enemies
- David kills Goliath (1022 BC)
- Samuel anoints David as king
- Saul's armies chase David
- David becomes an outlaw
- David marries Abigail and Ahinoam
- Nabal refuses hospitality to David
- David spares Saul's life
- Abner, cousin of King Saul, supports Saul's son Ishbosheth until insulted
- David rules in Hebron 7 years and 6 months (1011 BC)
- Six sons born to David, including Absalom and Adonijah
- David made king of Judah at age 30 in Hebron; Ishbosheth (Saul's son) made king of Israel by Abner
- King Saul and son Jonathan die in battle with Philistines (1011 BC)
- Samuel dies (1013 BC)
- David lives among the Philistines
- David spares Saul's life a second time

(continued below)

- Ishbosheth murdered by own generals
- David marries four more wives and takes several concubines, has more children
- David made king of Israel; conquers Jerusalem and makes it his capital; rules 33 years (1005 BC)
- David orders the ark of the covenant to be returned to Shiloh from Kiriath Jearim
- David defeats the Philistines at Baal Perazim
- Celebration when the ark returns; Michal scorns David's fervor
- God promises that David's kingdom will last forever
- David averts plague by a sacrifice to God on what would later be the Temple Mount
- Absalom rebels against his father and dies
- David kills Uriah, marries Bathsheba, and repents. Solomon is born (996 BC)
- David takes Jonathan's son Mephibosheth into his household
- David consolidates kingdom by victories over Philistines, Moabites, Arameans, Edomites, and Ammonites
- David dies, leaves kingdom to son Solomon (971 BC)

Saul and David by Rembrandt

David by Caravaggio

Death of King Saul by Elie Marcuse

David and Uriah by Rembrandt

David with the Head of Goliath by M. Stanzione

ESTHER

Chosen For a Time Such As This

When the opposition seems unbeatable, does God care? Am I alone in this world, with its suffering, injustice, and pain? Where can I go to resign when life becomes too tough? How can I risk my reputation, comfort, and future to rescue others?

These are questions that come up in the life of Esther.

It's easy to dismiss Queen Esther as a lucky young woman who won the heart of the king. But realistically, she was a woman with a tragic background and dangerous secret that could cost her life and her family's. She was married to a king who destroyed peoples' lives on a whim and had a history of killing people close to him. Worse still, the king's favorite counselor and chief advisor was a mortal enemy of Esther's family. Esther had to keep a low profile, keeping her secret, hoping he wouldn't make the connection.

For Esther, life was unfair. But her story brings hope to all who face trouble by showing how God works even through the fears and dangers.

Character	Genealogy	Actions in History
King Ahasuerus (Xerxes)	Persian king Son of Darius I of the royal Persian line	The king in the Book of Esther Invaded Greece, but later defeated by Greece Assassinated by courtiers
Queen Vashti	Queen of King Xerxes May be Amestris, daughter of Otanes	Loses her position as queen for disobeying the king's orders
Mordecai	Son of Jair (Esther 2:5) of the first royal line of Israel (Kish/Saul 1 Sam. 9:1)	Raised his cousin Esther Prevents the assassination of the king Becomes the king's main advisor
Esther	Mordecai's cousin	Lost both of her parents; raised by her cousin. Wins over the king to become queen in a dangerous time Saves the Jewish people from genocide
Haman	Born of the royal line of the Amalekites (line of King Agag) an important detail.	King's main advisor Plots the destruction of all the Jews in the Persian Empire Is hung on the gallows

The Missing Character

Yet the missing character in the book of Esther is the one who has the largest role: God, conspicuous by his absence, who uses the actions of the human characters to shape all of history.

- God worked through the Persian king's own weaknesses to preserve the Jewish people.
- God worked through the courage of Mordecai and Esther to keep the Jewish people from harm and redeem a family name (1 Samuel 9:1; 15).
- God overturned Haman's evil plans, and fulfilled a 500-year-old prophecy of judgment on the Amalekites (Haman's ancestors) (1 Samuel 15:1–3).

Pomp in the Persian Palace

This story takes place in the Persian royal court in Susa—a world of power where decisions, obsessions, and whims of the people with power in this world affect thousands. The book of Esther presents a childish, whimsical, unpredictable, and dangerous King Xerxes who acts in a drunken stupor, thoughtlessly punishes his own queen, is easily swayed by advisers

Susa

Susa (Shushan in the Old Testament) is an ancient city in Iran today. Some of the oldest written records referenced this city. As Empires appeared and disappeared, Susa became Akkadian, Babylonian, Assyrian, Persian, Macedonian, Parthian, Roman, and Muslim.

In the 6th century BC, King Cyrus' son, Cambyses II, transferred the capital of the Persian government from Pasargadae to Susa. His son, Darius I (Xerxes' father), extended and improved a road from Susa to Asia Minor in the West and to India in the East. This road was known as the "Royal Road." The road was crucial for Imperial communication and commerce. Several centuries later the Royal Road became part of the "Silk Road" that joined the West to India and China.

---

around him, and is a danger to his people. However, these very qualities generate not only the main crisis in the book, but also its solution.

The book opens with Queen Vashti refusing to obey the king who wants to parade his beautiful wife in front of his banquet guests. On the urging of his advisors, the king deposes Vashti, leaving himself without a queen. Vashti's act of defiance sets up a series of events that will include conspiracy, pride, lies, murderous plots, unexpected heroism, and deliverance. A beleaguered, young Jewish woman is placed in a position of power and responsibility. The future of her people, endangered by a vindictive and ancient enemy of God's people, Haman, the Agagite, is in her hands. But, where is God in all of this? Are the Jews in Persia, and in many other places of the ancient world, all alone?

Persia

Persia became the dominant power of the ancient world in the 6th century BC. Under the leadership of Cyrus the Great, the Persian Empire (also known as the Achaemenid Empire) conquered Babylon in 539 BC. Besides being a brilliant warrior and conqueror, Cyrus was also a great politician. He created a policy to send people previously conquered in Babylonian and Assyrian times back to their homelands.

The Bible portrays Cyrus as God's instrument to free and restore the Jews to the Promised Land (Ezra 1:1–6, 6:1–5; Isaiah 44:23–45:8; 2 Chronicles 36:22–23).

Thus, a group of Jews returned to Jerusalem to rebuild the walls and the temple around 515 BC. Other Jews, like Mordecai and Esther, remained in Persia.

The Persians remained in power until 330 BC when Alexander the Great, the Macedonian conqueror, defeated the armies of Darius III and occupied Persepolis, the capital of the Persian Empire.

The "Cyrus Cylinder" proclaims Cyrus as the legitimate king of Babylon. It also describes how Cyrus won the respect and favor of the Babylonian priests when he restored the temples in Babylon.

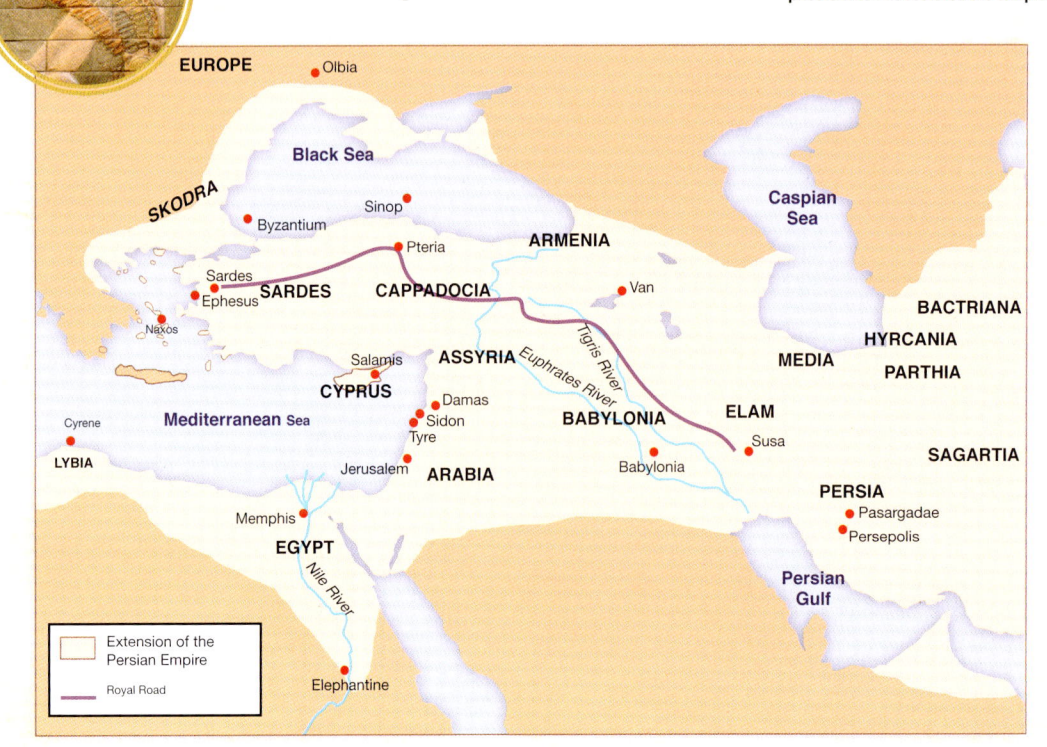

> **What's In A Name?**
>
> The books of Daniel and Esther both depict life for Jews in exile. They show that Jews in prominent places had both Hebrew and Babylonian names.

Hebrew Name	Meaning	Alternate Name	Meaning
Daniel	God is my judge	Belteshazzar	Bel protect his life. (Bel is another name for Marduk.)
Hadassah	Myrtle	Esther	Star
(No Jewish name mentioned)		Mordecai	Related to the Babylonian chief god Marduk

One Queen, Two Identities

After Vashti is stripped of her crown, the king finds a new queen: a young, beautiful woman whose identity seems irrelevant at the time. Her name is Esther. On Mordecai's instructions, Esther hides her Jewish identity and successfully blends into the Persian culture. The king is so pleased with his new queen that he throws a great banquet in her honor and proclaims a holiday throughout all the provinces.

Beauty Secrets

Everything we know about Esther's personality is derived from her actions and the responses of people around her. The expression "won his favor" (2:9, 15) is a clue to Esther's personality. The common expression is for someone to "find favor" with a king. However, Esther "won" the king's favor, showing Esther as active and purposeful. She is no passive and powerless observer in this story; rather, she shows herself to be daring, intelligent, and strong despite having been orphaned in her youth.

But before Esther won the king's favor, she won the favor of the man in charge of all the virgins. Hegai "quickly" provided Esther with the diet and beauty treatments required, and even advanced her to the best spot in the harem! Clearly, Esther showed pleasing qualities that wore well with those who mattered. But the depth of her ability to choose wisely and to trust worthy advice is shown in her willingness to rely on Hegai's advice as to what to bring with her when it was Esther's turn to go in to the king. And the payoff is big—the king is so pleased that he crowns Esther as his new queen.

In the dangerous atmosphere of the Persian court, where conspiracies were thick and executions routine, Esther's apparent serenity stands out. She "won the favor of everyone who saw her." Her life must have seemed charmed—until the royal shoe dropped.

> **King Xerxes (486-465 BC)**
>
> - Called Ahasuerus in the Bible
> - Known for his war against the Greeks: Despite his famous loss at the Battle of Thermopylae in 480 BC (the basis for the famed Leonidas of Sparta and his 300 warriors), Xerxes led his armies to sack Athens.
> - A year later, however, the Greeks expelled the Persian army from the Greek islands to Asia Minor.
> - Much of the information about this war comes from the accounts of the historian Herodotus.

> **Why Were the Jews in Persia?**
>
> In 722 BC the powerful king of Assyria, Sargon II, conquered and destroyed Samaria. Almost two hundred years later, Nebuchadnezzar, king of Babylon, conquered the kingdom of Judah.
>
> From 597 BC through 586 BC, Nebuchadnezzar systematically undermined Judah until he destroyed Jerusalem and its temple.
>
> To avoid rebellion and exert complete dominance, both Assyria and Babylonia deported people. By uprooting people from their land and their gods, they were easier to control. Some of the Jews who were taken from their homes during these years went to Persia.
>
> God's presence in the Jerusalem temple was a direct source of assurance and security for the Israelites, God's chosen people. If God was with them and dwelt among them, who could dare challenge them? However, the Babylonians not only conquered them but also destroyed their temple. Because every region had its own local gods, wars were also representations of divine wars. In conquering Judah, the Babylonians could claim that their god, Marduk, was superior to the Jewish God, Yahweh—a tremendous spiritual blow to the Jews (see for example 2 Kings 18:31–35).
>
> Exiled Jews not only lost their homes and their land, but also the certainty of God's presence. In light of this desperation and spiritual grief, the words of the prophet Isaiah echo powerfully: "Comfort, comfort my people, says your God" (Isaiah 40:1).
>
> When King Cyrus allowed the Jews to return to Jerusalem about 70 years later, an event Isaiah prophesied as God's own action (Isaiah 44:28–45:13), many who had already begun a new life in exile stayed in Babylon and Persia.

Why did Mordecai Refuse to Bow?

The text does not specify the reasons for Mordecai's refusal.

Possible reasons:

- Mordecai's religious conviction that only God deserves praise, or
- A reflection of the ancient enmity between the Amalekites and Israelites. Mordecai's refusal provides the excuse for Haman's hatred and homicidal plans.

Intrigue in the Persian Court

Esther's cousin Mordecai, a Jew from the tribe of Benjamin, holds a high post at the royal residence. Mordecai overhears two guards plotting to kill the king, which he reports to Queen Esther who exposes the plot. The Bible relays this event without giving it much importance, but it turns out to be crucial in the climax of the story. Not only does the event determine Mordecai's future, it shows the intolerant reaction that the king has to betrayal and deception—he hangs the two guards on gallows.

Because of Mordecai's position of high visibility in the royal residence, Haman, an Amalekite and the king's closest advisor, notices Mordecai. Haman is a vain and conceited man and the mortal enemy of the Jews. Haman determines that everyone should treat him as royalty. However, Mordecai refuses to bow down before him. Haman persuades the king to approve an edict he has written to annihilate all the Jews—men, women, and children—in every province of Persia.

A Queen's Courage

When Haman's plan for the Jews' destruction becomes public, Mordecai laments, and the Jews join him. Mordecai turns to Queen Esther to save the Jews by pleading with the king. Mordecai gives this message to Esther: "And who knows but that you have come to royal position for such a time as this."

Esther requests that Mordecai and the Jews join her in a three-day fast, after which she submits to whatever is to happen: "I will go to the king, even though it is against the law. And if I perish, I perish" (Esther 4:14, 16). Esther's memorable words are born from faith and fear. She is afraid of the unpredictable nature of the king who could legally have her executed for approaching him without being called. She has faith that someone above the powerful king himself is in control. In either case, these words show Esther's courage and willingness to risk her life for her people.

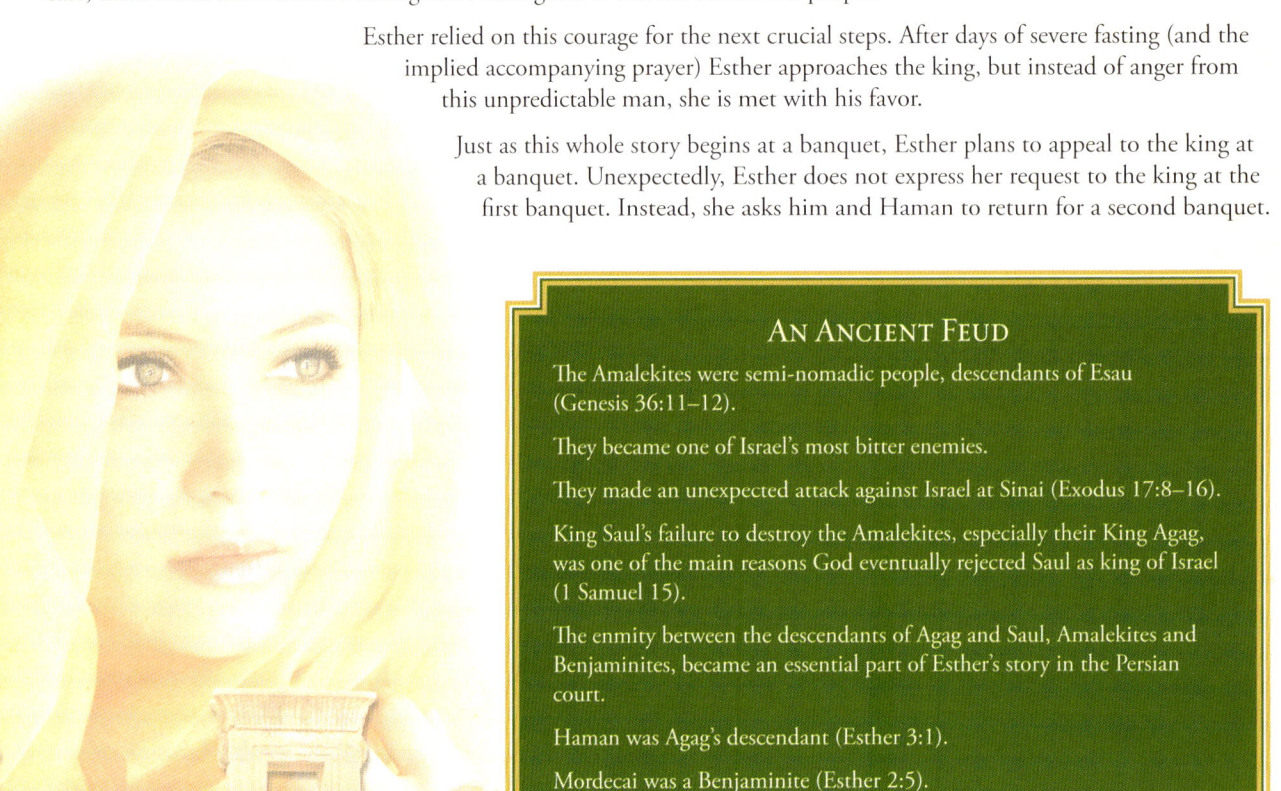

Esther relied on this courage for the next crucial steps. After days of severe fasting (and the implied accompanying prayer) Esther approaches the king, but instead of anger from this unpredictable man, she is met with his favor.

Just as this whole story begins at a banquet, Esther plans to appeal to the king at a banquet. Unexpectedly, Esther does not express her request to the king at the first banquet. Instead, she asks him and Haman to return for a second banquet.

An Ancient Feud

The Amalekites were semi-nomadic people, descendants of Esau (Genesis 36:11–12).

They became one of Israel's most bitter enemies.

They made an unexpected attack against Israel at Sinai (Exodus 17:8–16).

King Saul's failure to destroy the Amalekites, especially their King Agag, was one of the main reasons God eventually rejected Saul as king of Israel (1 Samuel 15).

The enmity between the descendants of Agag and Saul, Amalekites and Benjaminites, became an essential part of Esther's story in the Persian court.

Haman was Agag's descendant (Esther 3:1).

Mordecai was a Benjaminite (Esther 2:5).

Fasting Turns to Feasting

The repetition of Esther's banquets parallels the king's banquets earlier in the story.

The King's Banquets	Esther's Banquets
The king calls Queen Vashti to the banquet, but she refuses to come.	Esther invites the king and Haman to a banquet; they agree to go.
The king becomes furious and listens to bad advice.	The king is pleased and generous toward Esther.
The king rejects Vashti as his queen.	The king confirms Esther as his queen by his willingness to grant her any favor. Esther invites the king and Haman to a second banquet.
Esther wins the king's favor to become queen.	Having the king's favor, Esther reveals her request and Jewish identity to the king. The king becomes furious and condemns Haman.
As a celebration, the king gives a great banquet in honor of Esther.	Queen Esther and her people are thus saved from Haman's evil plans. They celebrate with feasting and establish the Feast of Purim to commemorate the event.

Royal Humiliation

Between Esther's two banquets, another important event takes place. Haman's wife and friends advise him to build gallows and ask the king to hang Mordecai on them. Haman is so prideful and confident of his success that he builds the gallows, but Haman is doomed.

Meanwhile, back at the palace, the king has insomnia. To help him sleep, the king orders the chronicles of his reign to be read to him. By apparent coincidence, the chronicles contain the record of Mordecai exposing the plot to kill the king. When the king is reminded of this event, he wishes to follow tradition by rewarding the hero. Instead of deciding on his own how to reward Mordecai, the indecisive king looks around for someone to ask how to do this. Although Haman is actually approaching the king to request the execution of Mordecai, the king requests Haman's advice on how to honor a hero! In an ironic reversal Haman is bitterly humiliated when the king orders him to follow his own advice and honor Mordecai as a hero!

Haman returns home to receive a harsh warning from his wife and advisors: "Since Mordecai, before whom your downfall has started, is of Jewish origin, you cannot stand against him" (Esther 6:13). Before Haman can respond, the king's officers hurry him off to Esther's second banquet.

Such a reversal of fortune is an illustration of this prayer in the Bible: "He raises the poor from the dust and lifts the needy from the ash heap; he seats them with princes and has them inherit a throne of honor" (1 Samuel 2:8).

Character	Traits	Life Lessons
King Xerxes	Foolish, rash, and acts in fits of anger	"A wise man fears the Lord and shuns evil, but a fool is hotheaded and reckless" (Proverbs 14:16). "Everyone should be quick to listen, slow to speak and slow to become angry, for a man's anger does not bring about the righteous life that God desires" (James 1:19–20).
Esther	Humble, faithful, and courageous even though fearful	"The Lord preserves the faithful, but the proud he pays back in full. Be strong and take heart, all you who hope in the Lord" (Psalm 31:23–24). "Humble yourselves before the Lord and he will lift you up" (James 4:10).
Haman	Prideful and arrogant	"Pride goes before destruction, a haughty spirit before a fall" (Proverbs 16:18). "There is no wisdom, no insight, no plan that can succeed against the Lord" (Proverbs 21:30).
Mordecai	Dedicated, and was used as an instrument of justice	"The Lord works righteousness and justice for all the oppressed" (Psalm 103:6). "Rescue the weak and needy; deliver them from the hand of the wicked" (Psalm 82:4).

Irony and Despair

At Esther's second banquet, she chooses to express her request. When Esther reveals her Jewish identity and Haman's plot to destroy her and her people, the king's anger is not surprising. Haman realizes his doom at once.

The king leaves the room in a fit of rage. In the meantime, Haman realizes his only chance to escape alive. He falls over Esther in despair, seeking her favor. Haman had wanted all to bow down to him, now Haman is begging for his life. Haman's wife had already anticipated this "falling" (Esther 6:13). As this happens, the king enters the room.

The king accuses Haman of attempting to molest Esther. How could the king misunderstand Haman's intentions? Did he need a further reason to condemn him? This scene is parallel to the conspiracy Mordecai discovered earlier in chapter 2. There, the king made sure the information was correct before condemning the guards who had conspired against him. Here, Haman falling over the queen gives King Xerxes the perfect excuse to avoid investigation. In the ancient world, taking a king's wife or concubine was a claim to the throne (for example, that is what Absalom did with David's concubines in 2 Samuel 16:21–22). In another "coincidence," one of the servants happens to remember that Haman had built an enormous gallows to hang Mordecai. Ironically, Haman is hung on those very gallows.

Purim Celebrations Today

Purim today is a minor festival which many Jews no longer celebrate. For those who do celebrate it as a religious holiday, it is a joyous celebration of God's grace and liberation, with parties, food, and gifts. During the service at the synagogue, as the story of Esther is read, people hiss and boo every time Haman's name is mentioned and cheer when Mordecai's name is mentioned. There are four main traditions people observe for Purim:

- listening to a reading of the Book of Esther,
- giving of gifts—usually food, pastries, or other sweets,
- giving charity to the poor as a way to express gratitude to God,
- eating a special meal in community to celebrate God's saving actions.

One of the special foods for this festival is a pastry called *hamantaschen*. They are triangle-shaped cookies filled with fruit (prune, dates, apricot) or a mixture of poppy seeds. In some traditions, the name *hamantaschen* refers to Haman's hat (or ears) which fell when he was executed.

Human Choices and God's Sovereignty

Human choices are real and have consequences.	God works through human choices.
Human choices do not and cannot deter God's action or his plan.	God does not approve evil but may use it to further his ultimate plan of salvation and judgment for the world.
We are foolish to think we can thwart God.	Wisdom is shown in acting according to God's principles.

One More Request

Although the king's fury subsides after Haman's hanging (7:10), the original decree to destroy the Jews is still in force. Esther requests one more favor of the king. The request is similar to Haman's own request in chapter 3. The king's response is equally indifferent in both cases: he leaves the writing of the decree to someone else. Since "no document written in the king's name and sealed with his ring can be revoked" (8:8), the king allows Mordecai and Esther to write another edict to spare the Jews from destruction. Mordecai receives the king's signet ring, which grants him the same status that Haman previously enjoyed. Mordecai and Esther write the edict in the name of the king sealed with the signet ring. The narratives of the writing and communication of both edicts are parallel.

Each edict produces a reaction from the city of Susa—the Persian capital—and the Jewish people. In the first edict, "the city of Susa was bewildered" (3:15) and "there was great mourning among the Jews" (4:3). But upon news of the second edict, "the city of Susa held a joyous celebration" and for the Jews it was a time of "happiness and joy, gladness and honor" (8:15–16).

Chapter 9 commemorates the salvation of the exiled Jews in the Persian Empire. It recognizes the reversal of fortunes (9:1). The Jews moved from lament and mourning to rejoicing and celebration: "I will turn their mourning into gladness; I will give them comfort and joy instead of sorrow" (Jeremiah 31:13). This event became an annual festival, similar to the Passover. Although God saved his people on many occasions, only a few are remembered with festivals.

Important historical and cultural events in the 5th century BC (499–400 BC)		
Approx. Date	**Israel/Mesopotamia**	**Greece/Egypt/China**
500–450 BC	Judah continues in exile in Babylon and Persia. The first group of exiled Jews returns to Jerusalem with Ezra and Nehemiah (around 458 BC). Around 486 BC, Xerxes I of Persia makes Esther his queen. Xerxes I is assassinated in 465 BC. Persia continues its expansion to the West and faces the Greeks.	Confucius teaches throughout China around 495 BC. Egypt is under Persian rule. The Battle of Thermopylae between the Persians and the Spartan King Leonidas occurs in 480 BC. After the Greeks defeat the Persians, the First Peloponnesian War begins between Athens and Sparta in 457 BC. Lives of Pericles, Athenian politician; Sophocles, Euripides, Aristophanes, Greek dramatists; Herodotus, historian; Hippocrates, physician; Anaxagoras and Socrates, philosophers.
449–400 BC	This is where the Bible ends its history of Israel. Persia administers the land of Israel.	The Second Peloponnesian War begins in 431 BC. Sparta defeats Athens in 404 BC.

Reversal of Fortune

The great reversal in Susa is still remembered in the feast of Purim, which is celebrated between February and March. The word Purim comes from a Hebrew word meaning "lot" (pur). Ironically, Haman used the word first. Haman chose the date when the Jews would be destroyed by casting a lot (something like dice). On the very date that Haman had planned for the destruction of the Jews he lost his life, showing that coincidence does not exist, but God is in control of what happens. "The lot is cast into the lap, but its every decision is from the Lord" (Proverbs 16:33).

The story ends with a brief epilogue highlighting Mordecai's position in Persia. It reassures the reader that the Jews were safe and prosperous even in this distant land.

God's Presence and Absence

An important question arises when reading the book of Esther: Where is God in this story? The name of God or any explicit reference to him is missing. The apparent absence of God is more than an oversight. It is a theological point, one that is expressed through the literary medium. The Jews in exile had to answer crucial questions about themselves: Were they still part of God's people? Could they lay claim to God's promises to Abraham? Was God with them? In the past, God had manifested himself with power in miracles of salvation and liberation. Would God also act there in Persia, away from the land God had promised Abraham?

The book provides a series of events when things first fell apart and then came together. For the person of faith, those who know God's actions in history, God is present and active in the story. As shown above, there are different ways the writer reminds readers of God's actions: subtle references to Exodus, Joseph, and the Judges. One of the best clues, however, is Esther herself.

Throughout biblical history, God chooses the least likely person. The stories in the book of Judges show God choosing unlikely heroes: Ehud, Deborah and Jael, Gideon, and so on. Esther is a heroine because she acted in unexpected ways for her people. She surpassed everyone's expectations. Although the text does not explicitly state that her actions were born of faith, her obedient and courageous attitude, her willingness to follow Mordecai's advice to help the Jews, and her own wise choices demonstrate a person who knew how God acted in history. Esther stands in contrast to King Xerxes who in weakness relied on bad advice; Mordecai stands in contrast with Haman who devilishly offered bad advice.

God's presence and his behind-the-scenes activity are also known as "divine providence," that is, God's continuous care for his creation. As the exiled Jews wondered about God's presence, the Scriptures show that his presence and care were there all along. God fulfilled his promise to Abraham: "I will make you into a great nation, and I will bless you; I will make your name great, and you will be a blessing. I will bless those who bless you, and whoever curses you I will curse; and all peoples on earth will be blessed through you" (Genesis 12:2–3).

THE GREATEST REVERSAL

Although the reversal of fortunes in Esther was extraordinary, it was not the greatest reversal God has prepared. The greatest reversal came in the most unexpected way: in a humble king who was born in a barn, who rode a donkey, who lived with the poor, ate with tax collectors, became a friend to prostitutes, and died a humiliating death on the cross. In Jesus Christ, God produced the greatest reversal of history since creation itself. He is creating a new people, changing lives, and using humble, Esther-like people to bring about even more reversals. God defeated an arrogant, evil enemy who thought himself victorious. And one day this great reversal will end with a wonderful climax: a new heaven and a new earth (Revelation 21:1). In that day, God "will wipe every tear from their eyes. There will be no more death or mourning or crying or pain, for the old order of things has passed away" (Revelation 21:4).

Although God is never truly absent (for the Spirit is always present), often in moments of grief and suffering one feels as if God were far away. At the moment of greatest need and suffering on the cross, Jesus lamented God's absence (Matthew 27:46). Jesus, in his full humanity, also experienced and suffered God's apparent absence.

The book of Esther is a reassurance, not only for the Jews in exile, but also for Christians who "are still in the world … but are not of the world" (John 17:11, 15). An assurance that even when God seems to be absent from our world or suffering, he is ever present, interested, and ready to act. The book of Esther affirms in narrative form what the Apostle Paul affirmed in his letter to the Romans:

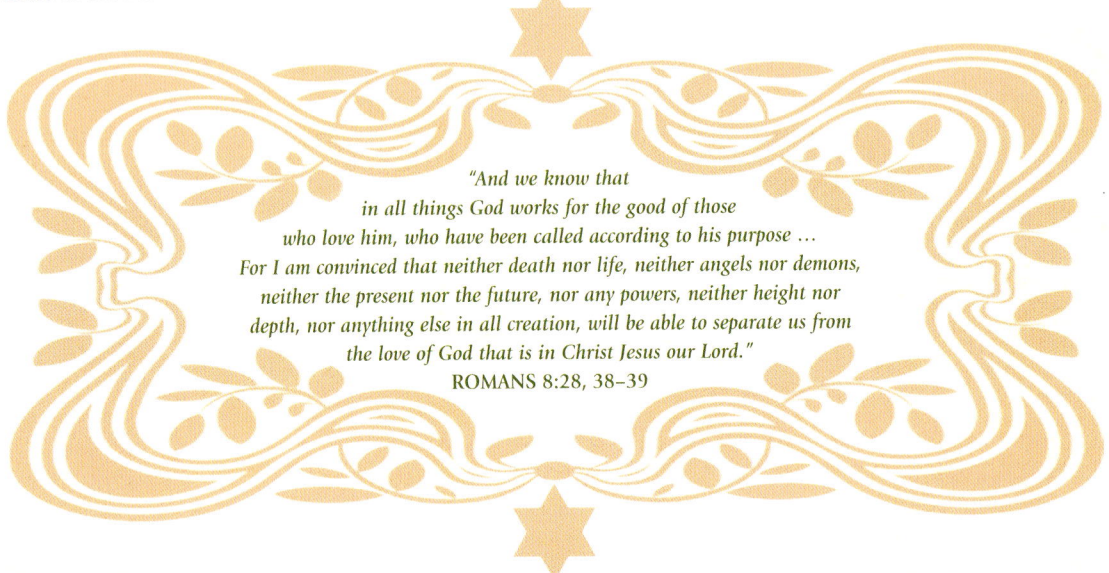

> *"And we know that in all things God works for the good of those who love him, who have been called according to his purpose … For I am convinced that neither death nor life, neither angels nor demons, neither the present nor the future, nor any powers, neither height nor depth, nor anything else in all creation, will be able to separate us from the love of God that is in Christ Jesus our Lord."*
> ROMANS 8:28, 38–39

COURAGE FOR DANGEROUS TIMES

Esther: Orphan, despised minority, exiled captive, beauty queen, trophy wife. Yet what defined Esther and gave her a place in history was the faithfulness and courage of her character, as shown in action. What lessons might we search out from her elegant story?

Esther was faithful and courageous in dangerous times.
Think of the last time you felt afraid. What did you do in response to your fear?
Why do you think God allows us to feel afraid and face danger?

Power is a noticeable theme in the book of Esther.
How have you seen people use and abuse their power?
What kinds of power do you have in your life?
What can you do to make sure you are using power wisely and not harmfully?

The book of Esther contains many reversals of fortune and power.
What reversals have you experienced in your own life?
In what ways was God working through those changes?
What do the reversals in the book of Esther teach us about hope?

RUTH

FROM TRAGEDY TO TRIUMPH

Life can throw us unexpected and painful surprises. For many of us, or for people we love, life can change in a single moment: a tragic car accident, an ill-timed jump into a pool, a catastrophic tornado or hurricane, or a broken relationship that drags us and others through horrible and sad experiences. Even worse, one terrible event might bring about another. As the saying goes, "when it rains, it pours." When events overturn our lives, we can get lost in grief and hurt. We might even experience a loss of identity and lose sight of those things that make us who we are. It is a time of disorientation.

The Old Testament story of Ruth and Naomi explores the problems of loss and identity. The answers the book offers contain much wisdom for our lives today. The book of Ruth is a love story. It is a love story between Ruth and Boaz, and one that illustrates the love between God and his people. It is a story that portrays God and his unfailing love and ceaseless loyalty.

In capable hands, stories are powerful tools. They appeal to both our emotions and our intellect. In the story of Ruth we encounter loss and suffering, disappointment and disorientation, uncertainty and bitterness. But we also find good news; we find love, commitment, perseverance, hope, and God's powerful and tender hand throughout. It is a story about transformation, about God turning our "wailing into dancing" (Ps. 30:11).

SCENE 1:

A TRAGIC STORY IN A FOREIGN LAND
(Ruth 1:1—22)

WHAT'S IN A NAME? "In the days when the judges ruled . . ." marks the setting for the story (Ruth 1:1). It sends the readers back to a time when "Israel had no king; everyone did as they saw fit" (Judg. 21:25). Israel's social and spiritual life was a mess. The time of the judges was known for its cycle of disobedience, repentance, God's intervention, gratitude, and back to disobedience. Although the text does not say that the famine was a punishment from God, the mention of the days of the judges makes this connection possible.

Whatever the case, we find a man from Bethlehem—the name *Bethlehem* means "house of bread"— leaving town and heading to the foreign land of Moab because of the famine. Already we know that things are not the way they are supposed to be. The "house of bread" is running out of bread. The Hebrew word for *bread* and *food* is the same.

The names of the man and his family increase the likelihood that we are in for a surprising story. The man's name, *Elimelek*, most likely means "my God is king." In those times, one of the main functions of a king was to provide security and food for his people. A good king made sure his people did not suffer hunger. Moreover, the names of Elimelek's sons suggest that the story will take a tragic turn. *Mahlon* means something equivalent to "sickly" and *Kilion* to "weakly." With those names, we suspect that they won't be in the story for too long. Elimelek's wife's name seems to be the only good news; *Naomi* means "pleasant." But in a story that promises surprises, we can anticipate a great surprise for Naomi as well.

DEATH AND THE AFTERMATH

In three short verses, we read that Elimelek died and, after ten years, so did Mahlon and Kilion. "And Naomi was left without her two sons and her husband" (Ruth 1:5). Before moving on, however, let's pause to fully appreciate the full effect of those few words.

In the cultural world during the times of the Old Testament, women were valued only by their connection to a man. Unmarried women derived their value from their fathers and married women from their husbands. Their security and safety depended on the husband's ability to provide for them. When a married woman lost her husband, as Naomi did, her value declined steeply, and her safety and security depended on her sons. When Naomi lost her sons as well, she became destitute. Now she was on a social level below servants. Making matters worse, she was a foreigner in a kingdom other than her own, one of the lowliest of the low.

The turn of fortunes for Naomi is total and paralyzing. Her life is overturned. It reminds us of another biblical character whose life was overturned: Job. However, Naomi was a woman; her life is even worse off than Job's because she has no one to turn to for help. "The LORD's hand has turned against me!" (Ruth 1:13).

A QUESTION OF LOYALTY

Naomi is not the only one in this position. Naomi's daughters-in-law, Ruth and Orpah, are in a similar predicament. They are also widows. Although the text never states it, Ruth and Orpah do not or cannot have children—ten years of marriage to Naomi's sons did not produce children for either woman. By cultural tradition, both women were attached to Naomi, their mother-in-law, to share her fate. Naomi, however, graciously releases them from their cultural duty and encourages them to go back to their mothers, to at least have the possibility of a future. After some argument, Orpah decides to go back. Ruth, however, decides to stay with her mother-in-law. It is a courageous decision, and one that comes from a deep love, commitment, and loyalty to Naomi. Naomi calls this love *hesed* ("kindness;" Ruth 1:8), a Hebrew word that is more often used to describe God's love, commitment, and loyalty toward Israel.

> DON'T urge me to leave you or to turn back from you. Where you go I will go, and where you stay I will stay. Your people will be my people and your God my God. Where you die I will die, and there I will be buried. May the LORD deal with me, be it ever so severely, if even death separates you and me. —Ruth 1:16–17

Ruth leaves her home, her identity, and her possibility of a favorable future, and joins Naomi in what could only be a future filled with more suffering. Yet, her actions are just what Naomi needs. Naomi leaves Moab, and when she is back in Bethlehem she says, "I went away full, but the LORD has brought me back empty. Why call me Naomi? The LORD has afflicted me; the Almighty has brought misfortune upon me" (1:21). Naomi changes her name; she is now "Mara," which means bitter (1:20).

THE LIFE OF DESTITUTION

Returning to Bethlehem must have been a very difficult decision for Naomi to make. All that she was had died in Moab. But she heard that "the LORD had come to the aid of his people by providing food for them" in Bethlehem (Ruth 1:6). Naomi understood that life for her back in her village of Bethlehem would be better. God commanded the Israelites to protect the weakest people in the community: "Do not deprive the foreigner or the fatherless of justice, or take the cloak of the widow as a pledge. Remember that you were slaves in Egypt and the LORD your God redeemed you from there. That is why I command you to do this" (Deut. 24:17–18; also Ex. 22:22). The second chapter of Ruth opens with a hopeful reminder: "Naomi had a relative on her husband's side, a man of standing . . . whose name was Boaz" (2:1).

However, life for Ruth in Bethlehem would not be any easier: She is female, a foreigner, barren, and widowed. Yet her commitment was firm and exemplary. She took it upon herself to care for her sorrowful mother-in-law. "As it turned out" (2:3), the text tells us, perhaps with a knowing smile and a wink, that Ruth just happened to be getting her grain in a plot of land that belonged to Boaz.

> LEARN to do right; seek justice. Defend the oppressed. Take up the cause of the fatherless; plead the case of the widow. —Isa. 1:17

SCENE 2:

A NEW LIFE, A NEW HOPE
(Ruth 2:1—23)

BOAZ, A WORTHY MAN These three Hebrew words, *ish gibbor hayil*, are used to describe Boaz in Ruth 2:1. Translated sometimes as "a man of standing" or "a worthy man," these words offer clues to the character of Boaz. The first part of the expression *ish gibbor* means "man mighty in," and *hayil* can mean "strength, power, ability, honor, wealth," depending on the context. In this social context, the expression means a man strong in wealth, ability, and honor. In other words, Boaz is a man well respected and known for his character and leadership. The name *Boaz* probably means "in strength." Socially, Boaz stands galaxies away from Ruth's own social status.

We also learn about Boaz's spiritual character when he arrives at his field and greets his servants. Boaz is a pious and well-liked person; his servants' love for him suggests that he is a fair and honest person. He is so in touch with his servants that he even notices a new person following his harvesters. He approaches Ruth and makes an offering that speaks volumes about his character. Boaz greets his servants with, "The LORD be with you!" (2:4). Indeed, the Lord's presence becomes evident in Boaz's own righteous and compassionate character toward his servants and Ruth. Boaz makes offers to Ruth worthy of his character:

- Permission to stay in his field,
- Permission to be with his servants,
- Protection from the men in the field,
- Provision to share in the water of his workers.

Although the first offer fulfills the command to provide for the poor (Lev. 19:9; 23:22; Deut. 24:19), Boaz went far beyond the requirements of the law. Ruth's social condition places her below even the poor Israelites following the harvesters. Not only that, but providing his protection to her from the men reminds us that women then, as often is the case today, are easy targets for abuse and violence. However, Boaz offered more than protection; he made Ruth, for all practical purposes, part of his household. Again, Ruth was socially far below Boaz's servants, but now she is to share in their water. Further, Boaz invites Ruth to his own table to share his bread. It is more than a generous gesture; it is a righteous and compassionate deed.

However, Boaz is not finished with showcasing his character. Unknown to Ruth, he orders his servants to leave extra grain, and even stalks of wheat, for Ruth to pick up. Ruth ends up with about thirty pounds of grain to take home! According to documents from Babylon around that time, harvesters would take home one or two pounds a day. Ruth took home more than ten times the salary of a harvester! In addition, she took home leftover cooked grain for Naomi. While the great amount of grain Ruth brought back home was impressive, for a hungry Naomi the sight of already cooked grain was a blessing beyond words. Ruth's care and commitment soothed Naomi's bitterness and grief.

A DEEP LOVE Why did Boaz act in such a way toward Ruth? The answer, in part, is that he acted from his own commitment and character. The answer is also found in his own words. Ruth bows down with her face to the ground—as a person in her social standing would be expected—and asks, "Why have I found such favor in your eyes that you notice me—a foreigner?" (Ruth 2:10). Boaz answers, "I've been told all about what you have done for your mother-in-law since the death of your husband . . ." (2:11). Boaz is moved to compassion because of Ruth's own loyalty and commitment to Naomi. Ruth's love and commitment to Naomi exemplify the attitude that God's people should have toward those in need. Ruth's unrelenting and selfless love toward Naomi enraptured Boaz.

In the times of the Bible, marriage was more an economic than a romantic affair. Boaz had nothing to gain from courting a foreign woman from the lowest rung of the social ladder. And that is exactly what makes Boaz's actions even more extraordinary—a man doing what is right without expecting anything in return! Boaz's loving actions were a response to Ruth's own loving commitment and loyalty to Naomi. Although not at the same social level, Ruth is his match on a spiritual level.

WHOSE HESED?

With great joy, Naomi receives Ruth's gifts and cries out: "Blessed be the man who took notice of you!" (Ruth 2:19). Naomi had bitterly complained that God's noticing her had brought much affliction (1:21). When she learns that the man's name is Boaz, a light comes on in her mind: "He has not stopped showing his kindness to the living and the dead" (2:20). Who is the "he" referring to? Boaz or the Lord? It's not clear, though it probably refers to both. In Boaz's *hesed* Naomi recognizes the Lord's *hesed*.

> **HESED** Most of the time in the Old Testament, *hesed* is used in connection to a covenant, such as marriage, as it is here in the book of Ruth. It means that people are willing to fulfill their covenant obligations and go beyond them for the sake of an important relationship. *Hesed*, then, suggests taking loyalty, commitment, compassion, and love a step beyond what is simply required.

After so much heartbreak and bitterness, Naomi finds comfort through the loving and compassionate acts of Ruth and Boaz. Although the text does not say it this way, we can recognize that God has reached out and touched Naomi through Ruth and Boaz. We would expect God to use his people this way. Boaz, after all, is an Israelite of impeccable character and reputation. But Ruth . . . well, notice the way Ruth is introduced in this chapter: "And Ruth the Moabite . . ." (2:2) and "She is the Moabite who came back from Moab . . ." (2:6). She is a Moabite, one of Israel's most ferocious enemies, and a pagan—remember that Naomi asked her to return to her gods and her family (1:15). Indeed, Boaz behaves the way all Israelites should. Ruth, although not from Israel, also behaves as an Israelite should!

SCENE 3:
A DECISIVE ENCOUNTER
(RUTH 3:1—18)

A PLAN FOR RUTH As she realizes that God is blessing her, Naomi's grief is diminished. But Naomi is still empty, and Ruth's future is still precarious. They are still poor, widowed, childless, and, in Ruth's case, a foreigner. With her renewed hope, Naomi reciprocates Ruth's *hesed* with a plan of her own. What will happen to Ruth if Naomi dies? Her prospects are even grimmer without her mother-in-law. Having witnessed the righteous character of her relative Boaz, Naomi makes a rather risky plan. Ruth is to approach Boaz in the middle of the night, after a time of celebration following the harvest, while he sleeps outside the city, where the threshing floor was most likely located. With any other man, such a plan would be a recipe for disaster. However, relying on Boaz's righteous character, Naomi is sure that Ruth will be safe.

> **RUTH AND PROVERBS**
> In the Hebrew Old Testament, the book of Ruth follows the book of Proverbs. By being there, the book of Ruth connects the last poem in Proverbs—"the wife of noble character" in Proverbs 31:10–31—and Ruth. The poem in Proverbs begins with the words *eshet hayil*: "A wife of noble character who can find?" (Prov. 31:10). The answer is Ruth. Ruth is the *eshet hayil*, the woman of noble character.

NAOMI'S LOYALTY Naomi explains her plan to Ruth and concludes: "He will tell you what to do" (Ruth 3:4). Ruth replies, "I will do whatever you say" (3:5). With this plan, Naomi is showing her *hesed* to Ruth: Naomi is seeking a husband for Ruth—a husband would assure a future for Ruth. However, Naomi needs to include the land in the marriage deal to entice a man such as Boaz to marry Ruth. By giving up her rights to the land, Naomi is taking a great risk. Once married, Ruth and the land would belong to Boaz. Naomi could end up with nothing, she could be completely destitute. Yet, Naomi knows Ruth's character and trusts in her *hesed*. Now more than ever, Naomi's future is tied to Ruth's. Filled with risks, this plan depends on Ruth's *hesed* and, as it turns out, on Boaz's *hesed* as well.

RUTH AND BOAZ

However, Ruth does not follow Naomi's instructions entirely. Instead, after waking up Boaz, she says, "Spread the corner of your garment over me, since you are a guardian-redeemer of our family" (Ruth 3:9). Boaz does not react in anger to Ruth's daring actions. He replies, "The LORD bless you, my daughter. This kindness [*hesed*] is greater than that which you showed earlier . . ." (3:10). It is not completely clear to what Boaz is referring by the earlier *hesed*. However, something Ruth has done has caused a great impression on Boaz.

Boaz Pouring Six Measures of Barley into Ruth's Veil (Rembrandt)

Ruth's request to "spread the corner of your garment" is a term that readers should recognize. In Ezekiel, the prophet used the image of marriage to illustrate God's relationship with Israel. The prophet used the same expression, "I spread the corner of my garment over you . . ." (Ezek. 16:8) as a symbolic gesture for the marriage covenant. Ruth is asking Boaz to marry her—a very daring request from a woman to a man. However, the words Ruth uses reflect Boaz's own words back in his field in Ruth 2:12: "under whose *wings* [God's] you have come to take refuge." (The words *wings* and *corner* are the same word in Hebrew.) Being covered by Boaz's garment represents God's own covering of Ruth. However, Ruth not only requests Boaz to marry her, but she goes beyond her own needs and future and requests that Boaz also redeem (buy back) Elimelek's land for Naomi, which would then provide a secure future for Naomi. Ruth's ability to think beyond herself and consider her mother-in-law's needs shows her commitment to Naomi.

Ruth's requests to Boaz include two important social protections in the law: the levirate marriage and the guardian-redeemer. These two ancient practices had a very practical social and theological purpose: to assure both the safety of descendants and the possession of ancestral family land. Ancient Israelites derived much of their identity as God's people from these two social realities. Sons were to carry the family name and the land, which was the concrete expression of God's promises to Abraham. To this point, Ruth's explicit identity has been that of a foreign woman who accompanies her Israelite widowed mother-in-law. To the reader, it has become increasingly clear that Ruth behaves just as an Israelite should. In chapter 3 of Ruth, it is also clear that Boaz shares that view, since he has praised her *hesed* twice now. Furthermore, it has become clear to others in the city that Ruth is more than a foreigner: "All the people of my town know that you are a woman of noble character" (3:11). "Noble character" translates from a Hebrew expression that connects Ruth with Boaz: *eshet hayil*. Boaz was first introduced in the book as an *ish gibbor hayil*. Once again, the text presents Ruth at the same spiritual level as Boaz, an extraordinary claim in a male dominated world!

AN UNEXPECTED RESULT

Although Boaz promises to do as Ruth has requested, Boaz unexpectedly informs her that a closer relative has the rights of the guardian-redeemer (Ruth 3:12). However, Boaz assures Ruth that if the nameless relative is not willing to exercise his right, Boaz will do it. As a visible assurance of his promise to Ruth, Boaz gives her "six measures of barley" (3:15) to fill her shawl. Symbolically, Ruth and Naomi had come to Bethlehem with empty hands, but now Ruth's hands are full. Naomi responds with caution and wisdom: "Wait, my daughter, until you find out what happens" (3:18).

LEVIRATE MARRIAGE AND GUARDIAN-REDEEMER

Levirate Marriage: A provision in the Mosaic law which guaranteed that the lineage of a man will continue. The nearest kinsman would marry the widow of a man who dies without a son (Deut. 25:5–10). The term *levirate* comes from a Latin word *levir*, which means "brother-in-law." In addition, this law provided protection for a widow who could be in danger to become indigent.

Guardian-Redeemer: Also known as "Kinsman-Redeemer." When an Israelite man experienced hard times, his nearest relative was required to help him. The Guardian-redeemer would buy the land of the needy relative to prevent it from becoming the possession of someone outside the clan (Lev. 25:25).

SCENE 4:

FROM EMPTINESS TO FULLNESS
(RUTH 4:1–15)

RESOLUTION AT THE GATES After the private conversation that Ruth initiated, the scene moves again to the public sphere. In the public sphere, Ruth and Naomi are voiceless and powerless. Boaz becomes their voice. He is a man of strength, of noble character, of great standing in the community. However, rather than bullying others to get his way, or using his own social capital to accomplish his plans, Boaz acts with wisdom. Boaz trusts in God's *hesed*. Although not explicitly affirmed, God's presence throughout the story is apparent. When Boaz goes up to the town gate, the nameless guardian-redeemer happens to come along. God is working behind the scenes, so this turn of events is not merely luck.

The names of the main characters are important in the story. However, the relative "guardian-redeemer" remains nameless. This nameless Israelite is willing to redeem the land that belonged to Elimelek, Kilion, and Mahlon, possibly because of the financial benefits that come with it. However, Boaz reminds him, "On the day you buy the land from Naomi, you also acquire Ruth the Moabite, the dead man's widow" (Ruth 4:5). Notice how Boaz presents Ruth. To this point, Boaz has spoken of Ruth with much admiration and praise: her demonstration of *hesed* toward Naomi is noteworthy, and she is described as a woman of noble character, one who any Israelite male would be blessed to marry. But here, Boaz introduces her as "the Moabite," a foreigner who belongs to one of Israel's most hated enemy kingdom.

And she is also described as "the dead man's widow," not only a foreigner—and, although not explicitly said, also childless. Presented this way, Ruth is not a desirable partner but a financial liability. The nameless relative relinquishes his right to redeem Naomi's land. Although not doing anything illegal or immoral, this relative fails to do *hesed* to Naomi. While obeying the law, he was not willing to walk the extra mile that *hesed* would demand.

REMOVING a sandal was a symbolic act that signaled a change of status. When people expressed pain, they would tear their clothing, and changing into rough clothing would symbolize their low emotional state. When women became widows, such as Naomi and Ruth, they would wear clothing that reflected this new social status. And before going to see Boaz, Ruth changed her clothing to indicate her new status as one who is open for marriage. Boaz subsequently covers Ruth as a symbol for marriage.

In the public sphere, Boaz forced the hand of the nameless relative. By means of what seems to have been a formalized ritual, the relative transfers all rights to Boaz. This transfer was made official with an offering of clothing. Here, at the gate, the piece of clothing is a sandal. This symbolic act formalizes the transaction, and the elders witness it: "We are witnesses" (4:11) and bless the foreign woman, "May the LORD make the woman who is coming into your home like Rachel and Leah . . ." (4:11). The elders praise Ruth at the gate, just as Proverbs affirms, "Honor her for all that her hands have done, and let her works bring her praise at the city gate" (Prov. 31:31).

FROM EMPTINESS TO FULLNESS Boaz married Ruth, and "the LORD enabled her to conceive, and she gave birth to a son" (Ruth 4:13). This is a story of redemption through *hesed*. God could have done wonders with Naomi and Ruth; he could have come in an awesome storm and talked to them, as he did with Job. He could have sent a powerful prophet, as he did with the widow of Zarephath and the prophet Elijah. But he didn't. Instead, quietly behind the scenes, God allowed his people to represent him. Boaz's *hesed* represented God's own *hesed*. Boaz's loving, courageous, compassionate, and righteous actions represented God. And Ruth's own courageous, loving, daring, and loyal actions, along with her commitment to Naomi's God, show a way to go beyond the written law and seek the kingdom of God and its righteousness. Ruth becomes a model for what *hesed* looks like—not just for women, but for all of God's people.

Naomi is no longer "*Mara*"; she is no longer bitter or empty. Now, "Naomi has a son!" (4:17). Naomi's identity has radically changed. Ruth's identity is equally changed. She is no longer a foreign widow. She is now married to a man of noble character; she is a mother; and she is being compared to great women of Israel: Rachel, Leah, and Tamar (4:12). Ruth is now an Israelite woman, a woman of noble character, the mother of Obed, the ancestor of the great King David, and, eventually, of the Messiah Jesus (Matt. 1:5–16). God's *hesed* transforms and renews people!

GOD'S HESED "This is how God showed his love among us: He sent his one and only Son into the world that we might live through him" (1 John 4:9). God's love is so much more than a feeling or an emotion—it is an action. The letter of John teaches us as much. We know about God's immense love in that he *sent* his own Son to give us life. That is the main quality of *hesed*. It is action that is born from commitment, loyalty, compassion, and love. If Ruth, Boaz, and Naomi illustrate it for us, Jesus Christ perfects it with his obedience and sacrifice. God's *hesed* in Christ gives us new life, makes us a new creation, and enables us to imitate Ruth, Boaz, Naomi, and, especially, Jesus. May our *hesed* be like that of Ruth, Boaz, Naomi, and Jesus!

WE LOVE *because he first loved us. Whoever claims to love God yet hates a brother or sister is a liar. For whoever does not love their brother and sister, whom they have seen, cannot love God, whom they have not seen. And he has given us this command: Anyone who loves God must also love their brother and sister.* —1 John 4:19–21

Psalms

Central to the Lives of God's People

In the psalms, we find words that express the deepest longings of our hearts: the aching of our souls when we experience loss, the exuberant joy of knowing ourselves forgiven, and the deep gratitude of God's amazing grace. God's people have sung, recited, memorized, and shared the psalms for thousands of years. The psalms are central in the lives of God's people.

The psalms are songs of praise, thanksgiving, lament, wisdom, blessing, and more. They provide us with models for our own spiritual lives. When pain has robbed us of words and meaning, the psalms provide us with words to scream to God for help and solace. When joy has filled our hearts so thoroughly, the psalms help us express our gratitude and our praise to God who is the fountain of all goodness.

However, the psalms do not give us step-by-step instructions for how to pray and give praise to God. Instead, the psalms *show* us how to praise and pray. As the fourth-century theologian Athanasius famously wrote, "Most of Scripture speaks *to* us; the Psalms speak *for* us."

The book of Psalms is for all of God's people. Although the psalms are important for our individual spiritual lives, they are the songs and prayers of a community, God's community. If we are to engage in the life of the kingdom of God, we must learn the language, the character, and the values of the kingdom of God.

The psalms are filled with teachings about God: who God is and how he relates to his people and nations. In their teachings, the psalms anticipate and prefigure the coming of God's promised Messiah, the one who would bring justice and righteousness to the world.

The book of Psalms can transform our minds by teaching us new and exciting things about our awesome God; it can transform our hearts by giving us words to understand strong and complex feelings; and it can transform our spirits by pointing us to the right way to praise God through our words and actions.

Background

The book of Psalms is a collection of collections. These collections were put together at different times and for purposes we might never know. One hundred and sixteen psalms have a title. It is likely that the titles were not part of the original writings and were added at later dates. However, these titles do provide helpful information. Each title reveals some details about a psalm's author, historical background, melody, use during worship, and other information.

Names for Psalms
The English word "psalms" comes from the title used in the Greek translation of the Old Testament, called the Septuagint. The Greek word *psalmos* was used to translate the Hebrew word *mizmor*, which could mean "song." The Hebrew title of the book of Psalms *tehillim* means "praises."

Authors of the Psalms
According to the titles, some of the named psalm authors are: David (73 times), Asaph (12 times), the sons of Korah (11 times), Solomon (2 times), Jeduthun (4 times), and Heman, Etan, and Moses (1 time each).

Dates of the Psalms
The poems were collected over a long period. Most were composed between the time of David (around 1000 BC) and the time of Ezra (450 BC).

In the times when the Scriptures were written, most people could not read and write. Yet the psalms still were important in people's lives. The psalms were sung (81:1–2; 144:9; 147:7), and they played a critical role in the worship at the temple (47:1; 118:27; 132:7; 149:3).

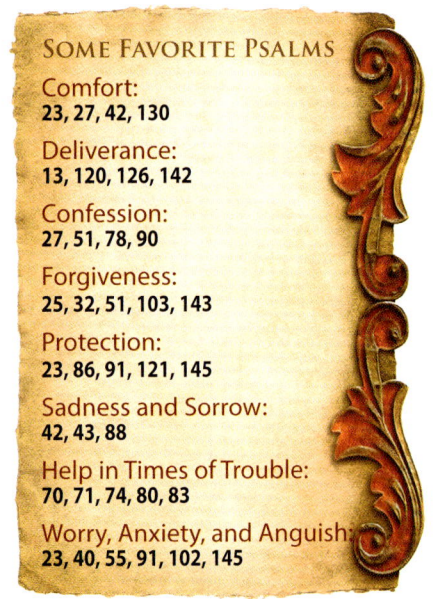

SOME FAVORITE PSALMS

Comfort:
23, 27, 42, 130

Deliverance:
13, 120, 126, 142

Confession:
27, 51, 78, 90

Forgiveness:
25, 32, 51, 103, 143

Protection:
23, 86, 91, 121, 145

Sadness and Sorrow:
42, 43, 88

Help in Times of Trouble:
70, 71, 74, 80, 83

Worry, Anxiety, and Anguish:
23, 40, 55, 91, 102, 145

The Psalm and the Psalter

Psalms are not only individual songs or prayers. They also have been placed together in one collection. When the many songs and prayers were put together, along with an introduction (Ps. 1) and a conclusion (146–150), the book of Psalms became a learning tool for God's people.

Scholars do not fully understand the way the individual psalms were placed in the Psalter (another name for the book of Psalms). However, we can make a few important observations that can help us understand the psalms as a collection.

Monks of Ramsey Psalter, England, c. 1310

The Collection Is Divided into Five Books.

The five-book division seems to connect the Psalter with the Pentateuch—the first five books of the Bible. One of the main functions of the Pentateuch (in Hebrew, the *Torah*), was to instruct the Israelites how to be God's people. The psalms are also meant to be a book of instruction. They instruct us how to worship God, how to address God when we experience suffering or joy, and how to recognize the feelings that move us toward or away from God. The book of Psalms instructs God's people to be wise in all areas of life: spiritual, emotional, and moral—both individually and as a people.

The Beginning and the Ending

Psalms 1 and 2 form a two-step introduction to the whole book. Two blessings frame this introduction: Ps. 1:1, "Blessed is the one who…" and Ps. 2:12, "Blessed are all who take refuge in him." These two psalms, a wisdom song and a royal song, set the tone of the psalms as a collection. For God's people, who would be conquered by the Babylonians and taken into exile for 70 years, the psalms became a way to relearn their identity as God's people. The psalms, with their powerful movement from grief to joy, from lament to praise, teach wisdom for life. The psalms show that trust in God's goodness and faithfulness, even in times of suffering and grief, leads people to a new vision and understanding of life at the other side of suffering, which is a life of praise as Psalm 150 shows.

Each of the Five Books Ends with a Doxology.

A doxology is a prayer or song that praises God for his power and glory. At its core, the psalms are songs that teach us how to bring glory to God. The doxologies move from praising God (Ps. 41:13; 72:19; 89:52) to inviting all the people to join in the celebration (Ps. 106:48) to that wonderful closing psalm that has become an example of praise and celebration of who God is (Ps. 150).

Book I	Ps. 1–41	Prayers of lament and expressions of confidence in God.
Doxology	Ps. 41:13	Praise be to the LORD, the God of Israel, from everlasting to everlasting. Amen and Amen.
Book II	Ps. 42–72	Communal laments; ends with a royal psalm.
Doxology	Ps. 72:19	Praise be to his glorious name forever; may the whole earth be filled with his glory. Amen and Amen.
Book III	Ps. 73–89	Intense and bleak prayers of lament and distress.
Doxology	Ps. 89:52	Praise be to the LORD forever! Amen and Amen.
Book IV	Ps. 90–106	Answers to the bleakness of book III. The theme of "The Lord Reigns."
Doxology	Ps. 106:48	Praise be to the LORD, the God of Israel, from everlasting to everlasting. Let all the people say, "Amen!" Praise the LORD.
Book V	Ps. 107–150	This book declares that God is in control, will redeem his people, and praises God's faithfulness and goodness.
Doxology	Ps. 150	…Praise the Lord!

The Psalms Show a Movement from David to God.

The first three books in the Psalter highlight God's covenant with David. The last two books emphasize God's kingship. The Scriptures have not rejected David's kingship. On the contrary, the theological point of the psalms is that God will be faithful to his promise to David: to always have one of his descendants on the throne of Israel (2 Sam. 7:5–16). However, instead of a human king, God himself would fulfill the promise to David. This shift suggests that hope should not be placed on human institutions but on God's merciful and mighty acts. The teaching about the coming of the Messiah arises from this view of God's kingship.

King David, Westminster Abbey Psalter c. 1200

Types of Psalms—Knowing the Genres in the Psalms

A genre is a particular kind of writing—or painting, or music, for example—that shares specific elements of content and form. Most of the time we read the psalms in a devotional way. This type of reading is refreshing for our spirits and leads us closer to God and other fellow believers. However, other times we may want to explore a given psalm more deeply. In those times, knowing about its genre will help us in our spiritual exploration. Each main genre below lists a sample of representative psalms:

The Hymn of Praise

- The beautiful and glorious songs of praise to God characterize these psalms. These hymns highlight God's character and deeds, such as his goodness, majesty, and virtue (Ps. 8; 19; 29; 33; 65; 100; 145), or his righteous kingship over all of creation (47; 93–99).
- The psalmist acknowledges that God is great and worthy of praise. These psalms praise God as creator (Ps. 8; 18; 104; 148), as protector and benefactor of his people (66; 111; 114; 149; 199), and as the Lord of history (33; 103; 113; 117; 145–147).

Psalms of Lament

- The psalms of lament outnumber any other type of psalm. This fact might reflect the messiness of life, or the many reasons for suffering and sadness. However, the psalms do not typically end in lament. They move from lament to praise, from grief to joy.
- The conclusion of the psalms, the magnificent hallelujah songs (Ps. 146–150), reflect that with God, all tears will be dried, all sufferings will turn to joy, and all injustices will receive the proper and righteous response.
- There are individual prayers of lament (13; 22; 31; 42–43; 57; 139; etc.) and community laments (12; 44; 80; 85; 90; 94).
- These prayers provide us with the language to ask God to intervene in our favor. They might include a plea to God for help, the specific cause of the suffering, a confession of faith or innocence, a curse of the enemies, confidence in God's response, and a song of thanksgiving for God's intervention. Prayers of lament may include one or more of these elements.

Songs of Thanksgiving

- These songs focus on thanking God for his answer to a specific request. The request is not always explicit in the song, though it seems that they are connected to laments.
- Songs of thanksgiving can also be individual (32; 34; 92; 116; 118; 138) or communal (107; 124).

Detail, Psalter of St. Gallen, c. 890, Latin

🔸 Songs Related to the Temple

- Some songs were to remind the community of their covenant with God (Ps. 50; 81). These covenant renewal celebrations occurred in the temple.
- Other songs, royal psalms, make mention of King David or his descendants (2; 18; 110). They point to God as the King and the temple as his throne.
- Songs of Zion celebrate God's presence with his people (46; 84; 122). It appears that the singing of these psalms took place during the worship at the temple in Jerusalem.

🔸 Teaching Psalms

- Songs have a unique way of teaching the people who hear and sing them.
- The wisdom psalms use traditional wisdom themes—for example, the fear of the Lord and advice for a good life—to guide and shape the view of those singing them (37; 49; 73).
- Closely related to the wisdom psalms, other psalms praise the wonders of God's law and encourage God's people to obey it and delight in it (1; 19; 119).

🔸 Other Genres

- Psalms of Confidence (11; 23; 63; 91; 121).
- Psalms of Creation (8; 104; 148).
- Songs of Zion (46; 48; 76; 84; 122).
- Historical Psalms (78; 105; 106; 135; 136).
- Royal Psalms (2; 18; 20; 21; 45; 72; 101; 110).
- Wisdom Psalms (1; 37; 49; 73; 112; 127; 128; 133).

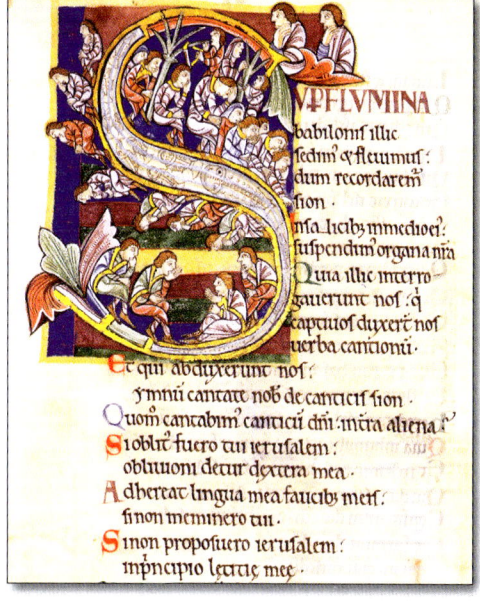

Psalm 136 from St. Albans Abbey, England, 12th Century

Reading the Psalms as Poetry

Poetry expresses deep and complex feelings and truths that may lie beyond normal speech. Short lines, powerful and vivid images, and conciseness characterize Hebrew poetry. However, interpreting a poem is like explaining a joke. Poetry is not supposed to be explained, but experienced. We understand a poem, then, when our emotions and our wills are moved as the poem desires: to joy, to compassion, to forgiveness, to repentance, to comfort, and so on. Analysis of biblical poetry is only a tool that allows us to enter into the world of the poem. However, understanding does not happen until we allow ourselves to experience the emotional and spiritual effects of each poem.

🔸 Reading Poetry

Most English poetry relies on rhyme and meter, as well as images and wordplay, to communicate the message. Old Testament poetry does not rely on rhyme, and there is a long-standing argument among scholars on whether Hebrew poetry has a meter or not. Nevertheless, the two most important characteristics of Hebrew poetry are terseness and parallelism.

🔸 Terseness

Terseness is the ability to express many complex ideas with only a few words. It is the most outstanding characteristic of Hebrew poetry. Typically, there are two or three short lines that make up a stanza. The ways in which those poetic lines relate to each other are an important tool for the poet's message.

🕊 Parallelism

As we read Old Testament poetry, we are struck by how much repetition there is. That is because poetic lines have parallelism. Parallelism means the second line of the verse repeats or advances the thought of the first line in some way. Determining how this movement occurs allows us to understand the sense and meaning of the poem.

There are different kinds of parallelism. Knowing that there is parallelism might be more important than knowing all the different kinds of parallelism. However, recognizing the main types of parallelism will illustrate how Hebrew poetry works.

Similar Parallelism

In similar parallelism, the second line can explain, specify, focus, or intensify the thought of the first line.

> A *You have searched me, Lord,*
> B *and you know me.* (Ps. 139:1)

A and B are the two lines that make up the first verse. The affirmation of the first line, that God has searched the poet, is further explained in the second line, B. When God searches for us, it is not as when we do a Google search. It means that God knows us, an intimate knowledge that grows in a relationship.

> A *The LORD Almighty is with us;*
> B *The God of Jacob is our fortress.* (Ps. 46:7)

Nonnberg Psalter Initial, c. 1255, Germany

The confession in the first line is extraordinary and is equivalent to Immanuel, which means "God is with us" and is one of Jesus' names! The second line explains what that powerful statement means. We know that God is with us because the God of Jacob is our fortress. It is an affirmation of trust and commitment.

Contrasting Parallelism

In contrasting, or antithetical parallelism, the second line moves the thought by offering a contrast with the first line.

> A *Some trust in chariots and some in horses,*
> B *but we trust in the name of the LORD our God.* (Ps. 20:7)

The verse contrasts two kinds of trust: one in human strengths that seem desirable and the other in the name of the Lord, which is another way to say the fame or reputation of God. The contrast emphasizes the point of the entire psalm: because of God's faithfulness and power, the safety of God's people, including the king, is assured.

Complementary Parallelism

In some poems, the following lines complement the thought or idea of the first line.

> A *Have mercy on me, my God,*
> B *have mercy on me,*
> C *for in you I take refuge.* (Ps. 57:1)

> A *I called to the LORD, who is worthy of praise,*
> B *and I have been saved from my enemies.* (Ps. 18:3)

In both examples, the last lines finish the thought. In the first example, the third line gives the reason for mercy; it is called a motivational clause, in which the psalmist gives reasons for God to act. In the second example, the second line makes the result of the calling explicit: salvation.

Ways to Read the Psalms

Reading the Bible does not require advanced studies, but we should understand that there are different ways to read the Bible that produce different results. Reading devotionally, theologically, and communally are three different manners with three different goals.

Reading Devotionally

Reading devotionally has the goal of deepening and enriching our relationship with God, individually and as a group. It is the time when we tell God what is in our hearts and minds, and when we pay attention to what God has in mind for each of us. It is a time for loving communication between God and us.

Reading devotionally means reading prayerfully. Some people combine their reading with their prayer. The psalms are ideal for this type of devotional reading. Choose a psalm, for example, Psalm 23. And, as you read it, use the words of the psalm to pray to God:

"The Lord is my shepherd . . ." *You, Lord, are my shepherd.* "I lack nothing . . ."
Thank you, God, that I lack nothing; for you have given me all that I need . . . And so on.

An important part of a devotional reading is memorization. For hundreds of years, believers have memorized the Scriptures, especially the psalms. Memorization is a tool that God uses to speak to us. When we are grasped by sorrow, despair, anguish, fear, or temptation, all of those memorized verses will come back to us. God speaks to us through them in unexpected ways. They become anchors for our wandering minds and hearts. The words of God dwell in our minds and hearts, shaping and transforming us: "I remembered my songs in the night. My heart meditated and my spirit asked . . ." (Ps. 77:6).

Reading Theologically

With in-depth study of the Scriptures, we attempt to understand the larger historical, literary, and theological connections and ramifications of a text or book of the Bible. It is an important intellectual activity with a helpful role in the life of the church.

The importance of in-depth Scripture reading is clear every Sunday when pastors preach. Their insights and wisdom come from a careful and deep study of the Scriptures. However, this type of Bible reading is not only for pastors or scholars. All Christians must learn how to examine the Scriptures deeply and carefully. Good study will open new windows and understandings about the Word, God, and the world. The two main reasons for honing our in-depth Bible study skills are:

1. The Holy Spirit can more easily transform our minds and hearts in deep, powerful ways.

2. We can recognize when truth is distorted, twisted, or denied.

Reading the Bible theologically means that we pay attention, to whatever degree possible for each of us, to the history, the literature, and the theology of the book and the text we are studying. With the aid of other tools, you should also learn some history of and about the events the Bible describes. This history study will give you a context for understanding the biblical writings. Learn to pay attention to the literary side of the Scriptures—in the case of the psalms, its poetry.

We can begin to make theological connections. What does the text teach us about God, about humanity, about the world? Are there any theological connections with other parts of the Scripture? How do we read that particular psalm in light of Christ's cross and his resurrection? Are there any connections between the teachings of the psalm and that of the New Testament?

Reading Communally

Reading in groups can enhance our understanding and foster spiritual communion with others. Two ways the psalms have been used in community are in prayers and in songs. For most of the history of the church, the psalms have been part of worship services, shaped the prayers of communities, and transformed people by providing the vocabulary of faith through hymns.

Singing the psalms shapes the spiritual life of God's people, and the act of singing involves our whole beings: it forces us to be fully attentive, engages us with others singing around us, captures and transforms our emotions, and makes our bodies (voice, eyes, breathing, and body posture) full participants. Singing the psalms is a discipline too valuable for the church to forget or ignore.

Reading Some Important Psalms

Psalm 13

How long, Lord? Will you forget me forever?
    How long will you hide your face from me?
How long must I wrestle with my thoughts
    and day after day have sorrow in my heart?
    How long will my enemy triumph over me?
(Ps. 13:1–2)

This is a song of lament. The psalmist inquires with great urgency of God, "How long, Lord?" The psalm begins with six piercing questions. Readers who know that parallelism plays a part in the composition of the psalm can better appreciate the important ways these questions relate to each other.

The questions move from the simple, initial question of "how long"; to asking God to stop hiding from the psalmist; to expressing the root problem: the threat of an enemy. The psalm does not give any details about the dangers the psalmist faced. However, the cry for help is easy to relate for most anyone.

The questions connect God's absence with the suffering of the psalmist. However, the answer to his suffering lies in God, and that is the basic confession of the psalm. "Although I'm in trouble, I trust in God's goodness," the psalmist is saying. So, the psalmist asks God to be present: "Look on me and answer . . ." The psalmist's solutions "look, answer, and give light" progressively move the psalm toward a final solution: to receive God's light "or I will sleep in death" (13:3). Giving light here is a metaphor for life. Light is the basis of natural life; God's light, then, is the basis for our lives, both physical and spiritual.

In addition, the psalmist offers motivations for God's action. If God does not act promptly, the psalmist's enemy will boast of the victory. God's name, his honor and reputation, will be tarnished if that happens. Moses argued similarly with God after the golden calf event in the desert (see Ex. 32:11–14).

The psalm ends in a beautiful and powerful expression of trust and confidence. The basis for trusting God is his "unfailing love" (Ps. 13:5). Because of this trust in God's goodness, the psalmist ends with a commitment to praise God. In six short and beautiful verses, the psalmist has shown to us the movement from grief to joy, from danger to salvation, from lament to praise.

Psalm 23

The Lord is my shepherd, I lack nothing.
    He makes me lie down in green pastures,
he leads me beside quiet waters,
    he refreshes my soul.
He guides me along the right paths
    for his name's sake. (Ps. 23:1–3)

Perhaps the most well known and loved of all the psalms, Psalm 23 holds a special place in people's minds and hearts. Present in the psalm are two main images: the shepherd and the host. In our experience, those two images do not seem to go together well. However, when the psalm was composed, a shepherd was the protector and caretaker of both his sheep and of a traveler passing by. Hospitality while travelling the wilderness is crucial for life. God is portrayed as both the caring shepherd and a hospitable host.

In the first verse, the second phrase, "I lack nothing" states the result of the first phrase. Because "The Lord is my shepherd," we can say that, "I lack nothing." The next three verses elaborate on what it means to lack nothing. In a beautiful and memorable play with the imagery of shepherding life, the psalmist conveys the reasons for his complete confidence. In Old Testament times, "shepherd" was a metaphor for king. The psalmist's statement of trust, then, is for God as King. And the Shepherd-King provides for all the needs of the wanderer traveler.

As a gracious host, the Shepherd provides the full protection and welcoming that his tent—his house—can offer. Unlike the temporary safety and welcome that people can offer, the divine host offers a permanent, full, and certain safety and welcome to those who place trust in him.

Psalm 100

*Shout for joy to the L*ORD*, all the earth.*
  *Worship the L*ORD *with gladness;*
  come before him with joyful songs.
*Know that the L*ORD *is God.*
  It is he who made us, and we are his;
  we are his people, the sheep of his pasture. (Ps. 100:1–3)

> **HESED**
>
> Most of the time in the Old Testament, *hesed* is used in connection to a covenant, such as marriage. It means that people are willing to fulfill their covenant obligations and go beyond them for the sake of an important relationship. *Hesed*, then, suggests taking loyalty, commitment, compassion, and love a step beyond what is simply required.

This is a hymn of praise celebrating God's faithfulness to his covenant. The psalm begins with a call to celebrate. This is an exuberant sort of celebration (the kind of celebration that rock stars or sports heroes often get). And it is a call for all the earth to join in the celebration.

"Shout for joy" is a general celebration of joy; "worship the LORD" is a more specific kind of celebration: the worship that happens at the temple, for example. "Come before him" is another way of saying: enter the temple, in the case of Jerusalem. The celebration of God happens on God's own terms. And, finally, "know that the LORD is God." Knowing refers to the intimate knowledge that spouses or close friends possess, and that grows in relationships. This relationship begins by understanding who we are in relationship to God: he is the creator and we are the creatures. But—and this is one of the amazing statements of the psalm—God's people are God's sheep. They are under the special protection of God!

The second part of the psalm is parallel to the first part, another three commands that explain what to do once one is at the temple: "Enter his gates . . . give thanks . . . and praise his name." The movement plays on the relationship between thanksgiving and praise. Praise arises from thanksgiving. And gratitude arises from recognizing who God is. We know who God is by what he has done. The last two poetic lines explain it: "the LORD is good . . ." We also know that the lines are parallel. So we can conclude that being good means that "his love endures forever" (the Hebrew word used here is *hesed*). Further, "the LORD is good" also means that God is faithful to his promises. Because he is faithful, we can rest assured that we are safe in God's hands (Ps. 100:4–5).

The Psalms and the New Testament

When Jesus said that all of the Scriptures spoke of him, he specifically mentioned the Psalms (Luke 24:44). It is not surprising then to find that the New Testament writers quote many of the Psalm's texts. The table shows some of these important quotations and what they say about the Messiah.

Psalm	What It Says of Jesus
2:1–12	Jesus is the Messiah, King and Son of God.
16:1–11	Jesus will rise from the dead.
22:1–31	Jesus will be forsaken, mocked, become thirsty, be pierced in hands and feet, have his clothes divided and gambled over, but conquer death to God's everlasting praise.
31:1–24	Jesus will commit his spirit into the hands of God and gain victory over those who oppress him.
40:1–17	Jesus will become human to fulfill the law for us just as it was written.
41:9–13	A close friend will betray Jesus, but Jesus will triumph in the end.
45:6–7	Jesus is crowned above all others and worshiped as God.
69:7–21	Because of his zeal, his own people will despise Jesus. He will be given gall and vinegar.
72:1–19	Jesus as David's son will be king forever.
110:1–6	Jesus will rule at God's right hand as Lord and High Priest.
118:1–29	Jesus will gain victory over his enemies and death. Although he is rejected, God will establish him as the one "who comes in the name of the Lord" (Ps. 118:26).

Psalm 23

Psalm 23 is one of the dearest passages of the Bible. It is a beautiful reminder that the Lord is caring and compassionate. It reminds us that, like sheep, we depend on God's care and provision.

PSALM 23	THE SHEPHERD'S CARE	APPLICATION
The LORD is my shepherd.	Sheep are able to recognize their shepherd. Care for sheep means ownership of them.	I am like a sheep under God's care. I belong to him.
I shall not be in want.	Sheep may wander off in search of "greener pastures." A stray sheep becomes easy prey for predators.	God meets my deepest needs.
He makes me lie down in green pastures.	Sheep will not rest until they are free from predators, pests, hunger, and conflict with other sheep. The shepherd's protection is crucial for sheep to rest.	God makes me free to rest.
He leads me beside quiet waters.	Sheep will not drink from waters moving too swiftly because they are not good swimmers, laden down with heavy woolen coats. Shepherds lead them to still waters.	I can drink deeply of God's Holy Spirit who is water to my thirsty soul.
He restores my soul.	Sheep may become "cast," stuck on their backs, unable to get up. A sheep struggling to get up can quickly become dehydrated in the summer sun or become prey for wild animals. The shepherd helps the sheep stand up again.	God cares for and keeps my heart and mind.
He guides me in paths of righteousness for his name's sake.	Sheep are creatures of habit. By overgrazing they will destroy their own pastures. They must be led to new pastureland. Only shepherds know the best way to get their sheep there.	God will lead me on the right path because of his great promise.
Even though I walk through the valley of the shadow of death, I will fear no evil, for you are with me.	Valleys on the way to high pastureland often have the best grass, but those valleys can also be places of dark danger for sheep.	God knows and deals with my fears about the deadly dangers of life.
Your rod and your staff, they comfort me.	Sheep need to learn to trust their shepherd. The shepherd's rod protects and disciplines; it guides and saves.	God's discipline and guidance make me feel safe.
You prepare a table before me in the presence of my enemies.	Often shepherds must prepare the pasture to remove poisonous plants. Predators often wait at the margins of the tableland for a chance to attack.	God provides for my hunger, even when my enemies surround me.
You anoint my head with oil.	Flying insects often plague sheep in summer. Oil is a natural bug repellant that also aids in the healing of skin.	God takes care of my bodily needs.
My cup overflows.	The good shepherd is willing to take the sheep to better grazing and water sources even if it means cost and danger.	My provision from God is abundant.
Surely goodness and love will follow me all the days of my life.	Sheep can aid in the fertility of the land, transforming wilderness into parkland and fertile fields. The good shepherd makes blessing follow his sheep.	God's goodness and grace will be with me my whole life.
And I will dwell in the house of the LORD forever.	Sheep, after spending the summer in high pastures, are taken back to the shepherd's property in the fall and winter.	I shall live eternally with God.

Shepherd Imagery in the Bible

OLD TESTAMENT

- God is the Shepherd (Gen. 49:24; Ps. 23; 80:1).
- God's appointed leaders are undershepherds (Ezek. 34).
- Many people in the Old Testament were shepherds by trade, like Abel, Abraham, Isaac, Rachel, Jacob, Moses, and David.
- Foreign leaders were sometimes called shepherds when their leadership impacted God's people (Isa. 44:28).
- The prophets depicted the distress of Israel without leadership or with bad leaders in terms of a flock without a shepherd (Ezek. 34:1–10; Zech. 10:2; 13:7).
- The prophets used shepherd imagery to point to the Messiah to come (Ezek. 34:22–24; 37:24; Isa. 40:11; Zech. 13:7; see also Matt. 26:31; Mark 14:27).

NEW TESTAMENT

- Jesus is our Chief Shepherd (1 Peter 5:3–4).
- Jesus is our Good Shepherd (John 10:1–30).
- Jesus is our Great Shepherd (Heb. 13:20).
- Jesus had compassion on the large crowds who came out to see him because they were "like sheep without a shepherd" (Matt. 9:36; Mark 6:34).
- Jesus used sheep and shepherds in his parables (Matt. 12:11–12; 18:12–14; 25:31–46).
- Jesus commissioned his disciples to care for his sheep (Matt. 10:6, 16; John 21:16–17).
- Jesus is the lamb of sacrifice (John 1:29; Acts 8:32; 1 Peter 1:19; Rev. 5:6).
- Elders are shepherds under Christ (1 Peter 5:2).

SHEPHERD'S DUTIES	JESUS' ACTIONS
Leads the sheep to safe pasture and water.	Calls disciples to follow wherever he leads (Matt. 4:18–22; John 10:4–9).
Protects the sheep from predators, pests, parasites, other sheep, and natural dangers.	Warns, intercedes, and rescues (Mark 8:15; John 17:12–15; Matt. 20:28; John 10:15).
Feeds the sheep, including removing poisonous plants and providing access to foliage on high branches or after a snowfall.	Feeds the crowds. He himself is the bread of life (Matt. 14:13–21; 15:32–39; John 6:22–71).
Cares for the weak or sick lambs.	Cares for the weak and sick (Matt. 14:14, 34–36).
Disciplines wayward sheep and retrieves the lost.	Rebukes his disciples and finds those who have lost their way (Matt. 14:29–31; 16:23; Luke 22:31–34).
Protects cultivated land and crops from the sheep.	Guides his disciples in the way of caring about others (Luke 6:27–36).
Prevents over grazing.	Teaches his disciples to be wise and harmless (Matt. 10:16).

Proverbs: A Guide to Godly Living

"An apple a day keeps the doctor away..." We all have heard or used some of these pithy sayings at one point or another. They express popular wisdom about the world that anyone can understand and apply. Their content expresses an observation about nature or society or advice concerning behavior or making choices.

People understand that following the advice of these wise sayings will help one to live a better life. Part of their effectiveness lies in their brevity—they are easy to remember. These sayings are most effective when we quote them at the right moment and in the right circumstances.

> Proverbs are short, memorable sayings that generalize on human experience to communicate an experiential truth.

Although we all recognize that these bits of wisdom are helpful, they are not universal or always applicable. While generally "an apple a day keeps the doctor away," we all know that some serious illnesses require immediate medical attention. In other words, we all recognize the limits of popular wisdom.

Who Wrote the Book?

- Proverbs 1:1, 10:1, and 25:1 affirm that King Solomon, King David's son, was the main author.
- Proverbs 25:1 also affirms that "the men of Hezekiah king of Judah" copied them.
- The book also recognizes other contributors: Wise men (22:17; 24:23), Agur (30:1), and Lemuel (31:1). Nothing is known about these writers.
- We read in 1 Kings 4:32 that Solomon wrote three thousand proverbs.

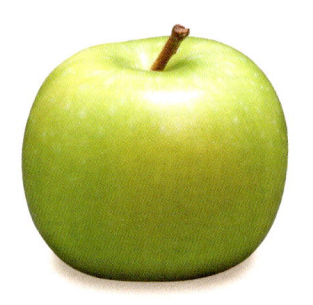

wisdom

Wisdom is often defined as "the ability to make godly choices." In the Bible, wisdom is tightly connected to creation. The way God created the universe has a direct effect on the way nature and society behave. In an important sense, wisdom is the ability to see life and the world the way God sees them. Wisdom is practical knowledge that allows people to live fully.

proverb

Proverb is a short, memorable saying that communicates an observation of the world or experience that helps one live better. The Hebrew word behind it is *mashal*. Among its meanings are: to rule and to compare or liken. The wisdom of proverbs helps wise people to master the art of godly living, as well as to discern how our lives and our behavior are connected with God's creation.

fear of the Lord

The Bible is clear that "the fear of the Lord is the beginning of knowledge" (1:7). In the Bible, the starting point of wisdom and its end-goal are an all-embracing relationship with God, the Lord of the covenant. The fear of the Lord is not a sense of terror but of reverence. In other words, it is a deep sense of who God is and who we are in relation to him. It is a deep understanding that God is the creator, sustainer, savior, judge, and owner of the whole universe. This knowledge is a relational knowledge that affects our behavior. The psalmist explains, "The Lord delights in those who fear him, who put their hope in his unfailing love" (Ps. 147:11). Fearing the Lord, then, takes the form of trust: trust in God's faithfulness to his promises as creator, redeemer, savior, and judge.

How Is the Book Arranged?

The structure of the book gives us an overview of the content and themes. The main sections of the book of Proverbs are:

1. Introduction to the book (1:1–7)
2. Instructions and warnings (1:8–9:18)
3. First collection of Solomon's proverbs (10:1–22:16)
4. First collection of the words of the wise (22:17–24:22)
5. Second collection of the words of the wise (24:23–34)
6. Second collection of Solomon's proverbs (25:1–29:27)
7. The words of Agur (30)
8. The words of Lemuel (31:1–9)
9. Poem of the virtuous woman (31:10–31)

Main Themes in the Book of Proverbs

Wisdom
We can read the whole book as an appeal to choose wisdom over all other things.

God created wisdom (8:22–23)	*The Lord brought me forth as the first of his works, before his deeds of old; I was appointed from eternity, from the beginning, before the world began.*
God used wisdom to create the universe (8:24–31)	*Then I was the craftsman at his side. I was filled with delight day after day, rejoicing always in his presence.*
God reveals and is the source of wisdom (2:6–7; 30:5–6)	*For the Lord gives wisdom, and from his mouth come knowledge and understanding (2:6–7).*
The beginning of wisdom is "fear of the Lord" (1:7; 2:5; 9:10; 10:27; 14:27; 15:16, 33; 16:6; 19:23; 22:4; 23:17)	*The fear of the Lord is the beginning of knowledge, but fools despise wisdom and discipline (1:7).*
Wisdom is desirable over all things (4:7–9; 8:10–11)	*Choose my instruction instead of silver, knowledge rather than choice gold, for wisdom is more precious than rubies, and nothing you desire can compare with her (8:10–11).*

2 Understanding Humanity
Wisdom teaching is directed to all people. Proverbs is an invitation to accurately identify the source of all wisdom, neither over- nor underestimating human wisdom. In the book of Proverbs we learn about humans:

Humans are God's creation (29:13)	*The poor man and the oppressor have this in common: The Lord gives sight to the eyes of both.*
Humans delude themselves (12:15; 14:12; 16:2; 25; 28:26)	*There is a way that seems right to a man, but in the end it leads to death.*
The heart is central and reveals humanity's true character (27:19)	*As water reflects a face, so a man's heart reflects the man.*
Humans are inherently foolish (22:15)	*Folly is bound up in the heart of a child, but the rod of discipline will drive it far from him.*

3. Description of a wise person

Wisdom is not something easily taught. As with many important things, it is easier to show what a wise person looks like than describe wisdom. Wise people are recognized by their:

Character	
They are righteous (13:5–6; 12:17)	The righteous hate what is false, but the wicked bring shame and disgrace. Righteousness guards the man of integrity, but wickedness overthrows the sinner (13:5–6).
Loyal (16:6)	Through love and faithfulness sin is atoned for; through the fear of the LORD a man avoids evil.
Humble (3:5, 9; 8:17; 28:13; 21:4)	He who conceals his sins does not prosper, but whoever confesses and renounces them finds mercy (28:13).
Teachable (12:1, 15; 3:1; 10:14; 15:12; 17:10; 18:15)	The heart of the discerning acquires knowledge; the ears of the wise seek it out (18:15).
Self-controlled and not rash (17:27; 14:29, 30; 19:2)	A man of knowledge uses words with restraint, and a man of understanding is even-tempered (17:27).
Forgiving (10:12; 17:9; 14:9; 20:22; 24:29)	Do not say, "I'll do to him as he has done to me; I'll pay that man back for what he did" (24:29).
Thoughtful (13:16; 14:8, 15, 16; 22:5)	A simple man believes anything, but a prudent man gives thought to his steps. A wise man fears the LORD and shuns evil, but a fool is hotheaded and reckless (14:15–16).
Is honest (12:22)	The LORD detests lying lips, but he delights in men who are truthful.
Does not boast (27:2)	Let another praise you, and not your own mouth; someone else, and not your own lips.
Does not reveal secrets (17:9; 20:19)	He who covers over an offense promotes love, but whoever repeats the matter separates close friends (17:9).
Does not slander (6:12)	A scoundrel and villain, who goes about with a corrupt mouth.
Is peaceful (12:16)	A fool shows his annoyance at once, but a prudent man overlooks an insult.

Speech	
Words have power (10:11; 12:18)	Reckless words pierce like a sword, but the tongue of the wise brings healing (12:18).
Limits of words (14:23; 28:24; 26:18–19)	Like a madman shooting firebrands or deadly arrows is a man who deceives his neighbor and says, "I was only joking!" (26:18–19).

Relationship with Wife	
He recognizes she is from God (18:22; 19:14)	Houses and wealth are inherited from parents, but a prudent wife is from the LORD (19:14).
Acknowledges as his crowning glory (12:4; 31:28)	He who finds a wife finds what is good and receives favor from the LORD (12:4).
Is faithful to her (5:15–20; 6:29)	Drink water from your own cistern, running water from your own well. Should your springs overflow in the streets, your streams of water in the public squares? Let them be yours alone, never to be shared with strangers. May your fountain be blessed, and may you rejoice in the wife of your youth (5:15–18).

Relationship with Children	
Acknowledges the need for wisdom in their lives (1–9)	My son, do not forget my teaching, but keep my commands in your heart, for they will prolong your life many years and bring you prosperity (3:1–2).
Recognizes children's natural condition (22:15)	Folly is bound up in the heart of a child, but the rod of discipline will drive it far from him.
Children can be trained (19:18; 22:6)	Train a child in the way he should go, and when he is old he will not turn from it (22:6).
Recognizes that foolish children are in danger and wisdom can help (20:20)	If a man curses his father or mother, his lamp will be snuffed out in pitch darkness.
Loves children and disciplines them (13:24)	He who spares the rod hates his son, but he who loves him is careful to discipline him.

Relationships with Other People	
Chooses kind friends (22:24–25)	Do not make friends with a hot-tempered man, do not associate with one easily angered, or you may learn his ways and get yourself ensnared.
Values and is loyal to friends (27:10; 17:17)	Do not forsake your friend and the friend of your father, and do not go to your brother's house when disaster strikes you—better a neighbor nearby than a brother far away (27:10).
Behaves fairly and justly with all (3:27–28)	Do not withhold good from those who deserve it, when it is in your power to act. Do not say to your neighbor, "Come back later; I'll give it tomorrow"—when you now have it with you.
Is considerate (25:17)	Seldom set foot in your neighbor's house—too much of you, and he will hate you.
Lives in peace (3:29; 25:8–9)	Do not plot harm against your neighbor, who lives trustfully near you (3:29).

Possessions	
Recognizes the proper value of money (30:7–9; 11:4)	Wealth is worthless in the day of wrath, but righteousness delivers from death (11:4).
Wisdom is better than riches (15:16; 16:8, 16; 22:1)	How much better to get wisdom than gold, to choose understanding rather than silver! (16:16).
Honors God with possessions and recognizes that blessings come from God (3:9–10; 10:22; 14:24)	Honor the Lord with your wealth, with the firstfruits of all your crops; then your barns will be filled to overflowing, and your vats will brim over with new wine (3:9–10).
Recognizes that foolish behavior leads to poverty (6:6–11; 10:4–5; 21:17; 26:13–15), as do injustice and oppression (13:23; 16:8; 22:16)	He who loves pleasure will become poor; whoever loves wine and oil will never be rich (21:17). He who oppresses the poor to increase his wealth and he who gives gifts to the rich—both come to poverty (22:16).
Is generous with possessions (3:27–28; 11:24; 28:27; 29:7)	The righteous care about justice for the poor, but the wicked have no such concern (29:7).
Is kind to animals (12:10)	A righteous man cares for the needs of his animal, but the kindest acts of the wicked are cruel.

A good man leaves an inheritance for his children's children,
but a sinner's wealth is stored up for the righteous.

4 Kingship

In the world of ancient Israel, the king represented the people. Kings were meant to model attitudes, behaviors, and character that all people should display in their lives. Jesus, the King of kings, plays this role when he shows us what it means to be God's children. Thus, the king should:

Know his place (21:1)	The king's heart is in the hand of the Lord; he directs it like a watercourse wherever he pleases.
Be wise (8:15–16)	By me kings reign and rulers make laws that are just; by me princes govern, and all nobles who rule on earth.
Be righteous (25:5)	Remove the wicked from the king's presence, and his throne will be established through righteousness.
Be just (28:8; 29:4, 14)	If a king judges the poor with fairness, his throne will always be secure (29:14).
Have self-control (31:1–7)	[D]o not spend your strength on women, your vigor on those who ruin kings. "It is not for kings, O Lemuel—not for kings to drink wine, not for rulers to crave beer (31:3–4).
Be compassionate (31:8–9)	"Speak up for those who cannot speak for themselves, for the rights of all who are destitute. Speak up and judge fairly; defend the rights of the poor and needy."
Be surrounded by godly people (16:13; 22:11)	He who loves a pure heart and whose speech is gracious will have the king for his friend (22:11).

> **genre** Genre refers to the sorting of written texts into categories. Separating texts in genres is helpful for understanding the ways different texts work internally, as well as the settings in which they were used. For example, we have different expectations from a letter from a bank than we do a letter from a loved one. Each type of letter produces certain expectations and prompts a specific response.
>
> The Bible contains different genres: narrative, prophecy, poetry, wisdom, apocalyptic literature, gospel, letters, history, and others. Each general genre is subdivided into smaller types. Wisdom, for example, is subdivided into proverbs, instructions, speeches, and advice. Knowing the genre helps us know the intention for the text.

Wisdom Literature

As "an apple a day" illustrates, proverbs do not occur exclusively in the Bible. The book of Proverbs is an example of a wider category of wisdom literature. In ancient Egypt and Mesopotamia, wisdom played an important role. In those societies, wisdom belonged to the royal court. Wise teachers instructed their royal students for important positions within the kingdom. From scribes to nobles, wisdom taught the proper—wise—behavior in the court, correct speech, and an understanding of society and the world that allowed them to serve the ruler effectively.

Wisdom Literature in the Bible

The book of Proverbs is an example of a wider category of wisdom books in the Old Testament.

Wisdom Books	Wisdom Themes in Other Books
• Job • Proverbs • Ecclesiastes	• Song of Songs • Psalms (for example, 1, 19, 34, 49, 78, 119) • Genesis (1–2, 37–50) • Amos and Isaiah • Daniel

Biblical wisdom literature shares themes, vocabulary, and genres with this international wisdom tradition. The chart shows some important differences between the wisdom of the Bible and that of the world around ancient Israel.

	Egypt and Mesopotamia	Old Testament
Focus	Anthropocentric (human-centered) The main interest was on finding ways for people to be successful in life. Material success was emphasized.	Theocentric (God-centered) The main focus is on the God who created with order. Success in life is connected to human relationship with God.
God	Since these societies were polytheistic, their wisdom depended on a personal god or a number of other gods. Each god provided some wisdom.	The Bible declares that the Lord alone is God. God is the source of all wisdom because he himself created wisdom and created the universe with wisdom.
Audience	The main audience for wisdom teachers were court officials and royalty.	Wisdom is meant for all people. Although Proverbs emphasize "sons," the other wisdom books make it clear that wisdom is for all.
Goal	Help civil servants to be effective and successful in their work and life in general.	Teach people to love wisdom by having a correct relationship with God, by understanding the order with which God created the universe, and by recognizing the limits of human wisdom.

Parallelism

Parallel lines are an important feature of biblical proverbs. English proverbs normally have one line—"a penny saved is a penny earned." Hebrew proverbs normally have two lines—"A fool finds pleasure in evil conduct, but a man of understanding delights in wisdom" (10:23).

The sense of the proverb is found in the interplay of these lines.

Parallelism means that the second line of the verse advances the thought of the first line in some way. Determining how this movement occurs allows us to understand the sense and meaning of the proverb. There are different kinds of parallelism; the following examples are the most common types of parallelism in the book of Proverbs.

Kings take pleasure in honest lips; they value a man who speaks the truth (16:13).	In this example, we find these parallels: 1. Kings are the main subject of the whole verse. 2. Taking pleasure is parallel to value. However, valuing something is a step beyond merely taking pleasure. 3. Honest lips is parallel to a man who speaks the truth. Although both expressions mean the same, the second one further specifies what honest lips are. 4. Some call this type of parallelism synonymous parallelism.
A fool finds pleasure in evil conduct, but a man of understanding delights in wisdom (10:23).	1. This verse presents a contrast which provides the parallelism. 2. A fool is contrasted with a man of understanding. 3. Another parallel is the action of each person: one finds pleasure whereas the other delights. The two concepts are closely related, though the first one seems more impulsive. 4. The true contrast is on what each one finds delight in: the fool finds pleasure in evil conduct, while the man of understanding delights in wisdom. 5. The final contrast is the key to the verse. Like the rest of Proverbs, the book invites its readers to delight in wisdom. Some call this contrasting parallel antithetical parallelism.
Better a meal of vegetables where there is love than a fattened calf with hatred (15:17)	1. Another important form of parallelism is often called "better than" proverbs. 2. These proverbs explain why wisdom is superior to folly. 3. In the book of Proverbs, riches can be a blessing from God. But not all riches are desirable. When riches are accompanied by hatred, then poverty with love is preferable.

Lady Wisdom and Lady Folly

The function of the book of Proverbs is to persuade and instruct. First, the book invites readers to make a decision. The choice is not only a rational one; it involves desires and emotions, as well as intelligence and discernment. The writer attempts to capture the reader's will by appealing to the imagination.

In the first nine chapters, the book addresses a "son." For young men, the choice of the right woman is life changing. Proverbs invites its readers to make an equally life-changing choice. Choosing wisdom over folly changes people's lives in a powerful way.

> Although the book addresses men only, as was traditional in ancient societies, its lessons are meant for all of God's people.

Wisdom and Folly are characterized as women. The readers "hear" from both Lady Wisdom and Lady Folly. Their invitations become alternatives between life and death. When reading the book of Proverbs, we must allow it to touch our emotions and our wills. We must allow ourselves not just to choose Lady Wisdom but also to love and pursue her.

Proverbs in Context

Although we can read each proverb separately, biblical proverbs were placed, by divine will, in a specific book context. Proverbs is part of a larger conversation with the other "wisdom books." Proverbs, Job, and Ecclesiastes balance and complement each other's views about wisdom, God, creation, humanity, and every important topic of the Bible.

A superficial reading of the book of Proverbs could suggest that the world functions with a perfect retribution theology: good things happen to good people, and bad things happen to bad people. As tempting as that might be to believe, the story in the book of Job calls us to be cautious. While Job's three friends argue individually that God rewards the righteous and punishes the wicked, Job continues to defend his own innocence. As readers, we know from the introduction in chapters one and two that Job is being used and abused by Satan, with God's authorization.

Job pleads for an audience with the creator. When he gets one, Job does not receive answers but a series of questions from God. God shows that he alone is wise; Job humbly recognizes the limits of his own wisdom, and declares, "Surely I spoke of things I did not understand, things too wonderful for me to know" (Job 42:3). At the end, God justifies and restores Job. He also rebukes Job's friends for their foolishness. Just as the book of Proverbs is an invitation to fall in love with Lady Wisdom, the book of Job is a reminder that we should not fall in love with our own wisdom.

Proverbs Today

Should we read the Proverbs today? Yes! And not only should we read them, but we need to allow the beauty and desirability of Lady Wisdom to captivate our imaginations and wills. The consequences of our efforts will be evident in:

1. Life
2. Health
3. Riches
4. Fulfillment and satisfaction
5. Relationships
6. Joy
7. Peace
8. Hope
9. Knowledge of and love for the world
10. Greater appreciation of God's wisdom in our lives

We will also be able to know and relate better to Jesus, "who has become for us wisdom from God…" (1 Cor. 1:30). In Jesus, God reveals the extent, depth, and power of his wisdom.

NEW TESTAMENT

THE GOSPELS SIDE BY SIDE

Why Do We Need Four Gospels?

Because the four Gospels contain different accounts of the same or similar events in the life of Jesus, readers of the Gospels have often sought to compare and contrast these accounts by placing them next to each other. These side-by-side comparisons attempt to harmonize the work of the four Evangelists and so are often called "Gospel Harmonies."

FOUR POINTS OF VIEW

Gospel	Symbol	Viewpoint	Audience	Jesus the Son of God
Matthew	Man	Palestinian Jewish	Jewish world	Is the Messiah King of Israel
Mark	Lion	Hellenistic Jewish	Greek-speaking world	Is the Power of God in the world
Luke	Bull	Greco-Roman	Gentile world	Is the Ideal Man of God
John	Eagle	Heavenly	Whole world	Is the Word of God

Why are there four Gospels instead of just one? One answer is that it takes four points of view to get the whole story about Jesus. Some might argue that one authoritative story should be enough. However, God chose to reveal himself using four Gospels. The Gospel of John begins with these words: "In the beginning was the Word … (vs. 1) and the Word became flesh … (vs. 14). In other words, God chooses as his preferred method of communication to speak to humans by means of the human. This is true of the Bible and it is supremely true of Christ whom we are told is God in the flesh (John 1:14–18). So then, the Gospels are, like Jesus, both a Divine work as well as a human work. They have real human authors and one divine Author. They give details that might be difficult to understand, but they are never truly contradictory. They have four different points of view on the history of Jesus but only one Divine conclusion as to his identity as the Son of God.

Harmony of the Gospels

EVENT	MATTHEW	MARK	LUKE	JOHN
The genealogy of Jesus	1:1–17		3:23–38	
Jesus' birth and childhood	1:18–2:23		1:5–2:52	
John the Baptist's ministry	3:1–12	1:1–8	3:1–18	1:19–34
Christ's public ministry and first Passover	3:13–4:12	1:9–14	3:21–4:13	1:35–4:42
Christ's ministry in Galilee	4:12	1:14–15	4:14–15	4:43–54
His rejection at Nazareth and move to Capernaum	4:13–22; 8:14–17	1:16–34	4:16–41	
His first ministry tour and second Passover	4:23–12:14	1:35–3:6	4:42–7:50	5:1–47
His second ministry tour	12:15–13:58	3:7–6:6	8:1–56	
His third ministry tour	9:35–11:1; 14:1–12	6:6–29	9:1–9	
Ministry to his disciples and third Passover	14:13–18:35	6:30–9:50	9:10–56	6:1–71
Ministry in Judea			10:1–13:21	7:1–10:39

The Gospels Side by Side

EVENT	MATTHEW	MARK	LUKE	JOHN
Ministry beyond Jordan	19:1–20:34	10:1–52	13:22–19:27	10:40–11:54
The last week (Passover/Easter)	21:12–28:20	11:1–16:20	19:28–24:53	11:55–21:25
Arrival in Bethany and Mary anoints Jesus' feet	26:6–13	14:3–9	19:28	11:55–12:11
Triumphal entry	21:1–11	11:1–11	19:29–44	12:12–19
Second cleansing of the temple; barren fig tree cursed	21:12–13; 18–22	11:12–18	19:45–48	
Greeks seek Jesus; fig tree withered	21:19–22	11:19–25	21:37–38	12:20–50
Jesus' authority challenged	21:23–22:46	11:27–12:37	20:1–44	
Denouncing the scribes and Pharisees	23:1–39	12:38–40	20:45–47	
Widow's offering		12:41–44	21:1–4	
The Olivet discourse	24:1–25:46	13:1–37	21:5–36	
Crucifixion predicted	26:1–5	14:1–2	22:1–2	
Judas's bargain	26:14–16	14:10–11	22:3–6	
Preparation and the Passover	26:17–30	14:12–26	22:7–20	13:1–14:31
Discourse and high priestly prayer				15:1–17:26
Gethsemane	26:36–46	14:32–42	22:39–46	18:1
Betrayal, arrest, and trial	26:47–56	14:43–52	22:47–53	18:2–14
Jesus condemned to death and Peter's denial	26:57–75	14:53–72	22:54–65	18:15–27
Formal condemnation after dawn	27:1–2	15:1	22:66–71	
Judas' suicide	27:3–10			
Jesus' first time before Pilate	27:11–14	15:1–5	23:1–5	18:28–38
Jesus before Herod the Tetrarch			23:6–12	18:39–19:16
Jesus' second time before Pilate	27:15–26	15:6–15	23:13–25	
Soldiers mock Jesus	27:27–31	15:16–23	23:26–33	19:16–17
The crucifixion	27:32–49	15:21–36	23:26–43	19:18–29
Jesus' death	27:50–56	15:37–41	23:44–49	19:30–37
Jesus' burial	27:57–66	15:42–47	23:50–56	19:38–42
Earthquake and tomb opened	28:1–4			
Visit of women at dawn	28:5–8	16:1–3	24:1–8	20:1
Women report to the apostles; Peter and John visit the tomb			24:9–12	20:2–10
Jesus appears first to Mary Magdalene		16:9–11		20:11–18
Jesus appears to other women; the guards report to the rulers	28:9–15			
Jesus appears to two on the road to Emmaus		16:12–13	24:13–32	
Jesus appears to Peter			24:33–35	
Jesus appears to ten, Thomas absent		16:14	24:36–43	20:19–25
Jesus appears to the eleven, Thomas present				20:26–31
Jesus appears to seven on the sea of Galilee				21:1–25
Jesus appears to about five hundred at an appointed mountain in Galilee	28:16–20	16:15–18		
Jesus appears to his brother James—1 Corinthians 15:7				
Jesus appears to his apostles again, his ascension		16:19–20	24:44–53	
Jesus appears to Paul—1 Corinthians 15:8				

Miracles of Jesus

The Gospel of John records the least number of miracles. Most of John's miracle accounts are not in the other Gospels. John seems to have intentionally included new material that had not previously been written down. At the same time John's focus is more on Jesus' words, his teaching, rather than on the miraculous signs Jesus did. Perhaps conscious of his readers' desire for miracle stories, John adds to his Gospel the words, "I suppose that even the world would not have room for the books that would be written" about Jesus' many other deeds (John 21:25).

MIRACLE	MATTHEW	MARK	LUKE	JOHN
Water into wine				2:1–11
Official's son healed				4:46–54
Healing of demoniac in the synagogue		1:21–28	4:33–37	
Healing of Peter's mother-in-law	8:14–17	1:29–31	4:38–39	
Many healed at sunset		1:32–34	4:40–41	
Miraculous catch of fish			5:4–11	
Healing of a leper	8:2–4	1:40–45	5:12–16	
Healing of a paralytic	9:2–8	2:1–12	5:17–26	
Healing at Bethesda				5:2–15
Withered hand healed in a synagogue	12:9–14	3:1–6	6:6–11	
Many healed	12:15–21	3:7–12	6:17–19	
Centurion's servant healed	8:5–13		7:1–10	
Widow's son raised at Nain			7:11–17	
Demon-possessed man healed	12:22–23	3:20–21		
Calming of the storm	8:23–27	4:36–41	8:23–25	
Demonic legion cast out	8:28–34	5:1–20	8:26–39	
Healing of the woman with the flow of blood	9:20–22	5:24–34	8:42–48	
Raising of Jairus' daughter	9:23–26	5:35–43	8:49–56	
Healing of two blind men	9:27–31			
Healing of a mute demoniac	9:32–34			
Many healed, feeding of five thousand	14:13–21	6:30–44	9:10–17	6:1–14
Walking on water and calming of the storm	14:22–33	6:45–52		6:16–21
Syro-Phoenician woman's daughter healed	15:21–28	7:24–30		
Deaf mute healed		7:31–37		
Many healed, feeding of four thousand	15:29–39	8:1–10		
Blind man of Bethsaida healed		8:22–26		
Healing of demoniac boy	17:14–19	9:14–29	9:37–43	
Healing of the man born blind				9:1–7
Crippled woman healed on Sabbath			13:10–13	
Healing of a man with dropsy on the Sabbath			14:2–6	
Jesus raised Lazarus				11:38–44
Ten lepers cleansed			17:11–14	
Healing of two blind men near Jericho	20:29–34	10:46–52	18:35–43	
Many healed in the temple	21:14			
Healing of the severed ear			22:51	
Resurrection	28:1–20	16:1–19	24:1–53	20:1–31
Miraculous catch of fish				21:1–8

Galilee and Judea

Jesus began his public ministry in Galilee, in the northern region. He spent much, if not most of his time there. Jesus frequented Judea and Jerusalem for the required religious festivals, but it seems he only spent significant time there late in his ministry (Luke 9:51). John affirms that his safety was compromised in Judea, and that it was only under cover that Jesus made his way to Jerusalem (John 7:1–10).

Yet, even this seeming insignificant fact about Christ's life was foretold in Scripture. Matthew 4:12–17 shows us that Isaiah had prophesied hundreds of years in advance that Christ's brilliant light would shine forth in Galilee (Isaiah 9:1–2).

Jesus' Last Week

The Gospel writers center much of their attention on the last week of Jesus' ministry. About a fourth to a half of the Gospel's material has to do with the incidents surrounding Christ's death and resurrection. This should tell us of the importance of this week in their minds. It holds the key to the central issue of the church and of all history, for in that last week, the life and death of the whole world and the whole of human history were at stake. Without the death and resurrection of Jesus there is no hope, nor can there be any salvation.

Jesus' Passovers

One way to measure the length of Jesus' public ministry is by counting the number of Passovers the Gospels record. Since the Passover festival only happened once a year, counting the Passovers gives a rough idea of how long Jesus' ministry lasted. The Gospels suggest that Jesus' public ministry continued for at least three years. Notice, John is the writer most concerned to give us the details about the festivals in Jesus' life.

FEAST	EVENT OR TEACHING	SCRIPTURE
First Passover	Jesus went to the Passover. He cleansed the temple, talked with Nicodemus and ministered in Judea for a while.	John 2:13–25
Second Passover	Jesus went to the "feast" (probably Passover) and healed the man at the pool of Bethesda.	John 5:1–47
Third Passover	Jesus delivered his "Bread of Life" teaching. However, he did not go to Passover because of a threat to his life in Judea.	John 6:4–7:1
Tabernacles (Booths)	Jesus went secretly for reasons of security. Teaching in the temple, he encountered opposition from the religious leaders. Jesus claimed to be the "Light of the World." He healed the man born blind near the pool of Siloam.	John 7:2–9:41
Hanukkah (Dedication)	Jesus attended the feast. He spoke of his "sheep." Again he escaped stoning.	John 10:22–42
Last Passover/ Last Supper	Jesus went to the Passover and the last week of his life took place.	Matthew 26:17; Mark 14:12; Luke 22:7; John 12:1

Tracking Jesus' Moves

The use of this kind of harmony is also helpful to get a picture of Jesus' movements.

PLACE	EVENT OR TEACHING	SCRIPTURE
Bethlehem	Birth of Jesus	Mt. 1:24–25; Lk. 2:1–7
Egypt	Flight from Herod	Mt. 2:13–15
Nazareth	Early childhood	Mt. 2:19–23; Lk. 2:39
Jerusalem	Passover celebration	Lk. 2:41–52
Jordan River	Baptism of Jesus	Mt. 3:13–17; Mk. 1:9–11; Lk. 3:21–23; Jn. 1:29–34
Wilderness	Temptation of Jesus	Mt. 4:1–11; Mk. 1:12–13; Lk. 4:1–13
Going to Galilee	Calling of Philip and Nathaniel	Jn. 1:43–51
Cana in Galilee	First miracle	Jn. 2:1–11
Capernaum	Family stay	Jn. 2:12
Jerusalem	First Passover	Jn. 2:13–25
Judea	Baptizing new disciples	Jn. 3:22
Returning to Galilee	Jesus goes through Samaria	Jn. 4:1–4
Samaria	Jesus talks to the women at the well	Jn. 4:5–42
Cana in Galilee	Healing of official's son and the beginning of Jesus' Galilean ministry	Jn. 4:43–54; Mt. 4:12; Mk. 1:14–15; Lk. 4:14–15
Nazareth	Rejection at Nazareth	Lk. 4:16–30
Capernaum	Move of ministry base	Mt. 4:13; Mk. 1:21; Lk. 4:31
Galilee	Preaching tour	Mt. 4:23–25; Mk. 1:32–39; Lk. 4:42–44
Jerusalem	Second Passover	Jn. 5:1–47
Galilee	The parable of the Sower and Seed	Mt. 13:1; Mk. 4:1; Lk. 8:1–4
Gennesaret	Healing of multitudes	Mt. 14:34–36; Mk. 6:53–56
Tyre and Sidon	Faith of the Canaanite woman	Mt. 15:21–28; Mk. 7:24–30
The Region of the Decapolis	Healing of deaf and dumb man, feeding of the 4000	Mt. 15:29–38; Mk. 7:31–8:9
Galilee	Teaching and healing	Mt. 15:39–16:5; Mk. 8:10–26
Caesarea Philippi	The question of Jesus' identity	Mt. 16:13–20; Mk. 8:27–30; Lk. 9:18–21
Galilee and Capernaum	Jesus tells of his death a second time, the half-shekel tax	Mk. 17:22–27; Mk. 9:30–50
Jerusalem	Feast of Tabernacles	Lk. 9:51; Jn. 7:2–10
Various places in Judea	Preaching tour	Lk. 10:1–24
Jerusalem	Feast of Dedication (Hanukkah)	Jn. 10:22–23
Across the Jordan	Preaching tour	Mt. 19:1; Mk. 10:1; Lk. 13:22; Jn. 10:40–42
Between Galilee and Samaria	Ten lepers healed	Lk. 17:11–19
Jericho	Jesus heals blind men	Mt. 20:29–34; Mk. 10:46–52
Bethany	The raising of Lazarus	Jn. 11:1–53
Ephraim	Jesus stays with his disciples	Jn. 11:54
Bethany, Jerusalem and places in the vicinity	Jesus' last week (Passover/Easter)	Mt. 26:6–28:15; Mk. 14:3–16:11; Lk. 19:28–24:49; Jn. 11:55–20:31
Galilee	Appears to his disciples	Mt. 28:16–20; Mk. 16:15–18; Jn. 21:1–23
Mount of Olives	Jesus' ascension	Mk. 16:19–20; Lk. 24:50–53

Israel During Jesus' Time

Jesus' three-year ministry occurred all over the ancient cities. From Syria to Judea, Jesus brought the gospel's powerful words and actions.

Harmonies Through History

Over the years, people have created different types of "Gospel Harmonies." These are some of the main types of harmonies:

- **Synthetic Harmonization:** One approach is to cut out any variation in similar accounts and replace it with preferred wording to create a kind of "official version."

- **Sequential Harmonization:** This type attempts to bring together two or more versions of an event by keeping both. The separate details are seen as separate incidents within the same story.

- **Parallel Harmonization:** A final approach may be to show two or more versions next to each other for comparison and contrast.

Gospel harmonies began to be produced early in the history of the church. Concern for accuracy and a full account of the gospel message became important for the church as it strove to remain faithful. These early harmonies bear witness to the church's use of the four canonical Gospels. Already by the post-apostolic age, the authority of the four to the exclusion of other texts is recognized.

AUTHOR	TITLE	DATE
Justin Martyr	Evident in his writings	Second Century
Tatian	Diatesseron	Second Century
Unknown	Dura-Europas Harmony	Second Century
Eusebius of Caesarea	Sections and Canons	Third Century
Augustine	Consensus of the Gospels	Fourth Century
Andreas Osiander	Gospel Harmony	Sixteenth Century

The Gospels as Biography

The four Gospels are best understood as biographies about the life and times of Jesus. However, there are important differences between modern and ancient biographies. The main difference is the notion of historical sequencing.

MODERN BIOGRAPHIES	ANCIENT BIOGRAPHIES
Biographies written today place a premium on sequencing. The events of the subject's life are typically narrated in the order in which they happened. Beginning with the birth of the individual, relevant events and information are viewed in sequential order up to the death of the subject. While chapters may present different phases in the subject's life, these phases are arranged in the order in which they are supposed to have happened.	Ancient biographers had a general commitment to an historical sequence. They did not feel the need to place every detail in their writings in the exact order in which it happened. Much more emphasis is given to developing an accurate picture of the character of the subject. Deeds and happenings are seen as illustrative of that character no matter when they occurred.

THE GOSPELS AS BIOGRAPHIES

Luke 7:36–50 is an example of the non-sequential nature of ancient biographies. This passage is Luke's account of the woman who anoints Jesus' feet. Matthew, Mark and John tell this event as part of Jesus' arrival at Bethany just before the events of Easter week (see Harmony Chart). Despite Luke's care as an accurate historian (Luke 1:1–4), he places this event much earlier in Jesus' ministry—that is, if we read Luke like we would read a modern biography. Some have tried to resolve the difficulty by suggesting that there were two such events, two times when various women anointed Jesus' feet. But the details of Luke's account too closely resemble the other Gospel accounts to make it a separate incident. It is much more likely that Luke (and so the Holy Spirit) was simply using this event out of historical sequence to illustrate the Pharisees and their lack of faith in contrast to the faith of the centurion (Luke 7:2–10).

The Synoptic Gospels and John

The word "synoptic" means "seen together." It refers to the first three Gospels: Matthew, Mark and Luke. When seen together, these Gospels often reveal related accounts in very similar language. Scholars agree there is some relationship between these three books. The exact nature of this relationship has been the subject of much debate. It seems that these three authors either read one another or some common source, which explains why so much of their substance and language are the same.

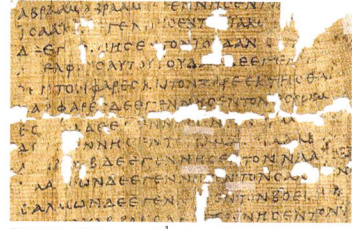

The Gospel of John, however, is different than the first three Gospels. John uses material that the other writers do not have. The wording of some of the stories is different. John often added details that the others do not include. For example, the name of the woman who washed Jesus' feet with her hair (John 12:3) or that he beat Peter in a foot race to the empty tomb on Easter Sunday (John 20:4). Many of these details have a personal tone.

Papyrus 1, also known as P[1], shows a fragment of the Gospel of Matthew. The fragment, housed in the University of Pennsylvania Museum, dates to around AD 250.

The Synoptic Gospels Compared to John
Three Examples

THE GOSPEL TEXT	EVENT	DESCRIPTION
Matthew 3:11–12; Mark 1:7–8; Luke 3:15–18	John the Baptist's introduction of Jesus	General and generic language is used about the crowds.
John 1:24–44		John names specific individuals who become disciples of Jesus through John the Baptist.
Matthew 14:13–21; Mark 6:30–44; Luke 9:10–17	Feeding of the 5000	Dialogue with Jesus is attributed to the disciples as a group.
John 6:1–14		John names specific individuals who speak.
Matthew 28:1–10; Mark 16:1–11; Luke 24:1–12; John 20:1–18	The Resurrection	Individuals are named in all accounts to a greater or lesser extent.
		John is specific about the actions of Mary Magdalene, Peter and himself (the unnamed disciple).

The First Gospel

Because the first three Gospels so closely resemble each other, the question has long been asked, "Who wrote first?" Many modern scholars are inclined in favor of Mark as being the first Gospel in print. This is due in part to the brevity of the work and the fact that most of Mark's material can also be found in Matthew and Luke. The idea is that if Mark wrote first, Luke and Matthew might have read his work and added their own material in their writing. Early tradition holds that Mark became associated with Peter and that his Gospel might be a kind of "Memoirs of Peter." Its rapid-fire style seems like Peter's way of recounting Jesus' life.

Others are convinced, however, that none of the Gospels that exists today was the first to be in print. These scholars believe that there was an earlier writing that the authors of the present Gospels (Matthew, Mark and Luke) drew upon as a reference work. Papias, an early Christian and disciple of the Apostle John, wrote, "Matthew put together the sayings in the Hebrew language, and each one interpreted them as best he could" (in Eusebius, Ecclesiastical History 3.39.16). Since Matthew was a tax collector (Matthew 9:9), he was a good pick to be the scribe among the disciples. So this tradition may bear some weight. It may be that Matthew recorded much of what happened in Jesus' ministry in the native tongue of Palestine. This document may later have been translated into Greek and used by him and the other synoptic writers to produce our present Gospels.

Medieval manuscript known as Aachen Gospels, folio 13r, made around AD 820.

The Gospels as we now have them were first written in Greek, which was the popular common language of the Roman world. It is entirely possible that Matthew made the first record in Aramaic, but that Mark drafted the first Gospel in Greek drawing on Matthew's record and adding what he had heard from Peter. Luke and Matthew (in present form) would then have been written. John wrote his account after the others had been in circulation for some time.

Genealogy of Jesus

The Gospel of Luke
Luke lists the genealogy from Jesus to Adam
Luke 3:23–38

The Gospel of Matthew
Matthew lists the genealogy from Abraham to Jesus
Matt. 1:1–16

Luke (Adam to Terah):
Adam, Seth, Enosh, Kenan, Mahalalel, Jared, Enoch, Methuselah, Lamech, Noah, Shem, Arphaxad, Cainan, Shelah, Eber, Peleg, Reu, Serug, Nahor, Terah

Matthew	Luke
Abraham	Abraham
Isaac	Isaac
Jacob	Jacob
Judah and Tamar ♀	Judah
Perez	Perez
Hezron	Hezron
Ram	Ram
Amminadab	Amminadab
Nahshon	Nahshon
Salmon and Rahab ♀	Salmon
Boaz and Ruth ♀	Boaz
Obed	Obed
Jesse	Jesse
King David and Uriah's wife (Bathsheba) ♀	David
King Solomon	Nathan
King Rehoboam	Mattatha
	Menna
King Abijah	Melea
	Eliakim
King Asa	Jonam
King Jehoshaphat	Joseph
King Jehoram	Judah
	Simeon
King Uzziah	Levi
King Jotham	Matthat
	Jorim
King Ahaz	Eliezer
King Hezekiah	Joshua
	Er
King Manasseh	Elmadam
King Amon	Cosam
	Addi
King Josiah	Melki
King Jeconiah	Neri
Shealtiel	Shealtiel
Zerubbabel	Zerubbabel
	Rhesa
Abiud	Joanan
	Joda
Eliakim	Josek
	Semein
Azor	Mattathias
	Maath
Zadok	Naggai
	Esli
Akim	Nahum
	Amos
Elihud	Mattathias
	Joseph
Eleazar	Jannai
	Melki
Matthan	Levi
	Matthat
Jacob	Heli
Joseph, the husband of Mary ♀	Joseph
JESUS	**JESUS**

Legend
♀ = Female
☐ = Names common in both genealogies

The Twelve Disciples

Who Are the Twelve Disciples?

THEIR BACKGROUNDS
- They were twelve Jewish men whom Jesus called to follow him during his three-year ministry on earth.
- The twelve disciples were from the Galilee region in the north except for Judas Iscariot, who was from Judea in the south.
- Their occupations ranged from fisherman to tax collectors and revolutionaries.
- Some were married (Mark 1:29–31; 1 Cor. 9:3–6).
- Some were well-versed in Scripture (John 1:46).

THEIR PURPOSE
- After being baptized by John the Baptist and spending forty days in the wilderness, Jesus started teaching and many people started following him.
- After a night of prayer and meditation, Jesus chose twelve men out of all those who were following him.
- These twelve men would be Jesus' main focus of instruction.
- These disciples were selected to let the world know of God's love, that God sent Jesus to redeem the world (John 17:23).

THEIR MISSION
- These are the twelve men who, for the most part, would prove to be valuable companions to Jesus.
- Their instruction and conversations would become the teachings, knowledge, and instruction for the church that would later grow and spread.
- Jesus knew their personalities, both strong and weak.
- Jesus knew that these men would disappoint him, desert him, deny him, and betray him.
- Jesus knew that these men, once filled with the Holy Spirit, would be the first witnesses of the gospel, carrying God's message of redemption to Judea, Samaria, and the ends of the earth.
- The twelve tribes of Israel were blessed in order to be a blessing to all nations. In a similar way, these twelve men, along with all disciples of Jesus who follow their lead, were to bless all nations (Gal. 3:8). Followers of Christ are commanded to go out and make disciples of all nations, baptizing them in the name of the Father, the Son, and the Holy Spirit (Matt. 28:19).

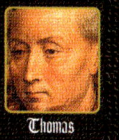

Being a Disciple of Christ

BEGINNING THE JOURNEY: COUNT THE COST
- Jesus said that whoever wants to follow him, that person must deny himself and take up his cross. He said that if one wants to save his life he will lose it, but if he loses his life for Jesus and for the gospel, he will save it.
- When Simon Peter, James, and John encountered Jesus, they pulled their boats up on shore, left everything and followed him.

FOLLOWING CHRIST TOGETHER: FELLOWSHIP
- Jesus prayed that his followers would be brought to complete unity.
- The followers of Jesus were not to give up meeting together and were to encourage one another.

SERVING CHRIST AND OTHERS
- Jesus said that whoever wants to become great among his disciples must be a servant, just as Jesus himself did not come to be served, but to serve, and "to give his life a ransom for many."

FAILURES AND FORGIVENESS
- When Jesus was arrested all the disciples deserted him and fled, and Peter denied knowing him because he feared for his life.
- Later Jesus said that the disciples would receive power when the Holy Spirit came to them and that they would share the good news in Jerusalem, and in all Judea and Samaria, and all over the earth.

IN THE POWER OF THE SPIRIT
- Jesus promised the disciples that he would send the Holy Spirit to them, and that the Holy Spirit would guide them and provide them with gifts that would help them carry out their mission.
- Paul wrote to the Corinthian church informing them that there is only one Spirit, but different kinds of gifts. There is only one God, but several kinds of good works.

Mark 8:34–35; 14:71–72; Luke 5:11; John 16:5–16; 17:23; Heb. 10:25; Matt. 20:26–28; 26:56; Acts 1:8; 1 Cor. 12:4–12

The Twelve Disciples

Peter | James, son of Zebedee

	Peter	**James, son of Zebedee**
Other Names	• Simeon bar Jona (Simon, son of Jona) • Cephas ("rock" or "stone") • Simon Peter • Simon	• Son of Zebedee • Boanerges (Son of Thunder) • "James the Elder" • "James the Great"
General Information	• Son of Jona and born in Bethsaida (John 1:42–44) • Lived in Capernaum (Matt. 8:5–14) • Fisherman (Matt. 4:18) • Brother of Andrew (Matt. 4:18) • Partner with James and John (Luke 5:10) • Married (Matt. 8:14) • One of the pillars of the Jerusalem church (Gal. 2:9) • Boldly preached, healed, and ministered to Jews and Gentiles after Pentecost (Acts 2–12) • Imprisoned by Herod for preaching and rescued by an angel of the Lord (Acts 12:3–19) • Wrote 1 Peter and 2 Peter	• Son of Zebedee. (Matt. 4:21) • Son of Salome. (Matt. 27:56; Mark 16:1) • Fisherman with his father and his brother (Matt. 4:18–22) • Brother of John (Matt. 4:21) • Partner with Peter (Luke 5:10) • Put to death by the sword by Herod Agrippa I. The only one of the twelve disciples whose death for his faith was recorded in Scripture (Acts 12:2)
Personality & Character	• Impulsive (Matt. 14:28), yet cowardly (Matt. 14:30; 26:69–74) • Hot tempered (John 18:10), yet tenderhearted (Matt. 26:75) • Insightful (Matt. 16:16), yet dense (Matt. 16:21–23) • Courageous and solid after Pentecost (Acts 5:27–30)	• Vengeful and fiery (Luke 9:54) • Selfish and conceited (Mark 10:35–37) • Committed to Christ and courageous to the end (Acts 12:2)
Encounters with Jesus	• Was called to be a fisher of people (Matt. 4:19) • Left everything to follow Jesus (Luke 5:11) • One of the three disciples in the core group of disciples (Mark 5:37; 9:2; 13:3; 14:33) • Simon said Jesus is the Christ, Son of the living God. Jesus names him Peter (rock) and said, "Upon this rock I will build my church, and the gates of Hell will not prevail against it." (Matt. 16:16–19) • Was reprimanded because he refused to accept that Jesus had to die (Matt. 16:23) • Witnessed Jesus' Transfiguration (where Jesus' divinity was revealed) (Mark 9:2–8) • Was sent to prepare the upper room for the Last Supper (Luke 22:8) • Jesus predicted that Peter would deny knowing him three times (Luke 22:31–34) • Was with Jesus in the Garden of Gethsemane (Matt. 26:36–46) • Jesus instructed Peter after his resurrection (John 21:15–19)	• Was called to be a fisher of people (Matt. 4:19) • Left everything to follow Jesus (Luke 5:11) • One of the three disciples in the core group of disciples (Mark 5:37; 9:2; 13:3; 14:33) • Jesus named him and John "Sons of Thunder" (Mark 3:17) • Was rebuked with his brother John for requesting God to rain fire on a Samaritan village (Luke 9:54–55) • Witnessed Jesus' Transfiguration (where Jesus' divinity was revealed) (Mark 9:2–8) • Jesus responded to James's and John's request to sit at his right and left in the kingdom (Mark 10:35–43) • Was with Jesus in the Garden of Gethsemane (Matt. 26:36–46) • Witnessed the miraculous catch of fish on the Sea of Galilee after Jesus' resurrection (John 21:2–7)
Key Lesson	God can forgive sins and strengthen the faith of those who love him.	Stand firm in the face of persecution.
Stories	• Papias (second-century Christian) recorded that Mark served as Peter's scribe and wrote the Gospel of Mark based on Peter's testimony. • According to some stories, Peter asked to be crucified upside down. Peter may have been crucified during the reign of Nero in Rome. • Symbols for Peter are sometimes keys, representing the keys to the kingdom of heaven (Matt. 16:19)	• Some claim he was the first bishop in Spain. • Symbols of James sometimes include the bishop's hat and the sword, which is in reference to his martyrdom.

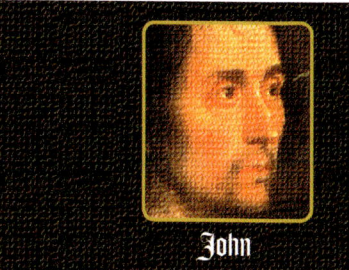

The Twelve Disciples

John | Andrew | Philip

John	Andrew	Philip
• Son of Zebedee • "The Evangelist" • Boanerges (Son of Thunder) • "The Revealer" • "The Beloved Disciple" (The disciple whom Jesus loved)	• "Protokletos" (First Called)	• None
• Son of Zebedee (Matt. 4:21) • Son of Salome (Matt. 27:56; Mark 16:1) • Fisherman with his father and his brother (Matt. 4:18–22) • Brother of James (Matt. 4:21) • Partner with Peter (Luke 5:10) • One of the pillars of the Jerusalem church (Gal. 2:9) • Healed and preached (Acts 3–4; 8) • Exiled to the island of Patmos (Rev. 1:1, 9) • Wrote the Gospel of John, 1, 2, and 3 John, and Revelation.	• Son of Jona (John 1:42) • Born in Bethsaida (John 1:44) • Lived in Capernaum with Peter (Mark 1:29) • Fisherman (Matt. 4:18) • Brother of Simon Peter (Matt. 4:18) • Disciple of John the Baptist (John 1:35–40) • Listed as one of Christ's twelve disciples (Matt. 10:2–4; Mark 3:16–19; Luke 6:14–16) • The name Andrew derives from Greek, meaning "manly."	• Born in Bethsaida (John 1:44) • Well versed in Scripture (John 1:45–46) • Listed as one of Christ's twelve disciples (Matt. 10:2–4; Mark 3:16–19; Luke 6:14–16) • The disciple Philip is often confused with Philip the evangelist found in Acts. • The name Philip derives from Greek, meaning "he who loves horses." • Philip probably spoke Greek (John 12:20–21)
• Vengeful and fiery (Luke 9:54) • Judgmental (Mark 9:38) • Selfish (Mark 10:35–37) • Bold, loving and compassionate after Pentecost (Acts 4:13; 1 John 4)	• Enthusiastic about Christ (John 1:35–42) • Inquisitive (John 1:35–38) • Resourceful (John 6:8–9)	• Practical (John 6:7) • Helpful (John 12:20–21) • Literal and confused (John 14:8)
• One of the three disciples in the core group of disciples (Mark 5:37; 9:2; 13:3; 14:33) • Suggested that driving out demons could only be performed by those who follow Jesus and his disciples (Mark 9:38) • Witnessed Jesus' Transfiguration (where Jesus' divinity was revealed) (Mark 9:2–8) • Was sent to prepare the upper room for the Last Supper (Luke 22:8) • Reclined next to Jesus during the Last Supper (John 13:23) • Was given the responsibility at the cross to take care of Mary, Jesus' mother (John 19:26–27) • Ran ahead of Peter to see Jesus' empty tomb and expressed faith by "seeing and believing" (John 20:2–8) • Witnessed the miraculous catch of fish on the Sea of Galilee after Jesus' resurrection (John 21:2–7)	• First to follow Jesus (John 1:35–40) • Called to be a fisher of people (Matt. 4:19) • Sent out on a mission to the Jews to preach "the kingdom of heaven is at hand," heal the sick, cleanse the lepers, raise the dead, and cast out demons (Matt. 10:5–8) • Informed Jesus that several Greeks wanted to see him (John 12:20–22) • Told Jesus of the boy with five loaves of bread and two fish (John 6:8–9) • Was present when Jesus appeared to the disciples after the resurrection (John 20:19–25) • Was present for the Great Commission when Jesus sent his disciples to all nations (Matt. 28:16–20) • Witnessed Jesus being taken up into heaven (Acts 1:8–9)	• The third disciple Jesus called (John 1:43) • Brought Nathanael (Bartholomew) to Jesus (John 1:45–46) • Jesus tested him regarding the feeding of the multitude (John 6:5–7) • Informed Jesus that several Greeks wanted to see him (John 12:20–22) • Asked Jesus to show him the Father (John 14:8–9) • Was present at the Last Supper (Matt. 26:20)
God's love, evident in Jesus Christ, saves, transforms, and unites all believers.	Go out and eagerly share the good news about Jesus Christ.	All the knowledge in the world does not compare to the truth found in Jesus.
• Some stories suggest that John was released from exile on the island of Patmos and returned to Ephesus (Turkey today). • Stories suggest that John died in Ephesus around AD 100. • Symbols of John sometimes include the eagle (Rev. 4:7) and a book.	• Some suggest that Andrew preached in Greece, Asia Minor, and Russia. • A seventh-century story suggests that Andrew was crucified on an X-shaped cross by a Roman proconsul. • The symbol for Andrew is sometimes the X-shaped cross.	• Tradition suggests that Philip lived and preached in Scythia (Ukraine today). • Some stories suggest that Philip was crucified on a tall cross at Hierapolis of Phrygia (Turkey today). • Symbols for Philip sometimes include loaves of bread (John 6:5–7) and a tall cross.

The Twelve Disciples

	Bartholomew	**Matthew**	**Thomas**
Other Names	• Nathanael	• Levi • Levi the son of Alphaeus	• Didymus (Twin) • Judas Thomas • "Doubting Thomas"
General Information	• Born and/or raised in Cana of Galilee (John 21:2) • Well versed in the Hebrew Scriptures (John 1:46) • Listed as one of Christ's twelve disciples (Matt. 10:2–4; Acts 1:13) • The name Bartholomew derives from Greek, meaning "son of Tolmai." • The name Nathanael derives from the Hebrew, meaning "God has given."	• Son of Alphaeus (Mark 2:14) • From Capernaum (Mark 2:1–17) • Tax collector in Galilee (Matt. 9:9) • Possible brother of James son of Alphaeus (Mark 3:18) • Listed as one of Christ's twelve disciples (Matt. 10:2–4; Acts 1:13) • Wrote the Gospel of Matthew • The name Matthew derives from Hebrew, meaning "gift of God."	• He was a twin (John 20:24) • Listed as one of Christ's twelve disciples (Matt. 10:2–4; Mark 3:16–19; Luke 6:14–16)
Personality & Character	• Skeptical (John 1:46) • Honest (John 1:47) • Faithful (John 1:49)	• Penitent (Matt. 9:9; 10:2) • Hospitable (Matt. 9:10)	• Inquisitive (John 14:5) • Doubtful (John 20:24–25) • Courageous (John 11:16) • Faithful (John 20:24–29)
Encounters with Jesus	• Jesus told Nathanael that he was an honest Israelite and informed him that he saw him sitting under the fig tree (John 1:47–48) • Nathanael said that Jesus was the "Son of God" and "King of Israel" (John 1:49) • Jesus enlightened Nathanael with what to expect (John 1:50–51) • Witnessed the miraculous catch of fish and ate breakfast with Jesus after his resurrection (John 21:2–7)	• Matthew left his tax collector booth to follow Jesus (Matt. 9:9) • Matthew invited Jesus over to dine with him and his corrupt friends (Matt. 9:10) • Sent out on a mission to the Jews to preach "the kingdom of heaven is at hand," heal the sick, cleanse the lepers, raise the dead, and cast out demons (Matt. 10:5–8) • Was present at the Last Supper (Matt. 26:20)	• Courageously encouraged disciples to go to Bethany (John 11:16) • Asked Jesus how to know where Jesus was going (John 14:5) • Doubted Jesus' resurrection, saying he would have to touch his wounds in order to believe (John 20:25) • Affirmed that Jesus was Lord and God (John 20:28) • Witnessed the miraculous catch of fish and ate breakfast with Jesus after his resurrection (John 21:2–7)
Key Lesson	Believers are called to test all things with Scripture and remain true to its principles.	Jesus Christ is for everyone, even sinners and outcasts.	Jesus can overcome doubts and lead believers to faithfulness.
Stories	• Some suggest that Bartholomew ministered to Asia Minor and India and the Armenian church claims Bartholomew as their founder. • Tradition suggests that Bartholomew was flayed alive in Armenia. • The symbol for Bartholomew is sometimes a blade.	• Some stories suggest that Matthew ministered to Persia, Macedonia, Syria, Parthia, Media, and Ethiopia, bringing the good news to kings. • Some stories suggest that Matthew died a martyr. • The symbol for Matthew is sometimes a bag of coins in reference to his occupation as a tax collector before he encountered Jesus.	• Stories suggest that Thomas traveled to India and founded the Christian church there. • Some suggest Thomas was killed by a spear for his faith, and was buried in India. • Some say Thomas was a carpenter. • Symbols for Thomas include the spearhead and the T-square.

The Twelve Disciples • 225

James, son of Alphaeus	Thaddaeus	Simon the Zealot	Judas Iscariot
• James the son of Alphaeus • "James the Younger" • "James the Less"	• Jude • Judas the son of James • Lebbaeus	• Simon the Cananaean	• "Judas the Betrayer" • Judas the son of Simon
• Son of Alphaeus. (Mark 3:18) • Possible brother of Matthew (Levi) the tax collector, also the son of Alphaeus (Mark 2:14) • Listed as one of Christ's twelve disciples (Matt. 10:3; Acts 1:13) • James the son of Alphaeus is often confused with James the brother of Jesus (who wrote the book of James) or James the brother of John.	• Son of James (Luke 6:16) • Listed as one of Christ's twelve disciples. (Matt. 10:2–4; Acts 1:13) • The Aramaic meaning of both Thaddaeus and Lebbaeus is the same, "beloved" or "dear to the heart." • The name "Judas" derives from the Hebrew name Judah, meaning "praise." • Jude is sometimes confused with Judas the brother of Jesus, Judas Barsabbas, and Judas Iscariot.	• Was a Zealot. (Matt. 10:4; Mark 3:18; Luke 6:15; Acts 1:13) • Listed as one of Christ's twelve disciples (Matt. 10:2–4; Acts 1:13) • The name Simon derives from the Hebrew name Shimon, meaning "hearing." • The word "Cananaean" derives from an Aramaic word meaning "zealous one."	• Treasurer for the group of disciples; was a thief (John 12:5–6; 13:29) • Betrayed Jesus, felt remorse, threw the blood money in the temple and hanged himself. The chief priest used the money to purchase the potter's field, fulfilling prophecy (Matt. 27:3–10). • Purchased the Field of Blood and fell headlong and "burst open" (Acts 1:18–20) • Was replaced by Matthias who was added to the eleven apostles (Acts 1:26)
• Unknown	• Inquisitive (John 14:22) • Confused (John 14:22)	• Patriotic (Matt. 10:4) • Loyal (Mark 3:18) • Passionate (Luke 6:15) • Sacrificial (Acts 1:13)	• Greedy (Matt. 26:14–16) • Deceitful (Matt. 26:25) • Treacherous (Matt. 26:47–50) • Remorseful (Matt. 27:3–5)
• Selected as one of Christ's twelve disciples (Matt. 10:2–4; Luke 6:14–16) • Sent out on a mission to the Jews to preach "the kingdom of heaven is at hand," heal the sick, cleanse the lepers, raise the dead, and cast out demons (Matt. 10:5–8) • Was present at the Last Supper (Matt. 26:20) • Was present when Jesus appeared to the disciples after the Resurrection (John 20:19–25)	• Selected as one of Christ's twelve disciples (Matt. 10:2–4; Acts 1:13) • Sent out on a mission to the Jews to preach "the kingdom of heaven is at hand," heal the sick, cleanse the lepers, raise the dead, and cast out demons (Matt. 10:5–8) • Asked Jesus how he would reveal himself to his followers and not to the world (John 14:22) • Was present at the Last Supper (Matt. 26:20)	• Selected as one of Christ's twelve disciples (Matt. 10:2–4; Acts 1:13) • Sent out on a mission to the Jews to preach "the kingdom of heaven is at hand," heal the sick, cleanse the lepers, raise the dead, and cast out demons (Matt. 10:5–8) • Was present at the Last Supper (Matt. 26:20) • Was present for the Great Commission and Jesus' Ascension into heaven (Matt. 28:16)	• Selected as one of Christ's twelve disciples (Matt. 10:4; Luke 6:16) • Jesus referred to Judas as the devil (John 6:70–71) • Criticized Mary for anointing Jesus with expensive perfume (John 12:4–8) • Conversed with Jesus during the Last Supper (Matt. 26:23–25; John 13:27–28) • The devil entered his heart at the Last Supper (John 13:2) • Betrayed Jesus for 30 pieces of silver (Matt. 26:14–16; 47–51)
All followers of Jesus can still accomplish the work of God without being in the limelight.	Jesus will reveal his truths to believers who follow him.	One should be willing to sacrifice his or her politics to follow Jesus.	Not all who claim to follow Jesus are faithful to him and his goals.
• Some suggest that James, son of Alphaeus, belonged to the revolutionary group known as the Zealots. • Tradition suggests that James was crucified in the Sinai or in Persia, or stoned to death in Jerusalem.	• Some suggest that Thaddaeus belonged to the revolutionary group, the Zealots. • Some scholars believe that Thaddaeus authored the book of Jude, although most believe the author is Judas, the brother of Jesus. • The symbol for Thaddaeus is sometimes a gold ship with silver sails before a red horizon, which is a reference to the ship he took on missionary journeys.	• One story suggests that Simon was the bridegroom at the wedding in Cana. • Some stories suggest that Simon was a missionary to Persia. • The symbol for Simon is sometimes a fish resting on a book, which is a reference to Simon fishing for people.	• Judas was possibly from Kerioth in Judea. • Some scholars suggest that Judas was a member of the Zealot sect known as the Sicarii, who were dagger-bearing assassins.

Other Disciples in the New Testament

Other Followers of Jesus	Apostles, Evangelists and Teachers	Important Leaders
Cleopas: Follower of Jesus who spoke with Jesus on the road to Emmaus (Luke 24:18)	**Apollos**: Missionary (Acts 18:18–27; 1 Cor. 1:12; 3:4–6, 22; 4:6; 16:12; Titus 3:13)	**Ananias**: Disciple and healer (Acts 9:11)
James: Brother of Jesus, leader of Jerusalem church, and author of James (Matt. 13:55–56; Acts 12:17)	**Aquila**: Teacher and missionary (Acts 18; Rom. 16:3; 1 Cor. 16:19; 2 Tim. 4:19)	**Archippus**: Leader of house church (Col. 4:17; Philem. 2)
Joanna: Follower of Jesus (Luke 8:3; 24:10)	**Barnabas**: Missionary, apostle, and partner with Paul (Acts 4:36; 9–15; 1 Cor. 9:6; Gal. 2:1, 9, 13; Col. 4:10)	**Aristarchus**: Missionary and fellow prisoner with Paul (Acts 19:29; 20:4; 27:2; Col. 4:10; Philem. 24)
Joseph of Arimathea: Follower of Jesus (Matt. 27:57; John 19:38)	**Junia**: Apostle (Rom. 16:7)	**Epaphras**: Preacher, fellow worker and prisoner with Paul (Col. 1:7; 4:12; Philem. 23)
Joseph Barsabbas: Follower of Jesus (Acts 1:23)	**Luke**: Physician, worker, and prisoner with Paul, and author of Luke (Col. 4:14; 2 Tim. 4:11)	**Epaphroditus**: Fellow worker with Paul (Phil. 2:25; 4:18)
Judas (Jude): Brother of Jesus and author of the book of Jude (Matt. 13:54–55; Mark 6:3; Jude 1)	**Mark (John Mark)**: Missionary, cousin to Barnabas, and author of the Gospel Mark (Acts 12; 1 Peter 5:13)	**Judas Barsabbas**: Prophet (Acts 15:22–35)
Lazarus: Friend and follower of Jesus (John 11–12)	**Paul (Saul)**: Apostle, missionary, and author of Romans to Philemon (Acts to Philemon; 2 Peter 3:15)	**Lucius of Cyrene**: Prophet and teacher in the church at Antioch (Acts 13:1)
Mary, the mother of James and Joseph: Follower of Jesus (Matt. 27:55; 28:5–7)	**Philip the Evangelist**: Deacon and missionary (Acts 6:5; 8)	**Manaen**: Prophet and teacher of the church in Antioch (Acts 13:1)
Mary of Bethany: Friend and follower of Jesus (Luke 10:38–42; John 11–12)	**Priscilla**: Teacher and missionary (Acts 18; Rom. 16:3; 1 Cor. 16:19; 2 Tim. 4:19)	**Mnason**: An early disciple (Acts 21:16)
Mary Magdalene: Follower of Jesus (Matt. 27–28; Mark 15–16; Luke 8:2; 24:10; John 20)	**Silas**: Missionary (Acts 15–18; 2 Cor. 1:19; 1 Thess. 1:1; 2 Thess. 1:1; 1 Peter 5:12)	**Philemon**: Leader of a house church (Philem. 1)
Matthias: Follower who replaced Judas Iscariot (Acts 1:15–26)	**Stephen**: Deacon, missionary, preacher, and martyr (Acts 6–8; 11:19; 22:20)	**Phoebe**: Deacon and helper of Paul (Rom. 16:1–2)
Salome: Follower of Jesus (Mark 15:40)	**Timothy**: Pastor and teacher (Acts 16–20; Rom. 16:21; 1 Cor. 4:17; Phil. 2:19–22; 1 and 2 Timothy)	**Simeon (Niger)**: Prophet and teacher in the church at Antioch (Acts 13:1)
Susanna: Follower of Jesus (Luke 8:3)	**Titus**: Pastor and teacher (2 Cor. 2:13; 7:6; 8:6–23; 12:18; Gal. 2:1–3; Titus 1:4–5)	**Tychicus**: Pastor and fellow worker with Paul (Eph. 6:21; Col. 4:7)

Parables of Jesus

Stories Jesus Told

Jesus' parables are among the most read and loved sections of the Bible. Just as in the times of Jesus, the parables are filled with vivid images and touch the readers in powerful ways. In short, the parables have been an important source of wisdom, instruction, and solace for Christians everywhere.

In the following pages, we will understand what parables are, what they do in the Gospels, and why they matter so much to us today. We will also learn some general suggestions for reading the parables fruitfully.

What Are Parables?

Parables are stories that fulfill a specific function in a specific way. Parables are extended analogies. In other words, parables are extended comparisons between two objects. This comparison seeks to identify similarities or highlight differences to explain or clarify something about one of the objects. Some parables are extended similes or extended metaphors, others are brief allegories. This means that in our reading of the parables, we must be careful to not interpret the metaphors, similes, and allegories beyond what the Bible itself allows.

Characteristics of Jesus' Parables

Jesus' creative stories were:

- Brief
- Simple and repetitive
- Composed of items, examples, or experiences from his audience's daily experience
- Meant to have major and minor points
- Engaging for listeners at different levels
- Shocking, surprising, challenging, appealing, and relevant
- Often connected to the Old Testament and the kingdom of God

Function of Parables in Jesus' Ministry

Jesus' chief message was the arrival of God's kingdom to the world. Jesus' life, ministry, death, and resurrection bear witness to the reality and power of the kingdom. The parables also bear witness to this coming kingdom.

Although the parables were an important teaching tool for Jesus' ministry, their importance goes beyond instruction. Like the prophets of the Old Testament, Jesus used the parables as a way to confront people with God's word.

Parables are stories that demand a response. More than simply instructing, Jesus seeks from his audience a response to the coming of the kingdom. To do that, the parables are designed to provoke emotions, reactions, repentance, and recognition of who Jesus is and what the coming of the kingdom means.

The parables are an invitation to those who belong to God to strengthen their faith and knowledge. For those who have rejected God, the parables become confirmation of their unbelief. Like Isaiah before him, Jesus knew his message would present opposition, skepticism, and hostility. Because the parables appeal to our emotions and will, their message often produces a strong reaction in us.

Word Pictures

Metaphor: Comparison of two objects, emphasizing a specific similarity or similarities. When the psalmist affirms that "God is my rock" (Ps. 18:2, 31; 42:9), we should not understand that God is literally a rock. Rather, the psalmist is comparing a specific characteristic of rocks with a specific characteristic of God. That is, just as rocks are solid and strong, so is God.

Simile: Like a metaphor, a simile is a comparison between two objects. However, the comparison is more evident, which makes the comparison more emphatic and vivid. Similes use the words *as* and *like* to make the comparison between the two objects obvious. When the psalmist writes, "man is like a breath," (Ps. 144:4) the comparison is direct and clear. The parables of the kingdom of God that begin with "the kingdom of God (or heaven)" are examples of similes.

Allegory: An allegory is an extended metaphor. It refers to stories, poems, images, and words that convey meanings beyond the literal one. An example of an intended allegory in the New Testament is found in Gal. 4:21–31, in which Sarah and Hagar stand for two covenants.

Parables in the Gospels

	Parable	Matthew	Mark	Luke
1	A Lamp on a Stand	Matt. 5:14–16	Mark 4:21–22	Luke 8:16–17; 11:33–36
2	The Wise and Foolish Builders	Matt. 7:24–27		Luke 6:47–49
3	New Cloth on an Old Garment	Matt. 9:16	Mark 2:21	Luke 5:36
4	New Wine in Old Wineskins	Matt. 9:17	Mark 2:22	Luke 5:37–38
5	The Sower	Matt. 13:3–9	Mark 4:2–9	Luke 8:4–8
6	The Weeds	Matt. 13:24–30		
7	The Mustard Seed	Matt. 13:31–32	Mark 4:30–32	Luke 13:18–19
8	The Yeast	Matt. 13:33		Luke 13:20–21
9	The Hidden Treasure	Matt. 13:44		
10	The Pearl	Matt. 13:45–46		
11	The Net	Matt. 13:47–50		
12	The Lost Sheep	Matt. 18:12–14		Luke 15:3–7
13	The Unmerciful Servant	Matt. 18:23–35		
14	The Workers in the Vineyard	Matt. 20:1–16		
15	The Two Sons	Matt. 21:28–32		
16	The Tenants	Matt. 21:33–45	Mark 12:1–12	Luke 20:9–19
17	The Wedding Banquet	Matt. 22:2–14		
18	The Ten Virgins	Matt. 25:1–13		
19	The Talents	Matt. 25:14–30		
20	The Growing Seed		Mark 4:26–29	
21	The Absent Householder		Mark 13:34–37	
22	The Creditor and the Two Debtors			Luke 7:41–43
23	The Good Samaritan			Luke 10:30–37
24	A Friend in Need			Luke 11:5–13
25	The Rich Fool			Luke 12:16–21
26	The Watchful Servants			Luke 12:35–40
27	The Faithful Servant	Matt. 24:45–51		Luke 12:42–48
28	The Barren Fig Tree			Luke 13:6–9
29	The Place of Honor			Luke 14:7–11
30	The Great Banquet			Luke 14:16–24
31	The Cost of Being a Disciple			Luke 14:25–35
32	The Lost Coin			Luke 15:8–10
33	The Prodigal Son			Luke 15:11–32
34	The Shrewd Steward			Luke 16:1–13
35	The Rich Man and Lazarus			Luke 16:19–31
36	The Obedient Servant			Luke 17:7–10
37	The Persistent Widow			Luke 18:1–8
38	The Pharisee and the Tax Collector			Luke 18:9–14
39	The Ten Minas			Luke 19:11–27
	Total Parables in each Gospel	20	8	27
	Unique Parables in each Gospel	10	2	17

Parables of Jesus • 229

TITLE	SUMMARY	COMMENTS
1 *A Lamp on a Stand* Matt. 5:14–16 Mark 4:21–22 Luke 8:16–17; 11:33–36	Jesus declared that his followers are the light of the world. He then asks them not to hide their light, but rather put it on a stand to be effective.	Christians are called to be light in a darkened world. This involves living according to Christ's commandments and allowing our lives to reflect Jesus' love, obedience, humility, and forgiveness.
2 *The Wise and Foolish Builders* Matt. 7:24–27 Luke 6:47–49	At the conclusion of the Sermon on the Mount (Matt. 5:1–7:29), Jesus contrasts those that understand and do his words with those who do not. A wise person builds upon a rock and endures the storms; a foolish person builds upon sand and suffers loss.	Jesus stresses the importance of having a sure and steady foundation. Scripture tells us that Jesus alone is that worthy foundation (1 Cor. 3:11).
3 *New Cloth on an Old Garment* Matt. 9:16 Mark 2:21 Luke 5:36	Jesus explains the danger of patching a garment with new cloth. Once washed, the new cloth would shrink and make the tear worse.	The parable challenges its audience to understand the newness of Jesus' message. Jesus did not come to get rid of the law but to fulfill it. By fulfilling it, Jesus extends the meaning of the law (love your enemies, for example). The ritual-and-sacrifice faith of the Old Testament would not make room for this type of change. What Jesus offers, then, is a whole "new cloth."
4 *New Wine in Old Wineskins* Matt. 9:17 Mark 2:22 Luke 5:37–38	Jesus refers to the fact that wineskins stretch as the wine they contain ferments. If a wineskin is used again, it is unable to stretch any further and breaks.	As in the parable of the new cloth on the old garment, this parable also challenges its audience to understand the newness of Jesus' message. Jesus did not come to get rid of the law but to fulfill it. By fulfilling it, Jesus extends the meaning of the law (love your enemies, for example). The ritual-and-sacrifice faith of the Old Testament would not make room for this type of change. What Jesus offers, then, is a whole "new wineskin."
5 *The Sower* Matt. 13:3–9 Mark 4:2–9 Luke 8:4–8	A farmer spreads seed that falls into four types of soil. Seed that falls on hard soil is eaten by the birds. Seed that falls on rocks springs up quickly, but withers due to lack of root. Seed that falls in weeds is overtaken. Seed that falls in good soil produces much fruit.	This parable includes an explanation of the four soils as symbolic of the responses of people who hear the proclamation of the kingdom of God. The parable challenges its audience to receive the word about the kingdom of heaven, be focused on that message, and grow. A true hearing of the message of the kingdom of God becomes a productive hearing and productive living.
6 *The Weeds* Matt. 13:24–30	A farmer sows good seed but his enemy comes in the night and plants weeds also. The farmer decides to allow them both to grow, planning to separate them at harvest time.	This parable explains the co-existence of believers and unbelievers until the Lord's return (Matt. 13:36–43).

TITLE	SUMMARY	COMMENTS
7 *The Mustard Seed* Matt. 13:31–32 Mark 4:30–32 Luke 13:18–19	The kingdom of heaven is compared to the mustard seed. This seed, the smallest known to Jesus' audience, becomes so great a bush that birds build their nests in it.	The kingdom does not come as a powerful mustard tree; rather, it arrives as a small seed that grows and provides shade and refuge. The kingdom of God is already present in the ministry of Jesus, but its fullness will only happen when Jesus comes back.
8 *The Yeast* Matt. 13:33 Luke 13:20–21	The kingdom of heaven is compared to yeast which, when put in dough, spreads throughout the entire mixture, causing it to expand.	The yeast is symbolic of the growing influence of the kingdom of God on the world (Matt. 28:19–20).
9 *The Hidden Treasure* Matt. 13:44	The kingdom of heaven is compared to a found treasure that is so desirable that a man sells all he has to acquire it.	Jesus announces the presence of the kingdom of heaven and invites his audience to rejoice in finding it.
10 *The Pearl* Matt. 13:45–46	The kingdom of heaven is compared to a pearl buyer who finds such a desirable pearl that he sells all he has to purchase it.	In this parable, Jesus urges his audience to recognize the value of the kingdom of heaven in their midst.
11 *The Net* Matt. 13:47–50	The kingdom of heaven is compared to a net that draws in both good (which is kept) and bad (which is burned).	This parable illustrates the separation of believers from unbelievers when Jesus returns (Matt. 25:32–46).
12 *The Lost Sheep* Matt. 18:12–14 Luke 15:3–7	When a sheep gets lost, the shepherd searches for the missing sheep and rejoices when he finds it.	The parable invites readers to participate in seeking and to join in celebrating the finding of the lost.
13 *The Unmerciful Servant* Matt. 18:23–35	A king, at his servant's pleading, forgives him of a great debt, which he could never repay. This same servant then imprisons a fellow servant who could not repay a much smaller debt. In response, the king has the first servant imprisoned.	We should be forgiving of others, realizing the great debt we have been forgiven by Christ (Ephesians 2:13).
14 *The Workers in the Vineyard* Matt. 20:1–16	A vineyard owner hires workers at 6 am for a day's wages to work in his vineyard. At 9 am, noon, 3 pm and 5 pm he hires additional workers. At 6 pm, he pays them all a full day's wages. The first workers feel cheated, but the owner reminds them that he paid them exactly what they agreed to.	The parable challenges the audience to understand that the way God treats people is not based on human standards of justice. The parable emphasizes God's mercy as the basis for salvation as it forces listeners to confront issues of envy, a sense of superiority, and jealousy.
15 *The Two Sons* Matt. 21:28–32	A man has two sons, whom he asks to work in his vineyard. The first says he will not, but later regrets it and goes to work. The second says he will work, but does not. The first son is the one that did the father's will.	A contrast of sinners who repent and are saved versus hypocrites who say the right things but do not do them (Ezek. 33:31–32).

Title	Summary	Comments
16 *The Tenants* Matt. 21:33–45 Mark 12:1–12 Luke 20:9–19	A landowner prepares a vineyard and rents it out to farmers while he goes far away. At harvest time, he sends servants to collect the "rent" (first fruits) but the farmers treat the servants shamefully. He finally sends his son, whom they kill. He will therefore destroy the wicked farmers and rent the vineyard to others.	This is one of the most difficult parables to interpret. The parable does not say that God has rejected the Jewish people as a group. It is an indictment against the Jewish leaders who rejected John the Baptist and Jesus. The parable demands from its audience that they reject, in turn, those leaders and follow Jesus.
17 *The Wedding Banquet* Matt. 22:2–14	A king prepares a wedding feast for his son and sends for the guests, who all give poor excuses for not attending and even murder his servants. The king destroys those people and invites others to the feast.	An indictment of the Jewish leaders' treatment and rejection of the prophets and Jesus. The offer of salvation is now open to all that will trust in Christ (Acts 28:28).
18 *The Ten Virgins* Matt. 25:1–13	Ten bridesmaids await the arrival of the bridegroom, but only the five that were wise enough to prepare with extra oil for their lamps were ready when he arrived and went with him.	The parable urges people to be ready and prepared for Christ's imminent return.
19 *The Talents* Matt. 25:14–30	Before going on a long trip, a man gives each of his three servants a different sum of his money to invest. Two double the money they were given and are rewarded; the third buries his for no profit and loses his reward.	At his return, Christ expects Christians to have used the gifts and opportunities he has given them (Col. 1:10). The central issue of the parable is faithfulness. The parable exhorts its audience to remain faithful disciples of Jesus in the time before his return.
20 *The Growing Seed* Mark 4:26–29	The kingdom of God is compared to seeds that grow to maturity. We do not understand the process of growth the seed experiences. However, when the fruit is ripe, it is harvested.	The parable conveys confidence and comfort to its audience by assuring that the kingdom of God will find fulfillment in God's time. It also reminds us that this fulfillment is inevitable and does not depend on human efforts.
21 *The Absent Householder* Mark 13:34–37	Christ is compared to a homeowner who goes on a trip and leaves his servants in charge. The servants must not be caught idle upon his return.	This brief comparison calls all believers to be ready for the return of Jesus. Being ready means that Christians are occupied with the matters and issues of the kingdom of heaven. Christ has left Christians to do his work in the world as salt and light. Our joy is to be found faithful upon his return (Matt. 5:13).
22 *The Creditor and the Two Debtors* Luke 7:41–43	A creditor forgives two debtors. One is forgiven an amount ten times greater than the other is. Christ confirms that the one that was forgiven the larger amount will love the creditor more.	As we come to understand more and more how great a debt we have been forgiven, we will love Christ more (Mark 12:30).

Title	Summary	Comments
23 **The Good Samaritan** Luke 10:30–37	A Jew traveling to Jericho was beaten, robbed, and left for dead. Both a priest and a Levite passed him by, but a Samaritan (hated by the Jews) rescued the man and ensured his recovery.	As a response to, "Who is my neighbor?" Jesus shows that life in the kingdom of God requires us to love our neighbors, even our enemies. The parable is a call to action; love is not only a matter of feelings or thoughts but of actions.
24 **A Friend in Need** Luke 11:5–13	A man goes to his neighbor late at night to ask for bread for a friend who has arrived from a long journey. Although the neighbor initially refuses, he eventually gives in to end the knocking at his door.	This is an encouragement to Christians to continue in prayer with perseverance and hope because God hears prayers and responds.
25 **The Rich Fool** Luke 12:16–21	A rich man has a harvest that will last him many years so he decides to "eat, drink, and be merry." God calls him a fool because that same night he will die and not enjoy his riches.	This brief parable reminds us that wisdom attends to the things of God, while foolishness concerns itself only with this life. We have very little control over life and our own success. God is the source of life, all that we need for that life, and satisfaction with our life.
26 **The Watchful Servants** Luke 12:35–40	A homeowner is pleased when he returns unexpectedly and finds his servants are ready to receive him at any time. Whether it is the master or a thief, the servants ought to be ready for each.	Jesus did not reveal the time of his second coming. Yet, he expects his servants, all Christians, to be ready to receive him when he comes back. The church is ready by doing the work of the kingdom of God and by remaining holy and faithful to Christ.
27 **The Faithful Servant** Luke 12:42–48 Matt. 24:45-51	A master will reward the servant that cares for his duties in the master's absence. Conversely, a master will punish the servant who willfully disregards his duties during his master's absence.	The parable urges its audience to right and wise living. Wisdom, in this parable, is living with the end in mind.
28 **The Barren Fig Tree** Luke 13:6–9	A vineyard owner becomes frustrated because a fig tree has not produced in three years. He commands that it be cut down, but his servant asks for one more year to nurture it.	The parable demands a response to the privilege of being God's people: Christians must "bear fruit." Bearing fruit in Luke means to live in obedience to God's will. This includes being witnesses, loving our neighbor, doing justice and loving mercy.
29 **The Place of Honor** Luke 14:7–11	When someone is invited to a feast, that person is wise to choose a humble place.	The parable confronts its audience with our natural desire to be noticed, loved, and exalted. Yet, Jesus reminded his audience that a wise person understands his own value and place in the kingdom of God (Phil. 2:3).

Parables of Jesus • 233

Title	Summary	Comments
30 **The Great Banquet** Luke 14:16–24	A man prepares a great feast for many people, but when he summons them they have a number of poor excuses for not attending. The man instead invites all the poor and disadvantaged in the city.	Salvation and the blessings of God are received by those who gladly accept and appreciate his good gifts (James 1:17).
31 **The Cost of Being a Disciple** Luke 14:25–35	It is wise to consider the cost before undertaking an important task. A person ensures sufficient funding for a building project. A leader ensures his military might is sufficient before engaging in war.	The parable urges its audience to carefully consider the cost of following Christ: surrendering our all to him and choosing his will over our own (Mark 8:34–35).
32 **The Lost Coin** Luke 15:8–10	A woman loses one of ten coins and looks diligently until she finds it. When it is found, she rejoices greatly.	Christ seeks those that are lost, and the inhabitants of heaven rejoice every time a person is saved (John 3:16).
33 **The Prodigal Son** Luke 15:11–32	A man with two sons is asked by the younger for his share of the family money. The son goes off and lives a riotous life until his money is exhausted. While working feeding pigs, he decides to go back and ask to be one his father's servants, since they were well cared for. His father sees him coming home while he is still far away and runs to him, kisses him, and treats him as an honored guest and son.	This parable challenges its audience to identify with the three main characters of the parable: The father, whose love allows him to move beyond his anger and disappointment and welcomes back his son; the older brother who, despite being a good son, is unable to move beyond his anger and welcome his once lost brother; and the younger son, who is able to move beyond his rebellion and pride and return to his father with humility and repentance. God, our Father, is compassionate and greatly rejoices when we return to him. God accepts all people, regardless of their past and actions, when they humbly come back to him with repentance.
34 **The Shrewd Steward** Luke 16:1–13	A steward is accused by his master of mishandling goods. The steward makes deals to reduce the amount owed by each of his master's debtors so that they will take care of him if he is dismissed.	This parable looks to what is wise living in light of the second coming. A wise person handles worldly wealth for the kingdom of God. No one can serve two masters: "God and Money" (Luke 16:13). The parable challenges us to use all of our resources to the service of the kingdom of God.
35 **The Rich Man and Lazarus** Luke 16:19–31	A rich man and a beggar (Lazarus) from his gates both die; Lazarus goes into Abraham's bosom (Paradise) and the rich man to torment in hell. The rich man asks Lazarus to bring him water (but he cannot pass) and to warn his brothers (but they would not believe).	This parable challenges its audience's notion of who has God's favor. Although the rich man felt confident that God was with him, God favored Lazarus. The problem with the rich man in the parable is not his wealth. Rather, the problem is wealth that ignores poverty and suffering.

	Title	Summary	Comments
36	**The Obedient Servant** Luke 17:7–10	A master expects a servant to perform his assigned duties. No additional reward is necessary.	Christians should not seek to be rewarded for their obedience. Rather, we should serve him out of love.
37	**The Persistent Widow** Luke 18:1–8	A widow continuously pleads for justice from an uncaring judge. He grants her desire simply to spare himself her persistent requests.	The parable emphasizes God's patience toward his people, the assurance that God will act on their behalf, and the need to live with faithfulness and readiness for Jesus' return. The parable also shows the importance of persistence and perseverance. It is an invitation to ask God for what we need. It promises that a loving God is far more likely to respond positively to the perseverance of his people's requests than would an uncaring judge.
38	**The Pharisee and the Tax Collector** Luke 18:9–14	A Pharisee goes to the temple and prays boastfully about his works, how good he is, and how much better he is than the publican (tax collector). The tax collector humbly bows his head and asks God to forgive him of his sins.	This powerful, short parable makes an important implied conclusion: "righteous acts without compassion and love are not considered righteous by God."[1] It forces its audience to recognize that when we exclude anyone from God's grace, we run the risk of excluding ourselves from God. God honors and uplifts the humble but rejects the arrogant.
39	**The Ten Minas** Luke 19:11–27	Before traveling afar, a master gave each of his three servants ten minas (about three month's wages) to invest. One servant profited ten minas and another servant five. As a reward, the first was made ruler of ten cities, the second ruler over five. A third servant refused to invest the money because he feared his master; his mina was given to the servant who gained ten minas.	At his return, Christ expects Christians to have used the gifts and opportunities he has given them (Col. 1:10). The central issue of the parable is faithfulness in the way we use the gifts God has given to us. The parable exhorts its audience to remain faithful disciples of Jesus in the time before his return.

Interpretation of Parables

Parables can be difficult to understand.

- One problem is the chronological and cultural gap between Jesus and us. The parables are expressed with objects and experiences of daily life: parenthood, seeds and grains, trees and animals. However, these are things not always accessible for people today.
- A great deal of the effectiveness of the parables lies in their evocative power. The parables remind people of their lives and important things in their lives. Parables in the Bible are effective because the original audiences "get them." Interpreting parables is like *getting* jokes; explaining a joke kills the joke. As modern readers, we may be too far removed from the original context to "get" the parables. Thus, we need to explain parables in such a way that we do not kill their effectiveness on today's audience.
- When we take the meaning of the Bible beyond what the Bible means, we often *allegorize*. Allegorization is the practice of turning into allegory what was *not* intended to be an allegory. An often-quoted example is Augustine's interpretation of the parable of the Good Samaritan. For Augustine, the man traveling represents Adam, Jerusalem is the heavenly city, Jericho stands for our mortality, the robbers are the devil and his angels, the priest and Levite are the priesthood and ministry of the Old Testament, the good Samaritan is Christ, the inn is the church, and so on. We can know whether a parable is an allegory if the Bible itself interprets it as an allegory. For example, in the parable of the Tenants in Matthew 21:33–45, the gospel writer suggests an allegorical parable. The audience of the parable understand that Jesus is referring to the prophets, which Jesus supports with his quote from Psalm 118. Although the landowner (God), the servants (the prophets), and the son (Jesus himself) do have an allegorical meaning, we should not extend the allegory to other elements of the story. The watchtower, for example, should not be allegorized, nor the journey. They are only support elements for the parable.

Following are general suggestions for interpreting parables. These suggestions are useful for understanding how parables work and what they mean. As an example, we read the parable of the lost sheep in Matt. 18:12–14 and Luke 15:4–7.

1. *Read the parable carefully and more than once. Read it in more than one translation.*
2. *Notice the structure of the parable.*
   - The structure of the text helps us discern what is important to the gospel writer. It helps us know where the main point is.
   - In the parable of the lost sheep, because Matthew emphasizes the action of seeking, the main point—the lost sheep—is right in the middle of the parable. Since Luke focuses on the joy that the finding causes, the main point of the parable is at the end.
   - Often, the main point of parables tends to be at the end of the story, but every parable must be interpreted on its own.
3. *Pay attention to the context of the parable.*
   - The evangelists present the parable to different audiences. In Matthew, Jesus tells the parable of the lost sheep to the disciples, whereas in Luke, Jesus speaks to the Pharisees.
   - Because the parables challenge listeners to do or change something, identifying the parable's audience is important in order to understand its meaning.
4. *Interpret what is given and not what is omitted.*
   - The fact that the shepherd leaves behind ninety-nine sheep should not prompt us to ask any "what ifs." Any dangers that the ninety-nine sheep may face are imaginary and not part of the parable. We must interpret only what is present in the parable.
   - The parable should not be used to define the salvation Jesus offers. The parable itself does not teach that God is a shepherd, though that is an image the Bible uses elsewhere.
   - Jesus' own interpretation of the parable makes it clear that the shepherd stands as a metaphor of God. However, we should not extend the metaphors and seek meaning for the hills or the one hundred sheep.

5. *Identify the main points and any secondary ones.*
   - The parable challenges its hearers to understand the value of all people, especially those who are lost.
   - It shows that just as a shepherd goes out of his way to find one lost animal and rejoices when he rescues his sheep, so does God rejoice when lost people are found by him.
   - Seeking the lost sheep and the joy of finding it are the main points of the parable.
6. *Detect the important cultural details in the parable that need explaining.*
   - The image of the shepherd was common in Jesus' times and instantly connected listeners with the Old Testament and the patriarchs.
   - But there's a twist: Shepherds were practical, and people assumed that a shepherd would not risk ninety-nine to save one. It is precisely this reversal of expectation that makes the parable so compelling. Sheep were valuable assets. Risking ninety-nine sheep for one is not a practical choice.
   - So Jesus used the expected to show something about God's character to bring his audience up short: God loves us so much he will risk everything for just one.

Studying the Parables

Choose a parable to study. (You might want to start with The Pharisee and Tax Collector, The Good Samaritan, or The Rich Fool.) Study the parable by yourself or with a group.

Step one: Read the parable three times.

Step two: Examine the structure. How many parts does the parable have? Draw a simple outline of the parable.

Step three: Note the context. To whom is Jesus telling this parable? What is the setting? Did some event or question prompt Jesus to tell this parable?

Step four: Look up cultural and historical questions. When you read the parable, what questions about biblical culture or historical setting came to mind? (For example: What is a Pharisee? Who were the Samaritans? What did it mean for someone in Jesus' time to own large barns?) Write down your questions and look for answers using Bible dictionaries and commentaries.

Step five: Find the main point. What is the lesson to be learned for Jesus' audience? If a question or challenge prompted Jesus to tell the parable, how does this parable address that?

Step six: Consider how the parable can strengthen your faith and knowledge of God. Do you see similarities between the events or characters described in the parable and today's society or your own life? What does this parable teach you about God? What does it motivate you to do?

Endnote
1 Snodgrass, 473

Suggested Books
The Parables of Jesus. J. M. Boice. Moody Press, 1983.
How to Read the Bible for All Its Worth. G. D. Fee and D. Stuart. Zondervan, 1981, 2003.
The Hermeneutical Spiral. G. R. Osborne. IVP, 1991.
Stories with Intent. K. R. Snodgrass. Eerdmans, 2008.

Herod's Temple – 20 BC–AD 70
Aerial view showing outer courts

Herod's Temple • 237

Living quarters for priests were within this colonnaded enclosure

Rooms within walls

F. Sanctuary

Written descriptions of Herod's Temple appear in history but must be interpreted by each artist. No two drawings look exactly alike.

D. Israel Court *(for Jewish men) under colonnades*

Chamber of hewn stone (possible Sanhedrin council room)

Laver

E. Priests' Court

Altar

Chamber of the hearth

Nicanor Gate

Lepers' court

(cutaway view)

Levite choirs performed on steps

Pharisee and Tax Collector
Lk 18:10-14

Oil Storage

C. Women's Court

Wood Storage

Nazarites Court

Widow's Offering
Mk 12:42

Beautiful Gate

Lame man healed
Acts 3:6-8

Chel (Rampart)

Chel

"No entry" laws were posted in 3 languages

Soreg — a low wall surrounding Temple (location uncertain) with 13 places of entry

Soreg

Triumphal Entry
Mt 21:15

B. Sacred Enclosure

No Gentiles permitted inside of Soreg boundary

A. Gentiles' Court

HEROD'S TEMPLE

Herod's Temple • 239

Palm Sunday to Easter
Walking with Jesus Each Day

2. Clearing of the temple MONDAY
Matt. 21:10–17; Mark 11:15–18; Luke 19:45–48

The next day he returned to the temple and found the court of the Gentiles full of traders and money changers making large profits as they gave out Jewish coins in exchange for "pagan" money. Jesus drove them out and overturned their tables.

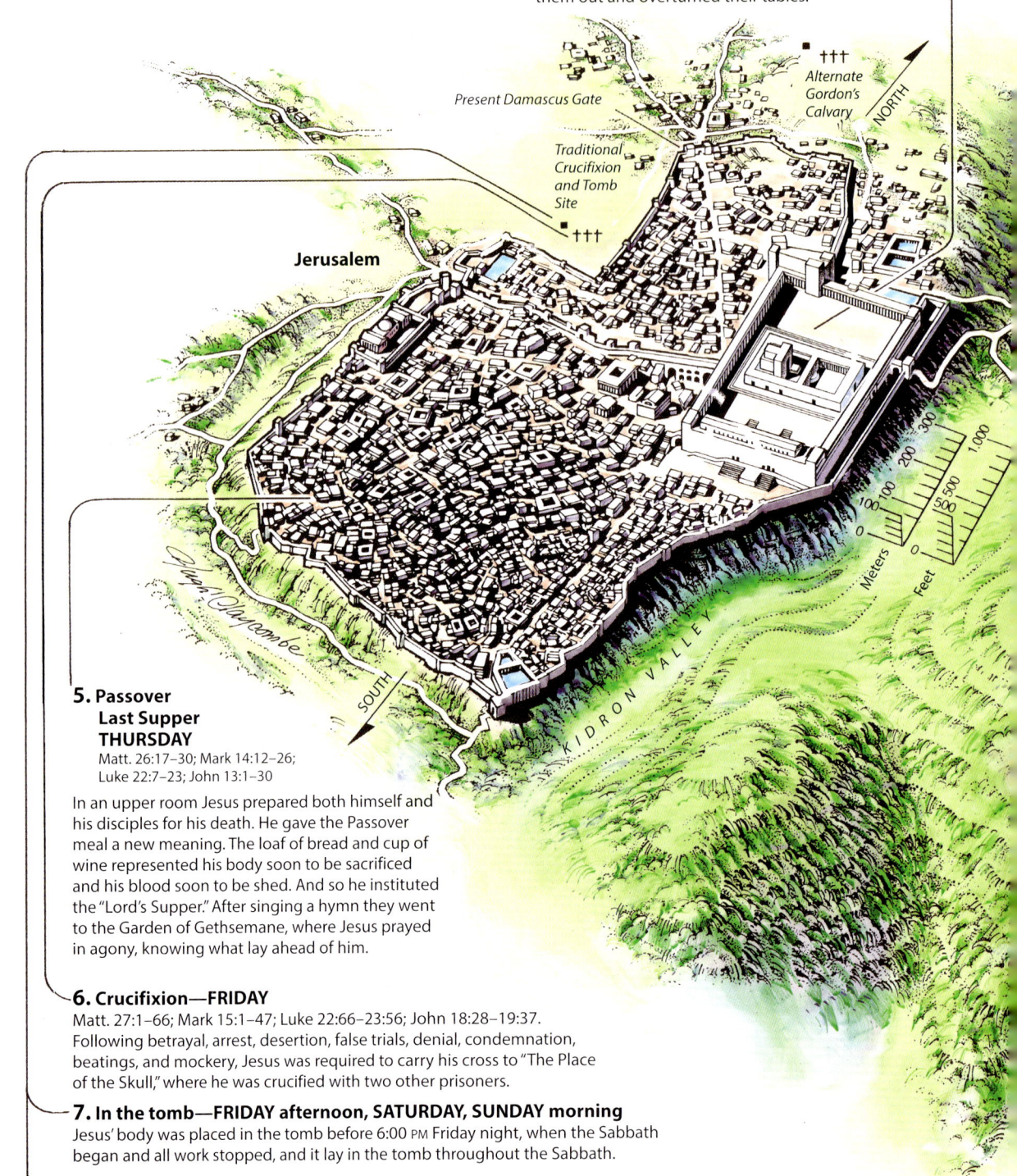

5. Passover Last Supper THURSDAY
Matt. 26:17–30; Mark 14:12–26; Luke 22:7–23; John 13:1–30

In an upper room Jesus prepared both himself and his disciples for his death. He gave the Passover meal a new meaning. The loaf of bread and cup of wine represented his body soon to be sacrificed and his blood soon to be shed. And so he instituted the "Lord's Supper." After singing a hymn they went to the Garden of Gethsemane, where Jesus prayed in agony, knowing what lay ahead of him.

6. Crucifixion—FRIDAY
Matt. 27:1–66; Mark 15:1–47; Luke 22:66–23:56; John 18:28–19:37.
Following betrayal, arrest, desertion, false trials, denial, condemnation, beatings, and mockery, Jesus was required to carry his cross to "The Place of the Skull," where he was crucified with two other prisoners.

7. In the tomb—FRIDAY afternoon, SATURDAY, SUNDAY morning
Jesus' body was placed in the tomb before 6:00 PM Friday night, when the Sabbath began and all work stopped, and it lay in the tomb throughout the Sabbath.

8. Resurrection—SUNDAY Matt. 28:1–13; Mark 16:1–20; Luke 24:1–49; John 20:1–31
Early in the morning, women went to the tomb and found that the stone closing the tomb's entrance had been rolled back. An angel told them Jesus was alive. Jesus appeared to Mary Magdalene in the garden, to Peter, to the two disciples on the road to Emmaus, and later that day to all the disciples but Thomas. His resurrection was established as a fact.

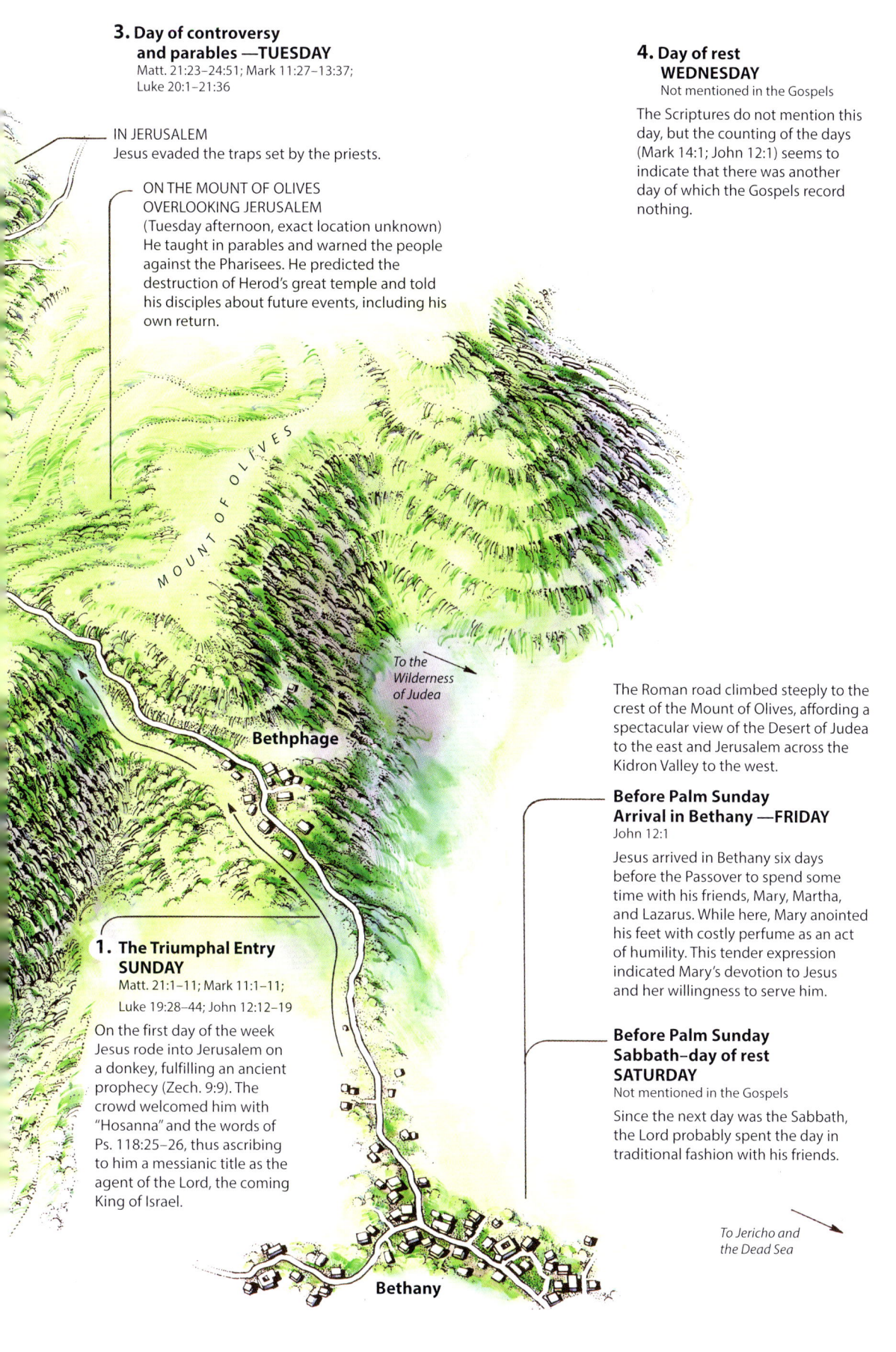

Palm Sunday to Easter • 241

3. Day of controversy and parables —TUESDAY
Matt. 21:23–24:51; Mark 11:27–13:37; Luke 20:1–21:36

IN JERUSALEM
Jesus evaded the traps set by the priests.

ON THE MOUNT OF OLIVES OVERLOOKING JERUSALEM
(Tuesday afternoon, exact location unknown) He taught in parables and warned the people against the Pharisees. He predicted the destruction of Herod's great temple and told his disciples about future events, including his own return.

4. Day of rest WEDNESDAY
Not mentioned in the Gospels

The Scriptures do not mention this day, but the counting of the days (Mark 14:1; John 12:1) seems to indicate that there was another day of which the Gospels record nothing.

To the Wilderness of Judea

Bethphage

The Roman road climbed steeply to the crest of the Mount of Olives, affording a spectacular view of the Desert of Judea to the east and Jerusalem across the Kidron Valley to the west.

Before Palm Sunday Arrival in Bethany —FRIDAY
John 12:1

Jesus arrived in Bethany six days before the Passover to spend some time with his friends, Mary, Martha, and Lazarus. While here, Mary anointed his feet with costly perfume as an act of humility. This tender expression indicated Mary's devotion to Jesus and her willingness to serve him.

1. The Triumphal Entry SUNDAY
Matt. 21:1–11; Mark 11:1–11; Luke 19:28–44; John 12:12–19

On the first day of the week Jesus rode into Jerusalem on a donkey, fulfilling an ancient prophecy (Zech. 9:9). The crowd welcomed him with "Hosanna" and the words of Ps. 118:25–26, thus ascribing to him a messianic title as the agent of the Lord, the coming King of Israel.

Before Palm Sunday Sabbath–day of rest SATURDAY
Not mentioned in the Gospels

Since the next day was the Sabbath, the Lord probably spent the day in traditional fashion with his friends.

To Jericho and the Dead Sea

Bethany

Jesus' Hours on the Cross

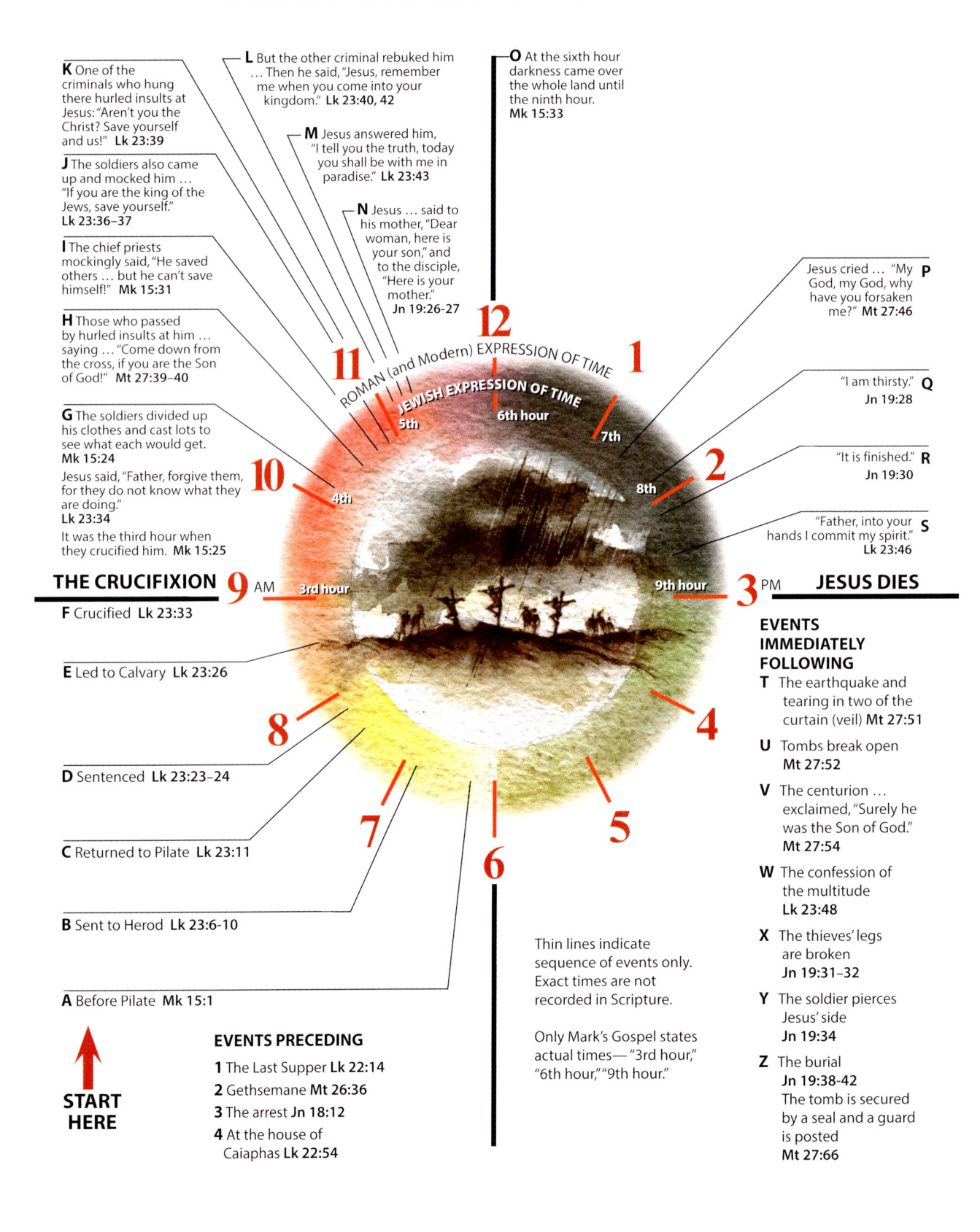

K One of the criminals who hung there hurled insults at Jesus: "Aren't you the Christ? Save yourself and us!" **Lk 23:39**

J The soldiers also came up and mocked him … "If you are the king of the Jews, save yourself." **Lk 23:36–37**

I The chief priests mockingly said, "He saved others … but he can't save himself!" **Mk 15:31**

H Those who passed by hurled insults at him … saying … "Come down from the cross, if you are the Son of God!" **Mt 27:39–40**

G The soldiers divided up his clothes and cast lots to see what each would get. **Mk 15:24**

Jesus said, "Father, forgive them, for they do not know what they are doing." **Lk 23:34**

It was the third hour when they crucified him. **Mk 15:25**

L But the other criminal rebuked him … Then he said, "Jesus, remember me when you come into your kingdom." **Lk 23:40, 42**

M Jesus answered him, "I tell you the truth, today you shall be with me in paradise." **Lk 23:43**

N Jesus … said to his mother, "Dear woman, here is your son," and to the disciple, "Here is your mother." **Jn 19:26-27**

O At the sixth hour darkness came over the whole land until the ninth hour. **Mk 15:33**

Jesus cried … "My God, my God, why have you forsaken me?" **Mt 27:46** **P**

"I am thirsty." **Jn 19:28** **Q**

"It is finished." **Jn 19:30** **R**

"Father, into your hands I commit my spirit." **Lk 23:46** **S**

ROMAN (and Modern) EXPRESSION OF TIME
JEWISH EXPRESSION OF TIME

THE CRUCIFIXION — 9 AM — 3rd hour

F Crucified **Lk 23:33**

E Led to Calvary **Lk 23:26**

D Sentenced **Lk 23:23–24**

C Returned to Pilate **Lk 23:11**

B Sent to Herod **Lk 23:6-10**

A Before Pilate **Mk 15:1**

START HERE

EVENTS PRECEDING
1. The Last Supper **Lk 22:14**
2. Gethsemane **Mt 26:36**
3. The arrest **Jn 18:12**
4. At the house of Caiaphas **Lk 22:54**

Thin lines indicate sequence of events only. Exact times are not recorded in Scripture.

Only Mark's Gospel states actual times— "3rd hour," "6th hour," "9th hour."

3 PM — JESUS DIES — 9th hour

EVENTS IMMEDIATELY FOLLOWING

T The earthquake and tearing in two of the curtain (veil) **Mt 27:51**

U Tombs break open **Mt 27:52**

V The centurion … exclaimed, "Surely he was the Son of God." **Mt 27:54**

W The confession of the multitude **Lk 23:48**

X The thieves' legs are broken **Jn 19:31–32**

Y The soldier pierces Jesus' side **Jn 19:34**

Z The burial **Jn 19:38-42** The tomb is secured by a seal and a guard is posted **Mt 27:66**

100 Prophecies Fulfilled by Jesus

Jesus' Birth

Prophecy	Old Testament References	New Testament Fulfillment
Be of the offspring of the woman; shall bruise the serpent's head	**Genesis 3:14–15** So the LORD God said to the serpent . . . "And I will put enmity between you and the woman, and between your offspring and hers; he will crush your head, and you will strike his heel."	**Galatians 4:4** But when the time had fully come, God sent his Son, born of a woman, born under law. **Hebrews 2:14** Since the children have flesh and blood, he too shared in their humanity so that by his death he might destroy him who holds the power of death . . . that is, the devil. **1 John 3:8** He who does what is sinful is of the devil, because the devil has been sinning from the beginning. The reason the Son of God appeared was to destroy the devil's work.
All nations shall be blessed through Abraham	**Genesis 18:17–18** Then the LORD said . . . "Abraham will surely become a great and powerful nation, and all nations on earth will be blessed through him." Also Genesis 12:3; 22:18; 26:4; 28:14	**Acts 3:25–26** "He said to Abraham, 'Through your offspring all peoples on earth will be blessed.' When God raised up his servant, he sent him first to you to bless you." Also Matthew 1:1, 17; Galatians 3:16
Be of the tribe of Judah	**Genesis 49:8–10** "Judah, your brothers will praise you . . . The sceptre will not depart from Judah, nor the ruler's staff from between his feet, until he comes to whom it belongs and the obedience of the nations is his." **Micah 5:2** "But you, Bethlehem Ephrathah, though you are small among the clans of Judah, out of you will come for me one who will be ruler over Israel, whose origins are from of old, from ancient times."	**Matthew 1:1–3** A record of the genealogy of Jesus Christ the son of David, the son of Abraham . . . Jacob the father of Judah and his brothers, Judah the father of Perez and Zerah. **Hebrews 7:14** For it is clear that our Lord descended from Judah . . . **Revelation 5:5** Then one of the elders said to me, "Do not weep! See, the Lion of the tribe of Judah, the Root of David, has triumphed. He is able to open the scroll and its seven seals."
Be born in the town of Bethlehem of Judea (Judah)	**Micah 5:2–5** "But you, Bethlehem Ephrathah, though you are small among the clans of Judah, out of you will come for me one who will be ruler over Israel, whose origins are from of old, from ancient times."	**Matthew 2:1–6** After Jesus was born in Bethlehem in Judea, during the time of King Herod, Magi from the east came to Jerusalem and asked, "Where is the one who has been born king of the Jews?"
Be born a king of the line of David	**Isaiah 9:7** He will reign on David's throne and over his kingdom. Also 2 Samuel 7:12–13 Jeremiah 23:5; 30:9	**Matthew 1:1** A record of the genealogy of Jesus Christ the son of David, the son of Abraham. Also Luke 1:32; Acts 13:22–23
A child to be born	**Isaiah 9:6** For to us a child is born . . . he will be called Wonderful Counselor, Mighty God.	**Luke 2:11** Today in the town of David a Savior has been born to you; he is Christ the Lord.
Be born of a virgin	**Isaiah 7:13–14** Then Isaiah said, "Hear now, you house of David! Is it not enough to try the patience of men? Will you try the patience of my God also? Therefore the LORD himself will give you a sign: The virgin will be with child and will give birth to a son, and will call him Immanuel (*God with us*)."	**Matthew 1:18–23** His mother Mary was pledged to be married to Joseph, but before they came together, she was found to be with child through the Holy Spirit. **Luke 1:26–35** God sent the angel . . . to a virgin pledged to be married to a man named Joseph, a descendant of David. The virgin's name was Mary.
Kings shall bring him gifts, fall down before him	**Psalm 72:10–11** The kings of Tarshish and of distant shores will bring tribute to him; the kings of Sheba and Seba will present him gifts. All kings will bow down to him and all nations will serve him.	**Matthew 2:1–11** After Jesus was born in Bethlehem in Judea, during the time of King Herod, Magi from the east came to Jerusalem . . . On coming to the house, they saw the child with his mother Mary, and they bowed down and worshiped him. Then they opened their treasures and presented him with gifts of gold and of incense and of myrrh.
Be born of the seed of Abraham	Genesis 17:7–8; 26:3–4	Matthew 1:1, 17; Galatians 3:16, 29; Hebrews 2:16
Be born of the seed of Isaac	Genesis 17:19; 21:12; 26:2–4	Matthew 1:2, 17; Romans 9:7; Hebrews 11:17–19
Be of the seed of Jacob; a star out of Jacob	Genesis 28:13–14; Numbers 24:17, 19	Matthew 1:2; Luke 1:33; 3:23–38
Be a firstborn son, sanctified	Exodus 13:2; Numbers 3:13; 8:17	Luke 2:7, 23
Be a rod out of the stem of Jesse	Isaiah 11:1–2	Matthew 1:6; Acts 13:22–23
Massacre of children	Jeremiah 31:15	Matthew 2:16–18
Have eternal existence	Micah 5:2	John 1:1, 4; 8:58; Colossians 1:15–19

Color Key

Prophecies more than 1,200 years before Jesus' birth are highlighted in green.
Prophecies more than 800 years before Jesus' birth are highlighted in yellow.
Prophecies more than 500 years before Jesus' birth are highlighted in blue.

Jesus' Life and Ministry

Prophecy	Old Testament References	New Testament Fulfillment
Be called out of Egypt	**Hosea 11:1** "When Israel was a child, I loved him, and out of Egypt I called my son."	**Matthew 2:13–15, 19–21** So he . . . took the child and his mother during the night and left for Egypt.
Be rejected by his brothers	**Psalm 69:8** I am a stranger to my brothers, an alien to my own mother's sons.	**John 7:3–5** Jesus' brothers said to him, "You ought to leave here . . . so that your disciples may see the miracles you do." For even his own brothers did not believe in him.
Rulers take council against him	**Psalm 2:1–2** Why do the nations conspire and the peoples plot in vain? The kings of the earth take their stand and the rulers gather together against the Lord and against his Anointed One.	**Matthew 12:14** But the Pharisees went out and plotted how they might kill Jesus. **Matthew 26:3–4** Then the chief priests and the elders . . . plotted to arrest Jesus in some sly way and kill him. **Matthew 26:47** Judas . . . arrived. With him was a large crowd armed with swords and clubs, sent from the chief priests and the elders of the people. Also Luke 23:11–12
Be rejected as capstone	**Psalm 118:22–23** The stone the builders rejected has become the capstone; the Lord has done this, and it is marvelous in our eyes.	**Matthew 21:42** Jesus said to them, "Have you never read in the Scriptures: "'The stone the builders rejected has become the capstone.'"
Was to enter the temple	**Malachi 3:1** "Then suddenly the Lord you are seeking will come to his temple; the messenger of the covenant, whom you desire, will come." Also Haggai 2:7, 9	**Matthew 21:12–16** Jesus entered the temple area and drove out all who were buying and selling there. Also Mark 11:11; Luke 2:25–47; 19:45–47
Call those who were not his people	**Isaiah 55:4–5** Surely you will summon nations you know not, and nations that do not know you will hasten to you. Also Hosea 2:23	**Romans 9:23–26** Even us, whom he also called, not only from the Jews but also from the Gentiles?
The King comes to Jerusalem riding on a donkey	**Zechariah 9:9** See, your king comes to you, righteous and having salvation, gentle and riding on a donkey, on a colt, the foal of a donkey.	**Mark 11:1–10** When they brought the colt to Jesus and threw their cloaks over it, he sat on it. Also Matthew 21:1–5; Luke 19:28–38; John 12:14–15
Be a "stone of stumbling" to the Jews	**Isaiah 8:14** And he will be a sanctuary; but for both houses of Israel he will be a stone that causes men to stumble and a rock that makes them fall. And for the people of Jerusalem he will be a trap and a snare.	**Romans 9:31–33** Israel. . . stumbled over the "stumbling-stone." As it is written: "See, I lay in Zion a stone that causes men to stumble and a rock that makes them fall, and the one who trusts in him will never be put to shame." **1 Peter 2:7–8** They stumble because they disobey the message—which is also what they were destined for.
Upon his coming, the deaf hear and the blind see	**Isaiah 29:18** In that day the deaf will hear the words of the scroll, and out of gloom and darkness the eyes of the blind will see. **Isaiah 35:5** Then will the eyes of the blind be opened and the ears of the deaf unstopped.	**Matthew 11:5** The blind receive sight, the lame walk, those who have leprosy are cured, the deaf hear, the dead are raised, and the good news is preached to the poor. Also Mark 7:37; Luke 7:19–22; John 9:39
Fulfill promises to Jews and be a light to the Gentiles	**Isaiah 42:6** "I will keep you and will make you to be a covenant for the people and a light for the Gentiles." **Isaiah 49:6** "I will also make you a light for the Gentiles, that you may bring my salvation to the ends of the earth."	**Luke 2:25–32** "A light for revelation to the Gentiles and for glory to your people Israel." **Acts 26:23** "That the Christ would suffer and, as the first to rise from the dead, would proclaim light to his own people and to the Gentiles."
A new everlasting covenant	**Jeremiah 31:31–34** "I will make a new covenant with the house of Israel and with the house of Judah. It will not be like the covenant I made with their forefathers . . . I will put my law in their minds and write it on their hearts." Also Jeremiah 32:37–40; 50:5	**Luke 22:15–20** "This cup is the new covenant in my blood." **Hebrews 10:15–20** "This is the covenant I will make with them after that time . . . a new and living way opened for us." Also Matthew 26:27–29; Mark 14:22–24; Luke 22:15–20; 1 Corinthians 11:25; Hebrews 8:8–12
Be a prophet like Moses, speaking God's words	Deuteronomy 18:15, 18–19	Matthew 21:11; Luke 7:16; 24:19; John 6:14; 7:40; Acts 3:18–22
Be hated without reason	Psalm 35:19; 69:4	John 15:24–25

Color Key

Prophecies more than 1,200 years before Jesus' birth are highlighted in green.
Prophecies more than 800 years before Jesus' birth are highlighted in yellow.
Prophecies more than 500 years before Jesus' birth are highlighted in blue.

Jesus' Life and Ministry

Prophecy	Old Testament References	New Testament Fulfillment
Come to do the will of God	Psalm 40:7–8	Matthew 26:39; Hebrews 10:5–9
Anointed by God	Psalm 45:6–7	Hebrews 1:8, 9
Have great zeal for God's house	Psalm 69:9	John 2:17
Care for the poor and needy	Psalm 72:12–14	Luke 7:22
Speak in parables with hidden meaning	Psalm 78:2	Matthew 13:10–16, 34–35; Luke 8:10
Will pray for his enemies	Psalm 109:4	Matthew 5:44; Luke 23:34
Be a priest after the order of Melchizedek	Psalm 110:4	Hebrews 5:1–6; 6:20; 7:15–17
People's hearts are hardened	Isaiah 6:9–10	Matt. 13:13–15; John 12:37–40; Acts 28:24–27
His ministry in Zebulun, Naphtali, and Galilee	Isaiah 9:1–2	Matthew 4:12–16
The government is on his shoulders	Isaiah 9:6	Matthew 28:18; 1 Corinthians 15:24–25
Someone will prepare for the coming of the Lord	Isaiah 40:3–5	Matthew 3:3; Mark 1:3; Luke 3:3–5; John 1:23
The Spirit of the Lord rests upon him	Isaiah 11:2; 42:1; 61:1–2	Matt. 3:16; Mark 1:10; Luke 3:22; 4:18; John 1:32; 3:34; Acts 10:38
Be a healer and savior, do miracles	Isaiah 35:4–6	Matthew 9:30; 11:4–6; 12:22; 20:34; 21:14; Mark 7:32–35; John 9:1–7; 11:47
Be a shepherd who tends his sheep	Isaiah 40:10–11	John 10:11; Hebrews 13:20; 1 Peter 2:25
Be a servant of God	Isaiah 42:1–4	Matthew 12:16–21
The Redeemer to come out of Zion	Isaiah 59:16–20	Romans 11:26–27
Nations shall walk in the light of the Lord	Isaiah 60:1–3	Matthew 4:16; Luke 2:32; John 12:46
Anointed to preach liberty to the captives	Isaiah 61:1–2	Luke 4:16–21; Acts 10:38
His Spirit poured out upon people	Joel 2:28–32	Acts 2:16–23
David's house shall be restored	Amos 9:11–12	Acts 15:16–18
God shall dwell among his people	Zechariah 2:10–13	John 1:14; Revelation 21:3
A new priesthood established	Zechariah 3:8	1 Peter 2:5, 9; Revelation 1:6, 5:10
Messenger sent to prepare the way before him	Malachi 3:1	Matthew 11:10; Mark 1:2–4, 7; Luke 7:27–28
Prophet sent before the day of the Lord	Malachi 4:5–6	Matthew 11:13–14; Mark 9:11–13; Luke 1:17; 7:27–28

Color Key

Prophecies more than 1,200 years before Jesus' birth are highlighted in green.
Prophecies more than 800 years before Jesus' birth are highlighted in yellow.
Prophecies more than 500 years before Jesus' birth are highlighted in blue.

Jesus' Death and Resurrection

Prophecy	Old Testament References	New Testament Fulfillment
Be Passover sacrifice with no bone broken	**Exodus 12:46** It must be eaten inside one house; take none of the meat outside the house. Do not break any of the bones. **Numbers 9:12** They must not leave any of it till morning or break any of its bones. When they celebrate the Passover, they must follow all the regulations. Also Psalm 34:20	**John 19:31–36** But when they came to Jesus and found that he was already dead, they did not break his legs. . . . These things happened so that the scripture would be fulfilled: "Not one of his bones will be broken."
Be hung upon a tree as a curse for us	**Deuteronomy 21:23** Be sure to bury him that same day, because anyone who is hung on a tree is under God's curse. You must not desecrate the land the LORD your God is giving you as an inheritance.	**Galatians 3:13** Christ redeemed us from the curse of the law by becoming a curse for us, for it is written: "Cursed is everyone who is hung on a tree."
Be thirsty during his execution	**Psalm 22:15** My strength is dried up like a potsherd, and my tongue sticks to the roof of my mouth; you lay me in the dust of death.	**John 19:28** Later, knowing that all was now completed, and so that the Scripture would be fulfilled, Jesus said, "I am thirsty."
Be accused by false witnesses	**Psalm 27:12** Do not hand me over to the desire of my foes, for false witnesses rise up against me, breathing out violence. **Psalm 35:11** Ruthless witnesses come forward; they question me on things I know nothing about.	**Matthew 26:60** Many false witnesses came forward. **Mark 14:55–61** Then some stood up and gave this false testimony against him.
Be struck on the head	**Micah 5:1** They will strike Israel's ruler on the cheek with a rod.	**Matthew 27:30** They spat on him, and took the staff and struck him on the head again and again.
Have hands and feet pierced	**Psalm 22:16** Dogs have surrounded me; a band of evil men has encircled me, they have pierced my hands and my feet. **Zechariah 12:10** "They will look on me, the one they have pierced, and they will mourn for him as . . . for a firstborn son."	**Matthew 27:35** They had crucified him. Also John 19:18, 34–37 **John 20:25–29** "Unless I see the nail marks in his hands . . . and put my hand into his side, I will not believe it." . . . Then he said ". . . Reach out your hand and put it into my side."
Have soldiers cast lots for his coat	**Psalm 22:18** They divide my garments among them and cast lots for my clothing.	**John 19:23–24** This garment was seamless . . . "Let's not tear it," they said to one another. "Let's decide by lot who will get it." Also Matthew 27:35; Mark 15:24; Luke 23:34
Be given gall and vinegar (sour wine)	**Psalm 69:20–22** They put gall in my food and gave me vinegar for my thirst.	**Matthew 27:34** There they offered Jesus wine to drink, mixed with gall; but after tasting it, he refused to drink it. Also Matthew 27:48; Mark 15:23; 15:36; Luke 23:36; John 19:29
Be beaten and spat upon	**Isaiah 50:6** I offered my back to those who beat me, my cheeks to those who pulled out my beard; I did not hide my face from mocking and spitting.	**Matthew 26:67** Then they spat in his face and struck him with their fists. Others slapped him. **Matthew 27:26–30** They spat on him, and took the staff and struck him on the head again and again. Also Mark 14:65; 15:15–19; Luke 22:63–65; John 19:1
Be betrayed by a friend	**Psalm 41:9** Even my close friend, whom I trusted, he who shared my bread, has lifted up his heel against me. **Psalm 55:12-14** If an enemy were insulting me, I could endure it; if a foe were raising himself against me, I could hide from him. But it is you, a man like myself, my companion, my close friend, with whom I once enjoyed sweet fellowship as we walked with the throng at the house of God.	**Matthew 26:14–16** Then one of the Twelve . . . the one called Judas Iscariot . . . went to the chief priests and asked, "What are you willing to give me if I hand him over to you?" **Matthew 26:23** Jesus replied, "The one who has dipped his hand into the bowl with me will betray me." Also Matthew 26:47–50; Luke 22:19–23, 48; John 13:18–30; 18:2–5
Be despised and rejected	**Isaiah 53:2–3** He was despised and rejected by men . . . Like one from whom men hide their faces he was despised, and we esteemed him not.	**Luke 17:25** But first he must suffer many things and be rejected by this generation. **Luke 23:18** "Away with this man! Release Barabbas to us!" Also Matthew 26:67; John 1:11
Be accused and afflicted, but did not open his mouth	**Isaiah 53:7** He was oppressed and afflicted, yet he did not open his mouth; he was led like a lamb to the slaughter, and as a sheep before her shearers is silent, so he did not open his mouth.	**Matthew 27:12** When he was accused by the chief priests and the elders, he gave no answer. **Luke 23:9** He plied him with many questions, but Jesus gave him no answer. Also Matthew 26:62–63; 27:14; Mark 14:61; 15:5; John 19:9
Commit his spirit into God's hand	**Psalm 31:5** Into your hands I commit my spirit; redeem me, O LORD, the God of truth.	**Luke 23:46** Jesus called out with a loud voice, "Father, into your hands I commit my spirit." When he had said this, he breathed his last.

Color Key

Prophecies more than 1,200 years before Jesus' birth are highlighted in green.
Prophecies more than 800 years before Jesus' birth are highlighted in yellow.
Prophecies more than 500 years before Jesus' birth are highlighted in blue.

100 Prophecies Fulfilled by Jesus • 247

Jesus' Death and Resurrection

Prophecy	Old Testament References	New Testament Fulfillment
Be buried with the rich	**Isaiah 53:9** He was assigned a grave with the wicked, and with the rich in his death, though he had done no violence, nor was any deceit in his mouth.	**Matthew 27:57–60** There came a rich man from Arimathea, named Joseph, who had himself become a disciple of Jesus. he asked for Jesus' body, . . . and placed it in his own new tomb.
Be numbered (crucified) with transgressors	**Isaiah 53:12** He poured out his life unto death, and was numbered with the transgressors.	**Matthew 27:38** Two robbers were crucified with him. Also Mark 15:27–28; Luke 22:37; 23:32–33
The thirty pieces of silver buy the potter's field	**Zechariah 11:12–13** So they paid me thirty pieces of silver. . . . I took the thirty pieces of silver and threw them into the house of the LORD to the potter.	**Matthew 27:3, 6–10** Judas . . . returned the thirty silver coins to the chief priests and the elders . . . they decided to use the money to buy the potter's field.
Be sold for thirty pieces of silver	Zechariah 11:12	Matthew 26:14–15
Be Passover male lamb, without blemish, slain, with blood applied as protection from judgment	Exodus 12:1–11 Isaiah 53:7	John 1:29–36; 1 Corinthians 5:7–8; 1 Peter 1:18–19; Revelation 5:6–13; 7:14; 21:22–27; 22:1–4
Be lifted up, just as Moses lifted up a serpent	Numbers 21:8–9	John 3:14–15
Be raised from the dead	Psalm 16:8–11	Luke 24:6–8; John 20; Acts 1:3; 2:32; 13:34–37; 2 Timothy 2:8
Conquer death through his resurrection	Psalm 16:8–11; 49:15; 86:13	Acts 2:24–36; 13:30–39; 1 Corinthians 15:3–4
Feel forsaken by God	Psalm 22:1	Matthew 27:46; Mark 15:34
Be mocked and insulted by many	Psalm 22:7–8, 17	Matthew 27:31, 39–43; Mark 15:29–32; Luke 23:35–39
Friends stand afar off	Psalm 38:11; 88:18	Matthew 26:56–58; 27:55; Mark 15:40; Luke 23:49
Ascend on high	Psalm 68:18	Luke 24:51; Acts 1:9; Ephesians 4:8
Reproaches of others fall on him	Psalm 69:9	Romans 15:3
Another to succeed Judas	Psalm 109:7–8	Acts 1:16–20
Be a Son who is given	Isaiah 9:6	John 3:16; Romans 8:32
Swallow up death in victory	Isaiah 25:8	1 Corinthians 15:54–57
Be mistreated, hardly recognized	Isaiah 52:14	Hebrews 5:8; 1 Peter 2:21
Bear our griefs and carry our sorrows	Isaiah 53:4–5	Matthew 8:17; Romans 5:6–8
Be wounded for our transgressions	Isaiah 53:5	1 Corinthians 15:3; 2 Corinthians 5:21; 1 Peter 3:18
Be led as a lamb to the slaughter	Isaiah 53:7	John 1:29, 36; Acts 8:28–35; 1 Peter 1:19; Revelation 5:6
Be sinless and without guile	Isaiah 53:9	1 Peter 2:22
Make intercession for the transgressors	Isaiah 53:12	Luke 23:34 "Father, forgive them for they know not what they do."
Be made into an offering for sin	Isaiah 53:10, 11	Acts 10:43; 13:38–39; Romans 3:21–26; 4:5-8; Ephesians 1:7; 1 Peter 2:21–25; 1 John 2:2
Be "cut off" at a specific time after Jerusalem wall is rebuilt, before the temple is destroyed	Daniel 9:24–26; Zechariah 9:9	Matt. 21:1–5; 1:15; 24:1–2; Luke 19:37–38; John 12:13–15
His body would be pierced	Zechariah 12:10	John 19:34–37
Shepherd smitten, sheep scattered (deserted by his followers)	Zechariah 13:6–7	Matthew 26:31, 56; Mark 14:27; John 16:32

Color Key

Prophecies more than 1,200 years before Jesus' birth are highlighted in green.
Prophecies more than 800 years before Jesus' birth are highlighted in yellow.
Prophecies more than 500 years before Jesus' birth are highlighted in blue.

Jesus' Titles and Attributes

Prophecy	Old Testament References	New Testament Fulfillment
"I Am" (Jehovah)	Exodus 3:13–15	John 8:24; 13:19
A Prophet like Moses	Deuteronomy 18:18–19	John 1:21; 6:14; Acts 3:22–23; Hebrews 3:1–6
The throne of David established forever	2 Samuel 7:12–13, 16, 25–26; Psalm 89:3–4, 36–37; Isaiah 9:7; 1 Chronicles 17:11–14, 23–27	Luke 1:32–33; Acts 2:29-36; 2 Timothy 2:8; Hebrews 1:8
The promised Redeemer	Job 19:25–27; Psalm 130:7–8 Isaiah 59:20	Galatians 4:4–5; Titus 2:13–14
The Son of God	Psalm 2:7	Matt. 3:17; 8:29; 16:16; Mark 1:11; Luke 1:32, 35; Acts 13:33; Hebrews 1:5; 5:5; 2 Peter 1:17
Delights to do God's will	Psalm 40:8	John 4:34; 6:38
A King known for righteousness, anointed	Psalm 45:1–7	Hebrews 1:8–9
Seed of David	Psalm 89:3–4	John 7:42; Acts 13:22–23
The firstborn over all creation	Psalm 89:27	Romans 8:29; Colossians 1:15
Never changing, everlasting	Psalm 102:24–27	Hebrews 1:10–12; 13:8
David's son; David's Lord at God's right hand	Psalm 110:1	Matthew 22:41–45; Mark 12:35–37; 16:19; Acts 7:56; Romans 1:3; Ephesians 1:20; Hebrews 1:3
A Priest according to the order of Melchizedek	Psalm 110:4	Hebrews 5:5–6, 10; 6:20; 7:1–22
The Chief Cornerstone	Psalm 118:22–23	Matthew 21:42; Mark 12:10–11; Luke 20:17; Acts 4:10–12; Ephesians 2:20; 1 Peter 2:4–7
The way of repentance for all nations	Isaiah 2:2–4	Luke 24:47
Immanuel, God with us	Isaiah 7:14; 8:8–10	Matt. 1:21–23; John 1:14; 14:8–11; Colossians 2:9
A stone of stumbling, a rock of offense	Isaiah 8:14–15	Matt. 21:42–44; Romans 9:32, 33; 1 Peter 2:6–8
The light which has shone out of darkness	Isaiah 9:1–2	Matthew 4:14–16; Luke 2:32; John 1:4–5
Prince of Peace	Isaiah 9:6	John 14:27; Acts 10:36; Romans 5:1; Ephesians 2:14; Col. 1:20
Full of wisdom, power and righteousness	Isaiah 11:1–10	Acts 10:38; 1 Corinthians 1:30; Ephesians 1:17; Colossians 2:2–3
The key of the house of David is upon his shoulder	Isaiah 22:21–25	Revelation 3:7
The stone in Zion, a sure foundation	Isaiah 28:16	Romans 9:33; 1 Peter 2:6
God's elect Servant, in whom he delights	Isaiah 42:1–4	Matthew 12:17–21; Philippians 2:7
Spirit of the LORD shall rest on him	Isaiah 61:1	Matthew 3:16; Luke 4:18
The Righteous Branch	Jeremiah 23:5–6; 33:15–16	Romans 3:22; 1 Cor. 1:30; 2 Cor. 5:21; Philippians 3:9
The Good Shepherd	Ezekiel 34:23–24; 37:24	John 10:11; Hebrews 13:20; 1 Peter 2:25
The enthroned High Priest	Zechariah 6:12–13	Hebrews 7:11–28; 8:1–2
Sun of Righteousness; the Dayspring; our Light	Malachi 4:2–3	Luke 1:78; Ephesians 5:14; 2 Peter 1:19; John 8:12; Revelation 2:28; 22:16

Color Key

Prophecies more than 1,200 years before Jesus' birth are highlighted in green.
Prophecies more than 800 years before Jesus' birth are highlighted in yellow.
Prophecies more than 500 years before Jesus' birth are highlighted in blue.

Evidence for the Resurrection

The Bible teaches that Jesus is the Son of God, and that he was crucified and died for the forgiveness of sin, was resurrected from the dead, and lives today.

Over the centuries, skeptics have developed several objections to the resurrection of Jesus and have proposed several alternative theories about what actually happened to the body of Jesus Christ. Many believe that Jesus' resurrection is too difficult to prove beyond a reasonable doubt. Here is evidence to answer those doubts.

Skeptics' Objections	Answers
Objection 1 Jesus was a mythological figure.	Evidence for Jesus Christ comes from many written documents from the first century, including 39 ancient sources in addition to the New Testament and early church leaders. An early statement of faith was probably written 8–20 years after the death of Jesus. The creed states that Jesus "was buried, and that he rose again the third day according to the Scriptures" (1 Cor. 15:3–8). Most critical historians agree that documents take more than 20 years to become corrupted by mythological development.
Objection 2 Jesus was just a man.	Evidence supports that Jesus was all he claimed to be. For over three years, Jesus performed many miracles and signs such as controlling the weather, walking on water, giving sight to the blind, healing the lame and diseased, casting out demons, and raising people from the dead. These miracles convinced people of his day that Jesus was all he claimed to be. More than one hundred prophecies found in the Old Testament were fulfilled in Jesus Christ. Jesus predicted he would suffer, die, and rise again, months before his crucifixion. C.S. Lewis wrote in *Mere Christianity* that Jesus could not only be a good man. Because of Jesus' teachings, he could only be the Son of God, a liar, or a madman.
Objection 3 Jesus' followers made it all up.	Evidence suggests that such a deception is highly unlikely. People will not knowingly die for a lie. The disciples were not fearless liars who wanted to fool the world. After the crucifixion, the disciples fled in fear for their lives. However, once they saw, touched, and spoke with the risen Lord, their lives were transformed. Furthermore, all of Jesus' followers doubted the resurrection until Jesus physically appeared to them; then they believed.
Objection 4 The witnesses were unreliable.	All four Gospels agree that the first eyewitnesses to the proof of Jesus' resurrection were women. On the surface, this does not seem like a major proof for the resurrection. The significance of these eyewitnesses lies in understanding the role of women in first century Judea. During the time of Jesus, a woman's testimony was considered worthless. In fact, a woman was not allowed to serve as a witness in court. If early believers wanted to fabricate the resurrection, they would have come up with witnesses who had political and religious influence in their community, not women who weren't even considered reliable witnesses. The greatest weapon against these early eyewitnesses would have been to produce the body of Jesus. The silence of those who opposed Christianity while Jesus' followers preached about the empty tomb only confirmed the fact that the tomb really was empty and its vacancy could not be explained otherwise.
Objection 5 The resurrection is not important.	The physical resurrection of Jesus Christ is important only if it is true. If Jesus did not rise from the grave, then the unbeliever is no worse or better off than before. However, if Jesus did rise from the dead, then it is reasonable to believe that everything Jesus claimed is true. If what Jesus claimed is true, then he died for the sins of the world and one receives eternal life by believing in Jesus.

Evidence for the Resurrection

Skeptics' Objections	Answers
Theory 1 — The eyewitnesses hallucinated.	It is very unlikely, if not impossible, that more than 500 people had the same hallucination. Those who saw Jesus after his death did not expect to see him and were surprised by his being there. Psychiatrists agree that hallucinations require expectation. A psychiatric study performed in 1975 suggests that the content of the hallucination "reflects the efforts [of the one experiencing the hallucination] to master anxiety to fulfill various wishes and needs."
Theory 2 — Jesus did not die on the cross.	If Jesus did not die, the Roman soldiers would have failed in their duties. Jesus had to survive massive blood loss, torture, and a stab wound in his side, and roll the stone away (which normally would take several men to accomplish). Witnesses saw that when Jesus was stabbed in the side, water mixed with blood poured out, medically indicating that Jesus had already died. According to studies of first century tombs, the tomb was likely sealed by a 2,000-pound rolling stone that fit in a sloping track, which would have been impossible for a sole individual to move from the inside of the tomb.
Theory 3 — Jesus' body was stolen.	The enemies of Jesus took several steps to prevent the disciples from stealing the body, such as sealing the stone and providing a guard of soldiers to watch the tomb. The soldiers at the tomb would not sleep for fear of death. During the crucifixion, the disciples were cowards who had abandoned Jesus. One disciple denied that he knew Jesus to a young servant girl. The disciples did not understand his purposes, or the importance of the resurrection. These men did not have the courage to pass by the guard at the tomb, silently move the extremely large stone, rob the grave, and leave undetected.
Theory 4 — Everyone went to the wrong tomb.	The women observed where Jesus' body was laid only a few days earlier. After hearing the report from the women, Peter and John ran to the tomb without directions from the women. It is unlikely that Peter and John would make the same mistake as the women. If Jesus' body were still in its correct tomb, his enemies could have produced the body immediately. Even if everyone went to the wrong tomb, Joseph of Arimathea, the owner of the tomb, would have corrected them.

On Pentecost, 50 days after the resurrection of Jesus, Peter addressed the crowd and specifically pointed out:
- Everyone there knew that Jesus of Nazareth was a man accredited by God by miracles and signs (Acts 2:22).
- Everyone there knew that Jesus was crucified, and that his death was by God's set purpose (Acts 2:23).
- Everyone there knew that David spoke about the resurrection of Jesus nearly 1,000 years before (Acts 2:24–31).
- Everyone there was a witness to the fact that Jesus was raised to life (Acts 2:32).

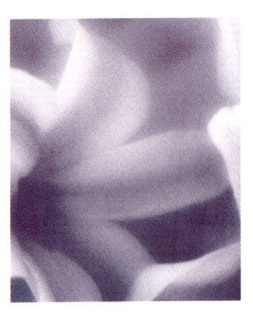

Women of the Bible: New Testament

The New Testament is about Jesus. His character shows very clearly in relation to the people around him. When dealing with hypocrites, he was strong. When dealing with children, he was tender and loving.

Following are portraits of the women with whom Jesus related during his earthly ministry, as well as women in the early church who worshiped the ascended Jesus. These women showed great faith and human faults; they were forgiven women, friends and disciples, and leaders in the church. Their short stories give us examples for our own relationships with the risen Lord.

Elizabeth

Mary, mother of Jesus

Mary Magdalene

Martha and Mary

Woman with the Flow of Blood

the Bent-Over Woman

the Forgiven Woman

the Canaanite Woman

the Samaritan Woman

Priscilla, Lydia, Phoebe, and Dorcas

ELIZABETH

Biblical References	Luke 1
Location and Dates	Jerusalem, around 7-4 BC
Key Events	• Childless wife of Zechariah, a priest in the temple in Jerusalem • Received a message from God saying she would have a son • Mother of John the Baptist, the prophet or "forerunner" of Jesus • Relative of Mary, the mother of Jesus

Key Story

The Gospel of Luke begins not with the story of Jesus' birth but with an unusual couple: Zechariah, a priest in the temple in Jerusalem, and his wife Elizabeth. Their story starts like the story of Abraham and Sarah. The first parallel Luke notes is a painful reality: Elizabeth, like Sarah, was barren and elderly. God uses the lives of these women to show that he is the God of life and miracles.

After a 400-year silence from God since the closing of the Old Testament, an angel from God surprised Zechariah during his service in the temple. The angel promised a child to the old couple. Like Abraham and Sarah, Zechariah found it difficult to believe the words of the angel. Even though Zechariah was a priest in the temple, he could not believe that God was again speaking to his people. But his unbelief does not stop God: Elizabeth became pregnant.

In Elizabeth's view, God restored her and gave her a new beginning. However, God's plans go beyond her; he was about to restore humanity through the birth of Jesus Christ. Just as God changed Elizabeth's sadness into joy, God was about to produce an unexpected reversal for humanity. Elizabeth's son, John, who became John the Baptist, prepared the way for such a change.

Elizabeth not only experienced God's special favor, she was also the first person in the gospel of Luke about whom we read that she "was filled with the Holy Spirit" (Luke 1:41). She and the baby in her womb were the first ones to recognize Jesus, still in Mary's womb, as the promised Messiah.

Insights from Her Story

- God demonstrates that there is nothing impossible for him.
- He transforms childlessness into fertility; he brings life where there is none.
- He shows that he is faithful to his promises. As he had promised to the Patriarchs and through the prophets, God now begins the process of restoring his people, and the whole world.
- Elizabeth and her unborn baby's recognition that Mary's baby was the Messiah was possible by the presence of the Spirit in them.

MARY, MOTHER OF JESUS

BIBLICAL REFERENCES	Luke 1
LOCATION AND DATES	Nazareth, around 7-4 BC
KEY EVENTS	• A young, virgin woman, engaged to Joseph • God chose her to be Jesus' mother • Called "blessed among women" • Submitted to God's will and sang a beautiful prayer • Became another of Jesus' disciples

KEY STORY

Mary was a very common, simple, young woman who would have passed unnoticed at any other moment. Scripture's focus is not about who she was, since the Scriptures say little about her; it is about what happened to her and her response to such an amazing event. The Bible simply says she is forever "blessed among women."

In a dark time when God's silence felt unending, his people had been under the oppression of the powerful Roman Empire, and the people's faith was in great need of renewal, a light shone in the least expected place: the village of a young couple-to-be, Joseph and Mary. The New Testament pays very little attention to this couple. They were engaged to be married (Matthew 1:18), they were from the little northern town of Nazareth, probably from a poor family, since they offered the sacrifice of the poor—two doves and two pigeons—rather than the required lamb (Leviticus 12:8). The Gospel of Luke's focus is Mary. The angel Gabriel descended to give Mary some extraordinary news: the Savior was coming, and Mary was to be his mother.

This unexpected news gives us a chance to read about Mary's extraordinary character. At this time in Israel's history, the people had little faith that God was involved with them. There had been no prophets in Israel for 400 years. Compare the priest Zechariah's reaction to the hopeful attitude in Mary's response: "I am the Lord's servant. May it be to me as you have said" (Luke 1:38). Mary was willing and quick to submit to God. Her response was written in Luke 1:46-55.

Although the Bible mentions Mary on two other occasions, during the wedding at Cana (John 2:1-12) and requesting time to talk to Jesus (Luke 8:19-21), the Scriptures do not report that she had a prominent part in Jesus' earthly ministry. Perhaps this is because the Gospels are about Jesus' ministry. Acts 1:14 is the last appearance of Mary in the Bible. She is shown with the other disciples. Mary, Jesus' mother, was above all else a follower of Jesus.

INSIGHTS FROM HER STORY

- Mary's humble acceptance of God's will is an example for God's people.
- The presence of the Holy Spirit allowed Mary to recognize that God was about to do something marvelous.
- Her humility is also shown after Jesus' death in her willingness to wait alongside the disciples as just one of them (Acts 1:14), not demanding special treatment.

Martha and Mary

Biblical References	Luke 10:38-42; John 11:1-3, 17-45
Location and Dates	Bethany, AD 26–30
Key Events	• Sisters of Lazarus, whom Jesus raised from death • Close friends of Jesus • Mary sat at Jesus' feet; Martha actively served and was hospitable • Martha echoed Peter's confession: "I believe you are the Christ, the Son of God, who was to come into the world" (John 11:27) • Mary washed Jesus' feet with expensive perfume

Key Story

When thinking about Jesus' earthly ministry, it is easy to forget that he too was human, with human needs. He walked far on hot days, was thirsty, and became tired. In such moments, friendship and loving companionship must have been precious to him. Besides his quiet moments of prayer and intimacy with his Father, Jesus also found friendship in people like Mary, Martha, and Lazarus.

The Gospels tell of several interactions between Jesus and at least one of these women. The first shows Jesus visiting at their home. Mary sat at his feet listening to the Master talk. The expression used to describe her actions is unusual when one of the parties is a woman. Tradition forbade rabbis to instruct women. While Mary sat listening to his teachings, Martha was busy being hospitable to Jesus. In frustration at Mary's lack of help, Martha asked Jesus to intervene. Jesus' gentle response shot to the heart of the matter: Only one thing was truly necessary, and Mary had made a good choice.

The Gospel of John describes two emotional interactions between Jesus and these two women. In one, Jesus came to Bethany, the village where Mary, Martha and Lazarus lived, after having learned that Lazarus was sick. Once again Martha was on the go, running to meet Jesus before he came into town. Her confession is both powerful and beautiful. After Jesus identified himself as the resurrection and the life, Martha confessed: "I believe that you are the Christ, the Son of God, who was to come into the world" (John 11:27).

Later on, as Jesus continued with his ministry, he returned to Bethany and visited his friends, Mary, Martha and Lazarus. Once again, Martha was serving dinner and attending the guests. Mary took perfume and cleaned Jesus' feet with it. That action was often associated with burials. Her act of love and gratitude becomes an announcement of Jesus' death.

Insights from Her Story

- Martha and Mary are examples of two important characteristics in the Christian life: Willingness to serve and hunger for God's instructions. The choice is, then, not between being like Mary or like Martha, for both are required: "Love the Lord with all your heart… and your neighbor as yourself" (Mark 12:30-31) However, loving God is a necessary first.

- In addition to being disciples, the sisters were also Jesus' friends. Yet, they fully recognize who Jesus is: Martha's confession and Mary's foot washing show their deep love and commitment to Christ.

Mary Magdalene

Biblical References	Luke 8:1-3; Mark 15:40-47; John 19:25; 20:1-18
Location and Dates	Galilee, AD 26–30
Key Events	• Belonged to the larger group of Jesus' disciples • Healed of possession by seven demons • Present at the time of Jesus' death • First to talk to the Lord after the resurrection • First disciple commissioned to tell about Jesus' resurrection

Key Story

Who is the real Mary Magdalene?

• She appears to be connected to a wealthy northern city, Magdala, which the Roman armies destroyed.

• Traditionally, Mary Magdalene has been mistakenly associated with the sinful woman in Luke 7:37-39. However, careful study of the text does not support this connection.

• Luke 8 introduces her as a woman who had been cured of evil spirits.

Mary was a follower of Jesus, one of the larger group of disciples who traveled with him. She was one of the many women who supported the Lord in his travels and sufferings. In fact, the four gospels show her present at the time of the death of Jesus. She was also among the women who went to the tomb to anoint the body of Jesus for burial, and she was the first person to speak to the resurrected Jesus.

It is a special experience; one unparalleled by that of any other disciple: she was the first disciple commissioned to tell the amazing good news of the risen Jesus. Some have suggested that Gnostic writings claimed that Jesus was married to Mary. There is no evidence of such a thing, and the Scripture makes it clear that, although Jesus did have a close relationship with Mary, it was one of Teacher (Rabbi) and disciple.

However, Jesus' relationship with Mary was unusual for that culture. Rabbis did not disciple women. Women were not permitted to study the Law, and associating with women was potentially a cause for impurity. But even more shockingly, relating to a woman who had been possessed by impure spirits was an unthinkable action by a man of God.

Insights from Her Story

🌿 Mary Magdalene exemplifies a person who left everything to follow Jesus. She became a friend, travel companion, supporter, and disciple of Jesus.

🌿 When all the disciples abandoned Jesus during his crucifixion, Mary Magdalene stayed there, alongside the other women.

The Woman with a Flow of Blood

Biblical References	Mark 5:21-34 (Matthew 9:18-22; Luke 8:40-48)
Location and Dates	West of Galilee Lake, AD 26–30
Key Events	• Suffered from a disease for twelve years • Was considered "impure," unfit for participation in religious rituals • Lost everything trying to find a cure • Was healed by touching Jesus' garment

Key Story

While Jesus was in Galilee, a synagogue ruler named Jairus met him with an urgent request to come and heal his daughter. Jesus agreed to come to Jairus' house. At this point, there is a curious interruption—an anonymous woman who had suffered a disease for twelve years breaks into the narrative. This sick woman was banned from any ritual activity, from any contact with others who did not wish to be unclean. Not only was this woman a religious and social outcast, she was also a poor woman who lost everything trying to find a cure. But she had heard of this Jesus who performed miracles. In a desperate act of courage, under the anonymity of a crowd, she touched the garments of this miracle healer, hoping that act would be enough to receive the healing she deeply hoped for. And she was right. A mere touch brought that healing.

However, in her moment of greatest happiness, Jesus sensed what happened and asked who touched him. Rather than trying to run away, the woman came forward with the truth. Instead of the anger and punishment she expected, she met Jesus' gentleness and grace: "Daughter," he said. For a person shunned from society, such a tender address must have come as a cup of sweet, refreshing water. This miracle worker addressed her as a human being, as a person with dignity and worth. Jesus was revealing himself as so much more than a miracle worker—he is the very Lord of Creation, the Great Healer, and the Savior of humanity.

Insights from Her Story

- Like this woman, we can find healing if we dare to touch Jesus and allow him to touch us. Just as Jesus restored her health, dignity, and the possibility of a future, Jesus offers to us the same wholeness.

	THE BENT-OVER WOMAN
BIBLICAL REFERENCES	Luke 13:10-17
LOCATION AND DATES	Galilee, AD 26–30
KEY EVENTS	• Bent over by a spirit for eighteen years • Went to synagogue the same day Jesus was teaching • Jesus called her forward to heal her • Jesus restored her physically and socially: she was a daughter of Abraham

KEY STORY

The Bible states that this woman was not suffering from the bending of age. It was a bending produced unnaturally. A spirit had afflicted her for eighteen years. Her condition was probably understood as a result of spiritual impurity, perhaps from a hidden and hideous sin. So her very presence in the synagogue may have taken courage.

As Jesus taught in the synagogue, he noticed the woman and called her forward. He healed her. Healing someone on the day of rest was against tradition. The reaction from the leader of the synagogue was criticism: If you can be healed on the other six days, why choose the holy day?

Jesus turned this awkward moment into a moment for teaching about God's grace and mercy. Jesus healed her and more: He also restored her sense of being, her value and rightful place among God's people. Traditionally, Israelite men were identified as "sons of Abraham." Jesus went beyond this tradition and applied the title to the woman, calling her "a daughter of Abraham." This woman, now whole, becomes an illustration of what is to come for those who enter the Sabbath of the Lord (Hebrews 4). We are all bent over by the weight of our burdens and our desires, but Jesus makes us whole; he leads us into a true Sabbath rest.

INSIGHTS FROM HER STORY

- This story illustrates what Jesus said in words before: The Sabbath was made for people, not people for the Sabbath (Mark 2:27). Jesus' care for this woman surpassed the traditions concerning the Holy Day. Indeed, although the day continued to be holy, God's work of restoration, bringing God's people to the true Sabbath (rest, wholeness), was Jesus' ministry. Just as he fully restored her health, he also restored her rightful place among God's people as a daughter of Abraham, a daughter of the promise!

The Forgiven Woman

Biblical References	John 8:2-11
Location and Dates	Jerusalem, AD 26–30
Key Events	• Accused of adultery • Brought before Jesus • Received Jesus' forgiveness and invitation to a changed life

KEY STORY

Jesus was teaching at the temple courts. Some religious leaders barged in, making a great commotion, bringing a frightened woman along. From the perspective of the religious leaders, the moment was a perfect opportunity for trapping Jesus. The trap was clever: if he agreed with them, he would break Roman law; if he disagreed with them, he would break Jewish law. Whether justice would be served with the woman or not is not what mattered; catching Jesus was the goal.

The woman was accused of adultery. It was a most dangerous charge with a deadly consequence. We do not know if the charge was truthful nor why the other party in the crime was absent. The Law required both the man and the woman to stand trial and punishment (Leviticus 20:10). We already know what Jesus thought about the Law: "Has Moses not given you the law?" (John 7:19); the answer is: obey it! He did not repeat the reminder, nor engage them in a legal debate. He simply responded: "If any one of you is without sin, let him be the first to throw a stone." Jesus skillfully turned the dilemma around: if they did not throw stones, they showed that they were inadequate to judge the woman. If they did throw the stone, they would be pretending to be without sin and not in need of the Law. Everyone went away.

The woman could have fled: her life was saved. Yet she remained standing. What could she have expected from this man writing on the ground? He engaged her in conversation, "Woman, where are they? Has no one condemned you?" "No one, sir," were the only words she said. Jesus replied: "Then neither do I condemn you." Judgment belongs to Jesus (John 5:22).

Insights from Her Story

- The woman gets a glimpse of Jesus' grace and mercy. The Law required that the woman to be put to death. We do not know if she was really guilty or not. Jesus' gentleness shows that there is no sin he could not forgive. Forgiveness allows new possibilities, the opportunity of a second chance. In Jesus, everyone can get a second (and a third and fourth) chance for a future and a new life.

	THE CANAANITE WOMAN
BIBLICAL REFERENCES	Matthew 15:21-28 (Mark 7:24-30)
LOCATION AND DATES	Region of Tyre and Sidon, AD 26–30
KEY EVENTS	• Persistently cried out for Jesus' help • Her daughter suffered from demon-possession • Courageously engaged Jesus in a conversation • Jesus rewarded her faith by healing her daughter

KEY STORY

Matthew 10 tells how Jesus commissioned and sent his apostles to preach the coming of the kingdom of heaven. He instructed them: "Do not go among the Gentiles or enter any town of the Samaritans. Go rather to the lost sheep of Israel" (10:5-6). Later on, after attending the crowds, Jesus and his disciples retreated far to the north for some peace and quiet. There they found a woman disturbing the peace with her cries for help in healing her demon-possessed daughter. Jesus' unresponsiveness was unusual. The apostles desired to rid themselves of the screaming woman and appealed to Jesus to send her away. Jesus repeated what he already told them, "I was sent only to the lost sheep of Israel."

However, it was not the disciples who responded but the woman herself, begging Jesus to help. And still Jesus' answer to her petition is puzzling: "It is not right to take the children's bread and toss it to their dogs." At this point the woman has been ignored, looked upon as a nuisance, and clearly rejected. However, although she could have walked away dejected or angry, she instead demonstrated great courage and wit, offering a response to Jesus: "Yes, Lord, but even the dogs eat the crumbs that fall from their masters' table." According to Mark, "because of her answer" Jesus granted her petition. Matthew's account builds on Mark's by understanding her ingenuity and wit as expressions of a great faith, which Jesus commended and rewarded: "Then Jesus answered, 'Woman, you have great faith! Your request is granted.' And her daughter was healed from that very hour" (Matthew 15:28).

THE CANAANITES

This story in Matthew is the only place in the New Testament that uses the name Canaanites. Who were the Canaanites?

- The inhabitants of Canaan, the land that God promised to Abraham (Genesis 15:15).
- A name used to describe sea merchants (Isaiah 23:8; Zechariah 14:21; Ezekiel 16:29).
- Later it became closely associated with the Phoenicians, people who lived by the Mediterranean Sea and were well known for being sea merchants.
- Matthew uses the name Canaanite as a way to make it very clear to the reader that the woman was not a Jew.

INSIGHTS FROM HER STORY

- The faith and perseverance of this woman is a reminder that the good news of Jesus is for every person, everywhere. Her faith also contrasts with the lack of faith of the Jewish leaders. Sometimes Jesus found more faith outside of the people of God.

THE SAMARITAN WOMAN

Biblical References	John 4:1-42
Location and Dates	Samaria, AD 26–30
Key Events	• She came out to draw water from Jacob's well • Jesus revealed to the woman that he is the promised Messiah • Went back to town to tell of her discovery • People believed in her testimony and came to Jesus

KEY STORY

We read that Jesus "had to go through Samaria" (John 4:4). The necessity was not geographical, since most Jews would have crossed the Jordan River. This meeting was, in fact, a divine appointment: Jesus went out of his way to go through Samaria for this conversation.

Jesus sat by a well during the heat of the day. Some people have thought that because the woman came out to draw water at noon she must be hiding from the other women. It is just as probable that the woman had run out of water while cooking and had a pressing need for water.

The woman was surprised when Jesus talked to her, requesting some water. The surprise arises from a double awareness: she was a Samaritan and a woman. Jesus was breaking two old traditions at once: teachers of the law did not talk to women in public, and practicing Jews did not relate to Samaritans, since both activities could cause impurity. Yet, the woman proved to be quite daring in questioning Jesus and in her openness for conversation.

It is easy to assume that the woman divorced five husbands, but this is not likely, as the culture allowed only men to file for divorce. It is possible that: 1) each husband died, or 2) she was caught in the Old Testament marriage laws that pass a widow from brother to brother, or 3) possibly that some husbands divorced her and some died. In any case, it is likely that this woman was deeply hurt. Her desire for this conversation and her thirst for something more demonstrate her need for Jesus. The fact that Jesus pointed out her affair with a man who was not her husband showed the woman that Jesus was more than just a teacher: he was a prophet. Yet, he is much more than that. The following dialogue makes this even clearer: Jesus revealed to her that he is the Messiah, the Savior of the world (John 4:42).

The Samaritan woman went to bear witness of the Messiah to the people in her town. Remarkably, the people believed her and came to Jesus. Despite the disciples' bewilderment, Jesus accepted the invitation of the people and stayed two more days with them.

THE SAMARITANS

- The Samaritans were a group of Israelites in the northern region, between Galilee and Judea, West of the Jordan River.
- Although not Jewish, they were the result of the intermarriage between Israelites and Assyrian deportees from other places.
- Although they observed the Law of Moses, they did not consider some of the other Old Testament books as authoritative.
- Their profound hatred of the Jews is first recorded in Nehemiah 4.
- The level of hostility between both groups was extremely high.

INSIGHTS FROM HER STORY

- Jesus did not let social barriers or taboos stop him from reaching out to people.
- Because of her interaction with Jesus she became a courageous witness to her town, bringing others to Jesus.

Four Women of the Early Church

PRISCILLA

Acts 18 tells that Priscilla and Aquila, a Jewish couple living in Rome, had become Christians. After the Emperor Claudius expelled all Christians from Rome, Aquila and Priscilla ended up in the port city of Corinth, where they became acquainted with the Apostle Paul, who was also in the profession of tent-making. Paul lived with them during his stay in Corinth. Both Priscilla and Aquila came with Paul to Ephesus.

As Paul continued in his traveling, Aquila and Priscilla stayed back in Ephesus to work with the church there. Although the exact nature of their work there is not clear, they were active leaders of the church. Acts recounts a special story about a young and fervent Jew from Alexandria, Apollos, who became a point of contention for the Apostle Paul in 1 Corinthians 3. While in Ephesus, Priscilla and Aquila took on the task to instruct him in "the way of God more adequately" (Acts 18:26).

LYDIA

Lydia bears the honor of being the first recorded European convert to Christianity. Her place of origin was an important commercial city in what is now Turkey. She was a dealer of purple fabrics, which were used for expensive robes. After God's miraculous intervention ("the Lord opened her heart…"), Lydia's home became the central base for Paul's work in Philippi.

DORCAS

Dorcas, also known as Tabitha (Acts 9:32-43), was a Christian in the church near Joppa, an important ancient seaport. Dorcas was much loved because of her generous and compassionate heart. She became sick and died. However, urged by the church in Joppa, the Apostle Peter came by and raised Dorcas from the dead. Dorcas' life is a beautiful illustration of God's love and power in favor of those who love him (Romans 8:28).

PHOEBE

Phoebe is mentioned only once in the New Testament. At the end of his letter to the Romans, Paul introduces Phoebe (apparently a gentile name) who was a *diakonos* of the church (that is, a deaconess). It is the same term that Paul applies to himself (1 Corinthians 3:5; 2 Corinthians 6:4) and Timothy. She may be the one bringing Paul's letter to the church in Rome. Paul's introduction makes it clear that Phoebe was a respected, committed member of the church, who had provided valuable help to the Apostle Paul.

The LIFE of the APOSTLE PAUL

Shipwrecked.
Attacked by murderous mobs.
Beaten. Starved. Imprisoned.
Betrayed by friends.
All to serve the one thing
he sought to destroy, Christianity.

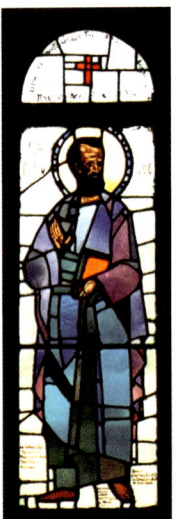

Who was Paul?
Paul was an arch-enemy of Christianity, who amazingly became the greatest Christian missionary of all time. He authored more books of the Bible than anyone else and is called the "Apostle to the Gentiles."

Stained glass window in Philippi

Background
Paul came from a well-respected family in Asia Minor (Turkey today) where his father was an official. He excelled in his studies and became a devout Pharisee. As a young man Paul—whose Jewish name was Saul—was sent to Jerusalem to study under the great teacher Gamaliel. He hated Christians and participated in the first execution of a Christian leader, a man named Stephen. Paul was determined to murder all those who followed Jesus, not just in Jerusalem, but elsewhere (Acts 7:54–8:3).

What was a Pharisee?
The Pharisees were a group of Jewish religious leaders who believed a person must keep every one of the traditions of Judaism, as well as the biblical commandments. The Pharisees were respected, but were legalistic. Jesus condemned them for being self-righteous and hypocritical (Matthew 23). Pharisees plotted to kill Jesus because of his popularity and claim to be God.

How did Paul become a Christian?
Paul asked the chief priest in Jerusalem to give him authorization to arrest any follower of Jesus in Damascus (about 100 miles away). On his way from Judea to Damascus, a light from heaven blinded him. He fell to the ground and a voice said, "Saul, Saul, why do you persecute me?" He answered, "Who are you?" The voice said, "I am Jesus, the one you are persecuting. Get up! Go into the city, and you will be told what to do." Paul was told to go to a house and wait for a Christian man named Ananias to come restore his sight (Acts 9:1-12).

What did other Christians think?
The Lord spoke to Ananias, and Ananias was afraid. He knew Paul's reputation, but went to the house anyway. The Lord said that Paul was chosen to take the Lord's name to Gentiles, their kings, and to the Jews. Ananias placed his hands on Paul and his sight was restored. Paul was filled with the Holy Spirit and was baptized. He started speaking in synagogues and convincing people that Jesus was the Messiah. People were amazed and confused. The believers back in Jerusalem refused to believe he had changed until one of their leaders, Barnabas, vouched for him (Acts 9:13-28).

What did the Pharisees think?
Because the Lord, had spoken to him, Paul kept preaching in the synagogues in Damascus, saying that Jesus was the Son of God. He gave proofs from the Scriptures to show that Jesus was the fulfillment of the Bible prophecies. To the Jews, this was blasphemy and they were outraged. They plotted to kill Paul as he walked out of the city gates. Paul learned of the plot. His friends put him in a basket and lowered him down the city wall to escape (Acts 9:20-25).

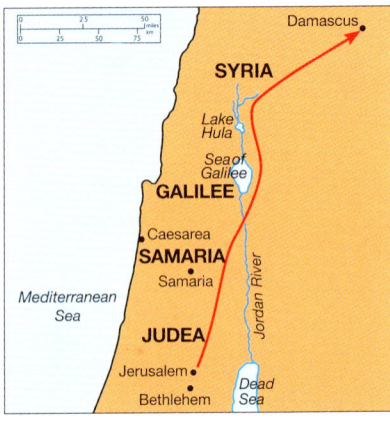

Life as a Fugitive?
Instead of hiding out, Paul went to Jerusalem and boldly preached in the synagogues. He tried to convince people about Jesus. He preached fearlessly and debated at every opportunity. He received death threats and the Christians brought him out of Jerusalem. He went back home to Tarsus (Acts 9:28-30).

Is Jesus for the Jews Only?
During the early years of Christianity, most of the converts were Jewish. Jesus' disciples preached only to Jews. Yet as Jewish people scattered throughout the Roman Empire, they told their neighbors about Jesus. Many of these Gentiles (non-Jews) became followers of Jesus too (Acts 11:19-21).

Barnabas Finds Paul
Barnabas went to Tarsus and together he and Paul preached to non-Jewish people. At the city of Antioch, these believers were first called Christians. A famine hit Jerusalem and the Christians wanted to send relief to their fellow believers. They sent Barnabas and Paul back to Jerusalem with gifts. When their mission was accomplished, Barnabas and Paul, along with a young man named John Mark, headed back north to start a missionary journey throughout Asia Minor (Acts 11:22-30).

Persecuted for Jesus Christ

"Everyone who wants to live a godly life in Christ Jesus will be persecuted..."
—2 Timothy 3:12

- Stoned and left for dead
- Beaten with rods three times
- Whipped with 39 lashes five times
- Attacked by angry mob
- Death threats

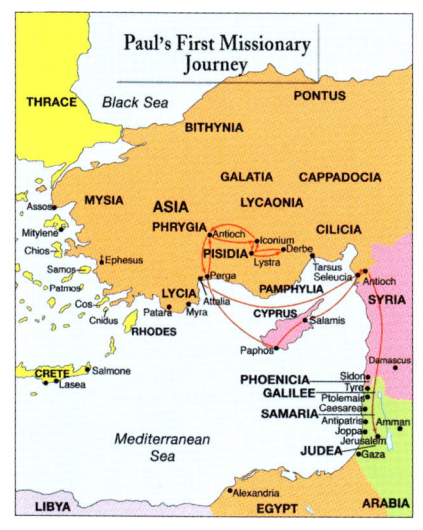

The Life of the Apostle Paul • 263

Paul's First Missionary Journey AD 47-49
Acts 13:1–14:28

Travelers: Paul, Barnabas, John Mark
Main route: Cyprus and Turkey
Cities/places: (1400 miles)

1. Antioch in Syria: The Holy Spirit sets apart Paul and Barnabas for the missionary ministry. John Mark goes along as their helper.

2. Sailed from Seleucia to Salamis and Paphos (on Cyprus): Paul confronts a sorcerer named Elymas and blinds him. (From this point the Bible calls him Paul, rather than Saul.)

3. Perga in Pamphylia: John Mark deserts the group and returns to Jerusalem.

4. Antioch of Pisidia (Turkey today): Paul preaches his longest recorded sermon, and many respond. Jewish leaders drive them out of the city. The Lord calls Paul to focus his ministry on Gentiles. The Gentiles are glad and many become believers.

Early Cave Church in Antioch

5. Iconium: More plots force them to flee.

6. Lystra: When Paul heals a lame man, the townspeople think he and Barnabas are Greek gods. Jews from Antioch stir up the crowd, and Paul is stoned and left for dead.

7. Derbe: Paul preaches and many disciples are added to the church.

8. Lystra, Iconium, Antioch of Pisidia, Pamphylia, Perga, Attalia: On the return trip, Paul and Barnabas appoint elders in the churches they had planted.

9. Antioch (Syria): Paul remains there for a while, reporting what God had done. Paul writes Galatians.

10. Jerusalem, via Phoenicia and Samaria: In AD 49, Paul and Barnabas report to the leaders of the Jerusalem church. This meeting is known as the Jerusalem Council (Acts 15:1-35).

Paul's Second Missionary Journey AD 49-51
Acts 15:36–18:22

Travelers: Paul, Silas, Timothy, Priscilla and Aquilla, Luke
Main route: Syria, Turkey, Greece, Jerusalem
Cities/places: (2800 miles)

1. Antioch in Syria: Paul and Barnabas decide to visit the churches again, but disagree about who should go with them. Paul doesn't want to take John Mark because he left them on their first trip. Barnabas takes John Mark with him to Cyprus; Paul takes Silas.

2. Syria and Cilicia: Paul and Silas take a letter from the Jerusalem church for the churches in this region.

3. Derbe, Lystra, Iconium: While visiting these churches, Timothy joins them.

4. Troas: While in this seaport, Paul has a vision of a man from Macedonia calling him to come help them. Acts 16:10 uses the word "we," indicating that Luke was with Paul.

Diana (Artemis), the goddess of Ephesus

5. Samothrace, Neapolis, Philippi: Lydia, a wealthy businesswoman, is converted in the Macedonian city of Philippi, and the group stays in her house. When a fortune-telling slave girl is converted, her owners start a riot, and Paul and Silas are thrown in jail. In the middle of the night, as they are singing, there is an earthquake and their chains fall off. The jailer is converted. When the magistrate discovers Paul and Silas are Roman citizens, he apologizes and they are escorted out of town.

An earthquake rocked the jail in Philippi.

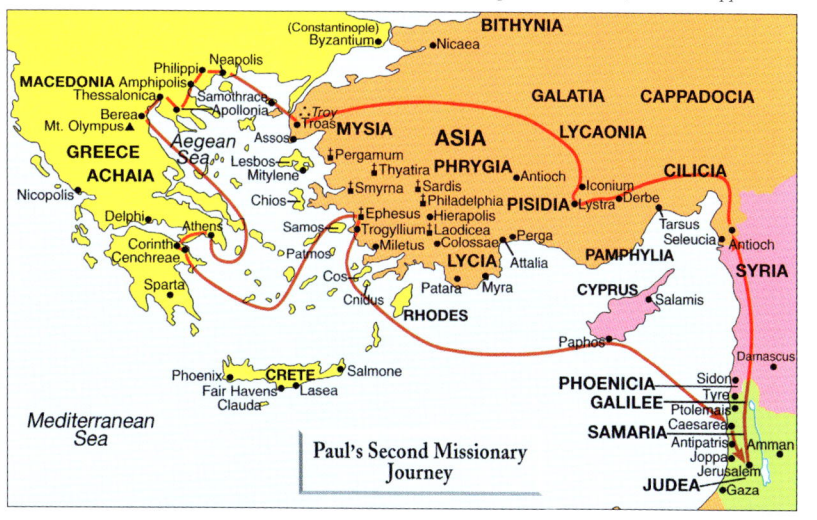

264 • The Life of the Apostle Paul

6. Amphipolis, Apollonia, Thessalonica: Jews in Thessalonica try to have Paul and Silas arrested after they gain some converts.

The Lion of Amphipolis, built 200 years before Paul's visit

7. Berea: The people in the synagogue receive the message eagerly. Silas and Timothy stay here while Paul goes on.

8. Athens (Mars Hill, or Areopagus): Paul sees an altar to an unknown god, and preaches to the thinkers of Athens. A number of them believe.

9. Corinth: Paul meets Aquila and Priscilla, who join him. People try to get Paul arrested, but the authorities refuse. He writes 1 and 2 Thessalonians here.

Paul preached at Mars Hill in Athens

10. Cenchrea: He gets his hair cut because he had taken a vow (Acts 18:18). No more details are given.

11. Ephesus: Paul leaves Priscilla and Aquila here.

12. Caesarea in Syria, Jerusalem, Antioch in Syria: After visiting these churches, Paul returns to his home base of Antioch.

Corinth. Paul wrote to the Corinthian Christians while he was in Ephesus.

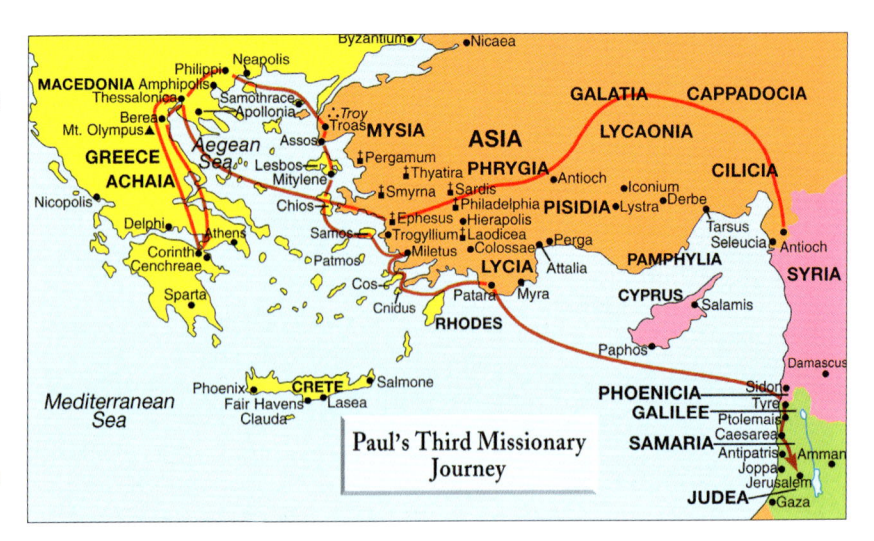

Paul's Third Missionary Journey

Paul's Third Missionary Journey AD 52-57
Acts 18:23–21:16

Travelers: Paul, Timothy, Luke, others
Main route: Turkey, Greece, Lebanon, Israel **Cities/places: (2700 miles)**

1. Region of Galatia and Phrygia: Paul decides to visit the churches again.

2. Ephesus: Paul stays here two years. He writes 1 Corinthians. So many people convert that the silversmiths who manufacture idols start a riot.

3. Macedonia and Greece (Achaia): Paul writes 2 Corinthians and Romans.

4. Philippi (Macedonia) and Troas: While Paul is preaching, a young man falls asleep, falls from a third-story window, and dies. Paul revives him.

5. Assos, Mitylene (near Chios), Samos, Miletus: Elders from Ephesus meet the ship at Miletus; Paul tells them he expects to be imprisoned in Jerusalem.

6. Cos, Rhodes, Patara, Tyre: Disciples warn Paul not to go to Jerusalem.

7. Ptolemais and Caesarea: A prophet predicts that Paul will be imprisoned and handed over to the Gentiles.

8. Jerusalem: The missionaries report to the church leaders, who urge Paul to participate in a purification ritual at the temple to counteract rumors that Christianity is anti-Jewish.

Columns in the open air market where Paul preached in Ephesus

When Bad Things Happen to Good People

"Endure hardship with us like a good soldier of Christ Jesus."
—2 Timothy 2:3

- Shipwrecked three times and floated 24 hours
- Criticized by other Christians 
- Under arrest for two years without a trial 
- Bitten by a viper

The Life of the Apostle Paul • 265

Paul's Journey to Rome
AD 57-62, Acts 21:17–28:31

Travelers: Paul, Roman guards, Luke, others
Main route: Israel, Lebanon, Turkey, Crete, Malta, Sicily, Italy
Cities/places: (2250 miles)

1. Jerusalem (Acts 21:27–22:30): The Roman commander arrests Paul to save him from a Jewish mob. When the commander learns of a death threat against Paul, he orders an armed escort to take him to Caesarea.

2. Antipatris and Caesarea (Acts 23:23–26:32): Paul is tried before Felix, the governor of Judea. Felix leaves Paul in prison for two years, and he is tried again before Festus, who was appointed governor after Felix. The Jews try to get Paul transferred to Jerusalem where they plan to have him killed. Paul demands his right as a Roman citizen and appeals his case to Caesar. King Agrippa visits Festus, and Paul appears before him as well.

The Colleseum in Rome was built four years after Paul's death

3. Sidon: The centurion in charge of Paul lets him visit with friends here. Then Paul boarded a ship, and set sail for Italy.

4. Myra, Cnidus, Fair Havens (Crete): Paul recommends that the ship stay in safe harbor, but the centurion orders the ship to sail on.

5. Clauda and the Island of Malta (shipwrecked): After a two-week storm, the ship is wrecked near the island of Malta. Everyone on the ship makes it to shore after the shipwreck. While putting wood on a campfire, Paul is bitten by a venomous snake, but it does not harm him.

6. Syracuse (Sicily), Rhegium, Puteoli: Paul stays with believers for seven days.

7. Appii Forum, Three Taverns: Paul is met by Christians from Rome.

8. Rome: Paul remains under house arrest for two years, where he writes Ephesians, Colossians, Philemon, and Philippians.

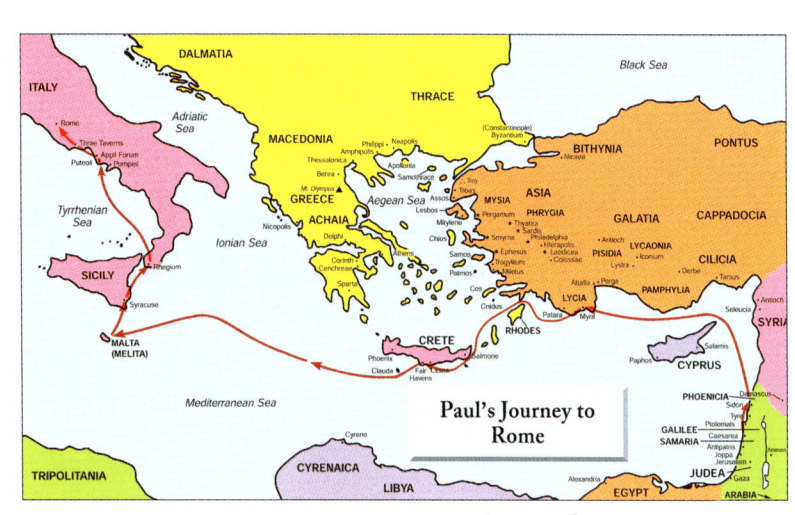

Paul's Journey to Rome

Paul's Other Journeys
AD 62-68

Paul was released after two years of house arrest and traveled again.

Cities/places: (order unknown)
Macedonia (1 Timothy 1:3)
Troas and Miletus (2 Timothy 4:13, 20)
Crete (Titus 1:5)
Planned to go to Spain (Rom.15:28) Nicopolis (Titus 3:12)
Back to Rome: Execution

Ruins of the forum in Philippi where Paul preached

Paul's Death
Paul was beheaded in Rome, in AD 68, while Nero was the emperor of Rome.

God's Strength and Paul's Personality

Paul was a strong, driven person, even before he became a Christian; yet when the Lord chose him to preach the Gospel throughout the world, Paul knew he could not rely on his own power to face the angry mobs, the miles of travel, and the other hardships.

Paul prayed for strength, courage, and boldness. He prayed that people would listen to the Lord's message and be saved. He asked the Lord for safety and for more opportunities to tell about Jesus Christ. Paul asked others to join in the struggle by praying for him. He was grateful for their faithful love and support. He knew that he was weak and needed God's power (Acts 9:15, 2 Corinthians 12:9, Ephesians 6:20, Philippians 1:19).

"I can do all things through Christ who strengthens me."
—Philippians 4:13

"I have fought the good fight, I have finished the race, I have kept the faith. Now there is in store for me the crown of righteousness, which the Lord, the righteous Judge, will award to me on that day—and not only to me, but also to all who have longed for his appearing."
—2 Timothy 4:7-8

Letters Written by Paul and their Message

Letter Key Verse	To	Where Written	When Written	Theme
Galatians 5:22, 23	Church at Galatia	Antioch in Syria	AD 49	Free in Christ Through Faith
1 Thessalonians 5:16-23	Church at Thessalonica	Corinth	AD 51	Letter to New Christians
2 Thessalonians 3:4-6	Church at Thessalonica	Corinth	AD 51	Persevere Until Christ Returns
1 Corinthians 13:4, 5	Church at Corinth	Ephesus	AD 56	Addresses Problems in the Church
2 Corinthians 12:9	Church at Corinth	Macedonia	AD 56	Paul's Authority Against False Teachers
Romans 12:1, 2a	Church at Rome	Corinth	AD 57	Salvation: Righteousness from God
Ephesians 2:8, 9	Church at Ephesus	Rome	AD 60/61	The Church and Body of Christ
Colossians 2:9, 10	Church at Colossae	Rome	AD 60/61	Christ Is Everything
Philemon 17-19	Philemon, a friend at Colossae	Rome	AD 60/61	Brothers in Christ
Philippians 2:14, 15	Church at Philippi	Rome	AD 62	Joy at All Times
1 Timothy 4:12, 13	Timothy, leader of Church at Ephesus	Macedonia	AD 62/63	Caring for the Church
Titus 3:4-7	Titus, leader of Church in Crete	Corinth	AD 63	Living in Faith
2 Timothy 3:15-17	Timothy, leader of Church at Ephesus	Rome	AD 67	Paul's Last Words

The LIFE of the APOSTLE PAUL Time Line

AD 5 — Dates are approximate

- Born an Israelite, from the tribe of Benjamin, a Roman citizen in Tarsus of Celicia, given the Hebrew name of Saul (Acts 7:58; 22:25-29). AD 5
- Receives the best of Roman education in Tarsus; studies under the Jewish scholar Gamaliel. AD 10-30

AD 30

- Persecution of Christians. AD 30-35
- Watches with approval the stoning of Stephen (Acts 7:57-60). AD 32 or 33

AD 35

AD 40

- Paul's conversion (Acts 9:1-19). AD 37
- Begins to preach about Christ in the synagogues (Acts 9:20-25). AD 37
- Goes to Jerusalem, but the Christian leaders are suspicious of him. (Acts 9:26-29; Galatians 1:18-19). AD 37
- When the Christians hear about a plot to kill him, they send him to Syria and Celicia (Acts 9:30; Galatians 1:21). AD 37-46
- Spends three years in Arabia, then returns to Damascus (Galatians 1:17; Acts 9:23). AD 37-40

AD 45

- **First Missionary Journey** AD 47-49
- Barnabas takes Paul to Syrian Antioch, where they minister for a year (Acts 11:25, 26). AD 46
- When a prophet predicts a famine will hit Jerusalem, the Christians collect contributions and send them to Jerusalem with Barnabas and Paul (Acts 11:27-30; 12:25). AD 47

AD 50

- **Second Missionary Journey** AD 49-51
- Jerusalem Council (Acts 15:1-35) AD 49
- Galatians letter written AD 49
- Appears before Gallio AD 51
- 1 & 2 Thessalonians written AD 51

AD 55

- **Third Missionary Journey** AD 52-57
- In Ephesus AD 53-55
- 1 & 2 Corinthians letters written AD 56

AD 60

- **Journey to Rome** AD 57-62
- Arrested in Jerusalem AD 57
- Romans letter written AD 57
- In prison in Caesarea AD 57-59
- Shipwreck AD 59
- Philemon letter written AD 60-61
- Ephesians letter written AD 60-61
- Colossians letter written AD 60-61
- Philippians letter written AD 62
- 1 Timothy letter written AD 62-63
- Titus letter written AD 63
- Released from prison AD 62-63

AD 65

- 2 Timothy letter written AD 67
- Imprisoned again in Rome AD 67
- Paul's death AD 64 or 68?

THE ARMOR OF GOD

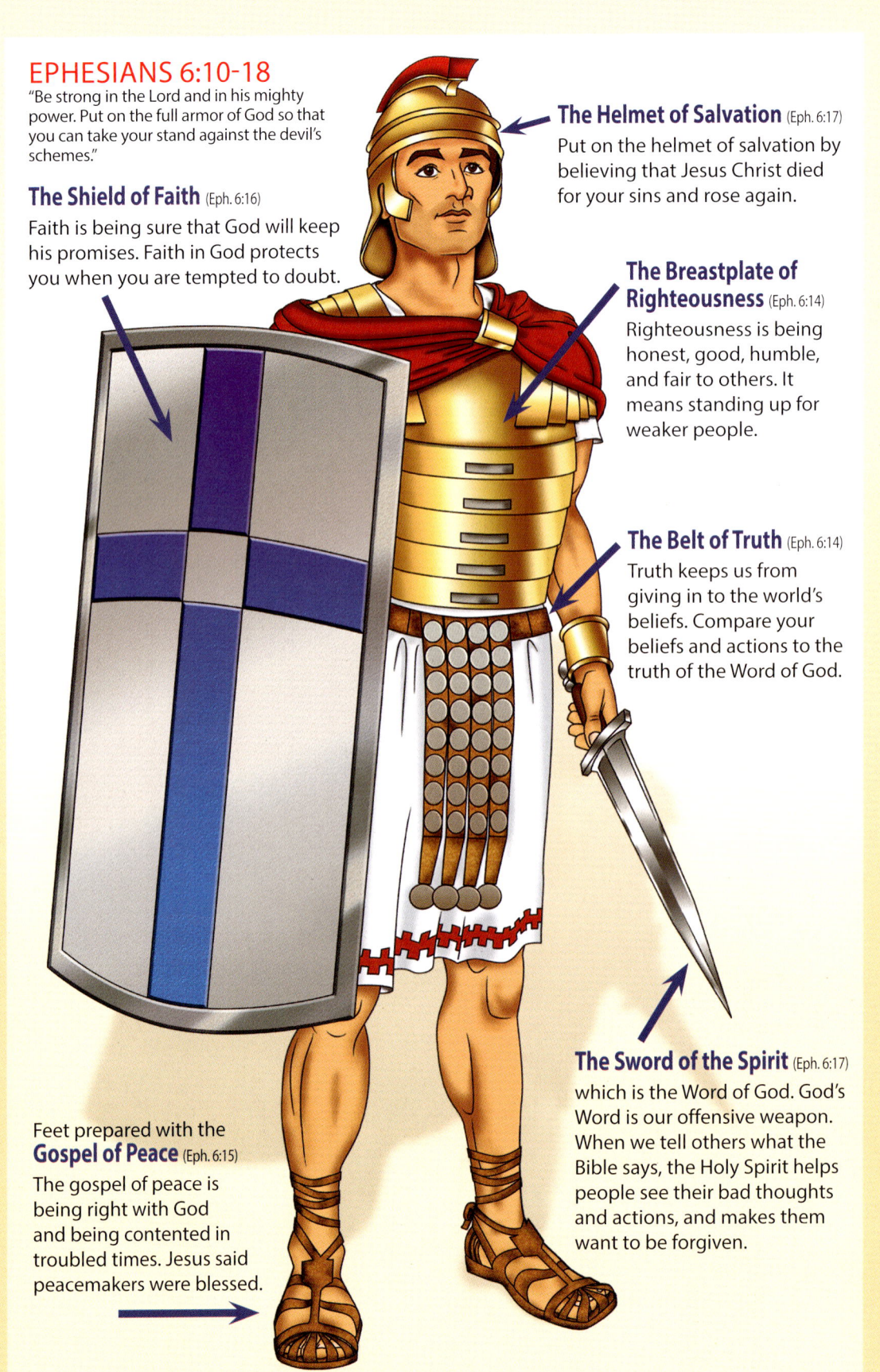

EPHESIANS 6:10-18
"Be strong in the Lord and in his mighty power. Put on the full armor of God so that you can take your stand against the devil's schemes."

The Shield of Faith (Eph. 6:16)
Faith is being sure that God will keep his promises. Faith in God protects you when you are tempted to doubt.

The Helmet of Salvation (Eph. 6:17)
Put on the helmet of salvation by believing that Jesus Christ died for your sins and rose again.

The Breastplate of Righteousness (Eph. 6:14)
Righteousness is being honest, good, humble, and fair to others. It means standing up for weaker people.

The Belt of Truth (Eph. 6:14)
Truth keeps us from giving in to the world's beliefs. Compare your beliefs and actions to the truth of the Word of God.

The Sword of the Spirit (Eph. 6:17)
which is the Word of God. God's Word is our offensive weapon. When we tell others what the Bible says, the Holy Spirit helps people see their bad thoughts and actions, and makes them want to be forgiven.

Feet prepared with the **Gospel of Peace** (Eph. 6:15)
The gospel of peace is being right with God and being contented in troubled times. Jesus said peacemakers were blessed.

The Love Chapter: 1 Corinthians 13

What Love is	How to Love	Scripture
Patient	Be willing to wait for God's perfect timing. Have self-restraint. Control your impulses.	Isa. 40:31; Rom. 15:1; James 1:4
Kind	Ask, "What would this person like?" "What does she need?" Speak softly and be caring.	Prov. 25:11; Isa. 58:6–7; Eph. 4:32
Does not envy	Be content with what you have. List your blessings. Be happy for others' good.	Ex. 20:17; 1 Cor. 3:3; Phil. 4:11–12
Does not boast	Be humble. Don't brag. Give credit to others.	Ps. 34:2; 49:6–7; Phil. 3:1–8
Not proud	Don't think you are better than other people. Be modest. Don't be arrogant or overbearing.	John 13:14–15; 1 Cor. 8:1; Phil. 2:2–8
Not rude	Be courteous and kind. Be gracious. Use good manners.	Num. 12:3; 1 Peter 4:9; 5:5
Not self-seeking	Think of others first. Give someone else first choice. Don't be greedy and selfish.	John 15:13; Acts 20:35; 1 Cor. 10:24
Not easily angered	Think the best of people. Don't jump to conclusions. Ask questions and listen.	Matt. 5:22; Rom. 15:2; James 1:19
Keeps no record of wrongs	Forgive the "wrongs." Remember the "rights." What did Jesus do?	Matt. 6:12; John 8:11; Gal. 6:1
Does not delight in evil	Don't watch or read evil things. Turn away from gossip. Don't gloat when others fall.	Prov. 11:13; Matt. 5:29; Gal. 6:1
Rejoices with the truth	Be happy about good things. Spread good news. Tell the truth to yourself and others.	Isa. 60:1; Eph. 4:25; Phil. 1:18
Always protects	Protect the helpless and weak. Protect yourself against temptation. Defend the name of Jesus.	Prov. 4:14–15; James 1:27; 1 Peter 3:15
Always trusts	Trust is believing God's promises. Pray about everything and trust him. Believe that all things work for good.	Isa. 14:24; Rom. 8:28; Phil. 4:6
Always hopes	Never give up. Remember God doesn't give up on you. Expect good things from God.	Rom. 5:10; Eph. 6:13; 1 John 3:3
Always perseveres	Be persistent. Keep on praying. If God is for you, who can be against you? Be faithful to God and others.	Rom. 8:31; James 5:16; 1 Peter 4:8
Never fails	Love never fails. God's love never fails. Pray for a loving heart like his.	John 13:35; 15:9; 1 Cor. 13:13

Fruit of the Spirit — Galatians 5:22–23

Fruit	Definition	Description	Greek Word	Scriptures
Love	Seeks the highest good of others	Love is not based on emotions or feelings. It is a decision to be committed to the well being of others without any conditions or circumstances.	*agape* (ah-**gah**-pey)	1 John 4:7–12
Joy	Gladness not based on circumstances	Joy is more than happiness. It is not based on financial success, good health, or popularity. By believing in God, obeying his will, receiving his forgiveness, participating in fellowship with other believers, ministering to others, and sharing the gospel, believers will experience joy.	*chara* (**kah**-rah)	1 Peter 1:8–9
Peace	Contentment, unity between people	Peace is a state of assurance, lack of fear, and sense of contentment. It is fellowship, harmony, and unity between individuals. Peace is freedom from worry, disturbance, and oppressive thoughts.	*eirene* (eh-**rey**-ney)	Phil. 4:6–7
Patience	Slow to speak and slow to anger	Patience is a slowness in avenging wrongs. It is the quality of restraint that prevents believers from speaking or acting hastily in the face of disagreement, opposition, or persecution. Patience is bearing pain or problems without complaining.	*makrothumia* (mah-krow-**thew**-me-ah)	James 5:8–9
Kindness	Merciful, sweet, and tender	Kindness is an eagerness to put others at ease. It is a sweet and attractive temperament that shows friendly regard.	*chrestotes* (krey-**stah**-teys)	Prov. 11:16–17
Goodness	Generous and openhearted	Goodness is the selfless desire to be openhearted and generous to others above what they deserve.	*agathosune* (ah-**gah**-thow-**soo**-ney)	Gal. 6:9–10
Faithfulness	Dependable, loyal, and full of trust	Faithfulness is firm devotion to God, loyalty to friends, and dependability to carry out responsibilities. Faith is the conviction that even now God is working and acting on our behalf.	*pistis* (**piss**-tiss)	Prov. 3:3 Rev. 2:10
Gentleness	Humble, calm, non-threatening	Gentleness is a humble, non-threatening demeanor that derives from a position of strength and authority, and is useful in calming another's anger. Gentleness is not a quality that is weak and passive.	*prautes* (prah-**oo**-teys)	Prov. 15:1 1 Peter 3:15
Self-control	Behaving well	Self-control is to restrain our own emotions, actions, and desires, and to be in harmony with the will of God. Self-control is doing God's will, not living for ourselves.	*egkrateia* (eg-**krah**-teh-ee-ah)	Prov. 29:11 Titus 2:11–12

Jesus' Example of the Fruit of the Spirit

Love	Jesus said, "As the Father has **loved** me, so have I **loved** you. Now remain in my **love**." John 15:9
Joy	Jesus said, "I am coming to you now, but I say these things while I am still in the world, so that they may have the full measure of my **joy** within them." John 17:13
Peace	Jesus said, "**Peace** I leave with you; my **peace** I give you. I do not give to you as the world gives. Do not let your hearts be troubled and do not be afraid." John 14:27
Patience	The apostle Paul wrote, "I was shown mercy so that in me, the worst of sinners, Christ Jesus might display his immense **patience** as an example for those who would believe in him and receive eternal life." 1 Tim. 1:16
Kindness	"And God raised us up with Christ … in order that in the coming ages he might show the incomparable riches of his grace, expressed in his **kindness** to us in Christ Jesus." Eph. 2:6–7
Goodness	"[God] saved us through the washing of rebirth and renewal by the Holy Spirit, whom he poured out on us **generously** through Jesus Christ our Savior." Tit. 2:5–6
Faithfulness	"But Christ is **faithful** as the Son over God's house. And we are his house, if indeed we hold firmly to our confidence and the hope in which we glory." Heb. 3:6
Gentleness	Jesus said, "Take my yoke upon you and learn from me, for I am **gentle** and humble in heart, and you will find rest for your souls." Matt. 11:29
Self-control	"When [Jesus' accusers] hurled their insults at him, **he did not retaliate**; when he suffered, **he made no threats**. Instead, he entrusted himself to him who judges justly." 1 Peter 2:23

Bad Fruit Gal. 5:19–21; Col. 3:5–9

Acts of the sinful nature:

- Sexual immorality
- Impurity
- Idolatry
- Debauchery
- Factions
- Hatred
- Drunkenness
- Jealousy
- Lust
- Filthy language
- Witchcraft
- Envy
- Selfish ambition
- Orgies
- Greed
- Fits of rage
- Slander
- Anger
- Evil desires
- Malice
- Deceit

The Seven Churches of Revelation

To the Church	Your Strengths	Your Faults	Instruction	Promise
Loveless Ephesus Rev. 2:1–7	Hard work. Patient endurance. Reject evil. Persevere.	You have forsaken your first love.	Repent and do the works as you did at first.	You will eat from the tree of life.
Suffering Smyrna Rev. 2:8–11	Endure your suffering and poverty, yet you are rich.	None	Remain faithful even when facing prison, persecution, or death.	I will give you the crown of life. You will not be hurt by the second death.
Worldly Pergamum Rev. 2:12–17	Loyalty to Christ. Refuse to deny him.	Tolerates cults, heresies, idolatry, and immorality.	Repent.	Hidden manna and a stone with a new name on it.
Wrong Doctrine Thyatira Rev. 2:18–29	Deeds, love, faith, service. Patient endurance. Constant improvement.	Tolerates cult idolatry and immorality.	Judgment coming. Repent. Hold fast until I come.	I will give you authority over the nations and gift of the morning star.
Spiritually Dead Sardis Rev. 3:1–6	Some have kept the faith.	Church is dead.	Wake up, repent. Turn to Jesus again. Strengthen what little remains.	Faithful will walk with Jesus and not be blotted out of the book of life.
Spiritually Alive Philadelphia Rev. 3:7–13	Kept my word. Have not denied my name.	None	I have placed before you an open door. I will keep you from the hour of trial.	I will make you a pillar in the temple of my God.
Complacent Laodicea Rev. 3:14–22	None	Neither hot nor cold. You rely on riches but don't realize your wretched condition.	Turn from indifference and repent.	I will invite those who overcome to sit with me on my throne.

Background Information

Ephesus: The City of Change
Ephesus was colonized by the Greeks no earlier than 1200 BC and was located near the Aegean Sea, providing a major harbor and caravan gateway for trade to all of Asia Minor and beyond. By the first century, Ephesus was already an established city, predominant in the Roman province of Asia Minor and home to the Roman governor. Besides becoming a city of great wealth, it was noted for the Celsus library, established in the second century. The Ephesians worshiped Diana, the Roman goddess of nature and fertility, identified with the Greek goddess Artemis. At the present day, Ephesus has all the appearance of an inland city, caused by natural changes in the coastline. Paul founded the church at Ephesus.

Smyrna: The City of Life
Smyrna, a thriving seaport city now called Izmir, is about 35 miles (56 km) north of Ephesus. Founded as a Greek colony more than 1,000 years before Christ, it paralleled Ephesus in wealth, beauty and commerce. Proud of being the city of the poet Homer, it was filled with the pagan temples of Apollo, Asclepia, Aphrodite, Cybele, Emperor Tiberius, and Zeus. Although it was a free city, it gave full allegiance to the Roman Empire which ordered Polycarp, the Bishop of Smyrna, to be burned at the stake in Rome. The temple of Athena, dating back to the seventh century BC, was the most important building of that period. It was famous for its superb school of medicine. Although the origin of the city is not mentioned in the Bible, the church in Smyrna was probably founded by believers from Ephesus.

Pergamum: The City of Authority
Pergamum, founded no later than 399 BC, became the capital city of the Roman province in Asia giving the traveler the impression of a royal city, the home of authority. Located about 60 miles (97 km) north of Smyrna and 15 miles (24 km) from the Aegean Sea, Pergamum was a center of learning, medicine, and religious books. The library, rivaling the Alexandrian library, drew many princes, priests, and scholars. Noted for marble carving, it excelled the other six cities in architectural beauty. They worshiped Zeus Olympus, the savior-god; Athena, patron goddess of Athens; the Roman Emperor, as god; Dionysus, god of vegetation; and Asclepius, god of healing. The animal cult worship of the god-Serpent and the god-Bull were also practiced. Some scholars believe that Gaius, addressed by John in the book of 3 John, was the first Bishop of Pergamum.

Thyatira: Weakness Made Strong
Thyatira, a small town about 35 miles (56 km) southeast of Pergamum, was founded by the general Seleucid Nicator under Alexander the Great in about 300 BC. Military garrisons greatly strengthened the city which was noted for commerce and guilds such as tanners, coppersmiths, potters, and purple dyers. Objects of worship included the emperor, the Thyatiran war hero, Tyrimnos, and trade guild gods, for example, bronzesmiths worshiped the goddess of war, Pallas Athena. How the church was established is unknown, but "Lydia, a seller of purple, of the city of Thyatira," came to the Lord under Paul's ministry in Philippi (Acts 16:14–15).

Sardis: The City of Death
The city of Sardis was founded in about 1200 BC and became the capital of the Lydian kingdom located 30 miles southeast of Thyatira. It stood on a lofty plateau above the Hermus valley. Sardis was twice defeated, once by King Cyrus of Persia (359 BC), and again by Antiochus III of Syria (218 BC). The wealth of the Lydian kings arose from trade and the commerce with the East. An impressive acropolis housed a temple dedicated to the goddess Artemis. Goddesses Artemis and Cybele were commemorated on local coins. Two hundred years after Christ's birth, Sardis lay in decay. Today Sardis is a small village called Sart. When and how the church there was started are unknown.

Philadelphia: The Missionary City
The city of Philadelphia, founded by King Attalus of Pergamum (140 BC), was located in the Hermus River valley about 28 miles (45 km) southeast of Sardis. An earthquake destroyed the city in AD 17; however, it was rebuilt by Emperor Tiberius. Famous for its grape industry, Philadelphia was also noted for textiles and leather goods. It became a strong fortress city and was called the "Gateway to the East." Although Dionysis was the major pagan god, people also worshiped sun and serpent gods. Philadelphia, the last of the Byzantine cities, was finally captured by the Turks in 1390. Christians lived there until the early 1900s. When and how the church was established there is not known, but it prospered for many centuries.

Laodicea: The City of Compromise
The city of Laodicea was located on a fertile plain overlooking the Lycus River about 50 miles (80 km) southeast of Philadelphia. Laodicea, which became the capital of ancient Phrygia, was established by Antiochus II (261–246 BC) and named in honor of his sister-wife Laodice before their divorce in 253 BC. Located on a major trade route running from Ephesus to Syria, Laodicea accumulated great wealth. It was known for banking and the manufacture of expensive cloth made from soft black wool. Its medical school became famous for the development of an ear salve made of spice and Phrygian powder. Zeus Azeus and Men Karou were the main Phrygian gods. Cicero lived in Laodicea in 50 BC. Laodicea was so wealthy that when a massive earthquake destroyed the city in AD 60, it refused aid from Rome and rebuilt at its own expense. Most scholars believe that Epaphras started the church there (Col. 1:7; 4:12–13). Paul was aware of their spiritual struggles (Col. 2:1).

Revelation

Hope and Encouragement

The book of Revelation is an exciting yet often misunderstood book of the Bible. It was probably penned between 35 and 65 years after Jesus' resurrection. This text became a source of hope and encouragement for Christians facing persecution.

Points of Unity

Although the book of Revelation allows for many interpretations, all Christians seem to agree that:

1. The message of the book is relevant for Christians today, as it was for Christians in the times of the apostles;
2. The main purpose of the book is to provide *hope* and *encouragement* for believers of all times, especially in times of persecution or suffering;
3. The message of the book is clear on at least three points:
    - Christ is coming back and will judge humanity;
    - The powers of evil are doomed before Christ;
    - God promises a wonderful future for all who believe in Christ.

God Acting in History

Both the Old and New Testaments reveal God as Lord over history. Christians of all eras have believed that Jesus will return a second time, but not all Christians have agreed that Revelation is all about the second coming. Whether the visions in Revelation have been, are being, or have yet to be fulfilled is a matter of debate, but the spirit of the last chapter calling on Jesus to come quickly is something all Christians can agree upon—"Come, Lord Jesus!" (Revelation 22:20)

Following is a comparison of four different approaches to the book of Revelation.

Four Views	How Revelation Is Viewed	More About This View
Historicist	The book of Revelation is prophecy about church history from the time of John to the end of the world.	Historicists view the events in Revelation as symbolic descriptions of historical events throughout church history. (Some futurists also understand the Seven Churches [Revelation 1–3] in a historic manner, treating each church as descriptive of a particular era of church history.)
Preterist	The book of Revelation is prophecy that was fulfilled primarily in the first century AD.	"Partial Preterism" views most of Revelation as prophecy fulfilled in the first century AD, though final chapters of Revelation describe future events to occur at the end of time. "Full Preterists" contend that the return of Jesus described in Revelation 19 was spiritual and occurred in AD 70. Preterists are typically amillennialists or postmillennialists, though some historic premillennialists might fit in this category.
Futurist	Revelation is prophecy primarily about the future end of the world.	In the futurist view, all or nearly all of Revelation is yet to occur. Revelation is a prophecy that describes the end of time and the years leading immediately to the end. Dispensational premillennialists as well as some historic premillennialists interpret Revelation in this way.
Idealist	Revelation is a non-historical and non-prophetic drama about spiritual realities.	This perspective seems to have originated among ancient Alexandrian theologians, who frequently spiritualized and allegorized biblical texts, but this view also has contemporary followers.

Revelation	Revelation 1:1 "soon" 1:3 "near" 1:19 "what is" (Compare, 22:6,7, 12, 20)	Revelation 2:1–3:22 The Seven Churches of Asia Minor	Revelation 4:1–3 God on His Throne	Revelation 5:1–4 The Scroll	Revelation 6:1–17 The Seals
Historicist View	The prophecy began to be fulfilled close to the author's lifetime.	The prophecy begins with the seven actual churches in John's day and proceeds through history from there.	God is about to outline his rule over history: the first part of that history is revealed under the vision of the seven seals.	The scroll is the coming history of the church as God reveals it and is Lord over it.	The seals are the stages of church history, perhaps describing the church from the late first century AD to the late fourth century.
Preterist View	Near, soon, and quickly are taken literally.	The prophecy begins with the seven actual churches of Asia Minor. It then focuses on the land of Israel before AD 70.	God's courtroom in the heavenly temple is the scene. The Judge on his throne is about to hold court.	The scroll is God's bill of divorce against unfaithful Israel.	The seals describe the Roman war with the Jews which led to the destruction of Jerusalem (AD 70).
Futurist View	These words refer to the whole of the "last days" or to the quickness with which Jesus will return.	The prophecy begins with the seven churches, which were actual churches in John's day and may also symbolize the types of churches present in the last days.	God gives John a vision from his throne of the events which are to take place "after these things."	The scroll is either the title deed to the earth or God's prophetic message in Revelation.	The seals begin to describe the great tribulation, with each opened seal leading to a greater tragedy upon the earth.
Idealist View	Christ is always at hand, near and quick to save his people.	The book begins with the seven churches, which symbolize tendencies in the church that can occur in every age.	God gives John the heavenly viewpoint of the important truths about his power over all things and his care for the church.	The scroll is God's last will and testament, revealing his salvation plan for all time.	The seals are about recurring evils throughout history and God's authority over them.

Revelation	Revelation 7:1–8 The 144,000	Revelation 8:1–13 The Trumpets	Revelation 9:13–19 The Four Angels at the Euphrates	Revelation 10:8–11 The Little Scroll
Historicist View	The 144,000 is a symbolic number that represents the entire church.	The trumpets are the stages of church history, perhaps from about AD 400 until the fifteenth century (or to the present).	The four angels represent the four principalities of the Turkish empire. The Turks destroyed the last of the Roman empire in AD 1453.	The little scroll is the Bible at the time of the Reformation. It was sweet to those starved for God's Word, but bitter to those who wanted to control its information and keep it from common people.
Preterist View	The 144,000 may be the Jewish Christians who escaped the destruction of Jerusalem.	The trumpets are a vision of the Roman war with the Jews in the first century AD and extend the seals' description in further detail.	The four angels may represent the four legions of Roman soldiers stationed in Syria that Vespasian led against the Jews (around AD 70). The colors mentioned are Roman military colors.	The little scroll is the same divorce bill as in Revelation 5:1–4 but now unsealed and empty of contents, indicating that the judgments against Israel are now occurring.
Futurist View	The 144,000 are Jewish Christians in the last days.	The trumpets describe the events of the tribulation in the last days.	The four angels represent the armies of the Orient that will march against Israel in the last days. They will cross the Euphrates as a signal of war.	The little scroll represents the divine plan for the end of the ages, showing that the Word of God is both sweet and bitter to God's prophets and messengers.
Idealist View	The 144,000 are the true spiritual Israel: the church on earth.	The trumpets are about the cycles of human sin, consequences, and God's salvation.	The four angels represent the judgment of God that comes on evil when there is no more restraint, which is represented by the river Euphrates.	The little scroll is the gospel, which must and will be preached to all "peoples, nations, tongues, and kings."

	Revelation 11:1–2 The Temple	Revelation 12:13–17 The Persecuted Woman	Revelation 13:18 666	Revelation 14:14–16 The Son of Man with the Sharp Sickle
Historicist View	The measuring of the temple, the altar, and those who worship there points to God's evaluation of the church, the doctrine of justification by faith, and what constitutes true membership in the church, all of which were issues at the Reformation.	The woman is the true church under persecution. The "third of the stars" may refer to the division of the Roman Empire under three emperors in AD 313, or it may refer to post-Reformation divisions in Europe.	It may be the number of the word Lateinos and so refers to the Latin or Roman Catholic pope/papacy.	It is a vision of the end of the age when Christ will come and gather his own to himself.
Preterist View	The measuring of the temple and its rooms, like the eating of the scroll in chapter 10, mirror what happens in Ezekiel 40–47. Both indicate the destruction of the temple and the separation of the faithful (symbolized by the sanctuary) from the unfaithful (symbolized by the court).	The woman is faithful Israel that gave birth to Christ (the Child). The Dragon, Satan, persecuted the Messianic church, but she escaped the destruction of Jerusalem by heeding Jesus' words (Luke 21:20–22) and fleeing to the desert hills (the prepared place).	It is the number that the letters in the name "Nero Caesar" add up to.	It is a vision of the coming of Christ to gather and preserve his church from the judgment that was to befall Jerusalem.
Futurist View	The measuring of the temple refers to the nation of Israel and the temple that will be rebuilt in the last days. Israel has been restored but still awaits the rebuilding of her faith. This faith will center on the new temple and will eventually lead some Jews to faith in Christ.	The woman is Israel (sun, moon and stars, Genesis 37:9). The Child is Christ (rod of iron, Psalm 2:9). The Dragon is Satan behind the coming Antichrist. As the head of the revived "Roman Empire," the Antichrist will attack Israel.	It is the number of the future Antichrist—someone who will be like Nero back from the dead.	It is a vision of the coming harvest at the end of the age when Christ will separate the wicked for judgment.
Idealist View	The measuring of the temple and the leaving of the outer court indicates the division that has always been present between true believers and those who are Christians only in name. The trampling of the court signifies the way the unbelieving world corrupts the church, but this will only be for a short while.	The woman is Israel as the ideal symbol of all the faithful. The Child is Christ and the Dragon is Satan, the great persecutor of the Church in every age. The stars are the angels that fell with Satan at his rebellion. The seven heads and crowns speak of Satan's full political power and authority. The ten horns are military might.	It is the number of imperfection and human evil that leads to idol worship.	It is a vision of the last judgment and the coming of Christ at the end of the age.

Revelation	Revelation 15:1–4 The Song of Moses and of the Lamb	Revelation 16:10–11 The Fifth Bowl	Revelation 17:1–12 The Great Prostitute	Revelation 18:9–24 The Fall of Babylon
Historicist View	The song of final salvation from the slavery of the Roman Catholic religious and political power known as the papacy.	The bowl is the judgment upon the Roman Pope Pius VI that occurred when the French revolutionary forces stripped the Vatican and took the Pope captive in 1798. The Pope was forced to flee Rome again in 1848. This event was actually predicted using 1260 days as years (12:6).	The prostitute is the corrupt Roman Catholic Church, including false "Protestant" churches that have come out of her. Her political and religious influence is carried by the beastly Roman papacy and Western European culture.	The destruction of Papal Rome (Babylon) will be complete and utterly devastating. The consequences of preaching a false gospel, persecuting true believers and dabbling in power politics will bring her to this end. Many will mourn her loss but it will be final.
Preterist View	The song of salvation from and victory over the ungodly religious and political persecution that Christians suffered in Israel and the Roman world.	The bowl is the judgment that fell upon Rome in AD 69. In that single year, Nero committed suicide, three emperors were deposed, civil war set Roman against Roman, and the Temple of Jupiter Capitoline was burned to the ground, causing darkness during the day.	The prostitute is Jerusalem. Her political and false religious influence is carried by the Roman Empire (Beast). The seven heads are Rome and the first seven emperors, Nero (the sixth of the emperors) ruling at that time. The ten horns are the ten imperial provinces.	The destruction of Jerusalem (Babylon) is sudden and complete. The misery and the economic disaster is nearly indescribable and a source of great despair. To this day, the temple has never been rebuilt.
Futurist View	The song of salvation from the last-days persecution of the Antichrist and resulting judgment of God. Believers may experience some persecution but they will not have to endure God's wrath.	The bowl is the coming judgment upon the revived Roman Empire that will happen in the last days.	The prostitute is the symbol of a false religious system, a new world religious order. The religious coalition will have political influence tied to the power of the Beast (Antichrist) who is the head of the alliance (ten horns) of ten nations in Europe in the last days.	The destruction of the coming world religious, political and economic system—under the control of the Antichrist and the False Prophet—will be a crash of unparalleled dimension.
Idealist View	The song of salvation that all the redeemed have sung throughout history and will sing anew when Christ comes again.	The bowl shows what will happen and does happen to those who steadfastly oppose God. The judgments of darkness and sores recall the plagues of Egypt.	The prostitute is all false and corrupt religion that has allied itself with political power in order to dominate. God warns that such religion shall come to an awful end when true faith triumphs.	The destruction of Babylon reveals that God's judgment is complete and final. Whether it is Nineveh, Babylon, Rome or any other economic power that opposes God, it is destined to fail.

Revelation	Revelation 19:1–10 The Marriage of the Lamb and His Bride	Revelation 20:1–15 The Millennium	Revelation 21:1–27 The New Creation	Revelation 22:1–21 The Salvation and Healing of the Nations
Historicist View	The entire removal of false religion represented by Rome/Babylon will leave the faithful to accomplish the purpose for which Christ came—the evangelization of the rest of the world. All people will be invited to come into relationship (the marriage feast with God).	The millennium is viewed as Christ's present, spiritual reign in the lives of his people (amillennialism).	The new creation will come with Christ at his second coming, yet there is a real sense in which it has already arrived in the believer's heart. Christians live now as citizens of the New Jerusalem.	It is happening now and will finally be completed when Christ returns.
Preterist View	The entire book has been about faithfulness using the image of marriage: the divorce bill in chapter 5, the imagery of the persecuted woman and the prostitute. The book builds toward the marriage feast of Christ and his church.	In partial preterism, the millennium may be Christ's literal reign on earth (premillennialism) or a spiritual reign (postmillennialism and amillennialism). In full preterism, the millennium refers to Christ's spiritual return and reign, beginning in the first century (amillennialism).	The new creation is now and future. Since the destruction of the old Jerusalem, Christians are building the New Jerusalem here and now, wherever the gospel is believed, as well as expecting it in full when Christ returns.	It will continue as the gospel grows and spreads throughout the world. Jesus will finalize and renew all things when he comes.
Futurist View	The entire church is the bride of Christ whose marriage is announced and celebrated. This scene refers to events near the end of the world and history.	The millennium is the future, physical reign of Jesus Christ on earth (premillennialism).	The new creation will come when Christ comes again and ushers in the age to come.	It will continue until the great tribulation when the Antichrist will temporarily prevail. Christ in his second coming will triumph and usher in the final salvation and healing of all the faithful.
Idealist View	The entire sweep of sacred history may be seen through the lens of the ancient Jewish wedding tradition. The prophets announced the wedding. Jesus comes and betroths his bride (church), paying the dowry on the cross. When Jesus comes again, he will offer his bride a wedding feast.	The millennium is viewed as Christ's present, spiritual reign in the lives of his people (amillennialism).	The new creation is something God continually does with each new day. Yet there will come a day when Christ will personally return and make all things new.	It is what God has always been doing in the world—seeking and saving the lost. Christ will bring all things right when he returns.

1 Seven Messages to Churches
(Revelation 1:1–3:22)

INTRODUCTION (1:1–8)
Blessing 1
Vision of Christ

MESSAGES TO THE CHURCHES

1. **EPHESUS**
   Praise: Hard work, perseverance
   Criticism: Forgot first love
   Exhortation: Repent
   Reward: Right to eat from the tree of life

2. **SMYRNA**
   Praise: You are rich!
   Criticism: None
   Exhortation: Be faithful
   Reward: Not hurt by second death

3. **PERGAMUM**
   Praise: Remain faithful
   Criticism: Idolatry and sexual immorality
   Exhortation: Repent
   Reward: A white stone with a new name

4. **THYATIRA**
   Praise: Deeds, love and faith, and perseverance
   Criticism: Idolatry and sexual immorality
   Exhortation: "Hold on to what you have until I come"
   Reward: The morning star

5. **SARDIS**
   Praise: None
   Criticism: "You are dead"
   Exhortation: Wake up
   Reward: Be dressed in white, never blotted out from the book of life

6. **PHILADELPHIA**
   Praise: Deeds and faithfulness
   Criticism: None
   Exhortation: Hold on to what you have
   Reward: Become a pillar of the temple

7. **LAODICEA**
   Praise: None
   Criticism: You are lukewarm
   Exhortation: Be earnest and repent
   Reward: Will be seated with Christ

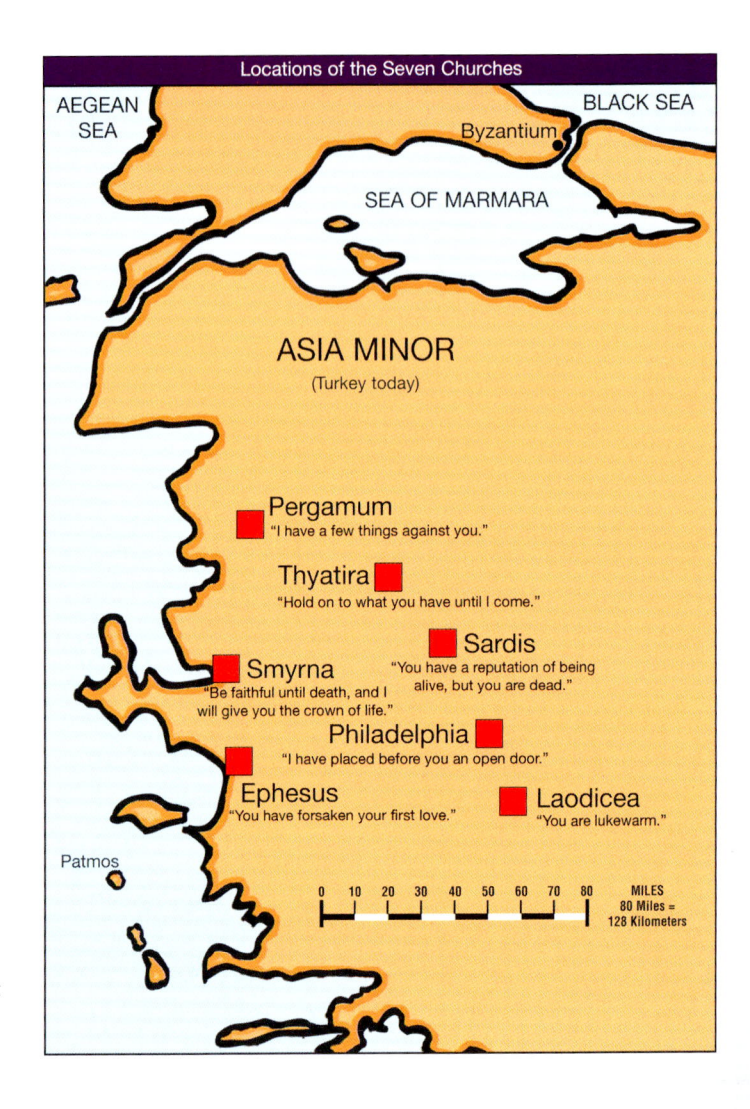

Locations of the Seven Churches

- **Pergamum** — "I have a few things against you."
- **Thyatira** — "Hold on to what you have until I come."
- **Sardis** — "You have a reputation of being alive, but you are dead."
- **Smyrna** — "Be faithful until death, and I will give you the crown of life."
- **Philadelphia** — "I have placed before you an open door."
- **Ephesus** — "You have forsaken your first love."
- **Laodicea** — "You are lukewarm."

ASIA MINOR (Turkey today)

80 Miles = 128 Kilometers

Book of Revelation

3. Seven Trumpets (Revelation 8:2–11:19)

1. **First Trumpet**—Hail, fire, blood
2. **Second Trumpet**—Fiery mountain in sea, 1/3 of sea becomes blood
3. **Third Trumpet**—star falls on 1/3 of rivers
4. **Fourth Trumpet**—1/3 of Sun, 1/3 Moon, 1/3 Stars

Interlude: Woe! Woe! Woe! (8:13)

5. **Fifth Trumpet**—Demon locust from the Abyss
6. **Sixth Trumpet**—Two-hundred-million demonic riders from the Euphrates

Interlude (10:1–11:14)
The Little Scroll: Promise for the church

7. **Seventh Trumpet**—"The kingdom of the world has become the kingdom of our Lord…" (11:15)

2. Seven Seals (Revelation 4:1–8:5)

Interlude:
Vision of Heaven (4:1–11)
Scroll with Seven Seals and the Lamb (5:1–14)

Opening of Seals (6:1–8:5)
1. **First Seal:** White Horse—*Conqueror*
2. **Second Seal:** Red Horse—*No peace*
3. **Third Seal:** Black Horse—*Famine*
4. **Fourth Seal:** Pale Horse—*Pestilence*
5. **Fifth Seal:** Martyrs under the altar
6. **Sixth Seal:** Earthquake, sun black

Interlude:
144,000 sealed (7:1–8)
The Great Multitude (7:9–17)

7. **The Seventh Seal:**
   It contains seven angels with trumpets (8:1–2)
   The angel with golden censer (8:3–5)

4. Seven Symbolic Histories (Revelation 12:1–14:20)

The Woman and the Dragon

SYMBOLIC HISTORIES

1. **HISTORY OF THE DRAGON (12:7–12)**
   Defeated
   The "ancient serpent"

2. **HISTORY OF THE WOMAN (12:13–17)**
   Persecuted by the dragon
   Defended by God

3. **THE SEA BEAST (13:1–10)**
   Ten horns and seven heads
   Blasphemer
   Has power to make war

4. **THE EARTH BEAST (13:11–18)**
   Two horns
   Deceiver
   666—The number of the beast

5. **THE 144,000 (14:1–5)**
   Marked with God's name
   Worshippers

6. **THE ANGELIC ANNOUNCERS (14:6–11)**
   First angel: "Fear God"
   Second angel: "Fallen! Fallen is Babylon the Great"
   Third angel: Warning against the mark of the beast

7. **THE HARVEST (14:14–20)**

5. Seven Bowls (Revelation 15:1–16:21)

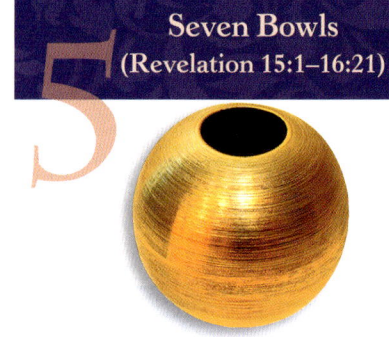

Commissioning of the Seven Angels with the Last Seven Plagues (15:1–8)

The Seven Bowls

1. **First Bowl**—Painful sores
2. **Second Bowl**—Turns sea into blood
3. **Third Bowl**—Turns rivers and springs of water into blood
4. **Fourth Bowl**—Sun burns people with fire
5. **Fifth Bowl**—Plunges kingdom of the beast into darkness
6. **Sixth Bowl**—Dries up the Euphrates; Armageddon
7. **Seventh Bowl**—Judgment against Babylon. "It is done!"

6. Seven Messages of Judgment (Revelation 17:1–19:10)

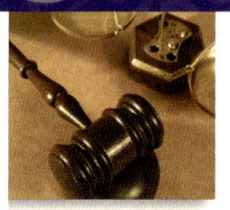

Judgment against Babylon

Description of symbolic characters

1. **First angelic message** (17:7–18)
   Explanation of the vision
2. **Second angelic message** (18:1–3)
   Announcement of the fall of Babylon
3. **Third angelic message** (18:4–8)
   Call to God's people; God's judgment on Babylon
4. **The kings of the earth** (18:9–10)
   Lament for the fall of Babylon
5. **The merchants of the earth** (18:11–17)
   Lament for the fall of Babylon
6. **The seafaring people** (18:18–19)
   Lament for the fall of Babylon
   Rejoice for God's judgment (18:20)
7. **Seventh angelic message** (18:21–24)
   Announcement of the final destruction of Babylon

7. Seven Visions (Revelation 19:11–22:5)

1. **First Vision** (19:11–16)
   Heaven opens and the white horse rider appears
2. **Second Vision** (19:17–18)
   Angel invites birds to "the great supper of God"
3. **Third Vision** (19:19–21)
   The beast and kings ready for war
4. **Fourth Vision** (20:1–3)
   The thousand years (millennium)
5. **Fifth Vision** (20:4–10)
   Thrones with judges and Satan's doom
6. **Sixth Vision** (20:11–15)
   Judgment of the dead
7. **Seventh Vision** (21:1–22:5)
   A vision of "a new heaven and a new earth."

Epilogue (22:6–21)

Jesus is coming back: "Amen. Come, Lord Jesus."

Terms in the Book of Revelation

666—Number of the beast, spelled out in Rev. 13:18 as *six hundred sixty-six*. Greek and Hebrew did not have written numbers. Instead, either they spelled out the number, or they wrote out the number using the letters in the alphabet. For example, the first letter of the alphabet might represent the number one, and so on. Many scholars point out that, in Hebrew, the number of Nero's name can be 666 if written using *Neron*, the Latin spelling of the name. (Nero reigned AD 54–68. He was the first emperor to engage in specific persecution of Christians.) A good approach to this issue is to remember that six is a symbol of incompletion; 666 indicated total imperfection.

144,000—Group of believers who endure the great tribulation (Rev. 7:14). Some believe that these persons are literally 144,000 Jews—12,000 from each tribe—who embrace Jesus Christ as their Lord (see Rev. 7:4–9). Others suggest that the terms "Israel" and "twelve tribes" often refer to Christians (Romans 9:6–8; Galatians 6:16; James 1:1). Therefore, the number would point to God's people (symbolized by twelve tribes, twelve apostles, or both) multiplied by 1,000 (a number that symbolizes an extreme multitude or length of time)—in other words, the full number of those who belong to God.

Abomination of desolation—An event that desecrates the temple in Jerusalem and is a signal to Jesus' followers that soon Jerusalem will be ruined. Mentioned in Matthew 24:15, it may refer to the destruction of the temple in AD 70 by the Romans, or Roman plans to set up a statue of the Emperor in the temple in AD 40, or some future event.

Antichrist—(from Greek, *antichristos*, in place of Christ) Anyone who denies what the apostles taught about Jesus Christ (1 John 2:18–22; 4:3; 2 John 1:7). Specifically, the antichrist is a Satanic counterfeit of Jesus Christ, described as "lawless" and as a "beast" (2 Thessalonians 2:3–8; Revelation 13:1–18; 17:3–17). The antichrist could be a specific person who rises to power during a time of tribulation or a symbol of false teachers and leaders who will arise when the end of the age draws near.

Armageddon—(from Hebrew, *Har-Megiddon*, Mount Megiddo) The city of Megiddo was located between the Plain of Jezreel and Israel's western coast. Deborah, Gideon, Saul, Ahaziah, and Josiah fought decisive battles near Megiddo—largely because the area around Megiddo is broad and flat. So the valley of Megiddo became the symbol of a point of decisive conflict. Some believe that a literal battle will occur near Megiddo near the end of time. Others view the reference to Armageddon as a symbol of an ultimate conflict between spiritual forces of good and evil.

Babylon—Revelation 17 presents the figure of a prostitute called Babylon riding upon a scarlet beast. The name is symbolic, yet interpretations vary:

1. Jerusalem: Jewish people assisted the Romans in their persecution of Christians after AD 64. The fall of Babylon could be a symbolic reference to the fall of Jerusalem in AD 70.

2. Rome: After AD 70, Jewish writers often referred to Rome as "Babylon."[1] The name may symbolize the political and religious powers in every age that attempt to defy God and to persecute His people.

3. One-world government and religion: Babylon may be a reference to a one-world government and one-world religion that will emerge near the end of time.

Beasts, two—Symbolic creatures described in Revelation 11:7 and 13:1–18.

The first beast: This creature rises from the sea and has ten horns and seven heads. The seven heads seem to point to Rome, the city known for its seven hills. Some interpreters understand this reference to Rome as a literal reference to a power that will arise from Rome near the end of time; others view it as a symbolic reference to the powers in every age that defy God's dominion and persecute God's people. The beast claims blasphemous names for itself—much like Domitian, emperor from AD 81 until 96, who demanded that he be addressed as "Lord and God." One of the horns seemed to have died but then returned to life—much like the false rumor that emerged after the death of Nero that he had come back to life.[2]

The second beast: This creature rises from the earth with horns like a lamb and a voice like a dragon—in other words, a satanic parody of Jesus Christ, the Lamb of God. Some interpreters understand this creature as a literal leader who will encourage people to worship the first beast. Others view the second beast as a symbol of any religion in any time period that focuses worshipers on anything other than Jesus Christ.

Final judgment—The event described in Rev. 20:11-15, when God resurrects all people, judges them from the great white throne, and delivers them to their eternal destinies.

Letters to the Seven Churches—After the opening vision (Chapter 1), John begins to write to the messengers (angels) of seven churches, Ephesus, Smyrna, Pergamum, Thyatira, Sardis, Philadelphia, and Laodicea. The messages review the churches' histories, give warnings and commands, and tells them to prepare for what is about to unfold. Scholars agree that these were actual messages to real churches in existence in John's day, though some see in the seven churches patterns that apply to the church in specific past, present, or future eras.

Mark of the beast—Indication of a person's allegiance to the teachings of the antichrist (Revelation 13:16–17). The people of God receive a similar mark, indicating their loyalty to Jesus (Revelation 7:3; 9:4; 14:1; 22:4). Some biblical students believe that the mark of the beast will be an actual mark, required by the antichrist. (Between the Old and New Testaments, some Jews were forced to be branded with the symbol of the god Dionysius.[3]) Other interpreters of Revelation understand the mark as a reference to someone's actions ("hand") and beliefs ("forehead"). "Hand" and "forehead" seem to carry this symbolic meaning in Exodus 13:9, 16.

Views of the Millennium—Chapter 20, the only direct reference in the Bible to a reign of Christ that lasts 1,000 years, is one of the most controversial sections of the Bible.

There are three basic views—Premillennialism, Amillennialism and Postmillennialism—that help to categorize the different interpretations.

- **Premillennialism** holds that Christ will return before the millennium. Jesus will rule the world and begin an age of peace and security. There are two varieties within this view: Historic Premillennialism and Dispensational Premillennialism.
  - *Historic Premillennialism* sees Christ's return at the end of the great tribulation. This time of tribulation may last seven years, or "seven" may symbolically refer to the completeness of this tribulation. The church will go through this time of trouble but endure to greet Christ when he comes.
  - *Dispensational Premillennialism* holds that the church will not endure the great tribulation. Christ will remove the church before that time or, alternatively, at some point before the worst experiences of the tribulation.
- **Amillennialism** is the view that the millennium is not a literal one thousand years. It refers to the period now in progress in which the gospel is spreading throughout the world and Christ is ruling at the right hand of God the Father.
- **Postmillennialism** asserts that there will be a period of great peace and security when the gospel has spread throughout the world and Christ reigns spiritually, through His people. After this time of one thousand years or so, Christ will return to end history.

Witnesses, two—Two beings described in Rev. 11:1–14 who speak the truth about God before being killed and then resurrected. (1) Some believe that these two witnesses are two people who will appear during the tribulation, near the end of time. (2) Others view them as two biblical prophets—perhaps Moses and Elijah—that have been resurrected to proclaim God's truth during the tribulation. (3) Others see the two witnesses as symbols of the Law and the Prophets—both of these testified about Jesus and yet, this testimony was rejected, even to the point of killing those that appealed to this testimony (for example, Stephen in Acts 7). If so, the "resurrection" of the two witnesses would point to a time of final vindication, a point at which God demonstrates that the Law and Prophets did indeed testify about Jesus Christ.

---

[1] G. K. Beale, *The Book of Revelation* (Grand Rapids, MI: Eerdmans, 1999), 19.

[2] G. E. Ladd, *A Commentary on the Revelation of John* (Grand Rapids, MI: Eerdmans, 1972), 178–179.

[3] 3 Maccabees 2:29.

BIBLE MAPS

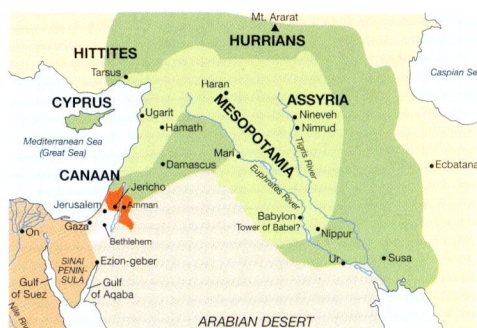

Middle East: Then

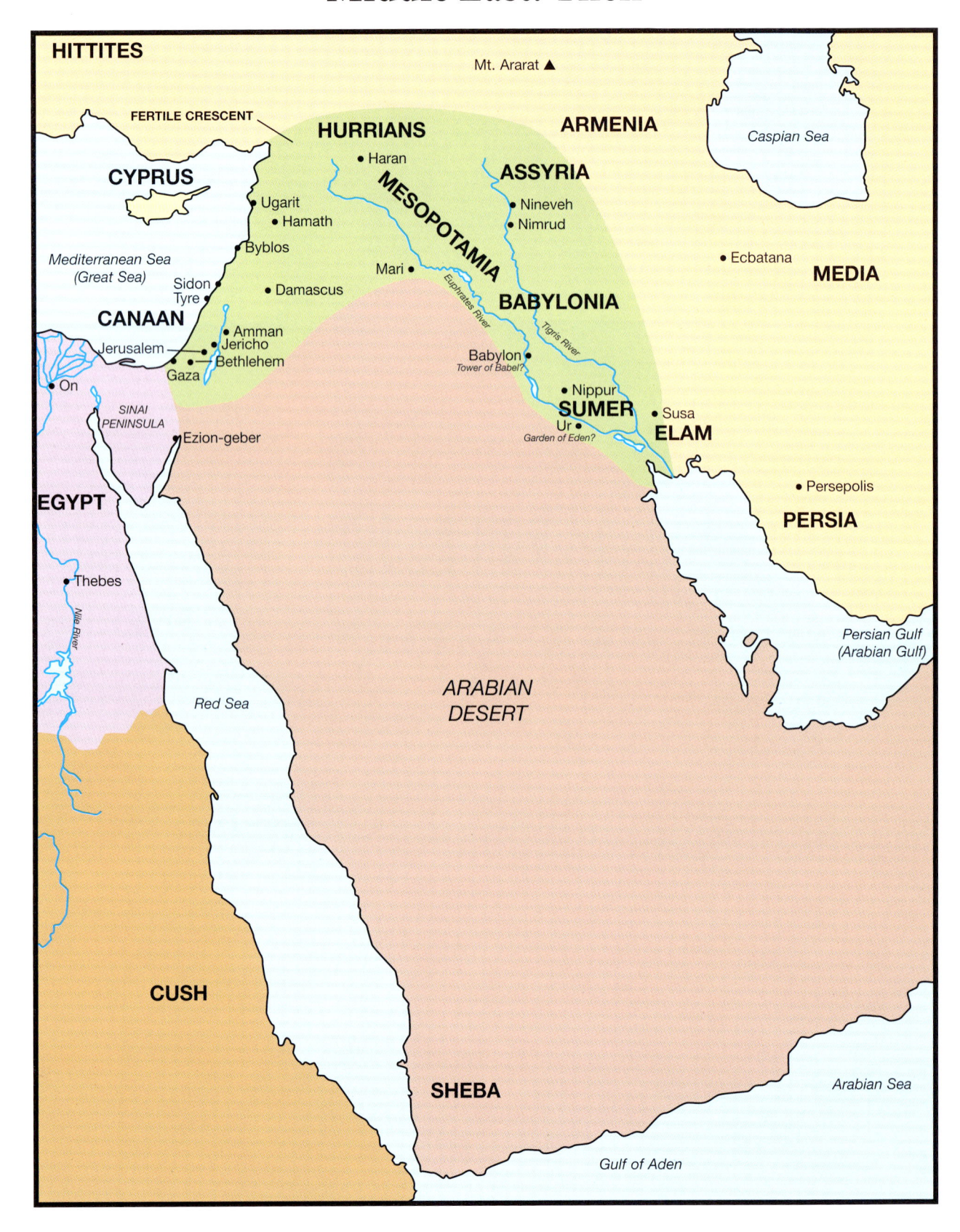

Middle East: Now

Ancient cities that exist today are underlined in red.

Holy Land: Then

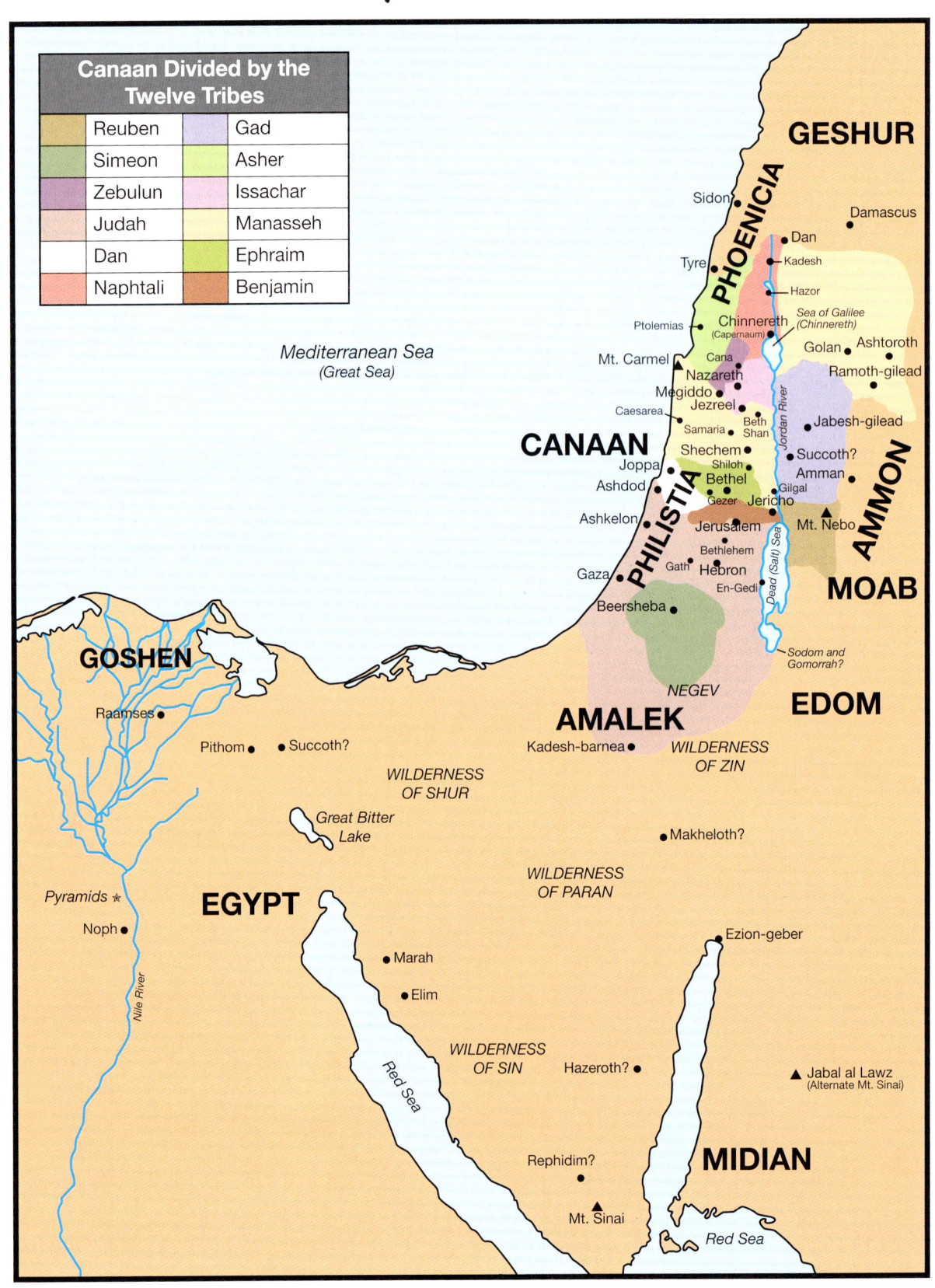

Canaan Divided by the Twelve Tribes

Reuben	Gad
Simeon	Asher
Zebulun	Issachar
Judah	Manasseh
Dan	Ephraim
Naphtali	Benjamin

Holy Land: Now

Ancient cities that exist today are underlined in red.

Holy Land: United Kingdom

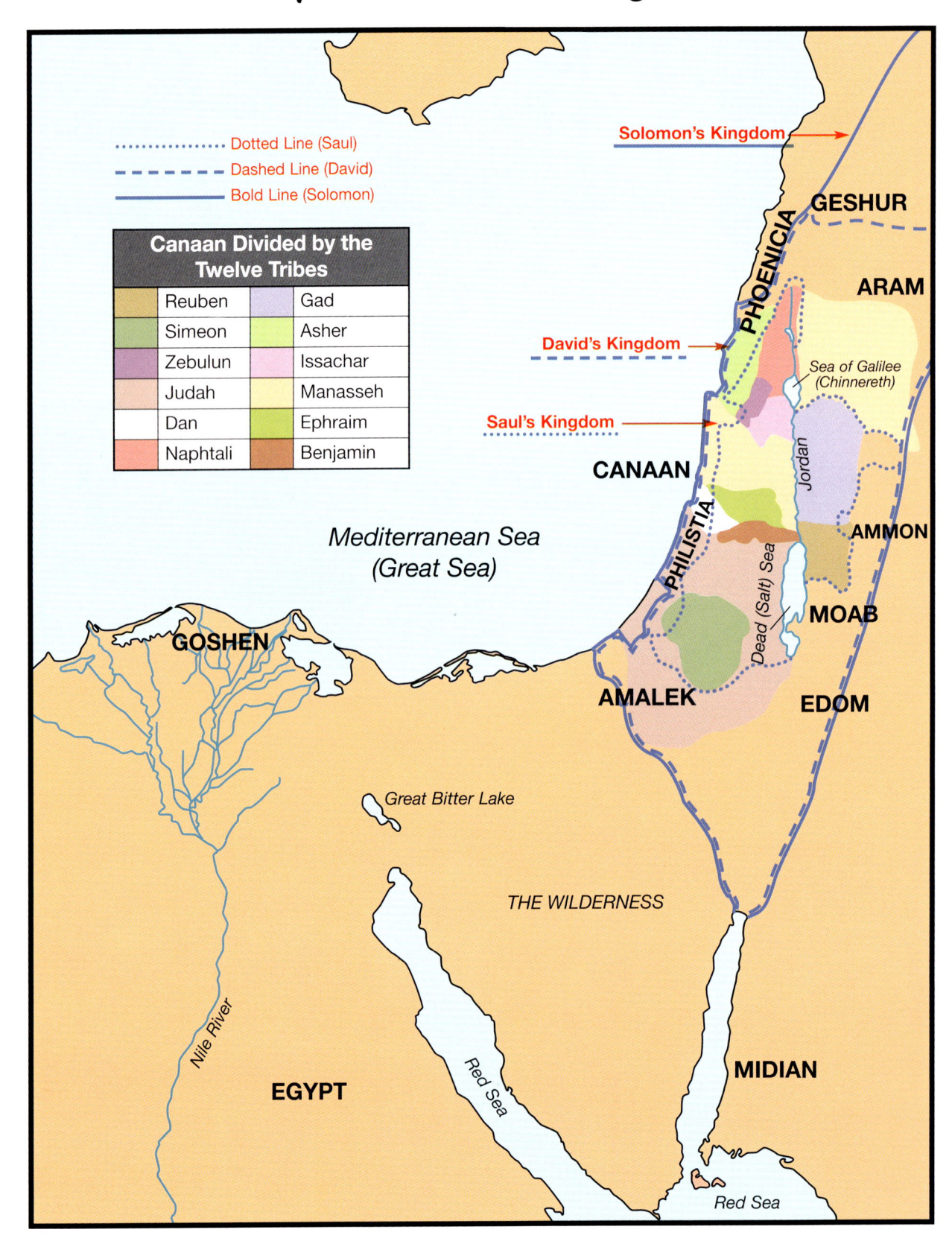

- ·········· Dotted Line (Saul)
- – – – – – Dashed Line (David)
- ————— Bold Line (Solomon)

Canaan Divided by the Twelve Tribes	
Reuben	Gad
Simeon	Asher
Zebulun	Issachar
Judah	Manasseh
Dan	Ephraim
Naphtali	Benjamin

Solomon's Kingdom
David's Kingdom
Saul's Kingdom

Phoenicia, Geshur, Aram, Sea of Galilee (Chinnereth), Jordan, Canaan, Philistia, Ammon, Dead (Salt) Sea, Moab, Amalek, Edom

Mediterranean Sea (Great Sea)

Goshen

Great Bitter Lake

THE WILDERNESS

Nile River

Red Sea

Egypt

Midian

Red Sea

Holy Land: Divided Kingdom

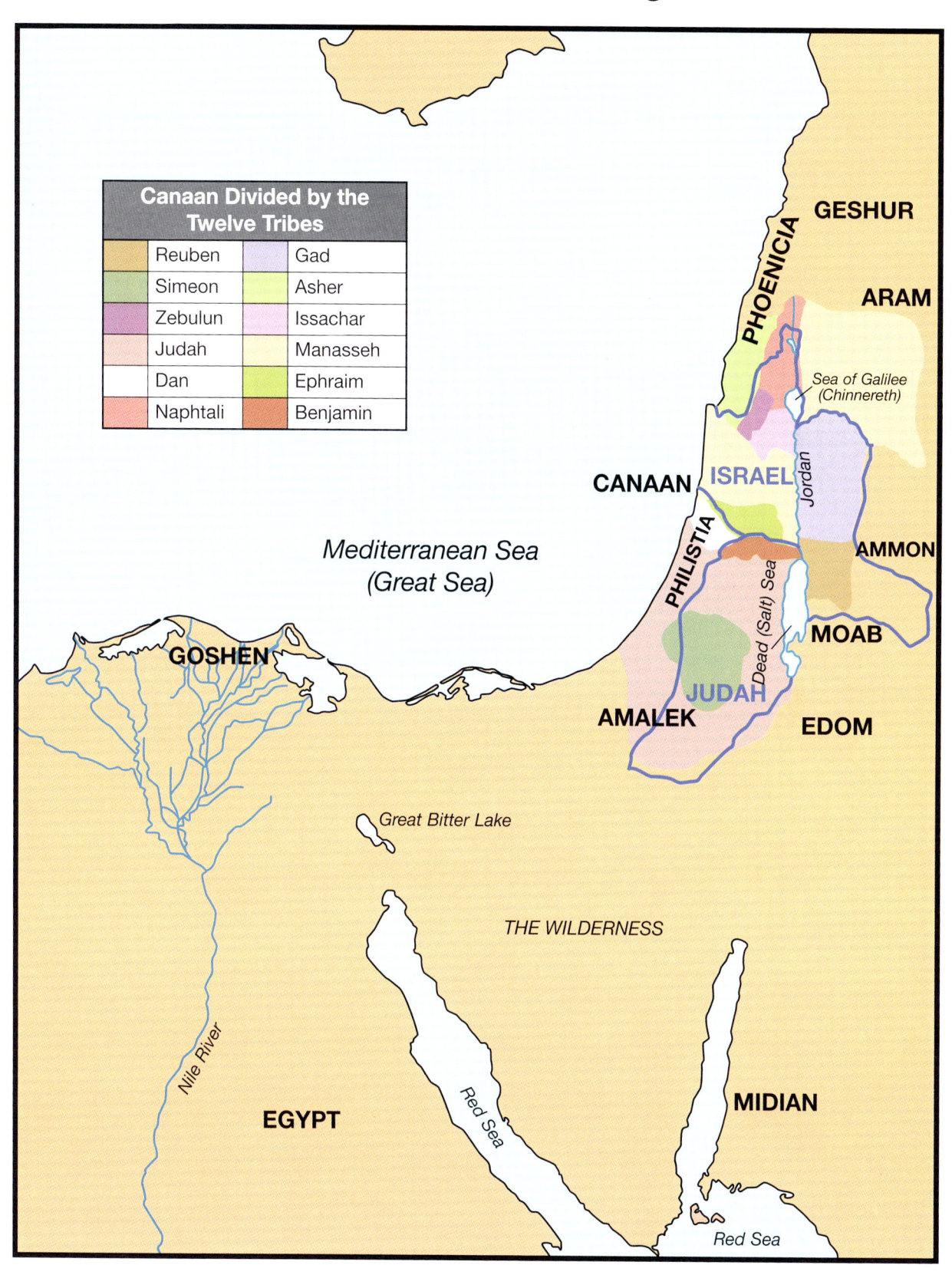

Canaan Divided by the Twelve Tribes	
Reuben	Gad
Simeon	Asher
Zebulun	Issachar
Judah	Manasseh
Dan	Ephraim
Naphtali	Benjamin

Expansion of the Assyrian Empire

- Existing Empire
- Expansion
- Israel
- Judah

King: Ashurnasirpal II (883 BC–859 BC)

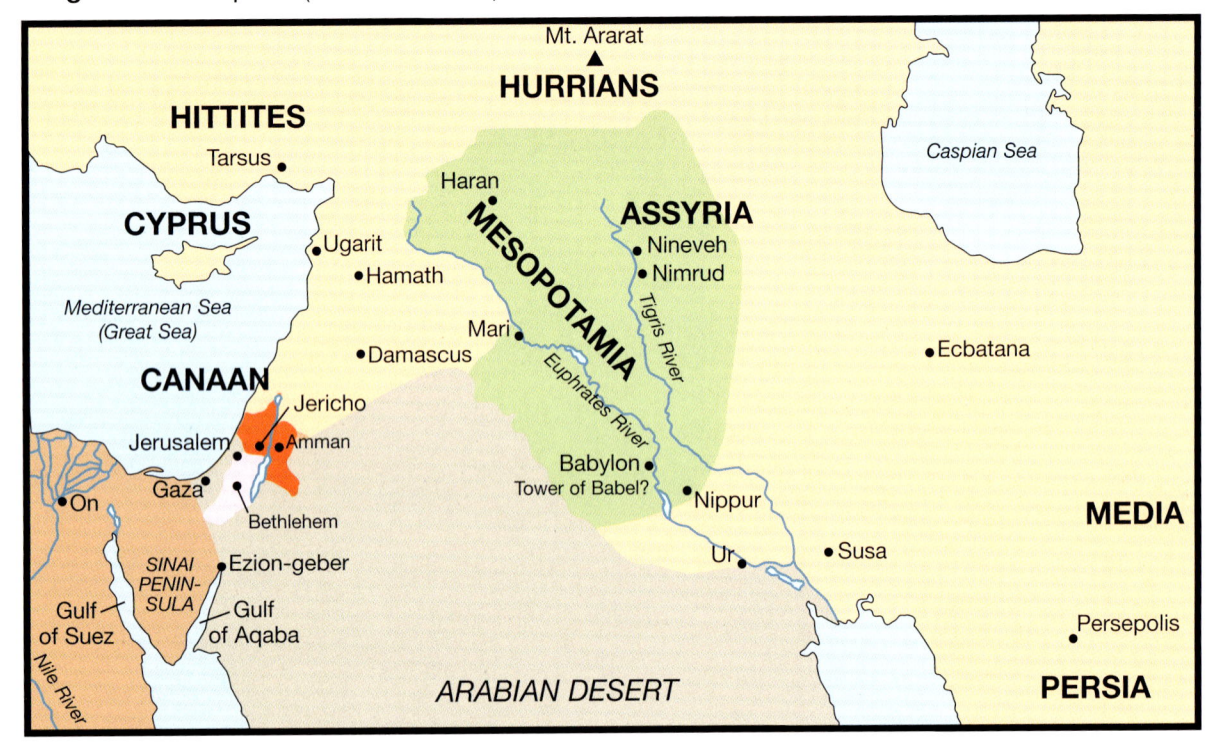

King: Shalmaneser III (858 BC–823 BC)

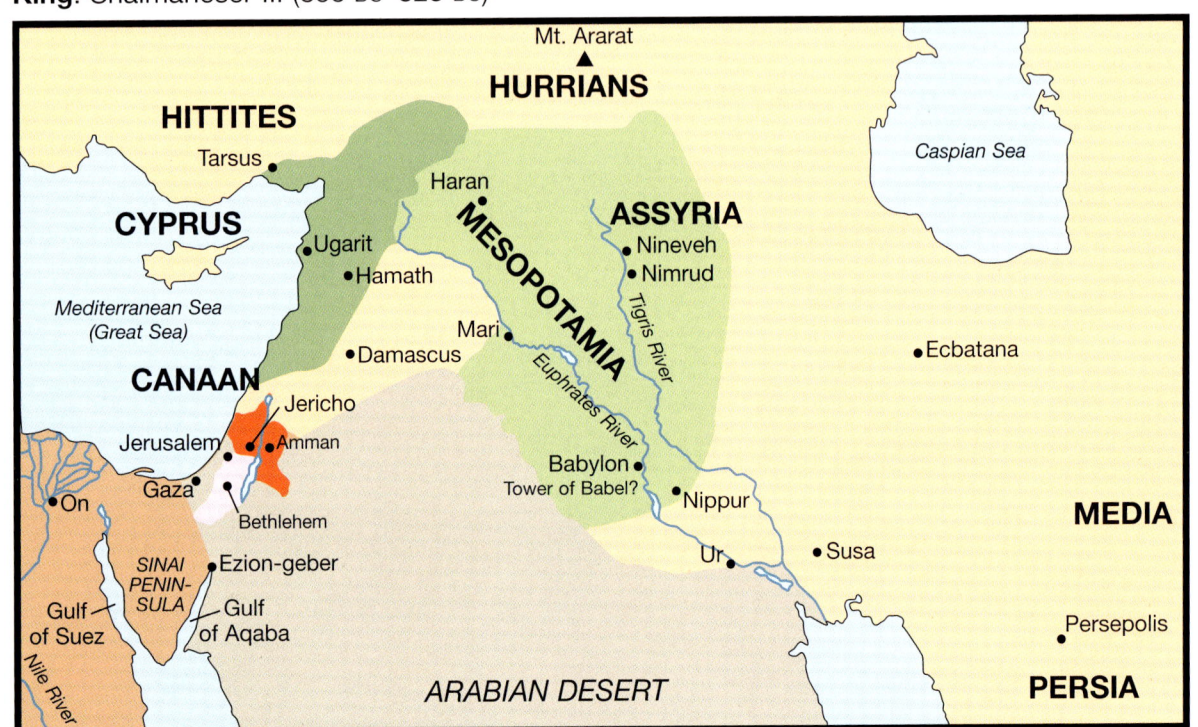

Expansion of the Assyrian Empire

☐ Existing Empire ☐ Expansion ■ Israel ☐ Judah

Kings: Tigleth-Pileser III (745 BC–727 BC) Sargon II (722 BC–705 BC) Israel falls to
Shalmaneser V (727 BC–722 BC) Sennacherib (705 BC–681 BC) Assyria 722 BC

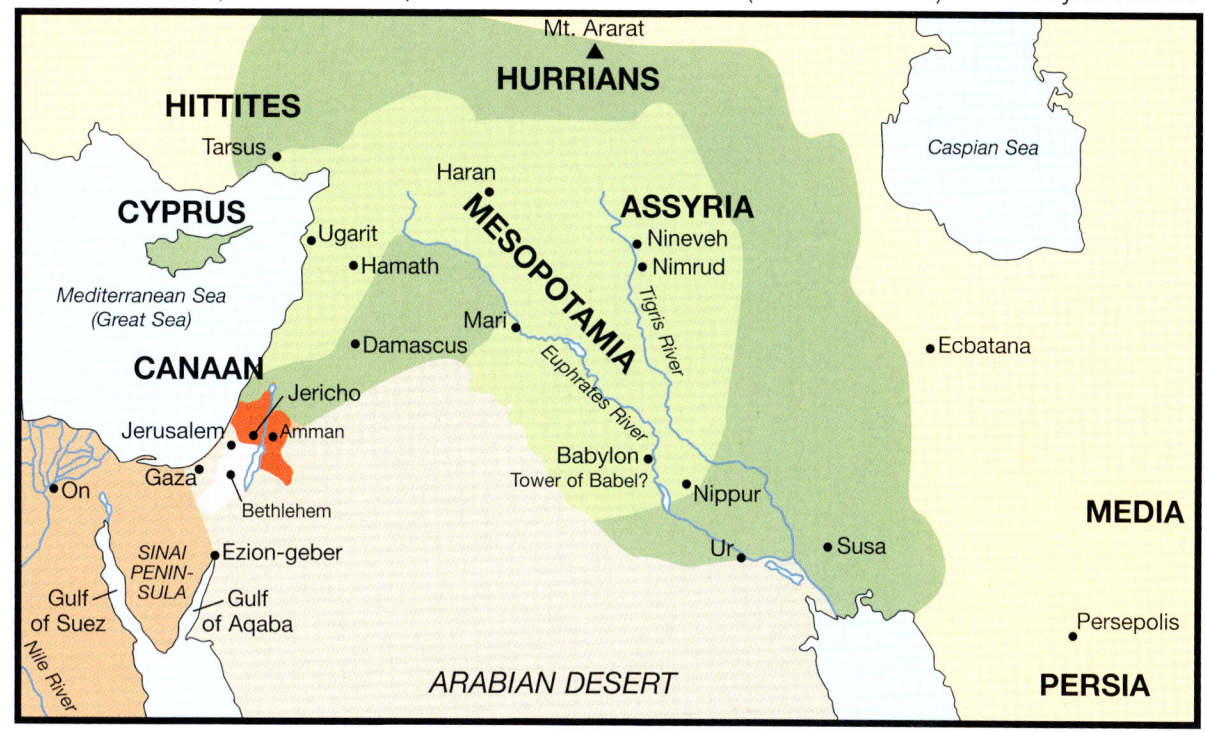

King: Esarhaddon (680 BC–669 BC) Ashurbanipal (669 BC–627 BC) Judah (vassal state)

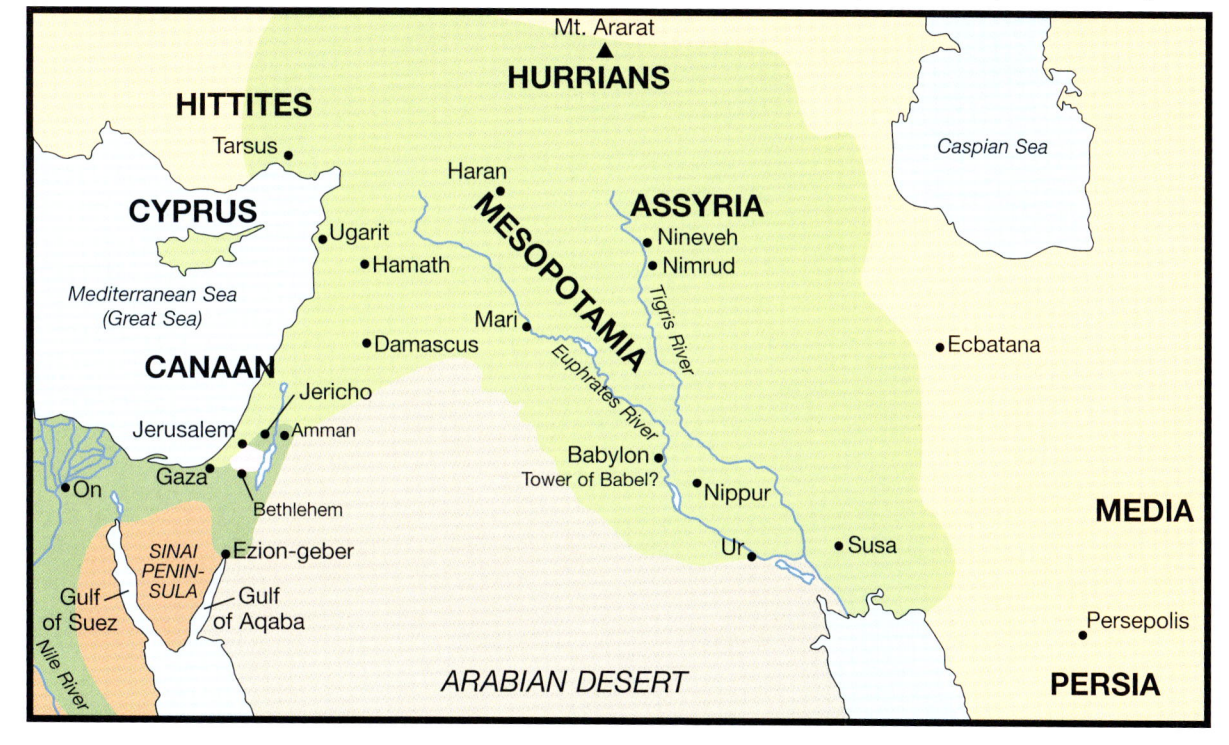

Babylonian and Persian Empires

- ▇ Babylonian Kingdom
- ▇ Persian (Median) Kingdom
- ▇ Arabian Desert

Babylonian Empire

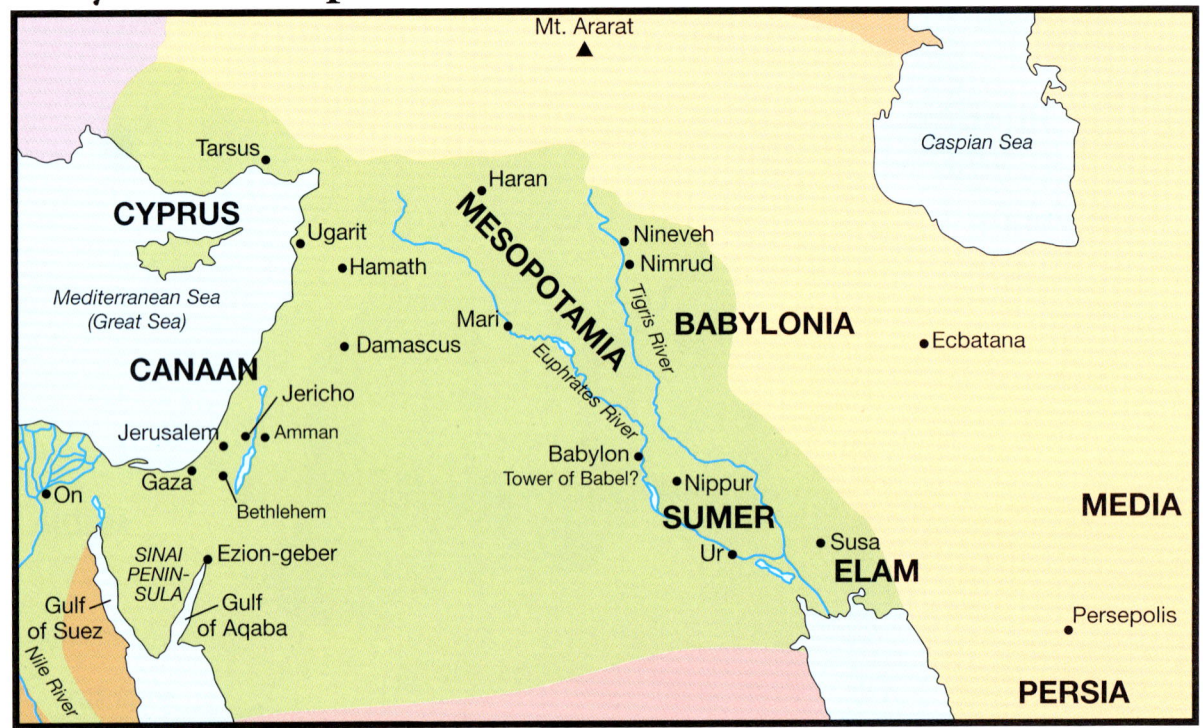

Persian Empire

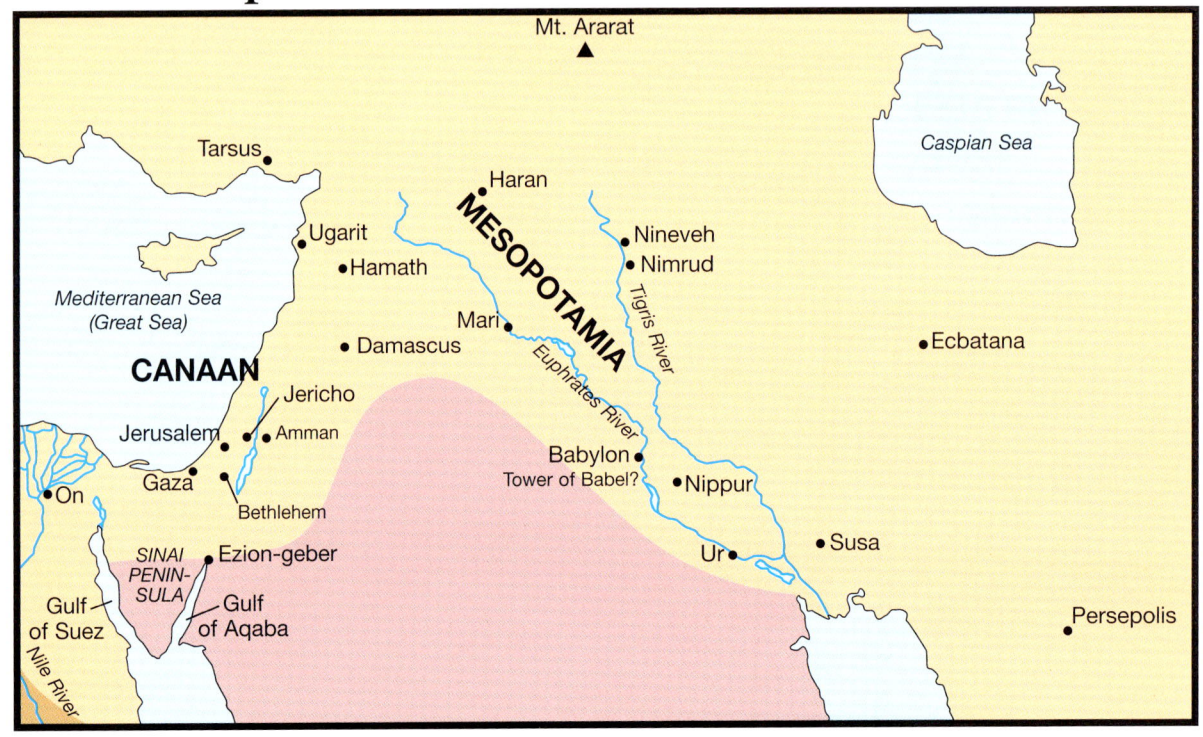

Middle East: Fascinating Facts and Figures

- The garden of Eden may have been in Iraq near the Tigris and Euphrates Rivers.

- Noah's ark may have landed on Mount Ararat in Turkey. Some people think it landed in the general area of the mountains of northern Iraq. (Genesis 6–8)

- The Tower of Babel may have been near Babylon. Ancient Babylon was in Iraq. It is believed that different languages started at the Tower of Babel. (Genesis 11)

- Abraham lived in Ur, which was the capital of the ancient kingdom of Sumer in Mesopotamia. Ruins of Ur are still in Iraq near the Euphrates River. (Genesis 11)

- God called Abraham to leave his father's home in Ur and go to a new land. The new land was Canaan, much of which is now called Israel. (Genesis 12)

- God promised Abraham and Sarah a son, Isaac, whose children would become a great nation. He made a covenant (solemn agreement) to be their God and to give them the land of Canaan. In return, they were to worship and obey him. (Genesis 15)

- God passed the blessing and inheritance from Abraham to Isaac to Jacob (Israel) and to Jacob's twelve sons. Jacob's twelve sons were the start of the twelve tribes of Israel. (Genesis 12, 15, 17, 21, 22, 25–27, 32, 35, 48, 49.)

- Instead of Joseph, his two sons—Manasseh and Ephraim—were "adopted" by Jacob and given the inheritance which was land for two tribes. The tribe of Levi was not given an area of land, but was spread throughout the other tribes.

- The Arabs came from Abraham's other son, Ishmael, of Hagar and from his sons of Keturah. Abraham loved Ishmael, but sent him and his mother away. God promised to make Ishmael a great nation, too, and gave him an inheritance outside the Promised Land of Canaan. (Genesis 16, 17, 21, 25)

- God trained Abraham and his family to trust and obey him through many problems. They were in Egypt about 400 years. God sent plagues on Egypt so Pharaoh would let his people go. Moses led the children of Israel through 40 years of wandering in the desert, much of the time on the Sinai Peninsula. (Book of Exodus)

- Moses wrote out the laws and a song for the Israelite people and gave them a blessing. Before Moses died, he saw the Promised Land from Mt. Nebo. (Deuteronomy 31–33)

- Joshua led Israel into the Promised Land. God told them to conquer the land, drive out the Canaanites, destroy the idols, and worship only God. (Book of Joshua)

- Joshua divided the land among the twelve Israelite tribes according to God's directions. He urged them to keep trusting God and to obey his commands. (Joshua 24)

- Daniel was "kidnapped" as a teenager and was taken to Iraq (Babylon) as a POW.

- Jonah went to northern Iraq (Nineveh).

Where Jesus Walked: Then

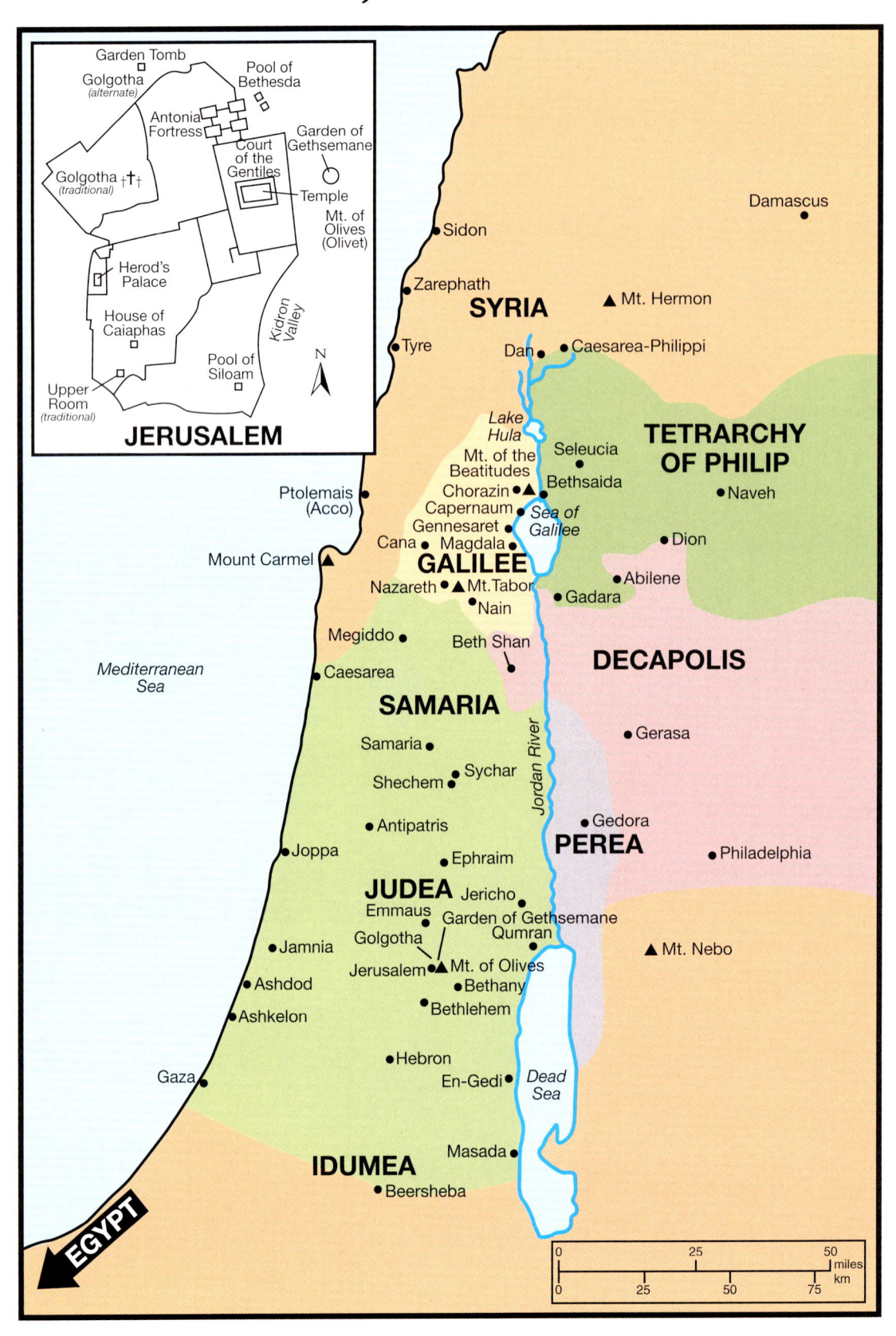

Where Jesus Walked: Now

World of the First Christians: Then

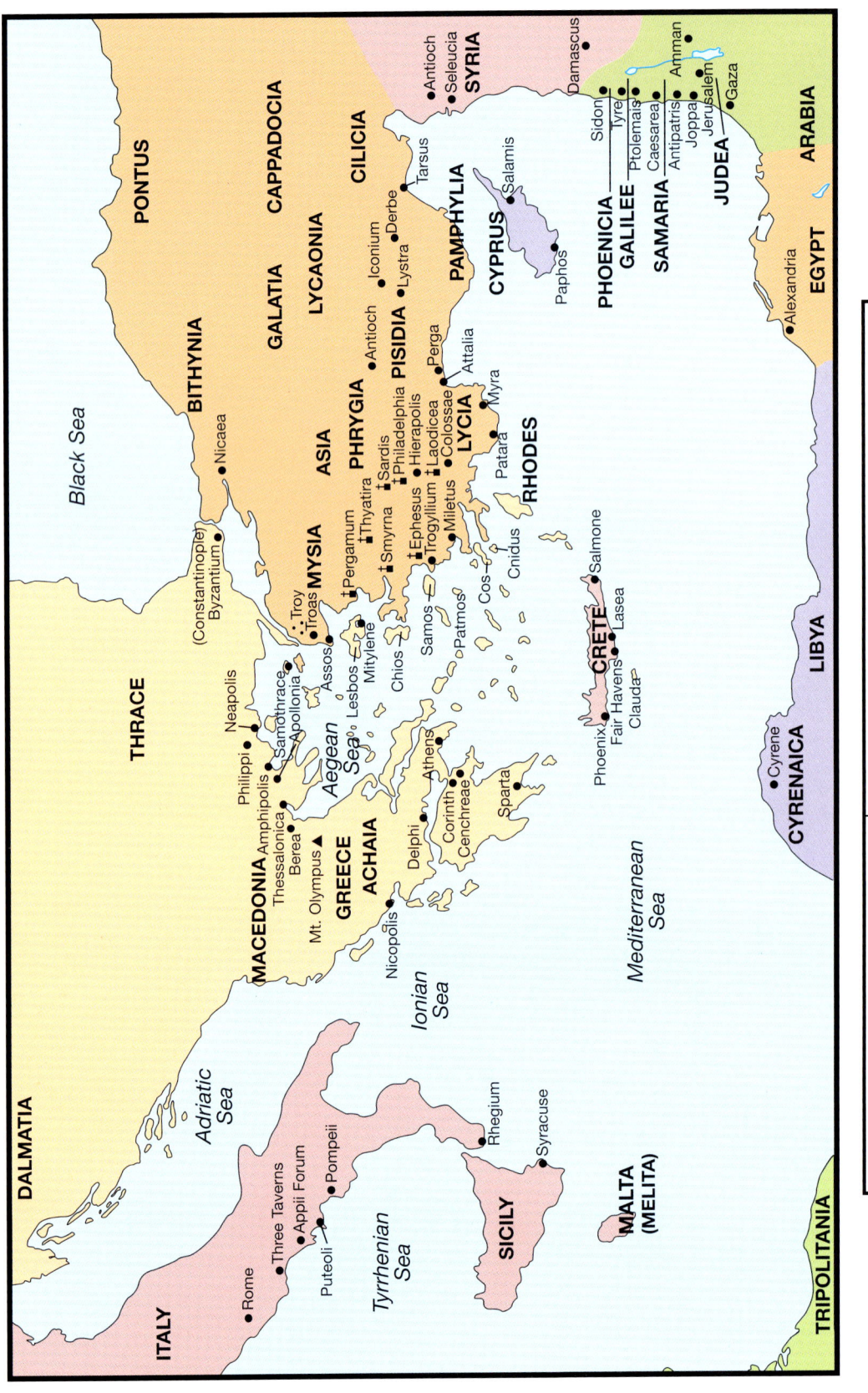

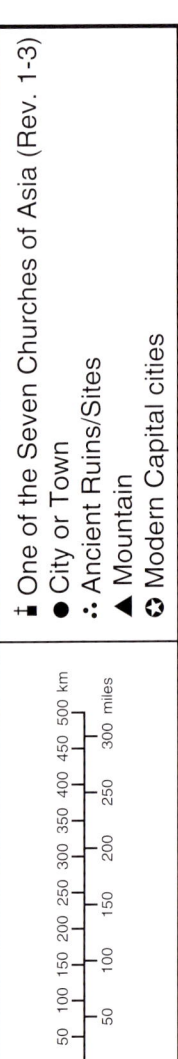

World of the First Christians: Now

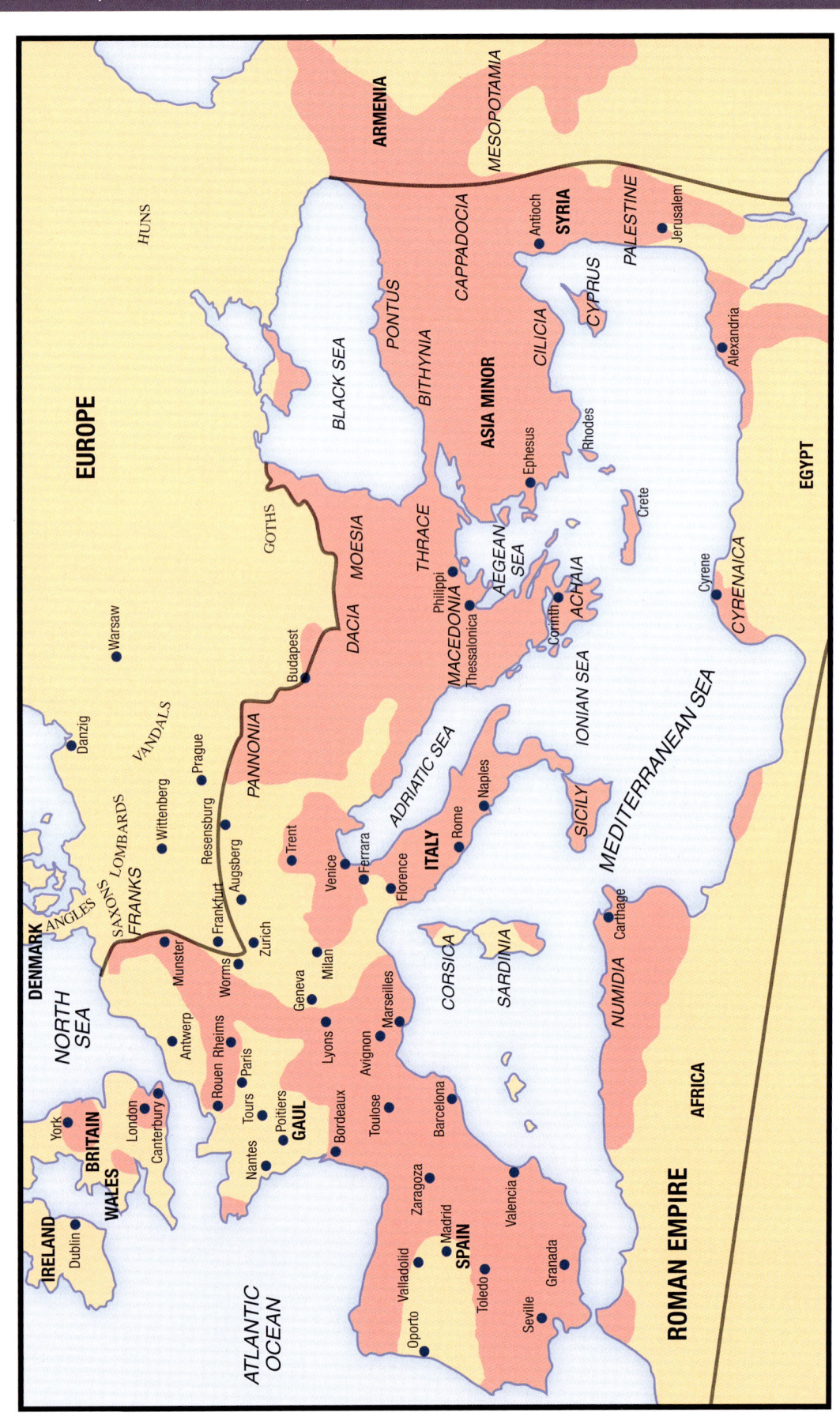

Expansion of Christianity

CHRISTIAN LIVING

FOLLOWING JESUS

SALVATION, SIN & FORGIVENESS

Welcome to God's Family!

Now that you believe in Jesus Christ, you are a "child of God" and you belong to a new family. The goal of this family is to serve God and to love people. Some people think that Christianity is a set of rules. It is really a relationship between a loving God and his beloved children (Romans 5:6-11).

Here are some of the most common questions that Christians have . . .

How Can I Be Sure that I'm Saved?

A The Bible tells us to: **Admit we have sinned** (Romans 3:23; 6:23; 1 John 1:10)

B **Believe in Jesus** (John 1:12)

C **Confess that Jesus is Lord** (Romans 10:9; Ephesians 2:8, 9)

Sometimes you may feel close to God, other times you may feel distant from him. Some people feel great joy and freedom from their problems when they first believe in Jesus. After a while, this joy may fade. This is normal.

Don't depend on your feelings. The Bible says, "*…if you confess with your mouth, "Jesus is Lord," and believe in your heart that God raised him from the dead, you will be saved*" (Romans 10:9).

Look for evidence of change. God now calls you his child, and has sent his Spirit to work inside you (John 1:12; 14:25, 26). As a follower of Jesus, you should see *progress*—not *perfection*—in your desire to obey and please Him (Ecclesiastes 7:20; Romans 7:14-25). For example, before you became a Christian you lost your temper or lied or hated people and it did not bother you. Now you have a deep desire to change and you regret your failures.

Hang in there! When you're discouraged by doubts and failures, remember that growth is a process. God has plans for you, and won't give up on you—ask for God's help. God promises to help you improve (Philippians 1:6).

Can God Forgive Me?

Yes! God can forgive any sin, no matter how terrible—cheating, murder, lying, infidelity, gossip, theft, selfishness. All people fail and disobey God. No one measures up. In fact the Bible says that no one can please God by good deeds. Good deeds aren't good enough.

God promises that he will forgive you. *If we confess our sins, he is faithful and just and will forgive us our sins and purify us from all unrighteousness* (1 John 1:9).

Jesus once told a story to his disciples, warning them that "good people" who think they are good enough for God are in more spiritual danger than humble people who recognize that they are unworthy and ask for forgiveness (Luke 18:9-14).

Confess your sins and forgive others. Though God has forgiven you, you'll still have struggles. Some consequences and scars from your past may remain. If you've wronged others, ask for their forgiveness and try to make amends (with counsel from mature believers). When others wrong you, God asks that you forgive them—not because they deserve it, but out of gratitude for the great gift you received from God (Colossians 3:13).

What If I Sin?

Don't be surprised by your struggles. Everyone has them. The Bible says … *for all have sinned and fall short of the glory of God, and are justified freely by his grace through the redemption that came by Christ Jesus* (Romans 3:23, 24).

Every follower of Jesus has certain vulnerabilities, whether it is losing your temper, materialism, envy, gossip, or pornography. People may persuade you to disobey God, or you may find yourself in tempting situations. The Bible says that before you accept Jesus, it is very difficult for you to resist temptation (Colossians 1:13). Even after deciding to follow Jesus, people still struggle with temptation and sometimes give into temptation. The good news is, once you've decided to follow Jesus, you will possess the desire to please God daily, and God will continue to help you resist temptation (Romans 7:21-25).

All people sin. When you do sin, it's not the end of your relationship with God. Confess your wrongs to God, and he will forgive you. Find Christian friends and support one another.

No matter what happens, God promises you a way to escape any spiritual danger. *No temptation has seized you except what is common to man. And God is faithful; he will not let you be tempted beyond what you can bear. But when you are tempted, he will also provide a way out so that you can stand up under it* (1 Corinthians 10:13).

PRAYER, BIBLE STUDY & CHURCH

How Do I Pray?

God wants to have a relationship with you! Prayer is simply "staying connected" with your heavenly Father by talking to him. It doesn't matter whether you're happy, puzzled, hurt, or in trouble; you can talk about anything with God. Trust that God wants the best for you. When you ask for things, God may say "yes," "no," or "not yet" (Romans 8:26-28).

God cares about you and will listen to you when you talk to him. *Do not be anxious about anything, but in everything, by prayer and petition, with thanksgiving, present your requests to God and the peace of God that passes all understanding will guard your hearts and minds in Christ Jesus* (Philippians 4:6, 7).

Where to pray. Jesus said you should find a secluded quiet place, and pray to God (Matthew 6:6). You can pray in your bedroom, car, or on a walk…anywhere. Try to set aside a special time each day to talk to God. Many people find that early morning is the best time to pray because there are fewer distractions. Start by praying for five to ten minutes and then increase the time you spend with God as your prayer life becomes more disciplined.

The Lord's Prayer. Jesus taught his disciples how to pray using the Lord's Prayer:

Our Father in heaven, hallowed be your name, your kingdom come, your will be done on earth as it is in heaven. Give us today our daily bread. Forgive us our debts, as we also have forgiven our debtors. And lead us not into temptation, but deliver us from the evil one.

The Lord's Prayer has four parts to help us remember:
- **PRAISE** Recognize that God is great and in charge. Remember, God loves you and knows what's best for you.
- **PROVIDE** Ask God to provide for you, your family, and friends. Ask for healing, courage, and wisdom for the problems you might have.
- **PARDON** Confess your sins and ask others for forgiveness. Remember to forgive people who have wronged you. Let God know that you are sorry for disobeying him and wronging other people. Ask for forgiveness; God promises to forgive you.
- **PROTECTION** We are constantly faced with temptation. Ask for God's protection and the strength to do what is right (Matthew 6:9-13).

How Do I Read the Bible?

Open It! In order to follow Jesus you need to know what he said and did.

Begin by reading the Gospels (stories of the life of Jesus):
- Matthew
- Mark
- Luke
- John

Apply It!
As you read, look for—
- An example to admire or avoid
- A command to obey
- A sin to confess
- A promise to embrace

With a mature believer, discuss the parts you don't understand. Read and pray (Acts 17:11).

Engage It! You may find it helpful to use a study Bible and take notes about what you read. It is important to read the Bible every day, because it has many passages that will give you encouragement. Memorizing these verses will be a big help to your life (Psalm 1:2; 119:15, 16).

It may be helpful to read:
- Genesis
- Proverbs
- Psalms
- Romans

Why is the Bible Important?
The Bible is the Word of God. It provides us with the wisdom needed in order to share with others the "good news" about Jesus. The Bible is useful for teaching others, recognizing incorrect teachings, and learning how to live as followers of Jesus day by day (2 Timothy 3:16, 17).

Do I Need to Go to Church?

A New Family. The church is made up of believers who become your family. The people at church care about you, support you, teach you, and encourage you.

The Lord wants believers to meet together. *And let us consider how we may spur one another on toward love and good deeds.*

Let us not give up meeting together, as some are in the habit of doing, but let us encourage one another—and all the more as you see the Day approaching (Hebrews 10:24, 25).

A Special Niche. The Bible describes the church as a building where you fit like a custom-cut stone (1 Peter 2:4, 5). Every player on a sports team is necessary and important to the team as a whole. In the same way, you are important to the church, and other believers need you. Your unique strengths and gifts will help others. You may not like or agree with every other believer, but no Christian is perfect and neither are you.

Be forgiving and live at peace with other followers of Jesus.
Be completely humble and gentle; be patient, bearing with one another in love. Make every effort to keep the unity of the Spirit through the bond of peace (Ephesians 4:2, 3).

A Larger Purpose. When Jesus went to heaven, he told his followers to love each other. In fact, he said that other people would know you were a follower of Jesus if you loved other Christians.

This is not always easy. Some people have personalities that are hard to love. Perhaps they are judgmental or grumpy. Jesus calls us to treat them kindly and gently and care for them.

FEARS, DOUBTS & TRUST

What About Fears and Doubts?

The Fear Factor. Do you ever worry about the future? How will I pay my bills? Will I ever get married? Will my children be safe? Will disaster strike? Life is better when we have someone strong and loving to lean on.

The Bible says that God will never abandon you. *"…the LORD your God goes with you; he will never leave you nor forsake you"* (Deuteronomy 31:6).

20 Questions. Real Christians *can* have doubts. At times, they may question whether God actually exists or doubt some of the claims of the Christian faith.

The Bible is full of questioners! Jesus' disciple Thomas was not present when Jesus first appeared to the other disciples after he rose from the dead. Thomas said that he would not believe unless he could see and touch the holes in Jesus' hands and put his hand in Jesus' side. Thomas might have had doubts about Jesus, but he kept his mind and heart open to the truth. When Jesus did appear to Thomas, Thomas exclaimed, "My Lord and my God." It was his search for the Truth that led Thomas into a faith that he had never had before (John 20:19-28).

Having doubts and questions may spur you to seek out answers, which can only bring you closer to God. In addition, believing something without checking the Bible may put you in spiritual danger. Doubts and questions help protect believers from being misled or becoming stagnant and inactive in their walk with Jesus.

Can God Be Trusted?

Why do bad things happen? A broken heart, an illness, a death in the family, a lost job.… Problems do come to followers of Jesus. Some hurts result from our own selfishness while others may result from the behavior of others. Bad things happen simply because we do not live in a perfect world and because God wanted to give us free will—the freedom to choose right and wrong (Romans 8:18-23).

> ***Is God really in control?*** Yes! God is with you, and he protects you more than you realize. When God does allow difficulties, it may be his way of disciplining you or strengthening you.

The Bible says that trials and sufferings help mold God's children into who God wants them to be. *Consider it pure joy, my brothers, whenever you face trials of many kinds, because you know that the testing of your faith develops perseverance. Perseverance must finish its work so that you may be mature and complete, not lacking anything* (James 1:2-4).

You may not recognize the purpose for problems in your life when they are occurring, but many times these trials could be part of a larger, unseen plan (John 9:1-3).

God has a good plan for you. *"For I know the plans I have for you," declares the LORD, "plans to prosper you and not to harm you, plans to give you hope and a future"* (Jeremiah 29:11).

Just before Jesus died on the cross, he earnestly asked God if it was possible to avoid it. However, Jesus ended his prayer by saying, "May *Your* will be done." Jesus also encouraged his followers to trust that God would take care of them (Matthew 6:25-34).

Why is the world such a mess?

If God condemns greed and injustice, why does it go on? Evil has polluted everything and everyone God created (Jeremiah 17:9). Some skeptics say that either God is not loving or He is not powerful enough to stop evil. The truth is that God puts up with evil, but only for a while, because he is waiting with patience and love for people to return to him. A day of final judgment will come, when God will punish evil (2 Peter 3:1-10). God will make everything right and fair in the end.

What's My Purpose in Life?

The Big Picture. You were created to serve God and love the people around you. When asked what the greatest commandment was, Jesus replied: *"Love the Lord your God with all your heart and with all your soul and with all your mind." This is the first and greatest commandment. And the second is like it: "Love your neighbor as yourself"* (Matthew 22:37-39).

Ultimately, the purpose in life for believers is to worship God in everything we do. In addition, we are to care about other people and tell them about Jesus.

God cares about everyone, and longs for each person to be saved (1 Timothy 2:3, 4).

How Do You Fit In? You have a unique role in God's kingdom. The Bible says that God is the potter and you are the clay–the work of his hands (Isaiah 64:8). God knew you before you were born, and created you to have special qualities and talents for serving him. He shaped your background and circumstances, both good and bad (Psalm 139; Ephesians 2:10). Often, God uses the painful situations of the past to help others. For example, a widow may someday help a friend or lead a ministry that helps others go through grief.

Day by Day. How will you know what God wants you to do at each moment? Start by reading the Bible and obeying its teachings. Do your normal everyday responsibilities with a cheerful attitude and look for ways to serve others (Psalm 100:2). Pray for guidance and understanding. Your goal is to hear God say, "Good job" (Matthew 25:21).

SPIRITUAL GIFTS, GIVING & SHARING

What Are Spiritual Gifts and Talents?

You already had God-given talents before you decided to follow Jesus. Now you can use them for His glory—whether playing the guitar during worship, serving food in a homeless shelter, fixing the pastor's computer, leading a Bible study, or rocking babies in the church nursery.

Now, as a believer, you receive special gifts from God's Spirit to help His kingdom. *Each one should use whatever gift he has received to serve others, faithfully administering God's grace in its various forms* (1 Peter 4:10).

You may have a gift for preaching, teaching, or showing mercy. You may be good at encouraging others or noticing their needs. People may ask you for wise advice. The Bible lists many gifts (Romans 12; 1 Corinthians 12; Ephesians 4). To find your gifts, ask others what they think your gifts might be. Pray and try different ways of serving God. Though some gifts may seem better than others, the Bible is clear that every gift is important and necessary (Romans 12:3-8). No one should feel too important or unimportant; all gifts are needed for God's people to function as a team (1 Corinthians 12:4-31).

What about Giving?

Why should I give? Jesus gave his life for you (1 Corinthians 6:19, 20). Now you *and* all you own belong to him (Psalm 24:1). God wants our love and gratitude. We demonstrate our devotion to God by giving. Giving to God demonstrates that we are following Jesus and making him our "Number One" priority (Matthew 6:24).

Where should I give? You can advance God's cause in the world in many ways. You might give cash, a car, a computer, even a cow! Pastors, Christian workers, and missionaries need salaries. Church and outreach programs need money for buildings, books, utility bills, and more. And poor people, in your church or across the world, need help just to survive.

How do I give? Before you donate, ask if the money will be used wisely. Support the church you attend, and perhaps other causes as God stirs your heart. Contribute regularly and generously. A tenth of your income is the standard set up in the Old Testament.

When giving is tough, pray for God's help. God does promise to reward you in his own way whenever you give humbly and generously (Malachi 3:8-10, Matthew 6:1-4).

When you give with a cheerful attitude, God will give you all that you need. *Each man should give what he has decided in his heart to give, not reluctantly or under compulsion, for God loves a cheerful giver. And God is able to make all grace abound to you, so that in all things at all times, having all that you need, you will abound in every good work* (2 Corinthians 9:7, 8).

How Do I Tell Others?

Start with your lifestyle. Actions speak louder than words! Jesus said that others will know Christians by their love for other people (John 13:35). Put other people's needs ahead of your own (Luke 10:27). With God's help, you can brighten your world with love and good deeds (Matthew 5:13-16).

Be prepared to talk about Jesus. You never know when someone may ask (1 Peter 3:15).

God cares about people so much that he sent Jesus to save them and give them eternal life in heaven. Jesus said that, "*God so loved the world that he gave his one and only Son, that whoever believes in him shall not perish but have eternal life*" (John 3:16).

It would be helpful to mention a few Bible verses, such as:
- Romans 3:23: *...for all have sinned and fall short of the glory of God.*
- Romans 5:8, 9: *But God demonstrates his own love for us in this: While we were still sinners, Christ died for us.*
- Romans 6:23: *For the wages of sin is death, but the gift of God is eternal life in Christ Jesus our Lord.*

Share what God has done in your life. God promises to help you (1 Corinthians 2:11-13).

Look for opportunities. People can't learn about Jesus unless someone tells them (Romans 10:13-15). Pray for chances to share. Bring God into conversations naturally, talking about how you deal with problems or worries. Notice when others express spiritual hunger, and let them know what you have experienced. Treat them with gentleness and love, even if they are not open to the message (Colossians 4:6).

Leave matters in God's hands. You can't force someone to follow Jesus. You are responsible to share with and pray for others who don't know Jesus. God's Spirit can turn the most unlikely people to His Truth (Romans 10:1).

RELIABILITY OF THE CHRISTIAN FAITH

Is the Bible Reliable?

More than myths. More than 100 archaeological finds have confirmed the accuracy of the Bible. For example, scholars dismissed the biblical description of the Hittite nation as fiction until they found evidence (Joshua 1:1-4). The Bible's descriptions of cities, rulers, and battles match other historical records.

The Bible is inspired by God and is useful for teaching and equipping followers of Jesus to do God's work. *All Scripture is God-breathed and is useful for teaching, rebuking, correcting and training in righteousness, so that the man of God may be thoroughly equipped for every good work* (2 Timothy 3:16, 17).

Accurately copied. Before the printing press, special scribes copied these texts by hand with an intricate checking system. The text of the Bible is better preserved than the writings of Plato and Aristotle. Discoveries like the Dead Sea Scrolls confirm their accuracy.

Is Following Jesus the Only Way to be Saved?

One way to God. Followers of Jesus claim to be a part of the one true religion and recognize the claims of Jesus as being true. Many people of other religions are good and moral people, but Jesus' own statements say that believing in him is the one and only way to be saved. In addition, the Bible is clear that being a moral person or doing good deeds is not enough to be saved.

Jesus said he was the only way to God. Jesus said, *"I am the way and the truth and the life. No one comes to the Father except through me"* (John 14:6).

Jesus said that he provides people with eternal life. Jesus said, *"I give them eternal life, and they shall never perish; no one can snatch them out of my hand"* (John 10:28).

Jesus claimed to be God. Jesus said, *"I and the Father are one"* (John 10:30).

Being a good, sincere person is not enough. The Bible says, *"For it is by grace you have been saved, through faith—and this not from yourselves, it is the gift of God—not by works, so that no one can boast"* (Ephesians 2:8, 9).

Is There Evidence for the Resurrection?

Jesus was a real person. At least 39 ancient sources *apart from the Bible* note his teachings, miracles, life, and death.

Many saw him dead, then alive. Some say Jesus merely fainted on the cross. Others say the people who saw him alive later were "hallucinating." But Jesus' enemies and the Roman soldiers who executed him were satisfied that he was dead. Then after three days, 500 people, as individuals and in groups, morning and evening, indoors and outdoors, over a period of 40 days, saw and touched him as he walked, ate, and preached (1 Corinthians 15:3-8).

His followers changed radically. Jesus' disciples turned from "common people" into bold preachers, bravely facing persecution.

Most died as martyrs for their faith (Acts 4:1-22; 12:1-3). People would not die for a religious belief if they knew that belief was a lie.

Why does it matter? Jesus' resurrection proved he was divine and that everything he taught and claimed is true.

The resurrection of Jesus showed the penalty for sin was paid. It displayed God's power over death, and the new life he offers. *Praise be to the God and Father of our Lord Jesus Christ! In his great mercy he has given us new birth into a living hope through the resurrection of Jesus Christ from the dead* (1 Peter 1:3).

Jesus is our hope, who lives forever to present us as clean and pure before God (Hebrews 7:12-25).

The Journey

When you chose to follow Jesus, you embarked upon a journey that has high mountain peaks and occasional low valleys. The final destination is eternal life with God in heaven. The good news is that you are not left alone as you travel. You are following Jesus and He promises not to leave you behind. You also have several travelers alongside of you to encourage you and help carry your load.

Key Verses to Memorize

If you confess with your mouth, "Jesus is Lord," and believe in your heart that God raised him from the dead, you will be saved. —Romans 10:9

If we confess our sins, he is faithful and just and will forgive us our sins and purify us from all unrighteousness. —1 John 1:9

For all have sinned and fall short of the glory of God, and are justified freely by his grace through the redemption that came by Christ Jesus. —Romans 3:23, 24

Do not be anxious about anything, but in everything, by prayer and petition, with thanksgiving, present your requests to God. And the peace of God, which transcends all understanding, will guard your hearts and your minds in Christ Jesus. —Philippians 4:6, 7

"For I know the plans I have for you," declares the LORD, "plans to prosper you and not to harm you, plans to give you hope and a future." —Jeremiah 29:11

Consider it pure joy, my brothers, whenever you face trials of many kinds, because you know that the testing of your faith develops perseverance. Perseverance must finish its work so that you may be mature and complete, not lacking anything. —James 1:2-4

The Great Commandment: *"Love the Lord your God with all your heart and with all your soul and with all your mind." This is the first and greatest commandment. And the second is like it: "Love your neighbor as yourself."* —Matthew 22:37-39

Each one should use whatever gift he has received to serve others, faithfully administering God's grace in its various forms. —1 Peter 4:10

God so loved the world that he gave his one and only Son, that whoever believes in him shall not perish but have eternal life. —John 3:16

For it is by grace you have been saved, through faith—and this not from yourselves, it is the gift of God—not by works, so that no one can boast. For we are God's workmanship, created in Christ Jesus to do good works, which God prepared in advance for us to do. —Ephesians 2:8-10

who i am in CHRiSt

because of what he has done

Because Jesus died, he can offer forgiveness. Because Jesus rose from the dead, he can give us life and victory. Forgiveness, life, and victory give us identity. We now live forgiven, abundant and victorious lives. Our lives are not perfect since we still experience pain and suffering. However, our hope is firm because it is based on Jesus' victory over death.

I am forgiven.

Eph. 1:6–8; Rom. 8:1, 38

All my sins are forgiven before God. God will not condemn me for:

- Bad things I have done.
- Good things I have left undone.
- Evil things I have said.
- Wrong things I have thought.

I am reconciled with God.

Rom. 5:10; 2 Cor. 5:18–19; Col. 1:21–22; Heb. 10:19–22

- I have been reunited with God.
- The anger that was between us is gone.
- Because of Jesus, I now have free access to God.

I am rescued.

Matt. 20:28; 1 Tim. 2:5–6

- I have been rescued from a life-threatening situation.
- Jesus paid the ransom for my life with his own life.
- Sin no longer holds my life hostage.

I am redeemed.

Eph. 1:13–14; Col. 1:14; Titus 2:14; Heb. 9:12; 1 Peter 1:18

- I have had my life debt covered, and my future holds an inheritance from God.
- My life is no longer a worthless debt to sin.
- I now look forward to rich meaning and purpose in God's future plan for me.

I am free.

John 8:32-36; Rom. 6:22–23; Gal. 4:7; 5:1

- I have been set free.
- I am no longer a slave to sin.

I am bought with a price and belong to God.

1 Cor. 6:19–20; 7:23

- I have been paid for by God.
- God owns me.
- I no longer belong to myself.
- My old way of life no longer owns me.

I am known by God.

Rom. 8:29; 2 Tim. 2:19

- I have been known and cared about all along.
- God has been watching out for me from the beginning.
- God has cared for me from day one.

I am chosen.

Rom. 8:30; Eph. 1:4; 1 Peter 2:9

- I have been hand picked by God.
- My salvation was not accidental. God intended it for me.
- God called me out for salvation, even though I do not deserve it.

I am justified before God.

Rom. 3:23–26, 5:1, 8:1, 30

- God has declared me innocent because of Christ.
- Jesus has won my case by paying my penalty for me.
- I have been acquitted of all my crimes.

I am accepted.

Rom. 15:7; Eph. 1:4-6; 1 Peter 2:10

- I have been welcomed by God.
- I am no longer rejected.
- I am no longer an outsider.

I am saved.

Rom. 5:8–10; 7:13–25; Eph. 2:1–10; Col. 1:13

I have been rescued:

- From God's just anger.
- From sin.
- From myself.
- From death.
- From Satan and a sinful system.

I am alive.

Rom. 6:11; 8:9–11; Eph. 2:4–5

- I have received new life from God.
- My spirit has been brought to life and will never be dead again.
- My body will be made new after I die and I will live forever.
- I have new meaning and purpose and a new way of looking at life.

I am loved.

Rom. 5:5; 8:39; 1 John 3:16; 4:19

- God deeply loves me.
- I know this because he has given me his most precious gift—his Son, Jesus.
- I know that I am loved because God's Spirit of love is in my heart.

I am taken care of.

John 6:37; Phil. 1:6; 4:19

- I am secure in God's hands.
- I will not be abandoned; God will complete his work in me.
- God will supply all that I need.

But how did we arrive here? Let's trace the story from the beginning…

who God created me to be

God created all things, visible and invisible. Because he is the creator, he is also the rightful owner of all things. In addition to being the rightful owner, God also rules over all of creation; his authority is final.

I am a creature.

Gen. 2:7

God made me.

- Like a potter, God crafted me.
- God made me with skill and intention.
- I am complex and complicated.
- I have God's life-breath in me.

I am like God.

Gen. 1:26–27

God made me more than just an animal.

- I am made in God's image.
- I am made to relate to God and others in love.

I am known.

Psalm 139; Jer. 1:5

God made me and knew me before I was born.

- God made me.
- God knew me while I was still in the womb.
- God knows me better than I know myself.

I am made to be God's caretaker of his creation.

Gen. 1:26–31; 2:15–17

God made me for caring responsibility.

- I am made to help God in his ruling of creation.
- I am made to care for his earth.

I am made to relate to his creation.

Gen. 2:19–24

God made me to relate to his entire creation.

- I am made to love humans just as God loves me.
- I am made to love and enjoy God's creatures and nature.

I am made for thankful, obedient worship to God.

Gen. 1:28–30; 2:16–17

God made me to glorify and enjoy him forever.

- I am made to praise God by doing what he intended for me.
- I am made to enjoy myself as I enjoy God.

image of God

In Genesis 1:27, the Bible says, "So God created man in his own image, in the image of God he created him; male and female he created them." What is the image of God? The Bible says that Jesus is the perfect image of God (see Col. 2:9 and Heb. 1:3). However, Christians have understood this concept in three different though complementary ways:

1. The qualities and attributes that distinguish humanity from the animals. Some of these qualities are: reason, will, personality, etc.

2. The ability to be in a relationship with God. This relationship constitutes the image of God in us.

3. The caring of God's creation is what demonstrates God's image in human beings.

It is possible that all three things are involved in what the image of God is. Humans are the image of God because they are able to relate to God, to each other, and to God's creation. In addition, humans represent God in this creation. When humans are reconciled with God, the abundant life that results allows the image of God to come through more clearly.

who i am on my own — when i ignored God and went my own way.

Although God made us to be his representatives in creation, humans rebelled and sinned against God. Because of sin, humanity is unable to relate to God, one another, and creation. Death, pain, and suffering entered the universe. Because of human disobedience, the whole creation was thrown into darkness and chaos. Our very existence was in danger. God's amazing grace and endless mercy allowed us to live. However, we live limited and twisted lives. This is also part of humanity's identity.

I was broken.
Rom. 3:10–18

Because of Jesus, I am…
Rom. 6:6; Gal. 2:20
- I am crucified with Christ.
- Jesus' body was broken for me.

I was living my life for myself.
Eph. 2:3

Because of Jesus, I am…
Rom. 6:4; Col. 2:12
- I am buried with Christ to my old life.
- Jesus' burial buried my old selfish life.

I was a sinner.
Rom. 3:23

Because of Jesus, I am…
Rom. 6:8; 1 Peter 2:24
- I am dead with Christ to sin.
- Jesus' death was the death of my sin.

I was a user and abuser of God's creation.
Rom. 1:21–25; 3:13–18; Eph. 2:2

Because of Jesus, I am…
Rom. 6:4; Col. 3:1
- I am raised with Christ to a new life.
- Jesus' resurrection raised me to a new relationship with God and his world.

I was not living by God's instructions.
Rom. 1:21–2:1

Because of Jesus, I am…
Rom. 13:8–10
- I am fulfilling God's law in Christ.
- Jesus' love for me makes me want to live his law of love.

God is the solution.

He chose for himself a people, those who would carry his name and be an example to all people. He gave us his word, in which he described his will for humanity and his creation. However, the ultimate solution is Jesus himself. Because he is both human and God, Jesus came to do what no other human could. His life, death, and resurrection created the bridge that allows us to be reconciled with God once again.

The cross is the climax of the biblical story. In the cross, all paths converge; all stories are given the possibility of a new direction. In the cross, God brings restoration, hope, and a new life for a creation groaning for redemption.

I was someone who worshiped my own way.
Rom. 1:25

Because of Jesus, I am…
Eph. 1:12–14
- I am glorifying God in Christ.
- Jesus' glorious victory makes me want to give all glory to God.

I was a mess.
Rom. 7

Because of Jesus, I am…
Phil. 1:6; Col. 2:9–10; Heb. 10:14
- I am complete in Christ.
- Jesus' perfect work has made my life complete. One day, when Jesus returns, he will make it perfect.

I was dead.
Eph. 2:1

Because of Jesus, I am…
Col. 2:13
- I am alive with Christ.
- Jesus' new life flows through me now.

I am…

We live in a culture of extremes. On the one hand, the culture around us emphasizes self-sufficiency and independence over the healthy emotional development of children. On the other, it attempts to bolster children's emotional health and self-worth by constant praise and a sense of entitlement. Both extremes have damaged children who grow up with a broken sense of self and lack of acceptance and love.

A realistic understanding of who we are gives us the chance for a healthy self-regard. The Bible gives us a correct understanding of who we are: people deeply flawed and sinful, deeply loved and redeemed by God, and equipped and empowered by the Holy Spirit to be and do as Christ would.

The Apostle Paul

The Apostle Paul is one of the great champions of the faith and worthy of imitation (1 Cor. 4:16). Paul candidly spoke about his past: a past full of pride and violence. He strongly contrasted the person he was, what he valued and what gave him meaning, with the person he became after his encounter with the risen Christ. His value, his goal and meaning for life were linked to Christ.

Paul before and after
Gal. 1:13–14; Phil. 3:4–6

before, I was…	now, I am…
born a Jew	an apostle of Christ
a Roman citizen	an apostle to the Gentiles
circumcised on the eighth day	a new person, all of my ancestry and ethnic background is worthless compared to the value of Christ
of the tribe of Benjamin	
a Pharisee	
persecutor of the church	a prisoner of Jesus
zealous for the tradition of my ancestors	a slave to everyone

I have been crucified with Christ and I no longer live, but Christ lives in me. The life I live in the body, I live by faith in the Son of God, who loved me and gave himself for me.

—Gal. 2:20

who i am and who i will be in CHRiST

The story of the Bible does not end on the cross. In fact, the cross opened new possibilities. The goal of the biblical story is not just the salvation of humanity through the gracious work of Jesus on the cross. God desires to redeem and restore all of his creation. The conclusion of this magnificent story is the creation of new heavens and new earth. All things will be made new! In that new creation, God will make things the way they should be.

I am a new creature.
2 Cor. 5:1–5, 16–19; Phil. 3:20-21

- I have had a total makeover of my mind and spirit and my new body is on order.
- My inner self has been recreated after a new model of human being—Jesus.
- My body will be made new after the pattern of Jesus' resurrected body.

I am born of God.
John 1:12–13; Rom. 8:29; 1 John 4:7

- I have been born into God's family.
- I am now a child of God after the likeness of Jesus.
- Jesus is the "firstborn" example from the dead of what I shall be in the resurrection.

I am adopted of God.
Rom. 8:15; Eph. 1:5; Heb. 2:10–12

- God has selected me to be his child.
- I am no longer an orphan.
- Jesus is my older brother.
- Because of him, I now share in the glory of being God's child.

I am a child of the promise.
Rom. 9:8; Gal. 4:23

- I am a child of Abraham, a promised child.
- I am a spiritual descendant of the father of faith.
- I am called to carry on this spiritual heritage in the world.

I am Jesus' friend.
John 15:15

- Jesus considers me his friend.
- I am a servant of Jesus Christ, yet he calls me friend.

I am a citizen of heaven.
Eph. 2:19; Phil. 3:20

- I belong with all those through history who have loved God.
- I am a member of God's heavenly kingdom.
- My true identity is with the people of God.

I am blessed with every spiritual blessing.
Eph. 1:3; 2:7
- I have all that can be had of God's treasures.
- I have been given unfathomable riches in Christ.
- It will take the rest of eternity to unfold all these blessings.

I am God's workmanship.
Eph. 2:10
- I am a work of art.
- I have been made by the most creative Artist ever.
- I am a poem of God's love.

I am a temple of the Holy Spirit.
1 Cor. 3:16; 6:19; 2 Cor. 6:16
- I have God living in me.
- I am God's house.
- I have been made holy for God to live in me.

I am a member of Christ's body.
Rom. 12:5; 1 Cor. 12:27
- I am connected in a living way to Jesus.
- I am a part of a living organism bigger than myself.
- I have a purpose and function in that body.

I am sealed.
2 Cor. 1:22; Eph. 1:13; 4:30
- I have God's royal seal upon me.
- I have God's seal of ownership.
- I have God's guarantee of a quality product in me.

I am made pure.
1 John 1:9, 3:3
- I am made clean.
- Christ's life and death purify me.
- I am being made holy for God by his Spirit working in me.

I am secure.
Rom. 8:28, 31–38
- I know that God works things for my good in all circumstances.
- I am free from all condemnation.
- I know that nothing can separate me from the love of God.

I am safe.
2 Cor. 1:21–22

I am safe because God has
- Anointed me.
- Set his seal of ownership on me.
- Put his Spirit in my heart as a guarantee.

I am victorious.
Rom. 8:37; 1 Cor. 15:57
- I cannot be beaten.
- I cannot be stopped by death, thanks to Christ.
- I shall be a winner in the end because God is for me.

I am going to live forever.
John 5:24; 6:47; 11:25-26; 17:3
- I will live on with God.
- My spirit shall not die but go to be with God.
- Even if my body dies, I will live again and get a new body in the resurrection.

I am in God's planned will as an heir of all creation.
Rom. 8:17, 32; Eph. 1:9–11
- I am going to inherit the universe with Christ.
- I know this because God has given all authority and power to Jesus and I belong to him.

> *Let the peace of Christ rule in your hearts, since as members of one body you were called to peace. And be thankful.*
> —Col. 3:15

---

the three R's— Reconciled, Ransomed, and Redeemed

Reconciled—to be reconciled means to be united again or to become friends again. Human sin and rebellion caused hostility between God and humanity. However, Jesus united us again in friendship with God by his death on the cross.

Ransomed—a ransom is a price that is paid for release; to be ransomed is to be freed at a cost. The Bible tells us that humanity was held hostage to sin, death and the Devil. Jesus' death was the ransom paid to free us from that slavery and reconcile us to God.

Redeemed—to redeem means to buy back again. Jesus' death paid the voucher, canceling the debt we owed.

a new mind

At the center of the good news about Christ is the transformation of individual lives. Paul tells us in Rom. 12:1–2 that this transformation involves the renewing of our minds. He goes on to say in Phil. 2:5–8 that this renewal is about having a new mind-set or attitude that Christ himself had. In other words, we are to identify with and take for ourselves Jesus' whole way of thinking and living.

who are we?

The Bible describes our encounter with God as a new birth (John 3:3). The apostle Paul extends this idea when he writes that we mature as Christians, and that we must, eventually, give up milk for solid food (Heb. 5:11–14). Just as children need to find their identities, we as spiritual children need to find our Christian identities as well.

Our identities begin with the recognition that we no longer belong to ourselves but to God. That is, we need to recognize that if Christ bought us at a high price, then we belong to him.

In the Scriptures, we learn who we are, where we came from, why we are here, and where we are going. When we read the stories of the Patriarchs in Genesis, we learn how God relates to us, imperfect people who long for him. When we read the Psalms, we learn a vocabulary of praise and petition. This vocabulary gives us words to praise God, to express our grief, and make our requests.

In the prophets, we learn what it means to be God's people in moments of difficulties and challenges, what it means to fail and receive God's grace and forgiveness. In the stories of the apostolic church, we see how the Holy Spirit guides and trains his church to carry on God's mission.

When we make ours the story of God's people, as told in the Bible and in the history of the church, our identity merges with that of God's people. In this process, we grow from infant believers to people mature in the faith. As we appropriate God's story with his people, we learn to teach others how to become part of this great story of salvation.

meaning of the word "Christian"

In Acts 11:25–26, Luke tells us that believers in Jesus were first called "Christians" at Antioch. The name obviously stuck, but what does it mean? *Christ* is the Greek term for the Hebrew *Messiah*, which means "anointed person." To be anointed in the Hebrew culture was to be set apart for some special service. It came to be associated in the prophetic writings of the Old Testament with God's promised savior of the line of king David—Jesus. The "ian" ending indicates belonging or membership. Christian means "one who belongs to Christ," or "one who is a part of Christ." Therefore, if a Christian is one who is connected to Christ, should it not be apparent in the way we act?

our identity—who we are, who I am—depends on the identity of God's people:

- I am a member of Christ's body;
- I am part of God's people;
- I am a child of God called to love him and his creation;
- I am a follower of Jesus because in him I am fully alive and willing to serve.

We are able to make this beautiful story ours only through the life, death, and resurrection of Christ. Through the Holy Spirit, we are renewed into the image of Jesus. By following his steps, we walk on the path of many believers before us, God's people, and we clear the path for those believers who are yet to come.

What the Bible Says About *Forgiveness*

Forgive us our sins, for we also forgive everyone who sins against us.—Luke 11:4a

With these familiar words in the Lord's Prayer, we are reminded that forgiveness should characterize our lives. But these few words, one might object, are a lot easier said than done. Forgiveness is one of the hardest things to do because the sins that need forgiving can be so damaging. They have wounded us so deeply that the mere idea of offering forgiveness to those who hurt us seems impossible. Forgiveness, in these cases, appears like letting people off the hook for their transgressions. The sharp pain in our hearts creates a barrier that prevents us from moving beyond our pain. Our pain and brokenness seem unending.

In the face of so much brokenness in ourselves and in our world, how should we respond? Should we deny it? Ignore it? Get even? Give up? God's Word says to forgive it. Forgiveness will never be easy. However, only through forgiveness can healing begin.

> "Forgiveness is God's invention for coming to terms with a world in which, despite their best intentions, people are unfair to each other and hurt each other deeply. He began by forgiving us. And he invites us all to forgive each other."
> —Lewis B. Smedes

Most of us can relate to many kinds of brokenness. Below are a few examples of situations in which forgiveness might be very difficult.

Areas	Sources of Brokenness
Emotional	• Abandonment by a father or mother • Infidelity, divorce, lying • Betrayal by a trusted friend or confidant
Physical	• Sexual or domestic abuse • Parental neglect of a child's physical needs • Assault or violence
Spiritual	• Misuse of authority by a church leader • Rejection or poor treatment by a church "family" • Major sins committed by a pastor • Private sins that damage a person's relationship with God
Financial	• Stealing, embezzlement, fraud • Failure to repay a debt or loan • Unfair loss of a job or employment discrimination
Social	• Name calling, insults, public humiliation • Loss of reputation from gossip and lies • Discrimination from prejudices, racism, or sexism • Bullying, cyber-bullying

Forgiveness Is Needed

Forgiveness exists because sin exists. Forgiveness is necessary because sin powerfully affects all areas of our lives. Forgiveness is not about ignoring evil, excusing it, or making light of it. On the contrary, forgiveness courageously faces sin and evil. Forgiveness acknowledges that a terrible wrong has been done and seeks to do something about it.

Sin Is Real

No one needs to look far to see that there is sin in the world. We are born into a world where harmful patterns of sin persist in societies, communities, churches, and families. We may not even be aware of our own contribution to the cycles of sin. Because sin is in the world and in us, we need forgiveness even more.

If we claim to be without sin, we deceive ourselves and the truth is not in us. If we confess our sins, he is faithful and just and will forgive us our sins and purify us from all unrighteousness. If we claim we have not sinned, we make him out to be a liar and his word is not in us.—1 John 1:8–10

SIN IS DESTRUCTIVE

Sin breaks our communion with God and destroys our relationships with others. The first human sin brought death into the world for all to suffer the consequences. When someone hurts us, our pain and our sin begin a cycle of anger, violence, resentment, and revenge that increases over time. Only forgiveness can allow us to break this cycle.

Therefore, just as sin entered the world through one man, and death through sin, and in this way death came to all people, because all sinned.—Romans 5:12

Once you were alienated from God and were enemies in your minds because of your evil behavior.—Colossians 1:21

What causes fights and quarrels among you? Don't they come from your desires that battle within you? You desire but do not have, so you kill. You covet, but you cannot get what you want, so you quarrel and fight.—James 4:1–2a

GOD TAKES SIN SERIOUSLY

Scripture tells us that God is merciful and forgiving, but it also makes clear that God does not tolerate sin. Because sin is so harmful, it demands divine judgment, not mere dismissal.

And he passed in front of Moses, proclaiming, "The Lord, the Lord, the compassionate and gracious God, slow to anger, abounding in love and faithfulness, maintaining love to thousands, and forgiving wickedness, rebellion and sin. Yet he does not leave the guilty unpunished; he punishes the children and their children for the sin of the parents to the third and fourth generation."—Exodus 34:6–7

Forgiveness Is Possible

If judgment of sin were the last word on the matter, we would all stay trapped in our guilt and brokenness. If vengeance for every offense were the only option, we would forever remain separated from our Creator. But thank God he has provided another way—the way of forgiveness. Forgiveness does not erase the past, but it gives us a chance for a better future.

GOD DESIRES TO FORGIVE

The Old Testament contains many examples of God sending punishment for sinful acts. However, his withholding of judgment was for the purpose of bringing the people back to God so he could forgive them and restore the broken relationship. Though our actions deserve judgment, God desires to be merciful.

If my people, who are called by my name, will humble themselves and pray and seek my face and turn from their wicked ways, then I will hear from heaven and I will forgive their sin and will heal their land.—2 Chronicles 7:14

Perhaps when the people of Judah hear about every disaster I plan to inflict on them, they will turn from their wicked ways; then I will forgive their wickedness and their sin.—Jeremiah 36:3

The Lord is compassionate and gracious, slow to anger, abounding in love. He will not always accuse, nor will he harbor his anger forever; he does not treat us as our sins deserve or repay us according to our iniquities. For as high as the heavens are above the earth, so great is his love for those who fear him; as far as the east is from the west, so far has he removed our transgressions from us.—Psalm 103:8–12

JESUS MADE FORGIVENESS POSSIBLE

In the New Testament, we see God's desire to forgive expressed most clearly in the life and death of his Son. Jesus' sinless life and voluntary death atoned for the world's sins. He bore the ultimate judgment of sin so we don't have to. God forgives us because he loves us.

Therefore, my friends, I want you to know that through Jesus the forgiveness of sins is proclaimed to you. —Acts 13:38

But God demonstrates his own love for us in this: While we were still sinners, Christ died for us. —Romans 5:8

In him we have redemption through his blood, the forgiveness of sins, in accordance with the riches of God's grace. —Ephesians 1:7

For he has rescued us from the dominion of darkness and brought us into the kingdom of the Son he loves, in whom we have redemption, the forgiveness of sins. —Colossians 1:13–14

Forgiveness Is Available

When we place our faith in Jesus, we are declared free from divine condemnation and we stand forgiven of our sin. Forgiveness, not judgment, is the final word.

> "Forgiving love is a possibility only for those who know that they are not good, who feel themselves in need of divine mercy... [who] feel themselves as well as their fellow men convicted of sin by a holy God and know that the differences between the good man and the bad man are insignificant in his sight."
> —Reinhold Niebuhr

I, even I, am he who blots out your transgressions, for my own sake, and remembers your sins no more. —Isaiah 43:25

Therefore, there is now no condemnation for those who are in Christ Jesus, because through Christ Jesus the law of the Spirit of life has set you free from the law of sin and death. —Romans 8:1–2

Peter replied, "Repent and be baptized, every one of you, in the name of Jesus Christ for the forgiveness of your sins. And you will receive the gift of the Holy Spirit." —Acts 2:38

All the prophets testify about him that everyone who believes in him receives forgiveness of sins through his name. —Acts 10:43

Forgiveness Is Ongoing

Forgiveness is not a one-time thing. We need to continue to ask God for forgiveness for the wrongs we commit even after our initial acceptance of Jesus. In response to such generous forgiveness, God entrusts us with the responsibility and privilege to mirror his love by forgiving those who sin against us.

Ask for Forgiveness as Often as Needed

As believers, we are made right with God through Jesus, yet old patterns of sin may still resurface. Sinful habits in our lives hurt others and impede a growing, vibrant relationship with God. We continue to be in need of God's forgiveness daily, and are instructed to ask forgiveness from anyone whom we have wronged.

My dear children, I write this to you so that you will not sin. But if anybody does sin, we have one who speaks to the Father in our defense—Jesus Christ, the Righteous One. He is the atoning sacrifice for our sins, and not only for ours but also for the sins of the whole world. —1 John 2:1–2

Therefore confess your sins to each other and pray for each other so that you may be healed. —James 5:16a

> "God's forgiveness is unconditional; it comes from a heart that does not demand anything for itself, a heart that is completely empty of self-seeking. It is this divine forgiveness that I have to practice in my daily life. It calls me to keep stepping over all my arguments that say forgiveness is unwise, unhealthy, and impractical. It challenges me to step over all my needs for gratitude and compliments. Finally, it demands of me that I step over that wounded part of my heart that feels hurt and wronged and that wants to stay in control and put a few conditions between me and the one whom I am asked to forgive."
> —Henri Nouwen

> Therefore, if you are offering your gift at the altar and there remember that your brother or sister has something against you, leave your gift there in front of the altar. First go and be reconciled to them; then come and offer your gift.
> —Matthew 5:23–24

Forgive Others as Often as Needed

God forgives us time and time again, and he calls us to do the same. There is no limit to how often or how many times we are to forgive others. God wants his forgiven people to be forgivers.

> If your brother or sister sins against you, rebuke them, and if they repent, forgive them. Even if they sin against you seven times in a day, and seven times come back to you saying "I repent," you must forgive them.—Luke 17:3–4

> Bear with each other and forgive one another if any of you has a grievance against someone. Forgive as the Lord forgave you. And over all these virtues put on love, which binds them all together in perfect unity.—Colossians 3:13–14

Ten Stories of Forgiveness

The Story	Reference	Key Verse
Esau forgave his brother Jacob after years of estrangement.	Genesis 25:19–34; 27:1–28:9; 32:1–21; 33	But Esau ran to meet Jacob and embraced him; he threw his arms around his neck and kissed him. And they wept (33:4).
Joseph forgave his brothers who betrayed him.	Genesis 37–50	You intended to harm me, but God intended it for good to accomplish what is now being done, the saving of many lives (50:20).
David asked for God's forgiveness for his adultery with Bathsheba.	2 Samuel 11:1–12:25; Psalm 51	Wash away all my iniquity and cleanse me from my sin. For I know my transgressions, and my sin is always before me (Ps. 51:2–3).
Out of love, a forgiven woman anointed Jesus' feet.	Luke 7:36–50	Therefore, I tell you, her many sins have been forgiven—as her great love has shown. But whoever has been forgiven little loves little (v. 47).
The Parable of the Prodigal Son	Luke 15:11–32	But while he was still a long way off, his father saw him and was filled with compassion for him; he ran to his son, threw his arms around him and kissed him (v. 20).
A tax collector begged for mercy while a Pharisee failed to see his own need for forgiveness.	Luke 18:9–14	But the tax collector stood at a distance. He would not even look up to heaven, but beat his breast and said, "God, have mercy on me, a sinner" (v. 13).
Jesus did not condemn a woman caught in adultery.	John 8:1–11	"Then neither do I condemn you," Jesus declared. "Go now and leave your life of sin" (v. 11b).
Jesus asked the Father to forgive those who crucified him.	Luke 23:32–43	Father, forgive them, for they do not know what they are doing (v. 34).
Jesus restored Peter who had denied him three times.	John 13:31–38; 18:15–27; 21:15–19	Jesus asked [Peter] the third time, "Do you love me?" He said, "Lord, you know all things; you know that I love you." Jesus said, "Feed my sheep" (21:17).
Stephen asked God to forgive those who were stoning him.	Acts 7:54–60	Then he fell on his knees and cried out, "Lord, do not hold this sin against them." When he had said this, he fell asleep (v. 60).

The Parable of the Unmerciful Servant — Matthew 18:21–35

Peter's Question: "Lord, how many times shall I forgive my brother or sister who sins against me? Up to seven times?" (v. 21). Peter probably thought his "seven times" suggestion was generous since the rabbis of the day taught that one should forgive only up to three times.

Jesus' Answer: "I do not say to you, up to seven times, but up to seventy times seven" (v. 22 NASB). If Peter is fishing for a cap on forgiveness, Jesus gives him an impossible limit, which is really no limit at all. Jesus explains why we should forgive with this story about a king and a servant who owes him a lot of money.

The Merciful King	The Unmerciful Servant
Is owed a massive debt of 10,000 bags of gold (v. 24). (This is a way of saying it is an incalculable sum, like saying "billions of dollars.")	Is owed a small debt (v. 28). (The debt the servant owes the king is about 600,000 times more than what the servant is owed by a fellow servant.)
Is moved to compassion by the servant's plea in which the servant promises to pay a debt which is clearly impossible for him to do (v. 26).	Becomes violent and chokes the servant who owes him, and refuses to listen when the servant pleads for mercy (v. 29).
Cancels the entire debt and lets the servant walk away a debt-free man instead of being sold into slavery as the law allowed (v. 27).	Throws his fellow servant into a debtor's prison (v. 30).

When the unmerciful servant's actions are exposed:

- The fellow servants are outraged and report his conduct to the king (v. 31).
- This time the king is moved to anger, not compassion (v. 34).
- The servant is called "wicked" by the king (v. 32).
- The king renews the debt and hands the servant over to jailers (v. 34).

The Lesson: "This is how my heavenly Father will treat each of you unless you forgive your brother or sister from your heart" (v. 35). Our debt to God is enormous, and his forgiveness is extravagant. In light of this, Jesus allows no excuse for withholding forgiveness from others.

Why Forgive?

FORGIVENESS FREES THE FORGIVER

Anyone who has been wronged knows that forgiveness is not easy. However, resentment and bitterness are damaging. If anger is allowed to fester it will spill over into other areas of life, destroying relationships and leading to a path of revenge.

> Make every effort to live in peace with everyone and to be holy; without holiness no one will see the Lord. See to it that no one falls short of the grace of God and that no bitter root grows up to cause trouble and defile many.—Hebrews 12:14–15

> Finally, all of you, be like-minded, be sympathetic, love one another, be compassionate and humble. Do not repay evil with evil or insult with insult. On the contrary, repay evil with blessing, because to this you were called so that you may inherit a blessing.—1 Peter 3:8–9

FORGIVE SO THAT YOU WILL BE FORGIVEN

If we want to be forgiven ourselves, we must extend that same forgiveness to others, allowing forgiveness to triumph over the desire to extract retribution.

> For if you forgive other people when they sin against you, your heavenly Father will also forgive you. But if you do not forgive others their sins, your Father will not forgive your sins.—Matthew 6:14–15

"Resentment is like a glass of poison that a man drinks; then he sits down and waits for his enemy to die."
—Author Unknown

"Forgiveness is unlocking the door to set someone free and realizing you were the prisoner!" —Author Unknown

And when you stand praying, if you hold anything against anyone, forgive them, so that your Father in heaven may forgive you your sins.—Mark 11:25

Do not judge, and you will not be judged. Do not condemn, and you will not be condemned. Forgive, and you will be forgiven.—Luke 6:37

Speak and act as those who are going to be judged by the law that gives freedom, because judgment without mercy will be shown to anyone who has not been merciful. Mercy triumphs over judgment.—James 2:12–13

Healing Relationships Requires Forgiveness

Often the key to healing relationships begins with forgiveness. God is working in the world to reconcile fallen humans to himself through Christ, and he calls us to be ministers of reconciliation in this broken world.

> "Without forgiveness, there's no future."
> —Desmond Tutu, Anglican Archbishop who opposed apartheid (racial segregation) in South Africa

All this is from God, who reconciled us to himself through Christ and gave us the ministry of reconciliation: that God was reconciling the world to himself in Christ, not counting people's sins against them. And he has committed to us the message of reconciliation. We are therefore Christ's ambassadors, as though God were making his appeal through us. We implore you on Christ's behalf: Be reconciled to God.—2 Corinthians 5:18–20 (See also Romans 5:6–11)

Once you were alienated from God and were enemies in your minds because of your evil behavior. But now he has reconciled you by Christ's physical body through death to present you holy in his sight, without blemish and free from accusation—if you continue in your faith, established and firm, and do not move from the hope held out in the gospel.—Colossians 1:21–23a

If anyone has caused grief, he has not so much grieved me as he has grieved all of you, to some extent—not to put it too severely. The punishment inflicted on him by the majority is sufficient. Now instead, you ought to forgive and comfort him, so that he will not be overwhelmed by excessive sorrow. I urge you, therefore, to reaffirm your love for him.—2 Corinthians 2:5–8

Forgiveness is a Testimony of God's Love

The world tells us to "get even" or "make them sorry!" God says something quite different. God's love for all people motivates us to love others as well—even the most unlovable! When we forgive, we demonstrate God's love for a sinful world.

> "We forgive with no strings attached; that may require us to forgive repeatedly. When we do, we shock the world with God's power at work within us."
> —Rebecca Nichols Alonzo, who, at age seven, witnessed her mother's murder

But I tell you: Love your enemies and pray for those who persecute you, that you may be children of your Father in heaven. He causes his sun to rise on the evil and the good, and sends rain on the righteous and the unrighteous. If you love those who love you, what reward will you get? Are not even the tax collectors doing that? And if you greet only your own people, what are you doing more than others? Do not even pagans do that? Be perfect, therefore, as your heavenly Father is perfect.—Matthew 5:44–48

Does Forgiveness mean Reconciliation?

A common reason people withhold forgiveness is that they think that forgiveness requires immediate and total reconciliation with the offender. People who have been hurt ask: If I forgive, does that mean I have to put myself back in the abusive situation? Must I force myself to be best friends again with the person who wronged me? Am I required to give the betrayer my full trust?

No, forgiveness is not the same as reconciliation. Forgiveness involves letting go of vengeance and hatred for being wronged. Reconciliation can be described as "restoration to harmony in relationship." One person can forgive, but it takes two people to restore a broken relationship. Forgiveness alone neither guarantees nor demands reconciliation. Often much more is needed before reconciliation can (or should) take place, for example: repentance, restitution of the wrong, gaining back trust, or evidence of genuine change. If forgiveness is taken to mean "going back" to the offender as if nothing ever happened, then people will end up only with a cheap imitation of reconciliation, far unlike the genuine harmony in a restored relationship described in Scripture (1 Thess. 5:11; Rom. 12:10).

> **DEALING WITH ANGER**
>
> Sometimes anger and bitterness prevent us from experiencing the freedom of forgiveness. The following steps can help us break free from the chains of anger.
>
> 1. Acknowledge God's complete forgiveness by grace (Col. 1:13–14).
>   *I am forgiven by the grace of God!*
> 2. Be willing to confess your bitterness and resentment to God (Ps. 51:10–12).
>   *God, forgive my bitter attitudes and my anger toward _____.*
> 3. Recognize that your anger is a violation of God's Word (Matt. 6:14–15) and choose to release the anger (Heb. 12:14–15).
>   *With the Holy Spirit's help, I choose to lay down this anger. I release my desire for revenge on _____.*
> 4. Follow the Holy Spirit's leading as to whether you need to speak to the person you need to forgive (James 2:12–13).
>   *God, I ask for your Spirit to guide me into what I should do next.*
>
> Go through these steps repeatedly until words become experience.

How to Forgive

PRACTICE FORGIVENESS BEFORE IT'S NEEDED

A runner who finishes a marathon has gotten into the habit of running long before the start of the race. In the same way, if we want to be able to forgive the big stuff, we have to get into the habit of forgiving the small stuff. Forgiveness, like other virtues, takes daily cultivation.

> "That is the whole lesson: the sins of others you see, but your own sin you fail to see. In repentance, recognize God's mercy toward you; in this way alone will you be able to forgive."
>
> —Dietrich Bonhoeffer, German pastor and theologian who was imprisoned and executed for his opposition to Nazism

Get rid of all bitterness, rage and anger, brawling and slander, along with every form of malice. Be kind and compassionate to one another, forgiving each other, just as in Christ God forgave you.—Ephesians 4:31–32

Above all, love each other deeply, because love covers over a multitude of sins. —1 Peter 4:8

EXAMINE YOUR OWN SIN

Recognizing our own need for God's forgiveness enables us to see our offender's need for mercy. The practice of the Lord's Supper (Communion) reminds us that we are all flawed and sinful people in need of forgiveness. Self-righteousness will breed an unforgiving heart, but through humility we can learn to extend mercy to others.

He who conceals their sins does not prosper, but the one who confesses and renounces them finds mercy.—Proverbs 28:13

But who can discern their own errors? Forgive my hidden faults.—Psalm 19:12

Then he took the cup, gave thanks and offered it to them, saying, "Drink from it, all of you. This is my blood of the covenant, which is poured out for many for the forgiveness of sins."—Matthew 26:27–28

GIVE UP YOUR RIGHT TO REVENGE

Anger is a natural response when we are harmed. But God's Word says to be careful that our anger does not result in taking revenge. We should not add sin upon sin, but leave the situation where it belongs—in God's hands. (See also 1 Thess. 5:15)

Do not say, "I'll pay you back for this wrong!" Wait for the LORD, and he will avenge you.—Proverbs 20:22

In your anger do not sin: Do not let the sun go down while you are still angry, and do not give the devil a foothold. —Ephesians 4:26–27

Bless those who persecute you; bless and do not curse.... Do not repay anyone evil for evil. Be careful to do what is right in the eyes of everyone. If it is possible, as far as it depends on you, live at peace with everyone. Do not take revenge, my friends, but leave room for God's wrath, for it is written: "It is mine to avenge; I will repay," says the Lord. On the contrary: "If your enemy is hungry, feed him; if he is thirsty, give him something to drink. In doing this, you will heap burning coals on his head." Do not be overcome by evil, but overcome evil with good.—Romans 12:14–21

Loving Your Enemies

Loving your "enemies" is to see them as fellow human beings who are loved by God and in need of his grace; but it is not to tolerate their abuse or invite them to hurt you again. The so-called "love" that ignores or allows such damaging sins is not really love at all.

Learn from Veteran Forgivers

There is no cookie-cutter way to forgive. Every situation is different. For instance, how to go about forgiving a close friend who has betrayed you will be different from how to forgive an unknown hit-and-run driver. We can gain wisdom in knowing how to deal with particular situations by taking note of Christians who have already walked the path of forgiveness. Their examples and guidance can give us a long-term view beyond the initial feelings of anger and pain.

> *Join together in following my example, brothers and sisters, and just as you have us as a model, keep your eyes on those who live as we do.*—Philippians 3:17

> *Brothers and sisters, as an example of patience in the face of suffering, take the prophets who spoke in the name of the Lord. As you know, we consider blessed those who have persevered. You have heard of Job's perseverance and have seen what the Lord finally brought about. The Lord is full of compassion and mercy.*—James 5:10–11

Let Forgiveness Take Time

The apostle Paul compares the Christian life to a race that we have not yet finished. This side of heaven we may not be able to forgive to the extent that we want to because we are still imperfect people in an imperfect world. What we are called to do is to continue moving forward and not to give up.

> *Not that I have already obtained all this, or have already arrived at my goal, but I press on to take hold of that for which Christ Jesus took hold of me. Brothers and sisters, I do not consider myself yet to have taken hold of it. But one thing I do: Forgetting what is behind and straining toward what is ahead, I press on toward the goal to win the prize for which God has called me heavenward in Christ Jesus. All of us who are mature should take such a view of things. And if on some point you think differently, that too God will make clear to you. Only let us live up to what we have already attained.*—Philippians 3:12–16

Pray for Your Enemies

It might sound cliché to say "just pray about it," but there is nothing trite about praying for someone who has wronged you. Such prayers can have a powerful effect on the person praying. By the power of God's Spirit in us, through prayer, God can miraculously change our hatred into love.

> *But I tell you: Love your enemies and pray for those who persecute you, that you may be children of your Father in heaven.*—Matthew 5:44–45a

> *In the same way, the Spirit helps us in our weakness. We do not know what we ought to pray for, but the Spirit himself intercedes for us through wordless groans.*—Romans 8:26

> *But [the Lord] said to me, "My grace is sufficient for you, for my power is made perfect in weakness." ... For when I am weak, then I am strong.*—2 Corinthians 12:9–10

Trust in God's Goodness

Placing a painful situation in God's hands is only possible if we allow ourselves to trust that God knows best. When we give it over to God, we will be surprised at the good he will bring out of any bad situation. The best example of God's goodness transcending evil is that of Jesus' death on the cross. What appeared to many to be the pointless crucifixion of an innocent man turned out to be the means whereby God provided forgiveness of sins for the world. Jesus trusted the Father that the way of forgiveness would be the best path.

> *To this you were called, because Christ suffered for you, leaving you an example, that you should follow in his steps. "He committed no sin, and no deceit was found in his mouth." When they hurled their insults at him, he did not retaliate; when he suffered, he made no threats. Instead, he entrusted himself to him who judges justly. "He himself bore our sins" in his body on the cross, so that we might die to sins and live for righteousness; "by his wounds you have been healed."*—1 Peter 2:21–24

"Forgiveness stretches out over time, but you have to start out with the will to forgive. But the bitterness may reenter your mind from time to time, and then you have to think about forgiveness again."

—An Amish mother whose daughter was killed when a gunman opened fire in a schoolhouse

"When we are powerless to do a thing, it is a great joy that we can come and step inside the ability of Jesus."

—Corrie ten Boom, concentration camp survivor

WHAT THE BIBLE SAYS ABOUT MONEY

Money is a big thing in the world's eye, but from God's view it's a small thing. It's what we *do* with this small thing that makes a big, eternal difference. God cares about our faithfulness with what he has entrusted to us—whether it's a lot or a little. Jesus praised the poor widow who gave generously to God out of her meager income (Mark 12:41–44). Her outward act of exceeding faithfulness mirrored an inward spiritual reality of a heart set on the things of God.

> *"Small things are small things, but faithfulness with a small thing is a big thing."*
> —Hudson Taylor, Missionary to China

Jesus tells us to invest in the kingdom of God so that we will find genuine treasures far better than the fleeting, insignificant riches of this world (Matthew 6:19–21). As we remain faithful to God in our use of money, he will prove faithful to care for us through all life's financial ups and downs. Jesus reassures us with these words: "Seek first [God's] kingdom and his righteousness, and all these things will be given to you as well" (Matthew 6:33).

ATTITUDES TOWARD MONEY

People may have different attitudes toward money based on personal experience or how they were raised. But whatever one's feelings are about money and possessions, they need to be evaluated in light of what the Bible says. Looking at the diagram below, how do you view money in your life?

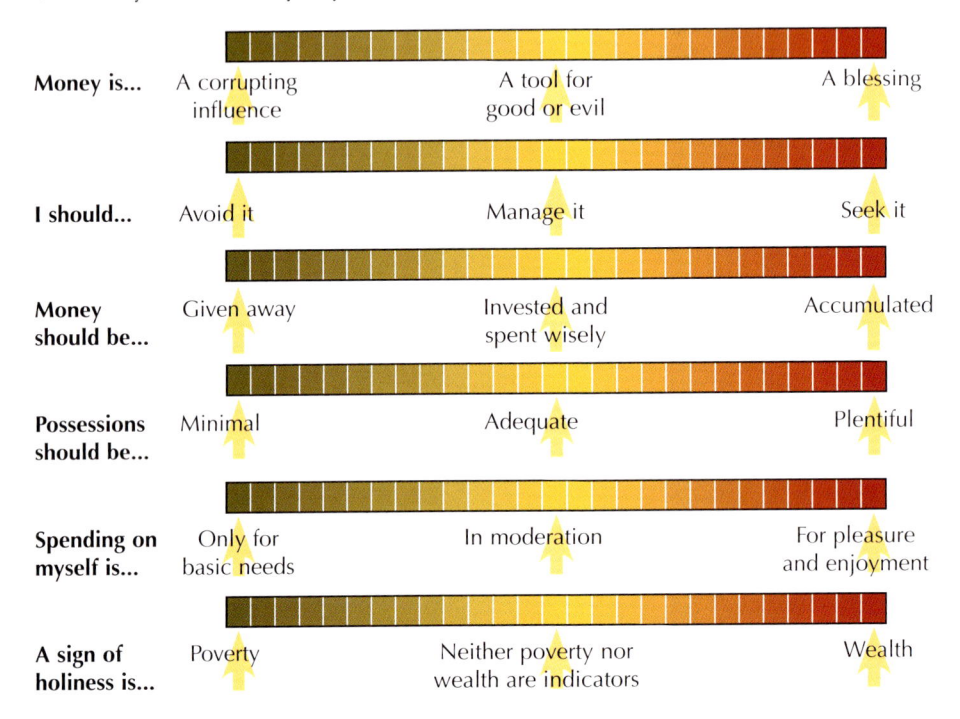

Money is...	A corrupting influence	A tool for good or evil	A blessing
I should...	Avoid it	Manage it	Seek it
Money should be...	Given away	Invested and spent wisely	Accumulated
Possessions should be...	Minimal	Adequate	Plentiful
Spending on myself is...	Only for basic needs	In moderation	For pleasure and enjoyment
A sign of holiness is...	Poverty	Neither poverty nor wealth are indicators	Wealth

FOR THE GLORY OF GOD

First Corinthians 10:31 says, "So whether you eat or drink or whatever you do, do it all for the glory of God." The use of money can be for the glory of God.

God Is the True Owner of Our Money.

In order to use money in ways that glorify God, it's important to first understand whose money it really is. God is the Creator and Owner of all things—including all money, property, and investments.

The earth is the LORD's and everything in it. —PSALM 24:1

Yours, O Lord, is the greatness and the power and the glory and the majesty and the splendor, for everything in heaven and earth is yours. Yours, O Lord, is the kingdom; you are exalted as head over all. —1 Chronicles 29:11

"The silver is mine and the gold is mine," declares the Lord Almighty. —Haggai 2:8

Faithfulness Will Be Rewarded.

God is the Owner, but we are his managers whom he has entrusted with the things of this world. We are accountable to the true Owner to be faithful in our financial transactions.

> *"The everyday choices I make regarding money will influence the very course of eternity."*
> —Randy Alcorn, Christian author

His master replied, "Well done, good and faithful servant! You have been faithful with a few things; I will put you in charge of many things. Come and share your master's happiness!" —Matthew 25:23

Honor the Lord with your wealth, with the firstfruits of all your crops; then your barns will be filled to overflowing, and your vats will brim over with new wine. —Proverbs 3:9–10

Give generously to [the needy] and do so without a grudging heart; then because of this the Lord your God will bless you in all your work and in everything you put your hand to. —Deuteronomy 15:10

Whoever can be trusted with very little can also be trusted with much, and whoever is dishonest with very little will also be dishonest with much. So if you have not been trustworthy in handling worldly wealth, who will trust you with true riches? And if you have not been trustworthy with someone else's property, who will give you property of your own? —Luke 16:9–12

Then the King will say to those on his right, "Come, you who are blessed by my Father; take your inheritance, the kingdom prepared for you since the creation of the world. For I was hungry and you gave me something to eat, I was thirsty and you gave me something to drink, I was a stranger and you invited me in, I needed clothes and you clothed me, I was sick and you looked after me, I was in prison and you came to visit me." —Matthew 25:34–36

God's Agenda Matters More than Ours.

Any money God has entrusted to us has the potential to be used for our selfish ends or for God's agenda. Evangelist Billy Graham said, "Give me five minutes with a person's checkbook, and I will tell you where their heart is." If you want your heart to be set on the things of God, get into the habit of placing your money into things God cares about.

Do not store up for yourselves treasures on earth, where moth and rust destroy, and where thieves break in and steal. But store up for yourselves treasures in heaven, where moth and rust do not destroy, and where thieves do not break in and steal. For where your treasure is, there your heart will be also. —Matthew 6:19–21

But Zacchaeus stood up and said to the Lord, "Look, Lord! Here and now I give half of my possessions to the poor, and if I have cheated anybody out of anything, I will pay back four times the amount." Jesus said to him, "Today salvation has come to this house, because this man, too, is a son of Abraham. For the Son of Man came to seek and to save what was lost." —Luke 19:8–9

From everyone who has been given much, much will be demanded; and from the one who has been entrusted with much, much more will be asked. —Luke 12:48b

BLESSINGS FROM GOD

God is the ultimate Owner of all things, but he is no miser. The Bible shows him to be a generous Father who gives blessings to his children because he loves them.

God Blesses His Children.

God gave his chosen people in the Old Testament a land of affluence. Abundance of wealth is portrayed (particularly in the Old Testament) as a blessing from God and considered to be evidence of God's favor.

You open your hands and satisfy the desires of every living thing. —Psalm 145:16

For the Lord your God will bless you in all your harvest and in all the work of your hands, and your joy will be complete. —Deuteronomy 16:15

If you, then, though you are evil, know how to give good gifts to your children, how much more will your Father in heaven give good gifts to those who ask him! —Matthew 7:11

God Gives Generously So We Can Give Generously.

Our Father's gifts to us are not for hoarding, but for giving as he gives.

Whoever sows sparingly will also reap sparingly, and whoever sows generously will also reap generously. Each man should give what he has decided in his heart to give, not reluctantly or under compulsion, for God loves a cheerful giver. And God is able to make all grace abound to you, so that in all things at all times, having all that you need, you will abound in every good work.... You will be made rich in every way so that you can be generous on every occasion, and through us your generosity will result in thanksgiving to God. —2 Corinthians 9:6–11

Share with God's people who are in need. Practice hospitality. —Romans 12:13

Trusting God Is at the Center.

At the core of receiving blessing and giving back generously is our trust in God. Trust is an expression of faith that God will come through for us. It may not be in the way we expect, but he will work all things together for good because of his abundant love.

I am not saying this because I am in need, for I have learned to be content whatever the circumstances. I know what it is to be in need, and I know what it is to have plenty. I have learned the secret of being content in any and every situation, whether well fed or hungry, whether living in plenty or in want. I can do everything through him who gives me strength.... And my God will meet all your needs according to his glorious riches in Christ Jesus. —Philippians 4:11–13, 19

THE DANGER OF MONEY

Money can be a blessing used to honor God, but allowing it to become an idol corrupts our lives and harms our walk with God. When we covet and cling to money instead of using money to serve God, we begin to serve money itself.

Serving Money Takes Us Away from God.

Jesus personified money as a rival master to our real Master. Like the rich young man who did not follow Jesus because it meant giving up his money, serving "master Money" will tear us away from allegiance to God (Matthew 19:16-22).

Still others, like seed sown among thorns, hear the word; but the worries of this life, the deceitfulness of wealth and the desires for other things come in and choke the word, making it unfruitful. —Mark 4:18–19

No one can serve two masters. Either he will hate the one and love the other, or he will be devoted to the one and despise the other. You cannot serve both God and Money. —Matthew 6:24

Then Jesus said to his disciples, "I tell you the truth, it is hard for a rich man to enter the kingdom of heaven. Again I tell you, it is easier for a camel to go through the eye of a needle than for a rich man to enter the kingdom of God." —Matthew 19:23–24

The Love of Money Leads to Destruction.

People who love money will do anything to get it. The grip that money can have over one's life can push one to resort to devious and exploitive means.

You want something but don't get it. You kill and covet, but you cannot have what you want. You quarrel and fight. You do not have, because you do not ask God. When you ask, you do not receive, because you ask with wrong motives, that you may spend what you get on your pleasures. —James 4:2–3

People who want to get rich fall into temptation and a trap and into many foolish and harmful desires that plunge men into ruin and destruction. For the love of money is a root of all kinds of evil. Some people, eager for money, have wandered from the faith and pierced themselves with many griefs. —1 Timothy 6:9–10

By your great skill in trading you have increased your wealth, and because of your wealth your heart has grown proud. —Ezekiel 28:5

Trust in God, Not Money.

Money's false promises are fleeting and ultimately unsatisfying. God's promises are eternal and always trustworthy.

Keep your lives free from the love of money and be content with what you have, because God has said, "Never will I leave you; never will I forsake you." —Hebrews 13:5

Money's False Promises	The Bible's Promises
SECURITY	Command those who are rich in this present world not to be arrogant nor to put their hope in wealth, which is so uncertain, but to put their hope in God, who richly provides us with everything for our enjoyment. —1 Timothy 6:17
POWER	So do not fear, for I am with you; do not be dismayed, for I am your God. I will strengthen you and help you; I will uphold you with my righteous right hand.... For I am the Lord, your God, who takes hold of your right hand and says to you, Do not fear; I will help you. —Isaiah 41:10, 13
PRIVILEGE AND SOCIAL STANDING	People will come from east and west and north and south, and will take their places at the feast in the kingdom of God. Indeed there are those who are last who will be first, and first who will be last. —Luke 13:29–30
SUCCESS	Has not God chosen those who are poor in the eyes of the world to be rich in faith and to inherit the kingdom he promised those who love him? —James 2:5
LOVE AND ATTENTION	The Lord your God is with you, he is mighty to save. He will take great delight in you, he will quiet you with his love, he will rejoice over you with singing. —Zephaniah 3:17
PEACE OF MIND	Come to me, all you who are weary and burdened, and I will give you rest. —Matthew 11:28
FREEDOM FROM CONSEQUENCES	Wealth is worthless in the day of wrath, but righteousness delivers from death. —Proverbs 11:4
HAPPINESS	Delight yourself in the Lord and he will give you the desires of your heart. —Psalm 37:4

WHY GIVE?

Giving Brings Freedom.

When we release our grip on money, we break free from the grip money has on our lives. Giving keeps us from spiraling down the destructive path of greed. If you want to be free from materialism and the love of money, start by giving.

Be on your guard against all kinds of greed; a man's life does not consist in the abundance of his possessions. —Luke 12:15

Whoever loves money never has money enough; whoever loves wealth is never satisfied with his income. —Ecclesiastes 5:10

What good will it be for a man if he gains the whole world, yet forfeits his soul? Or what can a man give in exchange for his soul? —Matthew 16:26

Giving Is Our Worshipful Obligation.

In the act of giving we worship God by acknowledging that it is ultimately God's money and it is his right to instruct us how to use it. Theologian Richard Foster suggests that rather than approaching the question of giving as "How much of my money should I give God?" we should ask, "How much of God's money should I keep for myself?"

"Will a man rob God? Yet you rob me. But you ask, 'How do we rob you?' In tithes and offerings. You are under a curse—the whole nation of you—because you are robbing me. Bring the whole tithe into the storehouse, that there may be food in my house. Test me in this," says the Lord Almighty, "and see if I will not throw open the floodgates of heaven and pour out so much blessing that you will not have room enough for it." —Malachi 3:8–10

Then he will say to those on his left, "Depart from me, you who are cursed, into the eternal fire.... For I was hungry and you gave me nothing to eat, I was thirsty and you gave me nothing to drink, I was a stranger and you did not invite me in, I needed clothes and you did not clothe me, I was sick and in prison and you did not look after me." They also will answer, "Lord, when did we see you hungry or thirsty or a stranger or needing clothes or sick or in prison, and did not help you?" He will reply, "I tell you the truth, whatever you did not do for one of the least of these, you did not do for me." Then they will go away to eternal punishment, but the righteous to eternal life. —Matthew 25:41–46

And do not forget to do good and to share with others, for with such sacrifices God is pleased. —Hebrews 13:16

Giving Makes Us Trust God.

Stockpiling money may be a sign of trusting in money rather than God. Giving helps focus one's eyes back on God, seeking him as the first priority and relying on him to supply our needs.

And why do you worry about clothes? See how the lilies of the field grow. They do not labor or spin. Yet I tell you that not even Solomon in all his splendor was dressed like one of these. If that is how God clothes the grass of the field, which is here today and tomorrow is thrown into the fire, will he not much more clothe you, O you of little faith? So do not worry, saying, "What shall we eat?" or "What shall we drink?" or "What shall we wear?" For the pagans run after all these things, and your heavenly Father knows that you need them. But seek first his kingdom and his righteousness, and all these things will be given to you as well. Therefore do not worry about tomorrow, for tomorrow will worry about itself. Each day has enough trouble of its own. —Matthew 6:28–34

Giving Is a Fundamental Part of Following Jesus.

Following Jesus requires earthly sacrifice for heavenly gain. Christian author Randy Alcorn said, "The more holdings we have on earth, the more likely we are to forget that we're citizens of another world … and our inheritance lies there, not here."

And anyone who does not carry his cross and follow me cannot be my disciple.… Any of you who does not give up everything he has cannot be my disciple. —Luke 14:27, 33

Give to everyone who asks you, and if anyone takes what belongs to you, do not demand it back. Do to others as you would have them do to you. —Luke 6:29b–31

I tell you the truth, at the renewal of all things, when the Son of Man sits on his glorious throne, you who have followed me will also sit on twelve thrones, judging the twelve tribes of Israel. And everyone who has left houses or brothers or sisters or father or mother or children or fields for my sake will receive a hundred times as much and will inherit eternal life. —Matthew 19:28–29

Giving is a Privilege.

Whether we have been blessed with much or with little, we can be part of God's plan. Financial giving is one of many ways to do the Lord's work. As God has blessed you, you can bless others.

And now, brothers, we want you to know about the grace that God has given the Macedonian churches. Out of the most severe trial, their overflowing joy and their extreme poverty welled up in rich generosity. For I testify that they gave as much as they were able, and even beyond their ability. Entirely on their own, they urgently pleaded with us for the privilege of sharing in this service to the saints. —2 Corinthians 8:1–4

We have different gifts, according to the grace given us. If a man's gift is prophesying, let him use it in proportion to his faith. If it is serving, let him serve; if it is teaching, let him teach; if it is encouraging, let him encourage; if it is contributing to the needs of others, let him give generously. —Romans 12:6–8a

All the believers were one in heart and mind. No one claimed that any of his possessions was his own, but they shared everything they had.… There were no needy persons among them. For from time to time those who owned lands or houses sold them, brought the money from the sales and put it at the apostles' feet, and it was distributed to anyone as he had need. —Acts 4:32–35

Giving Comes from Love

Missionary Amy Carmichael said, "You can give without loving, but you cannot love without giving." God gave generously to us out of his great love, and we give generously out of our love for others.

This is how we know what love is: Jesus Christ laid down his life for us. And we ought to lay down our lives for our brothers. If anyone has material possessions and sees his brother in need but has no pity on him, how can the love of God be in him? Dear children, let us not love with words or tongue but with actions and in truth. —1 John 3:16–18

Suppose a brother or sister is without clothes and daily food. If one of you says to him, "Go, I wish you well; keep warm and well fed," but does nothing about his physical needs, what good is it? In the same way, faith by itself, if it is not accompanied by action, is dead. —James 2:15–17

PROVERBS ABOUT MONEY

Proverb	Scripture
BRIBERY	A greedy man brings trouble to his family, but he who hates bribes will live. —Proverbs 15:27
	A wicked man accepts a bribe in secret to pervert the course of justice. —Proverbs 17:23
DEBT	Do not be a man who strikes hands in pledge or puts up security for debts; if you lack the means to pay, your very bed will be snatched from under you. —Proverbs 22:26–27
	The rich rule over the poor, and the borrower is servant to the lender. —Proverbs 22:7
DILIGENCE	Lazy hands make a man poor, but diligent hands bring wealth. He who gathers crops in summer is a wise son, but he who sleeps during harvest is a disgraceful son. —Proverbs 10:4–5
ENVY	A heart at peace gives life to the body, but envy rots the bones. —Proverbs 14:30
FRAUD	Food gained by fraud tastes sweet to a man, but he ends up with a mouth full of gravel. —Proverbs 20:17
GENEROSITY	He who is kind to the poor lends to the Lord, and he will reward him for what he has done. —Proverbs 19:17
	A generous man will himself be blessed, for he shares his food with the poor. —Proverbs 22:9
HOARDING GOODS	People curse the man who hoards grain, but blessing crowns him who is willing to sell. —Proverbs 11:26
HONESTY IN BUSINESS	The wicked man earns deceptive wages, but he who sows righteousness reaps a sure reward. —Proverbs 11:18
	A fortune made by a lying tongue is a fleeting vapor and a deadly snare. —Proverbs 21:6
MODERATION	Do not wear yourself out to get rich; have the wisdom to show restraint. —Proverbs 23:4
PATIENCE	Dishonest money dwindles away, but he who gathers money little by little makes it grow. —Proverbs 13:11
REPUTATION	A good name is more desirable than great riches; to be esteemed is better than silver or gold. —Proverbs 22:1
STINGINESS	A stingy man is eager to get rich and is unaware that poverty awaits him. —Proverbs 28:22
SUCCESS	Humility and the fear of the Lord bring wealth and honor and life. —Proverbs 22:4
	Whoever trusts in his riches will fall, but the righteous will thrive like a green leaf. —Proverbs 11:28
TRUE WEALTH	How much better to get wisdom than gold, to choose understanding rather than silver! —Proverbs 16:16
WORK	He who works his land will have abundant food, but he who chases fantasies lacks judgment. —Proverbs 12:11

HOW TO HONOR GOD WITH MONEY

1. Ask God to help you depend on him instead of money.

> You say, "I am rich; I have acquired wealth and do not need a thing." But you do not realize that you are wretched, pitiful, poor, blind and naked. I counsel you to buy from me gold refined in the fire, so you can become rich.... Those whom I love I rebuke and discipline. So be earnest, and repent. Here I am! I stand at the door and knock. If anyone hears my voice and opens the door, I will come in and eat with him, and he with me. To him who overcomes, I will give the right to sit with me on my throne. —Revelation 3:17–21a

> But remember the Lord your God, for it is he who gives you the ability to produce wealth. —Deuteronomy 8:18a

2. Stay focused on what matters most.

Better a little with the fear of the Lord than great wealth with turmoil. Better a meal of vegetables where there is love than a fattened calf with hatred. —Proverbs 15:16–17

Jesus replied: "Love the Lord your God with all your heart and with all your soul and with all your mind. This is the first and greatest commandment. And the second is like it: Love your neighbor as yourself." —Matthew 22:37–39

3. Remember that God is always faithful.

He who did not spare his own Son, but gave him up for us all—how will he not also, along with him, graciously give us all things? —Romans 8:32

"For I know the plans I have for you," declares the Lord, "plans to prosper you and not to harm you, plans to give you hope and a future." —Jeremiah 29:11

4. Ask God for your needs.

Give me neither poverty nor riches, but give me only my daily bread. Otherwise, I may have too much and disown you and say, "Who is the Lord?" Or I may become poor and steal, and so dishonor the name of my God. —Proverbs 30:8–9

5. Ask for wisdom in financial matters.

If any of you lacks wisdom, he should ask God, who gives generously to all without finding fault, and it will be given to him. —James 1:5

6. Handle money honestly and responsibly.

Give everyone what you owe him: If you owe taxes, pay taxes; if revenue, then revenue; if respect, then respect; if honor, then honor. —Romans 13:7

7. Put your money to work for God's purposes.

Sell your possessions and give to the poor. Provide purses for yourselves that will not wear out, a treasure in heaven that will not be exhausted, where no thief comes near and no moth destroys. —Luke 12:33

8. Be ready to give freely.

If there is a poor man among your brothers in any of the towns of the land that the Lord your God is giving you, do not be hardhearted or tightfisted toward your poor brother. —Deuteronomy 15:7

9. Practice being content with what you have.

But godliness with contentment is great gain. For we brought nothing into the world, and we can take nothing out of it. But if we have food and clothing, we will be content with that. —1 Timothy 6:7–8

I have not coveted anyone's silver or gold or clothing. You yourselves know that these hands of mine have supplied my own needs and the needs of my companions. In everything I did, I showed you that by this kind of hard work we must help the weak, remembering the words the Lord Jesus himself said: "It is more blessed to give than to receive." —Acts 20:33–35

10. Praise God for his blessings!

Praise the Lord. Blessed is the man who fears the Lord, who finds great delight in his commands. His children will be mighty in the land; the generation of the upright will be blessed. Wealth and riches are in his house, and his righteousness endures forever. Even in darkness light dawns for the upright, for the gracious and compassionate and righteous man. Good will come to him who is generous and lends freely, who conducts his affairs with justice. —Psalm 112:1-5

DO'S AND DON'TS WITH MONEY

Don't	Do
Don't love it! Luke 16:13	**Love the Lord.** Deuteronomy 6:5
Don't think it will last. Jeremiah 17:11	**Only the things of God will last.** Matthew 19:21
Don't think it can save you. Psalm 37:16–17	**Remember that only God can save you.** Psalm 27:1
Don't serve it. Matthew 6:24	**Serve the Lord.** 1 Peter 5:2; Mark 12:41–44
Don't envy others who have it. Exodus 20:17	**Be content with what you have.** Luke 3:14
Don't hoard it. James 5:3–6	**Remember that God provides.** Job 1:20–21; James 4:13–15
Don't be foolish with it. Proverbs 17:16	**Use it wisely.** Proverbs 31:10–31
Don't think it can compensate for turmoil. Proverbs 15:16–17	**Find peace in God.** Romans 15:13
Don't rely on it. Psalm 62:10	**Rely on the Lord.** Proverbs 18:10–11
Don't think it can buy God's blessings. Acts 8:9–24	**Find blessings by living for God.** 2 Corinthians 6:10
Don't use it for fraud. Micah 2:2	**Repay your debts with it.** Psalm 37:21
Don't oppress people to get it. Proverbs 22:16; Amos 2:6–7	**Work to get it.** 2 Thessalonians 3:9–11
Don't steal it. Titus 2:9–10; Exodus 20:15	**Handle it justly.** Leviticus 25:14; Psalm 112:5
Don't give special honor to those who have it. James 2:2–6	**Give it to those in need.** Matthew 5:41–42
Don't use it dishonestly. Proverbs 13:11	**Be trustworthy with it.** Proverbs 11:1
Don't use it for evil. Ezekiel 8:12–13	**Honor God with it.** Proverbs 3:9–10
Don't extort it. Ezekiel 22:29	**Earn it.** Proverbs 13:4
Don't be greedy for it. Luke 12:15	**Give it intentionally.** 1 Corinthians 16:2
Don't worry about it. Matthew 6:34	**Know that God will take care of you.** Proverbs 15:25

What the Bible Says About Prayer

PRAYER IS AN IMPORTANT PART OF HOW WE RELATE TO GOD. Many religions recognize the need for prayer, but what does the Bible say about it? Does God hear all our prayers? Do some people get special access to God? Is there a prayer technique that will get you what you want? God's Word answers these questions, and also gives us guidance as we struggle with tougher questions such as, Why didn't God answer my prayer? Why should I pray at all?

Three Things to Know Before You Pray

1. **GOD CARES FOR YOU.** Because of God's unfailing love for us, we can bring anything and everything in our hearts to God in prayer. Prayer is a safe place of trust.

   Cast all your anxiety on him because he cares for you.—1 Peter 5:7

   I trust in God's unfailing love for ever and ever.—Psalm 52:8

2. **GOD HEARS YOUR PRAYERS.** God Almighty is listening. Because we are his beloved children, no prayer is too small for him to hear.

   He will respond to the prayer of the destitute; he will not despise their plea.—Psalm 102:17

   How gracious he will be when you cry for help! As soon as he hears, he will answer you.—Isaiah 30:19

   For the eyes of the Lord are on the righteous and his ears are attentive to their prayer.—1 Peter 3:12a

3. **YOU CAN PRAY WITH CONFIDENCE.** You don't have to be a prayer giant to come confidently to God in prayer. As believers, we can all equally approach God because of our unique standing in Jesus.

   In him [Jesus] and through faith in him we may approach God with freedom and confidence.—Ephesians 3:12

   Let us then approach God's throne of grace with confidence, so that we may receive mercy and find grace to help us in our time of need.—Hebrews 4:16

What Is Prayer?

At its base, prayer is talking with God. We can pray alone or in a group; silently or aloud; using a written prayer or a spontaneous one. But to be in prayer is more than just speaking words. Scripture portrays a life of continual prayer, meaning a kind of openness toward God in all we do (1 Thess. 5:17). Our entire lives should be prayers to God, exhibiting the praise and love of our Creator and Savior.

Why Pray?

PRAYER IS IMPORTANT. God's Word instructs believers to make prayer a high priority. God wants to hear from his children.

Devote yourselves to prayer.—Colossians 4:2

I urge, then, first of all, that petitions, prayers, intercession and thanksgiving be made for all people.—1 Timothy 2:1 (Also see verse 8)

> Prayer should not be regarded "as a duty which must be performed, but rather as a privilege to be enjoyed, a rare delight that is always revealing some new beauty."—E. M. Bounds

PRAYER DRAWS US CLOSE TO GOD. In prayer, we worship, confess our sins, bring our requests to God, and wait and listen for him to speak. In short, we enter deeply and directly into relationship with God. Through communion with God, our hearts and minds will be changed to be more like our Lord, and we will grow to know his perfect will for our lives.

> "Prayer is a strong wall and fortress of the church; it is a goodly Christian weapon."
> —Martin Luther

> *Do not conform to the pattern of this world, but be transformed by the renewing of your mind. Then you will be able to test and approve what God's will is—his good, pleasing and perfect will.—Romans 12:2*

> *So all of us who have had that veil removed can see and reflect the glory of the Lord. And the Lord—who is the Spirit—makes us more and more like him as we are changed into his glorious image.—2 Corinthians 3:18 NLT*

PRAYER IS POWERFUL. God not only hears our prayers, but he is acting on them. Our prayer requests bring about real change in the world and in the lives of the people we pray for.

> *Ask and it will be given to you; seek and you will find; knock and the door will be opened to you. For everyone who asks receives; the one who seeks finds; and to the one who knocks, the door will be opened.—Matthew 7:7–8*

> *If you believe, you will receive whatever you ask for in prayer.—Matthew 21:22 (Mark 11:24; John 15:7, 16)*

> *And the prayer offered in faith will make the sick person well....*
> *The prayer of a righteous person is powerful and effective.—James 5:15–1*

> *Dear friends, if our hearts do not condemn us, we have confidence before God and receive from him anything we ask, because we keep his commands and do what pleases him.—1 John 3:21–22*

> Prayer as a relationship is probably your best indication about the health of your love relationship with God. If your prayer life has been slack, your love relationship has grown cold."—John Piper

PRAYER BRINGS PEACE. When we are at our wit's end, Scripture tells us to turn all those anxieties over to God who will give us peace of mind.

> *Do not be anxious about anything, but in every situation, by prayer and petition, with thanksgiving, present your requests to God. And the peace of God, which transcends all understanding, will guard your hearts and your minds in Christ Jesus.—Philippians 4:6–7*

PRAYER PROTECTS US. We have Almighty God on our side! Jesus showed believers the importance of praying for protection and deliverance. (Also see 2 Cor. 10:4; Eph. 6:10–18.)

> *Jesus' prayer for his disciples: My prayer is not that you take them out of the world but that you protect them from the evil one.—John 17:15*

> *The Lord's Prayer: And lead us not into temptation, but deliver us from the evil one.—Matthew 6:13*

> *Jesus warns his disciples: Be always on the watch, and pray that you may be able to escape all that is about to happen, and that you may be able to stand before the Son of Man.—Luke 21:36*

The Prayers of Jesus

Jesus took time to pray to God the Father. Jesus "often withdrew to lonely places and prayed" (Luke 5:16) and he would pray for long stretches of time (Luke 6:12).

JESUS:
- Prayed for his followers. John 17:9
- Prayed for the children. Matthew 19:13
- Praised the Father in prayer. Matthew 11:25
- Prayed for himself. John 17:1
- Prayed for Simon Peter. Luke 22:32
- Thanked the Father in prayer. John 11:41; Luke 24:30
- Asked the Father to forgive sinners. Luke 23:34a
- Prayed with his last words on the cross. Luke 23:46
- Prayed that his Father's will be done. Matthew 26:39; Luke 22:42

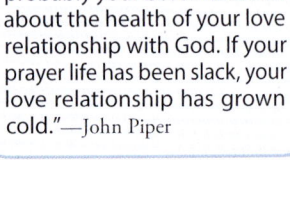

Four Kinds of Prayer

There are many types of prayer. Below are several main categories of prayer. A person may pray one or all of these in a single prayer time, and in any order. You can remember these categories with the acronym ACTS.

Adoration

Prayer, first and foremost, ought to be about worship. God alone is worthy of undiluted praise. That would be true even if God never gave us a thing, and that is why adoration is distinct from thanksgiving. Notice that the Lord's Prayer begins with "Our Father in heaven, hallowed be your name" (Matt. 6:9). Holding up God's name for praise is our prime duty in prayer. Examples: 1 Chron. 29:10; 2 Chron. 6:26–27; Luke 2:37.

Confession

"Forgive us our sins, for we also forgive everyone who sins against us" (Luke 11:4). Knowing that human sin blocks communication with God, Jesus taught his disciples to pray this way to make sure that there are no stumbling blocks between God and them. Examples: 2 Chron. 7:14; Dan. 9:4–19; 1 John 1:8–9.

Thanksgiving

Thanksgiving is praise for something God has done for us or given to us—or for what we trust him to do. The apostle Paul thanked God for the believers in Philippi: "I thank my God every time I remember you. In all my prayers for all of you, I always pray with joy because of your partnership in the gospel from the first day until now" (Phil. 1:3–5). Examples: Ps. 100:4; 107:1; 118:21; Matt. 14:19; Eph. 1:15–16; 1 Thess. 1:2; 5:16–18; 1 Tim. 4:4.

Supplication (Also called Petition)

Our heavenly Father wants his children to bring their requests to him (Phil. 4:6). Jesus taught, "If you, then, though you are evil, know how to give good gifts to your children, how much more will your Father in heaven give good gifts to those who ask him!" (Matt. 7:11). Intercession is a type of supplication where we pray for the needs and concerns of others. And we should not just pray for our friends, but also "...pray for those who persecute you" (Matt. 5:44). Examples: Gen. 24:12–15; 1 Sam. 7:8.

How to Pray

PRAY ALWAYS. We should live in a constant attitude of prayer. John MacArthur, a Christian author and pastor, explains that praying continually means "you live your life and your experiences of life with a constant, close connection to the Lord and are drawn into his presence through everything." (Also see Ps. 1; Josh. 1:8.)

> *Rejoice always, pray continually [or "pray without ceasing"], give thanks in all circumstances; for this is God's will for you in Christ Jesus.*—1 Thessalonians 5:16–18

PRAY ACCORDING TO GOD'S WILL. In all requests, we should keep the perspective that it is always "if the Lord wills." He is still in charge and knows best.

> *Now listen, you who say, "Today or tomorrow we will go to this or that city, spend a year there, carry on business and make money." Why, you do not even know what will happen tomorrow.... Instead, you ought to say, "If it is the Lord's will, we will live and do this or that."*—James 4:13–15

> *This is the confidence we have in approaching God: that if we ask anything according to his will, he hears us. And if we know that he hears us—whatever we ask—we know that we have what we asked of him.*—1 John 5:14–15

PRAY IN THE HOLY SPIRIT. Every time you pray, come with an open heart allowing God's Spirit in you to guide your prayers. Where we are inadequate, the Spirit knows exactly the right thing to say. (Also see Rom. 8:15–16; Eph. 5:18.)

> *And pray in the Spirit on all occasions with all kinds of prayers and requests. With this in mind, be alert and always keep on praying for all the Lord's people.*—Ephesians 6:18

> *But you, dear friends, by building yourselves up in your most holy faith and praying in the Holy Spirit, keep yourselves in God's love as you wait for the mercy of our Lord Jesus Christ to bring you to eternal life.*—Jude 20–21

We do not know what we ought to pray for, but the Spirit himself intercedes for us through wordless groans. And he who searches our hearts knows the mind of the Spirit, because the Spirit intercedes for God's people in accordance with the will of God.—Romans 8:26–27

> "Don't pray when you feel like it. Have an appointment with the Lord and keep it. A man is powerful on his knees." —Corrie Ten Boom

ASK IN FAITH—AND ALSO FOR FAITH. Faith may move mountains, but having that faith is often easier said than done. The Gospel of Mark tells a story of a father who wanted to fully believe that Jesus would answer his request to heal his son. The father cried out to Jesus, "I do believe; help me overcome my unbelief!" Even though this father had difficulty with faith, Jesus healed his son (Mark 9:14–29). Like this father, we too can pray for stronger faith.

Jesus replied, "Truly I tell you, if you have faith and do not doubt, not only can you do what was done to the fig tree, but also you can say to this mountain, 'Go, throw yourself into the sea,' and it will be done. If you believe, you will receive whatever you ask for in prayer."—Matthew 21:21–22

If any of you lacks wisdom, you should ask God, who gives generously to all without finding fault, and it will be given to you. But when you ask, you must believe and not doubt, because the one who doubts is like a wave of the sea, blown and tossed by the wind. That person should not expect to receive anything from the Lord.—James 1:5–7

PRAY IN JESUS' NAME. Jesus' death on the cross removed the "sin block" for all who believe. The lines of communication are now open for those who trust in Christ. This is what it means to pray in Jesus' name, for only through Jesus will any prayer be heard by God.

You did not choose me, but I chose you and appointed you so that you might go and bear fruit—fruit that will last—and so that whatever you ask in my name the Father will give you.—John 15:16

Until now you have not asked for anything in my name. Ask and you will receive, and your joy will be complete.—John 16:24

PRAY WITH A CLEAR MIND AND SELF-CONTROL.

The end of all things is near. Therefore be alert and of sober mind so that you may pray.—1 Peter 4:7

PRAY IN AGREEMENT WITH OTHER BELIEVERS.

Again, truly I tell you that if two of you on earth agree about anything they ask for, it will be done for them by my Father in heaven. For where two or three gather in my name, there am I with them.—Matthew 18:19–20

KEEP ON PRAYING. Persevere as you wait for the Lord to answer. Pray and don't give up.

Be joyful in hope, patient in affliction, faithful in prayer.—Romans 12:12

How Not to Pray

God does not expect us to be perfect to come to him in prayer, but he does expect us to be honest. Prayer should be the place where we meet God honestly and openly. The Bible tells us that the prayers that God does not accept are the prayers of hypocrisy.

PRAYERS THAT ARE SPOKEN TO PAT OURSELVES ON THE BACK (Luke 18:9–14).

"God, I thank you that I am not like other people—robbers, evildoers, adulterers—or even like this tax collector."—Luke 18:11

PRAYERS THAT ARE PRAYED ALL THE WHILE IGNORING GOD'S INSTRUCTIONS (Psalm 66:18–20). God cares more about whether we are following him and how we are treating others, rather than if we are simply "going through the motions" of prayer. Those prayers end up being empty and hindered (1 Peter 3:7).

If anyone turns a deaf ear to my instruction, even their prayers are detestable.—Proverbs 28:9

For I desire mercy, not sacrifice, and acknowledgment of God rather than burnt offerings.—Hosea 6:6

Prayers that are for selfish reasons. God knows all desires and no secret is hidden from him. Real prayer is an attitude of the heart (1 Thess. 5:16–18).

You desire but do not have, so you kill. You covet but you cannot get what you want, so you quarrel and fight. You do not have because you do not ask God. When you ask, you do not receive, because you ask with wrong motives, that you may spend what you get on your pleasures.—James 4:2–3

Prayers that are long and loud to get attention and admiration from other people (Mark 12:40; Luke 20:47).

And when you pray, do not be like the hypocrites, for they love to pray standing in the synagogues and on the street corners to be seen by others. Truly I tell you, they have received their reward in full. But when you pray, go into your room, close the door and pray to your Father, who is unseen. Then your Father, who sees what is done in secret, will reward you. And when you pray, do not keep on babbling like pagans, for they think they will be heard because of their many words. Do not be like them, for your Father knows what you need before you ask him.—Matthew 6:5–8

> "We may pray most when we say least, and we may pray least when we say most."
> —Augustine of Hippo

The Lord's Prayer   Matthew 6:9–13; Luke 11:2–4

When Jesus' disciples wanted to know how to pray, he taught them a prayer that is known today as "The Lord's Prayer." But this prayer is not so much Jesus' prayer as it is our prayer—it is how Jesus wants all his followers to pray.

The Seven Petitions

	Petition	Meaning
1	Our Father in heaven, hallowed be your name,	**God's holiness** comes first. We should set forth God's name as holy.
2	your kingdom come,	**God's sovereignty** is a fact affirmed by believers. We pray for the day when the world will see God's rule.
3	your will be done, on earth as it is in heaven.	**God's authority** extends over all his creation. We pray for his authority to be known and obeyed in all the earth.
4	Give us today our daily bread.	**God's providence** for our daily needs means that we may pray in faith that God will provide what we need or a way to obtain what we need.
5	And forgive us our debts, as we also have forgiven our debtors.	**God's forgiveness** of our sins (debts) is possible because of Jesus' sacrifice on the cross. We can expect to see God's mercy in our lives according to how merciful we are to others (Mark 11:25).
6	And lead us not into temptation,	**God's protection** from the things that will trip us up and undo us is something we need to ask for. Whether in trial or out of trial, we should seek God's protection.
7	but deliver us from the evil one.	**God's deliverance** from enemies and especially from death and the Devil are legitimate concerns. We can be confident in our prayers for deliverance because we are more than conquerors through Christ (Rom. 8:37).

Petitions 1–3 are "Your"; petitions 4–7 are "Us".

When God Says No

Anyone who has made prayer a part of his or her life knows that not everything asked for in prayer is granted. Prayer requests are just that, "requests," not demands or magic words that will make something happen. God hears our prayers and makes them effective, but he ultimately decides how to answer them—and sometimes that answer is no. "No" is one of the shortest yet hardest words to hear. But what does God's "no" mean? Often his "no" is not a "No way!" or "Forget about it," but rather it is, "No, I have something better in mind."

Moses *Deut. 3:23–27*
Moses asked to cross over the Jordan River to see the Promised Land. God said "No," but he let Moses view the land from the top of a mountain.

David 2 Sam. 7
King David asked to set up God's temple. God said "No," but promised to set up David's kingdom forever, and later allowed David's son, Solomon, to build God's temple.

> "God's answers are wiser than our prayers."—Unknown

Mary and Martha John 11
Mary and Martha asked Jesus to come quickly and heal their dying brother, but instead Jesus waited until their brother died. Then Jesus did something beyond their wildest expectations: he raised their brother from the dead! He answered their hearts' longing in a different way than what they had asked for.

Paul 2 Cor. 12:7–10
Paul pleaded three times for God to free him from a problem (the "thorn in his flesh"), but God did not remove it. However, through accepting the problem, Paul found that God's grace was sufficient for him and that power is made perfect in weakness. Paul found a greater meaning in his unanswered prayer.

Jesus Matt. 26:36–42; Mark 14:32–36; Luke 22:39–44; John 18:11
Jesus' prayer in the Garden of Gethsemane is the only prayer Jesus made that was denied. He prayed, that if it were possible, the suffering he was about to experience would be avoided. Yet he also prayed, "not my will, but yours be done." This example should teach us that there are some things we ask for—good as they may seem—that are not God's will for us. Jesus accepted the Father's will that he should suffer on our behalf. And just look at the powerful results: the forgiveness of sins and Jesus' resurrection from the dead! In Jesus' case, as in ours, the ultimate outcome from God will be life out of death.

When God Seems Silent

Sometimes we pray for change in our lives or the lives of our loved ones, and yet nothing happens. We do what we can, but God seems silent. From our perspective, our prayers may look like they are falling on deaf ears. Should we keep praying? Jesus addresses this important concern through two parables.

The Parable of the Friend in Need Luke 11:5–13
After Jesus teaches his disciples how to pray in the Lord's Prayer, he continues to instruct them through a story about a man who needs to borrow some food from a friend late at night for a visitor who is coming. Jesus says that the man will receive what he needs from his friend, not because his friend is so generous, but simply because of the man's persistence in asking.

The Lesson: God, who is far more generous than the friend, will surely supply our needs if we consistently ask him.

The Parable of the Persistent Widow Luke 18:1–8
"Jesus told his disciples a parable to show them that they should always pray and not give up" (v. 1). In this parable, a widow keeps coming back day after day to seek justice from a corrupt judge. Though the judge does not care about the woman's concern, he gets tired of her bothering him so he grants her justice.

The Lesson: If even a corrupt judge grants persistent requests, how much more will God who is just and cares for us bring about justice in our lives when we continue to call on him.

Waiting for God to Answer

As we pray for all the things we want and need and hope for, we must remember that prayer is learning what God wants for our lives. When we make God our top priority in prayer, our will begins to align with his will. As we stay connected to God, he will transform our hearts to his will (See John 15).

> But seek first his kingdom and his righteousness, and all these things will be given to you as well.—Matthew 6:33 (Luke 12:31)

> Take delight in the Lord, and he will give you the desires of your heart.... Be still before the Lord and wait patiently for him.—Psalm 37:3–7a

> One thing I ask from the Lord, this only do I seek: that I may dwell in the house of the Lord all the days of my life, to gaze on the beauty of the Lord and to seek him in his temple.—Psalm 27:4

The Who, What, Where, When and Why of Prayers in the Bible

The Bible provides us with many examples of all kinds of people praying for all sorts of things—in all imaginable situations! These examples show us that we can pray anytime and anywhere.

Who prayed?

- A national leader (Moses) *Ex. 32:11–13, 31–32; Num. 14:13–19*
- A child (Samuel) *1 Sam. 3:10*
- A military commander (Joshua) *Josh. 7:6–9*
- A weak man, once strong (Samson) *Judg. 16:28*
- A childless wife (Hannah) *1 Sam. 1:10–11*
- Priests *2 Chron. 30:27*
- Foreigners from distant lands *2 Chron. 6:32–33*
- An elderly widow (Anna) *Luke 2:36–38*
- A man on his deathbed (Hezekiah) *Isa. 38:2–3*
- A prophet (Isaiah) *Isa. 6:8*
- A king and musician (David) *Ps. 139*
- A grieving man (Jeremiah) *Lam. 3*
- A rebellious man (Jonah) *Jon. 2:2–9*
- Frightened sailors *Jon. 1:14*
- An elderly priest (Zechariah) *Luke 1:13*
- A blind beggar (Bartimaeus) *Mark 10:47*
- Jesus' family (his brothers and mother) *Acts 1:14*
- The Son of God *John 17*
- A seeking Gentile (Cornelius) *Acts 10:31*
- Widows *1 Tim. 5:5*
- Worshipers in heaven *Rev. 11:15–18*

Why did they pray?

- Were afraid for their life (Moses) *Ex. 17:4–5*
- Felt betrayed by God (Moses) *Num. 11:10–15*
- A sister was ill (Moses for Miriam) *Num. 12:13*
- Feared enemy nations (Joshua) *Josh. 6–8*
- Wanted revenge (Samson) *Judg. 16:28*
- Experienced life-changing disasters (Job) *Job 1:20–21*
- Were thankful to God for a child (Hannah) *1 Sam. 2:1–10*
- Saw God fulfill his promise (Solomon) *1 Kings 8:23–53*
- Didn't know what to do (Jehoshaphat) *2 Chron. 20:1–12*
- Couldn't go on anymore (Elijah) *1 Kings 19:4*
- Had a big decision and move to make (Nehemiah) *Neh. 2:4*
- Were very depressed *Ps. 116:3–4*
- A boy was demon possessed (Jesus' teaching) *Mark 9:29*
- Were thankful for other believers (Paul) *Eph. 1:16; 1 Thess. 1:2*
- Had new church leaders appointed *Acts 6:6; 14:23*
- A woman had died (Peter for Tabitha) *Acts 9:40–42*
- A father was ill (Paul for Publius' father) *Acts 28:8*
- Were awaiting the Lord's return (John) *Rev. 22:20*

What did they pray for?

- To spare a wicked city (Abraham for Sodom) *Gen. 18:23–25*
- A bride (Abraham's servant) *Gen. 24:12–14*
- Protection from a brother (Jacob) *Gen. 32:9–12*
- Their grandsons (Jacob) *Gen. 48:15–16*
- Someone else to do the work (Moses) *Ex. 4:13*
- To see God (Moses) *Ex. 33:18*
- To see the Promised Land (Moses) *Deut. 3:23–25*
- A child to be raised from the dead (Elijah for a widow's son) *1 Kings 17:21*
- Parenting instructions (Samson's father) *Judg. 13:8*
- A sign from God (Gideon) *Judg. 6:17–18*
- More sunlight (Joshua) *Josh. 10:12*
- A son (Hannah) *1 Sam. 1:11*
- To know what God wants them to do (David) *2 Sam. 5:19–23*
- Thunder and rain (Samuel) *1 Sam. 12:16–17*
- Forgiveness for adultery and murder (David) *Ps. 51; 2 Sam. 12:16*
- Wisdom (Solomon) *1 Kings 3:9*

- A heart wholly devoted to God *Ps. 86:11*
- Fire from heaven (Elijah) *1 Kings 18:36–38*
- Success (Jabez) *1 Chron. 4:10*
- Protection for their city (Hezekiah) *2 Kings 19:14–19*
- Strengthened hands (Nehemiah) *Neh. 6:9*
- Revival *Ps. 85:6–7*
- Protection from Satan (Jesus) *John 17:15*
- New believers to receive the Holy Spirit (Peter and John for believers in Samaria) *Acts 8:15*
- To speak God's Word with boldness (Apostles) *Acts 4:24–30; Eph. 6:19–20*
- Salvation of the Jews (Paul) *Rom. 10:1*
- That other believers would do right *2 Cor. 13:7*
- That the eyes of one's heart may be opened *Eph. 1:18*
- Government leaders *1 Tim. 2:1–2*
- Good health (John for Gaius) *3 John 1:2*
- The gospel to be spread *2 Thess. 3:1*

Where did they pray?

- Outdoors (Abraham's Servant) *Gen. 24:11–12*
- On the battlefield (Joshua) *Josh. 7:6–9*
- At the altar (Solomon) *2 Chron. 6:12–14*
- In their room (Daniel) *Dan. 6:10*
- In bed *Ps. 63:6*
- Inside the belly of a whale (Jonah) *Jonah 2:2–9*
- On a mountainside (Jesus) *Luke 6:12; 9:28*
- At the temple (Pharisee and tax collector) *Luke 18:10*
- From prison (Paul and Silas) *Acts 16:25*
- On the beach (disciples) *Acts 21:5*

When did they pray?

- At midnight *Ps. 119:62; Acts 16:25*
- Three times a day (Daniel) *Dan. 6:10*
- All through the night (Samuel) *1 Sam. 15:11*
- Every morning *Ps. 5:3*
- At fixed times daily *Ps. 55:17*
- Very early in the morning (Jesus) *Mark 1:35*
- While nearly drowning (Peter) *Matt. 14:30*
- While being crucified (Thief on the cross) *Luke 23:42*
- While being martyred (Stephen) *Acts 7:59–60*
- During a period set apart for prayer *1 Cor. 7:5*

How did they pray?

- Sitting (David) *2 Sam. 7:18*
- Standing (Solomon) *1 Kings 8:22 (Also Mark 11:25)*
- Kneeling (Peter) *Acts 9:40 (Also Dan. 6:10; Eph. 3:14; 1 Kings 8:54)*
- Facing Jerusalem (Daniel) *Dan. 6:10*
- In whispers *Isa. 26:16*
- In silence (Hannah) *1 Sam. 1:13*
- In a loud voice (Ezra) *Ez. 11:13*
- Looking up (Jesus) *John 11:41*
- With face to the ground (Jesus) *Matt. 26:39*
- With hands toward heaven (Solomon) *1 Kings 8:22 (Also Ps. 28:2)*
- With bitter weeping (Hezekiah) *Isa. 38:2–3*
- With tears and crying (Ezra) *Ezra 10:1 (Also Jesus; Heb. 5:7)*
- With joy! (Paul) *Phil. 1:4*
- As a group (believers) *Acts 1:14*
- Alone (Jesus) *Matt. 14:23*
- In unison (believers) *Acts 4:24*
- Earnestly! (Paul, Silas, and Timothy) *1 Thess. 3:10*

> "No learning can make up for the failure to pray. No earnestness, no diligence, no study, no gifts will supply its lack." —E.M. Bounds

Heaven

Why is Heaven Important?

Heaven is more than just hope for a better future. It is at the heart of God's plan for all creation. It is also at the center of the human heart.

The common experience of losing loved ones, and the eventual loss of our own lives, make the issue of heaven one with which everyone must wrestle. We wonder what happens when we die, when our loved ones die. Have we lost them forever? Are they in a better place? Will we see them again someday? What is life after death like? What is heaven like? Can we even know something about heaven?

Heaven is a source of hope, guidance, and meaning for every believer.

Heaven gives:

- Hope for our future destination and strength for life in the present
- Guidance for living as God's people today
- Meaning by giving us the certainty that there is more to life than this world

In the following pages, we will answer some of the most common questions about heaven. We will also broaden our perspective about heaven. We will realize that heaven is not only about hope but also about faith and love.

What do we mean by *heaven*?

In popular culture, and for many believers, heaven evokes images of cloudy, ghost-like existence, or angelic beings floating about among the clouds. This image comes directly from the radical separation of the physical and spiritual worlds. Some of the misconceptions are:

Popular View of Heaven
- A place for disembodied, ghost-like beings
- A place where people sing all the time
- A place up by the clouds
- A place everyone goes after death
- A place where all beings live as angels

Biblical View of Heaven
However, the final destination of believers is not an ethereal place like that. The final destination of all believers is *the renewed heavens and earth* anticipated in Revelation 21. A very physical, concrete future awaits us when Christ comes back.

What happens when people die?

When one experiences the loss of a loved one, the pain of the loss makes it difficult to focus on the ultimate destination. The immediate concern is *what has happened to my loved one? Is my loved one in heaven?*

What will happen to me when I die?
Although some of the details remain hidden, we know that:

- Our life and future are secure in God's hands (Ps. 34:6; 91:4; Is. 25:4; Rom. 8:37–39).
- We go to a place of waiting in the presence of God (1 John 3:2–3). Many theologians call this period between our deaths and Jesus' return the *intermediate state*.
- It is not a permanent place; the whole creation waits for the final redemption at the end of time.
- It is not a place up by the clouds; we do not know where it is, but it is where Jesus is present.

Can we be sure what happens after we die? Yes!
- Believers will enjoy the blessing of God's presence (1 John 3:2–3; Rev. 21:22).
- Believers from all of history wait in joy and peace, but with longing, for the return of Christ (Rev. 6:9–10).
- As believers, we will join them at some point.
- When God renews all things, we will all dwell together in the new heavens and the new earth (Rev. 21–22).

What can we know about heaven?

The answer is not as much as we would like; however, we can know just enough to be confident that:

- We can trust in God's promises.
- We will be with God and our loved ones.
- God will do something awesome with his creation.

How do we know anything about heaven?

- The only completely valid source of knowledge about heaven is the Bible. The Bible has direct and indirect information about heaven—over 600 verses in the Bible mention *heaven*.
- The Bible is the rule with which we can decide if other information is valid.
- However, for the most part, people's ideas about heaven come mainly from literature, movies, and television. Media has shaped much of our imagination and knowledge about heaven. Not all of this knowledge is accurate.
- A non-biblical understanding of the world has informed much of what popular culture knows about heaven.
- It mainly portrays heaven as boring and unappealing.

Although sin has profoundly affected creation, God never called creation evil. It is under a curse. However, Jesus came to lift that curse and turn it into blessing. God is redeeming all of creation. At the end of time, God will renew all things to their original intention.

Understanding God's original plan for his creation helps us understand our final destination as well.

A non-biblical understanding of the universe

Behind the cloudy, ethereal idea of heaven lies the old Gnostic belief that the physical world is evil and the spiritual is good. Thus, one must focus on the spiritual to escape this evil world. This is not a biblical idea. It ignores some basic biblical facts:

A biblical understanding of the universe

1. God made the whole universe and called it *very good* (Gen. 1:31).
2. Satan is a spiritual being and is evil—thus, not all *spiritual* is good and not all *physical* is evil.
3. God promises a renewed heaven and earth at the end of time (Rev. 21).

What Was God's Original Intent for Creation?

God created the whole universe for his own glory and relationships. He intended all his creatures to relate to each other, to nature, and to himself in harmony. Humanity's main and great goal in life is to glorify God (Isa. 60:21; 1 Cor. 6:20; 10:31) and enjoy him forever (Phil. 4:4; Rev. 21:3–4).

Human sin twisted God's original intentions. However, because of God's grace and faithfulness, his plans would not be frustrated. He planned to rescue his creation from the effects of sin (Rom. 8:18–27). Through the saving work of Jesus on the cross, people can find peace with God and each other. Through the same process, believers can begin the reconciliation with one another and nature.

Neos and Kainos

Greek has two different words for the idea of *new*. *Neos* is a newness of time; *kainos* is a newness of quality. A *neos* object would mean that the object did not exist and now is there. A *kainos* object means that the object was there but its quality has changed: it is better, it is made different. In this sense, the *new heavens and earth* in Revelation 21:1 are not *neos* but *kainos*. That is, God will renew, transform, improve, and refresh his creation. It will be a *kainos* heaven and earth.

What is the renewed heaven and earth?

This process will have a glorious ending when Christ returns. He will renew all things (Rev. 21:1). It will not be a different creation or a non-creation. It will be *this* creation renewed; God will restore his creation to its original glory and purpose. As if to close the circle, what God began at Eden he will fulfill in Revelation. Not everything will be the same. Some things from the biblical idea of Eden will continue in the renewed creation; others will end.

We do have glimpses of heaven, even if many things are not clear. We can see it in the love we experience for and from people, in the majesty of nature's beauty and power, in the generosity and kindness of people in times of need, in the smile of a happy baby, in the loyalty and warmth of our pets, in the tenderness and wisdom of old age, and in moments of deep emotional and spiritual connections with our loved ones and God.

What is our hope for the future?

Our hope for the future is firmly rooted in God's faithfulness. We can trust that God will do what he has promised us because he has been faithful in the past. We can safely conclude that many features and characteristics of this world will continue in the renewed creation. Of course, there will be things that will end as well. Based on biblical testimony, we can identify many things that will continue and some that will not.

What Will Continue	What Will End

• Physical bodies
• Emotions (relationships)
• Nature
    Daily cycles
    Weather
    Animals—including pets
• Many activities, such as:
    Work (Gen. 2:15)
    Learning (1 Cor. 13:12)
    Science
    Art (Rev. 14:2–3)
    Entertainment
	• No evil
	• No curse
	• No brokenness, emotional or physical
	• No more sin
	• No death
	• No marriage
	• No more suffering or sadness
	• No war
	• No famine
	• No need for temples

"This is the will of Him who sent Me, that of all that He has given Me I lose nothing, but raise it up on the last day."
—John 6:39 (*NASB*)

Besides referring to people, this text also refers to God's creation. The neuter pronoun *it* (Greek *auto*) would seem to extend Jesus' mission from people to all of creation (see Romans 8:19–22 and Colossians 1:20). Jesus' words in John 6:39 are a guarantee that no good thing shall be lost, but rather shall have some new and fulfilled form in the renewed creation. Everything good belongs to Christ, who is the life of the whole world as well as the life of every believer (John 6:33, 40). All things good in this world will continue to exist in the next, but they will be transformed and improved in the renewed creation.

Why does Jesus' resurrection matter?

Jesus' resurrection gives us a good idea of what heaven may look like. The Apostle Paul makes it clear that our future is tied to Jesus' own resurrection (1 Cor. 15:12–34). He concludes, "And if Christ has not been raised, your faith is futile…" (15:17).

- Because Christ has been raised from the dead, our hope is true and secured.
- Christ is the firstfruits or first example of all who will be raised into new life (15:20).
- Our future includes a *resurrected body*; that is, it will be a physical reality. Our future resurrected bodies will be like Jesus' own resurrected body (1 Cor. 15:42–49).
- The women and the disciples recognized Jesus after his resurrection (Matt. 28:9, 17).
- Jesus' body was physical (Lk. 24:39). Jesus ate with his disciples (Lk. 24:41–43). Yet, it was not a body like ours. The Apostle Paul uses two ways to explain this difference:
  1. Just as different animals have bodies suited for their environment (for the sea, the air, and the ground), so our resurrected bodies will be suited for the renewed creation (1 Cor. 15:39).
  2. There are also "natural bodies" and "spiritual bodies." Both Jesus' pre- and post-Resurrection bodies were physical; the difference is about perishability. That is, natural bodies die; spiritual bodies do not. Sin has polluted and damaged our natural bodies; our bodies die, decay, and are unfit for a future in God's presence. Just as God will renew this creation, also marred by sin, God will give us renewed bodies that will not be polluted by sin, will not decay, and will be fit to be in the presence of God.

Natural Bodies	Spiritual Bodies
Psychikos	*Pneumatikos*
Derived from *psyche*, meaning "soul"	Derived from *pneuma*, meaning "spirit"

The ending *ikos* is used in Greek to make an adjective, and it means "in reference to." It does not describe the material out of which something is made. Rather, it refers to the force that animates an object. In this case, *psychikos* refers to the human soul that animates our bodies. In the case of *pneumatikos*, it refers to the Spirit, God's Spirit, as the animating force (see, for example, Rom. 1:11 and Gal. 6:1). Thus, both kinds of bodies are physical. The difference is that a "natural body" dies and a "spiritual body" does not die.

Will we be able to recognize our loved ones in heaven?

Yes! When Jesus rose from the dead and appeared to his friends and disciples, they recognized him (Luke 24:39; John 20:27). There will be continuity between our bodies today and our resurrected bodies in the renewed creation.

I know that my Redeemer lives, and that in the end he will stand upon the earth. And after my skin has been destroyed, yet in my flesh I will see God; I myself will see him with my own eyes—I, and not another. How my heart yearns within me!—Job 19:25–27

What kinds of relationships will exist in heaven?

Emotions and relationships are a very important part of what it means to be human. There will be emotions and relationships in heaven, though they may not be exactly the same. They will be renewed emotions, emotions as they were meant to be from the beginning: joyful, satisfying, enriching, intimate, and refreshing.

There will be no sorrow, or regrets, or guilt. Rather, love, compassion, gentleness, tenderness, and other emotions will find new heights and depths in heaven. Relationships will be all we can imagine and more.

Will there be disabilities, injuries or deformities in heaven?

No. There will be no brokenness at all, either emotional or physical. God will renew our bodies; they will be beautiful and work as God intended them to. Because Jesus' injuries were present after his resurrection (Luke 24:39; John 20:27), many people think that martyrs, those who died for the name of Jesus, will wear their healed scars as badges of honor. Although it is possible, it remains, like so many other things about heaven, just speculation.

Will our bodies need food, clothing, and language in heaven?

Because we do not understand the nature of the future bodies, it is difficult to know whether they will need food, clothing, and languages. However, since our bodies will preserve much of their characteristics, we could imagine that language, food, and clothing will have very similar functions. The beautiful diversity of characters and gifts makes life more interesting. Each person reflects God's image in a way that none other can. Together, with our differences and similarities, with our talents and strengths, we reflect God's image as no individual human could.

Yet, there will certainly be differences as well. Now, differences in language, culture, and expression can be causes of deep, fierce divisions (Gen. 11:1–9). However, in the renewed creation, communication will be transparent. We will say what we mean, and people will fully understand us. This side of heaven, clothing can be used as a status symbol that can serve our pride. It is also used to cover our shame. There will be no shame in the renewed creation, nor will we have the need to boost our ego at the expense of others. Rather, clothing will not conceal but could reveal our inner being.

Will heaven be boring?

Definitely not! People may get the idea that heaven will be boring because we will worship God all day long in heaven. It is true—we will worship God non-stop! But let's revisit what we mean by *worship*.

Worship is not just the singing and praying part of Christian church services. Everything we do can be worship: from the moment we wake up, take our meals, relate to others, do our work, play games, and live life. Worship is not just an activity; it is primarily an attitude. Worship is the attitude that arises when we recognize who God is and who we are:

God	Human
He is the creator	We are the creatures
He is in control of our lives	We depend completely on God's grace and mercy
He is all powerful	We are limited and weak
He knows all things	We know imperfectly
He loves us unconditionally	We are just learning to love in the same way

Worship is the attitude that acknowledges God's presence at every moment in our daily lives, sometimes moving us to tears, sometimes to great joy, to repentance, to humility, to gratitude, to hard work, to commitment, to compassion, to love.

In the busyness of our lives, we often miss this reality: God is interested and active in our lives! We may go days or weeks without realizing that our words, actions, and thoughts have brought glory or sadness to God. This forgetfulness will find no place in the renewed creation; we will not miss God in our lives because he will dwell in our midst.

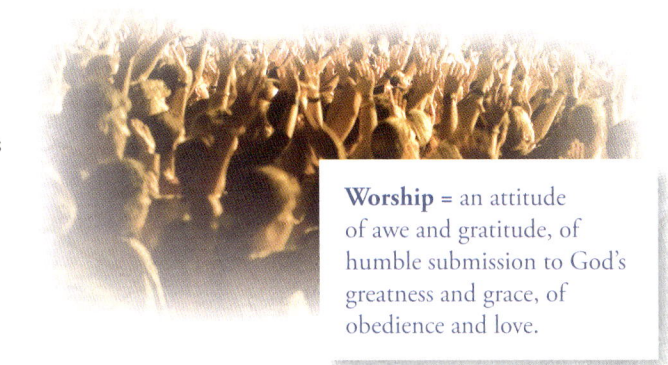

Worship = an attitude of awe and gratitude, of humble submission to God's greatness and grace, of obedience and love.

What will we do in heaven?

The Bible does not give many details about activities in heaven. But we can be sure that:

- God loves his creation. He proclaimed it good (Gen. 1:31).
- Nature itself reflects God's greatness and glory (Ps. 19).
- Nature will be renewed so it may fulfill God's purposes.

So it is at least possible that much of the new creation will be similar to what we experience now. The best things about this world will just become better in the renewed creation.

Will we have pets?

Our relationships with our pets are also important and meaningful. These relationships reflect the way God intended us to relate to animals in general: with love, respect, and companionship. Will God, then, resurrect our beloved pets? Yes, it is perfectly possible. We cannot be sure, since the Bible does not address this issue, but based on God's love for animals, their role as our companions, it is at least possible.

The wolf and the lamb will feed together, and the lion will eat straw like the ox, but dust will be the serpent's food. They will neither harm nor destroy on all my holy mountain.—Isaiah 65:25

Will there be work?

Because work can become an almost painful toil, we often wonder if rest means no more working. But remember that

- Work is also a form of worship;
- God meant for humans to help take care of his creation (Gen. 2:15).

Each person will develop and thrive with his or her own talents. We will no longer work in places that do not allow us to grow as individuals, or where our work might be unappreciated, or where we cannot possibly be happy.

God intended work to be a joyful activity. Rather than just making a living, work should be a way to fellowship with God by caring for his world. For this reason, we can be sure we will have plenty of interesting things to do in the renewed creation!

> *Whatever you do, work at it with all your heart, as working for the Lord, not for men, since you know that you will receive an inheritance from the Lord as a reward. It is the Lord Christ you are serving.*
> —Colossians 3:23–24

Will there be learning, science, sports, and arts?

As with work, we could imagine the same for learning, science, arts, and sports. The gifts and talents of painters, poets, athletes and scientists will be used simply to worship God.

So, what's so great about heaven?

Everything! Heaven is all we ever dreamt and more. In this life, we grow, reach our peak, and begin a slow descent until our life ends. Life in the intermediate heaven will be much better because we will be in God's presence. However, life in the renewed creation will be beyond our imagination.

It is true that we do not know many facts about the renewed creation, heaven, and even less about the intermediate state, intermediate heaven. However, what we read in the Bible and what we know about God give us great hope and joy.

> *Dear friends, now we are children of God, and what we will be has not yet been made known. But we know that when he appears, we shall be like him, for we shall see him as he is. Everyone who has this hope in him purifies himself, just as he is pure.*
> —1 John 3:2–3

The Ultimate Great Escape?

- Heaven is not an escapist idea.
- We do not think about heaven to escape this world's troubles—we think about heaven as a guide to live better in this world, to serve God with greater joy, and to show others God's great love.
- For many believers who suffer persecution for their faithfulness, and others who suffer in this life in indescribable ways, heaven is a great source of comfort.
- Knowing that God will make all things right one day gives us strength to continue life in faithfulness and obedience.

Who will be in heaven and how do we get there?

- In popular culture, it's common to believe that all people go to heaven, and, in some cases, they become angels. However, biblical testimony does not support either of these ideas.
- Just as we acknowledge the reality of heaven, we must recognize the reality of hell. We don't know very much about hell either, except that it exists, it is a place of punishment, and there is only one way to escape it. The other details are hidden from us.
- The Bible is clear, however, to specify who will go to heaven. Only those who have surrendered their lives to Jesus and who experience the renewal of their hearts will be allowed in God's presence.

> *For God so loved the world that he gave his one and only Son, that whoever believes in him shall not perish but have eternal life. For God did not send his Son into the world to condemn the world, but to save the world through him.*—John 3:16–17.

What is the New Jerusalem?

The book of Revelation provides another image of the renewed creation: the city of Jerusalem (Rev. 21:2). The city is described as a bride and its dimensions are detailed. Believers understand this text in different ways. Some understand the city to be a literal city, and the dimension an accurate representation of what the city will be like. The resulting picture is an enormous cube of about 1,400 miles per side.

Others take this image as a symbolic representation of God's people. Since the image of the bride ready to marry the Lamb occurs before, and it seems applied to God's people (Rev. 19:7), it is possible that the Holy City stands for God's holy people. It is perfectly possible that there will be no seas (21:1), or sun and moon (21:23). It is also possible that the language is symbolic— it says the "city does not need the sun or the moon…" not that they will not exist. If there is continuity between this creation and the renewed creation, as we have suggested, then the beauty of the sun and the moon will be present, even if not needed.

In any case, it is clear that:

- The renewed creation is God's work, since it comes from above.
- It is large enough to fit all of God's people and more.
- It points at the beauty and splendor of the renewed creation.
- God dwells in its midst.
- It closes the circle from Paradise in the Garden of Eden to the Holy City in the new heavens and new earth.

Original Creation (Genesis)	Renewed Creation (Revelation)
Heaven and earth created, 1:1	Heavens and earth renewed, 21:1
Sun created, 1:16	No need of sun, 21:23
The night established, 1:5	No night there, 22:5
The seas created, 1:10	No more seas, 21:1
The curse enters the world, 3:14–17	No more curse, 22:3
Death enters the world, 2:19	Death is no more, 21:4
Humanity is cast out of paradise, 3:24	Humanity is restored to paradise, 22:14
Sorrow and pain begin, 3:17	Sorrow, tears, and pain end, 21:4

Regarding knowledge of heaven, we must humbly recognize our limits.

The secret things belong to the Lord our God, but the things revealed belong to us and to our children forever.
—Deuteronomy 29:29

- Mystery requires faith to know that God is in control.
- We do not need to know everything.
- We know all that we need to be faithful and obedient.

LORD, TEACH US TO PRAY

Jesus' disciples had seen him pray many times. Sometimes he prayed all night and sometimes his prayers were just one sentence. But Jesus' followers made the connection between his intense prayer life and the power he showed in every aspect of life. They must have realized that prayer was the link. Finally, one disciple asked Jesus to teach them how to pray. Jesus gave them a deceptively simple, childlike prayer which has come to be known as the Lord's Prayer. This prayer is recorded in Luke 11:2–4 and Matthew 6:9–13. Matthew's version highlights seven key parts:

> *Our Father in heaven,*
> *hallowed be your name,*
> *your kingdom come,*
> *your will be done on earth as it is in heaven.*
> *Give us today our daily bread.*
> *Forgive us our debts,*
> *as we also have forgiven our debtors.*
> *And lead us not into temptation,*
> *but deliver us from the evil one.*
> —Matthew 6:9–13

In this pattern, Jesus provided his followers with guidelines for prayer based on the attributes or characteristics of God.

The two main sections of the prayer divide with the words "your" and "our."

1. The first part centers on God, putting God in his rightful place in our priorities. Only by focusing on the patient and loving Father can we find the attitude that puts our own needs in perspective.

2. The second part focuses on our needs—body, soul, and spirit—and the needs of others. In just three brief requests, Jesus targets all of human behavior and character and reminds us that we always need him. It's been said that if these three requests are prayed properly, nothing more need be said. Only in moment-by-moment dependence on God will we experience the good things God wants to provide.

The Lord's Prayer is a dangerous, life-changing prayer. Jesus' enemies eventually killed him for asserting his close tie to God through addressing God as Father. Until Jesus gave his followers the right to be called children of God, this would have been blasphemy.

Twenty-first-century Christians may take the privilege for granted, but the prayer is still a dangerous one. We do, in one sense, "take our lives in our hands" and offer them up again and again as sacrifice to the One who gave us all in the first place, receiving all of life in return.

THE LORD'S PRAYER

Rather than giving us a formula to repeat over and over, Jesus gave us a model prayer illustrating first of all what our relationship with God should be like (the total dependence of children on a loving Father), and also the three main purposes of prayer:

- To declare God's holiness
- To usher in God's kingdom
- To do God's will

Seven distinct parts emphasize seven of God's attributes that help to place all of our needs and desires in proper perspective.

	GOD'S ATTRIBUTE	FOCUS	PETITION
1	God's Love	God is a loving Father.	Our Father in heaven.
2	God's Holiness	God's name is holy.	Hallowed be your name.
3	God's Sovereignty	There is no one above God.	Your kingdom come.
4	God's Authority	God has the supreme authority.	Your will be done on earth as it is in heaven.
5	God's Providence	God is the source of everything we need.	Give us today our daily bread.
6	God's Mercy	Forgiveness is our greatest need.	And forgive us our debts, as we also have forgiven our debtors.
7	God's Protection	Trials prove our faith and develop our characters.	And lead us not into temptation, but deliver us from the evil one.

The Lord's Prayer • 347

Our Father in heaven (NIV)
Our Father which art in heaven (KJV)

GOD'S ATTRIBUTE

GOD'S FATHERLY LOVE

WHAT DOES IT MEAN?

God is a loving and compassionate Father who gives life to, provides for, and protects those who trust him. Like a caring human father, God wants a close relationship with his children. Addressing God as "Our Father" plunges the person praying into a relationship. A child approaching a loving father knows that father will give careful attention to the child's requests and will be lovingly inclined towards the child's best interests. The child knows the father will answer. This is how Jesus tells us to approach God—as trusting children of a patient, tender father.

SCRIPTURE

But to all who believed him [Jesus] and accepted him, he gave the right to become children of God. They are reborn—not with a physical birth resulting from human passion or plan, but a birth that comes from God.
—John 1:12–13 NLT

How great is the love the Father has lavished on us, that we should be called children of God! —1 John 3:1

Let us then approach the throne of grace with confidence, so that we may receive mercy and find grace to help us in our time of need.
—Hebrews 4:16

APPLICATION

During Jesus' time, people understood God to be awesome, majestic, and far away in the unreachable heavens. Though the Old Testament uses the metaphor of fatherhood when talking of God, no one would have dreamed of addressing God as Father in prayer. Jesus' use of the term *Pater*, meaning "Father," must have stunned his disciples. In fact, Jesus' use of the family name was so shocking to the religious leaders of his day that eventually he was accused of blasphemy and was crucified for identifying himself as God's Son.

Jesus taught his followers that they should address God as Father, and that their loving Father would care for all the needs of those who trust in him (Matt. 7:7–11). Then, not only did Jesus encourage that relationship of trust, but he willingly died a horrible death to purchase the right of believers in Christ to be called children of God! It's hard to comprehend that the God who has all the power in the universe will listen to our prayers because of the actions of his Son, Jesus.

Hallowed be your name (NIV)
Hallowed be thy name (KJV)

GOD'S HOLINESS

GOD'S ATTRIBUTE

WHAT DOES IT MEAN?

To *hallow* means to make holy. To hallow God's name means to honor it as holy and sacred. When we pray, we enter the presence of God with reverence, worship, and thanksgiving. We thank God not only for what he has done, but also for who he is. God's greatness and glory alone are worthy of praise and thankfulness. Thanksgiving recognizes that everything we have belongs to God, whether it be our talents, possessions, jobs, or children.

SCRIPTURE

Exalt the LORD our God and worship at his holy mountain, for the LORD our God is holy. —Psalm 99:9

You shall not misuse the name of the LORD your God, for the LORD will not hold anyone guiltless who misuses his name. —Exodus 20:7

So whether you eat or drink or whatever you do, do it all for the glory of God. —1 Corinthians 10:31

The earth is the LORD'S, and everything in it, the world, and all who live in it. —Psalm 24:1

APPLICATION

Traditionally, God's people, the Jews, never said or wrote the name of God. To do so was considered not keeping the name of God holy. God's name represents his character, his plan, and his will.

We often think of cursing as a common misuse of God's name, but what about attitudes of the heart? Lack of respect or indifference by one who professes love for God may be just as much a sin. Revelation 3:15–16 shows God's attitude toward indifference: "I know your deeds, that you are neither cold nor hot. I wish you were either one or the other! So, because you are lukewarm—neither hot nor cold—I am about to spit you out of my mouth."

Jesus encouraged his followers to use God's name in honorable ways and for purposes that deepen and endear our bonds to him. Part of showing reverence for the holy name of God is thanking him for who he is and for what he has done. Many psalms praise and worship God's holy name (see Psalms 100 and 148). Our greatest reverence, though, is shown by the stories our lives reveal. Our Father's name is most hallowed when we live in ways that attract others to him (Matt. 5:16).

Your kingdom come (NIV)
Thy kingdom come (KJV)

GOD'S ATTRIBUTE

GOD'S SOVEREIGNTY

WHAT DOES IT MEAN?

God has supreme power and authority over everything in heaven and earth. When we acknowledge God's sovereignty, we affirm and welcome his reign in our lives. We promise to live in ways that honor him. But God's kingdom is both here and now—and yet to come. During Jesus' life on earth, his ministry was "to proclaim freedom for the prisoners, to recover sight for the blind, to release the oppressed, and to proclaim the year of the Lord's favor" (Luke 4:18–19). When Jesus was around, people were freed from sickness, suffering, and pain. When Jesus returns to reign supreme, there will be no pain, suffering, or evil ever again. God will make everything right in the end.

SCRIPTURE

In the time of those kings, the God of heaven will set up a kingdom that will never be destroyed, nor will it be left to another people. It will crush all those kingdoms and bring them to an end, but it will itself endure forever.
—Daniel 2:44

And I heard a loud voice from the throne saying, "Now the dwelling of God is with men, and he will live with them. They will be his people, and God himself will be with them and be their God. He will wipe every tear from their eyes. There will be no more death or mourning or crying or pain, for the old order of things has passed away."
—Revelation 21:3–4

APPLICATION

Jesus said that the kingdom of God was near (Mark 1:15). When asked when the kingdom would come, Jesus said, "The kingdom of God does not come with your careful observation, nor will people say, 'Here it is,' or 'There it is,' because the kingdom of God is within you" (Luke 17:20–21). God's kingdom will be evident in the lives of those who make him their Lord. This petition asks the Lord to change our lives so that his goodness is always evident through us.

Some people have interpreted this prayer as an invitation to impact culture by passing laws calling people back to safer moral standards. But Jesus made it clear his church's mission is to lead people to himself. Jesus commissioned all disciples to proclaim that Jesus is King and Lord over all (Matt. 28:18–20). Our obedience to this commission helps spread God's kingdom throughout the world. This prayer can function as a petition for the strength and power we need to usher in God's kingdom on earth. When we focus on recognizing and embracing God's reign in this world, we help to make it visible.

Your will be done on earth as it is in heaven (NIV)
Thy will be done in earth, as it is in heaven (KJV)

GOD'S ATTRIBUTE

GOD'S AUTHORITY

WHAT DOES IT MEAN?

God's perfect will is always being done in heaven. But on earth, human free will results in selfishness, greed, and evil. In this part of the Lord's Prayer, we ask that God's will would take place on earth. More specifically, we pray for God's will to become our will. God calls each one of his children to live rightly and do good to others, caring for those around us as much as for ourselves. We pray that all people submit to the will of God over their own desires and faithfully love God and neighbors as themselves. Relationship with God depends on obedience to his will. God's will should be the context for everything we ask for, say, and do.

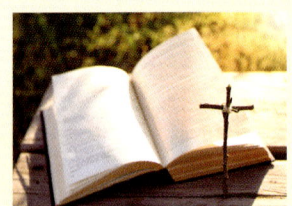

SCRIPTURE

Teach me to do your will, for you are my God; may your good Spirit lead me on level ground. —Psalm 143:10

Not everyone who says to me, "Lord, Lord," will enter the kingdom of heaven, but only he who does the will of my Father who is in heaven. —Matthew 7:21

Jesus prayed for his Father's will: "Yet not as I will, but as you will." —Matthew 26:39

For whoever does the will of my Father in heaven is my brother and sister and mother. —Matthew 12:50

APPLICATION

Philippians 2:3 says, "Do nothing out of selfish ambition or vain conceit, but in humility consider others better than yourselves." Our attitude should be like Jesus'. So often, when we come to God in prayer, we bring our own agendas. We want our will to be done, we want our wishes to be granted, and we want God to answer our prayers in a certain way. Often God's will differs from our own; in these situations, we need to trust God's will over our own desires.

For centuries, Christians have debated if God's will is done whether or not we pray. Some question, "Why pray if God knows everything we need before we ask?" Others have wondered whether God takes action at all if we don't initiate the request. While we trust in God's sovereignty and his ability to exercise his good will, we also trust his commands to exercise the muscles of our wills in prayer (Luke 18:1). We pray, believing in God's promises to respond in ways that are best for us. Though we often pray for changes in circumstance, the real work of prayer changes us from the inside out (Rom. 12:1–2). The more we talk with God, the more we find ourselves wanting to please him. Prayer often changes our circumstances, but more importantly, it changes us and our priorities.

Give us this day our daily bread (NIV)
Give us this day our daily bread (KJV)

GOD'S ATTRIBUTE

GOD'S PROVIDENCE

WHAT DOES IT MEAN?

God is able to provide for all our needs. Bread can represent not just food, but every physical thing we need. When we pray for our daily bread, we ask God to provide for our material, physical, emotional, relational, and spiritual needs for that day. Daily bread can include the daily needs of ministries, people, communities, leaders, family, friends, as well as personal needs. God commits himself to provide for his children, yet God knows more about what we need than we ourselves know. By praying for daily bread, we are not taking it for granted, but acknowledging that all our life depends on his mercy.

SCRIPTURE

But seek first his kingdom and his righteousness, and all these things will be given to you as well. Therefore do not worry about tomorrow, for tomorrow will worry about itself. Each day has enough trouble of its own. —Matthew 6:33–34

Then Jesus declared, "I am the bread of life. He who comes to me will never go hungry, and he who believes in me will never be thirsty."
—John 6:35

Every good and perfect gift is from above, coming down from the Father of the heavenly lights, who does not change like shifting shadows.
—James 1:17

APPLICATION

The phrase "this day" shows that we rely on God one day at a time. It is far too easy for us to forget that not only our talents, resources, and opportunities come from God, but also the next meal. Asking for what we need each day—even if it's already in our refrigerators—encourages a relationship with the One who gives all. He wants us to come to him not only with our big requests, but with our everyday requests as well. He wants us to remember and ask for his help with the most basic needs— disciplining our children, speaking to a spouse, growing spiritually, resolving a conflict with a friend, reuniting with family members, leading ministries, conducting an office meeting, and going to the movies.

So what if we ask for the wrong things—things that, while they may be good in themselves are not in God's plan for us? As a loving Father, God will always give us what is best for us, not necessarily what we want. What we receive will be what is right for us and fits God's greater goal of transforming us to be more like him.

*Forgive us our debts,
as we also have forgiven our debtors* (NIV)
*And forgive us our debts,
as we forgive our debtors* (KJV)

GOD'S ATTRIBUTE

GOD'S MERCY

WHAT DOES IT MEAN?

We ask God to forgive the wrong we have done as well as our neglect of the good things we should have done. But there is a catch: God will forgive us only as much as we forgive those who have injured us. God is merciful and he expects us to be also. If we refuse to forgive others, how can we expect God's forgiveness?

Debts vs. Trespasses

Several Greek words are used to describe sin. The Lord's Prayer in the gospel of Matthew uses the word *ophelema* which is rendered "debt" (Matt. 6:12). However, only two verses later, the gospel uses the word *paraptoma*, which is usually rendered "trespass" (Matt. 6:14). In all these cases, sin is what separates us from God, our friends, and our family. Without forgiveness—whether it be forgiving debts or forgiving trespasses—relationships suffer and redemption is not possible.

SCRIPTURE

If we confess our sins, he is faithful and just and will forgive us our sins and purify us from all unrighteousness. —1 John 1:9

For as high as the heavens are above the earth, so great is his love for those who fear him; as far as the east is from the west, so far has he removed our transgressions from us. —Psalm 103:11–12

No longer will a man teach his neighbor, or a man his brother, saying, "Know the Lord," because they will all know me, from the least of them to the greatest. For I will forgive their wickedness and will remember their sins no more. —Hebrews 8:11–12

APPLICATION

The New Testament uses five Greek words to talk about sin. The meanings range from slipping and falling (unintentional), "missing the mark" as an arrow misses the target, stepping across the line (intentional), "lawlessness" or open rebellion against God, and the word used in Matthew 6:12, which refers to a spiritual debt to God. This last aspect of sin is what Jesus illustrates in the following story.

Jesus told a parable about a man who owed a king over one million dollars. After the man begged for mercy, the king forgave the debt. Afterward, that same man demanded a few dollars from his neighbor. When his neighbor could not pay, the man had him thrown into prison. Once the king heard about it, he had the unmerciful man turned over to the jailers until he could repay the debt. Jesus finished by saying, "This is how my heavenly Father will treat each of you unless you forgive your brother from your heart" (Matt. 18:35). Jesus makes it clear that God will not show mercy to the merciless.

Sometimes we are unaware of our sins. Therefore, praying for forgiveness requires listening quietly in God's presence so that he may reveal to us our own acts of disobedience, our resentments, and our unresolved issues. Though as Christians we inevitably continue to sin, our lives ought to be characterized by a decreasing frequency of sin and an increased sensitivity to it.

The Lord's Prayer

And lead us not into temptation, but deliver us from the evil one (NIV)

And lead us not into temptation, but deliver us from evil (KJV)

GOD'S ATTRIBUTE

GOD'S PROTECTION

WHAT DOES IT MEAN?

We are taught to pray that we won't be tempted to do wrong. In a practical way, this is like praying that God will keep our minds off of tempting situations. People used to excuse bad behavior by saying, "The devil made me do it." But in reality, the devil cannot make us do wrong. We do it ourselves. God won't make us obey him, but he does give us the power to walk away from wrong choices. The Holy Spirit gives us strength to withstand temptation, avoid sin, and strive for holiness. Satan is constantly seeking to attack the hearts and minds of those who love God. The Lord provides us with the defenses we need to protect ourselves against the weapons of Satan. By praying for protection, we prepare each day for battle against evil.

SCRIPTURE

No temptation has seized you except what is common to man. And God is faithful; he will not let you be tempted beyond what you can bear. But when you are tempted, he will also provide a way out so that you can stand up under it. —1 Corinthians 10:13

Therefore put on the full armor of God, so that when the day of evil comes, you may be able to stand your ground. —Ephesians 6:13

In this you greatly rejoice, though now for a little while you may have had to suffer grief in all kinds of trials. These have come so that your faith—of greater worth than gold, which perishes even though refined by fire—may be proved genuine and may result in praise, glory and honor when Jesus Christ is revealed. —1 Peter 1:6–7

APPLICATION

The Greek word for "temptation" emphasizes the idea of testing or proving, rather than simply an enticement to sin. The Bible is clear that God is good and holy, and he would never lead us into sin. James 1:13–14 says that God does not tempt anyone, but each person is tempted by his own evil desire. So why do we pray this petition? Because it is better to avoid danger and all the trouble caused by sin than to have to fight and face the possibility of losing to it. Realistically, having the potential to do evil is part of being a human being. It gives us the opportunity to show what we are becoming. Genuine freedom requires that there be a choice between good and evil.

Yet, we also know that trials strengthen faith and character (1 Peter 1:6–7). Through our trials, we are driven closer to God through prayer and Scripture. We are reminded not to place our trust in ourselves. We learn to trust God more, and we gain the ability to help others in similar trials. So while human nature resists the realities of trials and temptations, the maturing Christian accepts the refining process they bring. All that is left is to throw ourselves on the Father who has promised not to leave us unprotected and exposed to attacks from the enemy (Satan), but to protect, deliver, and forgive.

WHAT ARE THE BEATITUDES?

The word *beatitude* comes from a Latin word (*beatus*) that means "happy" or "blessed." So the word beatitude is about some happiness or blessedness. What does it mean to be happy or blessed? The answer to this question is found in the context of the Beatitudes in Matthew 5.

The Beatitudes are the first part of Jesus' teachings called the Sermon on the Mount, (Matthew 5:1–7:29). In Matthew 4:17 Jesus began his ministry by announcing the coming of the kingdom of heaven: "Repent, for the kingdom of heaven is near." In Matthew 4:23–25, Jesus healed the sick throughout Galilee. This healing was a demonstration of the coming kingdom of heaven, of the fulfillment of God's promises through his prophets in the Old Testament. The teachings in the Sermon on the Mount, then, are descriptions and instructions for those living in the kingdom of heaven.

The Beatitudes are not imperatives; they are not commands the believer must fulfill to enter the kingdom of God. Rather, they are results of the coming of this kingdom. They are part of the Gospel, the good news that Jesus, the Messiah, has come. The good news is that God was about to intervene decisively in history and produce people like the ones described in the Sermon on the Mount.

Kingdom of God/Heaven

The expression "kingdom of heaven" only occurs in the Gospel according to Matthew. Why? Because the Gospel of Matthew appears to have been for a Jewish audience, Matthew avoids using the name of God—out of respect, Jews avoid pronouncing God's name.

- The idea of the kingdom uses an important metaphor in the Old Testament: God is King (Psalm 47:7). Kings in the ancient world had absolute power over their dominions. However, they also had responsibilities toward their subjects. Kings were supposed to:
  - *Provide protection for their territories and the people in them*
  - *Provide for the needs of their subjects*
  - *Maintain order in the kingdom, especially legal order*
  - *Represent the deity (in the Old Testament, God)—the king stood for God, representing his authority to the people*

Now and Future Kingdom

- In the New Testament, the kingdom of heaven is God's gracious rule. In other words, it is where God's will is done. The gospels make it clear that the kingdom was a present experience (Luke 11:20; 17:21). Jesus' miracles, teachings, and ministry are all manifestations of the kingdom.

- Yet, the rest of the New Testament, the apostolic letters, makes it also clear that the kingdom is a reality in the future. That is, the fullness of the kingdom will only be experienced when Jesus comes back at the end of times.

- Some theologians call these two realities about the kingdom of heaven the "already-not yet." The kingdom of heaven and the promises within it are *already* part of the church's experience. However, the fullness of the kingdom's power and influence is *not yet* experienced. Christ will bring about the fullness of the kingdom in his second coming.

The Beatitudes • 355

Beatitude 1

BLESSED ARE THE POOR IN SPIRIT, FOR THEIRS IS THE KINGDOM OF HEAVEN.

—Matthew 5:3

Meaning

The "poor in spirit" are those who recognize their need for God in all things. Like the poor and destitute who depend on others, the poor in spirit know that only God can save and protect them.

What the WORLD Says	What JESUS Says
The world and every kind of human-made religion value the "spiritual master," the guru, the great teacher. The idea is that if you know and do the right things, you can find your own spiritual salvation. People have their own answers to their problems, if they could only recognize it.	Jesus tells us that the opposite is true. The truly happy people are those who have recognized they are spiritually bankrupt before God. Their happiness consists in relying on God's strength because they know he cannot fail, and having the certainty that in the kingdom of God, the Messiah will be fully in charge (Isaiah 29:19).

Related Texts

"Once more the humble will rejoice in the Lord…" (Isaiah 29:19).

See also: Luke 6:20; Matthew 18:4; Isaiah 61:1.

Beatitude 2

BLESSED ARE THOSE WHO MOURN, FOR THEY WILL BE COMFORTED.

—Matthew 5:4

Meaning

"Those who mourn" refers to people wishing God to send his Messiah, hoping God will restore his kingdom and set the world right. Isaiah 61:2–3 tells of the coming Messiah who will "comfort all who mourn, and provide for those who grieve in Zion". These are people who understand the mess the world is in and wish for God's redemption. Their comfort consists in knowing that the Messiah has come and the redemption they have hoped for is about to occur!

What the WORLD Says	What JESUS Says
Today we avoid grief and pain. "How can a mournful person be happy?" The pursuit of happiness has become for us a goal above all goals. We have become very adept to hiding from pain and reality. Nothing is solved, but we can continue to pretend to be happy.	In stark contrast, Jesus asserts that the way to true happiness must come through a radical shift in thought, a change of mind that first makes us see ourselves as we really are—and our world as it really is—and mourn. Only after we recognize this sorrow can God comfort us. Knowing that the Messiah has come and offers redemption is the greatest comfort for those who mourn.

Related Texts

"As a mother comforts her child, so will I comfort you…" (Isaiah 66:13).

See also: John 14:1; John 16:20; Revelations 7:17; Isaiah 61:2; John 16:7.

Beatitude 3

BLESSED ARE THE MEEK, FOR THEY WILL INHERIT THE EARTH.

—Matthew 5:5

MEANING

This beatitude valludes to Psalm 37:11: "But the meek will inherit the land…." The Psalm is comparing the "evil" and "wicked" with the meek. In fact, Psalm 37:3, 5 seem to define what the psalmist means by the meek, "Trust in the Lord and do good…. Commit your way to the Lord; trust in him…." The prophet Zephaniah uses the same expression during a prophetic oracle of judgment: "…because I will remove from this city those who rejoice in their pride… But I will leave within you the meek and humble, who trust in the name of the Lord" (Zephaniah 3:11–12).

In addition, the word *meek* is an important adjective in the Bible. It is used to describe Moses in Numbers 12:3, and usually translated as "humble." Jesus describes himself with the same word in Matthew 11:29, "…for I am gentle and humble in heart…." The third Beatitude, then, refers to the meekness necessary to trust in God. It also refers to the attitude of God's servant: the meekness to serve God and do his will above our own.

Old Testament prophets communicated God's promise to restore the land to Israel. This promise was taken to be limited to the land that God originally promised to Abraham. But in the New Testament, the promise is extended It is a promise for "a new heaven and a new earth" (Revelation 21:1, 2 Peter 3:13). It is the new heaven and new earth that the meek will inherit.

What the WORLD Says	What JESUS Says
It is the proud and strong who will inherit the earth. Only the mighty have the power to seize the prize of ruling the planet. Only those who are clever and confident in themselves and their abilities have any hope of holding on to authority and dominion. "Nice guys finish last" describes this attitude that gentleness never gets you anywhere.	Although it may appear that meekness is a disadvantage according to the values of this world, it is a wonderful thing in the values of God. It is God's invitation to trust in him, to have the certainty that his plans and work will accomplish what he promised.

RELATED TEXTS

"For the Lord takes delight in his people; he crowns the humble with salvation" (Psalm 149:4).

See also: Psalm 37:3, 5, 11; 72:4; Isaiah 61:1; Numbers 12:3.

Old Testament Beatitudes

There are many beatitudes that occur in the Old Testament, some of which sound remarkably similar to Jesus' words.

- Psalm 41:1 says, "Blessed is he who has regard for the weak…" and we remember Jesus' beatitude about the merciful (Matthew 5:7).

- The book of Psalms opens with a blessing on righteous behavior: Jesus tells us that those who hunger and thirst for this righteousness shall be satisfied (Matthew 5:6).

- Psalm 32:1–2 presents a beatitude upon all whom the Lord has forgiven. The psalm goes on to speak of what it is like to confess utter dependence upon God. Jesus speaks of those who are poor in spirit as being blessed inheritors of the Kingdom of God.

- In Proverbs 8:34–35, personified wisdom says, "Blessed is the man who listens to me… for he who finds me finds life." Jesus ends the Sermon on the Mount by advising his hearers to take his words to heart. Then he reveals to them the consequences—it is a matter of life and death (Matthew 7:24–27).

Beatitude 4: BLESSED ARE THOSE WHO HUNGER AND THIRST FOR RIGHTEOUSNESS FOR THEY WILL BE FILLED.

—Matthew 5:6

Meaning

Just as poverty leads to hunger, the recognition of one's spiritual poverty leads to a hunger for righteousness. Jesus is talking to people who desire God's rule. It is a rule that brings justice for all. It is a reign in which God will satisfy the hungry and thirsty for righteousness. A fulfillment of God's promise in Isaiah 65:13, "My servants will eat…my servants will rejoice…."

What the WORLD Says	What JESUS Says
Hungering for things to be right is a fool's game. Nothing ever changes. It's fine to compromise and to set aside honor when doing what is right is inconvenient. It's all politics, so quit worrying about what is right, just go for what you need. You gotta look out for number one!	Jesus holds out the promise that those who are starved for righteousness will be satisfied. His kingdom is characterized by "righteousness, peace and joy in the Holy Spirit" (Romans 14:17).

Related Texts
See John 7:37; Isaiah 55:1–13; 65:13; John 6:48; Romans 14:17.

Blessings and Curses

Luke's gospel also contains a series of "woes" which are the opposites of the blessings (Luke 6:24–26).

- The woes describe the natural consequences to ignoring God's will. They tell us what we can expect if we do not live the way God desires.
- Here the blessings and curses are parallel, much the same as in Deuteronomy 28:1–19. At Mount Sinai, Moses set the covenant between God and the Israelites, laying out the natural consequences (both the blessings and the curses) of the people's responses.
- The parallel structure of the two passages gives the sermon in Luke's account the same authoritative feel of Moses' utterance. Jesus lays out its principles before his disciples and asks them the question, "Why do you call me, 'Lord, Lord,' and do not do what I say?" (Luke 6:46).
- It is clear Jesus claims authority for this teaching, and the Gospel of Matthew records the shock his hearers felt when faced with such claims (Matthew 7:28-29).

Righteousness

- **Righteousness in the Old Testament** was a relational concept.

    It described a legal relationship. That is, it was a relationship in terms of law, courts, judges, and so on (see Psalm 9:4; Psalm 15; Isaiah 5:7). In other words, it meant ethical or fair behavior.

    It described a covenant relationship. It is a description of God's relating and doing right toward his people; it was also the expected behavior of God's people toward God (see, Ezekiel 18:5–9, 25–32).

- **Righteousness in the New Testament** reflected the two-fold distinction in the Old Testament.

    The Apostle Paul expanded the legal sense of the concept. He applied it to Christ's work. Because of Jesus' atoning death on the cross (he died in our place), God makes right (justifies) sinners (Romans 4:5). Paul did not mean that God makes people righteous—that we can now only do what is right. Rather, he meant that God has applied Christ's righteousness—his perfect obedience and guiltlessness—to us, so we become "legally" (in the sense of a court proceeding) acquitted of the penalty of sin, which is death.

    In Matthew, Jesus was not using the "legal" sense of the concept. Rather, righteousness in the Sermon on the Mount goes back to the "covenant relationship" sense. That is, in the kingdom of heaven, relationships are restored: (1) relationship between God and humanity; (2) relationship between humanity and creation; and (3) relationships among humans. In the kingdom of heaven, people relate rightly, doing what is right in all relationships.

Beatitude 5

BLESSED ARE THE MERCIFUL, FOR THEY WILL BE SHOWN MERCY.

—Matthew 5:7

Meaning

Mercy is part of God's own nature. "The Lord, the Lord, the compassionate and gracious God, slow to anger, abounding in love and faithfulness…." (Exodus 34:6). Besides, God expects mercy from his people: "He has shown you, O man, what is good. And what does the Lord require of you? To act justly and to love mercy and to walk humbly with your God" (Micah 6:8). People who have experienced mercy and forgiveness are filled with gratitude. Their gratitude cultivates a merciful attitude in return.

What the WORLD Says	What JESUS Says
"We want justice!" "Take no prisoners" are the slogans of the proud, the strong and the careless. We like to condemn others to make ourselves feel better. Our world idolizes the arrogant and merciless in the sports world, the world of wealth and fame, and on the movie screen. "We are the champions—no time for losers." Mercy has become a liability—it is way too costly and will prevent the attainment of our goals.	Jesus again challenges the way the rest of the world thinks. Jesus lifts up mercy as an essential quality. In fact, mercy is what Jesus' life was all about—God's mercy to us. In many places Jesus makes the connection between giving mercy and receiving it (See Matthew 6:12–15, 18:21–35). It is not that we can buy God's mercy by our own acts of mercy, but that only those who know God's mercy can be truly merciful and receive God's most precious gift—eternal life.

Related Texts

See Psalm 86:15; Joel 2:13; Psalm 103:8, 145:8; Luke 6:36.

Beatitude 6

BLESSED ARE THE PURE IN HEART FOR THEY WILL SEE GOD.

—Matthew 5:8

Meaning

Seeing God is one of the greatest hopes of the believer (1 John 3:2–3). But only the pure in heart may receive this blessing. Purity of heart, the heart that desires only what God wants, is not the result of personal effort. In other words, a pure heart is not the same as maturity of Christian experience. A pure heart is clean of sin. Only Christ can clean us from sin. God must give a pure heart (Psalm 51:10). Although purity of heart is not something we work towards, it is something we desire and God grants.

What the WORLD Says	What JESUS Says
While our culture values things like pure air, pure water, pure food, it seems to devalue the pure heart. Some people insist on a "smoke-free" environment but do not mind a polluted heart.	True happiness begins in the presence of God. It is a hope that sustains and inspires those living in the kingdom of heaven. One of Jesus' constant criticisms of the Jewish leaders was their hypocrisy. That is, their desire to appear pure and holy, while being corrupted and impure inside. Jesus came to fulfill the promise in Ezekiel 36:25–27: "I will sprinkle clean water on you, and you will be clean… I will give you a new heart and put a new spirit in you…."

Related Texts

See Psalm 51:10; 1 John 3:2–3; Exodus 33:20; Psalm 24:3–4; Psalm 51; Hebrews 12:14; Revelation 22:1–4.

Beatitude 7: BLESSED ARE THE PEACEMAKERS FOR THEY WILL BE CALLED SONS OF GOD.

—Matthew 5:9

MEANING

This Beatitude brings together two important Old Testament concepts: peace and sons of God. Peace is a central characteristic of the kingdom of heaven. "The wolf will live with the lamb, the leopard will lie down with the goat, the calf and the lion and the yearling together, and a little child will lead them…" (Isaiah 11:6). Those who would normally be at war with each other will be in harmony. All things are made right and peace prevails. The Old Testament applies the title of "son of God" to the Messiah (Psalm 2:7). However, in the New Testament, the Apostle Paul explains that when we are in Christ, we "receive the full rights of sons;" in other words, we are made adopted children of God (Galatians 4:5).

What the WORLD Says	What JESUS Says
Peace at any price, Give peace a chance. Peace—the cessation of all conflict—has become what a world in war is desperately looking for. Some feel world peace would solve all problems; others are ready to buy peace at almost any cost. Many seek a personal peace through a variety of avenues—drugs, music, meditation, and others. Still, the cessation of conflict will not substitute for true peace, the kind of peace Jesus offers.	Jesus again challenges the way the rest of the world thinks. Jesus lifts up mercy as an essential quality. In fact, mercy is what Jesus' life was all about—God's mercy to us. In many places Jesus makes the connection between giving mercy and receiving it (See Matthew 6:12–15, 18:21–35). It is not that we can buy God's mercy by our own acts of mercy, but that only those who know God's mercy can be truly merciful and receive God's most precious gift—eternal life.

RELATED TEXTS
See Romans 12:18; Psalm 4:8; Isaiah 9:6; Romans 5:1.

Beatitude 8: BLESSED ARE THOSE WHO ARE PERSECUTED BECAUSE OF RIGHTEOUSNESS, FOR THEIRS IS THE KINGDOM OF HEAVEN.

—Matthew 5:10

MEANING

Just like the kingdom of heaven belongs to the poor in spirit, it also belongs to the ones persecuted because of righteousness. This verse is a reminder of God's prophets in the Old Testament. These were people who stood in for the right. They encountered opposition; they were mocked and harmed because they stood for what was right. But their reward is great. They truly enjoy the benefits of the kingdom of heaven.

What the WORLD Says	What JESUS Says
Principles are good, but not if they get you killed or cause you grief. Righteousness has little foundation in our world today. Standards for right and wrong are not defined by what God desires for our good. People get away with what they can.	Jesus made it clear to his disciples that persecution would occur: "If they persecuted me, they will persecute you also" (John 15:20). Often doing what is right leads people to feel lonely, isolated, and persecuted. However, Jesus promised that he would not leave these people alone. He sent the Holy Spirit to guide and comfort. Besides, he also promises that "Now is your time of grief, but I will see you again and you will rejoice, and no one will take away your joy" (John 16:22).

RELATED TEXTS
See 1 Peter 5:10; 1 Peter 3:14–15; Luke 6:22–23; John 15:18–21.

Other Beatitudes

BLESSED ARE THOSE WHO HAVE NOT SEEN YET HAVE BELIEVED.

—John 20:29

MEANING

Jesus is speaking about his resurrection. It is one thing to have seen the risen Christ as hundreds of his disciples did (1 Corinthians 15:6) and yet another to believe today based on the word of these eyewitnesses. There is a special blessing experienced by those who know that Christ has risen, based on the testimony alone.

What the WORLD Says	What JESUS Says
"Who really knows what happened back there 2000 years ago?" "People don't just get up from the dead. The whole thing was probably a hoax or a mistake." There is much skepticism about the events that eyewitness recorded in the Bible.	"I am the resurrection and the life" (John 11:25). We have the testimony of the Apostles (1 Corinthians 15:3-8), and the ministry of the Holy Spirit (John 15:26).

RELATED TEXTS

"Though you have not seen him, you love him; and even though you do not see him now, you believe in him and are filled with an inexpressible and glorious joy…" (1 Peter 1:8).

See also: John 1:12, 17:20–21; 1 Corinthians 15.

Other Beatitudes

IT IS MORE BLESSED TO GIVE THAN TO RECEIVE.

—Acts 20:35

MEANING

Giving, especially to those who are in need, will lead to happiness quicker than if we are only on the receiving end. The life that constantly takes without giving is a selfish life, and selfishness only leads to greater unhappiness. Meeting other peoples' needs is the road to a blessed life.

What the WORLD Says	What JESUS Says
"Get what you can now—after all, the one who dies with the most toys wins." No one's going to take care of you. If you're generous, you'll be taken advantage of. You have to make it on your own. Besides, you can't please everyone, so you have to please yourself. Charity is a scam, so get what you can, and take what you can get.	Jesus tells us that he came to serve, not to be served (Matthew 20:28). He came to give himself and calls us to the same lifestyle. It is easy to miss that this giving was a joy to him because he delighted to do what God had called him to (John 17:13). "A servant is not greater than his master" and we are blessed when we follow the Master's example (John 13:15–17).

RELATED TEXTS

"…And if you spend yourselves in behalf of the hungry and satisfy the needs of the oppressed, then your light will rise in the darkness, and your night will become like the noonday" (Isaiah 58:10).

See also: Matthew 6:1–4; Luke 6:38; 22:24–30.

BIBLE PROMISES FOR HOPE AND COURAGE

From the psalms and prophets of the Old Testament to the Gospels and letters of the New Testament, the Bible contains promises from God that can comfort us in times of pain, give us strength in times of weakness, and give us hope in times of despair.

God's love is revealed in every page of Scripture. Every promise made is a window into the heart of the Ever-Present, Sovereign, Almighty God.

I lift up my eyes to the hills—
  where does my help come from?
My help comes from the Lord,
  the Maker of heaven and earth.
He will not let your foot slip—
  he who watches over you will not slumber.
—Psalm 121:1-3

But those who hope in the Lord will renew their strength. They will soar on wings like eagles; they will run and not grow weary, they will walk and not be faint.
—Isaiah 40:31

Do not be anxious about anything, but in everything, by prayer and petition, with thanksgiving, present your requests to God. And the peace of God, which transcends all understanding, will guard your hearts and your minds in Christ Jesus.
—Philippians 4:6, 7

Jesus said, "Come to me, all you who are weary and burdened, and I will give you rest."
—Matthew 11:28

God's Promises

In His Word, God gave us promises that we can rely on when we need hope and comfort. These promises reveal to us the deepest nature of God and tell us who God is in relation to His people.

When we have problems or when we are afraid, we often begin to imagine the worst-case scenario. We forget that our loving Father holds us in His hands. When fear and doubt about God's faithfulness seem overwhelming, here's a way to refocus:

1. Choose to trust that God is bigger, smarter and more loving than you can imagine. God loves us, and He always keeps His promises. Read and reread God's promises to you. Fill your mind with them.

Trust in the Lord with all your heart and lean not on your own understanding, in all your ways acknowledge him, and he will make your paths straight.
—Proverbs 3:5, 6

2. Resist the temptation to worship the problem—it's a common form of idolatry! It's easy to get so focused on a problem so that we talk about it endlessly instead of praying about it and focusing on God's ability to handle it.

Cast all your anxiety on him because he cares for you.
—I Peter 5:7

3. Regain your joy and peace: Focus on God—on who He is and what He has done for you—and worship Him. Keep His ability, not the problem's overwhelming nature, in the forefront of your mind.

*I lift up my eyes to the hills—
where does my help come from?
My help comes from the Lord,
the Maker of heaven and earth.
He will not let your foot slip—
he who watches over you will not slumber.*
—Psalm 121:1-3

4. Pray, thank God, and let Him take care of it!

Do not be anxious about anything, but in everything, by prayer and petition, with thanksgiving, present your requests to God. And the peace of God, which transcends all understanding, will guard your hearts and your minds in Christ Jesus.
—Philippians 4:6, 7

Loneliness

The Lord your God is with you, he is mighty to save. He will take great delight in you, he will quiet you with his love, he will rejoice over you with singing.
—Zephaniah 3:17

The Lord is close to the brokenhearted and saves those who are crushed in spirit. —Psalm 34:18

Jesus said, "And surely I am with you always, to the very end of the age." —Matthew 28:20

Yet I am always with you; you hold me by my right hand. —Psalm 73:23

For the Lord will not reject his people; he will never forsake his inheritance. Judgment will again be founded on righteousness, and all the upright in heart will follow it.
—Psalm 94:14, 15

Fear

The Lord is with me; I will not be afraid. What can man do to me? The Lord is with me; he is my helper. I will look in triumph on my enemies.
—Psalm 118:6, 7

Even though I walk through the valley of the shadow of death, I will fear no evil, for you are with me; your rod and your staff, they comfort me.
—Psalm 23:4

The Lord himself goes before you and will be with you; he will never leave you nor forsake you. Do not be afraid; do not be discouraged. —Deuteronomy 31:8

Jesus said, "Peace I leave with you; my peace I give you. I do not give to you as the world gives. Do not let your hearts be troubled and do not be afraid."
—John 14:27

Worry

Do not be anxious about anything, but in everything, by prayer and petition, with thanksgiving, present your requests to God. And the peace of God, which transcends all understanding, will guard your hearts and your minds in Christ Jesus. —Philippians 4:6, 7

Cast all your anxiety on him because he cares for you.
—1 Peter 5:7

So do not worry, saying, "What shall we eat?" or "What shall we drink?" or "What shall we wear?" For the pagans run after all these things, and your heavenly Father knows that you need them. But seek first his kingdom and his righteousness, and all these things will be given to you as well. Therefore do not worry about tomorrow, for tomorrow will worry about itself. Each day has enough trouble of its own. —Matthew 6:31-34

Contentment

Wait for the Lord; be strong and take heart and wait for the Lord. —Psalm 27:14

God is not unjust; he will not forget your work and the love you have shown him as you have helped his people and continue to help them. We want each of you to show this same diligence to the very end, in order to make your hope sure. We do not want you to become lazy, but to imitate those who through faith and patience inherit what has been promised.
—Hebrews 6:10-12

Naked I came from my mother's womb, and naked I will depart. The Lord gave and the Lord has taken away; may the name of the Lord be praised.
—Job 1:21

I know what it is to be in need, and I know what it is to have plenty. I have learned the secret of being content in any and every situation, whether well fed or hungry, whether living in plenty or in want. I can do everything through him who gives me strength.
—Philippians 4:12, 13

Security

For you created my inmost being; you knit me together in my mother's womb. I praise you because I am fearfully and wonderfully made; your works are wonderful, I know that full well. My frame was not hidden from you when I was made in the secret place. When I was woven together in the depths of the earth, your eyes saw my unformed body. All the days ordained for me were written in your book before one of them came to be.
—Psalm 139:13-16

But those who hope in the Lord will renew their strength. They will soar on wings like eagles; they will run and not grow weary, they will walk and not be faint.
—Isaiah 40:31

For God did not give us a spirit of timidity, but a spirit of power, of love and of self-discipline.
—2 Timothy 1:7

He who began a good work in you will carry it on to completion until the day of Christ Jesus.

—Philippians 1:6

Strength and Courage

The Lord is my light and my salvation—whom shall I fear? The Lord is the stronghold of my life—of whom shall I be afraid? —Psalm 27:1

Be strong and courageous. Do not be afraid or terrified because of them, for the Lord your God goes with you; he will never leave you nor forsake you. —Deuteronomy 31:6

So do not fear, for I am with you; do not be dismayed, for I am your God. I will strengthen you and help you; I will uphold you with my righteous right hand. —Isaiah 41:10

Be strong and very courageous. Be careful to obey all the law my servant Moses gave you; do not turn from it to the right or to the left, that you may be successful wherever you go. Do not let this Book of the Law depart from your mouth; meditate on it day and night, so that you may be careful to do everything written in it. Then you will be prosperous and successful. —Joshua 1:7, 8

Comfort

He heals the brokenhearted and binds up their wounds. —Psalm 147:3

For the Lamb at the center of the throne will be their shepherd; he will lead them to springs of living water. And God will wipe away every tear from their eyes. —Revelation 7:17

Even though I walk through the valley of the shadow of death, I will fear no evil, for you are with me; your rod and your staff, they comfort me. —Psalm 23:4

Jesus said, "Blessed are those who mourn, for they will be comforted." —Matthew 5:4

Peace and Joy

Jesus said, "Peace I leave with you; my peace I give you. I do not give to you as the world gives. Do not let your hearts be troubled and do not be afraid." —John 14:27

Jesus said, "Come to me, all you who are weary and burdened, and I will give you rest." —Matthew 11:28

Though you have not seen him, you love him; and even though you do not see him now, you believe in him and are filled with an inexpressible and glorious joy, for you are receiving the goal of your faith, the salvation of your souls. —1 Peter 1:8, 9

Until now you have not asked for anything in my name. Ask and you will receive, and your joy will be complete. —John 16:24

Now may the Lord of peace himself give you peace at all times and in every way. —2 Thessalonians 3:16

Assurance of Salvation

And this is the testimony: God has given us eternal life, and this life is in his Son. He who has the Son has life; he who does not have the Son of God does not have life. I write these things to you who believe in the name of the Son of God so that you may know that you have eternal life. —1 John 5:11-13

If you confess with your mouth, "Jesus is Lord," and believe in your heart that God raised him from the dead, you will be saved. —Romans 10:9

For God so loved the world that he gave his one and only Son, that whoever believes in him shall not perish but have eternal life. For God did not send his Son into the world to condemn the world, but to save the world through him. —John 3:16, 17

Hope

"For I know the plans I have for you," declares the Lord, "plans to prosper you and not to harm you, plans to give you hope and a future." —Jeremiah 29:11

Find rest, O my soul, in God alone; my hope comes from him. He alone is my rock and my salvation; he is my fortress, I will not be shaken. My salvation and my honor depend on God; he is my mighty rock, my refuge. Trust in him at all times, O people; pour out your hearts to him, for God is our refuge. —Psalm 62:5-8

I lift up my eyes to the hills—where does my help come from? My help comes from the Lord, the Maker of heaven and earth. He will not let your foot slip—he who watches over you will not slumber. —Psalm 121:1-3

Why are you downcast, O my soul? Why so disturbed within me? Put your hope in God, for I will yet praise him, my Savior and my God. —Psalm 42:11

For it is by grace you have been saved, through faith— and this not from yourselves, it is the gift of God—not by works, so that no one can boast.

—Ephesians 2:8, 9

Confusion

Dear friends, do not believe every spirit, but test the spirits to see whether they are from God, because many false prophets have gone out into the world. This is how you can recognize the Spirit of God: Every spirit that acknowledges that Jesus Christ has come in the flesh is from God.
—1 John 4:1, 2

So do not fear, for I am with you; do not be dismayed, for I am your God. I will strengthen you and help you; I will uphold you with my righteous right hand.
—Isaiah 41:10

The fear of the Lord is the beginning of wisdom; all who follow his precepts have good understanding. To him belongs eternal praise.
—Psalm 111:10

Do not conform any longer to the pattern of this world, but be transformed by the renewing of your mind. Then you will be able to test and approve what God's will is—his good, pleasing and perfect will.
—Romans 12:2

Guidance

But when he, the Spirit of truth, comes, he will guide you into all truth. He will not speak on his own; he will speak only what he hears, and he will tell you what is yet to come.
—John 16:13

I will lead the blind by ways they have not known, along unfamiliar paths I will guide them; I will turn the darkness into light before them and make the rough places smooth. These are the things I will do; I will not forsake them.
—Isaiah 42:16

If I rise on the wings of the dawn, if I settle on the far side of the sea, even there your hand will guide me, your right hand will hold me fast. If I say, "Surely the darkness will hide me and the light become night around me," even the darkness will not be dark to you; the night will shine like the day, for darkness is as light to you.
—Psalm 139:9-12

In his heart a man plans his course, but the Lord determines his steps.
—Proverbs 16:9

God's Goodness and Mercy

But I pray to you, O Lord, in the time of your favor; in your great love, O God, answer me with your sure salvation. Rescue me from the mire, do not let me sink; deliver me from those who hate me, from the deep waters. Do not let the floodwaters engulf me or the depths swallow me up or the pit close its mouth over me. Answer me, O Lord, out of the goodness of your love; in your great mercy turn to me. Do not hide your face from your servant; answer me quickly, for I am in trouble.
—Psalm 69:13-17

Who is a God like you, who pardons sin and forgives the transgression of the remnant of his inheritance? You do not stay angry forever but delight to show mercy.
—Micah 7:18

Grace and peace be yours in abundance through the knowledge of God and of Jesus our Lord. His divine power has given us everything we need for life and godliness through our knowledge of him who called us by his own glory and goodness. Through these he has given us his very great and precious promises, so that through them you may participate in the divine nature and escape the corruption in the world caused by evil desires.
—2 Peter 1:2-4

And we know that in all things God works for the good of those who love him, who have been called according to his purpose.
—Romans 8:28

God's Provision

The Lord is my shepherd, I shall not be in want.
—Psalm 23:1

Then Jesus declared, "I am the bread of life. He who comes to me will never go hungry, and he who believes in me will never be thirsty."
—John 6:35

He who did not spare his own Son, but gave him up for us all—how will he not also, along with him, graciously give us all things?
—Romans 8:32

> *Therefore I tell you, whatever you ask for in prayer, believe that you have received it, and it will be yours.*
>
> —Mark 11:24

God's Forgiveness

If we confess our sins, he is faithful and just and will forgive us our sins and purify us from all unrighteousness.
—1 John 1:9

When you were dead in your sins and in the uncircumcision of your sinful nature, God made you alive with Christ. He forgave us all our sins, having canceled the written code, with its regulations, that was against us and that stood opposed to us; he took it away, nailing it to the cross.
—Colossians 2:13, 14

Praise the Lord, O my soul, and forget not all his benefits– who forgives all your sins and heals all your diseases, who redeems your life from the pit and crowns you with love and compassion.
—Psalm 103:2-4

The Lord is compassionate and gracious, slow to anger, abounding in love. He will not always accuse, nor will he harbor his anger forever; He does not treat us as our sins deserve or repay us according to our iniquities. For as high as the heavens are above the earth, so great is his love for those who fear him; As far as the east is from the west, so far has he removed our transgressions from us.
—Psalm 103:8-12

Temptation

So, if you think you are standing firm, be careful that you don't fall! No temptation has seized you except what is common to man. And God is faithful; he will not let you be tempted beyond what you can bear. But when you are tempted, he will also provide a way out so that you can stand up under it.
—1 Corinthians 10:12, 13

Because he himself suffered when he was tempted, he is able to help those who are being tempted.
—Hebrews 2:18

Finally, be strong in the Lord and in his mighty power. Put on the full armor of God so that you can take your stand against the devil's schemes. For our struggle is not against flesh and blood, but against the rulers, against the authorities, against the powers of this dark world and against the spiritual forces of evil in the heavenly realms.
—Ephesians 6:10-12

Blessed is the man who perseveres under trial, because when he has stood the test, he will receive the crown of life that God has promised to those who love him.
—James 1:12

God's Presence

When you pass through the waters, I will be with you; and when you pass through the rivers, they will not sweep over you. When you walk through the fire, you will not be burned; the flames will not set you ablaze.
—Isaiah 43:2

The Lord is near to all who call on him, to all who call on him in truth. He fulfills the desires of those who fear him; he hears their cry and saves them.
—Psalm 145:18, 19

We are hard pressed on every side, but not crushed; perplexed, but not in despair; persecuted, but not abandoned; struck down, but not destroyed.
—2 Corinthians 4:8, 9

Anger

"In your anger do not sin": Do not let the sun go down while you are still angry, and do not give the devil a foothold.
—Ephesians 4:26, 27

My dear brothers, take note of this: Everyone should be quick to listen, slow to speak and slow to become angry, for man's anger does not bring about the righteous life that God desires.
—James 1:19, 20

Do not repay anyone evil for evil. Be careful to do what is right in the eyes of everybody. If it is possible, as far as it depends on you, live at peace with everyone. Do not take revenge, my friends, but leave room for God's wrath, for it is written: "It is mine to avenge; I will repay," says the Lord.
—Romans 12:17-19

A man of knowledge uses words with restraint, and a man of understanding is even-tempered. Even a fool is thought wise if he keeps silent, and discerning if he holds his tongue.
—Proverbs 17:27, 28

The Lord replied, "My Presence will go with you, and I will give you rest."

—Exodus 33:14

Understanding

If any of you lacks wisdom, he should ask God, who gives generously to all without finding fault, and it will be given to him.

—James 1:5

Trust in the Lord with all your heart and lean not on your own understanding; In all your ways acknowledge him, and he will make your paths straight.

—Proverbs 3:5, 6

"For my thoughts are not your thoughts, neither are your ways my ways," declares the Lord. "As the heavens are higher than the earth, so are my ways higher than your ways and my thoughts than your thoughts."

—Isaiah 55:8, 9

"This is what the Lord says, he who made the earth, the Lord who formed it and established it—the Lord is his name: 'Call to me and I will answer you and tell you great and unsearchable things you do not know.'"

—Jeremiah 33:2, 3

Sharing Your Faith

How beautiful on the mountains are the feet of those who bring good news, who proclaim peace, who bring good tidings, who proclaim salvation, who say to Zion, "Your God reigns!"

—Isaiah 52:7

Then Jesus came to them and said, "All authority in heaven and on earth has been given to me. Therefore go and make disciples of all nations, baptizing them in the name of the Father and of the Son and of the Holy Spirit, and teaching them to obey everything I have commanded you. And surely I am with you always, to the very end of the age."

—Matthew 28:18-20

"You are the salt of the earth. But if the salt loses its saltiness, how can it be made salty again? It is no longer good for anything, except to be thrown out and trampled by men. You are the light of the world. A city on a hill cannot be hidden. Neither do people light a lamp and put it under a bowl. Instead they put it on its stand, and it gives light to everyone in the house. In the same way, let your light shine before men, that they may see your good deeds and praise your Father in heaven."

—Matthew 5:13-16

Jesus said, "I tell you, whoever acknowledges me before men, the Son of Man will also acknowledge him before the angels of God."

—Luke 12:8

24 Ways to Explain the Gospel

Some concepts and ideas in the Bible are difficult to express in words. Things like love, forgiveness, sin, and others are very abstract and complex. Metaphors make abstract concepts easier to understand. By using common experiences—such as gardening, becoming ill, joining a family, becoming a citizen, or having debt—metaphors allow people to connect with the concepts at a personal level.

The gospel is about the good news of Jesus: Jesus has come to save us. It is important to explore, learn, appropriate, and use the illustrations the Bible itself uses to explain what Jesus accomplished on the cross.

What does "salvation" mean? How does the Bible explain it? How do we explain it to others? The following pages list twenty four illustrations of salvation in the Bible.

> A **metaphor** is a figure of speech in which a word or phrase, literally denoting one kind of object or idea, is used in place of another to suggest a likeness or analogy between them.
>
> An **illustration** is an example or instance that helps explain and make something clear.

Removing the Veil

The Bible is God's revelation to humans (2 Tim. 3:16). That means that in the Bible we meet and get to know who God is and what he has done. Revelation means that something hidden is unveiled so it is open to be seen. We can only know God if he lifts the veil from our eyes so we can know him and his actions.

- The Lord Jesus spoke about "the secrets of the kingdom of God" (Luke 8:10). The Apostle Paul wrote about the mysteries God revealed to us in Jesus (Rom. 16:25; Eph. 1:9; 3:6; Col. 1:26).
- These secrets and mysteries are now revealed in the Scriptures. However, not all mysteries are revealed (Deut. 29:29). God lifted the veil far enough to let us see: who God is, what he has done in history, Jesus' work of salvation, and our need for that salvation.

Metaphor	**NAVIGATION**	Jesus came to seek and save the lost. He promises to guide us to the right destination (Luke 19:10).
Positive	**FOUND**	• The lost have been returned (1 Peter 2:25). • The Good Shepherd seeks the lost sheep (Matt. 18:12). • Jesus came to save what was lost (Luke 19:10). • Joy in heaven for the found (Luke 15:1–7). • Joy over the lost who is found (Luke 15:11–32).
Negative	**LOST**	• We were lost (Isa. 53:6; Jer. 50:6; Mark 6:34).
Illustrations		• The sense of being lost, especially in a hostile environment, produces many and strong emotions: fear, anxiety, anger, and disappointment. • The final problem is that lost people are incapable of reaching their destination. • Jesus reorients us toward our correct destination: God's kingdom. When Jesus saves us, we begin to walk in the direction that will lead us to our final destination in God's presence.

Metaphor	**VISION**	Jesus promises to open our eyes so we can see him and God's wonders (Isa. 42:7).
Positive	**SIGHT**	• Jesus opened the eyes of his disciples (Luke 24:31). • Jesus came to give sight (Luke 4:18–19; John 9:39).
Negative	**BLINDNESS**	• Sin is blindness (John 9:39–41). • Blind guides lead others astray (Matt. 23:16–17). • People blinded to the gospel (2 Cor. 4:4).
Illustrations		• In the Bible, physical blindness was a metaphor for spiritual blindness. • Jesus used this metaphor to teach about the gospel (see John 9) • In the ancient world, only the "gods" were able to heal blindness. • Jesus restores both physical and spiritual sight to people. • Spiritual blindness has different causes: fear, unbelief, pride, greed, hatred, and egocentrism. Spiritual blindness prevents us from seeing God's doings in the world.

Metaphor	**PURITY**	Jesus promises to cleanse us completely from our sins (Heb. 9:14).
Positive	**PURE/CLEAN**	• Jesus purifies his people (Titus 2:14). • Jesus' blood purifies us from sin (1 John 1:9).
Negative	**IMPURITY/ DIRTY**	• Jesus did not call us to be impure (1 Thess. 4:7). • We were slaves to impurity (Rom. 6:19).
Illustrations		• Cleanliness and dirtiness are daily experiences in life. The idea of cleaning something to make it acceptable is easy to visualize. • We clean our homes, our clothing, our bodies to make them presentable and pleasant for others. • Sin corrupts and makes people impure. • People cannot make themselves clean of this pollution on their own. • However, God cleans us with Jesus' blood to make us acceptable, pleasant to himself.

Sin
- Disobeying God's law in deed or attitude is a common definition of sin. The Bible uses illustrations to explain the meaning of sin.
- One of these illustrations is the idea of missing the mark. The most common words for sin in the Old and the New Testaments have the basic meaning of someone missing the mark. When people disobey, rebel, or act on their iniquity, their actions and thoughts miss the mark of God's Law. Acting or thinking in a way that contradicts God's Law leads us in a path away from God.

Metaphor	**KNOWLEDGE**	Jesus gives us the knowledge of God to be saved, to grow and mature, and live a life that pleases God (1 Tim. 2:4; 2 Tim. 2:25).
Positive	**UNDERSTANDING**	• Jesus gives the knowledge of salvation (Luke 1:77). • The Spirit gives understanding of what Christ has done (1 Cor. 2:12). • We have wisdom from God (Eph. 1:8, 17; Col. 2:2–3; James 1:5).
Negative	**IGNORANCE**	• Lack of knowledge causes destruction (Hos. 4:6). • Life apart from God is a life of ignorance (1 Peter 1:14). • Foolishness separates us from God (Jer. 5:21; 10:8; Titus 3:3).
Illustrations		• The knowledge the Bible refers to here is not only mental knowledge. It also means intimate knowledge. It is a knowledge that affects the mind and the heart. • To truly get to know a person, reading a biography, hearing from other people, or spending a few minutes with a person is not enough. One needs time and energy to develop a relationship. After that time, one knows the other person. • It is not only book knowledge that allows us to know God and obtain salvation; we need deep, relational knowledge of Jesus. • The Holy Spirit gives us this knowledge primarily through the Scriptures, prayer, and fellowship with other believers.

Metaphor	**MILITARY**	Jesus has promised to give us lasting peace (John 14:27).
Positive	**PEACE**	• Peace with God through faith in Jesus (Rom. 5:1) • Jesus destroyed barriers of hostility (Eph. 2:14–22). • Jesus has defeated the powers of this world (1 Cor. 15:24–28). • Believers are also victorious (Rom. 8:31–39).
Negative	**WAR**	• We were God's enemies (Rom. 5:10; Col. 1:21). • We were under the dominion of darkness (Col. 1:12–14). • We were followers of the Devil and his ways (Eph. 2:1–7).
Illustrations		• Life often feels like a battle: a battle with our own struggles and sin (Rom. 7:21–25), with external influences and pressures. • Yet, Jesus' victory on the cross has defeated all the powers that bind and limit humanity: sin and death are defeated; Satan and his hosts are defeated. • Jesus' death on the cross was D-Day for God's people. In the famous day in World War II, the Allies overtook the beaches of Normandy and changed the course of the war. Jesus mortally wounded Satan and sealed his fate.

Metaphor	**AGRICULTURAL**	By being connected to Jesus, God's people have new life, can be fruitful, and have an abundant life.
Positive	**CONNECTION**	• God is portrayed as a caring gardener (Isa. 5:1–7). • Jesus allows us to be saved by grafting us into the tree to become part of his people (Rom. 11:24). • God's people are like trees planted by streams of water (Ps. 1:3). • Only by being connected to Jesus, the true vine, can we bear fruit (John 15:1–8).
Negative	**SEPARATION**	• By pruning Israel, God allowed Gentiles to become part of God's people (Rom. 11:17–21). • People without Jesus are like chaff that the wind blows away (Ps. 1:4). • No one can bear fruit apart from Jesus (John 15:4–6).
Illustrations		• Gardening has become a more common urban activity—and continues to be vital in rural communities. Grafting and pruning are common activities in gardening. • Gardeners, professional and amateur, understand how important pruning is for the care and productivity of plants. • Like a gardener caring for his plants, God cares for his people. • God takes each of us, lifeless chaff, and grafts us into the tree of his people to give us new life. • Being saved is like being a plant, which is cared for and fruitful, in God's garden.

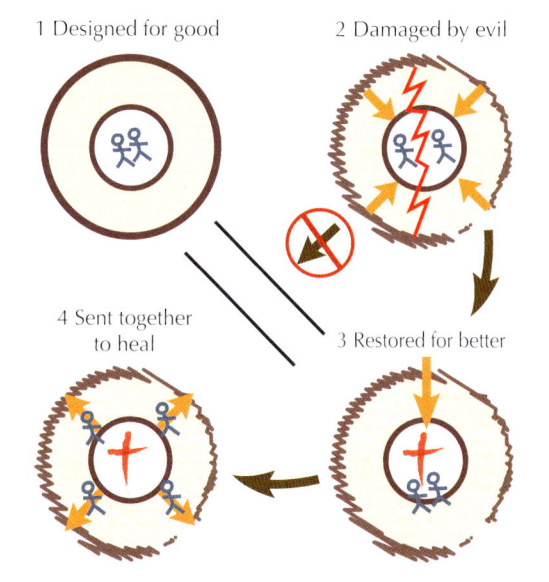

1 Designed for good
2 Damaged by evil
4 Sent together to heal
3 Restored for better

James Choung's Four Circles illustration shows God's original intention for his creation. God made humans to be and do good. However, sin affected our ability to do good. We became self-centered and enslaved to sin. Our sin breaks our relationship with God, nature, and one another.

Jesus came to restore humanity. His death on the cross liberated us from the slavery of sin and death.

Being free from sin, believers can become ambassadors of God. God is sending believers to heal relationships by preaching the good news of Jesus to a lost humanity.

Humans cannot move from circle 2 to 4 because sin has opened a gap that separates God from humans. Only through Christ is it possible to reach God.

Metaphor	**FAMILY**	Through Jesus, believers become children of God and can call him, "Abba, Father" (Gal. 4:6).
Positive	**ADOPTION**	• Christians become part of God's family (Rom. 8:15; Eph. 1:5). • Have the full rights of a son (Gal. 4:5). • Receive the assurance that God will resurrect believers' bodies.
Negative	**ORPHAN**	• The orphan, along with the widow and the poor, are the most vulnerable and needy in society (Deut. 10:18; James 1:26–27). • Life apart from God is like that of an orphan: full of uncertainty, danger, and lack of love (Hos. 14:1–3).
Illustrations		• Orphans are some of the most neglected, unprotected, and unloved people in societies throughout history. • Family connections were decisive for survival and a chance to succeed. • Christians call God "Father" because God has adopted us into his family. • The word *Abba* is a close affectionate term like *daddy*. • Now, regardless of who our family is, whether they are good or not, we all have one, good Father.

Metaphor	**LEGAL**	In Jesus we find complete forgiveness so God "will tread our sins underfoot and hurl our iniquities into the depths of the sea" (Micah 7:19).
Positive	**FORGIVENESS**	• Sins are forgiven forever (Jer. 31:34; Heb. 8:12). • Forgiveness comes from God's grace (Eph. 1:7). • God desires for everyone to be forgiven (1 Tim. 2:4).
Negative	**CRIME AND PUNISHMENT**	• A compassionate but just God (Num. 14:18) • God punishes sin (Lam. 3:39). • God is the ultimate judge (Prov. 24:12; Rom. 14:12).
Illustrations		• Most people, at one point in their lives, have had to deal with a legal issue—a parking ticket, a dispute in court, the selling of a home, or other more serious cases. • While not pleasant, we understand that the legal requirements and process is necessary and healthy. • The Bible uses this metaphor to show both the necessity and the rightness of Jesus' ministry of forgiveness and eventual judgment. • The legal consequences of sin are so big and eternal that we cannot deal with it on our own. Jesus is the only person who can and has done something about it. • His death on the cross has made it possible for us to receive God's forgiveness. • The Bible presents Jesus' work as an advocate on our behalf. He is our "defense lawyer" (Heb. 7:25; 1 John 2:1).

Metaphor	**BIOLOGY**	Jesus promises us a new and abundant life (John 10:10).
Positive	**LIFE**	• Abundant life (John 5:24–26) • Bread of life (John 6:35) • God wants us to be fruitful (John 15:8; Col. 1:10).
Negative	**DEATH**	• Deserving death (Rom. 1:32) • Death through Adam (Rom. 5:12–14) • Sin causes lack of fruit (Gen. 3:16–19; Luke 3:9; John 15:2).
Illustrations		• Death is a human reality. But Jesus offers life, eternal life. • As a metaphor, death represents the end of all possibilities and hope. People live as if they were dead, without hope and separated from God. • Jesus offers abundant life. Jesus offers a new opportunity to live life like God intended it from the beginning. • Jesus raised Lazarus from the dead (John 11). Besides being a miracle, it also illustrates what Jesus can and does for people: He gives new life. • As we receive new life, God wants us to be fruitful and share this new life with the people around us.

Metaphor	**AMBULATORY—RELATED TO WALKING**	Jesus promises to walk alongside us: "And surely I am with you always, to the very end of the age" (Matt. 28:20).
Positive	**STANDING/ WALKING**	• Walking on the path of righteousness (Prov. 8:20; 12:28) • The path of life revealed (Acts 2:28; Ps. 16:11) • Jesus keeps us from falling (Jude 1:24).
Negative	**FALLING/ STUMBLING**	• Those burdened by sin stagger and fall (Isa. 3:8). • Those who do not know Christ will stumble over him (Rom. 9:32, 33; Isa. 8:14). • Unbelief in Jesus causes us to fall (1 Peter 2:8; Luke 20:18).
Illustrations		• Walking in God's paths is a common metaphor in the Bible. • Walking brings to mind the idea of movement and journey, the satisfactions and benefits of traveling as well as the difficulties involved in it. • As we walk, we learn, grow, and move forward. • However, walking requires a direction, lest it becomes a mere wandering. • One way to understand sin is that one misses the mark, or one's destination. • Jesus gives us a new orientation. • The Holy Spirit is our compass, and the Scriptures our map. • Only by walking alongside Jesus can we reach God, our true destination.

24 Ways to Explain the Gospel

Metaphor	**LIGHT**	Jesus is the light that shines on our path toward God (John 12:46).
Positive	**LIGHT**	• Jesus is the light of the world (John 8:12). • Jesus' light shines in our hearts (2 Cor. 4:4–6). • Children of light (Eph. 5:8). • Jesus has rescued us from darkness (Col. 1:13). • Putting aside the deeds of darkness (Rom. 13:12).
Negative	**DARK**	• People living in darkness have seen a great light (Matt. 4:16). • Humans have loved darkness (John 3:19).
Illustrations		• A campfire in the wilderness provides light, warmth, safety, and sustenance. • The light helps campers to find their way back to the camp. It provides warmth for the night. It keeps wild animals away. It cooks food and purifies water. • In a similar way, Jesus provides us with guiding light, warmth, safety, and sustenance for our journey of life.

Metaphor	**HEALTH**	Jesus promises to be our physician and heal our minds, hearts, and souls (Mark 2:17).
Positive	**HEALING**	• Through Jesus' sacrifice, we are healed from our sins (Isa. 53:5; 1 Peter 2:24). • Prayer and confession to be healed (James 5:16) • God forgives our sins and heals our illness (Ps. 103:3).
Negative	**ILLNESS**	• Sickness (Matt. 9:2, 5; 1 Peter 2:24)
Illustrations		• The common experience of illness offers many possibilities to illustrate Christ's work. • "It is not the healthy who need a doctor but the sick…" Jesus used these words to describe his own ministry. The prophet Isaiah had promised: "No one living in Zion will say, 'I am ill'; and the sins of those who dwell there will be forgiven" (Isa. 33:24). • There are illnesses that our body can fight off alone. There are others, however, that require help. There are personality faults and character issues that one can deal with. There is a deep, moral problem, called sin, that only one physician can cure: Jesus.

Metaphor	**TRUTH**	Jesus offers the only truth that can lead us to God (John 14:6).
Positive	**CORRECT/ TRUE**	• Salvation as knowledge of the truth (1 Tim. 2:4) • The gospel is the word of truth (Eph. 1:13; John 17:17). • The truth of the gospel makes us free (John 8:32). • The Holy Spirit leads us to the truth (John 16:13).
Negative	**ERROR/FALSE**	• False prophets deceive and lead astray (Ezek. 13:1–23; Matt. 24:11, 24). • False teachings lead to destruction (2 Peter 2:1–2).
Illustrations		• Traveling without a map can lead to an exciting adventure or a disastrous end. A map is helpful when we follow its instructions. A correct map will lead us faithfully. An incorrect map will lead us astray. • The words of the gospel lead us correctly to our final destination.

Metaphor	**RELATIONSHIP**	Jesus promises to be more than our master. He promises to be our friend (John 15:15).
Positive	**FRIEND**	• Jesus gave his life for his friends (John 15:13). • We show our friendship through our obedience (John 15:14).
Negative	**ENEMY**	• We were God's enemies (Rom. 5:10; Col. 1:21); in Jesus, we are reconciled with God. • Jesus will defeat his enemies (1 Cor. 15:25).
Illustrations		• Sin has created a gap between God and humans. • This gap is enmity between God and us. • Jesus became a bridge that allows us to walk over to God. • Then, we can have a relationship with God as his friends.

People (Sinful) — God (Holy)

This drawing illustrates how Jesus' work on the cross allows sinful people to begin a relationship with God and be rescued from eternal death.

Metaphor	**ECONOMIC**	Jesus bought each believer at a price; the sale is final (1 Cor. 6:20; 7:23).
Positive	**PAYMENT**	• Offered himself as ransom (payment) on our behalf (Matt. 20:28; Heb. 9:15) • His sacrifice on the cross paid in full the debt that sin caused.
Negative	**DEBT**	• Sin caused a "debt" with God—Jesus cancels this debt (Col. 2:14). • The price for redemption is high (1 Peter 1:19).
Illustrations		• Difficult economic times make the burden of debts a very concrete reality. Although we often ignore it, the burden of sin is much heavier. • Getting rid of the huge weight of financial debt would allow people to start over, be wiser, and live better. Similarly, when Jesus lifts the weight of sin from us through his death, we are free to live life to the fullest. Jesus offers the opportunity to live without the burden of sin so we can live the abundant life that Jesus promises.

Redemption
- Redemption refers to the payment one offers for the deliverance of someone or something.
- In the ancient world, redemption was related to the freedom of prisoners of war and slaves. In this sense, God redeemed Israel from Egypt with power.
- The New Testament uses this metaphor to explain what Jesus accomplished on the cross. Jesus redeemed us from the power of sin and evil. His blood was the price he paid to make us free. The price for our freedom from sin and death was too high for any human to pay. Jesus alone was able to make the only and final payment for our redemption. Jesus' redemption is a free offer to every person.

Metaphor	**FREEDOM**	Jesus has promised to make us free from all bondage (John 8:36).
Positive	**DELIVERANCE**	To free us to: • New life (Rom. 6:4) • Freedom to serve (Gal. 5:1, 13) • Eternal life (John 10:28)
Negative	**SLAVERY**	To free us from: • Sin (Rom. 6:18) • The curse of the law (Gal. 4:3–5) • The fear of death (Heb. 2:14–15)
Illustrations		• Many things bind us: self-interest, addictions, broken relationships, anger and bitterness, destructive pasts, and debts. Sin captures our minds and hearts. Only a miracle can break those bonds. • Jesus breaks these bonds and gives us new life. This new life gives us the freedom to serve God, to become the people God wants us to be.

Metaphor	**NATIONAL**	Jesus allows us to become citizens of the kingdom of heaven.
Positive	**CITIZEN**	• Fellow citizens (Eph. 2:19) • Citizens of heaven (Phil. 3:20)
Negative	**ALIEN**	• Alien to a sinful world (1 Peter 2:11) • People looking for a country of their own (Heb. 11:13) • Longing for our real home (2 Peter 3:13)
Illustrations		• Being a citizen of a country provides identity, security, and rootedness. • Christians are citizens of God's kingdom. Our loyalties are to God and his will. • In a globalized world, where people move so fast and everywhere, the concept of citizenship takes new meanings. • Our identity, security and sense of community do not depend on the place or culture in which we were born. Rather, it depends on the values of the kingdom of God.

Citizenship in the Roman World
- The concept of Roman citizenship is the background for the Apostle Paul's use of citizenship as an illustration of salvation. The Apostle Paul was a Roman citizen by birth (Acts 22:25–29).
- Access to Roman citizenship was limited and difficult to obtain. Although many people achieved, earned, or were granted Roman citizenship, their citizenship was of a secondary kind. Even this secondary type of citizenship provided many rights and protections. In the Roman Empire, when slaves were freed, they became citizens.

Metaphor	**HUMAN DEVELOPMENT**	Jesus promises to complete the transforming work of maturity in each believer (Phil. 1:6).
Positive	**MATURITY**	• Parable of the Sower (Luke 8:14) • Becoming mature (Eph. 4:13) • Perseverance to maturity (James 1:4) • No longer foolish (Titus 3:3)
Negative	**IMMATURITY**	• Idols made by humans are foolishness (Jer. 10:8). • In need of teaching (Rom. 2:20–22) • Ignorance of God's will (Eph. 5:17)
Illustrations		• One of the effects of sin is that it stunts growth. God intended humans to live a full life. Sin does not allow us to reach our true potential. It makes people act like fools, in immature ways. • Sin has stunted our growth. Although we claim wisdom, our sin has made us fools (Rom. 1:22). • When Jesus cares for us, we become like trees planted by abundant waters that have the maturity to stand during droughts (Ps. 1:3).

Metaphor	**CREATION**	Jesus gives us the opportunity to be born again, to be a new creation. It is more than a fresh start. It is the right start (John 3:16–18).
Positive	**NEW CREATION**	• Jesus used the language of being born again (John 3:3, 7; 1 Peter 1:23). • Those born of God are children of God (1 John 3:9–10). • Christians are a new creation (2 Cor. 5:17; Gal. 6:15). • Jesus is presented as the second Adam (Rom. 5:15–17). • Jesus is the firstborn of the new creation (1 Cor. 15:27; 2 Cor. 5:17; Col. 1:15; Phil. 3:21).
Negative	**OLD CREATION**	• Sin transformed all of creation (Gen. 3:18; Rom. 8:22). • Sin entered through Adam's disobedience (Rom. 5:12–14). • This creation will pass and God will make all things new (Rev. 21:1; 2 Peter 3:13). • Nothing of the old creation can enter the kingdom of God (John 3:5).
Illustrations		• Jesus illustrated this point with a common object of his time: an unshrunk cloth to patch an old garment (Matt. 9:16). • The illustration is clear: when the garment is washed, the patch will shrink and tear the garment beyond repair. The old and the new do not mix with each other. • In the same way, God's grace requires a new heart (Ezek. 36:26). • Just as God makes us a new creation, God will make all things new one day (Rev. 21:1).

Creation to New Creation

Human Nature	What	When	Where	Who
Innocent	Good heart (Gen. 1:31)	In the beginning (past time)	In Eden (in paradise)	In Adam (our first parent)
Fallen	Corrupt heart (Gen. 3:19; 6:5,11,12; Rom. 3:9–19)	Upon the first sin (present time)	Upon the Earth (a wilderness outside Eden)	Upon all humanity
Redeemed	Transformed heart (Rom. 12:1–2)	At Christ's death and resurrection (present time)	At Calvary (outside the city of Jerusalem)	At conversion (all who are in Christ)
Perfect	Pure heart (Matt. 5:8; Heb. 12:14)	The age to come (future time)	The new heavens and earth (in the New Jerusalem)	God's people (believers in Christ, the last Adam)

For it is by grace you have been saved, through faith—and this not from yourselves, it is the gift of God—not by works, so that no one can boast.

—Ephesians 2:8–9

Metaphor	**RESCUE**	Jesus promises to rescue and keep us safe forever (Deut. 31:6; Heb. 13:5).
Positive	**SAVED**	• Jesus came to save the world (John 3:17). • Saves us from our sins (Eph. 2:1–9). • Saves us from God's just wrath (Rom. 5:9). • Saves us from death (Heb. 2:14–15). • Whoever believes in Jesus will not perish (John 3:16). • Jesus gives eternal life (John 10:28).
Negative	**PERISHING**	• God does not want anyone to perish (2 Peter 3:9). • Eternal Death (Matt. 7:13; 25:41, 46; Rev. 20:14–15) • Gehenna (Garbage Dump) (Matt. 5:22, 29, 30; 10:28; 18:9; 23:15, 33; Mark 9:43–47; Luke 12:5)
Illustrations		• Jesus speaks of the wicked perishing in "Gehenna." • Gehenna is another word for hell, but it was also the garbage dump of the city of Jerusalem, where garbage was continually burning. • Our sin had broken us and made us useless to God. • We were ready for the garbage dump. • Jesus came to rescue us from the never-ending trash pile. • Jesus' cross stands as a bridge that leads us to eternal safety.

Evangelism Plans

These four evangelism plans are ways to illustrate the gospel so its message is easier to understand. These four plans have helped millions of Christians around the world to bring the message of the gospel in a simple yet effective way.

Four Spiritual Laws (Campus Crusade for Christ)	▶ God loves you and offers a wonderful plan for your life (John 3:16; 10:10). ▶ Humans are sinful and separated from God. Thus, they cannot know and experience God's love and plan for their lives (Rom. 3:23; 6:23). ▶ Jesus Christ is God's only provision for humanity's sin. Through Jesus, you can know and experience God's love and plan for your life (Rom. 5:8; John 14:6). ▶ We must individually receive Jesus Christ as Savior and Lord; then we can know and experience God's love and plan for our lives (John 1:12; Eph. 2:8–9).
Bridge to Life (Navigators)	▶ The Bible teaches that God loves all humans and wants them to know him (John 10:10; Rom. 5:1). ▶ But humans have sinned against God and are separated from God and his love. This separation leads only to death and judgment (Rom. 3:23; Isa. 59:2). ▶ But there is a solution: Jesus Christ died on the cross for our sins (the bridge between humanity and God) (1 Peter 3:18; 1 Tim. 2:5; Rom. 5:8). ▶ Only those who personally receive Jesus Christ into their lives, trusting him to forgive their sins, can cross this bridge. Everyone must decide individually whether to receive Christ (John 3:16; John 5:24).
Steps to Peace with God (Billy Graham Crusade)	▶ Step 1. God's Plan ⇒ Peace and Life (Rom. 5:1; John 3:16; 10:10) ▶ Step 2. Humanity's Problem ⇒ Separation (Rom. 3:23; 6:23; Isa. 59:2) ▶ Step 3. God's Remedy ⇒ The Cross (1 Tim. 2:5; 1 Peter 3:18; Rom. 5:8) ▶ Step 4. Human Response ⇒ Receive Christ (John 1:12; 5:24; Rom. 10:9)
The Romans Road of Salvation	▶ Human Need (Rom. 3:23) ▶ Sin's Penalty (Rom. 6:23) ▶ God's Provision (Rom. 5:8) ▶ The Person's Response (Rom. 10:9)

Spiritual Gifts

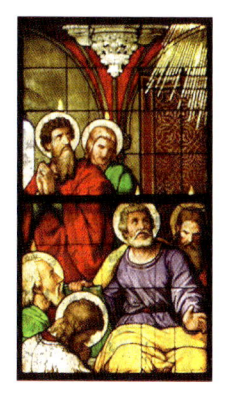

Gifts for Life

You've become a believer and, perhaps, even joined a church. Wonderful! Your wonderful and challenging journey has just begun. The church as God's people has existed for many hundreds of years. The church you're becoming part of has likely been around for a few years already. How do you, being new to Christianity and the different practices in your specific congregation, go about being an active member in the life of the church?

The good news is that God himself will help each believer fit into God's church. The way God does this is through the special empowering of the Holy Spirit. God not only promised to be with each of his people "to the very end of the age" (Matt. 28:20), but he also promised to give us all the tools we need to serve him and each other—"you will receive power when the Holy Spirit comes on you" (Acts 1:8).

Gifts for the Body

The apostle Paul used a helpful illustration to explain this important teaching. When he explained what the church is and how it works, he used the image of the body.

Paul taught in his letters that for the church to function correctly, each member of the "body" must perform a role. God prepared *ministries*. Ministries are activities believers do that serve and allow the church to grow and mature. These ministries exist for each believer. God empowers every believer that forms part of the church to participate in one or more of these ministries. Through the work of the Holy Spirit, God gives gifts—in the sense of "presents"—to each believer. These gifts are called "spiritual gifts" because they are directly connected to the work of the Holy Spirit. Through these gifts, the life and the ministry of the church occur.

Read on to discover presents from God that allow us to be active members of Christ's body.

> *"For just as each of us has one body with many members, and these members do not all have the same function, so in Christ we, though many, form one body, and each member belongs to all the others."*
>
> —Romans 12:4–5

GIFTS?

The English word *gift* has two meanings:

1. A special ability or talent—such as playing piano, learning languages, and so on.

2. Something that is given without a charge and freely—such as a *present* for a birthday.

These two definitions color the way we read the New Testament passage. For some of these ministries God did give special talents and abilities—for healings, miracles, or speaking in tongues. However, the emphasis of the New Testament is not on the abilities themselves but on how they function in the ministries (services) of the church.

As we think about the spiritual gifts, we must keep in mind that what makes them spiritual is that they come from the Holy Spirit. And what makes them a gift is that the Holy Spirit freely gives them to us so we can use them in serving the body of Christ. Spiritual gifts are not meant to be stored or publicized. They are meant to be *used* for the service of the body.

The Real Force—The Holy Spirit

Who is the Spirit?

The Holy Spirit is a person. The Spirit is God. Before his death and resurrection, Jesus promised his disciples to send the Spirit of truth, one who "will teach you all things and will remind you of everything I have said to you" (John 14:26). Jesus has not left his disciples alone. The Holy Spirit is with us.

What does the Spirit do?

Besides giving us comfort as we wait for Jesus' return, the Spirit is actively moving within our lives.

The Holy Spirit Acts in these Ways:

ADVOCATES (John 14:16)—"And I will ask the Father, and he will give you another advocate to help you and be with you forever." The Holy Spirit teaches, reveals, and interprets Jesus' words to his followers. The Holy Spirit is the divine presence with Jesus' followers.

CONVICTS (John 16:8–9)—"When he comes, he will prove the world to be in the wrong about sin and righteousness and judgment." The Holy Spirit will convince people of the need to repent from sin, that justice is only achieved through Christ, and that judgment of all humanity belongs to Jesus alone.

DRAWS TO CHRIST (John 16:14)—"He will glorify me because it is from me that he will receive what he will make known to you." The Holy Spirit leads people to Christ at all times.

TEACHES (John 14:26)—"But the Advocate, the Holy Spirit, whom the Father will send in my name, will teach you all things and will remind you of everything I have said to you."

SEALS (Eph. 1:13)—"And you also were included in Christ when you heard the message of truth, the gospel of your salvation. When you believed, you were marked in him with a seal, the promised Holy Spirit," Like a "seal of authenticity," the Holy Spirit marks us as God's property.

GUIDES (John 16:13)—"But when he, the Spirit of truth, comes, he will guide you into all the truth. He will not speak on his own; he will speak only what he hears, and he will tell you what is yet to come."

INTERCEDES (Rom. 8:26)—"In the same way, the Spirit helps us in our weakness. We do not know what we ought to pray for, but the Spirit himself intercedes for us through wordless groans."

EMPOWERS (Acts 1:8)—"But you will receive power when the Holy Spirit comes on you; and you will be my witnesses in Jerusalem, and in all Judea and Samaria, and to the ends of the earth."

These ministries identify the Holy Spirit's main function: to glorify Christ (John 16:14). Similarly, the primary function of our own ministries is *to glorify Christ*. The other critical function of our ministries—service—in the church is to allow the body to mature, to grow up. How do we reach this goal? Through the ministry of the Holy Spirit, especially his ministry of empowering believers, each Christian becomes an extension of God's own ministry among his people.

The Nurturing of the Body — Spiritual Gifts

One way the Holy Spirit empowers believers in the church is by creating ministries—opportunities to serve. Each believer contributes to the growth—both in numbers and in maturity—of the church. If the Holy Spirit is the "fire" that gives the body warmth and life, believers are the "members of the body" that keep it moving.

The Holy Spirit empowers believers to be part of these ministries. The spiritual gifts, then, are the tools we use to carry on those ministries. The function of the spiritual gifts is service. Paul's main interest in his letters to the early churches is to teach, guide, and help them to grow as the body of Christ.

FOUR LISTS of SPIRITUAL GIFTS in the BIBLE

EPHESIANS 4:11	ROMANS 12:6–8	1 CORINTHIANS 12:8–10	1 CORINTHIANS 12:28–30
Apostles Prophets Evangelists Pastor-teachers (or pastors and teachers)	Prophecy Service/serving Teaching Encouragement One who gives One who leads One who shows mercy	A word of wisdom A word of knowledge Faith Healings Workings of miracles Prophecy Distinguishing the spirits Kinds of tongues Interpretation of tongues	Apostles Prophets Teachers Miracles Healings Helps Guidance Speaking in tongues Interpreting tongues

Cessationism and Continuationism

One of the most debated issues in Christian theology is the question of what some people call the "extraordinary or miraculous" gifts of the Holy Spirit. These gifts are:

- APOSTLESHIP
- PROPHECY
- SPEAKING and INTERPRETING TONGUES
- WORKING of MIRACLES

MOST COMMON CHRISTIAN UNDERSTANDING of the GIFTS:

- Some believers hold firmly that these four gifts were limited to a period between Jesus' ascension and the death of the last Apostle, Jesus' beloved disciple John (about AD 90). People who hold this view are known as cessationists.
- Other Christians affirm the continuation of all of the gifts. They are continuationists.
- Many other believers would fall in an in-between category of being "open but cautious."
- Still other believers hold that some of the four gifts continue, while others have ceased.

Whatever view we take, we must remember that according to Paul, the spiritual gifts are meant to promote the unity of the body (1 Cor. 12:12; Eph. 4:12–13). In the letters of Paul, the unity of the body is necessary for the church's growth. The alternative, disunity and spiritual arrogance, tears down the church.

	Cessationists	Continuationists
DEFINITION	Cessation refers to the conviction that the extraordinary gifts that the Holy Spirit gives to the church ended with the closing of the apostolic age.	Continuation refers to the conviction that the Holy Spirit continues to grant extraordinary gifts to the church so it can continue its mission in the world.
MAIN POINTS	• The extraordinary gifts of the Holy Spirit were necessary to lay down the church's foundation—in other words, the teachings of the apostles. • Apostleship as a gift ended when the New Testament-era apostles died. Since the church has already been founded, the presence of apostles is no longer necessary. • Since the writings of the New Testament are finished, there is no need for new revelation. Thus, the gift of prophecy is no longer necessary. • Although God can and does do miracles, the gift of working of miracles by individuals has ended along with the gifts of apostleship and prophecy.	• Although the foundation work—for example, writing the New Testament—of apostles and prophets has ended, they had other functions—for example, planting new churches or bringing the gospel to people who've never heard it. • The extraordinary gifts of the Spirit aid the church in fulfilling its mission by providing encouragement, edification, and guidance. • Unlike prophecy as an office in the Old Testament, prophecy in the church is a gift that any believer can have, though some have a special gift in this area. Prophecy today does not reveal God's will the way the Scriptures did. Prophecy today communicates God's word to his people for encouragement, edification, and guidance. • Prophecy and all other gifts are dependent and subordinated to the authority of the Scriptures.

What is the Church?

The word *church* comes from a Greek word (*kuriaskos*) that means "belonging to the Lord." However, the most common word in the New Testament for *church* is *ekklesia*, which means "assembly, gathering." In the New Testament, it is used for the gathering of believers in specific places to worship and have fellowship together.

The church is made up of individuals. Yet, it is more than just the sum of individuals. It is a divine institution. The church is one (it is Christ's body) even if it can be found in many places and at different times. The church is universal. Christ's body is found throughout the world, and it is timeless. It contains all the people who have believed and those who will believe.

POWER and WEAKNESS

God empowers his people to carry on their ministries in the church. Spiritual gifts aren't only about the abilities one may have, but about what God is doing in and through the church and how we fit in. God is always active inside and outside the church. We must discern how he is active and ask him to empower us to be part of those activities.

The apostle Paul reminds us that our calling does not depend on who we are, what we have, and what we can do. God uses for his glory what we can offer. Yet, God is not limited to our personality and abilities. Surprisingly, according to Paul, God often calls us to serve him and others out of our weaknesses, even to the point of emphasizing that we are weak. It is in these cases that God's strength shines through our weaknesses. Paul concludes that, "For when I am weak, then I am strong" (2 Cor. 12:10). Paul teaches us that we must serve out of humility, dependence, and trust.

Description of Gifts

APOSTLE
1 Cor. 12:28–29; Eph. 4:11

We can speak of more than one kind of apostle in the New Testament. The first kind refers to those Jesus called and set apart, who witnessed his life and ministry. They are the first twelve disciples, although it also includes people like Paul and James (see 1 Cor. 9:1; 15:5–9; Gal. 2:9). A different type of apostle includes those who were especially appointed as missionaries to spread the gospel—for example, Barnabas (Acts 13:2–3; 14:14) and Silas (Acts 15:40; 1 Thess. 1:1, 2:6).

MIRACLES
1 Cor. 12:10, 28–29

For the apostle Paul, miracles existed to validate the message of the apostles—"I persevered in demonstrating among you the marks of a true apostle, including signs, wonders and miracles" (2 Cor. 12:12). Some examples of miracles in the New Testament are the judgment of Ananias and Sapphira (Acts 5:9–11) and the judgment of Elymas the magician (Acts 13:6–11). Many Christians believe that the need for these miracles for validation ended with the passing of the apostles. However, Christians affirm the possibility and existence of miracles from God today. Miracles strengthen the believers' faith. They build up the church.

EVANGELIST
Eph. 4:11

Though sharing the good news of the gospel is a privilege and responsibility of every believer, some people have the ability to present the message of salvation in a clear, simple, and engaging way. Those who fit in this ministry can provide leadership to all believers to carry on their task of evangelism.

TEACHING, PASTOR-TEACHER, and EXHORTATION
1 Cor. 12:28–29; Rom. 12:7-8; Eph. 4:11

Traditionally, the ministry of pastors is closely connected to that of teaching. In addition to caring for the members of each church, the other crucial role of pastors is to explain the apostolic teachings to believers. However, many people can thrive as teachers without having to become pastors. Teaching is a vital ministry of the body of Christ. Beyond giving information, teaching allows people to deepen their relationship with God. Furthermore, teaching equips believers to be aware of false teachings that they might encounter. Closely connected to other gifts, exhortation means that one comes alongside of someone with words of encouragement, comfort, consolation, and counsel to help them be all God wants them to be.

HEALINGS
1 Cor. 12:9, 28, 30

Connected to miracles, healings were also a demonstration of God's power that validated apostolic authority. The specific "office" of healer—if there was ever one—may have ended with the apostolic age. However, Christians continue to believe that God can and does heal as a response to prayer.

WORD of WISDOM and WORD of KNOWLEDGE
1 Cor. 12:8

We must understand these two gifts in the context of the whole letter. The Corinthian church seems to have struggled with being too impressed with, and attracted to, the more "flashy" gifts of tongues and prophecy. Although Paul does not deny their importance, he makes it clear that these gifts without love, wisdom, and knowledge are empty. Wisdom, the discerning and understanding of God's doings in the world and the way the world functions, is a critical ministry that allows all ministries and gifts of the church to work in harmony and unity. Knowledge allows believers to understand and explain God's revelation to others.

HELPING, SERVING, GIVING, and MERCY
1 Cor. 12:28, Rom. 12:7, 8

These different gifts are so closely related that some tend to assign them to the tasks of deacons. However, the overall context of these passages suggests that they are activities for all believers. These gifts are crucial for the maturity of the church. Service stands at the core of our calling. The practice of these gifts can be as varied as offering help to widows, orphans, and the poor, give aid for the daily activities in the church, and discerning when individuals or groups are in need of help to carry on their ministries.

FAITH
1 Cor. 12:9

This faith does not refer to "saving faith," which every believer has. Nor does it refer to the daily faith necessary for the Christian life (Eph. 2:8), which every believer is expected to exercise (Heb. 11). Rather, it refers to a faith that complements the other gifts and allows them to be daring and active. When the ministries of the church face odds that overwhelm most people, this ministry of faith challenges, encourages, and reminds people that we serve a powerful God who owns and controls all things.

LEADERSHIP and GUIDANCE
Rom. 12:8, 1 Cor. 12:28

Although traditionally these gifts have been related to the ministry of elders in the church, the context of the passages suggests that they are meant for all believers. These ministries are applicable to many areas of church life: goals for the church, teaching, evangelism, acts of mercy and service, and so on.

DISTINGUISHING BETWEEN SPIRITS
1 Cor. 12:10

In the context of the letter to the Corinthians, distinguishing (or discerning) between spirits may refer to two activities. One is the ability to recognize truth from error. In this sense, truth is a revelation from God, so this gift is the ability to discern when a prophecy actually comes from God. According to many believers, since God has stopped revealing his will in the same way he did in the Bible and since prophecies have stopped, this part of discerning is no longer necessary. However, the second activity is still important. It refers to the ministry that discerns when a teaching or a plan fits in with God's will, whether it comes from the leading of the Holy Spirit. It also includes the ability to discern when a new teaching contradicts the basic teachings of the Christian faith—for example, contradicts teaching on the Trinity, the person and ministry of Christ, the person and ministry of the Holy Spirit, the inspiration of the Scriptures.

TONGUES and INTERPRETATION of TONGUES
1 Cor. 12:10, 28, 30

The apostle Paul did not discourage speaking of tongues—in fact, he urged the Corinthian leaders to not forbid it (1 Cor. 14:39). However, Paul was correcting an error in the church. Some in the Corinthian church were too enchanted with the flashy gift of speaking in tongues. Paul reminds them that speaking in tongues without love is like a "resounding gong or a clanging cymbal." Paul's main concern is the edification of the church as a whole, as a body. He explains that speaking in tongues edifies the one speaking (1 Cor. 14:4). Thus, for the apostle Paul, speaking in tongues seems to be a secondary. Today, Christians are divided on whether the ministry of speaking in tongues has stopped or continues. Paul makes it clear that the unity of the body of Christ is far more important than speaking, or not speaking, in tongues.

Spiritual Gift Questionnaire

This questionnaire is one of many tools to help you discern where you fit in the church's many ministries. It can help you to either learn or confirm areas of affinity—areas that you naturally tend to focus on. But as with most spiritual gifts tests, it is not meant to definitively *tell* you what your gift is. Simply knowing your spiritual gifts is not the goal, but rather knowing how to serve God as a member of Christ's body and serve are the real goals.

- Ask God for guidance and wisdom to find your place in the church's ministry.
- Your life experience can be a good guide to find your interest and abilities.
- Be mindful of the needs of your church. Sometimes, God will call you to minister—serve—in places you might not prefer. The calling may be temporary or long term.
- Be ready, willing, and courageous. Obedience is challenging.
- Listen to the encouragement, wisdom, and guidance of other members of the body of Christ.
- Be prayerful about finding God's will for you.

For each question, choose a response between 0 and 3 as follows:

3 Consistently, almost always true   **2** Most of the time, usually true   **1** Some of the time, once in a while   **0** Not at all, never

---

1. ____ I am able to communicate effectively the message of salvation.
2. ____ I make critical decisions when necessary.
3. ____ I rejoice when meeting needs through sharing my possessions.
4. ____ I enjoy studying.
5. ____ I thrive when trusting God in difficult situations.
6. ____ I actively meet physical and practical needs.
7. ____ I can analyze events or ideas from different points of view.
8. ____ I naturally encourage others.
9. ____ I am acutely in tune with the emotions of other people.
10. ____ I am a cheerful giver.
11. ____ Yielding to God's will gives me great joy.
12. ____ It is very important for me to do things for people in need.
13. ____ I can identify those who need encouragement.
14. ____ I am sensitive to the hurts of people.
15. ____ I am sensitive to new truths and to how they apply to specific situations.
16. ____ I have experience with organizing ideas, resources, time, and people effectively.
17. ____ I am able to discern when sermons or teachings do not conform to the Scriptures.
18. ____ I can trust in God even in very difficult moments.
19. ____ I can discern where God wants a group to go and help it get there.
20. ____ I have the ability and desire to teach.
21. ____ I am sensitive to what people need.
22. ____ I have experience making effective and efficient plans for accomplishing the goals of a group.
23. ____ I can explain Scripture in simple and accessible ways.
24. ____ I spend time digging into facts.
25. ____ Sharing Christ with nonbelievers comes naturally to me.
26. ____ I can discern the motivation of persons and movements.
27. ____ I can delegate and assign meaningful work.
28. ____ I detect when people experience stress and distress.
29. ____ I desire to give generously and unpretentiously to worthwhile projects and ministries.
30. ____ I can relate God's truths to specific situations.
31. ____ I can organize facts into meaningful relationships.
32. ____ I can detect honesty when people share their religious experiences.
33. ____ I look for ways to encourage and comfort others around me.
34. ____ I am able to help people flourish in their ministries.
35. ____ I can make complex ideas and doctrines simple and accessible.
36. ____ I look for opportunities to establish relationships with non-believers.

Write your answer for each question, then add your answers for each gift. Pay attention to 2's or 3's. These are likely the gifts you are currently leaning toward.

GIFT	QUESTION NUMBER	YOUR ANSWER	TOTAL
Discernment	17		
	26		
	32		
Exhortation	8		
	13		
	33		
Evangelism	1		
	25		
	36		
Faith	5		
	11		
	18		
Giving	3		
	10		
	29		
Guidance	16		
	22		
	27		
Help/Serving	6		
	12		
	21		
Knowledge	4		
	24		
	31		
Leadership	2		
	19		
	34		
Mercy	9		
	14		
	28		
Teaching	20		
	23		
	35		
Wisdom	7		
	15		
	30		

Spiritual Disciplines

What are Spiritual Disciplines?

Understanding the power of sin over us will help us grasp the meaning and necessity for spiritual disciplines.

Sin

The Bible explains sin with several metaphors. Sin:

- Captures (Prov. 5:22; Heb. 12:1)
- Enslaves (Gen. 4:7; John 8:34; Rom. 7:14, 23; Gal. 3:22)
- Is deadly (Rom. 6:23; 5:12; Eph. 2:1)
- Is a sickness (Ps. 32:1–5; Isa. 53:5; Matt. 9:2, 5; 1 Peter 2:24)
- Is impurity (Zech. 13:1; Ps. 51:2; Isa. 1:18)
- Separates (Isa. 59:1–2; Eph. 2:12–16; 4:18)

Sin disguises itself as habits—that is, behaviors and thoughts that have become "second-nature." Many of the sins we commit come so naturally to us that we hardly notice them—whether they occur while driving on a busy freeway, having conversations about other people, abusing substances or other harmful things that may temporarily make us feel better. Habits require time and repetition to become entrenched. These habits enslave us, lead us to deadly consequences, make us sick, corrupt us, and ultimately separate us from God. We have to unlearn many of these behaviors and learn behaviors that are fit for the citizens of God's kingdom.

Spiritual disciplines are practices we do regularly that can help us change, with the power and grace of the Holy Spirit, our sinful habits into good habits that make us more like Christ and connect us closer to God.

Spiritual Disciplines and Salvation

We are saved by and through God's grace alone. We can do nothing to earn our salvation. Spiritual disciplines are not behaviors or practices that make us right with God in any way. They are tools that the Holy Spirit can use to renew our hearts. When we practice spiritual disciplines:

- We recognize that Jesus is the King of our lives.
- We acknowledge that we belong to him alone.
- We also seek to live out the fruit of the Spirit in our lives: love, joy, peace, patience, kindness, goodness, faithfulness, gentleness, and self-control (Gal. 5:22–23).

Spiritual disciplines *do not* help God to make our lives holy. Instead:

- They help us recognize God's callings and promptings in our lives, and identify those areas in our lives that still need to be renewed.
- They make us sensitive and humble to follow God's leading.
- They help us realize that we depend completely on God's grace at every moment and for everything.
- They train and equip us to respond in a worthy manner when life throws problems and storms at us.

> "God has given us the Spiritual Disciplines as a means of receiving His grace and growing in Godliness. By them we place ourselves before God for Him to work in us."
>
> —**Donald S. Whitney,** *Spiritual Disciplines for the Christian Life*

Spiritual Disciplines Should Be

- Instruments of God's grace which, through the Spirit, transform us daily into people who reflect Jesus' love, obedience, humility, and connection to God
- Activities that connect us deeply to other believers in our common desire to follow God's will
- A source of humility and dependence on God
- Experiences that enrich our lives and the lives of those around us
- Activities that occur in the context of God's whole body; spiritual disciplines, although often practiced alone, are not individualistic activities
- As much focused on building up God's body as building up each believer
- Practices that give us hope, despite our failings and limitations. We can hope that "he who began a good work in you will carry it on to completion until the day of Christ Jesus" (Phil. 1:6).
- Practices that permeate every area of our lives
- Disciplines that help us train for the life of faith, hope, and love to which Jesus has called us

Spiritual Disciplines Should Not Be

- Heavy loads of impossible, unrealistic, or unfair expectations for people
- Benchmarks to judge people's Christianity or maturity
- Individualistic attempts to be holy or perfect
- A measure of one's spiritual stature and strength
- A way to separate our "religiosity" from the rest of our lives
- A way to hide our sins with good works

Spiritual Disciplines and the Bible

Contemporary society is fascinated with spirituality. One can find all kinds of books about self-help or spiritual guidance and practices. How are Christian spiritual disciplines different from those offered in such books? The difference is simple, though profound.

Popular Spiritual Disciplines Are:	Biblical Spiritual Disciplines Are:
For self-improvement	For the spiritual maturity of each person and the community as a whole
For self-realization—the fulfillment of one's abilities and potential	For realization of the fruit of the Spirit in one's life
For self-sufficiency	For dependence on God and interdependence with other believers within God's body
Based on one's own work and dedication	Based on the work of the Spirit in our lives, the support and encouragement of all believers, and the effort of each believer.

His divine power has given us everything we need for life and godliness through our knowledge of him who called us by his own glory and goodness.... For this very reason, make every effort to add to your faith goodness; and to goodness, knowledge; and to knowledge, self-control; and to self-control, perseverance; and to perseverance, godliness; and to godliness, brotherly kindness; and to brotherly kindness, love. For if you possess these qualities in increasing measure, they will keep you from being ineffective and unproductive in your knowledge of our Lord Jesus Christ.—**2 Peter 1:3, 5–8**

The Apostle Peter is clear: God has given us all we need, and we must make every effort to grow.

Spiritual Practice

Practicing spiritual disciplines is not easy. Jesus reminded the disciples that believers would experience hatred and persecution (John 15:18–25). Spiritual disciplines help us get ready for difficult moments: moments of persecution, temptation, doubt, and grief.

Moreover, spiritual disciplines help us to deepen our relationship with God. God does not wish a shallow, "good morning–see you later," type of relationship. God wishes to be in deep, satisfying, loving, transforming, and challenging relationships with us, individually and as a community of believers. Spiritual disciplines build in us the attitudes, emotions, thoughts, and actions that will promote the kind of relationship that our hearts yearn for.

Below is a list of common spiritual practices, by no means comprehensive, which many Christians have practiced throughout the centuries.

> "A disciplined person is someone who can do the right thing at the right time in the right way with the right spirit."
>
> —John Ortberg, *The Life You've Always Wanted: Spiritual Disciplines for Ordinary People*

1. Bible Reading/Study
2. Prayer
3. Fasting
4. Worship
5. Service
6. Solitude
7. Discernment
8. Evangelism

From Bad to Good Habits

1. **Know** your bad habits.
   - Pray that God will help you see the specific areas of your life that need changing;
   - Pray that God will give you the courage, strength, and help to face those areas.
2. **Confess** your weaknesses to God with a humble and hopeful heart.
3. **Submit** to God's call to change. Surrender your efforts and receive God's grace. Trust that God is with you and is helping you.
4. **Be accountable.**
   - Find one or more people you trust and ask them to pray with and for you about a specific area in your life that needs changing;
   - Allow them to be God's instruments in your life for that specific area.
5. **Train** to substitute a bad habit—sin—with a good habit—virtue.
   - If prayer is difficult for you, find a person who will pray with you, or begin a praying group that meets once a week.
6. **Be persistent.** Bad habits take a long time to form; it takes an equally long time to break them and acquire new habits.
7. **Be graceful** toward yourself and others.
   - It is highly possible that you will experience failure.
   - Remember, you are not changing just for your sake; you are allowing God's Spirit to work in your life.
   - Jesus gave his life for you. You are that valuable; God will patiently wait for you to get up and continue walking every time you stumble and fall.
   - Do not obsess over the actual change; it is not your job. The Holy Spirit is the one who renews and transforms us. Focus on the growing relationship with God. Let God be God and do what he does best: give you new life.
8. **Be grateful** for all the things you already are and have.
   - Thank God for every small change that occurs;
   - Thank God for every time you get up after a fall;
   - Thank the people around you for helping you along.

I. Scripture Reading and Studying

Biblical Basis and Examples

- Moses read the word of God to the people and commanded that it be read publicly—Ex. 24:7; Deut. 31:9–13
- Joshua was commanded to meditate on God's word day and night—Josh. 1:8
- Kings of Israel were to study the Scriptures—Deut. 17:18–19
- The longest psalm is a psalm about the value of knowing God's word—Ps. 119
- Paul required his letters be read publicly—Col. 4:16; 1 Thess. 5:27
- Paul urged Timothy to study the Word of God and handle it with care—2 Tim. 2:15
- The Ethiopian was reading God's Word and he became a follower of Jesus—Acts 8:27–40
- Jesus read the Bible and taught it to the people—Luke 4:16–21
- Jesus said the value of studying the Bible was to see that it spoke about him—John 5:39
- God's word is supposed to be close to the mouths and hearts of believers—Deut. 30:11–14; 32:47; Ps. 1:2; Rom. 10:8–11; Col. 3:16

The Disciplines Today

Jesus said: "I am the vine; you are the branches. If a man remains in me and I in him, he will bear much fruit; apart from me you can do nothing" (John 15:5).

- Reading the Bible is the best way to stay connected to God.
- Scripture reading is the lifeblood of the church. The Bible equips, trains, and empowers believers to fulfill God's calling (2 Tim. 3:17; 2 Peter 1:3–11; Heb. 13:21).
- Scripture reading and studying involves different activities: memorization, reflection, and transformative study.

Memorization

- When scuba divers face problems under water, they rely on their previous training to find a way out. When we face temptation or sudden grief, our "training" will kick in.
- All those verses we have memorized will come back; God will speak to us through them in unexpected ways.
- One of the best ways to memorize something is by finding partners who help and challenge you to work together.

Reflection

- It is often called *meditation*. It means that we allow the Bible to settle in our minds and hearts.
- We do this by thinking about it all day long, wondering what a passage or a verse means for us throughout the day's activities.
  - Write a verse, or passage, on a small piece of paper and carry it along with you. If you are standing in line, waiting at a restaurant, or another short moment, take the paper out and think about how the text connects to your life at that specific moment.

Transformative Study

- Studying the Bible does not mean one becomes an expert in one passage or book. Studying the Bible means we dig deeply so we can be deeply transformed.
- The more we know about God, the more we can love him.
- God gave the Bible to the church. Reading and studying the Bible in community is most profitable.

- Traditionally, Christians have practiced this discipline by reading early in the morning, after meals, or before going to bed.
- Today there are many other opportunities for Bible reading, memorizing, and studying.
- The many hours we spend in transportation can be useful for listening to an audio recording of the Bible.
- The Internet is full of tools and helps for Bible reading and studying.

2. Prayer

Biblical Basis and Examples

- Many of the Psalms are prayers—for example, see Psalms 10, 59, 83, 86, and others
- The believer is to constantly be in an attitude of prayer—Luke 18:1; Eph. 6:18; Phil. 4:6; Col. 4:2; 1 Thess. 5:17; 1 Tim. 2:8
- Access to God through Jesus belongs to the believer—Heb. 4:16
- The manner of prayer calls for honest communication, not showy pretense or empty repetition—Eccl. 5:1–3; Matt. 6:5–7
- Prayer should not be done with an unforgiving attitude—Mark 11:25
- Prayer should be made in confident hope that God hears and knows our real needs—Matt. 7:7–11; Heb. 11:6

The Disciplines Today

- Prayer is commanded in the Bible. The discipline of prayer is a way to be obedient to this commandment.
- Often learning about the heroes of the faith is intimidating. Instead of being motivated, we might feel discouraged with the enormous challenge of their example.
- Who could fly a jet or run a marathon without much previous and rigorous training? No one is born knowing how to pray and being great at it.
- Learning to pray is a bit like learning to swim. It can only happen in the water, despite fears, insecurities, and doubts.
- Prayer requires *concentration* and *focus*.
  - Teaching ourselves to concentrate is one of the reasons we close our eyes.
  - But we need to close our ears and minds as well to the many distractions around us.
  - Spending a few minutes just to quiet mind and heart will help us achieve better concentration and focus.
- Prayer builds up our humility, dependence on God, and compassion for others.
- If praying on your own is difficult, make a "prayer date" with a friend you are comfortable with.
- Start by praying simple, short prayers—pray one minute, take a break and read or sing, then pray again.
- When you feel stuck, unmotivated, or without words—all very normal occurrences—pray a prayer from the Bible: a psalm, the Lord's Prayer (Matt. 6:9–13), Nehemiah's prayer (Neh. 1:5–11), Solomon's prayer (1 Kings 8:22–61).
- Your prayers do not have to be pretty—the Holy Spirit takes all of our prayers, pretty or not, and brings them before God the Father (Rom. 8:26–27).
- Make sure your prayers include, among other things, *praise* for God's greatness, *gratitude* for God's gifts, *petitions* for you and others, *confession* of your struggles and sins, and whatever the Spirit brings to your mind.
- The apostle Paul tells us to "pray continually" (1 Thess. 5:17). Is this even possible? Not immediately. Just as no one can run a marathon without training, no one can pray continually without training.
- Sometimes prayer is a "battleground." Prayer can be difficult and produce anxiety. Sometimes it is while praying that God reveals to us what needs changing, what needs to be done. Sometimes, prayer can be a painful mirror.
- Finally, our prayers are not primarily for changing God's mind about something; prayer changes our mind about who we are, what we need, and how we please God. Prayer is transformational.

3. Fasting

Biblical Basis and Examples

- The nation Israel fasted asking God's forgiveness—Judg. 20:26; 1 Sam. 7:6; Jer. 36:9; Ezra 8:21–23
- The city of Nineveh fasted asking God's forgiveness—Jonah 3:5–10
- Moses fasted when he received God's commandments—Ex. 34:28
- David fasted seeking God's forgiveness and guidance—2 Sam. 1:12, 3:35, 12:16–22
- Ezra fasted to ask God's forgiveness—Ezra 10:6
- Nehemiah fasted seeking God's favor—Neh. 1:4
- Daniel fasted seeking God's favor—Dan. 9:3, 10:2–3
- Anna fasted seeking God's favor and guidance—Luke 2:37
- Cornelius fasted seeking God's favor—Acts 10:30
- Paul fasted seeking God's guidance—Acts 9:9
- Jesus fasted in the wilderness seeking God's guidance—Matt. 4:2
- The manner of fasting is to be sincere, dedicated to God, without a public show—Matt. 6:16–18

The Disciplines Today

- Fasting may be the most neglected of all the spiritual disciplines today. It is easy to dismiss it as an old and quaint practice. But we miss an important and meaningful opportunity for spiritual growth.
- The central point of fasting is training for self-control (2 Peter 1:6; Gal. 5:23; 1 Peter 1:13).
- If we are to break the hold of habits—sin—in our lives, training for self-control is essential.
- Fasting is an effective approach to developing self-control because it deals with a very fundamental necessity of human existence: food.
- We need food to live; however, we can become enslaved by food—or other things we may need or simply want for our lives.
- If we are able to control things essential for life, we will be able to keep in check the things that are not essential for life.
- The practice of fasting fosters humility, reliance on God, compassion, gratitude, and self-control.
- Begin by fasting from food for a short period, such as skipping a meal. Build your fasting time up from there.
- As much as possible, use the time it takes to get or prepare food and eat it for prayer and Bible reflection.
- Fasting from food is the most obvious way to do it. However, you can also abstain from other things. For example, watching television (or other media) often consumes too much of our lives. That central place belongs to God alone.
- If you find you rely too much on caffeine to stay awake or for energy, it may be a good idea to fast from caffeine and be reminded that our dependence on God is sufficient.
- We can extend the same principle to many things around us: technology, music, sports, and so on.
- Internet, although a wonderful tool of communication, can absorb our time and attention in ways not even television could. Try a "media fast." Turning the computer off in order to be completely present in the lives of others has become a wonderful spiritual practice for many people today.

> "First, let [fasting] be done unto the Lord with our eye singly fixed on Him. Let our intention herein be this, and this alone, to glorify our Father which is in heaven."
>
> —(John Wesley, as found in the collection *Sermons On Several Occasions*)

4. Worship

Biblical Basis and Examples

- Worship must be to God and God alone—Ex. 20:1–6; Matt. 4:10
- Worship must be in Spirit and in truth—John 4:23–24
- Moses composed and taught a song about God to the people—Deut. 31:19–22; 32:1–47
- David danced in worship before the Lord—2 Sam. 6:14–16
- The entire book of Psalms is a book for worship—Ps. 8, 89, and 105 are examples
- Worship may be in a public place—Deut. 16:11; Luke 24:53
- It may be in a private residence—Acts 1:13–14; 5:42; 12:12; Rom. 16:5; Col. 4:15
- Worship may be done with instruments—Ps. 150
- It may be done in silence—Ps. 46:10; Hab. 2:20
- Worship may be done bowing or kneeling—Ps. 95:6
- It may be done upright or with hands raised—1 Tim. 2:8
- Paul tells believers to use psalms, hymns, and spiritual songs—Col. 3:16
- Believers are commanded to worship God regularly—Psalm 96:8–9; Heb. 10:25

The Disciplines Today

- Worship is more than an activity: it is an attitude—an attitude of awe and gratitude, of humble submission to God's greatness and grace, of obedience and love.
- Every activity and every relationship in our daily life can be a way to worship God.
- The spiritual discipline of worship is not limited to the activities we do on Sundays.
- We must train ourselves to recognize God's presence in the smallest of events and in the most casual of our relationships.
- This discipline will hone our humility, dependence on God, gratitude, obedience, and fellowship with God and our fellow believers.
- We can worship alone. However, worshiping with other believers has a way of connecting people in an incomparable way. Worship nurtures fellowship, promotes intimate relationships, and fosters the edification of Christ's body.
- Sunday worship is the best initial training ground for this discipline. As we continue developing this habit of worshiping God, we will see Sunday worship as the beginning of our worship, rather than as the only worship time.
- List your daily activities from dawn to bedtime. Reflect on how each of your activities and your attitudes toward them worship God. Sometimes they do not seem to worship God; is there any way you can make them worshipful?
- Take one event, activity, or relationship at a time and find ways it can bring worship to God. Perhaps all you need to do is dedicate the activity to God in prayer, or change an attitude toward a relationship that is difficult. Perhaps you need to stop an activity or event that does not glorify God.
- Just as prayer can occur all day long in the background of your mind and spirit, worshiping God occurs often unnoticed. If you make a habit of noticing and being mindful about God throughout your day, you will be able to express your joy, gratitude, sadness, frustration, anger, or love in different ways that bring worship to God.
- It is in this discipline that the previous disciplines are handy. You can express your worship through prayer, singing, or meditating on a Bible verse.

5. Service

Biblical Basis and Examples

- Jesus taught that true greatness is serving others—Matt. 20: 26–27; Mark 9:35
- Jesus illustrated the importance of service when he washed his disciples' feet —Mark 10:43–45; John 13:4–17
- Paul followed Jesus' example and taught the same—Acts 20:35; Rom. 15:1–3; 1 Cor. 10:24; 2 Cor. 4:5; Gal. 6:10
- Believers are to follow this example—Phil. 2:3–8; Eph. 2:8–10
- "… faith by itself, if it is not accompanied by action, is dead" (James 2:17)

> **"Resolved: that all men should live for the glory of God.**
>
> **Resolved second: that whether others do or not, I will."**
>
> —Jonathan Edwards

The Disciplines Today

- The discipline of service is not self-serving. Serving others to feel better, or to gain people's gratitude, becomes a self-serving activity. We give expecting nothing in return.
- Serving arises from our identity in Christ: we are his servants. Service is not what we do; it is who we are.
- Calling Jesus Lord means that we are his servants. Being a servant means that God called us to be of service.
- One of the ways to serve God is by serving people.
- Service is born of love and gratitude. It requires humility, strength, and love.
- Serving others can be exhausting and draining. One way to minimize this problem is by allowing the spiritual disciplines above to be the basis for our service. In addition, service in community also helps to minimize the problem of exhaustion and feeling burnt out.
- Like the other disciplines, training for service is a gradual process. The more we serve others, especially those with great need, the barriers that stay in our way of spiritual growth—pride, arrogance, indifference, fears, and insecurities—will slowly crumble.
- The practice of service begins by caring for one's own family (1 Tim. 5:8).
- Begin by serving those around you in small and unexpected ways. When they notice your service, be sure to give God the honor and the glory. Enjoy being a faithful servant (Matt. 25:21).
- Find ways to serve those with the greatest need in our society.
- Serving the people we like or feel comfortable with is easy. However, Jesus urges us to serve even if we are treated unfairly or unkindly.
- The apostle Peter (1 Peter 4:10–11) urges us to serve other believers in order to share in God's goodness. Service begins among Christians and extends to others as a way to show gratitude for God's own grace.
- In serving others, we become channels of God's love and compassion.
- When we serve others, we get to see Jesus' heart of love and compassion. Service becomes a spiritual experience beyond ourselves.

6. Solitude

Biblical Basis and Examples

- The prophets Moses, Elijah and Habakkuk retired to the wilderness to seek God's guidance—Ex. 3:1–6; 1 Kings 19:11–13; Hab. 2:1
- Jesus often withdrew to a solitary place to pray—Matt. 14:23; Mark 1:12, 35; Luke 5:16; 6:12; 9:18, 28
- Jesus taught the value of praying in private—Matt. 6:6
- Jesus advised the disciples to retire to a lonely place and rest—Mark 6:31
- The Apostle Paul went away to prepare for his ministry—Gal. 1:17

The Disciplines Today

- We live in a time of continuous visual and auditory stimulation: images and sound constantly come at us from many different sources.
- Often we miss God's voice and signals because we are distracted. We are busy people with busy lives.
- Just as our bodies need physical rest, our minds, hearts, and souls need intellectual, emotional, and spiritual rest.
- The problem with intellectual, emotional and spiritual rest is that they often require solitude and silence. We have grown so used to being surrounded by busyness, noise, and stuff that it is a great challenge to be in true solitude and silence.
- Like all disciplines, the habit of solitude takes time to form. It requires one step at a time.
- Begin by setting apart moments of quiet and reflection.
- Turn the radio off while driving in traffic. Allow that stressful time to be a moment of solitude, prayer, praise, and reflection.
- Solitude can be practiced by setting aside an hour, a day, a week, or any period of time that allows you to focus on God.
- Share with others the insights you gain during your moments of solitude. It will be an inspiration and example to others.

> "Here then I am, far from the busy ways of men. I sit down alone; only God is here."
> —John Wesley (1703–1791)

7. Discernment

Biblical Basis and Examples

- Discernment may include wisdom to understand the times—1 Chron. 12:32
- It may include wisdom to understand dreams—Gen. 41:25–39; Dan. 2:27–48
- It may include wisdom to make moral or judicial decisions—1 Kings 3:9–12
- Jesus told his followers to be wise but gentle—Matt. 10:16
- James tells believers to ask God for wisdom—James 1:5
- Discernment may at times run counter to prevailing human wisdom—1 Cor. 1:18–25
- It is useful to distinguish truth from falsehood and grow mature in the faith—Eph. 4:14; 2 Peter 2:1–22

The Disciplines Today

- Discernment is primarily a spiritual gift. However, all believers are called to be wise and discerning (Phil. 1:9–10).
- While some people in the church have a special gift for discernment, everyone in the church ought to be able to use discernment for at least two purposes:
  - To understand God's calling and will for our individual and collective lives.
  - To perceive and distinguish truth from falsehood.
- Discernment develops alongside the practice of all the previous spiritual disciplines.
- At a time when religions and pseudo-Christian cults are drawing away young people and uneducated Christians, correctly defining and recognizing beliefs is key.
- As a spiritual discipline, discernment depends entirely on the work of the Holy Spirit.
- We develop our ability to discern through prayer, Bible study and meditation, and fasting. As we become more sensitive to God's voice and promptings, our ability to discern God's plans and desires for our lives will increase.
- Discernment benefits greatly from the joint search for God's will within Christ's body. We are limited and imperfect beings; we are also skilled in self-deception. We may be convinced that God is leading in a specific direction. However, we could be deceiving ourselves. Having the joint discernment of God's people can keep us from this error.

Discernment: The Spirit-inspired ability to separate our imperfect will from God's perfect will in recognizing, judging, and choosing what is right, good, and pure from what is wrong, evil, and impure.

8. Evangelism

Biblical Basis and Examples

- Jesus charged his followers with the duty of spreading the gospel—Matt. 28:19–20
- The special ministry of evangelism is given to some—Eph. 4:11
- Peter tells believers to be ready to give a reasonable answer concerning the hope of the gospel—1 Peter 3:15

> "There is not a square inch in the whole domain of our human existence over which Christ, who is Sovereign over all, does not cry: 'Mine!'"
> —Abraham Kuyper, inaugural address at the dedication of the Free University of Amsterdam

The Disciplines Today

- Evangelism is a command for every person in the church.
- However, speaking about one's faith is not always a natural thing for many people.
- Practicing evangelism as a spiritual discipline will allow many Christians to grow more comfortable in sharing their faith.
- Just like our lives, all the spiritual disciplines are intimately related. They enrich each other and work in harmony.
- Evangelism feeds on all the spiritual disciplines mentioned above:
  - Scripture study: The more we know God, about God, and God's plans for humanity, the better we can share what God has done for us.
  - Prayer: Abundant life overflows our hearts and minds. The closer we are to God, the more life we can share with others.
  - Worship, fasting, and service can open doors to engage people in conversation about spiritual matters.
- We must also train ourselves to be God's instruments. It can be difficult to remember that we are not the ones convincing, transforming, or converting people. That is God's job. Our mission is to share with others what God has done. We do not "close the deal." Only God can do that.
- There are many evangelistic tools and programs that help believers obey Jesus' command to evangelize.
- Often, however, the best way to evangelize is by developing close relationships with people around us.
- Spiritual conversations are most natural in the context of close, intimate relationships.
- A spiritual conversation can be simply telling others your own story about when you first realized the importance of Jesus Christ in your life.

> "Evangelism is a natural overflow of the Christian life…. But evangelism is also a Discipline in that we must discipline ourselves to get into the context of evangelism, that is, we must not just wait for witnessing opportunities to happen."
> —Donald S. Whitney,
> *Spiritual Disciplines for the Christian Life*

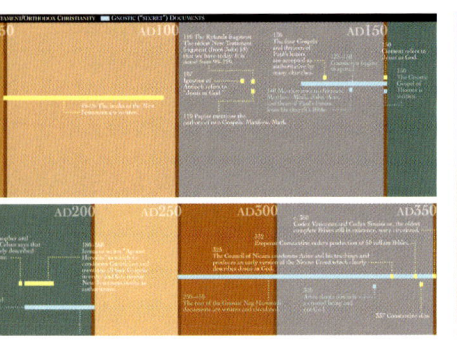

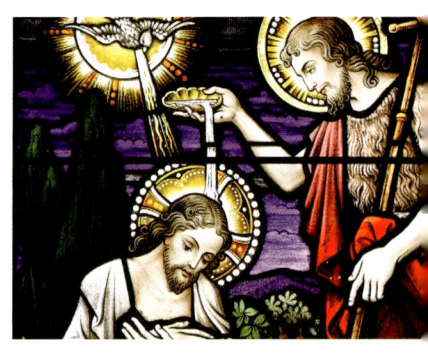

CHRISTIAN HISTORY AND DOCTRINES

Essential Doctrines

What Do Christians Believe?

What are the key doctrines of the Christian faith? The core teachings of the Bible have defined Christianity for 2,000 years. Virtually all Christians who seek to have a faith that is biblical hold to some form of these basic doctrines. Christians may not always agree on how they work out the details of their faith, but they should agree on the essential doctrines, these core truths.

> *"In essentials, unity; in non-essentials, liberty, and in all things, charity."*
> —*Rupertus Meldenius (1627)*

We can identify the essential doctrines of the Christian faith by looking at the core truth of the gospel, which is the salvation of humanity through the life, death, and resurrection of Jesus Christ. Salvation, as God has revealed to us through his Holy Scriptures, is defined as forgiveness of sins and everlasting life with God by confessing that "Jesus is Lord" and believing that God raised Jesus from the dead (Rom. 10:9). By examining the gospel message, we can identify fourteen doctrines that are necessary for salvation to be possible.

What Are the Essential Doctrines?

The essential doctrines of Christianity have to do with who God is, who Jesus is, and God's love for people and his desire to save them. There are fourteen essential salvation doctrines that have to be true in order for anyone to know God and be saved, and two more essential doctrines that define how we know about salvation.

Not all doctrines necessary for salvation are necessary for a person to believe in order to be saved. There is a distinct difference between what must be true in order for us to be saved and what must be believed in order for us to be saved. For instance, nowhere does the Bible say it is necessary to believe in the Virgin Birth in order to get into heaven; nonetheless, the Virgin Birth assures us that God took an active role in breaking the bonds of sin through his Son, Jesus.

There are certain essential doctrines that one may not believe and still be saved (for example, the Virgin Birth, Ascension of Christ, the Second Coming), and there are certain things one must believe in order to be saved. A person must believe that Christ died for sins and rose again (Rom. 10:9–11; 1 Cor. 15:1–6). One must "believe in the Lord Jesus Christ" (Acts 16:31). Since the word "Lord" (*kurios*) when it refers to Christ in the New Testament means "deity," one cannot deny the deity of Christ and be saved (Acts 2:21, 36; 3:14–16; 5:30–35; 10:39; 1 Cor. 12:3).

1. God's Unity

Explanation	There is only one God. He has always existed and will always exist. There is one—and only one—God, Creator of the universe.
What do I actually need to believe?	There is only one God.
What's at stake here?	Knowing the only true God (John 17:3).
Scripture	Deut. 6:4; Ex. 20:2–3; Isa. 43:10–11

2. God's Tri-unity

Explanation	While there is only one God, he exists eternally in three Persons. In the Bible, the Father is called God (2 Thess. 1:2); the Son (Jesus) is called God (John 1:1–5; 10:30–33; 20:28; Heb. 1:8; Phil. 2:9–11); and the Holy Spirit is called God (Acts 5:3–4; 2 Cor. 3:17). God is one substance, but three Persons in relationship. There are more than 60 passages in the Bible that mention the three Persons together.
What do I actually need to believe?	God is one essence, but three Persons.
What's at stake here?	The unity and relational nature of God.
Scripture	Matt. 3:16–17; 28:19; 2 Cor. 13:14

3. Human Depravity

Explanation	Since God is a personal Being, he wants personal relationships with human beings. Human depravity means that every human is spiritually separated from God, totally incapable of saving himself. When Adam sinned, he died spiritually and his relationship with God was severed. Additionally, all of Adam's descendants are "dead in trespasses" (Eph. 2:1). Without a new birth (being created anew) no one can enter life (John 3:3).
What do I actually need to believe?	We are sinful and cannot please God by our own good works alone. We can never be "good enough."
What's at stake here?	When we try to deal with the problem of separation and death on our own terms, we will fail, resulting in eternal separation from God.
Scripture	Rom. 3:10–12

4. Christ's Virgin Birth

Explanation	Jesus was born as a result of a miracle: Mary, Jesus' mother, became pregnant without ever having sexual relations. The doctrine of Jesus' Virgin Birth is not primarily about Mary's virginity and miraculous conception. Though this miracle fulfilled a preordained prophecy (Isa. 7:14), the reason it is essential has to do with God's supernatural intervention. Our sin is not merely something we do—it is who we are. It is inborn. Our depravity is transmitted to us from our parents (Ps. 51:5; 1 Cor. 15:22; Rom. 5:12–15). Because God interrupted the natural birth process in the case of Jesus, Jesus did not inherit a sin nature. In other words, Jesus not only did not sin, he had no inclination to sin even when tempted. He was perfect.
What do I actually need to believe?	Jesus became a human being through a supernatural conception in Mary's womb.
What's at stake here?	God's supernatural intervention in order to break the chain of sin.
Scripture	Matt. 1:18–23

5. Christ's Sinlessness

Explanation	Christ was born of a virgin, and he did not suffer the effects of a sin nature. Throughout his life Jesus remained sinless. Because of our sin, we could not have a relationship with God; but because Jesus did not sin he was perfectly able to represent us (stand in our place) before God.
What do I actually need to believe?	Jesus was perfect.
What's at stake here?	The ability of Christ to represent us before God and thus provide salvation for us.
Scripture	2 Cor. 5:21; Heb. 4:15; 1 Peter 2:22

6. Christ's Deity

Explanation	The only way for humans to be restored spiritually to God was for God to build a bridge across the gap of separation. So God, while retaining his full God nature, became a perfect man in Christ in order to bridge the chasm. If he is not both God and Man he cannot mediate between God and man (1 Tim. 2:5). Jesus Christ is the second Person in the Trinity.
What do I actually need to believe?	Jesus Christ is, in essence, God. He is divine, not just a good teacher or a righteous man.
What's at stake here?	Jesus' ability to save us.
Scripture	John 1:1; Col. 2:9; Heb. 1:8

7. Christ's Humanity

Explanation	Jesus was also fully human. Jesus got tired; he slept; he sweated; he got hungry and thirsty. Without being fully human, Jesus could not pay the price for human sin. He needed to be divine to have the power to save us, and he needed to be human in order to adequately represent us. Christ had to be both divine and human.
What do I actually need to believe?	Jesus Christ was fully human, as well as fully divine.
What's at stake here?	Confidence in Jesus' ability to fully represent humankind in atonement.
Scripture	John 1:14; Phil. 2:7–8; Heb. 2:14

8. Necessity of God's Grace

Explanation	Because of human depravity, we cannot save ourselves. It is by God's grace alone that salvation is possible. God is right to call humankind to account for sin. However, by his grace, undeserving people will be united in fellowship with him and avoid judgment. Without God's grace, no one could come into relationship with God. Relationship with God is peace, joy, and eternal life itself (John 17:3).
What do I actually need to believe?	God—and God alone—is able to rescue us.
What's at stake here?	Our relationship to God, eternal life.
Scripture	Eph. 2:8–9; John 15:5; Titus 3:5–7; Rom. 9:16

9. Necessity of Faith

Explanation	Faith is trusting that God can and will save us. No one can earn salvation. No amount of good works can ever repay the debt that is owed to God. However, by trusting in him and thankfully accepting his gift of salvation, we can be united with God. Faith is an act on our part, but it is not a work. Faith is trusting God to do what we could not do for ourselves (Eph. 2:8–9; Titus 3:5).
What do I actually need to believe?	That faith, not works, connects us to God.
What's at stake here?	Whether we want to be judged by what we deserve or with God's undeserved favor (grace).
Scripture	Heb. 11:6; Rom. 4:5

10. Christ's Atoning Death

Explanation	The penalty for sin is death—not only physical death (separation of the soul from the body), but also spiritual death (separation of ourselves from God). The penalty we owe to God was paid by Christ through his death on the cross. The acceptable payment had to be perfect, complete, and without fault. Christ, the perfect man, gave himself in our place, so that whoever believes in him will not die (physically and spiritually) but have everlasting life (John 3:16).
What do I actually need to believe?	Only Christ's sinless life, sacrificial death and bodily resurrection can bring us to God.
What's at stake here?	The unique nature of Jesus' work of salvation.
Scripture	Mark 10:45; 1 Peter 2:24; 3:18; John 14:6

11. Christ's Bodily Resurrection

Explanation	The atoning death of Christ paid for our sins, but the process was not complete until he had defeated death by being physically resurrected in the same body (John 2:19–21). Because Christ is the victor over death and the prototype of a new, glorified physical body, all of humanity will be resurrected and live forever in either heaven or hell.
What do I actually need to believe?	Jesus rose bodily from the grave.
What's at stake here?	The proof that Jesus conquered death.
Scripture	Luke 24:39; Rom. 4:25; 10:9

12. Christ's Bodily Ascension

Explanation	Christ died for our sins and was physically resurrected for our salvation. Then forty days later, he was taken up ("ascended") bodily into heaven. Because Christ has ascended to the Father, the Holy Spirit now guides us, shows us where we are wrong and comforts us when we hurt. Jesus' going to the Father means our life is kept safe in heaven with God.
What do I actually need to believe?	Jesus ascended, body and soul, to God.
What's at stake here?	The Holy Spirit's work in the life of the believer.
Scripture	Luke 24:50–51; John 16:7; Acts 1:9–10

13. Christ's Intercession

Explanation	Christ's bodily ascension allowed him to serve as our mediator (or high priest) before God. In God's presence, Christ prays continually on our behalf. Like a lawyer defends someone before a judge, so Jesus defends us before the bar of God's law and against the accusations of Satan (Rev. 12:10).
What do I actually need to believe?	Christ represents our best interests before God.
What's at stake here?	Assurance that my prayers are heard by God.
Scripture	Heb. 1:3; 4:15; 7:25; 1 John 2:1

14. Christ's Second Coming

Explanation	Just as Christ left the world physically, so he will return in the same manner. His second coming is the hope of the world. When he returns, dead believers will receive their resurrected bodies. Believers that are alive when he returns will not die, but will be transformed into immortal, physical bodies. Christ's bodily return to earth will be visible to all, and believers will rule with him in his kingdom and live with him forever. Those who do not believe will be separated from God's goodness forever.
What do I actually need to believe?	Jesus is coming again soon, and we should be ready.
What's at stake here?	Our hope of being together with Christ.
Scripture	Matt. 24:30; Rev. 22:12; Col. 3:3–4; Luke 12:40

After Jesus returns, believers will enter conscious eternal blessing and unbelievers will go into conscious eternal punishment. *Eternal Life*: John 14:1–3; Rev. 21:4. *Eternal Separation*: 2 Thess. 1:7–9; Rev. 20:11–15.

How Do We Know about Essential Doctrines?

We know about the essential doctrines through the Bible. However, the inspiration of Scripture as a doctrine is not necessary for salvation to be possible. People were saved before there was a Bible, and some people are saved without ever reading the Bible. The Bible is, however, the only divinely authoritative foundation that makes the plan of salvation knowable.

15. Inspiration of Scripture

In order for us to have a sure foundation for what we believe, God revealed his Word (the Bible) as the basis of our beliefs. God cannot err (Heb. 6:18) and neither can his Word (John 17:17). Without a divinely authoritative revelation from God, such as we have in the Scriptures, we could never be sure of the doctrines that are necessary for salvation.

16. Method of Interpretation

In addition, all the salvation doctrines are derived from the Bible by the literal method of interpretation—that is, Scripture is true, just as the author meant it. By applying the historical-grammatical method of interpretation to Scripture one can know which truths are essential for salvation.

Attributes of God

A Relationship with God

God created humanity for relationships: relationships with each other, with nature, and with God. However, human sin separated us from God, turning what should have been a loving relationship into one filled with hate and disobedience (Rom. 5:10). Yet, God has reached down to us to deliver us from sin and death because he wants to have a relationship with us. In Christ, God has built a bridge that allows us to relate to him.

Deep, meaningful relationships require knowledge of the other person. The more we know God, the more our love can grow and mature. Also, our obedience and service will spring forth from this knowledge and love of God.

Then, how do we get to know God? Our relationship with God begins and ends with Jesus. We get to know God as we know Jesus. His death and resurrection have given us direct access to God. We now know Jesus and God in two ways:

1. Through the work of the Holy Spirit in each believer
2. Through the revealed Word of God

> "This is what the LORD says: 'Let not the wise boast of their wisdom or the strong boast of their strength or the rich boast of their riches, but let the one who boasts boast about this: that they have the understanding to know me, that I am the LORD, who exercises kindness, justice and righteousness on earth, for in these I delight,' declares the LORD." —Jeremiah 9:23–24
>
> "Now this is eternal life: that they know you, the only true God, and Jesus Christ, whom you have sent." —John 17:3

It is good for us to be near unto God. It is eternity to know him intimately in our daily lives… That's the mark of believers. They know what joy there is in being near unto God, and they want nothing else.
—Abraham Kuyper, *Near Unto God*

Jesus: A Model of God's Attributes

God is spirit. We can discern some of his attributes in nature—for example, his power in the storms, his goodness in the bounty of the earth, his love in the loving actions of people around us. We also know about God's attributes through the Scriptures.

The book of Hebrews teaches us that "In the past God spoke to our ancestors through the prophets at many times and in various ways, but in these last days he has spoken to us by his Son, whom he appointed heir of all things, and through whom also he made the universe. The Son is the radiance of God's glory and the exact representation of his being, sustaining all things by his powerful word" (Heb. 1:1–3). Jesus models the attributes of God, especially the communicable attributes.

- Jesus showed his *love* for all people (Luke 7:47; Mark 10:21). His love is especially clear in his sacrifice: "This is how we know what love is: Jesus Christ laid down his life for us. And we ought to lay down our lives for our brothers and sisters" (1 John 3:16).
- Jesus demonstrated a life without sin (Heb. 4:15)—he was *holy*. His sacrifice on our behalf was perfect and sufficient because: "Such a high priest truly meets our need—one who is holy, blameless, pure, set apart from sinners, exalted above the heavens" (Heb. 7:26).
- Throughout his ministry, Jesus showed compassion and *mercy*: for the multitude (Matt. 9:36), for the unfortunate (Matt. 20:34), for Jerusalem (Matt. 23:37), for the leper (Mark 1:41).
- Jesus is *faithful*. He promised to be with us always (Matt. 28:20), and we can rest knowing that "the Lord is faithful, and he will strengthen you and protect you from the evil one" (2 Thess. 3:3). For this reason, we can be "confident of this, that he who began a good work in you will carry it on to completion until the day of Christ Jesus" (Phil. 1:6).

God's Attributes as a Window

Knowing who God is, his character and his nature, can be discovered through learning about his attributes. One way to think about God's attributes is by distinguishing between the attributes that belong only to God and the attributes that we also share with him—we share these attributes with God because he made us in his image. The first kind of attributes is called *incommunicable*, while the second kind is called *communicable*. In God, no attribute is more important than the others are. All of them, in conjunction, make God who he is.

INCOMMUNICABLE (THE ATTRIBUTES THAT ONLY GOD HAS)	COMMUNICABLE (THE ATTRIBUTES WE SHARE WITH GOD)
1. TRIUNE	1. LOVING
2. ONE	2. HOLY
3. TRANSCENDENT	3. GOOD
4. INFINITE	4. JUST
5. ETERNAL	5. JEALOUS
6. CREATOR	6. MERCIFUL
7. OMNIPRESENT	7. SOVEREIGN (AUTHORITY)
8. IMMUTABLE	8. OMNIPOTENT (POWERFUL)
	9. KNOWLEDGEABLE (OMNISCIENT)
	10. PATIENT
	11. FAITHFUL
	12. SPIRIT

The attributes of God provide us with a window through which we can contemplate who God is. As we contemplate and learn about God's character, we begin to grasp the glorious, loving, awe-inspiring, and holy person that is the only one worthy of our allegiance. Jesus modeled these characteristics in his life and ministry. By learning what they mean and how they apply to our lives, we can grow in our faith by being imitators of God.

> But the plans of the LORD stand firm forever, the purposes of his heart through all generations. —Psalm 33:11

> God is perpetually the same: subject to no change in His being, attributes, or determinations. Therefore God is compared to a Rock (Deut. 32:4, etc.) which remains immovable, when the entire ocean surrounding it is continually in a fluctuating state; even so, though all creatures are subject to change, God is immutable. Because God has no beginning and no ending, He can know no change. He is everlastingly 'the Father of lights, with whom is no variableness, neither shadow of turning' (James 1:17). —A. W. Pink, *The Attributes of God*

Attributes that Only God Has

1–2 Triune and One

While being one, God is triune. It's easy to see that these two attributes exist in tension with each other. We know both are correct, but it's not easy to understand how they exist together.

- God is *one*: "Hear, O Israel: The Lord our God, the Lord is one" (Deut. 6:4). God is one in two ways: There is no other being like God. And God is the only real God. Because God is one, he is the only being worthy of praise.

- God is *triune*. God is one being who exists in three persons. God the Father, God the Son, and God the Holy Spirit are three separate persons, but they all share the same divine being. This unity of persons is called the "Godhead." God is a person who desires to relate to his creation (Matt. 28:19; 2 Cor. 13:14; Eph. 4:4–6; Titus 3:4–6): "As soon as Jesus was baptized, he went up out of the water. At that moment heaven was opened, and he saw the Spirit of God descending like a dove and alighting on him. And a voice from heaven said, 'This is my Son, whom I love; with him I am well pleased'" (Matt. 3:16–17). We have a model for healthy personal relationships in the way the persons of the Trinity relate to each other.

REFLECTION

- How does knowing that God is in a relationship with the Godhead help you have a personal relationship with him?
- God is one. Does he have any competition for your love and loyalties? Are there other things or beings that are more important to you than God? Should that be the case?

3–4 Transcendent and Infinite

When trying to understand God, we must humbly keep in mind two other attributes of God: he's *transcendent* and *infinite*.

Transcendent means that he's beyond the universe and beyond our intelligence and imagination. This attribute means that we naturally have limits to how far our understanding of God can go. It also means that God is not united, or somehow connected, with the created universe. He is outside the universe. When God's face is hidden from his people (Ps. 13:1; 22:24; Isa. 8:17), we are reminded that God is beyond us and only accessible to us because he reaches first.

God is also beyond our understanding because he is *infinite*. This means that God is above our standards. He's not only wise or gracious; no one is wiser or more gracious than he is. It also means that God has no limits because he is beyond limits. This is an encouraging thought when we face troubles and trials: "I know that you can do all things; no purpose of yours can be thwarted" (Job 42:2; see 1 Kings 8:27; Job 5:9; Ps. 145:3).

REFLECTION

- God is so much greater than we are. He knows the future, he laid out the universe, and he planned our lives. Through Scripture, God has given us hints about what he is like, but it also says God's ways are mysterious and they are good beyond our imagination. How does this affect the way we worship God?

An infinite God can give all of Himself to each of His children. He does not distribute Himself that each may have a part, but to each one He gives all of Himself as fully as if there were no others. —A. W. Tozer

Attributes that Only God Has

5-6 ETERNAL AND CREATOR | 7 OMNIPRESENT | 8 IMMUTABLE

While being *infinite* refers to limits—and God has no limits—being *eternal* refers to time. God does not have a beginning or an end. Before all things were, God already existed: "'I am the Alpha and the Omega,' says the Lord God, 'who is, and who was, and who is to come, the Almighty'" (Rev. 1:8; Deut. 33:27; Ps. 90:1–2; Isa. 40:28; Jer. 10:10; Jude 25).

If God is eternal—he existed before anything else—it also means that God is *creator*. No one created God, but he created all things. God's existence doesn't depend on anything; he is free from obligation. God doesn't owe anything to anyone. We can trust that God always wants what is best for us because—unlike human authorities—God's loyalties are not compromised.

REFLECTION
- We all have experienced betrayal of one kind or another. Often, it happens when other people's commitments prevent them from keeping their word to us. However, God doesn't experience those conflicts of interest. Nothing will stop him from loving us. What keeps us from trusting God fully? What would our lives be like if we did?

As an *eternal* and *infinite* God, God is also not limited by space. God is *omnipresent*—God is present everywhere. God is present at all moments of our life. God is always accessible because he is always present. We can be strong and courageous because God will never leave our side. We can't hide from God or escape his rule over our lives. There is nowhere to run away from God. His love finds us everywhere: "No one will be able to stand against you all the days of your life. As I was with Moses, so I will be with you; I will never leave you nor forsake you" (Josh. 1:5; Ps. 33:13; Ps. 139:7–12; Jer. 23:24).

REFLECTION
- God often calls us to do things we'd rather not do—forgive, love, speak up, care for others. What happens when we try to ignore God and run from him?

Finally, since God is *eternal*, *infinite*, and *omnipresent*, we can be sure that he's always the same; he's *immutable*—God doesn't change. He will never become evil, or weak, or hateful, or cruel. No matter what happens to us or to our surroundings, we can depend on God, our firm foundation, to always remain the same. We can learn God's attributes, essence, nature, and we can trust that it will always be consistent and unchanged. God's nature is reliable and trustworthy.

These incommunicable attributes remind us what an awesome and glorious God we worship. Also, they show that although God is so far away from any of our common experience, he still reaches out to us, he still desires to relate to us in personal, intimate ways.

REFLECTION
- Find a rock and hold it in your hand. Squeeze it, knock on it, and try to bend it. The rock is pretty hard to move or change, but with enough pressure or heat it would probably change. God, however, doesn't change no matter what you do.
- How is God's changelessness a comfort to you?

Attributes that We Share With God

9 LOVING	10 HOLY	11 GOOD
The first communicable attribute—this means that we share that characteristic with God—is that God is *love*: "Whoever does not love does not know God, because God is love" (1 John 4:8; Jer. 31:3; John 3:16; 13:34). Because of human rebellion and sin, God could justly destroy us. Yet, because of his love, God has extended his grace and forgiveness to us. His love for us—and the love we see in the Godhead, among the persons of the Trinity—is an example of how to love: "We love because he first loved us" (1 John 4:19). God's love is best seen in Jesus: "But God demonstrates his own love for us in this: While we were sinners, Christ died for us" (Rom. 5:8).	While *love* drives God's grace, his *holiness* sets natural limits to how we can relate to him. It's not that God's love and holiness are in a struggle; rather, they complement each other. God is separated from sin and evil. Therefore, in our sinful state, we cannot approach God or even be near his holiness. Because of Jesus' sacrifice for us, we can now be in a relationship with God. The cross of Jesus bridged the chasm between us (a sinful people) and God (The Holy One). God expects us to be holy—"Be holy because I, the Lord your God, am holy" (Lev. 19:2; Ps. 99:9; Isa. 6:3; 1 Peter 1:15).	In God, we learn that love is more than a feeling: it's active and dynamic. The engine that moves love to action is God's *goodness*. We experience God's goodness in his love, patience, provision, and compassion. All good things in our lives come from God's goodness: "The Lord is good to all; he has compassion on all he has made" (Ps. 145:9; Ps. 25:8; Nahum 1:7; Rom. 2:4).

REFLECTION

- Bring to mind the name of one person you love or have been in love with at some point in your life.
- What are some things you expect or expected from that person?
- What are some things that person expects or expected from you?
- How does this type of love differ from the love of God? How is it the same?

REFLECTION

- Pour a tablespoon of oil in a glass of water. Watch to see if the oil mixes with the water. The water and the oil will always remain separate; the oil will not corrupt the pure water.
- "Holiness" means separate from sin. Why is God's holiness so important?

REFLECTION

- Write down five things you're grateful for and then thank God for his goodness and for blessing you with those five things.

Attributes that We Share With God

12 JUST

As *holiness* balances *love*, God's *justice* balances his *goodness*. God is *just* because he judges with fairness and always does the right thing. God will judge the whole world (Rev. 20:13), and the wrongs will be righted: "The LORD within her is righteous; he does no wrong. Morning by morning he dispenses his justice, and every new day he does not fail, yet the unrighteous know no shame" (Zeph. 3:5; Ps. 33:5; Ps. 97:1–3; Isa. 42:1).

REFLECTION

- When Christ comes again, he will right the wrongs: He will judge those who have cheated us and been cruel to us, but he will also look at our lives and judge our selfish and self-righteous behavior toward others. All of our hidden deeds will be made known. All of our worst thoughts will be revealed. When you go to the Lord in prayer, what do you need to be forgiven for?

13 JEALOUS

Because of our sin, we reject God. Yet, he's the only being worthy of praise—as seen in the incommunicable attributes. In our rebellion, we offer our allegiance to idols and make God secondary. God is *jealous*. God does not share his glory with anyone or anything. God wants first place in our lives. He wants our loyalty over any other thing—even good things such as family, friends, church group, and country: "Do not worship any other god, for the Lord, whose name is Jealous, is a jealous God" (Ex. 34:14; Deut. 4:24; Zech. 8:2; James 4:5).

REFLECTION

- It's easy to allow family, friends, hobbies, and recreation to take first place in our lives. Even good things, such as career, church activities, and loyalty to country, can get in the way of following God. Make a list of the 10 things you spend the most time and money on and rank them in order of importance. What would be the most difficult ones to give up?

14 MERCIFUL

Although *justice* demands that "the wages of sin is death," God's *mercy* paves the way for "the gift of God [which] is eternal life in Christ Jesus our Lord"(Rom. 6:23). God is *merciful*. Out of his love and goodness, God's mercy holds rightful judgment against sin and evil to allow the salvation of those who come to him in faith: "But in your great mercy you did not put an end to them or abandon them, for you are a gracious and merciful God" (Deut. 4:31; Neh. 9:31; Dan. 9:9; Rom. 9:14–18).

REFLECTION

- Read Matthew 18:21–35.
- Reflect on a time you withheld mercy from someone or someone didn't show you mercy. How did this lack of mercy affect your life?
- How does God's mercy affect whether or not you show mercy to someone else?

Attributes that We Share With God

15 SOVEREIGN (AUTHORITY)	16 OMNIPOTENT (POWERFUL)	17 KNOWLEDGEABLE
God is *sovereign*. This means that God rules the universe and that he is not ruled by anything or anyone. Also, it means that nothing is beyond God's control: evil, death, blessings, relationships, all things happen within his authority. God has absolute *authority*, while humans have a limited authority in different areas of life. As a *sovereign God*, he provides faithfully for his creatures, in general, and for his people, in particular: "How great you are, Sovereign LORD! There is no one like you, and there is no God but you, as we have heard with our own ears" (2 Sam. 7:22; Ps. 33:8–11; Isa. 46:9–11; Dan. 4:32–35).	Being the creator of all things gives God the authority to be king. God is *all-powerful—omnipotent*. God has the power to do whatever he pleases, but he never contradicts his nature. He can meet our needs and can help us through any trial, no matter how overwhelming or impossible to overcome it may be. Unlike God who can do all things, humans have power limited by our condition as creatures. With the same power that raised Jesus from the dead, God will also raise us from the dead and give us victory (2 Cor. 4:13–14; Phil. 3:10; 1 Peter 1:5; Gen. 18:13–14; Isa. 40:25–26; Jer. 32:17).	As you pray to God, know that he already knows what you need. God knows all things—he is *omniscient*. God knows the past, the present, and the future. God knows our hearts. He knows what we think, say, and do. Nothing is a surprise to God. Nothing catches him off guard. Whereas God knows all things, humans have a limited knowledge. Our knowledge is limited by our condition as creatures. "Nothing in all creation is hidden from God's sight. Everything is uncovered and laid bare before the eyes of him to whom we must give account" (Heb. 4:13; 1 Sam. 2:3; Ps. 139:1–6; 147:5; 1 John 3:20).
REFLECTION • When the storms of life seem to overwhelm you and all seems lost, what do you think Jesus would want to tell you?	**REFLECTION** • Make a list of all the obstacles in your life that seem impossible to overcome. • Pray that our omnipotent God will take care of each of the items in your list.	**REFLECTION** • In what way does God's knowledge of every person and every situation comfort you? • How does knowing that God knows everything about you—that you can't hide from God—help you grow closer to him?

Attributes that We Share With God

18 PATIENT

God is *just* and *holy*, and he will judge all people; however, God is *patient* and slow to carry out his righteous judgment. God waits patiently for his people to repent and come back to him. God sent his only Son, Jesus, to atone for our sins and appease that judgment and condemnation. Now, God waits patiently for people to turn to Christ in faith: "And he passed in front of Moses, proclaiming, 'The Lord, the Lord, the compassionate and gracious God, slow to anger, abounding in love and faithfulness'" (Ex. 34:6; Ps. 86:15; Jonah 4:2; 2 Peter 3:8–9).

REFLECTION

- Read the Parable of the Lost Son (Luke 15:11–31). This parable illustrates God's love and patience for the lost.
- Which son do you most identify with and why?
- What are some ways you can exercise the attribute of patience?

19 FAITHFUL

God is *faithful*. In our relationships, we're afraid to become vulnerable and allow someone to take advantage of us. However, God is faithful to his word. He'll do just as he said. He'll never take advantage of us. We can trust that God will be faithfully good to us, show mercy and forgiveness to us, and do justice in the world. When we are in trouble, we can completely rely on God's promises, because God is faithful: "Praise be to the Lord, who has given rest to his people Israel just as he promised. Not one word has failed of all the good promises he gave through his servant Moses" (1 Kings 8:56; Deut. 7:9; Ps. 57:10; 1 Thess. 5:24).

REFLECTION

- How has God shown his faithfulness in your life despite your failures?
- How have you responded to God's faithfulness?

20 SPIRIT

Finally, it is important to remember that God is spirit. It means, first, that God does not have a body. When the Bible speaks of God's face, hands, or any "body language," it is using comparison with our bodies that we can understand and relate to. It also means that God is the source of all life. Whereas God is spirit, humans have both a spirit and a body. "God is spirit, and his worshipers must worship in the Spirit and truth" (John 4:24; 1:18; Acts 17:24; 2 Cor. 3:17; 1 Tim. 1:17; 6:16).

REFLECTION

- How does creation point you toward the invisible God?
- How has the physical human being, Jesus Christ, helped you develop your relationship with God, who is spirit?

Creeds and Heresies

Where Did the Creeds Come From?

As the gospel spread in the first centuries after Jesus' death and resurrection, people wondered about the beliefs of this new religion. Like today, believers then needed quick, accessible answers to questions. Early Christians formulated simple creeds that expressed essential Christian beliefs. These creeds served at least three purposes:

1. *Explanation of the faith.* Creeds are basic, memorable statements of belief.

2. *Training of believers.* Creeds help believers understand who they are, what they believe, and how they should act as Christians. They are like posts that delimit the boundaries of what it means to be, to believe, and live as Christians.

3. *Identification and correction of false teachings:* Even in the first century AD, false teachers abounded—teachers who claimed to follow Jesus but who promoted a message about Jesus that differed radically from the historical accounts proclaimed by apostolic eyewitnesses. Early Christian creeds helped believers to distinguish the truth about Jesus from the alternative perspectives presented by false teachers.

What Does a Christian Believe?

Early Christians struggled to keep their faith rooted in the historical truth about Jesus Christ—a truth first proclaimed by apostolic eyewitnesses, then passed on through oral traditions, and recorded in the New Testament writings. By providing brief summaries of the truth about Jesus, creeds promoted unity and identity among believers in Jesus Christ.

Religious Persecution

Jesus Christ is the fulfillment of God's promises to the people of Israel. For this reason, Christianity was not simply another Jewish sect like the Pharisees and Sadducees. Early Christian writings, including the earliest of the creeds, clearly reflect efforts to demonstrate that Christian faith consummated and fulfilled the Old Testament promises of a Messiah. Eventually, this radical claim led to a separation between the church and mainstream Judaism. Some Jewish religious leaders persecuted believers in Jesus. One of these religious leaders—Saul, later known as Paul—eventually trusted Jesus as his Lord and Messiah.

Political Persecution

The early church also experienced persecution from the Roman Empire. The Romans were tolerant of other people's religions to a point; because of their respect for ancient and venerable traditions, the Romans even tolerated the Jewish religion. As persecution drove believers away from Jerusalem, it became clear that Christianity was not simply another Jewish sect, and the Romans began to demand that Christians worship the Roman emperor. Christians refused to worship the Emperor and declared that Jesus alone is Lord. Christians' refusal to worship the Emperor was one reason for the vicious Roman persecution in the latter half of the first century. The powerful influences of pagan culture—both in the state religion of emperor worship and in the growing presence of Gnosticism—made it all the more important to articulate clearly what Christians ought to believe. Identifying God as the sole Creator of all things and declaring Jesus as the only Lord became an important confession for the early church.

Confessing the Good News

Jesus' life and ministry challenged Jewish expectations and hopes. The radical call to be transformed by the power of the Holy Spirit and live a different life is not easy to digest. New Testament writers had to stretch their knowledge and understanding. These Spirit-inspired authors presented the truth about Jesus in ways that could be understood not only by Jewish people but also in the broader Greco-Roman world and beyond. The New Testament writings and the creeds of early Christianity answered some of the challenges of the Greco-Roman world.

Today, the creeds still give us identity as Christians. They tell us the following and much more:

- What does it mean to be a Christian?
- Why is it important to believe in the Trinity?
- Why is it important that Jesus is fully God and fully human?
- What unites us as believers?

The Apostle Paul emphasizes "one Lord, one faith, one baptism" (Eph. 4:2). When we recite the creeds, we agree with them; and this agreement joins us in one Lord—the God of the Bible, revealed to humanity as one God in three persons—and one faith: the confession of our common belief. The creeds identify us as the church, the called-out people of God.

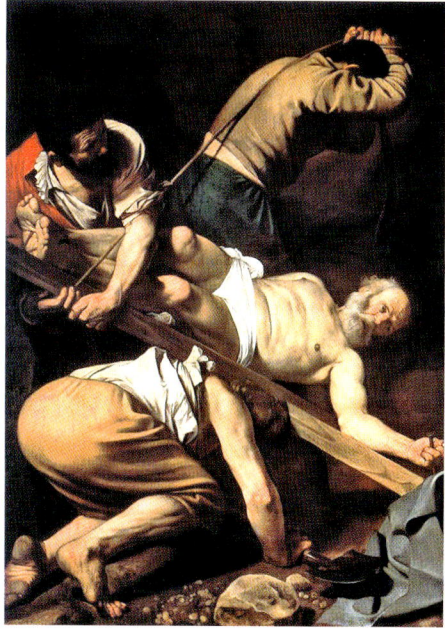

Caravaggio: Crucifixion of St. Peter, Santa Maria del Popolo, Rome

Key Words

KEY WORD	MEANING	EXPLANATION
DOCTRINE	From the Latin word *doctrina*, meaning "teaching, learning."	A doctrine is a belief that a group holds as true. Christian doctrines organize and explain the beliefs the church learns from the Bible.
CREED	From the Latin word *credo*, meaning "I believe."	Creeds are simple summaries of beliefs. They are easy to memorize and flexible to teach.
CONFESSION	From the Latin word *confiteri*, meaning "acknowledge."	Like creeds, confessions are an active acknowledgement of the church's faith and teachings. Often, "confessions of faith" include not only creedal declarations but also statements that summarize the unique teachings of a particular denomination or group of believers.
HERESY	From the Greek word *hairesis*, meaning "choice."	It refers to teachings that contradict another teaching that has been accepted as the norm. Many heretics in the early church began as believers trying to understand difficult teachings about the Trinity (three persons in one perfect divine unity) and the Incarnation (the embodiment of God the Son in human flesh).
ORTHODOX	From the Greek words *ortho*, "straight," and *doxa*, "belief, opinion."	Irenaeus coined the word *orthodox* to characterize his own teachings, which most other Church Fathers agreed with, and the word *heresy* to define those of his adversaries.

Note: The text of the Apostles' Creed and the Nicene Creed are modified from *Creeds of Christendom, Vol. 1* by Philip Schaff.

Creeds in the Bible

The Bible is a confessional document. It is God's revelation of God's plans for humanity. It also includes human responses to God's revelation: praises (psalms), confessions (for example, Naaman's and Peter's in 2 Kings 5:15 and Matthew 16:16), petitions, and creeds. To treat the Bible as a confessional document means that Christians affirm (confess) its teachings as truthful. These confessions identify Christians as God's people.

BIBLE	SUMMARY	IMPORTANCE TODAY
Deuteronomy 6:4–5 (Shema) Hear, O Israel: The Lord our God, the Lord is one.	In the midst of peoples with many gods, the Shema sets the Israelites apart. It expresses the basic belief about the uniqueness of God.	We live in a world in which many different gods claim people's allegiance. The confession of the Shema sets Christians apart by their belief in the one true God.
Romans 10:9 If you confess with your mouth, "Jesus is Lord," and believe in your heart that God raised him from the dead, you will be saved.	This passage is a brief summary of a basic Christian belief: the confession that Jesus is Lord as a public testimony of faith.	This text declares the Lordship of Jesus. Jesus is both our one God and our Master. He has proven his divinity and power through his resurrection.
1 Corinthians 15:3–4 For what I received I passed on to you as of first importance: that Christ died for our sins according to the Scriptures….	This confession about Jesus' resurrection captures the centrality of the resurrection for the believer.	As the Apostle Paul wrote, if Jesus was not raised from the dead, our faith is in vain (15:17).

What Does a Christian NOT Believe?

Creeds are constant reminders of what is central to our faith. Creeds are also boundary markers that set the rules for intelligent, creative conversation about God and his creation. Like fences, creeds protect us from "heresy"—choosing to wander away from the historical testimony about the nature and workings of God found in Holy Scripture.

The creeds of the early church—the Apostolic, Nicene, Athanasian, and Chalcedonian creeds—were responses to heretical teachings. The heresies in the early church were, for the most part, related to our understanding of God and Jesus. Studying the creeds helps us understand the heresies of the past. By understanding those heresies, it is easier to avoid repeating them today.

The Apostles' Creed

The Apostles did not write the Apostles' Creed. No one knows for certain when this creed was written. References to and quotation of similar statements—known as the "Rule of Faith"—can be found in writings as early as the second century AD. The name "Apostles' Creed" means that the creed contains the Apostolic tradition. The Apostles' Creed is the most universal of all the creeds. Most Christian denominations continue to recite and teach it.

Early creedal statements were very helpful for new Christians in understanding their faith. These early creedal statements were used in baptism. New believers memorized and studied them before being baptized. It is quite possible that from these baptismal "formulas," the ancient church developed what we now call the Apostles' Creed.

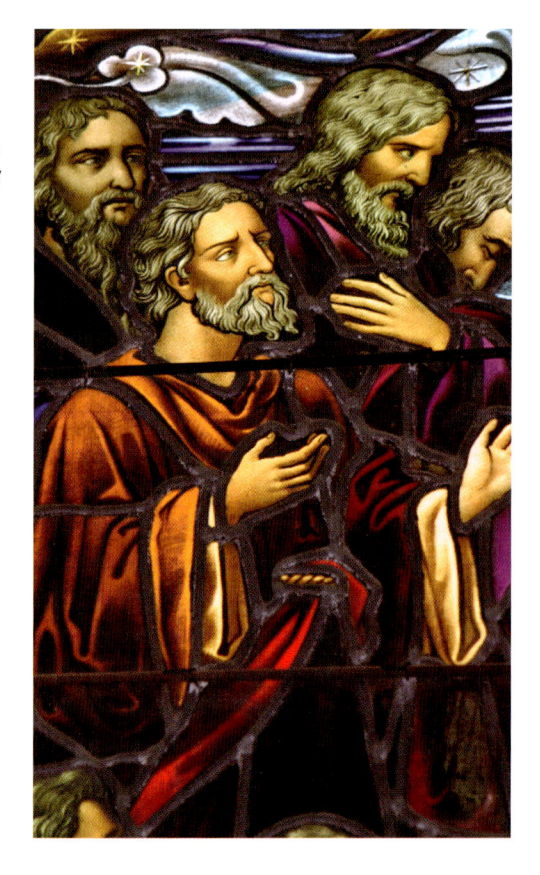

Creeds and Heresies • 411

APOSTLES' CREED	SUMMARY OF MEANING
I believe in… (Isa. 44:6)	The basic meaning of creed. It expresses the beliefs that unite all Christians. The words that follow preserve the teaching of the Apostles.
God, the Father Almighty (Isa. 44:6)	Not just belief in an impersonal force or in many gods, but rather, a deep trust in a personal, caring, loving God.
Maker of heaven and earth. (Gen. 1:1; John 1:1)	God is powerful. Just as God created the universe, God can heal, save, guard, comfort, and guide us. The whole universe is his.
And in Jesus Christ, his only Son, (John 9:38; 20:28)	We believe Jesus is the promised Messiah. Believing in God is also believing in Jesus.
Our Lord; (Phil. 2:9–11)	No nation, no king, no Caesar comes first: only Jesus is Lord. He has all authority and power; only he deserves praise and worship.
Who was conceived by the Holy Spirit, and born of the Virgin Mary; (Luke 1:35)	Jesus' birth and life were a miracle. By being fully human, Jesus has given us an example of life, taken upon himself the penalty of sin, and given us a new life and a new future.
Suffered under Pontius Pilate, (Luke 23:23–25)	Many have blamed Jews for Jesus' death. The Creed makes it clear that Pilate decided Jesus' death. Jesus died an innocent man. Pilate's injustice contrasts with God's justice; Pilate's arrogance contrasts with Jesus' humility.
Was crucified, died, and buried (1 Cor. 15:3–4)	These events really happened. Jesus' crucifixion and death were not merely staged; Jesus' death was real and a sad necessity for our sake.
He descended into hell; (1 Peter 3:18–19)	The meaning of this line is not clear; some think it refers to 1 Peter 3:19: "He went and preached to the spirits in prison." It is also possible to translate this line as "he descended to the dead," emphasizing the reality of Jesus' death. The phrase was not in the oldest available copy of the creed.
On the third day he rose from the dead; (1 Cor. 15:4)	Jesus' resurrection is fundamental. His resurrection points to the fulfillment of all justice and the hope for all believers. Jesus is the "firstborn from among the dead" (Col. 1:18).
He ascended into heaven and is seated at the right hand of the Father; (Luke 24:51)	Ascending to heaven and sitting at the right hand of the Father demonstrate Jesus' authority over the whole creation.
From thence he will come to judge the living and the dead. (2 Tim. 4:1; John 5:22)	Jesus' second coming will not be like a humble lamb. He will return like a triumphant king and judge. With his authority, he will judge all of creation. Christians rest assured that there is "no condemnation for those who are in Christ Jesus" (Rom. 8:1).
I believe in the Holy Spirit, (John 15:26; 16:7–14)	Jesus promised to send us a comforter, guide, equipper, and advocate. The Holy Spirit is God's presence in our midst.
The holy catholic church, (Gal. 3:26–29)	God has called his people out of sin and death; it is a group separated (holy) and from the whole world and throughout all time (catholic, or universal). The church is a people bought with the precious blood of Jesus on the cross.
The communion of saints, (Heb. 10:25)	In Jesus, all believers from all places and all times are brothers and sisters; we all share the same fellowship, the same Spirit, and the same Lord. We, who were many, are now one people in Jesus.
The forgiveness of sins, (Heb. 8:12; Luke 7:48)	Sin had broken our relationship with God, with creation, and with one another. Jesus has reconciled us with God, freeing us from our sin and death.
The resurrection of the body, and the life everlasting. (1 Thess. 4:16; John 10:28)	Unlike the Gnostics who viewed every physical reality as evil, Christians believe that they will receive new bodies and a new creation. Jesus' resurrected body was real (he could eat and could be touched); our resurrection bodies will also have a physical nature. And we will live with Jesus forever in a new creation.

Heresies in the Early Church

HERESY	SUMMARY	COMMENTS
DOCETISM First Century	This heresy denies the reality of Jesus' human nature. Jesus only *appeared* to be human. (The word *docetism* is derived from a Greek word meaning "appearance.") Docetism was imported directly from Gnosticism into Christianity.	Today many people deny Jesus' divinity and consider him just a human. But Christians who focus only on Jesus' divinity and ignore the physical reality of Jesus' resurrection fall into a mild form of docetism.
EBIONITISM First Century	Ebionites denied Jesus' divinity and proposed the full continuity of the Old Testament Law. In other words, Christians should still submit to the Old Testament Law. Ebionites rejected Paul's teachings.	This heresy is significant because it prompted the church to define itself as distinct from Judaism, though still connected to the Old Testament.
ADOPTIONISM Second Century	Adoptionism claims that Jesus was born as (only) a human. Later, he became divine when God adopted him. This common position among Gnostics is a form of *Monarchianism*.	The Bible clearly shows that Jesus is God. Adoptionism arises from a misplaced respect for God's uniqueness. The idea that God became human is very difficult to understand. Today, some scholars still teach adoptionism as a way to understand Jesus as a human being who became divine in a *metaphorical* way.
MANICHEANISM Second Century	A heresy fusing Christian, Zoroastrian and Buddhist beliefs in a religion that was very popular and widespread until around the AD 600's. Mani called himself the Paraclete who would complete the work of people like Zoroaster, Plato, Buddha, and Jesus.	Manicheanism is important because it spread Gnosticism in the West and in Christianity (Augustine was a Manichean before becoming a Christian). Mani did not believe in a personal God; good and evil were equal but opposing forces.
MARCIONISM Second Century	Marcion made a radical break between Christianity and the Old Testament. Marcion proclaimed himself a follower of Jesus but rejected Paul's writings and anything that sounded like the Old Testament.	Today, many Christians who ignore the Old Testament are functional Marcionites. Whatever our doctrinal differences may be, the church confesses that the whole Bible, both Old and New Testaments, is the Word of God.
MODALISM Second Century	Modalism teaches that God takes on different modes of being at different times. In the Old testament God manifested himself as the Father. In the New Testament, God manifested himself as the Son. In the Church age, God manifests himself as the Holy Spirit.	Modalism attempts to make sense of the difficult doctrine of the Trinity. However, it is inconsistent with biblical testimony. Some people today continue to hold to a form of modalism. Though they identify themselves as Christians, they understand God in modalist terms.
MONTANISM Second/Third Century	Montanists emphasized the spiritual gift of prophecy. Montanus, the founder, believed he received direct revelation from God through the Holy Spirit. Church fathers were divided concerning his teachings. However, Montanus's followers were more radical, claiming their prophecies were superior to the Bible. They also identified their three leaders with the Father, the Son, and the Holy Spirit. The church condemned their teachings and their legalistic way of life.	This heresy reminds us of the importance of the Holy Spirit. It also warns us of the excesses of some prophetic claims. Some Christians believe the Holy Spirit continues to give the gift of prophecy in our times. However, such prophecy must depend on biblical revelation to be valid.

HERESY	SUMMARY	COMMENTS
APOLLINARIANISM Fourth Century	The idea that Jesus had a full human body and soul, but no human reason. Instead, the divine *logos* was Jesus' rationality. Apollinaris, Bishop of Laodicea, could not understand the union of two very different natures, human and divine. He attempted to preserve the divine glory by separating the human and the divine.	This view is based on a semi-Gnostic understanding of reality: the "soul" is good; the "material world" is bad. A rejection of the world as God's good creation can lead one to this position.
ARIANISM Fourth Century	Arianism argues that Jesus does not share the same essence with God, and thus does not share in the same divine nature with eternity and authority. The Nicene, Chalcedonian, and Athanasian Creeds are primarily responses to this heresy.	This heresy prompted the church to define its understanding of Christ. The question of Jesus' nature, divine or not, is directly related to his work of salvation.
MACEDONIANISM Fourth Century	A heresy similar to Arianism, also denying that Jesus is the same *essence* of God the Father, although affirming Jesus as eternal. In addition, believers denied the divinity of the Holy Spirit.	Despite the strong condemnation from the Nicaea Council, the rise of this heresy shows the extension and powerful effect of the Arian heresy in Christianity. It extended the doubts from the nature of Jesus to the nature of the Holy Spirit.
PELAGIANISM Fourth Century	Pelagius taught that sin had not affected human nature at all. Adam's sin set a "bad example," which people choose to follow or not. Christ came to offer a "good example" of life. Salvation means choosing to follow Jesus' example.	Pelagianism represents a conscious rejection of God's grace-filled action to save humans and reconcile people with himself. A milder form, called semi-Pelagianism, suggests that we cooperate with God for our justification.
NESTORIANISM Fifth Century	Nestorius attempted to explain Jesus' incarnation by suggesting that Jesus has two separate natures: a human and a divine nature. However, the separation is so extreme that it would appear that Jesus had both two natures and two persons: a divine nature for one "person" and a human one for another "person."	Nestorianism was a reaction to the teaching that Jesus had only one nature (Apollinarianism is an example of this teaching). This teaching caused a great split in Christianity.

TRADITION When contemporary Christians speak of *tradition*, they may mean a human teaching that is not found in the Bible; in this sense, traditions cannot have the same authority as the Bible.

The early church did not use the word *tradition* in this way. The Apostle Paul wrote, "Stand firm and hold to the teachings [or *traditions*] we passed on to you, whether by word of mouth or by letter" (2 Thess. 2:15). *Tradition* meant the handing down of the Apostles' teachings. For the earliest church, the Scriptures were the Old Testament books—the New Testament did not yet have a final form.

Around one hundred years after the death of Jesus, Gnostics produced many writings similar to those in our New Testament; some of those writings claimed to have apostolic authorship—these writings are called the "Gnostic Gospels." The church realized the need to identify and make official the writings that faithfully contained the Apostles' teachings. This became urgent when the influential heretic Marcion questioned the authority of most writings that church fathers accepted.

MARCIONISM Marcion was born around AD 85 and was condemned around AD 144. Marcion rejected the Old Testament. He taught that the God of the Old Testament was angry and vengeful. He taught that the Old Testament God had nothing to do with the God of the New Testament, who is loving and forgiving. Marcion even threw out all writings that agreed, quoted, or referenced the Old Testament! Marcion rejected the Epistle of James and all the other books except Luke and the Pauline epistles. Marcion had rejected the full Apostolic teaching, so the church rejected Marcion's teachings.

Gnosticism

One ancient and important heresy that still thrives today is Gnosticism. The word *Gnosticism* is derived from the Greek word *gnosis*, meaning "knowledge." Gnosticism emphasized secret knowledge and secret rituals. Salvation consisted of experiencing the secret knowledge and rituals.

Ancient Gnosticism incorporated many beliefs from different religions. As Christianity spread throughout the Roman Empire, Gnostics quickly adopted some Christian practices and terminology. However, Gnosticism completely contradicts Christianity and opposes the biblical understanding of creation and God himself.

In the first two centuries AD, Justin Martyr, Irenaeus, Tertullian, Eusebius, and many others challenged specific forms of Gnosticism and wrote powerful critiques to demonstrate how Gnosticism contradicted biblical Christianity. Partly due to the Gnostic heresy, these three areas became critical for the early church to define:

- The books of the New Testament
- Salvation
- The nature and work of Jesus

TOPIC	GNOSTIC BELIEF	BIBLICAL BELIEF
Cosmogony (Origin of the universe)	A form of pantheism—a belief that identifies God with the universe. God and creation are one. The material world flows out of the divine essence. However, this god is not the God of the Bible, but a fallen god.	God created all things. The Creator and the creation are separate.
Cosmology (Nature, order, and function of the universe)	God is real, but the material world is an illusion. The material world is evil. The human soul, a remnant of the divine, is imprisoned in the body, which is part of the evil world. Humans have forgotten about their divine inner being.	The material world is as real as God. The world is not evil—God called it *good* and *blessed* it.
Origin of Evil	One dominant form of Gnosticism was based on the myth of Sophia, who lusted after the "First Father." Matter is the fruit of her sin. The physical world is evil.	Human sin originates with pride and disobedience. Creation is not evil, although it has been corrupted as a result of human sin.
Salvation	Salvation comes through experiential knowledge—a secret knowledge that teaches one how to escape the evil of a physical world. Its ultimate goal is a return to the original condition of being one with the First Father. In Christian-influenced Gnosticism, Jesus is the one teaching this secret knowledge. The knowledge of people's divine inner being is the main secret knowledge.	God is rescuing humanity through the work of Jesus, not through any special, hidden knowledge.
Jesus	Jesus is not really a human at all; he just appeared to be one. He was an *aeon*, an intermediary between the real world (the world of the spirit) and this evil reality, the material world.	He is the second person of the Trinity. He was incarnated as a real, full human, who atoned for the sins of humanity on the cross.

Gnosticism became such an influential belief system that it has continued to appear over the centuries in people's ideas about God and the world. Much of today's popular spirituality is Gnostic in its orientation.

THE NICENE CREED

The greatest doctrinal challenge to the church arose internally. Arius, a priest in Alexandria, suggested that if God begat Jesus, then Jesus had an origin. As such, Jesus did not share in the same divine essence with the Father. Therefore, Jesus was a lesser god.

In AD 325, Constantine called the leaders of the church to participate in a council—that is, an assembly of bishops. They met in the city of Nicaea, in present-day Turkey. The Council of Nicaea, made up of about 300 participants, overwhelmingly voted against the Arian teachings—ancient documents suggest that only three bishops refused to sign their agreement. The council expressed its views about God, Jesus, and the church in the Nicene Creed.

A CHRISTIAN EMPIRE

In AD 313, Constantine became the sole ruler of the Roman Empire. His Edict of Milan, put into effect in 313, granted full tolerance to all religions of the Empire. Constantine fought hard to gain stability for the Empire. Scholars have debated much whether Constantine really converted to Christianity—and if so, at what age he did. Whatever the case, Constantine became the protector and, in time, promoter of Christianity throughout the Empire.

During Constantine's reign, the Arian controversy threatened to divide Christianity and bring chaos to the Empire. Constantine understood that a divided Christianity would also divide the Empire. To keep his Empire together, he needed to keep Christianity together. From a political standpoint, the Nicaea Council solved and prevented a schism in Christianity and the Roman Empire.

ATHANASIUS AND THE TRINITY

Athanasius was one of the most active opponents of Arius' teachings. His persistence and clear mind helped the church to clarify its positions and write it in a creed, the Nicene Creed.

Athanasius' teachings are summarized in the Athanasian Creed. While it is likely that Athanasius did not write it, the creed contains his teachings and main ideas. The Athanasian Creed begins by affirming, "This is what the catholic [or universal] faith teaches: we worship one God in the Trinity and the Trinity in unity. We distinguish among the persons, but we do not divide the substance [or essence]." After unpacking these ideas, the creed concludes, "So that in all things, as aforesaid, the Unity in Trinity and the Trinity in Unity is to be worshipped."

NICENE CREED	MEANING	COMMENTS
We believe in one God, the Father Almighty, Maker of heaven and earth, **and of all things visible and invisible.**	As in the Apostles' Creed, the foundation of the Christian faith is the uniqueness of God. He alone is God. The Father is a distinct person, or individual reality, within the Godhead. In addition, God created *all* things. He is not created, but the Creator.	In Gnosticism, the God of the Bible is just the *demiurge*, an evil god who brought about the material world. This god is himself created.
And in one Lord Jesus Christ, the only-begotten **Son of God, begotten of the Father** before all worlds, **Light of Light, very God of very God, begotten, not made, being of one substance with the Father; by whom all things were made;**	The creed affirms Jesus' • Lordship: The same title applied to God the Father in the Old Testament. • Equality: Jesus is as much God as the Father. They share the same divine *essence*. Thus, Jesus is eternal. • Distinctness: Although they share the same essence, Jesus is a *person* distinct from the Father.	In the New Testament, Jesus' Lordship is directly connected to his divinity. He is not Lord simply because he earned it; rather, he is Lord because he is God. Arius tried to understand the Incarnation, but his approach ignores the broad context of the Scriptures.
Who for us, and for our salvation, came down from heaven, **and was incarnate** by the Holy Ghost of the Virgin Mary, **and was made man;** he was crucified for us under Pontius Pilate, **and suffered,** and was buried, **and the third day he rose again,** according to the Scriptures, **and ascended into heaven,** and sits on the right hand of the Father; **from thence he shall come** again, with glory, **to judge the living and the dead;** whose kingdom shall have no end.	The creed emphasizes both Jesus' divinity and humanity. • The image of coming down from heaven shows his divinity. • His miraculous virgin birth shows his humanity. • His suffering and death on the cross, again, show his full humanity. • His resurrection and ascension show his perfect work of salvation on behalf of humanity. • His final judgment shows his authority over the whole creation.	Heresies about Jesus denied either his full divinity or his full humanity. • Denying Jesus' divinity removes his ability to save humanity from sin and death. Jesus is reduced to being a *model* of perfection. • Denying Jesus' humanity removes his ability to intercede and represent humanity in his death.
And in the Holy Spirit, the Lord and Giver of life, who proceeds from the Father, who with the Father and the Son together is worshiped and glorified, who spoke by the prophets.	The creed confirms the Bible's doctrine of the Trinity: The Holy Spirit is fully divine, of the same *essence* as the Father and the Son, and is a distinct person within the Godhead. In the sixth century, Western churches added "who proceeds from the Father *and the Son*." It is this last addition, known as the *filioque* (Latin for "and the Son") that has caused division and conflict between the Eastern Orthodox and Western churches.	The natural consequence of denying Jesus' divinity is that the Holy Spirit is not divine either. After the creed of AD 325, the heresy about the Holy Spirit arose as a follow-up to Arianism.
In one holy catholic and apostolic church; we acknowledge one baptism for the remission of sins; we look for the resurrection of the dead, and the life of the world to come. Amen. [NOTE: The words in italics were added after the First Council of Nicaea in AD 325. The Council of Constantinople made these additions in AD 381.]	One of the main purposes of the creed was to promote the unity of all believers in one universal church within the Apostolic tradition. Baptism represents this unity, as does the forgiveness of sins, the resurrection, and the world to come. These are all promises and hopes that link all Christians everywhere and at every time.	The Arian controversy threatened to split the young and growing church. The creed allows the possibility of unity of belief and practice. The word *catholic* means "universal," in the sense of the whole world. It refers, then, to the worldwide fellowship of all believers.

The Chalcedonian Creed

Understanding the incarnation of Jesus—the embodiment of God the Son in human flesh—was one of the greatest challenges for the early church. In AD 451 the Council of Chalcedon (located in today's Turkey) provided a clear statement of the Apostolic teachings concerning Jesus. The Chalcedonian Creed made it clear that Jesus is fully God and fully human, two natures existing in perfect harmony in one person.

Heresies about Christ Corrected in the Chalcedonian Creed

SUBJECT	HERETICAL POSITION	APOSTOLIC TEACHING
Nature of Christ	Arianism: Jesus was the first created being, similar to God, but not fully divine like the Father. Docetism: Jesus was only a divine being. He merely *appeared* human.	Christ is *fully* God and *fully* human.
Relationship of Christ's Two Natures	Nestorianism: No connection between Jesus' two natures. Practically, Jesus had two natures and was two persons. Eutychianism: The divine and human natures are fused into one nature.	Two natures, divine and human, and one person.

Why Do The Creeds Matter?

1. **Creeds help Christians to distinguish between essential and nonessential beliefs.** Not everyone who disagrees with you is a heretic! There are some beliefs on which Christians cannot compromise. On others, we can agree to disagree. The creeds—which focus on the essential beliefs that cannot be compromised—help us to distinguish between essential and nonessential beliefs.

2. **Creeds help Christians to focus their faith and worship on the issues that matter most.** The issues that the creeds emphasize—such as the Trinity, the character of God, the nature of Jesus, and the resurrection, for example—are the ones that the earliest Christians understood to matter most. These same beliefs can provide a unifying focus for contemporary Christians' teaching and worship.

3. **Creeds help Christians to articulate clearly how their beliefs differ from other teachings.** The apostle Peter commanded his readers always "to be ready to provide to anyone who asks a defense for the hope that is in you" (1 Peter 3:15-16). When it comes to giving a defense for our faith, the creeds are crucial! When someone asks what Christians believe about the resurrection of Jesus, the Apostles' and Nicene Creeds provide concise summaries of this core doctrine. When a child in Sunday school asks why Jesus came to earth, a teacher who remembers the Nicene Creed can tell the child immediately, "It was for us and for our salvation." If someone asks whether the virgin conception of Jesus really matters, the Christian who knows the creeds can immediately recall that, even for the earliest believers in Jesus, this was an essential doctrine.

Heresies Today

Many heresies—wrong beliefs—relate to two central biblical teachings: the Trinity and the Incarnation. Misunderstanding who God is will lead to misunderstanding what God has done and will do. Knowing the basic teachings of the church will help us identify and respond to heresies still existing today.

ANCIENT HERESY	WHAT IT LOOKS LIKE TODAY	CORRECT APOSTOLIC TEACHING	COMMENTS
GNOSTICISM	• Confusing God with his creation. Taking things and people as part of the divine. • Rejecting the physical world as evil. • Belief that salvation is inside every person. • Speaking about Jesus as a guru or only as a great teacher. • "Pop spirituality" based on Gnostic ideas. *The Secret, The Power of Now*, and many self-help teachings fall into this category.	• God is the Creator of all things. • The world is good, though corrupted through human sin. • Salvation is possible only through Jesus.	• Christians need to be careful not to reject this material world. Radical separation of the body and soul is not a biblical teaching. God loves the world he made. He blessed it. We should do likewise.
MARCIONISM	• Rejecting the Old Testament. • Rejecting anything that sounds too Jewish from the New Testament. • Completely divorcing the Old Testament from the New Testament.	• The Old and New Testaments together are the Word of God. • Some ideas and concepts in the Old Testament continued in the New. Others Jesus fulfilled and are no longer binding in the New Testament. • God reveals himself in both Testaments. But Jesus is the fullness of God's revelation to humanity.	• Sometimes Christians make too strong a distinction between the Law and the Gospel. • The New Testament revelation is more complete than the Old Testament revelation because of Jesus (Heb. 1:1–3). • The revelation of the New Testament depends on God's works and words in the Old Testament.
MONARCHIANISM	• Denying the Trinity. • Claiming one god with three functions: First appearing as Father, then as Son, and now as Holy Spirit. • Both forms are active: Adoptionism and Modalism.	• There is one God in three distinct Persons: God the Father, the Son, and the Holy Spirit. • All three persons participate in the divine nature but have distinct personalities. • All three are involved in God's work of Creation, redemption, and restoration.	• Some groups believe that only Jesus (of the three members of the Trinity) is God. This is a form of modalism. • Other groups, like the Jehovah's Witnesses, confess a form of adoptionism. They deny that Jesus is fully God. Rather, they may believe Jesus is an angel, a special divine being, but not God.
ARIANISM APOLLINARIANISM DOCETISM MACEDONIANISM NESTORIANISM	• Claims that Jesus was human only and became divine. • Claims that Jesus was only divine and merely appeared human. • Claims that Jesus was two persons with two natures in one being.	• Jesus is the second Person of the Trinity. • He is fully God and fully human. • He is one person with two natures, divine and human. The natures are joined, but not mixed.	• Jehovah's Witnesses and Mormons show clear examples of such errors. • It is possible to emphasize Jesus' divine character to the point of forgetting that he is fully human as well. Jesus suffered, was hungry, and was tempted like any other human.
MONTANISM	• Offering prophecy beyond what the Bible reveals. • Claiming greater authority than the Bible. • Making the Holy Spirit more important than Jesus. • Using prophetic gifts to abuse other Christians' trust and faith. • Misleading people through unverifiable prophecies.	• God has revealed his will in the Scriptures and in Jesus. • The Holy Spirit only testifies about Jesus. • Although there are gifts of prophecy, prophecies are still subject to the authority of the Bible. • Prophecies from God are for building up the church, not for personal gain.	• Most founders of current cults—like Jehovah's Witnesses, Mormonism, and Christian Science—have claimed to receive new revelations from God. • These revelations contradict the Bible. • The prophetic claims of groups like Heaven's Gate, Peoples Temple, and many others have had tragic consequences.

The Trinity

In the simplest of terms, Christians believe:

There is only one God, and this one God exists as one essence in three Persons.

The three Persons are:
- God the Father
- God the Son (Jesus Christ)
- God the Holy Spirit (also called the Holy Ghost)

Early Christians used this diagram to explain the Trinity. The Father, Son, and Holy Spirit are all God, but they are not three names for the same Person.

The Persons are distinct:
- The Father is not the Son.
- The Son is not the Holy Spirit.
- The Holy Spirit is not the Father.

God is one absolutely perfect divine Being in three Persons. His *being* is what God *is*, in relation to the universe he created. The three are called Persons because they relate to one another in personal ways.

When Christians talk about believing in one God in three Persons (the Trinity), they do NOT mean:

1 God in 3 Gods, or
3 Persons in 1 Person, or
3 Persons in 3 Gods, or
1 Person in 3 Gods

Rather, they mean:

1 God in 3 Persons

Therefore,
- The Father is God—the first Person of the Trinity.
- The Son is God—the second Person of the Trinity.
- The Holy Spirit is God—the third Person of the Trinity. (The title "Holy Ghost" is an older English expression for "Holy Spirit." Each is an acceptable translation of the phrase in the Bible.)

Why do Christians Believe in the Trinity?

The Bible clearly teaches that there is only one God, yet the Bible calls all three Persons "God."

There is only one God.
- "Hear, O Israel: The Lord our God, the Lord is one." (Deut. 6:4)
- "Before me no god was formed, nor will there be one after me." (Isa. 43:10)

The Father is God.
- "Grace and peace to you from God our Father and the Lord Jesus Christ." (1 Cor. 1:3; 8:6; Eph. 4:4–6)

The Son is God.
- The Word was God. Jesus is identified as "the Word." (John 1:1–5, 14)
- I and the Father are one. (John 10:30–33)
- Jesus' disciple Thomas addressed Jesus as "My Lord and my God." (John 20:28)

  Jesus did not tell Thomas he was mistaken; instead Jesus accepted these titles. Other people in Scripture, notably Paul and Barnabas, refused to accept worship as gods (Acts 14).

- "But about the Son he says, 'Your throne, O God, will last for ever and ever; a scepter of justice will be the scepter of your kingdom.'" (Heb. 1:6–8)
- "Therefore God exalted him to the highest place and gave him the name that is above every name, that at the name of Jesus every knee should bow, in heaven and on earth and under the earth, and every tongue acknowledge that Jesus Christ is Lord, to the glory of God the Father." (Phil. 2:9–11)

  Paul, the writer of Philippians, is saying about Jesus what Isaiah 45:23 says about the Lord, and then Paul concludes that Jesus is Lord, that is, the same Lord God of the Old Testament.

See these passages about Jesus' deity: Isa. 7:14; 9:6; John 1:1, 18; 8:58–59; 10:30; Acts 20:28; Rom. 9:5; 10:9–13; Col. 1:15–16; 2:9; Titus 2:13; Heb. 1:3, 8; 2 Peter 1:1; 1 John 5:20

The Holy Spirit is God.
- "'Then Peter said, "Ananias, how is it that Satan has so filled your heart that you have lied to the Holy Spirit? ... You have not lied just to human beings but to God."'" (Acts 5:3-4). This verse equates the Holy Spirit with God.
- Now the Lord is that Spirit. (2 Cor. 3:17)

  "The Lord" here refers to "the Lord" in the Old Testament verse (Ex. 34:34) Paul had just quoted in the previous verse (2 Cor 3:16).

More than 60 Bible Passages mention the three Persons together

- Matthew 3:16–17 "As soon as Jesus was baptized, he went up out of the water. At that moment heaven was opened, and he saw the Spirit of God descending like a dove and alighting on him. And a voice from heaven said, 'This is my Son, whom I love; with him I am well pleased.'"
- Matthew 28:19 "Therefore go and make disciples of all nations, baptizing them in the name of the Father and of the Son and of the Holy Spirit."
- 2 Corinthians 13:14 "May the grace of the Lord Jesus Christ, and the love of God, and the fellowship of the Holy Spirit be with you all."
- Ephesians 4:4–6 "There is one body and one Spirit, just as you were called to one hope when you were called; one Lord, one faith, one baptism; one God and Father of all, who is over all and through all and in all."

See also John 3:34–35; 14:26; 15:26; 16:13–15; Rom. 14:17–18; 15:13–17; 15:30; 1 Cor. 6:11, 17–19; 12:4–6; 2 Cor. 1:21–22; 3:4–6; Gal. 2:21–3:2; 4:6; Eph. 2:18; 3:11–17; 5:18-20; Col. 1:6-8; Thess. 1:1–5; 4:2, 8; 5:18–19; 2 Thess. 3:5; Heb. 9:14; 1 Peter 1:2; 1 John 3:23–24; Titus 3: 4-6; 1 John 4:13–14; Jude 20–21.

The Trinity

Misunderstanding #1 "The word 'Trinity' does not appear in the Bible; it is a belief made up by Christians in the 4th century."

Truth: It is true that the word "Trinity" does not appear in the Bible, but the Trinity is nevertheless a Bible-based belief. The word "incarnation" does not appear in the Bible either, but we use it as a one-word summary of our belief that Jesus was God in the flesh.

The word "Trinity" was used to explain the eternal relationship between the Father, the Son, and the Holy Spirit. Many Bible passages express the Trinity. False beliefs flourished during the early days of Christianity, and still do. Early Christians constantly defended their beliefs. The following early church leaders and/or writings all defended the doctrine of the Trinity long before AD 300:

Approximate Dates:

AD 96	**Clement**, the third bishop of Rome
AD 90–100	**The Teachings of the Twelve Apostles**, the "Didache"
AD 90?	**Ignatius**, bishop of Antioch
AD 155	**Justin Martyr**, great Christian writer
AD 168	**Theophilus**, the sixth bishop of Antioch
AD 177	**Athenagoras**, theologian
AD 180	**Irenaeus**, bishop of Lyons
AD 197	**Tertullian**, early church leader
AD 264	**Gregory Thaumaturgus**, early church leader

Misunderstanding #2 "Christians believe there are three Gods."

Truth: Christians believe in only one God.

Some people might believe that Christians are polytheists (people who believe in many gods) because Christians refer to the Father as God, the Son as God, and the Holy Spirit as God. But Christians believe in only one God. The Bible says there is only one God. But it also calls three distinct Persons "God." Over the centuries people have tried to come up with simple explanations for the Trinity. There are limits to every illustration, but some are helpful.

For example, it has been said that

God is not $1 + 1 + 1 = 3$
God is $1 \times 1 \times 1 = 1$

The Trinity is a profound doctrine that must be accepted by faith. Accepting a doctrine by faith does not exclude reason, but it also means that we cannot always apply the same logic that we use in mathematics. Without the Trinity, the Christian doctrine of salvation cannot stand. Some religious groups that claim to believe in the God of the Bible, but reject the Trinity, have an understanding of salvation that is based on good works.

St. Patrick is believed to have used the shamrock as a way of illustrating the Trinity. He asked, "Is this one leaf or three? If one leaf, why are there three lobes of equal size? If three leaves, why is there just one stem? If you cannot explain so simple a mystery as the shamrock, how can you hope to understand one so profound as the Holy Trinity?" Even though this is an overly simple way to explain the Trinity, some teachers find it helpful.

Misunderstanding #3 "Jesus is not God."

Truth: Jesus is God, the Second Person of the Trinity.

1. Jesus' own claims

- **He forgave sin.** We may forgive sins committed against us, but we cannot forgive sins committed against others. Jesus has the authority to forgive any sin. (Mark 2:5–12; Luke 5:21)
- **He accepted worship as God and claimed to deserve the same honor as the Father.** (Matt. 14:33; 28:17–18; John 5:22–23; 9:38; 17:5)
- **He claimed to be the divine Son of God,** a title the Jews rightly understood to be a claim to equality with God. (John 5:17–18; 10:30-33; 19:7)

2. Jesus and God share traits (see below)

Traits Unique to God	Traits of Jesus
Creation is "the work of his hands"—alone (Gen. 1:1; Ps. 102:25; Isa. 44:24)	Creation is "the work of his hands"—all things created in and through him (John 1:3; Col. 1:16; Heb. 1:2, 10)
"The first and the last" (Isa. 44:6)	"The first and the last" (Rev. 1:17; 22:13)
"Lord of lords" (Deut. 10:17; Ps. 136:3)	"Lord of lords" (1 Tim. 6:15; Rev. 17:14; 19:16)
Unchanging and eternal (Ps. 90:2; 102:26–27; Mal. 3:6)	Unchanging and eternal (John 8:58; Col. 1:17; Heb. 1:11–12; 13:8)
Judge of all people (Gen. 18:25; Ps. 94:2; 96:13; 98:9)	Judge of all people (John 5:22; Acts 17:31; 2 Cor. 5:10; 2 Tim. 4:1)
Only Savior; no other God can save (Isa. 43:11; 45:21–22; Hosea 13:4)	Savior of the world; no salvation apart from him (John 4:42; Acts 4:12; Titus 2:13; 1 John 4:14)
Redeems from their sins a people for his own possession (Ex. 19:5; Ps. 130:7–8; Ezek. 37:23)	Redeems from their sins a people for his own possession (Titus 2:14)
Hears and answers prayers of those who call on him (Ps. 86:5–8; Isa. 55:6–7; Jer. 33:3; Joel 2:32)	Hears and answers prayers of those who call on him (John 14:14; Rom. 10:12–13; 1 Cor. 1:2; 2 Cor. 12:8–9)
Only God has divine glory (Isa. 42:8; 48:11)	Jesus has divine glory (John 17:5)
Worshiped by angels (Ps. 97:7)	Worshiped by angels (Heb. 1:6)

Misunderstanding #4: "Jesus is a lesser God than the Father."

Truth: Jesus is co-equal with God the Father. People who deny this truth may use the following arguments and verses. (These heresies date back to Arius, AD 319.)

Verses wrongly used to teach that Christ was created

▶ **Colossians 1:15:** If Christ is "the first born of all creation," was he created?

Answer: "Firstborn" cannot mean that Christ was created, because Paul says that all of creation was made in and for Christ, and that he exists before all creation and holds it together (Col. 1:16–17). The "firstborn" traditionally was the main heir. In context Paul is saying that Christ, as God's Son, is the main heir of all creation (verses 12–14).

▶ **John 3:16:** Does "only begotten Son" mean Jesus had a beginning?

Answer: "Only-begotten" does not mean that Jesus had a beginning; it means that Jesus is God's "unique" Son. In Hebrews 11:17, Isaac is called Abraham's "unique" son, even though Abraham had other children (Gen. 22:2; 25:1–6). Jesus is God's unique Son because only Jesus is fully God and eternally the Father's Son (John 1:1–3, 14–18).

▶ **Proverbs 8:22:** Does this mean that Christ ("Wisdom") was "created"?

Answer: This is not a literal description of Christ; it is a personification of wisdom. For example, Christ did not dwell in heaven with someone named Prudence (verse 12); he did not build a house with seven pillars (9:1). This verse says in a poetic way that God used wisdom in creating the world (Prov. 3:19–20).

Verses wrongly used to teach that Jesus is inferior to the Father

▶ **John 14:28:** If "the Father is greater than" Jesus, how can Jesus be God?

Answer: In his human life on earth Jesus voluntarily shared our natural limitations in order to save us. After he rose from the dead, Jesus returned to the glory he had with the Father (John 17:5; Phil. 2:9–11). In that restored glory, Jesus was able to send the Holy Spirit and empower his disciples to do even greater works than Jesus did while he was here in the flesh (John 14:12, 26–28).

▶ **1 Corinthians 15:28:** If Jesus is God, why will he be subject to the Father?

Answer: Jesus humbly and voluntarily submits himself to the Father's will for a time (Phil. 2:5–11). But, as the pre-existent and eternal Son, he is co-equal with God the Father.

▶ **Mark 13:32:** If Jesus is God, how could he not know when he would return?

Answer: Jesus voluntarily lowered himself to experience the limitations of human life. Paradoxically, while Jesus continued to be God, he chose to limit his access to knowledge (John 16:30). Paradoxes like this (not contradictions) are exactly what we would expect if, as the Bible says, God chose to live as a real human being (John 1:1, 14).

> Irenaeus, early church leader (AD 177), writes, "Now the Church,...received from the apostles and their disciples its faith in one God, and the father Almighty, who made the heaven, and the earth, and the seas, and all that is in them, and in one Christ Jesus, the Son of God, who was made flesh for our salvation, and in the Holy Spirit, who through the prophets proclaimed the dispensations of God..."

Misunderstanding #5: "The Father, the Son, and the Spirit are just different titles for Jesus, or three different ways that God has revealed himself."

Truth: The Bible clearly shows that the Father, Son, and Holy Spirit are distinct persons.

Some people think that the doctrine of the Trinity contradicts the truth that there is only one God. They argue that Jesus alone is the one true God, and therefore that Jesus is "the name of the Father and the Son and the Holy Spirit" (Matt. 28:19), and not just the name of the Son. While it is certainly true that there is only one God, we must allow the Bible to define what this means. And the Bible makes it quite clear that the Father, Son, and Holy Spirit are distinct persons:

▶ The Father sends the Son (Gal. 4:4; 1 John 4:14)
▶ The Father sends the Spirit (John 14:26; Gal. 4:6)
▶ The Son speaks, not on his own, but on behalf of the Father (John 8:28; 12:49)
▶ The Spirit speaks, not on his own, but on behalf of Jesus (John 16:13–15)
▶ The Father loves the Son, and the Son loves the Father (John 3:35; 5:20; 14:31)
▶ The Father and the Son count as two witnesses (John 5:31–37; 8:16–18)
▶ The Father and the Son glorify one another (John 17:1,4–5), and the Spirit glorifies Jesus the Son (John 16:14)
▶ The Son is an Advocate for us with the Father (1 John 2:1; Greek, *parakletos*); Jesus the Son sent the Holy Spirit, who is another Advocate (John 14:16, 26)
▶ Jesus Christ is not the Father, but the Son of the Father (2 John 3)

In Matthew 28:19, Jesus is not identifying himself as the Father, Son, and Holy Spirit. He is saying that Christian baptism identifies a person as one who believes in the Father, in the Son whom the Father sent to die for our sins, and in the Holy Spirit whom the Father and the Son sent to dwell in our hearts.

Misunderstanding #6: "Jesus wasn't really fully God and fully man."

Throughout history many people have balked at the idea that Jesus is both fully God and fully man. They have tried to resolve this paradox by saying that Jesus was a mere man through whom God spoke, or that he was God and merely appeared to be human, or some other "simpler" belief. Admittedly the idea that in Jesus, God became a man, is difficult for us to comprehend. But the Incarnation—the truth that God became flesh—is the ultimate proof that nothing is too hard for God (Gen. 18:14; Luke 1:37). And this truth is clearly taught in the Bible.

> A simple illustration:
> Ice, Water, Steam
> All have the same nature, water.
> (But of course, the Father, Son, and Holy Spirit are God at the same time.)

The Bible clearly shows that Jesus was fully human

As a child, he grew physically, intellectually, socially, and spiritually (Luke 2:40, 52).

He grew tired; he slept; he sweat; he was hungry and thirsty; he bled and died; his body was buried (Matt. 4:2; 8:24; Luke 22:44; John 4:6–7; 19:28–42).

After he rose from the dead, he ate and drank with people and let them see his scars and touch his body (Luke 24:39–43; John 20:27–29; Acts 10:41).

The Bible also clearly shows that Jesus was fully God

Jesus did on earth what only God can do: he commanded the forces of nature (Matt. 8:23–27; 14:22–33), forgave sins (Mark 2:1–12); claimed to be superior to the Sabbath law (John 5:17–18); and gave life to whomever he pleased (John 5:19-23).

Paul said that God purchased the church with his own blood (Acts 20:28).

Paul also said that the rulers of this world unwittingly crucified the Lord of glory (1 Cor. 2:8).

All the fullness of God's nature and being resides in Jesus' risen body (Col. 2:9).

The Creeds

Early Christian theologians of the first two centuries wrote many works defending Christianity from several threats:

- Persecution from the Roman Empire. Until the early AD 300s, Christianity was illegal and often Christians were viciously persecuted.

- Heresies attacking basic Christian beliefs, especially the deity of Jesus Christ and the nature of God.

The Apostles' Creed was one of the earliest statements of faith Christian leaders crafted to clarify basic Christian beliefs. It emphasizes the true humanity—including the physical body—of Jesus, which was the belief the heretics of the time denied.

> *I believe in God, the Father almighty, Creator of heaven and earth, and in Jesus Christ, his only Son, our Lord, who was conceived by the Holy Spirit, born of the Virgin Mary, suffered under Pontius Pilate, was crucified, died and was buried; he descended into hell;*
>
> *on the third day he rose again from the dead; he ascended into heaven, and is seated at the right hand of God the Father almighty; from there he will come to judge the living and the dead.*
>
> *I believe in the Holy Spirit, the holy catholic Church, the communion of saints, the forgiveness of sins, the resurrection of the body, and life everlasting. Amen.*

The **Nicene Creed** was written by church leaders in AD 325, and was later expanded somewhat. It was written to defend the church's belief in Christ's full deity and to reject formally the teachings of Arius, a man who claimed that Jesus was a created, inferior deity.

> *We believe in one God, the Father, the Almighty, maker of heaven and earth, of all that is, seen and unseen.*
>
> *We believe in one Lord, Jesus Christ, the only Son of God, eternally begotten of the Father, Light from Light, true God from true God, begotten, not made, of one Being with the Father; through him all things were made. For us and for our salvation he came down from heaven; by the power of the Holy Spirit he became incarnate from the virgin Mary and was made man. For our sake he was crucified under Pontius Pilate; he suffered death and was buried; on the third day he rose again in accordance with the Scriptures; he ascended into heaven. He is seated at the right hand of the Father, he will come again in glory to judge the living and the dead, and his kingdom will have no end.*
>
> *We believe in the Holy Spirit, the Lord, the giver of life, who proceeds from the Father and the Son; with the Father and the Son he is worshiped and glorified; he has spoken through the prophets.*
>
> *We believe in one holy catholic and apostolic Church. We acknowledge one baptism for the forgiveness of sins. We look for the resurrection of the dead, and the life of the world to come.*

Note: The Greek word from which the word *catholic* is derived means "universal." The "catholic Church" means the ancient church that agreed with the whole of the apostles' teaching, as opposed to false teachers that followed a "secret revelation" or emphasized only one part of the first-century apostles' teachings.

Divine Attributes	Father	Son	Holy Spirit
Eternal	Rom. 16:26–27	Rev. 1:17	Heb. 9:14
Creator of all things	Ps. 100:3	Col. 1:16	Ps. 104:30
Omnipresent (capable of being all places at once)	Jer. 23:24	Eph. 1:23	Ps. 139:7
Omniscient (knows all things)	1 John 3:20	John 21:17	1 Cor. 2:10
Wills and acts supernaturally	Eph. 1:5	Matt. 8:3	1 Cor. 12:11
Gives life	Gen. 1:11–31 see also John 5:21	John 1:4 see also John 5:21	Rom. 8:10–11 see also John 3:8
Strengthens believers	Ps. 138:3	Phil. 4:13	Eph. 3:16

The **Athanasian Creed**, written about AD 400 and named after Athanasius, a great defender of the Trinity, says the three Persons are not three Gods, but only one.

> This is what the catholic faith teaches: we worship one God in the Trinity and the Trinity in unity.
>
> We distinguish among the persons, but we do not divide the substance.
>
> For the Father is a distinct person; the Son is a distinct person; and the Holy Spirit is a distinct person. Still the Father and the Son and the Holy Spirit have one divinity, equal glory, and coeternal majesty. What the Father is, the Son is, and the Holy Spirit is.
>
> The Father is uncreated, the Son is uncreated, and the Holy Spirit is uncreated. The Father is boundless, the Son is boundless, and the Holy Spirit is boundless. The Father is eternal, the Son is eternal, and the Holy Spirit is eternal.
>
> Nevertheless, there are not three eternal beings, but one eternal being. Thus there are not three uncreated beings, nor three boundless beings, but one uncreated being and one boundless being. Likewise, the Father is omnipotent, the Son is omnipotent, and the Holy Spirit is omnipotent. Yet there are not three omnipotent beings, but one omnipotent being.
>
> Thus the Father is God, the Son is God, and the Holy Spirit is God. But there are not three gods, but one God. The Father is Lord, the Son is Lord, and the Holy Spirit is Lord. There as not three lords, but one Lord.
>
> For according to Christian truth, we must profess that each of the persons individually is God; and according to Christian religion we are forbidden to say there are three Gods or three Lords.
>
> The Father is made of none, neither created nor begotten. The Son is of the Father alone; not made nor created, but begotten. The Holy Spirit is of the Father and of the Son; neither made, nor created, nor begotten, but proceeding.
>
> So there is one Father, not three Fathers; one Son, not three Sons; one Holy Spirit, not three Holy Spirits. And in this Trinity none is afore, nor after another; none is greater, or less than another.
>
> But the whole three persons are co-eternal, and co-equal. So that in all things, as aforesaid, the Unity in Trinity and the Trinity in Unity is to be worshipped.

The **Chalcedonian Creed**, written in AD 451 by church leaders to defend the faith against false teachings, says that Jesus is fully God and fully man.

> Therefore, following the holy fathers, we all with one accord teach men to acknowledge one and the same Son, our Lord Jesus Christ, at once complete in Godhead and complete in manhood, truly God and truly man, consisting also of a reasonable soul and body; of one substance (homoousios) with the Father as regards his Godhead, and at the same time of one substance with us as regards his manhood; like us in all respects, apart from sin; as regards his Godhead, begotten of the Father before the ages, but yet as regards his manhood begotten, for us men and for our salvation, of Mary the Virgin, the God-bearer (theotokos); one and the same Christ, Son, Lord, Only-begotten, recognized in two natures, without confusion, without change, without division, without separation; the distinction of natures being in no way annulled by the union, but rather the characteristics of each nature being preserved and coming together to form one person and subsistence, not as parted or separated into two persons, but one and the same Son and Only-begotten God the Word, Lord Jesus Christ; even as the prophets from earliest times spoke of him, and our Lord Jesus Christ himself taught us, and the creed of the Fathers has handed down to us.

Why Be Baptized?

Baptism is one of the most important practices in the life of the church. The need for baptism is something that most Christians recognize. Jesus emphasized the importance of baptism when he commanded his disciples to "Go and make disciples of all nations, baptizing them in the name of the Father and of the Son and of the Holy Spirit" (Matthew 28:19). Baptism reminds us of

- Jesus' death and resurrection
- Our relationship to God and one another through the Holy Spirit (Ephesians 4:4-6).

Committed Christians interpret baptism in different ways, but most Christians agree that baptism

- is central to the Christian faith;
- is not optional but a commandment;
- is often a way for people to show in public their commitment to God;
- unifies Christians as members of the same body;
- has no ultimate significance apart from faith in Jesus Christ.

Method of Baptism

Different methods are used in baptism—some groups sprinkle water on the forehead, others pour water from a pitcher over the whole head, and others dip or immerse a person's whole body in water.

- Those who practice believers' baptism believe that the practice of immersion (being completely covered with water) more fully displays the symbolic burial of the believer's old life. As believers go under and emerge from the water, they identify themselves with Jesus' sacrificial death, burial, and resurrection (Romans 6:3–4).
- Other modes of baptism developed in the early church—such as pouring (affusion) and sprinkling (aspersion)—are more practical during times of persecution, and also with infants. As a result, pouring and sprinkling are usually connected with churches that practice infant baptism and with places where Christianity is illegal.

Baptize

The term *baptism* comes from a Greek word. The verb *baptizo* means "to cover in water, wash, dip, baptize."

What Happens During Baptism?

Although baptism ceremonies may look quite different from group to group, there are more similarities than differences.

1. Water is always present, whether it is in the form of a natural body of water, a baptismal font, a baptistery, a pool, or simply a bowl of water.
2. A church leader asks a few questions to give opportunity for persons involved in the baptism to profess their faith outwardly, then asks the support of those present. In the case of infant baptism, those questions are for the parents and others present to make certain that the child will have Christian examples, support, and instruction to guide the child toward an eventual profession (public expression) of faith.
3. The leader sprinkles, pours, or immerses the person being baptized and says, "I baptize you in the name of the Father and of the Son and of the Holy Spirit."

Believer's Baptism vs. Infant Baptism

One of the main points on which Christian groups differ is about who can be baptized. The following table clarifies the emphasis in perspective that each tradition places on its understanding of baptism.

Note the difference in emphasis. Both traditions agree that the act of baptism itself does not save a person. Salvation comes through Christ alone by faith (Galatians 3:26–28; Ephesians 2:8–9). Christians disagree about whether a person must be able to communicate a desire for baptism and an understanding of its meaning (sometimes referred to as the "age of accountability").

Believer's Baptism	Infant Baptism
Emphasis on faith as a human response to God's grace	Emphasis on faith as a gift from God
Believer who trusts	God who acts
Obedience and faith of believer	Command and promise of God
Believer's witness to the world	Covenant and covenant community
Old Testament model of sacrifice	Old Testament model of circumcision

Those who advocate believer's baptism refer to Bible passages that reveal recognition and repentance as a sign of readiness for baptism, such as:

Peter replied, **Repent and be baptized,** *every one of you, in the name of Jesus Christ for the forgiveness of your sins. And you will receive the gift of the Holy Spirit.* (Acts 2:38)

Those who accepted his message *were baptized, and about three thousand were added to their number that day.* (Acts 2:41)

But **when they believed** *Philip as he preached the good news of the kingdom of God and the name of Jesus Christ, they were baptized, both men and women.* (Acts 8:12)

Those who advocate *infant baptism* point to covenantal promises that include children (Genesis 17:7) as well as instances in Scripture where entire households—including children and slaves—were baptized based on the faith of the head of the household, such as:

Early Debate

Some of the earliest writings from the church fathers show that a debate over baptism for believers vs. infants was underway within the first hundred years of Christianity's beginnings.

Tertullian (AD 145–220), early church leader, contended that baptism was for believers, arguing that a conscious choice should precede baptism. On the other hand, Cyprian (AD 200–258), bishop of Carthage in North Africa, supported infant baptism, which was becoming a dominant practice in some areas.

Then they spoke the word of the Lord to him and to all the others in his house. At that hour of the night the jailer took them and washed their wounds; then **immediately he and all his family were baptized.** (Acts 16:32–33. See also Acts 18:8; 1 Cor. 1:16.)

*Peter replied, Repent and be baptized, every one of you, in the name of Jesus Christ for the forgiveness of your sins. And you will receive the gift of the Holy Spirit. T***he promise is for you and your children and for all who are far off***—for all whom the Lord our God will call.* (Acts 2:38–39)

Underlying the issue of believers' vs. infant baptism is the question of whether baptism is *primarily* about the believer personally identifying with the sacrificial death and resurrection of Christ, or whether it is *primarily* about God initiating the believer into the covenant community. (Note: Both traditions include the other view; the distinction is made to show emphasis only.) Below are descriptions of the Old Testament models upon which each tradition is based.

The Old Testament Models

Sacrifice	Circumcision
Sacrifice was a conscious act of repentance for sin	Circumcision was the sign and seal of being initiated into God's covenant people
• Identification with the sacrifice for sin • Individual's conscious response to God is crucial. • The faith of the believer connects one to God, not the symbolic act alone	• Sign and seal of initiation • Included entire community • Individual's faith not crucial, as symbol points to God who gives faith • Individual, personal faith will follow God's action in covenant

Sacrifice was a conscious act of repentance for sin and thus, only believers in the God of Israel could bring a sacrifice to the altar of God. In sacrifice, the believer was to be identified with the death of the animal given on behalf of sins. Understood in this way, baptism is seen as identification with the death of Christ (Romans 6:3–4). In both the Old Testament act of sacrifice and the New Testament act of baptism, it is faith that connects the believer to God.

"Wade in the Water." Postcard of a river baptism in New Bern, North Carolina, around 1900.

Since **circumcision** was about God's command and promise in covenant relationship, it involved entire families and nations and included not only adults but also infants. The covenant ceremony included sacrifices and thus pointed to the need for cleansing and faith in God's actions on behalf of believers (Exodus 13:1–16; Leviticus 12:1–8). It also brought the individual into a covenantal relationship that made the need for sacrifice clear.

In circumcision, the immediate faith of an infant was not crucial since the effect of the symbol was to point to God who commands, promises, and gives faith in covenant relationship. Paul connected circumcision with baptism in Colossians 2:10–12: "You were circumcised with a circumcision not made with hands, … having been buried with him in baptism." (Circumcision took place eight days after birth.)

By looking at how the church has practiced baptism over the centuries, it is possible to understand the current variety of views about baptism.

Where Do the Differences Come From?

Growth of the Church

As the early church took root in different places in the Roman Empire, different traditions developed about baptism. The church grew somewhat like a plant (Matthew 13:31–32). The phases of growth may be outlined in three stages:

The Early Church (around AD 1–500)	The Middle Church (around AD 500–1500)	The Modern Church (around AD 1500 to today)
Marked by • Rapid expansion similar to the rapid growth from seed to shoot seen in plants. • Time of great danger when persecutions by Roman rulers and religious authorities threatened to destroy the tender plant (Matthew 13:1–23).	• Despite early threats, the church consolidated and grew into a mature tree. • Many different peoples and cultures found a place in the church's various branches.	• The church grew, broke open, and scattered its seeds throughout the world. • The first split took place between the Roman Catholic and Eastern Orthodox branches (AD 1054), but an even greater scattering occurred at the Reformation (c. AD 1500).

Methods of Baptism Throughout History

Historically, the method of baptism is related to the meaning and symbolism of the ordinance.

Tradition	Meaning	Mode
Initiation	• Meaning centered on the water as a sacramental symbol of God's cleansing.	• Mode of baptism is not critical; any method can be used. • The symbolic application of water is crucial. • Methods needed to be flexible during times of persecution.
Identification	• The act of immersion symbolizes identifying with Christ's death and burial, while rising out of the water symbolizes resurrection and eternal life.	• Emphasis is on outward expression of inward faith through immersion. • One of the main meanings of the Greek word *baptizo* is "to cover with water."
Infusion	• Infusion of the Spirit's power is highlighted.	• The activity of the Spirit is more important than the specific mode of baptism.

Scriptural Roots

During the growth of the church, baptism's various Scriptural roots were emphasized at different times.

Initiation: The word comes from a root meaning "to enter in." Those who are initiated into the church enter into the life of Christ's body.

"Therefore go and make disciples of all nations, baptizing them in the name of the Father and of the Son and of the Holy Spirit, and teaching them to obey everything I have commanded you. And surely I am with you always, to the very end of the age." —Matt. 28:19–20

See also: Acts 2:41; 8:12, 36–38; 1 Cor. 12:13

Identification: The word comes from a root meaning "to treat as the same."
Those who are identified with Christ inherit God's riches through Christ (Ephesians 2:6–7), as children of God, because Christ identified with us by being treated as sinful.

"Or don't you know that all of us who were baptized into Christ Jesus were baptized into his death? We were therefore buried with him through baptism into death in order that, just as Christ was raised from the dead through the glory of the Father, we too may live a new life." —Romans 6:3–4

See also: Gal. 3:26–27; Col. 2:9–14; 1 Peter 3:21

Infusion: The word comes from a root meaning "to pour into." Those who have been infused have had the Holy Spirit and his power poured into them. Many biblical passages mention the Spirit's involvement in the lives of believers.

"When they arrived, they prayed for them that they might receive the Holy Spirit, because the Holy Spirit had not yet come upon any of them; they had simply been baptized into the name of the Lord Jesus. Then Peter and John placed their hands on them, and they received the Holy Spirit." —Acts 8:15–17

See also: Matt. 3:11; Lk. 24:49; Acts 1:5; 2:1–4; 8:15–17; 10:44–47; 11:15–16; 19:1–6; 1 Cor. 12:1–31

- Expansion of Christianity in first century AD
- Expansion of Christianity in second century AD

Perspectives Throughout History

	INITIATION	**IDENTIFICATION**	**INFUSION**
The Early Church (before AD 500)	• Baptism is a corporate act of **initiation** into the community of God. • Baptism is seen as the act and sign that the Holy Spirit is planting faith and working in the life of the newly baptized. God initiates the person (1 Corinthians 12:13). • Baptism is a group act and may include clans, tribes and families, infants through adults on the model of circumcision.	• Baptism is an individual act of faith and personal **identification** with Christ. • Baptism is seen as a personal act of faith that expresses the repentance and conversion of believers as they identify with Christ (Colossians 2:12). • Baptism is an individual act of faith and is therefore to be restricted to believers who have professed their faith.	• Baptism is God's act of **infusion** of power for ministry. • Baptism is seen as the act of receiving the Holy Spirit sent by the Father and the Son to infuse the believer with power for ministry (Acts 1:8). • Baptism is an act of both God who gives his Spirit and the believer who receives the gift of the Spirit. Only those who can make use of the gift show the evidence of the Spirit's baptism.
The Middle Church (around AD 500–1500)	• Baptism as a corporate act of initiation becomes the dominant view. • The expansion of the church and the end of persecution pushes this majority view to the forefront as the church pursues a group identity.	• Identification through baptism is minimized as churches pursue unity and consistency of teaching. • At this time, the emphasis on group identity rather than individual identity makes this view secondary.	• The infusion tradition is minimized early, becoming associated with heretical groups. • Montanism, a heresy that emphasized ecstatic prophecy, may have understood baptism in terms of infusion.
The Modern Church (around AD 1500 to today)	• Baptism in this tradition is retained by the Reformed, Anglican, and Roman Catholic denominations. **Note:** The act of baptism itself does not save a person. Salvation comes through Christ alone by faith (Galatians 3:26–28; Ephesians 2:8–9).	• Identification becomes the focus among Anabaptists and other Protestant bodies in the free church tradition, and the Greek Orthodox Church. • The fragmenting of the tradition of initiation in the Reformation allows for the re-emergence of the tradition of identification. • With the rise of individualism and personal choice, this view flourishes among independent church groups.	• The tradition of infusion is downplayed at the time of the Reformation, but appears intermittently. • The scattering of the church results in the tradition of infusion resurfacing slowly and sporadically. • The rise of Pentecostal and Charismatic churches (late 1800s to present) brings this view to the church. Many such groups, however, identify infusion with the "second blessing"—usually demonstrated through speaking in tongues—rather than with water baptism (Acts 8:14-17). • Other churches today believe that the Holy Spirit's power is given upon conversion or water baptism, and that believers simply need to be aware of this power from God and use it.

Baptism, Ritual and Ceremonial Cleansing in the Bible

- Baptism is connected to Old Testament practices of cleansing and purification.
- Besides meaning "to cover with water," the Greek word *baptizo* also means "to wash or dip in water."
- Old Testament people saw little distinction between physical washing and ceremonial cleanliness—physical acts were spiritual acts as well.
- Old Testament purity laws pointed toward the spiritual cleansing that was to happen through Christ.
- Thus, baptism came to symbolize the washing away of sin.

Old Testament	New Testament
Aaron—Leviticus 16:4, 24; and other priests—Leviticus 8:6; 16:26, 28; Exodus 29:4; 30:18–21; 40:12, 31, 32; Numbers 19:7–10, 19; 2 Chronicles 4:6; elders, Deuteronomy 21:6; the people, Exodus 19:10, 14.	John the Baptist—Matthew 3:5–11; 21:25; Mark 1:4–5; 11:30; Luke 3:2–3, 12; 7:29; John 1:25–33; 3:23; 10:40; Acts 1:5, 22; 10:37; 11:16; 18:25; 19:3–4
Washing with water used—For clothes, Exodus 19:10, 14; burnt offerings, Leviticus 1:9, 13; 9:14; 2 Chronicles 4:6; infants, Ezekiel 16:4; hands, Deuteronomy 21:6; Psalm 26:6; feet, Genesis 18:4.	Jesus—Matthew 3:13–16; Mark 1:8–10; Luke 3:7–8; John 3:5, 25–26; 4:1
Conditions cleansed—Leprosy, Leviticus 14:8–9; discharge of blood, Leviticus 15:1–13; defilement by dead, Leviticus 17:15–16; Numbers 19:11–13.	Disciples—John 4:2; Matthew 28:19
Common purification for normal body functions—Leviticus 12:6–8; 15:16–30.	Paul—Acts 9:18; 1 Corinthians 1:13–17
Fire and water together as symbols of purification after battle—Numbers 31:19–24.	Church—Matthew 28:19; Acts 2:38, 41; 8:12–13, 36–38; 10:46–48; 16:14–15; 18:8; 19:5; 22:16

- People in the Old Testament did not baptize. However, some practices provide the background for the New Testament baptism. Purification rites and sacrifices in the Old Testament point to the need for cleansing of impurity, evil, and sin.
- In Christ, the functions of both water and blood came together.
  ▸ The blood of Christ cleans us from all sin and evil (1 John 1:7).
  ▸ The blood of Christ atones for our sins (Romans 5:9).
- Baptism symbolizes this cleansing in Jesus' blood (1 Peter 3:21)
	Moses, a type—1 Corinthians 10:1–2

	Initiation—1 Corinthians 12:13
	Identification—Romans 6:3–4; Galatians 3:27; Colossians 2:12
	Infusion—Matthew 3:11,16; Mark 1:8; Luke 3:22; 24:49; John 1:32–33; 3:5; Acts 1:5; 2:1–38; 8:15–17; 10:38–47; 11:15–16; 19:2–6
	Water a symbol for the cleansing by the Word and Spirit—Ephesians 5:26; Titus 3:5–6; 1 Peter 3:21

Purification with Water in the Old Testament

- The high priest ritually washed himself before his service on the Day of Atonement, as did the priest who released the scapegoat (Leviticus 16:3, 4, 26–28).
- John the Baptist, from the priestly line of Aaron (Luke 1:5–80), may have transformed the priestly rites of purification into baptism.
- At the time of John the Baptist's preaching, some groups were practicing baptism as a ritual of purification for all believers.
- The Qumran community that produced the Dead Sea scrolls appears to have been one such community.

Baptism and Water Cleansing in the Bible

What Was John the Baptist Doing?

Is the baptism of repentance that John the Baptist practiced the same baptism that is now practiced in the church? No. However, there are several similarities:

- Water is used as a symbol of purification and cleansing. (Matthew 3:5, 6, 11; 1 Peter 3:21)
- Repentance, turning away from the self-centered life to a God-centered one, is central. (Mark 1:4–5; Acts 2:38)
- The practice includes all manner of people, both genders, all levels of society. (Luke 3:7–14; Acts 16:25–33)

There are also important differences between John's baptism and Christian baptism:

John's Baptism	Christian Baptism
John the Baptist and his ministry were the last of the Old Testament order.	With the coming of Christ, a new order begins (Matthew 11:7–15; John 5:33–36).
The old order is not destroyed, but becomes the basis for the new.	The new order fulfills the old but is not identical to it.
John the Baptist pointed to the coming Messianic King.	Jesus the Messiah announces the coming of the Kingdom of God.

One Lord, One Faith, One Baptism (Ephesians 4:4-6)

There is one body and one Spirit—just as you were called to one hope when you were called—one Lord, one faith, one baptism; one God and Father of all, who is over all and through all and in all.

The Spirit of God has an end and goal for believers—to transform us into the image of Christ (Romans 12:1–2). We may be works in progress, but we are God's work (Ephesians 2:10).

The words of the Apostle Paul in Ephesians are a humbling reminder that baptism is an external symbol of our unity as believers. Our baptism, our faith, and our Lord unite us into one body: the church.

Jesus' desire for his church is revealed in his prayer for all believers in John 17:23, "May they be brought to complete unity to let the world know that you sent me and have loved them even as you have loved me." —John 17:23b

The Lord's Supper

What is the Lord's Supper?

In a simple way, the Lord's Supper is a meal that Jesus had with his disciples the night before he was crucified. Jesus commanded them to continue celebrating the supper. Years later, as an explanation of this practice, the Apostle Paul wrote to Christians in Corinth:

> *I received from the Lord what I also passed on to you: The Lord Jesus, on the night he was betrayed, took bread, and when he had given thanks, he broke it and said, 'This is my body, which is for you; do this in remembrance of me.' In the same way, after supper he took the cup, saying, 'This cup is the new covenant in my blood; do this, whenever you drink it, in remembrance of me.' For whenever you eat this bread and drink this cup, you proclaim the Lord's death until he comes* (1 Cor. 11:23–26).

The Lord's Supper is not a common meal. It is a time of fellowship, reflection, remembering, and spirituality. The Lord's Supper is related to how Christians understand who Jesus is and what he did in his earthly ministry. Understanding the meaning and importance of the Lord's Supper in the life of the church will help us to better understand Jesus' life and ministry.

Why do Christians celebrate the Lord's Supper?

We participate in the Lord's Supper because:

- Jesus commanded his followers to do it (1 Cor. 11:24–26).
- Just as a physical meal feeds and strengthens the body, celebrating the Lord's Supper feeds and strengthens the body of Christ, as a community and individually.
- It is a way to proclaim our hope in Christ's return and our forgiveness through his blood (1 Cor. 11:26). Every time we celebrate the Lord's Supper, we proclaim the Gospel and Jesus' return.
- It creates a strong bond of spiritual fellowship among believers (1 Cor. 10:17).
- The Lord's Supper is another form of worship (for many Christians, a special form of worship).
- It is a necessary time for reflection and introspection (1 Cor. 11:28).
- It teaches new believers about who Jesus is and what he did for us (1 Cor. 11:24–26) and refreshes seasoned believers.
- It fosters unity with Christ and among believers. Unity is one of the central messages of the celebration. This unity is symbolized in the one loaf of bread all share (1 Cor. 10:17).

Lord's Supper in History

In the first century, early Christians were persecuted by the Roman authorities. Some influential people in Rome even accused Christians of practicing cannibalism—eating human flesh! This accusation was related to the practice of the Lord's Supper. Christians talked about eating the body and drinking the blood of Christ as part of their rituals. Some uninformed Romans assumed that it was literally people eating people.

The Romans found the Christian celebration of the Lord's Supper strange and worrisome. Non-believers today are often similarly puzzled by the celebration. Imagine a person coming for the first time to a traditional Christian Sunday service, in which the Lord's Supper is served at the end after the sermon. What's the point of this practice? Why do we eat a little piece of bread and a tiny sip of juice? New believers may still have questions about the Lord's Supper after going through a beginner's class in church. Even lifelong Christians may be surprised to learn views of other groups of Christians.

What does it mean?

The Lord's Supper is important to our understanding of being Christ's church. It is meaningful in the following four areas:

- **Worship.** It is a way to worship Christ for his work, grace, love, and salvation. We participate with gratitude for Jesus' sacrifice for us.
- **Witness.** Participating in the Lord's Supper gives a testimony that Jesus died for our sins and resurrected in victory to give us eternal life, and that Jesus will return as a victorious king (Matt. 26:29; 1 Cor. 11:26).

- **Edification.** In the Lord's Supper, the Holy Spirit ministers to us individually and as Christ's body (1 Cor. 10:16). It is a time for mutual instruction, restoring broken relationships, forgiving past grievances, and repenting for offenses against others (1 Cor. 11:28–29).
- **Service.** The Lord's Supper is an occasion for Christians to serve each other, at the moment of the celebration itself as well as beyond the Lord's Supper. Remembering the sacrificial gift of Christ on the cross (the gifts of the bread and the wine) is a powerful motivation for us to "offer your bodies as living sacrifices, holy and pleasing to God" (Rom. 12:1). Just as we receive abundant gifts from the Lord, so do we extend this generosity unto others around us, starting with those closest to us (1 Tim. 5:8).

Names for the celebration

1. Breaking of the Bread (Acts 2:42; 1 Cor. 10:16)

- In the times of the Apostles, the expression was used for a meal in a family or a larger group.
- Jesus instituted the Lord's Supper at the end of a Passover celebration meal (Luke 22:13–16).
- Sharing a meal with others creates a sense of belonging and unity.

2. Holy Communion (1 Cor. 10:16)

- The Apostle Paul writes about "the communion of the blood" and "the communion of the body" of Christ. The Greek word he used in this verse is *koinonia*, which is a word that speaks of a two-sided relationship. It is variously translated as *communion, fellowship, participation or sharing.*
- Communion with whom? *First*, it refers to communion among believers, with each other, as Paul suggests in verse 17: "Because there is one loaf, we, who are many, are one body, for we all partake of the one loaf." *Second*, it refers to the believers' union with Christ.

3. Table of the Lord (1 Cor. 10:21)

- The Apostle Paul uses this expression to contrast the celebration of the Lord's Supper with the pagan sacrifices common in his time. The pagan celebrations included food sacrificed to their gods and abundant wine. Often these celebrations ended in drunkenness and debauchery.
- The Apostle Paul makes it clear that drunkenness does not have any place at the Lord's Table (1 Cor. 11:34). "You cannot drink the cup of the Lord and the cup of demons too; you cannot have a part in both the Lord's table and the table of demons" (1 Cor. 10:21).

4. Lord's Supper (1 Cor. 11:20)

- It refers to the historical event in which Jesus instituted this practice for his followers (Matt. 26:26–28).
- During this last meal, Jesus instructed his disciples about the Holy Spirit and their task after Jesus left them (John 13–16). At the end of the meal, Jesus established and commanded the celebration of the Supper.

5. Eucharist (1 Cor. 11:24)

- The word *eucharist* is a Greek word meaning "thanksgiving." It is a reference to the Apostle's teaching that Jesus gave *thanks* before giving the Apostles bread and wine (1 Cor. 11:24).
- The Corinthian Christians celebrated the Lord's Supper in the context of a group meal (also called "love feast," see 2 Peter 2:13; Jude 12). After the meal, the Christians from Corinth would celebrate the Eucharist by giving God thanks for the gifts of the Lord's Supper.

The Lord's Supper: Practice among Christians

Christian Unity in the Lord's Supper

One of the central purposes of the Lord's Supper is unity. The Apostle Paul wrote in 1 Corinthians 10:17: "Because there is one loaf, we, who are many, are one body, for we all partake of the one loaf." One of the main themes in First Corinthians is the unity of the church. Here, the Apostle suggests that the unity of all believers is expressed symbolically when we share together the Table of the Lord. In Christ, believers are one, like a loaf of bread.

Paul's conclusion about the oneness of all Christians agrees with Jesus' own prayer for the unity of the church: "Holy Father, protect them by the power of your name, the name you gave me, so that they may be one as we are one" (John 17:11; see, also, 17:20–23). The New Testament makes it clear that Christian unity is not an option but part of God's plan for his people.

Important Themes Christians Agree on

- *Jesus instituted the Lord's Supper* (Matt. 26:26–30; Mark 14:22–25; Luke 22:19–20; 1 Cor. 11:23–26). Jesus wants his disciples to celebrate the Lord's Supper.
- *The new covenant* (1 Cor. 11:25, Matt. 26:27–28, Mark 14:23–24). In the new covenant, God promised to write his law in our hearts (Jer. 31:32–34). It is based on Jesus' sacrifice on the cross, and it includes forgiveness and removal of sin and cleansing of our consciences (Heb. 10:2, 22).
- *Remembrance* (1 Cor. 11:24, Luke 22:19). The Lord's Supper allows Christians to remember and celebrate Jesus' birth, life and ministry, death and resurrection.
- *Thanksgiving, fellowship and unity* (1 Cor. 10:16 See also Matt. 26:26–27, Mark 14:22–23). It is gratitude for what God has done through Jesus, the new fellowship we now have with God and each other through Christ's sacrifice, and the unity of Christ's body.
- *The Lord's return* (1 Cor. 11:26 See also Matt. 26:29, Luke 22:16; 1 Cor. 16:22; Rev. 22:20). The Lord's Supper anticipates the celebration of the wedding supper of the Lamb (Rev. 19:9). Every time we participate in the Lord's Supper, we announce that Christ is coming back and has invited us to a glorious supper with him.
- *Separation from sin* (1 Cor. 10:21). Remembering Jesus' sacrifice gives us the opportunity to re-commit ourselves to God. Participating in the Supper requires us to examine our lives, confess our sins and ask God for forgiveness (1 Cor. 11:27–32).
- *A foretaste of heaven* (Matt. 26:29, Mark 14:25). The unity Christians can experience in the Lord's Supper as a special moment of celebration anticipates what life will be like with God in the new heavens and the new earth (Rev. 21:1–5).

Is Christ Present in the Wine and Bread?

One of the most controversial questions about the Lord's Supper is whether Jesus is present or not. For many Christians, Jesus is truly present at the moment of the consecration and celebration of the Lord's Supper. Because of this special presence of Christ, the Lord's Supper is a special tool and channel for God's grace.

Many other Christians believe that Jesus is neither *more* nor *especially* present in the Lord's Supper. Rather, Jesus is present always and in all moments of a worship service, including the Lord's Supper.

Christians have tried to explain in different ways how it is that Christ is present, or absent, in the elements of the Lord's Supper. The first three views attempt to explain how Christ is present in the Lord's Supper. The fourth view attempts to explain the main function of the Lord's Supper without appealing to Christ's presence.

Transubstantiation

If the participants really eat the body and drink the blood of Christ, how does it happen? Scholars used the idea of transubstantiation to avoid a crass materialism (that is, affirming that people eat actual flesh and blood) or pure intellectualism (the idea that the elements are merely a sign). These scholars made a distinction between *accident* and *substance*. The *substance* of a thing is that which makes the thing be what it is, and it is invisible to the eyes. The *accidents* of a thing are the visible characteristics of the thing: color, shape, weight, and so on. According to the theory of transubstantiation, the *accidents* of the bread and wine remain unchanged, but their *substance* changes into the body and blood of Christ. Thus, Catholic scholars speak of the substantial presence of Christ in the Eucharist. That means that Christ is present in the underlying reality of the elements. The bread and wine continue to be bread and wine (their *accidents*) while Christ's body and blood are present (their *substance*).

Consubstantiation

Martin Luther, the German Reformer, agreed that Jesus is really present in the elements of the Eucharist. However, he disagreed with the idea that the elements change in *substance*, as Catholics explained through transubstantiation. He argued that the full bread and wine are present alongside the body and blood of Christ. He called this *sacramental union*, and he refrained from giving any further explanations. Later Lutheran scholars used the concept of *consubstantiation* to explain Luther's understanding of *sacramental union*. They explained that the *substance* of Jesus' body and blood is present alongside the *substance* of the bread and wine.

Instrumental View

John Calvin disagreed with Catholic and Lutheran scholars about Christ's real presence in the Lord's Supper. For Calvin, Christ's presence in the Supper is real, but no change of the elements occurs. He also disagreed with Zwingli that Christ's presence is merely symbolic.

In his view, the biblical sacraments are instruments of the Holy Spirit to confer grace to believers. In addition, Calvin considered the doctrine of the union with Christ to be central in understanding faith in Christ. While our union with Christ is initiated in baptism, it is confirmed and sustained in the Lord's Supper. Through the elements of the Lord's Supper, the Holy Spirit unites us with the ascended Christ's body and blood, but not because Jesus descends into the bread and wine. Rather, the miracle of the Supper is that we are spiritually taken to heaven to commune with Christ.

Symbolic or Memorial View

Ulrich Zwingli was a pastor of the church in Zurich during the Reformation. Zwingli disagreed with the Catholic understanding of the Eucharist as well as with that of Martin Luther and John Calvin. Whereas they argued for the real presence of Christ in the communion—while explaining how that happens in different ways—Zwingli disagreed that there was a "real presence." His view, later known as a symbolic or memorial approach, says that the elements of the Lord's Supper are signs that point to the risen Christ. They function to make us observe, remember, proclaim, and worship this risen Christ.

Two Main Views

Sacrament

The Latin word *sacramentum*, which means "sacred oath," was the normal word used for translating the Greek word *musterion*, which means "mystery." In liturgical churches, such as the Catholic, Lutheran, Anglican, Reformed, it refers to the practices the Bible prescribes through which God's grace is specially received by the participants of the ceremonies. Protestant churches affirm only two sacraments: Baptism and the Lord's Supper. A sacrament is a witness to God's grace through Christ. In the sacramental view, the Lord's Supper is a divine instrument to bless and nurture believers with God's grace. The sacraments are tied to the Word of God in that the Word of God validates the sacraments. The sacraments, on the other hand, make the Word of God visible. Faith in the people participating is necessary so the sacraments can effectively communicate God's grace.

Ordinance

Ordinances are ceremonies that allow believers to express their faith. Many Christians believe that Baptism and the Lord's Supper are ordinances or external symbols of internal truths. Jesus commanded or ordered his followers to baptize and to celebrate the Lord's Supper. For this reason alone, the ordinances are very important. In this view, the main point of the Lord's Supper is commemorative. That is, in the Lord's Supper, the church commemorates—remembers, celebrates, and honors—Christ's work of salvation for us.

Main Views of the Lord's Supper

Sacramental View

	Presence of Christ	**Benefits of the ceremony**	**Administration of the ceremony**
Real Presence *Catholic* *Orthodox* *Some Anglicans*	• The bread and the wine change when priests consecrate them. • Catholics believe in *the real presence of Christ* in the elements; it is not just a symbolic or spiritual presence. • This change is considered a mystery—*sacramentum*, a miracle. • This change is explained with the philosophical concept of *transubstantiation*.	• The Eucharist re-presents (makes present) Christ's sacrifice on the cross. • It does not mean that Jesus is sacrificed again; rather, that Christ's sacrifice on the cross is made present in the Eucharist. • In the Eucharist, Christ's sacrifice on the cross is celebrated in a bloodless sacrifice. • Because Christ is present in the Eucharist, which also re-presents his sacrifice on the cross, the Eucharist becomes a channel of God's grace apart from the faith of the celebrant.	• Roman Catholics practice a closed communion. • Only ordained priests can consecrate the elements of the Eucharist. • Priests celebrate the Eucharist in the Mass daily. They encourage all Catholics to partake of the Eucharist at least once weekly. • Catholics in the state of mortal sin can participate in the Eucharist only after they have confessed and received forgiveness of their sin.
Sacramental Union *Lutheran* *Some Anglicans*	• Christ is present in the Eucharist. This presence is called *sacramental union*. • The body and blood of Christ are sacramentally (supernaturally) present alongside the bread and wine. • Rather than using the concept of transubstantiation to explain this union, many Lutherans use a similar concept: *consubstantiation*.	• Lutherans do not believe that the participant of the Eucharist offers a sacrifice to God that causes forgiveness of sin in itself. • Martin Luther affirmed that the sacrament offers a special benefit to the participants: forgiveness of sins, to the extent that it is connected to the participant's own faith, and confirmation of faith.	• Most Lutherans practice open communion. • Only ordained clergy can consecrate the elements of the Lord's Supper. • The Eucharist is offered weekly.
Real Spiritual Presence *Reformed* *Presbyterians* *Some Anglicans* *Some Baptists*	• Most Reformed people—or Calvinists—believe in *the real spiritual presence* of Christ in the Lord's Supper. • Although the elements do not experience any transformation, the presence of Jesus in the Lord's Supper is not simply spiritual or symbolic. It is real. • In the Lord's Supper, the Holy Spirit unites the believer with the risen Christ who is in heaven.	• The Lord's Supper is a sacrament and a means of grace. • Through the ministry of the Holy Spirit, believers are spiritually nourished and restored in a special way. • This view affirms the importance of faith in receiving the benefits of the sacrament. • The Lord's Supper is an expression and continuation of God's covenant with his people.	• Churches in the Reformed tradition practice open communion. • Only committed Christians can participate in the Lord's Supper. • The Lord's Supper has been traditionally celebrated either four times a year or the first Sunday of the month. Some churches celebrate it weekly. • Only ordained ministers can administer the Lord's Supper.

Ordinance View

	Presence of Christ	**Benefits of the ceremony**	**Administration of the ceremony**
Many Baptists *Pentecostals* *Most Contemporary Evangelicals* *Many non-denominational Churches* *Some Anglicans*	• These churches hold a view called the memorial view. • In this view, Christ is said to be either spiritually present or only symbolically present. • This view rejects the idea of a "real presence" of Christ in the Lord's Supper.	• The Lord's Supper commemorates Christ's sacrifice on the cross. • It benefits participants' spiritual growth in a similar way that renewing wedding vows may strengthen and nurture a marriage. • In this way, the Lord's Supper is another form of proclamation, like preaching or worshiping.	• Most practice open communion. • Only committed Christians can participate in the Lord's Supper. • Churches vary in how often they celebrate the Lord's Supper, such as weekly, monthly, or quarterly. • Some churches allow only ordained people to administer the Lord's Supper. Other churches allow lay leaders to administer the Lord's Supper.

The Orthodox Church holds a very similar view to that of the Catholic Church. The main difference is that the Orthodox view does not appeal to the idea of *transubstantiation* to explain the change in the elements. They are content to call it a mystery.

The Anglican Church is divided in their understanding of the Lord's Supper. High Church Anglicans prefer a view similar to that of the Catholic Church, while not appealing to transubstantiation as an explanation for Christ's real presence. Low Church Anglicans prefer either a more Reformed or Zwinglian view of the Lord's Supper.

Pentecostal churches also have a variety of understandings about the Lord's Supper. However, most of them prefer a Zwinglian understanding of the ordinance. In addition, they emphasize the role of the Holy Spirit in the Supper. For many Pentecostals, the celebration of the Lord's Supper can be a healing experience for the participants.

Quakers understand all of life as sacramental. Most Quakers do not practice the Lord's Supper because they consider that every meal is equally holy

Practical Questions

Why is it important?

- The simple fact that Jesus commanded us to observe it makes it important.
- Participating in this celebration allows us to deepen our relationship with Jesus and with other believers. The better and more deeply we understand Jesus' death on the cross on our behalf, the more we know Jesus' heart, the more we are willing to follow and obey him. Sharing in the meal together as one also promotes unity and love among believers.
- Participation also requires personal reflection and confession of one's sins. The Lord's Supper is an incomparable time for self-evaluation, confession, and repentance.
- The Lord's Supper is a crucial moment for Christian fellowship. It is a moment in which we proclaim we are one in Christ and bear witness as a body that our Lord and Savior has risen and will come back one day.

Open Communion
Many churches allow all Christians—that is, baptized believers from any background—to participate in the celebration of the Lord's Supper.

Closed Communion
Other churches limit who can take the Lord's Supper to members of a specific denomination. They believe that participants should share the same beliefs about the sacraments and the church.

How often should we celebrate the Lord's Supper?

- The Bible does not clearly indicate how often.
- The early church seems to have celebrated the Lord's Supper every time they met to share meals together. It is not clear if that occurred daily, weekly, or on a different schedule.
- The frequency of the celebration depends on our understanding of the Lord's Supper. The central issue is that all believers participate in the celebration, understand its importance, and grow in their relationship with Christ and other believers.

Is there one right way to do it?

No. But there are some elements included in all valid celebrations of the Lord's Supper. Below are some biblical guidelines for meaningful worship:

Before the Lord's Supper

- The Apostle Paul encourages us to examine ourselves before partaking in the Lord's Supper (1 Cor. 11:28). He encourages us to identify sin, bitterness, anger, hatred, or any other feeling or attitude and bringing it before God. Repentance is necessary before participating in the Lord's Supper. He gives warnings that all Christians ought to pay attention to before partaking in the Lord's Supper:

So then, whoever eats the bread or drinks the cup of the Lord in an unworthy manner will be guilty of sinning against the body and blood of the Lord. Everyone ought to examine themselves before they eat of the bread and drink from the cup. For those who eat and drink without discerning the body of Christ eat and drink judgment on themselves. That is why many among you are weak and sick, and a number of you have fallen asleep (1 Cor. 11:27–30).

- Once we have confessed our sins and asked God for his forgiveness, we must come in faith to the Table of the Lord believing that because of Jesus' sacrifice, God offers us his forgiveness. We must end our prayer with the certainty of God's forgiveness. Our eating and drinking of the bread and wine is our witness that we are forgiven.
- Although the Lord's Supper is a solemn moment, it is also a moment of thanksgiving, celebration, and great joy. We are remembering and celebrating Christ's wonderful work of redemption! We are also celebrating our unity with Christ through the Holy Spirit and with each other.

During the Lord's Supper

- We do not have specific instruction in Scripture for how we are to celebrate the Lord's Supper. We only have the words of Jesus and Paul, which often the ministering person will repeat right from the Bible.
- Different churches celebrate the actual Supper differently. Traditionally, many churches use individual cups of grape juice and small pieces of bread, which are distributed among the celebrants. Once all the bread and wine are distributed, the celebrants eat the bread and drink the juice together as a way to emphasize the unity of the church. Other churches prefer to use a chalice with juice or wine and a whole loaf of bread.

After the Lord's Supper

- The celebration of the Lord's Supper reminds us who we are in Christ (the church is Christ's body). With this conviction in mind, we should go out into our lives to live out this reality. We should seek to reflect Christ in our daily lives, pursue reconciliation where relationships are broken and bring peace where unrest exists.
- The Lord's Supper reminds us that Jesus will come back as a victorious King. Our lives are shaped by this knowledge: despite trials and sufferings, we can live in hope that our Lord and Savior is coming back. For this reason, all believers can boldly proclaim, Maranatha! "Come, Lord Jesus" (Rev. 22:20).

Passover & the Lord's Supper

The Passover began when God freed the Hebrew people from slavery in Egypt (Exodus 12). Unleavened bread and the Passover lamb were eaten to commemorate this event.

Jesus transformed the Hebrew Passover meal into what is known as the Lord's Supper. It was during Passover that Jesus celebrated the first Communion with his disciples, using the imagery of bread and wine to point to himself as the real Passover Lamb of God.

How did the early church celebrate the Lord's Supper?

The early church left some instructions about what was important. The chart below lists instructions and suggestions for how to apply those words today.

The Didache: The word *didache* is a Greek word meaning "teaching." Here it is used to refer to an ancient Christian document known as *The Teaching of the Twelve Apostles*. Written some time soon after the time of the apostles, this book gives instruction on the Christian way of life. It contains a short section on the Eucharist.

Early Church: The Didache	Suggestions
"Do not let anyone eat or drink of your Eucharist except those who have been baptized in the name of the Lord. For the statement of the Lord applies here also: *Do not give to dogs what is holy*."	• Think about your baptism. • Remember the words of Scripture that talk about how you were baptized into Jesus' death (Rom. 6:3–4). • Know that when you became a believer, you died to the old life and were born into a new and holy one.
"On the Lord's day, when you have been gathered together, break bread and celebrate the Eucharist. But first confess your sins so that your offering may be pure. If anyone has a quarrel with his neighbor, that person should not join you until he has been reconciled."	• Think about where you have gotten off track from God's plan for your life. • Have you hurt or argued with someone recently? (Matt. 5:23–24).
"Celebrate the Eucharist as follows: Say over the cup: 'we give you thanks, Father, for the holy vine of David, your servant, which you made known to us through Jesus your servant. To you be glory for ever.'"	• Think about the cup of wine and how it stands for the blood of Jesus. • Think how God will keep all his promises to you because of Jesus!
"Over the broken bread say: 'we give you thanks, Father, for the life and the knowledge which you have revealed to us through Jesus your servant. To you be glory for ever. As this broken bread scattered on the mountains was gathered and became one, so too, may your Church be gathered together from the ends of the earth into your kingdom. For glory and power are yours through Jesus Christ for ever.'"	• Think about how Jesus' body was broken like the bread. Now think how you are a part of Jesus' body, you are like an individual piece of bread. • Think now how someday God will gather all those fragments together from all around the world just like the fragments were gathered up from Jesus' miracles (Matt. 16:8–12). • Think about how your new life is kept alive by Jesus, the Bread of Life. • Ask yourself if you are hungry. Remember Jesus promised to satisfy those who hunger for God (Matt. 5:6).

Meals and the Bible

Is it a coincidence that two of the main celebrations in the Bible, the Passover in the Old Testament and the Lord's Supper in the New Testament, are centered on meals? Many of our fondest memories and relationships tend to be formed around the sharing of food. Meals allow us to develop relationships with others; God invites us into a special relationship with him, our deepest relationship. We get to know God during these special meals in a special way. When we share a meal with others with gratitude to God, we humbly recognize our dependence on God's goodness. Meals address basic human needs: food for hunger and water for thirst. In our daily meals, we remember and are thankful for God's goodness and provision for our lives. Because food and drink are so close to our most basic needs, they become exceptional images for our most basic spiritual needs: forgiveness of sin, reconciliation with God and with other people, and spiritual nourishment.

Four Views of the End Times

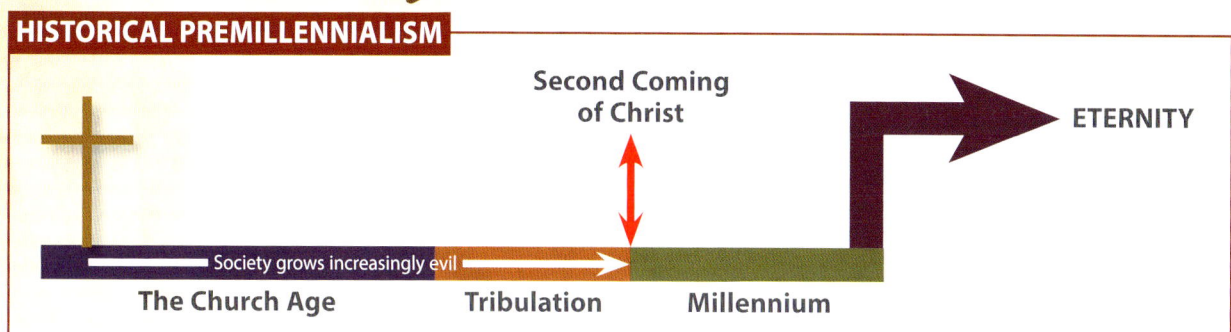

HISTORICAL PREMILLENNIALISM

Timeline: The Church Age (Society grows increasingly evil) → Tribulation → Second Coming of Christ → Millennium → ETERNITY

What is historical premillennialism?
It is the belief that Christians will remain on the earth during the great tribulation, which will purify the churches by rooting out false believers. The second coming of Christ will precede the millennium, which is a literal, future event. God's promises of land and blessings to Abraham and his offspring were conditional promises based on their obedience. The church has replaced the nation of Israel as God's covenant people. God has maintained a covenant of grace throughout the Old and New Testaments with all who trusted in him. These believers—embodied today in the church—are the true Israel (Rom. 9:6–8; Gal. 6:16).

What Scriptures seem to support this view?
The revealing of the Antichrist precedes Christ's return (2 Thess. 2:3–4). The tribulation will root out false members from the churches (Rev. 2:22–23). The saints are on earth during the tribulation (Rev. 13:7). God's promises to Abraham and his offspring were conditional (Gen. 22:18; 2 Chron. 33:8; Isa. 1:19–20; Jer. 7:6–7). The New Testament frequently uses "Israel" and "the twelve tribes" to refer to Christians (Matt. 19:28–29; Rom. 9:6–8).

When has this view been popular?
It seems to have been the earliest view of the end times among Christians who lived just after the apostles, but it faded with later church fathers. Supporters included many early church fathers such as Lactantius, Irenaeus, Justin Martyr, and possibly Papias. Modern supporters include David Dockery, John Warwick Montgomery, George R. Beasley-Murray, Robert Gundry, and George E. Ladd.

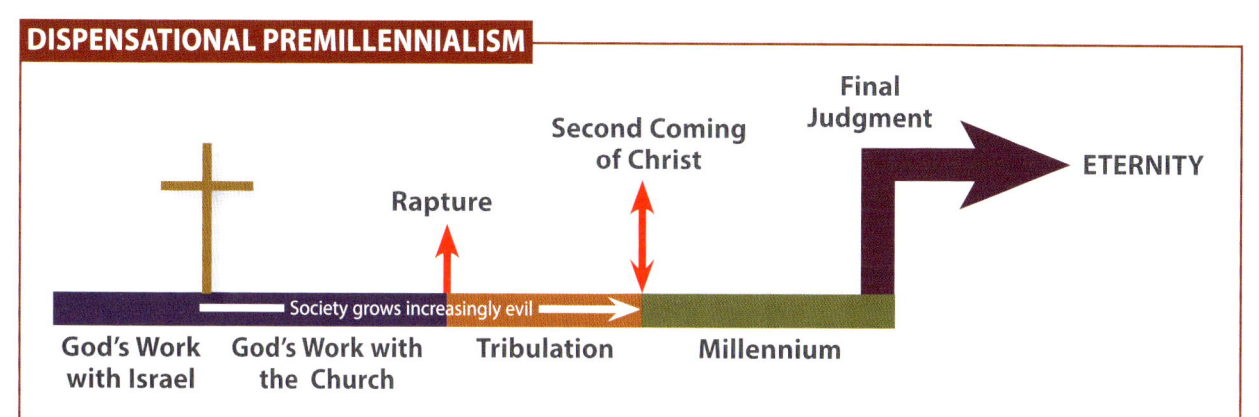

DISPENSATIONAL PREMILLENNIALISM

Timeline: God's Work with Israel → God's Work with the Church (Society grows increasingly evil) → Rapture → Tribulation → Second Coming of Christ → Millennium → Final Judgment → ETERNITY

What is dispensational premillennialism?
It is the belief that Jesus will come back to earth after a seven-year tribulation and will rule during a thousand-year millennium of peace on earth. God will still give to the nation of Israel the land described in Genesis 15:18. All references to Israel in Revelation refer to the nation of Israel. Most who hold this view are "pre-tribulationists"; they understand Revelation 4:1–2 to refer to the rapture. The rapture is the event when Christ removes Christians from the earth before the great tribulation begins. The rapture and the second coming of Jesus are two separate events. Others who hold this view are "mid-tribulationists"; they believe the rapture will occur during the tribulation.

What Scriptures seem to support this view?
God will remove Christians before the tribulation (1 Thess. 5:9; Rev. 3:10). God's promises to Abraham and his offspring were unconditional (Gen. 15:7–21). The church is not specifically mentioned between Revelation 4 and 19.

When has this view been popular?
This view emerged in the 1800s among the Plymouth Brethren. It increased in popularity in the late 1800s and remains widespread today. Supporters include J. Nelson Darby, C.I. Scofield, Harry A. Ironside, Gleason Archer, Donald G. Barnhouse, Hal Lindsey, Chuck Smith, John MacArthur, Charles Ryrie, Charles Stanley, Norman L. Geisler, and Tim LaHaye.

AMILLENNIALISM

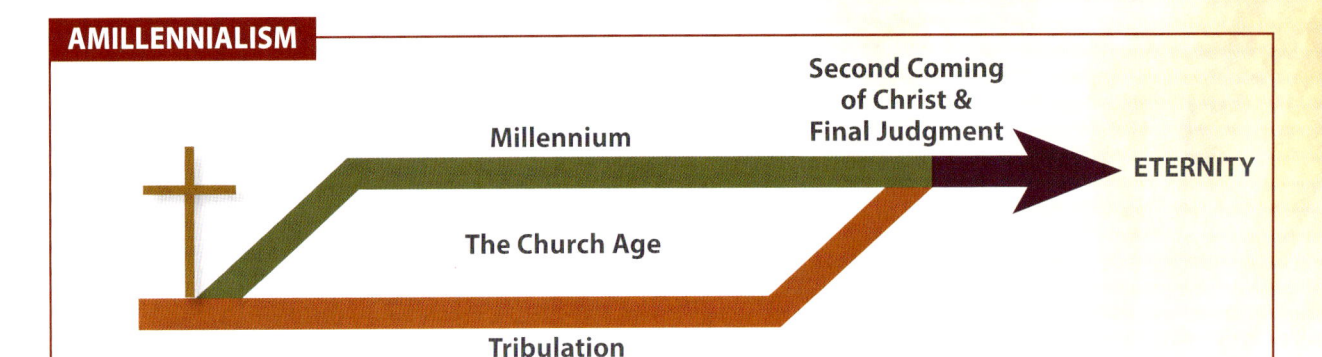

What is amillennialism?
It is the belief that the millennium is the spiritual reign of Jesus in the hearts of his followers. The "first resurrection" in Revelation 20:5 is not a physical restoration from the dead, but a spiritual resurrection (regeneration). Christ's triumph over Satan through his death and resurrection restrained the power of Satan on earth (Rev. 20:1–3). Persecution of Christians (tribulation) will occur until Jesus comes again, as will the expansion of God's kingdom (the millennium). When Christ returns, he will immediately defeat the powers of evil, resurrect the saved and the unsaved, judge them, and deliver them to their eternal destinies. Most references to Israel in Revelation are symbolic references to the people of God on earth.

What Scriptures seem to support this view?
The Bible frequently uses the number 1,000 figuratively (Ps. 50:10; 90:4; 105:8; 2 Peter 3:8). The first resurrection could refer to the spiritual resurrection of those who trust Christ (Rev. 20:4; Rom. 11:13–15; Eph. 2:1–4). The second coming of Christ and the resurrection of the saved and the unsaved will occur at the same time (Dan. 12:2–3; John 5:28–29). The saints are on earth during the tribulation (Rev. 13:7).

When has this view been popular?
It became popular in the fifth century and has remained widespread throughout church history. Augustine was possibly was the first amillennialist. Martin Luther and John Calvin held this view. Other supporters include E.Y. Mullins, Abraham Kuyper, G.C. Berkouwer, Herschel Hobbs, Stanley Grenz, and J. I. Packer.

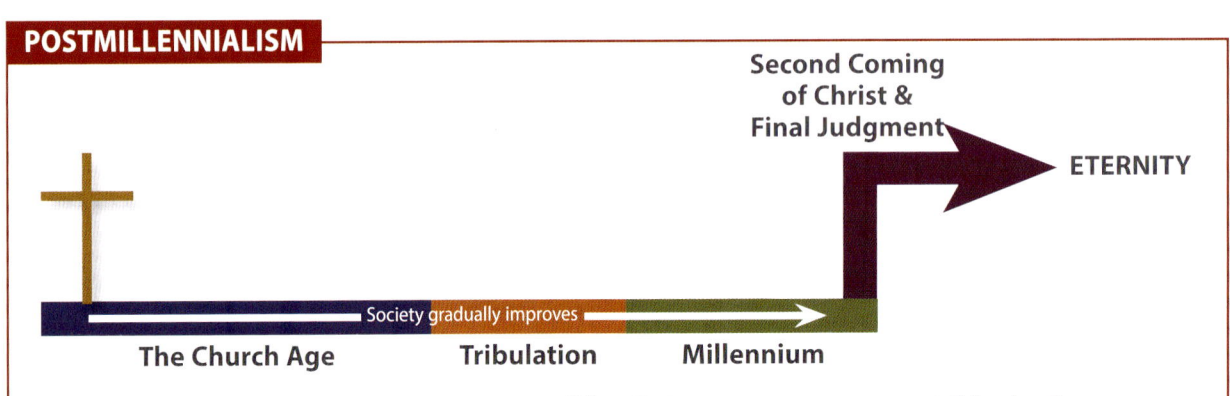

POSTMILLENNIALISM

What is postmillennialism?
It is the belief that the second coming of Christ will occur after the millennium, which represents a long time period when, through the preaching of the gospel, most of the world will submit to Jesus. Satan will have no power over the earth, and evil regimes will collapse (Rev. 19:19–20:3). Christ will rule the earth through his Spirit and through his church. He will not, however, be physically present on the earth. The resurrection depicted in Revelation 20:4 represents the spiritual regeneration of people who trust in Jesus Christ. The second coming of Christ, the final conflict between good and evil, the defeat of Satan, the physical resurrection of all people, and the final judgment will occur together, immediately after the millennium (Rev. 20:7–15).

What Scriptures seem to support this view?
Every ethnic group will receive the gospel before the second coming (Matt. 24:14; Mark 13:10). The second coming of Christ and the resurrection of all people will occur at the same time (Dan. 12:2–3; John 5:28–29).

When has postmillennialism been popular?
The earliest writer who was clearly postmillennialist was Joachim of Fiore (1135–1202). Earlier leaders such as Eusebius, Athanasius, and Augustine may have also been postmillennialists. During the missionary expansion of the 1800s, this view increased in popularity. But in the early 1900s, a world war and economic depression raised questions about whether the world was becoming a better place, and postmillennialism diminished in popularity. Supporters include Jonathan Edwards, B.B. Warfield, Augustus H. Strong, Charles Hodge, R.L. Dabney, Loraine Boettner, and R.C. Sproul.

Four Views of the End Times

	Dispensational Premillennialism	Historical Premillennialism	Amillennialism	Postmillennialism
Will Jesus return physically?	Yes	Yes	Yes	Yes
When will Jesus return?	After a 7-year tribulation; before the millennium.	After tribulation; before the millennium.	Anytime; a detailed time frame is not important.	After the millennium.
Do the rapture and second coming of Christ occur at the same time?	No, they are events separated by either 7 years (pre-tribulation rapture) or 3½ years (mid-tribulation rapture).	Yes	Yes	Yes
Will there be a great tribulation?	Yes	Yes	The tribulation occurs any time Christians are persecuted or wars and disasters occur.	Tribulation is either the first-century Jewish-Roman War or the ongoing conflict between good and evil prior to millennium.
Will Christians suffer during the tribulation?	Christians are either raptured before the tribulation (pre-tribulation rapture) or 3½ years into the tribulation (mid-tribulation rapture).	Yes, Christians will go through the tribulation and endure suffering and persecution for the cause of Christ.	Yes, Christians will suffer and endure persecution until Jesus returns; persecution will increase in the end.	Yes, Christians are called to share the gospel, and tribulation will occur when that gospel is opposed.
Will there be a literal 1,000-year millennium?	Yes, after the 7-year tribulation, Christ will return and reign for 1,000 years.	Yes, after the tribulation, Christ will return and reign for 1,000 years.	No, the millennium refers to the reign of Christ in the hearts of his believers.	No, the millennium refers to a period of peace when the gospel reaches all people.
Who is saved?	Christians only	Christians only	Christians only	Christians only
Is the modern state of Israel relevant to the prophecies in Revelation?	Yes	No	No	No
When was this view most held?	Became popular about 1860. Has increased in popularity.	The earliest view of the end times, emerging at the end of the first century.	Popularized in AD 400. Continues to be accepted today.	May have been popular as early as AD 300. Less popular today.

Christian History Time Line

AD 1

4? BC Birth of Jesus Christ in Bethlehem of Judea.

AD 29? Beginning of Jesus' public ministry, about age 30. He preaches, does miracles and claims to be God.

AD 33? Jesus crucified, resurrected, and appears to more than 500 disciples at one time (1 Cor. 15:6). Jesus gives his followers the Great Commission (Matt. 28:19). After 40 days, he ascends into heaven (Acts 1:3, 9).

33 Pentecost: the Holy Spirit descends on the disciples in Jerusalem. Some 3,000 people become Christians. They spread the gospel throughout the Roman Empire (Acts 2:8).

35 Stephen, the first Christian martyr, is stoned to death in Jerusalem. Believers scatter through Judea, Samaria.

35 Conversion of Paul. He goes on three missionary journeys starting in AD 48 to preach to Jews and Gentiles. He writes 13 letters (epistles) to the new churches.

41 Conversion of Roman centurion, Cornelius. Peter and other Christians evangelize Gentiles. Followers of Christ first called Christians at Antioch.

44 Christians are persecuted under King Herod Agrippa. James is executed, Peter is imprisoned. Famine strikes Judea; Christians in Antioch send relief.

45-100 The Gospels (Matthew, Mark, Luke, John) and other New Testament books are written.

49-50 Council of Jerusalem agrees with Paul that Gentile converts are not required to follow Jewish law. Paul's work with Gentiles recognized.

53 Jews expelled from Rome. Jewish believers Priscilla and Aquila flee.

64 Great fire in Rome blamed on Christians. Emperor Nero tortures and kills thousands of Christians.

67-68? Peter and Paul taken to Rome. Paul evangelizes while under house arrest. Both executed under Nero.

66-70 Jewish revolt against Romans. Emperor Titus destroys the temple in Jerusalem. Jews and Christians flee to all parts of the empire, including Alexandria, Carthage, and Rome. Antioch becomes the center for Christianity.

71-81 Colosseum in Rome built. Christians thrown to beasts.

81 Roman persecution of Christians under Domitian. Jews oust followers of Jesus from synagogues.

85-150 Writings of apostolic fathers (early church leaders) Barnabas, Clement of Rome, Ignatius, Polycarp.

90 Rise of Gnostic heresies within the church. Some Gnostics deny Jesus' humanity (Docetism), saying that he merely appeared to have a body. Gnostics claim to have secret knowledge beyond divine revelation and faith.

Christianity spreads to Egypt (Mark), Sudan (Ethiopian eunuch), Armenia (Thaddaeus, Bartholomew), France, Italy, Germany, Britain, Iraq, Iran, India (Thomas), Greece, Yugoslavia, Bosnia, Croatia (Titus), Asia Minor (Turkey today), Albania, Algeria, Libya, and Tunisia.

AD 100

c. 100 Death of John, the only one of Jesus' 12 disciples to die a natural death. All others are martyred.

c. 107 Martyrdom of Ignatius, bishop of Antioch, who wrote letters of encouragement to the early churches.

c. 125 Gnosticism spreads.

132-135 Second Jewish rebellion. Jerusalem destroyed. Most of the population dies or flees.

c. 144 Marcion is excommunicated for heresy. He taught that there was no connection between the Old and New Testament, between the God of the Jews and the God of the Christians. He rejected the Old Testament. The heresy persists in some areas for several centuries.

c. 155 Justin Martyr, theologian, writes his first Apology, a rebuttal to Greek philosophers.

Early Christians create this mosaic floor in a church in Galilee to depict Jesus' miracle of the loaves and fishes.

Polycarp, bishop of Smyrna and disciple of the apostle John, is burned at the stake at age 86. Polycarp refers to Old and New Testament books as "Scriptures."

c. 156 Montanus of Phrygia preaches a form of religious extremism called Montanism.

c. 180 Irenaeus of Lyons, student of Polycarp and great theologian, writes *Against Heresies*. He lists 20 New Testament books as *canonical* (officially accepted and recognized as authoritative).

193 Roman persecution under Septimius Severus.

196 Easter controversy concerning the day to celebrate Christ's resurrection. Western Christians prefer Sunday; eastern Christians prefer linking Easter with the Jewish Passover regardless of the day of the week.

197 Christianity sweeps the empire. Tertullian writes, "There is no nation indeed which is not Christian."

The Apostles' Creed and the *Didache* (an important document describing Christian beliefs, practices, and church government) are written during this century.

By AD 200 the church recognizes 23 New Testament books as canonical, but it is unlikely these are collected yet into one volume.

Christianity expands to Morocco, Bulgaria, Portugal, and Austria. Widespread conversion to Christianity in North Africa.

AD 200

200 The Scriptures now are translated into seven languages, including Syriac and Coptic (Egyptian).

Christians in Egypt viciously persecuted, thousands martyred.

215 Clement of Alexandria, theologian, dies.

c. 220 Origen, theologian and student of Clement, founds a school in Caesarea. He writes many works, including commentaries on most of the New Testament books. Origen writes, "The gospel of Jesus Christ has been preached in all creation under heaven."

235-270 Roman persecution under several emperors. Christianity grows rapidly.

Carthage becomes a major center for Christianity in Africa.

c. 242 Manichaeism originates in Persia (Iran today). This dualistic heresy denies the humanity of Christ, and reappears in different forms over the centuries.

261 First church buildings erected as rectangular shaped basilicas. Previously Christians met in homes.

The Madaba map, a mosaic from the 500s, shows basilicas built by early Christians in Jerusalem.

During this century, monasticism begins in Egypt: eremitical (individual hermits) and cenobitic (religious groups or orders).

287 Mass conversion of Armenia under Gregory the Illuminator; King Tiridates makes Christianity the state religion.

c. 292 Diocletian divides Roman Empire into East and West. Regions are different culturally and politically. Rome's influence wanes in the East.

295 Some Christians refuse military service and are executed. Galerius begins to doubt that Christians in the army will obey orders. He persuades Diocletian to expel Christians from the Roman legions.

The phrase "catholic" is used to mean all churches that agree with the whole apostolic teaching, as opposed to the heretical groups that follow a "secret revelation" or knowledge based on one teaching.

Christianity expands to Switzerland, Sahara, Belgium, Edessa, Qatar, Bahrain (Assyrian Church), Hungary, and Luxembourg.

AD 300

303-304 Violent persecution of Christians under Diocletian. Scriptures burned; thousands killed.

311-411 Donatist schism in North Africa. Christians who stayed faithful during Diocletian's persecution oppose leniency toward those who lapsed.

312 Constantine (emperor of the western provinces) sees a vision of the cross of Jesus that he credits for giving him victory in battle.

Constantine legalizes Christianity. His mother, Helena, a devout Christian, goes to the Holy Land to locate key places in Jesus' life, and builds many churches.

313 Edict of Milan (Toleration). Constantine and Licinius (emperor of the eastern provinces) agree to end the persecution of Christians, but it continues in the East.

320 Arius claims that Jesus Christ is a created being and not God by nature. His beliefs are called Arianism.

324 Eusebius writes *Church History*.

325 Council of Nicaea is convened in response to numerous heresies. It condemns Arianism and produces an early version of the Nicene Creed—a clear definition of the Trinity.

330 Constantine establishes the capital of the empire at Byzantium and renames it Constantinople.

337 Constantine baptized a few days before death.

339 Severe persecution of Christians in Persia (Iran).

346 Death of Pachomius, father of monasticism in the East and founder of the monastery at Tabennisi, Egypt.

350 Eastern church is mostly Arian. Arianism spreads to the Goths.

361 Emperor Julian the Apostate attempts unsuccessfully to restore paganism to the Roman Empire.

364 Basil, bishop of Caesarea, opposes Arian teachings.

367+ Canon of the New Testament slowly collected and confirmed. Books recognized as authoritative by Athanasius, bishop of Alexandria, in the East, and the Council of Carthage in the West.

c. 376 Goth and barbarian invasions of the Roman empire begin.

381 Council of Constantinople I finalizes the Nicene Creed and condemns heresies about Jesus.

391 Theodosius makes Christianity the official religion.

398 John Chrysostom, great orator, becomes bishop of Constantinople.

Christianity expands to Afghanistan and Ethiopia.

AD 400

395-430 Augustine, bishop of Hippo (N. Africa), authors numerous theological works including City of God and arguments against Donatists, Pelagians, and Manichaeans. His writings dominate Christian theology in the West for centuries.

405 In Bethlehem, Jerome finishes translating the Old and New Testament into Latin after 23 years of work. The Vulgate, as it is known, is the Bible used for the next 1,000 years.

410 Arian Visigoths sack Rome.

428 Nestorius, patriarch of Constantinople, teaches that there are two distinct Persons in Jesus Christ (Mary is mother of the human part only), therefore some of Jesus' actions were human and some were divine.

431 Council of Ephesus condemns Nestorianism and Pelagianism (which claims man can attain salvation by works). The council defines Mary, Jesus' mother, as Theotokos, "bearer of God" to show that Jesus is one person with two natures—fully human and fully divine.

432 Patrick evangelizes Ireland. Over the next 30 years most of the country has been converted.

440 Leo the Great becomes pope. He persuades Attila the Hun to spare a weakened Rome.

451 Council of Chalcedon focuses on the divine and human natures of Christ. It confirms Pope Leo's *Tome* and condemns Appolinarianism, Nestorianism, and Monophysitism (also known as Eutychianism, which denies the humanity of Christ). Copts of Egypt and Ethiopia divide, the majority form monophysite or "One Nature" churches.

Early Christians commemorate this location on the Mt. of Olives, as the place where Jesus wept over Jerusalem.

476 Fall of the western Roman Empire. Emperor ousted. This marks the beginning of the Middle Ages.

496 Clovis, king of the Franks, converts to Christianity.

499 By the end of this century, the Scriptures have been translated into 13 languages.

Christianity spreads to Western No. Africa, the Isle of Man, San Marino, Liechtenstein, the Caucasus, Ireland, and tribes in Central Asia.

AD 500

500 Syrian Orthodox church establishes a monophysite monastery in Ethiopia.

520 Irish monasteries flourish as centers of learning, spiritual life, and training for missionaries to other parts of the known world.

Nestorians gain converts throughout Asia and continue to influence religious life for many centuries.

The monastery of St. George of Koziba in the Judean Wilderness is built in 480.

525 Christianity spreads throughout the Middle East, including the Arabian Peninsula (Saudi Arabia, Yemen, and Oman today).

529 Monk Benedict of Nursia, founder of Monte Cassino Abbey in Italy, writes the *Rule*, a guide for monastic life. Benedict is considered the father of monasticism in the West.

545? Death of Dionysius Exiguus, a monk, who was the first to date history by the life of Christ, leading to the B.C. and A.D. designations. His calculations were off by at least four years.

553 Council of Constantinople, convened by Emperor Justinian, condemns the "Three Chapters," (the writings of several theologians including Theodore of Mopsuestia) for alleged heresies.

589 Third Council of Toledo. Visigoth king renounces Arianism, accepts church teachings.

590 High ranking Roman official, Gregory, resigns his post and donates his wealth to church relief efforts for the poor in 574. He is elected pope in 590. Known as Gregory the Great (or Gregory I), he institutes reforms and sends missionaries (including Augustine of Canterbury) to re-evangelize England, after Angle and Saxon pagans force Christian Britons to Wales. He also promotes liturgical music and the growth of monasticism. He is the first of the medieval popes.

597 Death of Columba, evangelist of Scotland and founder of an important monastery at Iona, Scotland.

Christianity spreads to North Yemen, Ceylon, Malabar, Nubia (Sudan), Channel Islands, and Andorra.

AD 600

600 Plainsong "Gregorian" chants begin to develop.

610? Muhammad declares himself to be Prophet of God, after claiming to receive divine revelations. He founds the religion of Islam. In 622, he is persecuted and flees (*hegira*) from his home in Mecca to the oasis of Medina. There he founds a Muslim community. In 630 he launches a military campaign and defeats his opponents in Mecca. His teachings and deeds are called the Qur'an (Koran). By Muhammad's death in 632, Islam has spread to much of Arabia.

632 Islam sweeps through Palestine and Syria. Muslims (those who follow Islam) conquer Jerusalem. By 640, Islam invades Egypt and North Africa, almost eradicating Christianity (which had numbered more than one million believers). Three hundred years later very few Christians remain in the region.

663 The Synod of Whitby aligns the English church with Rome for the next nine centuries.

676-709 Earliest Old English (Anglo-Saxon) translations and paraphrases of portions of the Bible are made by Caedmon and Aldhelm.

680-692 Eastern and Western churches drift further apart due to differences in church practices and expression of theology. On clergy celibacy: the Eastern church allows priests to be married, provided that they are married before ordination. The Western church discourages it.

688-691 The Dome of the Rock, gold domed shrine of Islam, is built on the Temple Mount in Jerusalem by caliph Abd al-Malik. Its ornate interior and location were designed to impress travelers. Some of the beautiful columns in the shrine are adorned with crosses, indicating that they were removed from Christian churches.

Christianity spreads to China, Andorra, Netherlands, Indonesia, Niger, and Mongolia. Christianity declines in Northern Africa.

AD 700

711 Muslim Moors invade Spain and Portugal, their first foothold in Europe. They are driven out in the 1200s.

716 Boniface, an English missionary, known as the "Apostle to the Germans," evangelizes southern and central German cities and establishes Benedictine monasticism.

720 Bede translates the Gospel of John into English; writes *Ecclesiastical History*.

The use of icons is debated throughout the East for 100 years. In 787 the Second Council of Nicaea decides in favor of those who venerated icons.

726 Controversy over the use of icons in the East. Emperor Leo condemns the veneration of sacred images and relics (supports *iconoclasm*, "image-breaking"). In 731, Pope Gregory III condemns iconoclasm and supports the veneration of icons.

732 Charles Martel defeats the Muslims in France, stopping the Muslim advance in Europe for 100 years.

754 A council of 300 Byzantine bishops endorse iconoclasm. The council is condemned by the Lateran synod of 769.

754 Pepin, son of Charles Martel, unites and rules the Franks. At the request of Pope Stephen II (III), Pepin invades Italy to defend it against Lombard invaders. Pepin gives conquered land to the church (called the Donation of Pepin) which establishes the papal states.

768-814 Charlemagne, son of Pepin, expands his empire through military conquest to almost all of what is now France, Germany, and Italy. He forces the German Saxons to convert.

787 Council of Nicaea II condemns iconoclasm (the belief that venerating sacred images is idolatry) and Adoptionism (belief that Jesus was not Son of God by nature). This is the last council that is recognized as binding by both the eastern and western churches.

Christianity spreads to Iceland, Pakistan, and East Germany.

AD 800

800 Charlemagne crowned Roman emperor by Pope Leo III. His administration reforms the law and church organization. He also encourages all monasteries to teach reading and writing. Through the influence of the scholar Alcuin, schools are founded and scriptoria set up to copy the Bible and Latin classics. This commitment to culture is known as the Carolingian Renaissance. The Western church's prominence begins to increase; the Eastern church's declines.

800 Egbert, king of the West Saxons, unifies England and becomes the first king.

814 Charlemagne dies.

829 Sweden is evangelized by Anskar, "Apostle of the North."

837 Christians in Egypt are persecuted and forced to wear 5-pound crosses around their necks.

843 Charlemagne's empire is split between his three grandsons.

845 Nestorians are persecuted in China.

846 Muslims attack Rome.

857 Photian Schism: communion between Eastern and Western church broken when Patriarch Photius of Constantinople (Orthodox Church) rejects the Roman pope's claim of primacy among the bishops of the East as well as the West.

861 Slavs are converted by Greek missionary brothers Cyril and Methodius, who translate the Scriptures and other works into the Slavonic language.

868 Count Vimara Peres drives Moors out of Portugal.

871 Alfred the Great, king of Wessex, translates portions of the Psalms, Exodus, and Acts into Old English (Anglo-Saxon).

876 Byzantine Empire retakes Italy.

Built near the Pools of Bethesda in Jerusalem, the Church of St. Anne is one of the finest examples of Crusader architecture.

Christianity spreads to Tibet, Burma, Denmark, Czechoslovakia, Sweden, and Norway.

AD 900

902 Muslims gain complete control of Sicily.

909 William, Duke of Aquitane, founds the Benedictine Abbey of Cluny, France, which becomes the center for reform under Abbot Odo (926).

950-999 Conversion of royalty across the empire, including Olga of Kiev, Miesko of Poland, and Stephen of Hungary.

962 Otto I, the Great, founder of the Holy Roman Empire, is crowned by Pope John XII. This empire continues until 1806.

988 Conversion of Vladimir of Kiev, grandson of Olga, to Eastern (Orthodox) Christianity. According to tradition, Vladimir considered other religions, but chose Orthodoxy because the splendor of the worship at the Church of St. Sophia in Constantinople convinced him that "God dwells there among men." Vladimir orders the population of Kiev to choose Christianity. He wipes out paganism, builds churches, and establishes schools. At his death, he donates all of his possessions to the poor.

996 In Egypt, Caliph El Hakim persecutes Copts, destroying thousands of churches and forcing people to convert to Islam.

The iconostasis of an Orthodox church separates the nave (the central area of the church) and the altar.

999 Leif Ericson converts to Christianity while in Norway. The next year he brings the gospel to his father's colony in Greenland.

Christianity in western North Africa virtually wiped out by Islam.

Christianity spreads to Hungary, Kiev (Russia today), Greenland, Bohemia, and Poland.

AD 1000

1000 Greek Catholicism (Melkite) introduced in Nubia.

1009 Nestorians convert northern Mongolians. Their beliefs spread to Persia (Iran today), India, and China.

1054 Great Schism between the church in the West and the East. Roman Cardinal Humbart, envoy of Pope Leo IX, excommunicates Patriarch Michael Cerularius in the Church of St. Sophia (Hagia Sophia) in Constantinople. Despite this, there is some cooperation between the Eastern (Orthodox) and Western (Roman Catholic) church against the Seljuk Turks.

1066 Normans (French Christians) conquer Britain, Sicily, and evangelize the Celts.

1071 Seljuk Turks (converts to Islam) from Central Asia conquer Persia (Iran today) and move west toward the Byzantine capital, Constantinople (Turkey today).

1073 Gregory VII (Hildebrand) becomes pope. He works to revive and reform the church. He prohibits simony (the buying or selling of church offices), sexual immorality in the clergy, and lay investiture (the custom of emperors and local rulers choosing local church leaders).

1096 Pope Urban II calls for volunteers for a crusade to repel the Turks: specifically to help Eastern Christians in Constantinople, to liberate the Church of the Holy Sepulchre in Jerusalem, and to reopen the Holy Land to Christian pilgrims.

Church of the Holy Sepulchre in Jerusalem. Considered by many scholars to be the location of Jesus' tomb.

1097-1099 The First Crusade. More than 70,000 people inspired by both noble and lesser motives, join the ranks and head for the Holy Land. In their zeal they slaughter Jews in Germany and pillage villages en route. They capture Jerusalem in 1099 and brutally massacre their opponents. They set up the Latin Kingdom of Jerusalem under Godfrey of Bouillon, and build castles and churches.

AD 1100

1115 Bernard founds a monastery at Clairvaux, which becomes the influential center of Europe.

1116 Peter Abelard, philosopher and theologian.

1122 Concordat of Worms focuses on the controversy over lay investiture. (Worms, pronounced "vormps," is a city in Germany.)

1123 Lateran Council ratifies the Concordat of Worms.

1129 The Knights Templar, an order of monastic soldiers sworn to protect Holy Land pilgrims, is recognized.

1130 Disputed election of Popes Innocent II and Anacletus II. Innocent becomes pope.

1139 Second Lateran Council focuses on pseudo-popes (popes elected by unauthorized councils).

1146 Second Crusade is preached by Bernard of Clairvaux in response to the Muslim conquest of Edessa, the crusader capital (Turkey today). The crusade, led by Louis VII of France and Emperor Conrad III of Germany, fails.

1150 Syrian Orthodox church reaches zenith.

College of Cardinals is established by pope.

1162 Thomas Becket becomes archbishop of Canterbury. A close friend of Henry II and chancellor of England, Becket resigns his chancellorship after conflicts with Henry over the power of the church and the throne.

1170 Becket is murdered by knights of Henry II.

1174 French merchant and reformer Peter Valdes gives his wealth to the poor and becomes an itinerant preacher, the beginning of the Waldensians. His beliefs are accepted by the church, but his practice of appointing ministers and preaching without permission draws criticism and eventually excommunication.

1177 Third Lateran Council denounces the Waldensians and Albigensians. (Albigensians were heretics that believed that Jesus was an angel with a phantom body, and therefore did not die or rise again.)

1187 Muslim general Saladin defeats Crusaders at the Horns of Hattin (Galilee) and captures Jerusalem.

The Horns of Hattin (flat mountain, center)

1189-1192 The Third Crusade, led by Richard I (the Lion-Heart) of England, Philip II of France, and Barbarossa the Holy Roman Emperor, captures Cyprus, Acre, and Jaffa. Richard negotiates access to Jerusalem for Christian pilgrims.

Christianity spreads to Finland.

AD 1200

1201 Pope Innocent III claims the right of the pope to oversee the moral conduct of heads of state and to choose rulers, including the emperor. The height of papal authority.

1202 Innocent III launches Fourth Crusade to defeat Egypt. After some setbacks, Crusaders defy the pope and sack Constantinople, center of the Orthodox church. A three-day massacre by the Crusaders alienates the eastern and western church for centuries.

1208 Church declares a crusade against Albigensians.

1209 Francis of Assisi gives away his wealth and starts group of traveling preachers (Franciscans).

1211 Mongol Genghis Khan, whose mother is a Nestorian, rises to power. Conquers China, Iran, and Iraq.

1212 Children's Crusade disaster. Thousands of children die at sea or are sold into slavery.

1212 Alfonso VII of Castile leads a coalition against the Moors and drives them out of Spain (the battle of Las Navas de Tolosa).

1215 Fourth Lateran Council condemns Waldensians and Albigensians; affirms doctrine of transubstantiation. In 1231, the Papal Inquisition is established.

1216 Dominican order forms, dedicated to spiritual reform.

1217 Fifth Crusade to defeat Egypt fails. Francis of Assisi crosses enemy lines to preach to the sultan.

The seaport Acre, the last Crusader stronghold, falls to Egyptian Mamluks in 1291.

1229 Crusaders recover Jerusalem by negotiation. In 1244 the Muslims recapture Jerusalem by force.

1255 Thomas Aquinas, the most influential medieval theologian, writes *Summa Theologiae*.

1266 Mongol leader, Kublai Khan, asks the pope to send 100 Christian teachers to baptize him and teach his people. The pope sends seven. In 1295 the Mongols begin to convert to Islam.

1274 Byzantine Empire rebuilt. Second Council of Lyon decrees unification of the eastern and western church, but unification is rejected in the East.

AD 1300

1302 Pope claims supremacy over secular rulers.

1302 Franciscans active in Mongol empire.

1309 The "Babylonian Captivity": for the next 70 years, the papacy resides in Avignon, France. The new pope favors French policies; convenes the Council of Vienne that abolishes the Order of Knights Templar and gives their wealth to King Philip IV of France.

1312-1324 Marsilius of Padua writes *Defensor pacis*, stating that the church should be ruled by general councils. He is condemned as heretical.

1348-1351 The Bubonic plague, also known as the Black Death, kills 33% of the people in Europe (about 40 million). People blame the disease (which is transmitted by fleas living on rats) on the Avignon papacy, the Jews, or personal immorality.

John Wycliffe

1371 John Wycliffe, English priest and diplomat, proposes that papal taxation and civil power should be limited. He challenges some church doctrines, including transubstantiation. He believes Scripture should be available to the people in their own language. People inspired by Wycliffe (derisively called "Lollards," meaning mumblers), translate the entire Bible into English (1382) from Latin, and call it the Wycliffe Bible.

1373 Julian of Norwich, English mystic.

1376 Catherine of Sienna, mystic, sees a vision calling the new pope, Gregory XI, to return the papacy to Rome, which he does in 1377.

1378 Great Papal Schism: Two or three popes at one time. The College of Cardinals elects an Italian pope, Urban VI, but later denies the validity of the decision and elects Clement VII instead. Urban remains in Rome. Clement goes to Avignon, France. The schism continues until 1417.

AD 1400

1408 In England, it becomes illegal to translate or read the Bible in English without permission of a bishop.

1413 Jan Hus of Bohemia (Czechoslovakia) writes *De Ecclesia*, which supports ideas popularized by Wycliffe.

1414-1418 Council of Constance rejects Wycliffe's teachings and burns Jan Hus at the stake as a heretic. It affirms that general councils are superior to popes (conciliarism), a decision later overturned. Pope Martin V is elected; the Great Papal Schism ends.

1418 Thomas À Kempis, a German monk, writes the *Imitation of Christ*, a devotional.

1431 Joan of Arc, a French peasant girl during the Hundred Years' War, sees visions and hears voices telling her to save France. She leads a successful military expedition at Orleans. Later she is taken prisoner, tried for witchcraft, and is burned. In 1456, the verdict is reversed.

Joan of Arc

1438 Council of Florence affirms the primacy of the pope over general councils. It declares reunion between the Roman and Orthodox churches, but is not accepted by the Orthodox.

c. 1450 Beginning of the Renaissance. The popes of the Renaissance (1447-1521) are notable more for their intrigues and quests for power than for their pastoral care or desire for reform.

1453 Ottoman Turks capture Constantinople and make the Church of St. Sophia (Hagia Sophia) a mosque. Scholars flee to the West with Greek literary and scientific manuscripts, including manuscripts of the Bible. These manuscripts help to revive classical learning during the Renaissance.

Plans to build a new St. Peter's Basilica in Rome begin, including efforts to raise funds for construction.

1456 Johann Gutenberg prints the Latin Vulgate, the first book printed using moveable metal type. The invention of printing makes the Bible accessible to more people who previously could not afford handmade copies, which cost a year's wage.

Page from the Gutenberg Bible

1479 The Spanish Inquisition begins at the initiation of King Ferdinand V and Queen Isabella of Spain, and is approved by the pope. It is established to investigate and punish heretics. It targets Jews, Muslims, and Protestants. Its cruel methods (torture, death by burning), secret trials, and favoritism toward the Spanish monarchy continue despite protests from Rome. The Franciscan and Dominican friars who serve as judges often misuse their power. It is finally suppressed in 1820. Catholics today condemn the methods used.

1492 Thousands of Jews are expelled from Spain.

The last of the Muslim regions of Spain falls to Ferdinand and Isabella. Muslims are forced to convert to Christianity.

Columbus discovers the Americas.

Peak of papal corruption: Rodrigo Borgia buys cardinals' votes and becomes Pope Alexander VI.

1493 Pope Alexander VI avoids war by dividing newly discovered lands in the Americas and Africa between Spain and Portugal. Vast colonizing of the New World by explorers for the next 150 years. Settlers wishing to exploit the land and the people conflict with missionaries (Dominicans, Franciscans, and Jesuits) who spread the gospel and advocate for the Indians.

1497-1498 Dominican friar Savonarola preaches reform. He encourages the people of Florence, Italy, to burn luxury items and return to a humbler Christian life. He sells church property and gives the proceeds to the poor. Despite his initial popularity with the common people, he is caught in a political conflict with Alexander VI and is excommunicated. His popularity wanes and later he is executed for heresy.

Christianity reaches Senegal, Guinea Bissau, Mauritania, Haiti, Dominican Republic, Kenya, and Equatorial Guinea.

AD 1500

1500 Decline of Christianity in China, Persia, Nubia (Southern Egypt and Ethiopia), and areas influenced by Islam.

Moscow claims to be the center of Christianity after the fall of Constantinople.

1503-1512 Pope Julius II commissions Michelangelo to finish painting the Sistine Chapel. In 1506, the foundation stone of St. Peter's Basilica is laid.

1512-1517 Council of Lateran V is held to address a variety of concerns, including church reform.

1516 Erasmus, priest and Greek scholar, publishes a Greek translation of the New Testament. Later editions of his Greek text form the basis of the *textus receptus* and are used by Martin Luther, William Tyndale, and the King James Bible (Authorized Version).

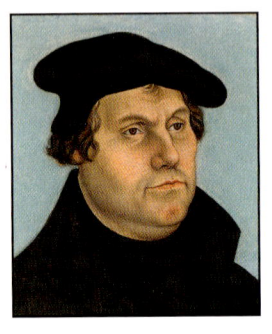

Martin Luther becomes convinced that faith alone justifies the Christian, not works (Eph. 2:8-9)—a doctrine supported by Augustine's writings.

1517 Martin Luther posts his Ninety-Five Theses on the door of the church in Wittenberg. They call for an end to abuses involved in methods of selling indulgences. The Protestant Reformation begins.

1519 Swiss Ulrich Zwingli spreads reform.

1522 Luther translates the New Testament into German.

1525 William Tyndale makes an English translation of the New Testament from Greek without permission and smuggles copies into England. He is burned at the stake.

1525 The Anabaptist movement, predecessor to Brethren and Mennonite churches, teaches believers' baptism only, democratic decision making, and separation of church and state.

1529 The term Protestantism becomes associated with Lutheranism, Zwinglianism, and Calvinism. Protestant characteristics: acceptance of the Bible as the only source of revealed truth, the doctrine of justification by faith alone, and the priesthood of all believers.

1530 Augsburg Confession adopted by Lutherans.

1534 Act of Supremacy makes British monarch Henry VIII head of the English church, breaking away from Roman Catholic control. The new "Church of England" (Anglican Church) sets forth a doctrinal statement: *The 39 Articles*.

1535 The Munster Rebellion. Anabaptists take over Munster and are slaughtered. Later, under the leadership of Menno Simons, the group adopts pacifism.

1536 John Calvin's *Institutes of the Christian Religion* explains Protestant beliefs, including predestination.

1537 The Matthew's Bible is the first English Bible published with the king's permission. On the last page of the Old Testament, the translator prints Tyndale's initials in 2 ½ inch letters to honor him. Many Bibles in common languages begin to appear.

1540 Ignatius Loyola's Society of Jesus (Jesuits) approved. They vow to evangelize the heathen.

1545-1563 Council of Trent (Catholic Counter-Reformation) condemns indulgence sellers, immorality of clergy, nepotism (appointing family members to church offices), and Protestantism.

1549 The Church of England's *Book of Common Prayer* unites most English churches in a middle route between Catholicism and Protestantism.

Jesuit Francis Xavier begins missionary efforts in the Indies and Japan: 100,000 converts attributed to him.

1555 Queen Mary Tudor restores Roman Catholicism to England, bans Protestant translations of the Bible, and persecutes Protestants. Many Protestants flee to Geneva, Switzerland, where they print the Geneva Bible (1560).

1558 Queen Elizabeth I becomes queen of England and Supreme Governor of the Church of England. She aims for a compromise between Catholics and Protestants. In 1570, she is excommunicated by the pope, and in turn persecutes Catholics.

1560 John Knox's Reformed church begins in Scotland.

1562 Heidelberg Catechism is formed. It is the most widely held Protestant doctrinal statement for centuries.

1568 Bishops Bible, Church of England translation.

1577 Formula of Concord defines Lutheran beliefs.

1582/1609 Catholic scholar Gregory Martin translates the Rheims-Douay Bible from the Vulgate (Latin) while in exile in France.

1596 Council of Brest-Litovsk. Most Orthodox in Kiev, Czechoslovakia, Hungary, and Polish Galatia (Uniat Churches) join communion with Roman Catholic church.

1598 Edict of Nantes grants freedom of worship to French Protestants (Huguenots) after 30 years of persecution. In 1685, the Edict is revoked by Louis XIV.

Christianity spreads throughout Thailand, Cambodia, Macao, South Korea, South America, and Africa through Catholic missionary efforts (through monastic orders), conquest, and colonization. Few Protestant efforts during the next 200 years.

AD 1600

1601 Jesuit missionary and scholar, Matteo Ricci, starts evangelizing China by befriending intellectuals in the emperor's court in Peking (Beijing). Ricci is one of the first missionaries to adopt the dress and customs of the land he seeks to evangelize. His methods are criticized by other Catholics as too tolerant toward the idolatrous Confucian custom of ancestor worship.

1603 Dutch Reformed theologian Jacobus Arminius's studies of the Epistle to the Romans lead him to doubt Calvin's doctrine of predestination. He sets forth doctrines that emphasize man's ability to choose Christ and Christ's death for all people (Arminianism).

1605 Gunpowder Plot fails. Catholic fanatics attempt to kill England's King James I and blow up the houses of Parliament in order to seize the government.

1609 The first Baptist church is founded in Amsterdam by John Smyth, who baptizes himself (by pouring).

1611 King James Version Bible (KJV), also known as the Authorized Version (AV), is published. King James I of England commissions 54 scholars to undertake a new Bible translation, which takes six years to complete. The scholars use the Bishops Bible and Tyndale's Bible as well as available Greek and Hebrew manuscripts. After slow initial acceptance, this becomes the most popular Bible for the next 300 years.

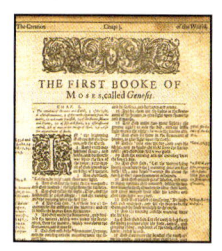

A page from the King James Bible, also known as the Authorized Version (even though it never received official royal authorization).

1618 Dutch Reformed Synod of Dort denounces Arminianism and responds to Arminius's five criticisms of Calvinism with five points of Calvinism. They are (using the mnemonic *tulip*): the **t**otal depravity of mankind (mankind's inability to choose Christ), **u**nconditional election, **l**imited atonement, the **i**rresistibility of grace, and the final **p**erseverance of the saints (an elect person cannot "lose" his salvation).

1622 Creation of the Congregation de *Propaganda Fide* for Roman Catholic missionary efforts.

1620-1630s Separatists reject the Church of England and sail to America on the *Mayflower*. Later Puritans, who wish to cleanse the church, arrive and start colonies.

1629 Orthodox Patriarch of Constantinople, Cyril Loukaris (Lucar), befriends Protestants and presents the earliest known copy of the Bible in Greek (*Codex Alexandrinus*, fifth century AD) to Charles I of England.

1630 Catholicism wiped out in Japan, thousands of martyrs.

Coptic and Syrian Orthodox churches decline.

1633 The Sisters of Charity founded by Vincent de Paul.

Galileo

1642 Death of Galileo, scientist, who agreed with Copernicus's theory that the earth moved around the sun. He was censured by the church and kept from teaching his views because his proofs were inadequate. The case was closed in his favor in 1992.

Power struggles between Charles I and the Parliament lead to civil war in England. Puritan member of Parliament, Oliver Cromwell, defeats the king's troops. Later, as Lord Protector, he seeks tolerance for many Protestant groups.

1646 Westminster Confession accepted as the statement of Presbyterianism in Scotland and England.

1647 Beginnings of the Quaker movement (the Society of Friends) under preacher George Fox.

1648 End of the Thirty Years' War. Catholics and Protestants given equal rights in most of the Holy Roman Empire.

1649 In America, Iroquois Indians destroy Huron Indians and their Jesuit mission.

1654 Conversion of Blaise Pascal, French mathematician and theologian.

1655 Waldensians break from Roman Catholicism and embrace Protestantism. Catholics launch persecutions.

1667 John Milton writes *Paradise Lost*.

1673 The British Test Act bans Catholics from holding public office unless they deny certain doctrines.

1678 John Bunyan's *Pilgrim's Progress* published.

1685 Edict of Nantes revoked. Huguenots flee France.

1689 English Parliament issues Toleration Act (tolerating all Protestant groups, but not Roman Catholics).

1692 Chinese emperor officially allows Christianity. Ricci's initial 2,000 converts multiply to 300,000.

1698 First missionary societies formed by Protestants.

Christianity spreads to Bermuda, Uruguay, Taiwan, Barbados, St. Kitts-Nevis, Laos, Montserrat, Antigua, Virgin Islands, Grenada, Anguilla, Belize, Gambia, Polynesia, Chad, Micronesia, Gabon, Bahamas, Benin.

AD 1700

1700 Slave trafficking from Africa increases.

1704 Pope Clement XI condemns "Chinese Rites," the mixture of Confucianism and ancestor worship with Christianity in China. Persecution against Christians begins; thousands are killed.

1705 Death of Philipp Jakob Spener, the "father of Pietism." Pietism emphasizes feelings, a personal religious experience, and living a life of intense devotion.

1706 First Presbyterian church in America. It is governed by a board of elders (presbyters).

1707 Isaac Watts writes more than 600 hymns in his life.

1721 Peter the Great appoints the Holy Synod to head the Russian Orthodox church, putting the church under the state's control until 1917.

1722 Count Nikolaus Ludwig von Zinzendorf welcomes fleeing Hussites from Moravia (Moravian Brethren) to live on his lands. The pietistic colony that forms, "Herrnhut," sends out missionaries to Africa, India, and the Americas.

1724 Greek Catholic (Melkite) church established in what is now Lebanon. Primarily located in Ethiopia and parts of Egypt, the Melkite church had accepted the Council of Chalcedon in 451, rejecting monophysitism.

1729 Jonathan Edwards, one of America's greatest preachers and theologians, preaches in Northampton.

Anglican minister John Wesley and his brother Charles are converted through contact with Moravians.

1738 Conversions of John and Charles Wesley. Their emphasis on living a holy life by doing specific spiritual disciplines each week is derided as "methodist." Eventually the descriptive is accepted with pride, and Methodism spreads rapidly in the Church of England.

Charles Wesley pens more than 6,000 hymns, including "And Can It Be" and "O For a Thousand Tongues to Sing," and "Hark, the Herald Angels Sing."

Freemasonry condemned by Pope Clement XII (and later popes). The pope forbids Catholics to join.

1739 George Whitefield, Anglican preacher, gives open-air evangelistic messages.

John Wesley travels throughout Britain on horseback, reportedly giving 40,000 sermons during his lifetime.

1740 The Great Awakening in New England, led by Whitefield. Revival spreads throughout colonial America.

1741-1742 George Frideric Handel writes the *Messiah*.

1759 Powerful Jesuit order suppressed. In 1773, it is dissolved by the pope. In 1814, Jesuits are reestablished.

1764 John Newton, former slave trader converts, writes "Amazing Grace."

1769 Serra founds the first of nine missions in California.

1771 John Wesley sends Francis Asbury to preach in America. The American Methodist Church becomes a separate organization in 1784.

1773 First independent Black Baptist church is established in America.

1780 "Sunday school" is developed in England by Robert Raikes out of concern for urban poor.

1781 Immanuel Kant's *Critique of Pure Reason*. Reason cannot deny the existence of God, the soul, or eternity.

1784 "Conference of Methodists" forms a group within the Church of England.

The Russian Orthodox send missionaries to Alaska.

1785 Korean Christianity expands, then is exterminated.

1789 The French Revolution results in a new government and a new religion hostile to Christianity, "The Cult of Reason." Thousands of Catholic and some Protestant clergy are executed. Ten years later the French invade Rome, and take Pope Pius VI prisoner to France.

1792 Second Great Awakening: revival sweeps New England for 30 years.

William Carey, often called the father of modern Protestant missions

1793 William and Dorothy Carey of England sail for India. Carey writes a significant work on the Great Commission and offers strategies for fulfilling it at a time when many Protestants believe that "when God pleases to convert the heathen, he'll do it without consulting you or me."

The Baptist Missionary Society and other missionary societies formed during this century.

1795 Many American churches, including the Baptists, begin to divide over the issue of slave holding.

1797 Methodists separate from the Church of England to form a distinct church.

Christianity spreads to Nepal, Seychelles, Falkland Islands, Turks and Caicos Islands, Pitcairn Island, Sierra Leone, Norfolk Island, and Tonga.

AD 1800

1801 French leader Napoleon Bonaparte reconciles with new pope temporarily (Concordat of 1801) and makes himself emperor in 1804. France reinvades Rome and takes Pius VII to France as a prisoner.

1807 William Wilberforce, member of Parliament and devout Christian, leads Parliament to abolish the slave trade in the British Empire. He and other Christians also address social problems including exploitative child labor, illiteracy, prison reform, education, and reinstating civil rights for Jews and Catholics.

1811 Thomas and Alexander Campbell's Restoration Movement gives rise to the Disciples of Christ and some Church of Christ groups.

1813 Adoniram and Ann Judson arrive in Burma.

Richard Allen, founder of the AME Church

1816 The African Methodist Episcopal Church (AME) is founded by Richard Allen, a free Black, in Philadelphia. In 1821, the African Methodist Episcopal Zion Church forms.

1822 Congregation for the Propagation of the Faith (reestablished by Pope Pius VII) spurs Roman Catholic missionary efforts in Ethiopia, Mongolia, North Africa (Charles Lavigerie, founder of the White Fathers) and Hawaii (Fr. Damien, works with lepers 16 years and dies of leprosy).

1827 John Nelson Darby of the Plymouth Brethren creates the first dispensational system (dividing history into spiritual eras or dispensations), which influences Cyrus Scofield's teachings of the 1900s.

1830 Friedrich Schleiermacher, the "Father of Liberal Protestant Theology," teaches that God is *within* human reality, not above it.

Joseph Smith, Jr., founds the Church of the Latter-day Saints (Mormonism), which denies the Trinity.

1833 Oxford Movement calls the Church of England to return to "high church" practices and doctrines.

1835 Charles Finney leads revival in New York.

1836 George Müller opens faith orphanage in England.

1840 David Livingstone, missionary, goes to Africa.

1844 Søren Kierkegaard's *Philosophical Fragments*.

The YMCA and YWCA (Young Men's/Women's Christian Association) form in London during the Industrial Revolution to introduce Christianity to new large populations in urban areas.

Adventist Movement begins with William Miller.

1854 Baptist preacher Charles H. Spurgeon draws such great crowds that a church is built for him in England.

Immaculate Conception dogma is pronounced by Pope Pius IX. It states that Mary, Jesus' mother, was free from original sin, a belief debated since the Middle Ages.

Dwight L. Moody

1855 Dwight L. Moody, shoe salesman in Chicago, converts and works with the YMCA. He develops a simple message of repentance and salvation and the work of the Holy Spirit ("higher life"). Moody, Finney, and singer Ira Sankey mark the beginning of "revivalism": revival meetings held in urban areas.

1859 Charles Darwin writes *Origin of the Species*.

1863 Seventh-day Adventist Church founded.

1864 Catholics in Korea persecuted by revolutionaries.

1865 Hudson Taylor begins China Inland Mission.

1865 After the U.S. Civil War, many former slaves join with other African-Americans to start denominations in America, including the Black Baptists and the Colored Methodist Episcopal Church (CME; later the C is changed to mean Christian).

1870 First Vatican Council (Roman Catholic) on faith and the church declares papal infallibility dogma.

1875-1879 Christian Science and Jehovah's Witnesses (Watchtower Bible and Tract Society) founded. Both deny Christ's deity.

1878 The Salvation Army is founded by William Booth and his wife, Catherine Munford, both Methodist preachers, to minister to the poor.

1880 Moody leads the nondenominational Northfield Conferences, which emphasize holiness, dispensationalism, missions, evangelism, and the Spirit-filled life.

1887 B.B. Warfield, Reformed theologian at Princeton.

1895 The five "fundamentals" of the faith are set forth by the Evangelical Alliance to define the line between fundamentalism and modernism (radical liberalism). They are the inerrancy of Scripture, the deity of Jesus, the Virgin birth, Jesus' death providing substitutionary atonement, Jesus' physical resurrection, and his imminent return.

1895 Turks massacre 300,000 Armenian Christians.

Christianity spreads to Botswana, Madagascar, Djibouti, Somalia, Zambia, Rwanda, Liberia, Samoa, Transkei, New Hebrides, Lesotho, Uganda, Hong Kong, and Pacific Islands.

AD 1900

1901 Amy Carmichael, Irish missionary to India for 53 years, starts work at Donavur for children in danger.

Boxer Rebellion: Chinese kill missionaries and converts.

Many revivalists now preach premillennialism.

1906 Azusa Street revivals, led by William Seymour, emphasize living a holy life demonstrated by Spirit baptism and evidenced by speaking in tongues. Beginnings of Pentecostalism.

Albert Schweitzer writes *Quest for the Historical Jesus*.

1909 Scofield Bible published. Cyrus Scofield links verses from various books of the Bible in an attempt to explain God's actions in human history—fitting history into seven distinct spiritual eras (dispensations).

1914 Assemblies of God, and later Church of God and Four-Square Gospel denominations, form in the wake of the Azusa Street revivals.

1917 Communism spreads anti-religious ideology through Europe, Asia, and Latin America. Christianity is eradicated from education and worship. Millions are imprisoned and killed.

1919 Karl Barth's *Commentary on Romans*. Birth of neo-orthodoxy, which challenges liberalism with an emphasis on the Bible and on God's transcendence.

1925 Billy Sunday, the "baseball preacher," preaches salvation and temperance revivals.

Scopes "Monkey" Trial (State of Tennessee v. John Scopes) on the teaching of evolution.

1930-1950 Many Protestant denominations split over issues involving modernism, higher life, or dispensationalism, including the Presbyterian Church in the USA and the Northern Baptist Convention.

1934 Wycliffe Bible Translators is founded by Cam Townsend. Wycliffe and other organizations translate the Bible into other languages. In 1914 there are portions of the Bible in 600 languages. By 1980, the Bible is translated into more than 1,600 languages.

1941 Rudolf Bultmann leads movement to "demythologize" the Bible.

1933-1945 Rise of Nazism, leading to World War II and the death of 6 million Jews and millions of Christians.

1945 Dietrich Bonhoeffer, Lutheran pastor and a leader of the underground church in Germany, is hanged for plotting to kill Adolph Hitler.

1945 Franciscan priest Maxmilian Kolbe, prisoner in Auschwitz, volunteers to die and is executed in place of a fellow prisoner.

1948 Discovery of the Dead Sea Scrolls, the oldest known copies of portions of the Bible (c. 100 BC).

Modern political State of Israel established.

1949 Organized Christian churches exist in every country in the world except for Afghanistan, Saudi Arabia, and Tibet, according to *World Christian Encyclopedia*.

Billy Graham, a Southern Baptist minister, preaches the largest crusade in history—1.1 million people in Seoul, Korea, in 1973.

Billy Graham's Los Angeles Crusade launches his ministry. Over the next five decades, he preaches to more people than any evangelist in history.

World Council of Churches formed by representatives from all major Christian denominations except the Roman Catholics.

1954 Scientology and Unification Church founded. Neither accepts the Trinity or the deity of Jesus Christ.

1950-1960s Explosion of Christianity in newly independent African countries. Approximately 200 million Christians by 1980.

1962 Second Vatican Council (Roman Catholic) accepts Protestants as "separated brethren," encourages translating and reading the Bible, revokes the excommunication of the Great Schism (1054), upholds papal infallibility and encourages services (the Mass) to be held in each common language rather than in Latin.

1963 C.S. Lewis, author of *Mere Christianity*, dies.

1964 Baptist minister Martin Luther King, Jr., receives Nobel Peace Prize for civil rights efforts.

1970s Many major national and international crusades held: Latin America (Luis Palau), worldwide Here's Life crusade (Campus Crusade), Korea (Billy Graham). Jesus Movement in the USA; charismatic movement.

Largest church in the world is now in Seoul, Korea.

1997 Death of Mother Teresa of Calcutta, Catholic nun, who spent 50 years caring for the poor and dying.

Pope John Paul II apologizes for the Roman Catholic Church's lack of moral leadership during the Holocaust.

1998 *The Jesus Film*, an evangelistic film, is seen by more than 5 billion people since 1979.

2004 *The Passion of the Christ* movie released. Depicts Jesus' suffering, death, and resurrection.

Persecution of Christians continues around the world.

Christianity spreads to the Antarctic. There are still 2,000 groups of people who have no portion of the Bible in their own language.

REFORMATION TIME LINE

Five hundred years ago, a monk in Germany made a list of 95 issues that he wanted the theologians of the Roman Catholic Church to discuss. Little did he know that his list, called the Ninety-Five Theses, would spark the Reformation, a movement that would split the church and form a new kind of Christianity: Protestantism.

The story really begins much earlier. Years of power struggles within the Church as well as between religious and civil leaders had weakened the reputation of the clergy. Early sixteenth-century popes sold government and church positions, made their illegitimate children cardinals in the church, authorized murder, and increased their families' fortunes by abusing their power. The Renaissance (1447-1521) brought education, wealth, and revitalization to the common people at the same time that greed, abuse of power, and immorality ran rampant in the Church. All these factors brought desire for reform to a boiling point.

The monk was Martin Luther, and his debate caused the boiling pot of discontent to erupt all over Europe. In Luther's wake, the new shape of Western faith was revealed, leading even later to a new kind of nation.

The Magna Carta

John Wycliffe

Jan Hus

The Pre-Reformation Period (1215–1515)

1215 • Signing of the Magna Carta, considered the founding document of English (and later American) liberties; English barons force King John to agree to a statement of their rights, including a fair trial decided by a jury

1295 • England's first Parliament is called (the parliamentary was the first form of government in which people other than the king could pass laws)

1302 • Pope Boniface VIII claims that the pope has supremacy over every human being, in his bull (sealed declaration) Unam Sanctam (Latin for "the One Holy," that is, the Church)

1312 • 1312-1324 Marsilius of Padua, while in Paris, writes Defensor Pacis; he is condemned as heretical

1338 • Electors of Holy Roman Empire declare that they can select an emperor without approval from the pope

1349 • Death of William of Ockham, English philosopher called "the first Protestant" who argued for the independence of church and state, claiming that the Church had absolute authority in spiritual matters only and denying the right of the pope to interfere in civil affairs

1370 • 1370-1371 John Wycliffe, English priest and diplomat, proposes limiting papal taxation and civil powers

• John Ball, outspoken English priest and follower of Wycliffe, preaches equality and freedom of all, "crazy notions" which would form the founding philosophy of two revolutions and a new nation many years later

1377 • Pope Gregory XI issues five bulls denouncing Wycliffe; Wycliffe placed under house arrest

1382 • Council known as Blackfriars Synod condemns Wycliffe's writings, followed by persecution of Wycliffites at Oxford, England

1408 • In England, it becomes illegal to translate or read the Bible in English without permission of a bishop

1413 • Jan Hus of Bohemia writes De Ecclesia, which supports ideas popularized by Wycliffe

1414 • Lollard Rebellion, led by Sir Jon Oldcastle, follower of Wycliffe and friend of the king, suppressed

---

A "bull" is a sealed declaration by a pope. The bull *"Unam Sanctam"* declares
1. There is only one true Church, outside of which there is no salvation; the church has one head, not two.
2. That head is Christ and His representative, the Roman pope.
3. There are two swords (forms of power), the spiritual and the temporal (earthly or civic). Spiritual power is borne by the Church, temporal power is borne for the Church under the direction of the clergy.
4. The spiritual authority (the pope) is above the temporal and has the right to direct and judge all civil authority; whoever resists the highest power ordained by God resists God Himself.
5. All people need be ruled by the pope in order to be saved.

Defensor Pacis proposes that:
1. All the Church's power comes from the community and from the emperor.
2. The Church has no temporal head— Peter had no more authority than the other Apostles did.
3. The pope's only power is in calling an ecumenical council whose decisions are higher than his.
4. The Church is subject to the state in everything.
5. The pope has no power except through permission of the emperor; instead, the emperor has power over the pope and the council.
6. All the Church's possessions belong by right to the emperor.

Later called "the morning star of the Reformation," John Wycliffe challenges some church doctrines, including transubstantiation. He believes Scripture should be available to the people in their own language. People inspired by Wycliffe (derisively called "Lollards," meaning mumblers), translate the entire Bible into English (1382) from Latin, and call it the Wycliffe Bible; this is the first translation of the Bible into English.

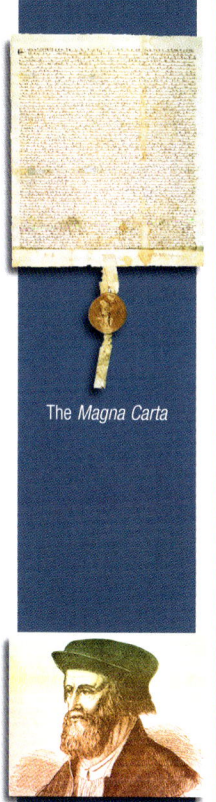

Reformation Time Line

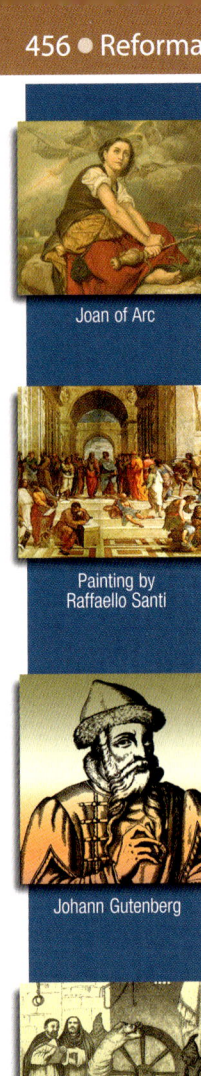

1415 • Council of Constance, Germany, condemns Wycliffe on 267 counts of heresy and demands that John Hus recant; Hus refuses and is burned at the stake

1417 • Sir Jon Oldcastle is burned at the stake

1428 • At papal command, the remains of Wycliffe are dug up, burned, and scattered on the river

1431 • Trial of Joan of Arc

> Joan, a French peasant girl during the Hundred Years' War, sees visions and hears voices telling her to save France. She leads a successful military expedition at Orleans. At about age 19, she is taken prisoner, tried for witchcraft, and burned. Twenty-five years later the verdict is reversed.

1450 • c. 1450 Beginning of the Renaissance

1456 • Johann Gutenberg prints the Bible (Latin Vulgate), the first book printed in Europe using movable metal type

> The popes of the Renaissance (1447-1521) are notable more for their intrigues and quest for power than for their pastoral care or desire for reform.

1478 • Spanish Inquisition persecutes Jews, Muslims, and heretics

> The invention of a printing press with movable metal type in Mainz, Germany, makes the Bible accessible to more people who previously could not afford handmade copies, which cost a year's wage.

1483 • Martin Luther, founder of the Reformation in Germany, is born in Eisleben, Germany

1484 • Ulrich Zwingli, founder of the Reformation in Switzerland, is born in Wildhaus in Switzerland

1494 • c. 1494 William Tyndale is born in Gloucestershire, England

1496 • Menno Simons, future Anabaptist leader, is born in Witmarsum, Friesland, today's Netherlands

1497 • 1497-1498 Dominican friar Savonarola preaches reform

> Savonarola encourages the people of Florence, Italy, to turn from lives of luxury and entertainment and toward serving Christ and following His example. He sells church property and gives the proceeds to the poor. Despite his initial popularity with the common people, he is caught in a political conflict with Pope Alexander VI and is excommunicated. His popularity wanes and later he is executed for heresy.

1502 • Erasmus, leader of German humanism, future priest, philosopher, writer, and Greek scholar, writes *Enchiridion* ("The Handbook of the Christian Soldier"), promoting a Christianity based on the Sermon of the Mount

• Papal bull orders the burning of any books questioning Church's authority

1505 • John Knox, the leader of the Scottish Reformation, is born in Haddington, Scotland

1506 • William Tyndale enters Magdalen College at Oxford, England; "singularly addicted to the scriptures," he reads the Bible in English to his fellow students

1507 • Martin Luther is ordained as priest and celebrates his first Mass

1509 • John Calvin—Swiss reformer, greatest of Protestant theologians, and perhaps, after St. Augustine, the most widely followed Western theologian—is born in France

> Later editions of his Greek text form the basis of the textus receptus and are used by Martin Luther, William Tyndale, and the King James Bible (Authorized Version) translators.

1512 • 1512-1517 Fifth Lateran Council is held in Lyons, France, to address a variety of concerns, including church reform

> Luther challenges the Church to a discussion on the subjects of penance, the pope's authority, and abuses in the selling of indulgences.

1515 • William Tyndale is ordained as priest but refuses to enter monastic orders

The Reformation Period 1516-1563

1516 • Erasmus publishes a Greek translation of the New Testament

1517 • Martin Luther posts his 95 theses on the door of the church in Wittenberg, Germany; the Protestant Reformation begins

> Indulgences are certificates that free their owners from performing the acts of penance that the church requires to show sorrow for certain sins. Indulgences are not intended to let people "buy forgiveness," but instead are supposed to express people's inner desire to turn from their sins. However, many medieval priests and popes distort the original intent of indulgences.

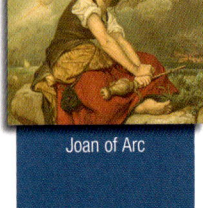

Joan of Arc

Painting by Raffaello Santi

Johann Gutenberg

The Spanish Inquisition

John Knox

Luther posts his 95 theses

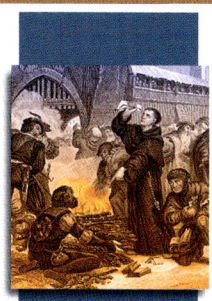

Reformation Time Line • 457

Luther burns the document

1518
- At a meeting in Heidelberg, Germany, Luther defends his theology; later he appears before Cardinal Cajetan at Augsburg, Germany, but refuses to recant; Frederick the Wise protects Luther from being handed over to Rome

> **Recant:** To take back or say one no longer has an opinion or belief, especially applied to matters of heresy.

1519
- Martin Luther questions papal infallibility (belief that the pope is preserved from error in matters of faith and morals) and begins New Testament sermon series, starting new era of preaching
- Ulrich Zwingli begins New Testament sermons, thus ushering in Swiss reformation

1520
- The pope publishes a bull giving Martin Luther 60 days to recant or be excommunicated; Luther burns the document

1521
- Martin Luther is excommunicated by the pope; at the Diet of Worms (city in Germany pronounced "vormps") Luther refuses to recant writings; the diet publishes an edict condemning him; Luther begins translating the Bible into German

> The Edict of Worms bans the reading or possession of Luther's writings. It condemns Luther as a heretic and an outlaw, permitting anyone to kill Luther without legal consequence. (The edict was not enforced.)

- Pope names King Henry VIII "Defender of the Faith" for attacking Luther's views of the sacraments
- Lutheran books appear in England
- First Protestant communion at Wittenberg, Germany
- 1521–1523 William Tyndale begins teaching and is arraigned on charges of heresy; translates Erasmus's *Enchiridion* into English

> In politics, a Diet is a formal assembly for purposes of debating issues and making decisions. The term comes from the Latin *dies*, "day." The word diet refers to the fact that these assemblies met on a daily basis.

William Tyndale

1522
- Luther introduces German-language worship services at Wittenberg

1524
- Erasmus publishes *On Freedom of the Will*, his famous attack on Luther's denial of free will

1525
- William Tyndale plans to print the New Testament in English but is discovered and escapes with only a few printed sections
- The Anabaptist movement, predecessor to Brethren and Mennonite churches, teaches believers' baptism only, democratic decision making, and separation of church and state
- Martin Luther marries former nun Katherine von Bora; writes *Bondage of the Will* (a response to Erasmus)

> Luther's work describes the absolute inability of humankind in our fallen state to act morally, a clear opposite to Erasmus' humanistic ideal.

Katherine von Bora

1526
- William Tyndale completes printing of the New Testament in Worms, Germany

> This is the first printing of the New Testament in English and the first English translation of the scriptures from the biblical Greek. The smuggled copies of his New Testaments soon spread throughout England.

- Cardinal Wolsey, Archbishop of York, attends public burning of "Lutheran" books
- Reformation reaches Sweden and Denmark where Protestant churches begin to appear

Erasmus

1527
- The city of Basel, Switzerland, orders corporeal punishment and confiscation of property for Christians who are baptized as adults and who shelter Anabaptists
- Martin Luther pens "A Mighty Fortress"; writes against Zwingli's views on the Lord's Supper
- Protestant university in Marburg, Germany, is founded
- 1527–1530 English seek to capture Tyndale; he keeps moving from place to place, continuing to translate the Bible

1528
- Erasmus publishes his English translations of the works of St. Augustine
- Thomas Bilney, Cambridge preacher and "Lutheran sympathizer," is dragged from his pulpit and imprisoned

Thomas More

Reformation Time Line

1529
- Sir Thomas More begins writing *Dialogue* against William Tyndale and Martin Luther
- King Henry VIII of England summons the "Reformation Parliament" and begins to cut ties with the Church of Rome
- At the Diet of Speyer (Germany) Luther's followers are first called Protestants (the term Protestantism becomes associated with Lutheranism, Zwinglianism, and Calvinism)
- Tyrolean Anabaptists flee to Moravia, region of the Czech Republic

> The Diet of Speyer declares that the previously unenforced Edict of Worms is now to be enforced. The Protestant princes profess their faith here for the first time in opposition to the edict.

> **Protestant Characteristics**
> - Acceptance of the Bible as the only source of revealed truth
> - Doctrine of justification by faith alone
> - Priesthood of all believers

1530
- Tyndale's translation of the first five books of the Old Testament into English appears in England
- Diet of Augsburg, Germany

1531
- William Tyndale refuses Henry the VIII's invitation to return to England
- Ulrich Zwingli urges civil war in Switzerland to force remaining Catholic districts to accept Protestantism; Zwingli is killed in battle of Kappel

> The Diet of Augsburg attempts to calm rising tension between Protestantism and Roman Catholicism. Luther, being an outlaw, cannot attend; Philipp Melanchthon—Luther's friend and collaborator on German Bible translation—presents the Augsburg Confession, a statement of Lutheran beliefs.

1532
- English clergy submits to Henry VIII, beginning process of declaring the king, rather than the pope, supreme authority over spiritual matters
- John Calvin starts Protestant movement in France; publishes his commentary on Seneca's De Clementia

1533
- Tyndale's translation of Erasmus's *Enchiridion* is printed
- John Frith, friend of Tyndale, burned at the stake
- Thomas Cranmer becomes Archbishop of Canterbury, ending debate on clerical celibacy (whether priests can marry) among Anglicans, as Cranmer is married
- The Church of England declared the officially established Christian church in England
- John Calvin labeled a heretic by Catholic officials, flees Paris, France
- Jacob Hutter joins Moravian group who become known as Hutterites

> Frith is first arrested for assisting Tyndale in the translation of the New Testament. He is released, arrested again, and tried for heresy. While imprisoned in the Tower of London, Frith writes the first Protestant views on the sacraments.

1534
- William Tyndale's revised New Testament is printed
- Luther completes a translation of the Bible into German, 13 years after he began

1534
- Act of Supremacy makes British monarch Henry VIII head of the English church, breaking away from Roman Catholic control
- Roman Catholic priest Ignatius Loyola founds Society of Jesus (Jesuits) in Paris to spread Counter-Reformation and to evangelize

> The new "Church of England" (Anglican Church) sets forth a doctrinal statement: The 39 Articles.

1535
- William Tyndale arrested by King Henry VIII's agent in Antwerp, Belgium, and imprisoned
- First complete Bible printed in English. Myles Coverdale, close friend of Tyndale, translates portions of the Old Testament not completed by Tyndale and publishes the "Coverdale Bible" (dedicated to Anne Boleyn, one of King Henry VIII's wives)

> The Counter-Reformation is the Roman Catholic Church's reaction to the Protestant Reformation. By addressing abuses, redefining doctrines and re-establishing the authority of the pope, the Catholic Church is reformed in many ways; but it is also solidified against Protestantism, ensuring that there will be no reconciliation between the branches. Interestingly, the Protestant challenge results in greater desire to end division dating to 1054 between Roman Catholic and Orthodox Churches.

King Henry VIII

Ulrich Zwingli

The burning of William Tyndale

John Calvin

Reformation Time Line

Menno Simons

Coverdale Bible page

The Chained Bible

John Knox

- The Münster Rebellion: Anabaptists take over the city of Münster, Germany and are slaughtered by Catholic residents previously expelled; later, under Menno Simons, Anabaptists adopt pacifism

1536
- After 15 months in prison, William Tyndale is strangled and burned at the stake for heresy
- Luther agrees to Wittenberg Concord defining the Lord's Supper in an attempt to resolve differences with other reformers, but the Swiss Zwinglians reject the document
- Denmark and Norway become Lutheran
- Erasmus dies
- Menno Simons becomes the Anabaptist leader in the Netherlands
- Henry VIII disbands 376 Roman Catholic monasteries and convents in England
- John Calvin's *Institutes of the Christian Religion* explain Protestant beliefs

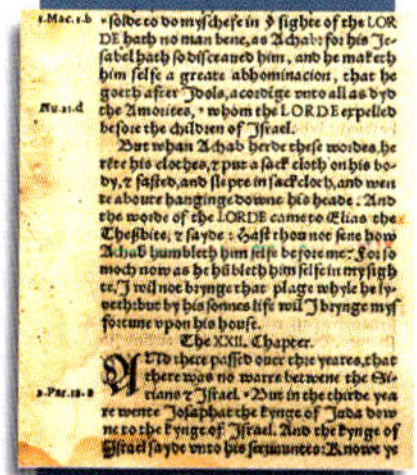

1537
- John Rogers publishes the second complete English Bible under the pseudonym "Thomas Matthew"

1538
- John Calvin is banished from Geneva, Switzerland, goes to Strasbourg, France

1539
- King Henry VIII requests publication of a large pulpit Bible; Archbishop of Canterbury Thomas Cranmer commissions Myles Coverdale for the job
- 1539–40 Menno Simons publishes the *Foundation of Christian Doctrine*, an important exposition of Anabaptist faith

1540
- In Rome, Pope Paul III recognizes the Jesuit order; the Jesuits become important figures in Counter-Reformation
- Conference at Worms fails to reconcile Protestants and Catholics

1541
- John Calvin establishes theocracy in Geneva, Switzerland, in which government leaders are also the religious leaders. John Knox starts the Calvinist Reformation in Scotland. Scottish Protestants become known as Presbyterians because elders ("presbyters") make decisions for churches, not one person.
- Conference of Regensburg, Germany, attempts to reach doctrinal agreement between Protestants and Catholics, but Luther and official Rome reject their work

1545
- 1545-1563 Council of Trent (Italy): Roman Catholic Counter-Reformation condemns the selling of indulgences, immorality of clergy, nepotism (appointing family members to church offices), and Protestantism

1546
- Martin Luther dies

1549
- The Church of England's *Book of Common Prayer* unites most English churches in a middle ground between Catholicism and Protestantism
- Jesuit Francis Xavier begins missionary efforts in the Indies and Japan: 100,000 converts to Christianity are attributed to him

---

Anabaptists ("re-baptizers" from the Greek) are Christians who believe that infant baptism is not valid; they "re-baptize" adults who had been baptized as infants. Distinctive principles include:
- Restoration of "primitive Christianity," including the rejection of oaths and capital punishment, and the refusal of roles in civil government.
- Belief in the absolute supremacy of the Bible as sufficient for faith, but with private inspiration playing an important part.
- Rejection of infant baptism and the doctrine of justification by faith alone (only).
- Holding of goods in common was to be the underlying principle of new Kingdom of God.

Two main accusations against Tyndale are the translation of the Bible into English and opposition to King Henry VIII's divorce. Tyndale's final words reportedly are, "Oh Lord, open the King of England's eyes."

The Wittenberg Concord (covenant) is signed by Reformed and Lutheran leaders to resolve different beliefs about the Real Presence of Christ's body and blood in the Eucharist.

The "Matthew's Bible" is the first English Bible published with the king's permission. On the last page of the Old Testament, the translator prints Tyndale's initials in 2-inch letters to honor him. Many Bibles in common languages begin to appear.

Geneva's city council ousts John Calvin over disagreement on the withholding of communion, moral censorship, and punishment by excommunication.

Coverdale's Bible, first English Bible authorized for public use, is chained to every pulpit—hence its common name, the Chained Bible. Henry VIII approves the "Great Bible." It is "sent abroad among the people" to be read by all and "set forth with the king's most gracious license." In addition, the king decrees that every church should have a reader so that even the illiterate can hear the Word of God. Three years after his martyrdom, William Tyndale's last prayer is granted (see note for 1536).

Reformation Time Line

1554 • Queen Mary Tudor, daughter of Henry VIII, restores Roman Catholicism to England, bans Protestant translations of the Bible, and persecutes Protestants

> John Rogers, Tyndale's assistant (aka "Thomas Matthew"), is the first to be burnt at the stake. Many Protestants flee to Geneva, Switzerland, led by Myles Coverdale and John Foxe. There under the protection of John Calvin, the Church of Geneva determines to produce a Bible to educate families while they continue in exile.

1555 • Peace of Augsburg (Germany) allows each ruler to determine religion of his region

1558 • Queen Elizabeth I becomes Queen of England and Supreme Governor of the Church of England; she attempts a compromise between Catholics and Protestants

> The Peace of Augsburg is a treaty signed between Charles V and Protestant princes; it establishes the first permanent legal basis for the dual existence of Lutheranism and Catholicism in Germany.

1560 • Publication of Geneva Bible in Switzerland; this is the first time a Bible is printed with verse divisions

• John Knox establishes Reformed church in Scotland

1562 • Heidelberg Catechism is formed; it is the most widely held Protestant doctrinal statement for centuries

1563 • John Foxe publishes *Acts and Monuments* ("Foxe's Book of Martyrs")

The Post-Reformation Period (1564-1689)

1564 • The term "Puritan" is first used for Protestants who want to "purify" the Church of England of ceremony and ritual not found in the Bible

• John Calvin dies

1568 • Bishops Bible, Church of England translation, is printed

1570 • Queen Elizabeth I is excommunicated by the pope, and in turn persecutes Catholics

1577 • Formula of Concord defines Lutheran beliefs in a statement of faith known as the *Book of Concord*

1582 • 1582-1609 Catholic scholar Gregory Martin translates the Rheims-Douay Bible from the Vulgate (Latin) while in exile in France

1598 • Edict of Nantes, France, grants freedom of worship to French Protestants (Huguenots) after 30 years of persecution

1601 • Dutch Reformed theologian Jacobus Arminius sets forth doctrines emphasizing man's ability to choose Christ and Christ's death for all people (Arminianism)

> Arminius' studies of Paul's Epistle to the Romans lead him to disagree with Calvin's doctrine of predestination, which claims that God's will determines ahead of time what the destiny of groups and individuals will be.

1605 • "Gunpowder Plot" fails in London, England

1611 • King James Version Bible (KJV), also known as the Authorized Version, is published

1618 • Dutch Reformed Synod of Dordt, the Netherlands, denounces Arminianism; responds to Arminius' five criticisms of Calvinism with five points of Calvinism

> Guy Fawkes and other Roman Catholic conspirators attempt to kill Protestant King James I and blow up the houses of Parliament in order to seize the government. Their aims are total revolution in the government and the installation of a Catholic monarch.

1620 • Separatists ("Pilgrims") reject the Church of England and sail to America on the Mayflower; later Puritans, who wish to cleanse the church, arrive in America and start colonies

> King James I of England commissions 54 scholars to undertake a new Bible translation, which takes six years to complete. The scholars use the Bishops Bible and Tyndale's Bible as well as available Greek and Hebrew manuscripts. After slow initial acceptance, this becomes the most popular Bible for the next 300 years.

1629 • Orthodox Patriarch of Constantinople, Turkey, Cyril Loukaris (Lucar), befriends Protestants and presents the earliest known copy of the Bible in Greek *(Codex Alexandrius,* fifth century AD) to Charles I of England

1637 • Antinomian Crisis in New England: Anne Hutchinson banished for antinomianism and heresy

> Antinomianism: The doctrine that faith in Christ frees Christians from obeying Old Testament moral law.

Queen Mary Tudor

Queen Elizabeth I

Huguenots persecuted

Jacobus Arminius

King James Bible page

Reformation Time Line

1642 • Power struggles between Charles I and the English Parliament lead to civil war in England ....

Puritan Member of Parliament, Oliver Cromwell, defeats the king's troops. Later as Lord Protector, Cromwell seeks tolerance for many Protestant groups.

1647 • Westminster Confession is accepted as the statement of Presbyterianism in Scotland and England

• Beginnings of the Quaker movement (the Society of Friends) under preacher George Fox

1648 • After the end of the Thirty Years' War, Catholics and Protestants are given equal rights in most of the Holy Roman Empire

1654 • Conversion of Blaise Pascal, French mathematician and theologian

1655 • Waldensians break from Roman Catholicism and embrace Protestantism; Catholics launch persecution

1670 • Secret Treaty of Dover between Charles II of England and Louis XIV of France intends to restore Roman Catholicism to England; the treaty, made without the knowledge of the British people, fails

1685 • Edict of Nantes of 1598 is revoked; Huguenots flee France

1687 • English king James II issues Declaration of Liberty of Conscience, suspending laws punishing religious dissenters

1698 • First missionary societies formed by Protestants

Oliver Cromwell

George Fox

Five points of Arminianism

1. **Free will or human ability**
   Free will consists of our ability to choose good over evil; we have the power to cooperate with God's grace or resist it.

2. **Conditional election**
   God's choice (election) determined by knowledge of what man would do (foreseen faith). Our choice of God, not God's choice of us, is cause of salvation.

3. **Universal redemption or general atonement**
   Jesus' death and resurrection made it possible for all to be saved, but is effective only for those who choose to accept it.

4. **Resistible grace**
   Our free will limits the Holy Spirit's ability to draw us toward salvation; God's grace can be resisted.

5. **Falling from grace**
   Salvation can be lost, as it requires our cooperation.

Five points of Calvinism

1. **Total depravity (inability)**
   Sin affects every part of human nature, resulting in our inability to choose good over evil. We must be regenerated by the Holy Spirit in order to believe.

2. **Unconditional election**
   God's choice (election) determined not by our foreseen response (faith); rather, faith and repentance are also gifts given by God. God's choice of us, not our choice of God, is the cause of salvation.

3. **Limited atonement**
   Jesus' death and resurrection actually saved the elect; it guarantees everything necessary for salvation, including the gift of faith.

4. **Irresistible grace**
   The Holy Spirit's call is irresistible; God's grace never fails to result in salvation for those to whom it is extended.

5. **Perseverance of the saints**
   Salvation cannot be lost, as it is completely powered by God; thus the elect will persevere (be preserved) to the end.

The Five Solas of the Reformation

Sola Scriptura	Scripture Alone
Soli Deo Gloria	For the Glory of God Alone
Solo Christo	By Christ's Work Alone are We Saved
Sola Gratia	Salvation by Grace Alone
Sola Fide	Justification by Faith Alone

Reformation Time Line

Map of the Reformation

Branches of the Reformation

Reformation Leaders	Branch	Denominational Offshoots	
Martin Luther Philip Melanchthon	Lutheran	Lutheran	
Ulrich Zwingli John Calvin John Knox	Reformed Tradition	Reformed Calvinist Presbyterian Puritan	Congregational United Church of Christ Baptist
Henry VIII Elizabeth I John Wesley	Anglican	Church of England Episcopal (Anglican) Methodist	
Conrad Grebel Jacob Huter Felix Manz George Fox Menno Simons Count Zinzendorf	Anabaptist	Swiss Brethren Mennonites Amish	Hutterites Quakers Moravian Brethren

THE GOSPELS: "LOST" & FOUND

The New Testament begins with four accounts of the life of Jesus Christ commonly known as "Gospels," a word that means "good news" or "victorious tidings." The Gospels According to Matthew, Mark, Luke, and John have been familiar to Christians for so many centuries that many believers have assumed these Gospels are the only retellings of the life of Jesus that ever existed. But there are more than a *dozen* other "Gospels," plus several supposed accounts of episodes from Jesus' life that aren't known by the name of "Gospel."

Some of these alternative "Gospels" have been familiar among scholars for centuries. Dan Brown's novel *The Da Vinci Code* popularized several "lost Gospels," including *Gospel of Philip*, *Gospel of Mary Magdalene*, and *Gospel of Thomas*. A couple of years later the *Gospel of Judas* was reconstructed and translated anew. The media implied that *Gospel of Judas* and other lost Gospels provide information about the historical Jesus that isn't included in the New Testament Gospels. Several writers and entertainment corporations were quick to turn a profit by sensationalizing the news of this reconstructed "Gospel." Indeed, the viewpoints found in the "lost Gospels" *do* differ from the New Testament Gospels.

According to New Testament Gospels	According to "Lost Gospels"
Jesus was fully human and fully divine	Jesus was a spirit who seemed human or a mere human uniquely inhabited by a divine spirit (Gnostic gospels)
Judas Iscariot willingly chose to betray Jesus	Jesus told Judas to betray him (*Gospel of Judas*)
The first miraculous sign that Jesus performed was turning water to wine at Cana	Jesus performed self-serving miracles throughout his childhood ("infancy Gospels")

How likely is it that the lost Gospels really tell us the truth about Jesus Christ? An open-minded look at the historical record quickly reveals that there is little reason to doubt the New Testament Gospels and great reason to reject the so-called "lost Gospels."

True or False?

What if the version of the life of Jesus that's found in the Bible isn't the right one? What if there were other accounts of his life and ministry? And what if none of these versions actually represents eyewitness testimony about Jesus? That's precisely what some scholars are teaching, not just on college campuses but in popular literature and on television.

Popular scholars such as Bart Ehrman and Elaine Pagels, whose books boast titles such as *The Gnostic Gospels*, *Lost Scriptures*, and *Lost Christianities*, make claims such as this one: "Many years passed before Christians agreed concerning which books should comprise their sacred scriptures.... In part this was because other books were available, also written by Christians, many of their authors claiming to be the original apostles of Jesus, yet advocating points of view quite different from those later embodied in the canon."[1]

Indeed, the viewpoints found in these writings, many of which are called "Gospels," *do* differ from the New Testament Gospels. In fact, many include descriptions of Jesus that directly contradict the Gospels according to Matthew, Mark, Luke, and John. Most significantly, the "lost Gospels" consistently depict the *nature of Jesus* in ways that disagree with the Gospels according to Matthew, Mark, Luke, and John. For example, the New Testament writings describe Jesus as fully divine and yet fully human (see, for example, Philippians 2:5-11). But, according to other writings, Jesus Christ was a spirit who merely *seemed* human. In others, such as *Gospel of Philip*, Jesus of Nazareth—a human being—was possessed by a Christ-spirit; then on the cross, this Christ-spirit abandoned the human Jesus.

So what's at stake when it comes to the lost Gospels? Nothing less than the nature of Jesus Christ, the essence of Christian faith! Simply put, if the authors of the lost Gospels were telling the truth, the perspective on Jesus that's found in the New Testament Gospels is false. Let's look together at the historical evidence, though, and see what we actually find.

The Gospels: "Lost" & Found

What are the "lost Gospels"?

The term "lost Gospels" usually refers to ancient writings that were excluded from the New Testament, even though they included *supposed* recollections of events and teachings from the life of Jesus. A few of these "lost Gospels" have lasted throughout the centuries. Others survive only in tiny fragments of papyrus or in brief quotations found in the writings of early Christian scholars. Several "lost Gospels" were discovered anew in the past 100 years. Copies of some texts—such as *Gospel of Philip*, *Gospel of Thomas*, *Gospel of Truth*, and *Coptic Gospel of the Egyptians*—were unearthed in 1945 in Egypt, near a village known as Nag Hammadi.

Truth about the New Testament Gospels

Why were the "lost Gospels" excluded from the New Testament?

The lost Gospels were excluded because they did not include reliable, eyewitness testimony about Jesus. Some scholars today depict this decision as having been made by powerful church leaders in the fourth century, three centuries after the books in the New Testament were written. One such scholar claims that a letter from a powerful bishop, Athanasius of Alexandria, established the list of authoritative books in AD 367. He claims, "Athanasius wrote his annual pastoral letter to the Egyptian churches under his jurisdiction, and in it he included advice concerning which books should be read as Scripture in the churches. He lists our twenty-seven books, excluding all others. This is the first surviving instance of anyone affirming our set of books as the New Testament. And even Athanasius did not settle the matter. Debates continued for decades, even centuries."[2]

(Courtesy of the Schøyen Collection, Oslo and London)

Earliest known fragment of *Acts of Paul*. When it was discovered that *Acts of Paul* was a fictional text, Christians rejected its authority.

Each fact in this summary is *technically* correct, but it leaves out several key truths, leaving readers with false impressions—such as, (1) until the late fourth century, there was no consensus about which Christian writings were authoritative and true, and (2) even then the church's standard was simply the authoritative statement of a powerful bishop.

So when *did* Christians agree on which writings were authoritative in their congregations? And what was the standard for these decisions? Hints of this standard can be found in first-century Christian writings. The basic idea was something like this: *Testimony that could be connected to eyewitnesses of the risen Lord was uniquely authoritative among early Christians.*[3] It was *not* one specific person or a powerful group in the early church that decided to include certain books in the New Testament. *From the beginning, authoritative testimony about Jesus Christ had to have its source in eyewitnesses of the risen Lord.* The lost Gospels were excluded by the fact that they could not be clearly connected to persons who walked and talked with Jesus; therefore, their testimony could not be considered authoritative or reliable.

When did Christians begin to treat the words of eyewitnesses as the most reliable testimony about Jesus?

Even while the New Testament books were being written, the words of people who saw and followed the risen Lord—specifically, the words and writings of the apostles—carried special weight in the churches (see Acts 1:21-26; 15:6—16:5; 1 Corinthians 4—5; 9:1-12; Galatians 1:1-12; 1 Thessalonians 5:26-27). After the apostles' deaths, Christians continued to cherish the testimony of eyewitnesses and their associates. Around AD 110, Papias of Hierapolis put it this way: "So, if anyone who had served the elders came, I asked about their sayings in detail—what Andrew or Peter said, or what was said by Philip or Thomas or James or John or Matthew or any other of the Lord's followers."[4] The people most likely to know the truth about Jesus were the ones who had encountered Jesus personally or the close associates of these witnesses. So, although Christians wrangled for several centuries about *which* writings were authoritative, it was something much greater than political machinations that drove their decisions. Their goal was to determine which books could be clearly connected to eyewitnesses of the risen Lord.

Why did only four Gospels make it into the New Testament if so many Gospels were available to early Christians?

Only four Gospels—the ones known to us as the Gospels according to Matthew, Mark, Luke, and John—could be clearly connected to firsthand accounts of the risen Lord. Unlike the "lost Gospels," each of the New Testament Gospels was written in the first century AD, at a time when the eyewitnesses of Jesus' ministry were still alive. (The earthly ministry of Jesus began around AD 28 and lasted until AD 30 or so.) What's more, it's possible to trace widespread awareness among

Christians that these Gospels represented eyewitness testimony back to the late first century, within a few years of the time when the last of the New Testament Gospels was written.

- Papias of Hierapolis—a church leader in the geographic area known today as Turkey, born about the time the Gospels were being written and a friend of Philip's four daughters mentioned in Acts 21:9[5]—received his information about the first two New Testament Gospels from the first generation of Christians. According to Papias, the primary source for Matthew's Gospel was the testimony of the Matthew, a follower of Jesus and former tax collector (Matthew 9:9).

- Papias also wrote that the author of Mark's Gospel had served as Peter's translator when Peter preached in the early churches. As such, what Mark recorded in his Gospel was the witness of Peter himself.

- About the same time as Papias recorded these recollections, a pastor named Polycarp of Smyrna referred to the words of the apostle Paul as "Scripture."

- In a mid-second-century document known as the Muratorian Fragment, an unknown church leader reports that Luke's Gospel came from Luke, the apostle Paul's physician, and that this Gospel included eyewitness accounts from people that Luke interviewed.[6]

- The Muratorian Fragment also makes it clear that the apostle John was the source for the Gospel that bears John's name.

- Also in the mid-second-century, another church leader—Irenaeus of Lyons—reported that he had received these same traditions about the four Gospels from Christians of the first and second centuries.[7]

This painting from the ruins of Pompeii depicts two methods for writing in the first century: The man holds a papyrus scroll while his wife holds a stylus and wax tablet.

So, from the first century onward, it seems to have been widely recognized that the Gospels now known by the names of Matthew, Mark, Luke, and John represented eyewitness testimony about the life and ministry of Jesus Christ. In contrast, *none* of the "lost Gospels" can be connected to firsthand testimony.

■ How do we know that Matthew, Mark, Luke, and John were really the sources of the Gospels that bear their names?

Consistent and reliable traditions have connected the names of Matthew, Mark, Luke, and John with these Gospels from the first century onward. Some scholars claim that the New Testament Gospels received their names in the same way that some of the "lost Gospels" received their titles—people wanted these writings to seem authoritative; so, they simply added names of eyewitnesses, even though these people really didn't write the Gospels at all. For example, one scholar puts it this way: "Sometime in the second century, when [Christians] recognized the need for *apostolic* authorities, they attributed these books to apostles (Matthew and John) and close companions of apostles (Mark, the secretary of Peter; and Luke the traveling companion of Paul)."[8]

The first problem with this skeptical line of thinking is that the Gospels According to Matthew, Mark, Luke, and John seem to have been connected with their authors as soon as the Gospels began to circulate widely. At this time, some people who knew the authors would still have been alive; under these circumstances, it would have been difficult to ascribe false names to the Gospels without someone protesting.

Tax collectors were known to carry pinakes, *books with wooden pages covered with wax. Notes were scratched into the wax using styluses.*

But there's another problem with the skeptics' claims: By the end of the first century, the four New Testament Gospels had circulated thousands of miles throughout the Roman Empire. In fact, a fragment of John's Gospel from early years of the second century—a portion known as the John Rylands Papyrus or P52–has been found in Egypt, hundreds of miles from the Gospel's point of origin in Asia Minor! Without rapid communication and without centralized church leadership, what would have happened if second-century Christians began ascribing false, apostolic names to the Gospels that had already spread this far from their places of origin? Most likely, each church would have connected a different author with each Gospel. Churches in Asia Minor might have ascribed a Gospel to the apostle Andrew, for example, while churches in Judea might have connected the same Gospel with Thaddeus or James or Jude. But, *in every titled manuscript copy of the four New Testament Gospels, no matter what part of the world in which it was used, each Gospel is connected to the same author.*

How did early Christians determine which writings really came from eyewitnesses?

These decisions were informed by a combination of *oral history, external and internal evidence.*

■ **Oral history:** Most of the knowledge about the origins of the New Testament books probably passed orally from one generation to another. From the first century onward, the names of Matthew, Mark, Luke, and John were connected with the four New Testament Gospels, and the writings of early Christians such as Ignatius of Antioch suggest that it would have been widely known that Paul wrote the epistles attributed to him.

(Courtesy of CSNTM.org)
Gospel According to John, around the tenth century AD.

■ **External evidence:** When no clear tradition was available to connect a book to an eyewitness, church members might explore *external evidence* about a book's origins. For example, a generation after the deaths of the apostles, a church leader near Rome considered which Christian writings should be viewed as authoritative. His conclusions can be found in a document known today as "the Muratorian Fragment." After listing the books that he viewed as authoritative, here's what this leader said that he had discovered regarding a popular book known as *The Shepherd*: "Hermas composed *The Shepherd* quite recently—in our times, in the city of Rome, while his brother Pius served as overseer.... While it should indeed be read, it cannot be read publicly for the people of the church—it is counted neither among the prophets (for their number has been completed) nor among the apostles (for it is after their time)."[9] Notice the reasons: This writing could not be added to the Old Testament prophets because the time of the Hebrew prophets had passed, and—with the deaths of the apostles—the time of the apostolic eyewitnesses had also ended. This teacher didn't forbid believers to read *The Shepherd*; he simply pointed out that the book should not serve as an authoritative text.

■ **Internal evidence:** Other times, Christians might conclude on the basis of *internal evidence* that a certain book did not represent eyewitness testimony. For example, in AD 199, a leading pastor named Serapion was told that a certain Gospel was "inscribed with Peter's name."[10] Since it bore the name of an apostolic eyewitness, Serapion allowed the Gospel to be used in the churches. When Serapion read *Gospel of Peter* for himself, however, he recognized he'd made a mistake. Although *Gospel of Peter* didn't directly contradict the New Testament Gospels, certain phrases in the book could be taken to imply that Jesus wasn't fully human. What's more, Serapion probably knew from oral tradition that John Mark had once served as Peter's translator and that the Gospel According to Mark represented the words of Peter; yet, the *Gospel of Peter* added many fanciful details that never appeared in Mark's Gospel—like a towering, talking cross that accompanied the risen Jesus out of the tomb. After comparing *Gospel of Peter* to "the writings handed down to us"—that was Serapion's term for the New Testament texts that were connected indisputably to eyewitnesses—Serapion concluded that *Gospel of Peter* did *not* represent the eyewitness testimony of Simon Peter, and he reversed his previous decision. As it turns out, Serapion was correct: The language and thought-patterns in *Gospel of Peter* have convinced most scholars today that the book was written a generation after Simon Peter's death.[11]

■ Why do we call the chosen books of the New Testament a "canon"?

The word "canon" comes from the Greek word *kanon,* which means "measuring stick," and these are the writings that "measure" Christians' faithfulness to Jesus Christ. It was not until the fourth century AD that the authoritative writings about Jesus Christ began to be known as a "canon." The idea of recognizing certain writings as authoritative, however, emerged much earlier, apparently in the first century. Each authoritative writing was expected to be connected to an eyewitness of the risen Lord, to be recognized in churches throughout the known world, and not to contradict other writings about Jesus. Although debates continued into the fourth century about a few writings—including the letters of Peter, John's second

> "*We,* brothers and sisters, receive Peter and the rest of the apostles as we would receive Christ himself. But those writings that are falsely ascribed with their names, we carefully reject, knowing that no such writings have ever been handed down to us."
>
> —Serapion of Antioch, late second century AD[12]

and third letters, and the letters of James and Jude—Christians universally agreed at least as early as the second century on the authority of at least nineteen of the books in the New Testament. From the beginning, Christians unanimously embraced at least the four Gospels, Acts, Paul's letters, and first epistle of John. (*See chart on page 50.*) Even if this handful of books had been the *only documents that represented eyewitness* testimony about Jesus, every vital truth of Christian faith would remain completely intact.

Truth about the "Lost Gospels"

■ Who wrote the "lost Gospels"?

No one knows for sure. Even though the names of Jesus' apostles and other companions are attached to several lost Gospels, no evidence exists to suggest that the authors of these texts even *could* have been eyewitnesses of the ministry of Jesus. In many cases, names such as "Mary" or "Philip" have been attached to these Gospels simply because these individuals are such prominent characters in the book. In a few cases—such as *Gospel of Thomas*, for example—the Gospel does actually claim to come from a prominent apostle or church leader, though it is clear from the language used in the book that the document was written long after the death of its namesake.

■ How are these writings different from the New Testament writings?

The "lost Gospels" were primarily fanciful accounts of Jesus' life, or they were written to promote a theology that contradicts the eyewitness testimony found in the New Testament. A few lost Gospels—for example, *Infancy Gospel of Thomas*, *Infancy Gospel of James*, and perhaps *Gospel of Peter*—seem to have been penned by well-meaning Christians who felt compelled to expand stories in the New Testament. Many parts of these writings don't directly contradict anything in the New Testament, but they tend to expand the New Testament accounts in fanciful and theologically problematic ways. For example, according to these writings, Jesus used his divine powers for his own benefit throughout his childhood. A couple of lost Gospels—such as *Gospel of the Lord* and *Gospel of the Ebionites*—were variations of the New Testament Gospels, edited to fit the theology of certain sects.

Inkwell discovered near the site where the Dead Sea Scrolls were copied.

The distinct theology of most of the "lost Gospels" was, however, *Gnostic*. From the perspective of most Gnostics, the deity who created the universe was not the true or supreme God; the creator of the physical world was an evil deity, a rebel against a higher and greater deity. Since they understood the cosmos to be the product of an evil deity, most Gnostics viewed everything physical—especially the role of women in reproduction—as evil; they also claimed that Jesus Christ only *seemed* human. According to Gnostics, Christ came to deliver humanity from the limitations of the physical world. As such, Gnostics were not typically interested in the actual, historical events of the life of Jesus; the Gnostics focused most of their attention on other-worldly sayings and myths, many of which depicted biblical villains as heroes and vice-versa.

■ How many lost Gospels are there?

If a Gospel is defined as an ancient retelling of the events and teachings of Jesus' life, there are fewer than thirty known Gospels. Most texts survive only in incomplete fragments. Here's a summary of many of the lost Gospels, most of which could not have been written by eyewitnesses:

■ *Gospel of Basilides (Gnostic writing, mid-second century AD)* Gnostic writing, now lost, mentioned by several early Christians.

■ *Gospel of the Ebionites (Ebionite writing, second century AD)* Surviving only in fragmented quotations in the writings of early Christians, *Gospel of the Ebionites* appears to have been a variation of *Gospel of the Hebrews*, edited to fit the theology of a sect known as "Ebionites." The Ebionites believed Jesus was a human being, adopted by God at his baptism.

■ *Gospel, Egerton (Fragments from an ancient document, second century AD)* Not actually a Gospel but a few fragments from an unknown source, the "Egerton Gospel" includes four stories about Jesus. Three of these stories appear, in varying forms, in the New Testament Gospels (Mk. 1:40–45; 12:13–17; Jn. 5:39–47; 10:33–39).

- **_Gospel of the Egyptians_ (Ancient writing, perhaps Gnostic, second century AD)** Presented as a dialogue between Jesus and a female disciple named Salome, _Gospel of the Egyptians_ encourages all believers to practice celibacy.

- **_Coptic Gospel of the Egyptians_ (Gnostic writing, late third century AD)** _Coptic Gospel of the Egyptians_ recounts a Gnostic myth in which Jesus is presented as a reincarnation of Seth, the third son of Adam and Eve.

- **_Gospel of Eve_ (Gnostic writing, probably third century AD)** Lost Gnostic writing, quoted by Epiphanius of Salamis. _Gospel of Eve_ was written at least a century after the time of Jesus. Seemingly also known as _Gospel of Perfection_.

- **_Gospel of the Hebrews_ (Christian writing, first century AD)** _Gospel of the Hebrews_ is truly a "lost Gospel"; it survives only in quotations found in the writings of early Christians. Many scholars believe _Gospel of the Hebrews_ represents an early, Aramaic summary of Jesus' life from the apostle Matthew—a summary that eventually became part of the document that now known as the Gospel According to Matthew. Also known as _Gospel of the Nazoreans_.

> "_Matthew_ composed his Gospel among the Hebrews in their language, while Peter and Paul were preaching the Gospel in Rome and building up the church there. After their deaths, Mark—Peter's follower and interpreter—handed down to us Peter's proclamation in written form. Luke, the companion of Paul, wrote in a book the Gospel proclaimed by Paul. Finally, John—the Lord's own follower, the one who leaned against his chest—composed the Gospel while living in Ephesus, in Asia."
>
> —Irenaeus of Lyons, mid- to late second century AD[13]

- **_Infancy Gospel of James_ (Christian writing, late second century AD)** An account, supposedly written by James, of the life of Mary. According to this document, Mary the mother of Jesus remained a virgin throughout her life.

- **_Acts of John_ (Docetic writing, late second century AD)** Supposed retelling of events from the life of the apostle John. Some copies of this text include comments that are _Docetic_—that is, they imply that Jesus Christ was not fully human—but these comments are not present in every version. It is possible that they were added later.

- **_Gospel of Judas_ (Gnostic writing, late second century AD)** Supposed account of the life of Jesus in which Judas Iscariot is portrayed as a heroic figure, commanded by Jesus to act as the betrayer.

- **_Gospel of the Lord_ (Marcionite writing, mid-second century AD)** Alteration of the Gospel According to Luke, edited to fit Marcion's theology.

- **_Gospel of Mary_ (Gnostic writing, late second or early third century AD)** Although frequently called _Gospel of Mary Magdalene_, the text of this document never indicates _which_ biblical Mary is the story's central character.

- **_Gospel of Matthias_ (Ancient writing, perhaps Gnostic, second century AD)** Lost document, known to many early Christians. This writing seems to have passed out of usage among Christians because (1) no clear evidence was available to suggest that the apostle Matthias actually wrote the book and (2) the book was used by heretical sects including the Gnostics.

- **_Gospel of Nicodemus_ (Forgery, fourth century AD)** Forgery that claimed to include Pontius Pilate's report to the emperor about Jesus. Also known as _Acts of Pilate_.

- **_Gospel, Oxyrhynchus_ (Christian writing, third century AD or earlier)** Not actually a Gospel but a tiny papyrus fragment from an unknown source, the "Oxyrhynchus Gospel" describes a confrontation between Jesus and the Pharisees. The events described in this fragment do not contradict any New Testament Gospels and seem to represent an expansion of the events described in Mark 7:1–23.

- **_Gospel of Peter_ (Christian writing, second century AD)** Although familiar to many early Christians, this text was rejected as an authoritative account of the life of Jesus because (1) it could not be clearly connected to the apostle Peter and (2) some passages in the book could be misconstrued to suggest that Jesus wasn't fully human.

- **_Apocalypse of Peter_ (Christian writing, second century AD)** An apocalyptic text that circulated with _Gospel of Peter_, _Apocalypse of Peter_ doesn't directly contradict any New Testament writings, but the book seems to have been written around AD 135, seventy years or so after the death of the apostle Peter.

- **_Coptic Apocalypse of Peter_ (Gnostic writing, late third century AD)** The _Coptic Apocalypse of Peter_ clearly denied that Jesus had a physical body, declaring that "the one whose hands and feet they nailed to the cross [was] only a fleshly substitute."

- **_Gospel of Philip_ (Gnostic writing, third century AD)** Not actually a gospel but a collection of brief excerpts from other Gnostic writings, _Gospel of Philip_ summarizes the views of the followers of the Gnostic leader Valentinus.

Beginning after the fire in Rome in AD 64, the Emperor Nero harshly persecuted Christians, killing significant leaders such as Peter and Paul. One of the motivations for writing the Gospels may have been the deaths—because of Nero's persecution—of key eyewitnesses of the life of Jesus.

■ ***Gospel of the Savior*** **(Gnostic writing, early third century AD)** Not actually a Gospel but a few fragments from an ancient document known as Papyrus Berlin 22220, *Gospel of the Savior* seems to have been a Gnostic adaptation of *Gospel of Peter*. Also known as *Vision of the Savior*.

■ ***Gospel of Thomas*** **(Gnostic writing, mid-second century AD)** Not actually a Gospel, but a collection of sayings attributed to Jesus. Most sayings in *Gospel of Thomas* are similar to statements found in the New Testament Gospels. A few, however, seem to represent an early form of Gnosticism. Although some sayings in the book can be traced to the first century AD, the book did not emerge in its final form until the middle of the second century.

■ ***Infancy Gospel of Thomas*** **(Christian writing, mid-second century AD)** An account of the childhood of Jesus, supposedly written by the apostle Thomas. In this text, the boy Jesus uses his miraculous powers for his own benefit. The author's style of writing and his lack of knowledge about Jewish traditions suggest that the book was written in the mid-second century AD, long after the death of the apostle Thomas.

■ ***Gospel of Truth*** **(Gnostic writing, late second century AD)** Unearthed at Nag Hammadi in the 1940s, *Gospel of Truth* is a Gnostic retelling of the creation story and of the life of Jesus. According to Irenaeus of Lyons, a disciple of a Gnostic teacher named Valentinus wrote *Gospel of Truth*, also known as *Gospel of Valentinus*.

■ Why are so many people so enthralled by the "lost Gospels"?

Perhaps people long to believe that there's some knowledge or experience of Jesus Christ that isn't available in the New Testament Gospels—and, in some sense, they're correct. There *is* experience and knowledge of Jesus Christ that isn't available simply by reading the New Testament Gospels. But this knowledge and experience certainly is not available in the unreliable myths found in the "lost Gospels." The full knowledge and experience that our souls crave is available when we not only *read about* Jesus Christ but also *personally commit our lives to* Jesus Christ, the One in whom we can be "made complete" and through whom we can enter into fellowship with the God who gives us his love in "far greater abundance than any of us could ask or think" (Colossians 2:9; Ephesians 3:20).

Notes

1. See Bart Ehrman, *Lost Christianities* (New York: Oxford University Press, 2003) 3-5. Hereafter, *Lost Christianities* will be cited as *LC*, followed by the page numbers.
2. *MJ* 36.
3. Ehrman places the emergence of this principle later and summarizes it in this way: Authoritative texts had to be "ancient" (from the time of Jesus) and "apostolic" (from the first followers of Jesus or their associates) (*LC* 242-243). As Ehrman notes, two other standards came into play later, those of catholicity (widespread usage among Christians) and orthodoxy (agreement with other Scriptures). I would contend, though, that—for the earliest Christians—the categories of *orthodoxy*, *apostolicity*, and *antiquity* were not distinguishable. All three categories were rooted in the assumption that eyewitness testimony was authoritative.
4. Quoted in Eusebius, 3:39
5. It was, according to Eusebius, from these prophetesses that Papias received some stories about the apostles (Eusebius 3:39).
6. Muratorian Fragment.
7. Eusebius, 5:8.
8. *LC* 235.
9. Translated from "Muratorian Canon in Latin": Retrieved October 28, 2006, from http://www.earlychristianwritings.com/text/muratorian-latin.html.
10. Eusebius, 6:12.
11. See *LC* 16. The beginnings of blaming the crucifixion on the Jewish people can be seen in the trial before Pontius Pilate in *Gospel of Peter*, suggesting a date after the expulsion of Christians from the synagogues in the late first century AD
12. Eusebius, 6:12; cf. Tertullian of Carthage, *De Praescriptione Haereticorum*, 3:20-21: Retrieved October 28, 2006, from http://www.tertullian.org/latin/de_praescriptione_haereticorum.html.
13. Eusebius, 5:8.

Author: Timothy Paul Jones, Ed.D

Excerpted material © 2007 Dr. Timothy Paul Jones. Excerpted from the book *Misquoting Truth: A Guide to the Fallacies of Bart Ehrman's Misquoting Jesus*. Published by InterVarsity Press (www.ivpress.com). All rights reserved. Reprinted by Permission.

EARLY LISTS OF AUTHORITATIVE CHRISTIAN WRITINGS

The Fragment of Muratori (mid-second century AD, Rome)	Codex Claromontanus (late third century AD, Egypt or North Africa)	Eusebius of Caesarea's Church History (early fourth century AD, Palestine and Asia Minor)	Letter of Athanasius (AD 367)
Accepted Matthew Mark Luke John Acts Romans 1 & 2 Corinthians Galatians Ephesians Philippians Colossians 1 & 2 Thessalonians 1 & 2 Timothy Titus Philemon 1 John 2 or 3 John (or both letters, counted as one) Jude Revelation Wisdom of Solomon [Epistle to the Hebrews and the letters of Peter not mentioned at all]	**Accepted** Matthew Mark Luke John Acts Romans 1 & 2 Corinthians Galatians Ephesians Philippians Colossians 1 & 2 Thessalonians 1 & 2 Timothy Titus Philemon Hebrews* James 1 and 2 Peter 1, 2, and 3 John Jude Revelation	**Accepted** Matthew Mark Luke John Acts Romans 1 & 2 Corinthians Galatians Ephesians Philippians Colossians 1 & 2 Thessalonians 1 & 2 Timothy Titus Philemon Hebrews 1 Peter 1 John Revelation*	**Accepted** Matthew Mark Luke John Acts Romans 1 & 2 Corinthians Galatians Ephesians Philippians Colossians 1 & 2 Thessalonians 1 & 2 Timothy Titus Philemon Hebrews James 1 and 2 Peter 1, 2, and 3 John Jude Revelation
Recognized but Questioned Apocalypse of Peter	**Recognized but Questioned** Apocalypse of Peter Epistle of Barnabas The Shepherd of Hermas Acts of Paul	**Recognized but Questioned** James Jude 2 Peter 2 and 3 John	**Recognized but Questioned**
Rejected Laodiceans Alexandrians The Shepherd of Hermas	**Rejected** (All other writings)	**Rejected** Apocalypse of Peter Acts of Paul The Shepherd of Hermas Epistle of Barnabas Teaching of Twelve Apostles Gospel of Peter Gospel of Thomas Gospel of Matthias Gospel of the Hebrews Acts of Andrew Acts of John	**Rejected** (All other writings)

> This chart shows that early Christians accepted the four Gospels according to Matthew, Mark, Luke, and John long before the critics claim, and that none of the so-called lost Gospels were *ever* accepted.

* indicates that this listing may have placed this writing in the list of questionable books

The Gospels: "Lost" & Found

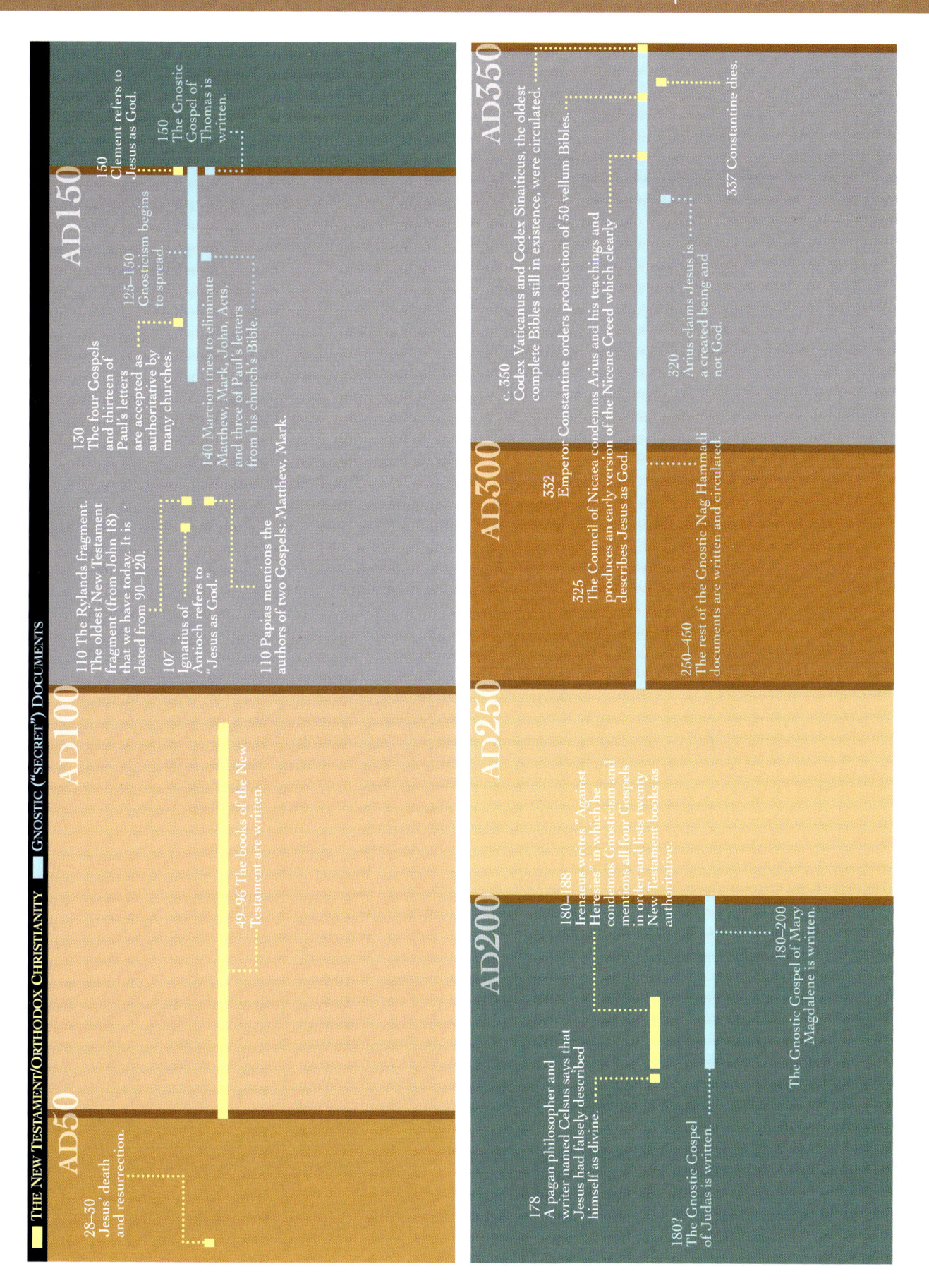

Legend:
- ■ The New Testament/Orthodox Christianity
- ■ Gnostic ("Secret") Documents

AD 50

28–30 Jesus' death and resurrection.

49–96 The books of the New Testament are written.

AD 100

107 Ignatius of Antioch refers to "Jesus as God."

110 The Rylands fragment. The oldest New Testament fragment (from John 18) that we have today. It is dated from 90–120.

110 Papias mentions the authors of two Gospels: Matthew, Mark.

AD 150

125–150 Gnosticism begins to spread.

130 The four Gospels and thirteen of Paul's letters are accepted as authoritative by many churches.

140 Marcion tries to eliminate Matthew, Mark, John, Acts, and three of Paul's letters from his church's Bible.

150 Clement refers to Jesus as God.

150 The Gnostic Gospel of Thomas is written.

AD 200

178 A pagan philosopher and writer named Celsus says that Jesus had falsely described himself as divine.

180? The Gnostic Gospel of Judas is written.

180–188 Irenaeus writes "Against Heresies" in which he condemns Gnosticism and mentions all four Gospels in order and lists twenty New Testament books as authoritative.

180–200 The Gnostic Gospel of Mary Magdalene is written.

AD 250

250–450 The rest of the Gnostic Nag Hammadi documents are written and circulated.

AD 300

325 The Council of Nicaea condemns Arius and produces an early version of the Nicene Creed which clearly describes Jesus as God.

332 Emperor Constantine condemns Arius and his teachings and orders production of 50 vellum Bibles.

AD 350

c. 350 Codex Vaticanus and Codex Sinaiticus, the oldest complete Bibles still in existence, were circulated.

320 Arius claims Jesus is a created being and not God.

337 Constantine dies.

CHRISTIANITY, CULTS, AND RELIGIONS

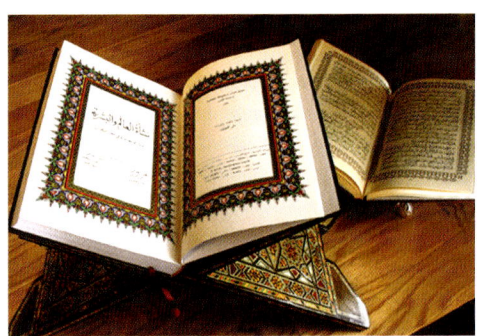

Christianity, Cults & Religions

How to Test Prophets

"If what a prophet proclaims in the name of the Lord does not take place or come true, that is a message the Lord has not spoken. That prophet has spoken presumptuously. Do not be afraid of him." —Deuteronomy 18:22

"Dear friends, do not believe every spirit, but test the spirits to see whether they are from God, because many false prophets have gone out into the world. This is how you can recognize the Spirit of God: Every spirit that acknowledges that Jesus Christ has come in the flesh is from God, but every spirit that does not acknowledge Jesus is not from God. This is the spirit of the antichrist, which you have heard is coming and even now is already in the world." —1 John 4:1–3

How to Recognize False Gospels

"But even if we or an angel from heaven should preach a gospel other than the one we preached to you, let him be eternally condemned! As we have already said, so now I say again: If anybody is preaching to you a gospel other than what you accepted, let him be eternally condemned!" —Galatians 1:8–9

How to Become a Christian

The Bible says God loved the world so much that he gave his only begotten Son, that whoever believes in him will not perish but have everlasting life (John 3:16). God loves you and wants a relationship with you. Here are God's promises:

A. **A**ll have sinned and come short of the glory of God (Romans 3:23; 6:23; 1 John 1:10).

B. **B**elieve on the Lord Jesus Christ, and you will be saved (Acts 16:31; John 1:12).

C. If you **C**onfess with your mouth the Lord Jesus, and believe in your heart that God raised him from the dead, you will be saved (Romans 10:9; Ephesians 2:8–9).

Biblical Christianity

Key Person or Founder, Date, Location	Jesus Christ. Founded about AD 30–33, in the Judean province of Palestine (Israel today), under the Roman Empire. Followers of Jesus Christ became known as Christians.
Key Writings	The Bible, written originally in Hebrew and Aramaic (Old Testament), and Greek (New Testament).
Who is God?	The one God is Triune (one God in three persons, not three gods): Father, Son, and Holy Spirit. Often the title "God" designates the first person, God the Father. God is a spiritual being without a physical body. He is personal and involved with people. He created the universe out of nothing. He is eternal, changeless, holy, loving, and perfect.
Who is Jesus?	Jesus is God, the second person of the Trinity. As God the Son, he has always existed and was never created. He is fully God and fully man (the two natures joined, not mixed). As the second person of the Trinity, he is coequal with God the Father and the Holy Spirit. In becoming man, he was begotten through the Holy Spirit and born of the Virgin Mary. Jesus is the only way to the Father, salvation, and eternal life. He died on a cross according to God's plan, as the full sacrifice and payment for our sins. He rose from the dead on the third day, spiritually and physically immortal. For the next 40 days he was seen by more than 500 eye-witnesses. His wounds were touched and he ate meals. He physically ascended to heaven. Jesus will come again visibly and physically at the end of the world to establish God's kingdom and judge the world.
Who is the Holy Spirit?	The Holy Spirit is God, the third person of the Trinity. The Holy Spirit is a person, not a force or energy field. He comforts, grieves, reproves, convicts, guides, teaches, and fills Christians. He is not the Father, nor is he the Son, Jesus Christ.
How to be Saved	Salvation is by God's grace, not by an individual's good works. Salvation must be received by faith. People must believe in their hearts that Jesus died for their sins and physically rose again, which is the assurance of forgiveness and resurrection of the body. This is God's loving plan to forgive sinful people.
What Happens after Death?	Believers go to be with Jesus. After death, all people await the final judgment. Both saved and lost people will be resurrected. Those who are saved will live with Jesus in heaven. Those who are lost will suffer the torment of eternal separation from God (hell). Jesus' bodily resurrection guarantees believers that they, too, will be resurrected and receive new immortal bodies.
Other Facts, Beliefs, or Practices	Group worship, usually in churches. No secret rites. Baptism and Lord's Supper (Communion). Active voluntary missionary efforts. Aid to those in need: the poor, widows, orphans, and downtrodden. Christians believe that Jesus is the Jewish Messiah promised to Israel in the Old Testament (Tanakh). Jesus said his followers would be known by their love for one another.

Christianity, Cults, and Religions

Jehovah's Witnesses (Watchtower Bible & Tract Society) | Mormonism (Latter-day Saints) | Seventh-day Adventism

	Jehovah's Witnesses	Mormonism	Seventh-day Adventism
Founder	Charles Taze Russell (1852–1916), later Joseph F. Rutherford (1869–1942). Began 1879 in Pennsylvania. Headquarters in Brooklyn, New York.	Joseph Smith, Jr. (1805–1844) organized what is now the Church of Jesus Christ of Latter-day Saints (LDS) in 1830 near Rochester, New York. Headquarters in Salt Lake City, Utah.	Primary organizers: James (1821–1881) and Ellen (1827–1915) White, Joseph Bates (1792–1872). Incorporated in 1863 in Michigan. Headquarters in Silver Spring, Maryland.
Writings	All current Watchtower publications, including the Bible (New World Translation only), Reasoning from the Scriptures, What Does the Bible Really Teach?; Watchtower and Awake! magazines.	The Book of Mormon, Doctrine and Covenants, Pearl of Great Price, plus the Bible (King James Version only or Smith's "Inspired Version") which is seen as less reliable. Authoritative teachings of Mormon prophets and other LDS "general authorities." Ensign and Liahona magazines.	The Bible, including Adventist paraphrase The Clear Word. Over 600 published titles by Ellen White, including The Desire of Ages and The Great Controversy. Sabbath School Bible Study Guide; SDA Bible Commentary. Adventist Review, numerous other magazines.
God	One-person God, called Jehovah. No Trinity. Jesus is the first thing Jehovah created.	God the Father was once a man, but "progressed" to godhood. He has a physical body, as does his wife (Heavenly Mother). No Trinity. Father, Son, and Holy Ghost are three separate gods. Worthy members may one day become "exalted" to godhood themselves.	God is comprised of a unity of three coeternal persons—Father, Son and Holy Spirit—who are one in motive and purpose, but not substance. God the Father is generally understood to possess a physical body. Both trinitarianism and anti-trinitarianism are believed in the church today.
Jesus	Jesus is not God. Before he lived on earth, he was Michael, the archangel. Jehovah made the universe through him. On earth he was a man who lived a perfect life. After dying on a stake (not a cross), he was resurrected as a spirit; his body was destroyed. Jesus is not coming again; he "returned" invisibly in 1914 in spirit. Very soon, he and the angels will destroy all non-Jehovah's Witnesses.	Jesus is a separate god from the Father (Elohim). He was created as a spirit child by the Father and Mother in heaven, and is the "elder brother" of all men and spirit beings (including Lucifer). His body was created through sexual union between Elohim and Mary. Jesus was married. His death on the cross does not provide full atonement for all sin, but does provide everyone with resurrection.	Ellen White says God the Father exalted Jesus to be his Son, thus provoking Lucifer's jealousy and a war in heaven. Jesus is our example to prove we can live sinlessly. His sacrifice on the cross did not complete the atonement; since 1844 he has been applying his blood in heaven in an ongoing "Investigative Judgment" after which he will return. Also identified as Michael the Archangel; most Adventist founders denied Jesus' deity.
Holy Spirit	Impersonal "holy spirit" is not God, but rather an invisible, active force from Jehovah.	The "holy spirit" is different from the "Holy Ghost." The "holy spirit" is not God, but is an influence or electricity-like emanation from God (or "light of Christ").	Originally thought to be a force or power from God, today the Holy Spirit is understood to be the third person of the Godhead.
Salvation	Be baptized as Jehovah's Witnesses. Most followers must earn everlasting life on earth by "door-to-door work." Salvation in heaven is limited to 144,000 "anointed ones." This number is already reached.	Resurrected by grace, but saved (exalted to godhood) by works, including faithfulness to church leaders, Mormon baptism, tithing, ordination, marriage, and secret temple rituals. No eternal life without Mormon membership.	Salvation by grace through faith, but maintained by commandment-keeping and repentance. Seventh-day (Saturday) Sabbath observance is the sign of the seal of God, Sunday worship is the mark of the beast. Satan is the scapegoat to be punished in the lake of fire for the sins of the saved.
Death	The 144,000 live as spirits in heaven. The rest of the righteous, the "great crowd," live on earth, and must obey God perfectly for 1,000 years or be annihilated.	Eventually nearly everyone goes to one of three separate heavenly "kingdoms," with some achieving godhood. Apostates and murderers go to "outer darkness."	Humans have no immaterial spirit, so at death the body goes into the ground and the breath goes to God. Nothing remains except in God's memory. At judgment, the lake of fire annihilates the wicked.
Beliefs/Other	Also known as the International Bible Students Association. Meet in "Kingdom Halls" instead of churches. Active members encouraged to distribute literature door-to-door. Once a year, Lord's Evening Meal (communion); only "anointed ones" may partake. Do not observe holidays or birthdays. Forbidden to vote, salute the flag, work in the military, or accept blood transfusions.	Secret temple "endowment" rituals and "celestial marriage" available only to members in good standing. Baptism on behalf of the dead. "Word of Wisdom" prohibits tobacco, alcohol, and caffeine drinks. Two-year missionary commitment encouraged. Tithing essential. Door-to-door proselytizing. Extensive social network. People of African ancestry denied full access to Mormon priesthood and privileges until 1978.	The SDA Church considers itself to be God's one, special remnant church. Old Testament clean/unclean meat laws observed. SDA "health message" includes abstinence from alcohol, tobacco, and caffeine and advocates veganism. Traditionalist SDAs believe wearing jewelry is sinful. Proselytizing programs include "Revelation seminars," health outreach.

Christianity, Cults, and Religions • 475

	Unification Church		Christian Science		Unity School of Christianity
Founder	Sun Myung Moon (1920–2012). Started "Holy Spirit Association for the Unification of World Christianity" (Family Federation for World Peace and Unification) in 1954 in Korea. Known in the U.S. as "Lovin' Life Ministries." Based in New York City.	**Founder**	Mary Baker Eddy (1821–1910). Founded 1875 in Massachusetts. Headquarters in Boston, Massachusetts.	**Founder**	Charles (1854–1948) and Myrtle (1845–1931) Fillmore. Founded 1889 in Kansas City, Missouri. Headquarters in Unity Village, Missouri.
Writings	*Divine Principle* by Sun Myung Moon, considered the "Completed Testament." *Outline of the Principle, Level 4*, and the Bible. (The Bible is "not the truth itself, but a textbook teaching the truth.")	**Writings**	*Science and Health, With Key to the Scriptures*; *Miscellaneous Writings*; *Manual of the Mother Church*; and other books by Mrs. Eddy. The Bible (not as reliable). *Christian Science Journal*, *Christian Science Sentinel*, and other official periodicals.	**Writings**	*Unity* magazine. *Lessons in Truth*, *Metaphysical Bible Dictionary*, the Bible (not as reliable, interpreted with "hidden" meanings).
God	God is both positive and negative. God created the universe out of himself; the universe is God's "body." God does not know the future, is suffering, and needs man (Sun Myung Moon) to make him happy. No Trinity.	**God**	According to Mrs. Eddy, God is an impersonal Principle of life, truth, love, intelligence, and spirit. God is all that truly exists; matter is an illusion. *Mary Baker Eddy*	**God**	Invisible impersonal power. "God" is interchangeable with "Principle," "Law," "Being," "Mind," "Spirit." God is in everything, much as the soul is in the body. No Trinity. The spirit is reality; matter is not.
Jesus	Jesus was a perfect man, not God. He is the son of Zechariah, not born of a virgin. His mission was to unite the Jews behind him, find a perfect bride, and begin a perfect family. The mission failed. Jesus did not resurrect physically. The second coming of Christ is fulfilled in Sun Myung Moon, who is superior to Jesus and will finish Jesus' mission.	**Jesus**	Jesus was not the Christ, but a man who displayed the Christ idea. ("Christ" means perfection, not a person.) Jesus was not God, and God can never become man or flesh. He did not suffer and could not suffer for sins. He did not die on the cross. He was not resurrected physically. He will not literally come back.	**Jesus**	Jesus was a man and not the Christ. Instead, he was a man who had "Christ Consciousness." "Christ" is a state of perfection in every person. Jesus had lived many times before and was in search of his own salvation. Jesus did not die as a sacrifice for anyone's sins. Jesus did not rise physically and will never return to earth in physical form.
Holy Spirit	The Holy Spirit is a feminine spirit who works with Jesus in the spirit world to lead people to Sun Myung Moon.	**Holy Spirit**	Holy spirit is defined as the teaching of Christian Science. Impersonal power.	**Holy Spirit**	The Holy Spirit is the law of God in action, the "executive power of both Father and Son." A "definite" thought in the mind of man.
Salvation	Obedience to and acceptance of the True Parents (Moon and his wife) eliminate sin and result in perfection. Those married by Moon and his wife drink a special holy wine containing 21 ingredients (including the True Parents' blood).	**Salvation**	Humanity is already eternally saved. Sin, evil, sickness, and death are not real.	**Salvation**	By recognizing that each person is as much a Son of God as Jesus is. There is no evil, no devil, no sin, no poverty, and no old age. A person is reincarnated until he learns these truths and becomes "perfect."
Death	After death one goes to the spirit world. There is no resurrection. Members advance by convincing others to follow Sun Myung Moon. Everyone will be saved, even Satan.	**Death**	Death is not real. Heaven and hell are states of mind. The way to reach heaven is by attaining harmony (oneness with God).	**Death**	Death is a result of wrong thinking. One moves to a different body (reincarnation) until enlightenment. No literal heaven or hell.
Beliefs/Other	Emphasis on mediumism (channeling) to contact the dead, "liberate" souls of one's ancestors. Mass marriages, based on different racial backgrounds, arranged and performed by Moon. Efforts to persuade churches to remove their crosses. Belief that Jesus bows down to Rev. Moon, who is the King of Kings, Lord of Lords, and the Lamb of God.	**Beliefs/Other**	Members use Christian Science "practitioners" (authorized professional healers who "treat" supposed illnesses for a fee) instead of doctors. Healing comes through realizing one cannot really be sick or hurt and that the body cannot be ill, suffer pain, or die since matter is an illusion. Attracts followers by claims of miraculous healing. Publishes *Christian Science Monitor* newspaper.	**Beliefs/Other**	Worship services in Unity churches. Counseling and prayer ministry ("Silent Unity") by phone and mail. It is reported that Unity receives millions of prayer requests annually. Unity devotionals, such as *Daily Word*, are used by members of other religious groups and churches. Millions of pieces of literature are printed each year.

476 • Christianity, Cults, and Religions

	New Age	Wicca	Scientology
Founder	Based on Eastern mysticism, Hinduism, and paganism. Popularized in part by actress Shirley MacLaine (1934–) in the 1980s and 1990s. Beliefs vary.	No one person. Roots in 19th-century Britain. Partly inspired by Margaret Murray (1863–1963) and organized by Gerald Gardner (1884–1964) in the 1930s to 1950s.	Founded by L. Ron Hubbard (1911–1986) in 1954 in California. Major headquarter facilities in California and Florida.
Writings	No holy book. Use selected Bible passages; *I Ching*; Hindu, Buddhist, and Taoist writings; and Native American beliefs. Writings on astrology, mysticism, and magic.	No holy books; however, many groups use *The Book of Shadows*, first compiled by Gardner and later expanded by him and other leaders. Other popular works include *A Witches' Bible* and *The Spiral Dance*.	*Dianetics: The Modern Science of Mental Health* and others by Hubbard. *The Way to Happiness*.
God	Everything and everyone is God. God is an impersonal force or principle, not a person. People have unlimited inner power and need to discover it.	The supreme being is called the Goddess, sometimes the Goddess and God, or goddess and horned god ("Lord and Lady"). The Goddess can be a symbol, the impersonal force in everything, or a personal being. Wiccans can be pantheists, polytheists, or both.	Does not define God or Supreme Being, but rejects biblical description of God. Everyone is a "thetan," an immortal spirit with unlimited powers over its own universe, but not all are aware of this.
Jesus	Jesus is not the one true God. He is not a savior, but a spiritual model and guru, and is now an "ascended master." He was a New Ager who tapped into divine power in the same way that anyone can. Many believe he went east to India or Tibet and learned mystical truths. He did not rise physically from the dead, but "rose" into a higher spiritual realm.	Jesus is either rejected altogether or sometimes considered a spiritual teacher who taught love and compassion.	Jesus is rarely mentioned in Scientology. Jesus was not the Creator, nor was he an "operating thetan" (in control of supernatural powers, cleared from mental defects). Jesus did not die for sins.
Holy Spirit	Sometimes considered a psychic force. Man is divine and can experience psychic phenomena such as contacting unearthly beings.	The Holy Spirit is not part of this belief. However, some Wiccans may refer to "Spirit" as a kind of divine energy.	The Holy Spirit is not part of this belief.
Salvation	Need to offset bad karma with good karma. Can tap into supernatural power through meditation, self-awareness, and "spirit guides." Followers use terms such as "reborn" to describe this new self-awareness.	Wiccans do not believe that humanity is sinful or needs saving. It is important for Wiccans to honor and work for the preservation of nature (which they equate with the Goddess).	No sin or need to repent. Salvation is freedom from reincarnation. One must work with an "auditor" on his "engrams" (negative experience units) to achieve the state of "clear." One then progresses up the "bridge to total freedom" to higher "Operating Thetan" states and eventual control over matter, energy, space, and time (MEST).
Death	Human reincarnations occur until a person reaches oneness with God. No eternal life as a resurrected person. No literal heaven or hell.	The body replenishes the earth, which is the Goddess's wish. Some Wiccans are agnostic about life after death, others believe in reincarnation. Some believe in a wonderful place called Summerland.	Hell is a myth, and heaven is a "false dream."
Beliefs/Other	Can include yoga, meditation, visualization, astrology, channeling, hypnosis, trances, and tarot card readings. Use of crystals to get in harmony with God (Energy), for psychic healing, for contact with spirits, and for developing higher consciousness or other psychic powers. Strive for world unity and peace. Emphasis on holistic health.	Wiccans practice divination and spell-casting, with most rituals performed in a circle. Many Wiccans are part of a coven (local assembly), though many others are "solitary." Covens meet for ritual and seasonal holidays, including the eight major holidays (such as Vernal Equinox, Summer Solstice, and Beltane). Wicca is an occultic "nature religion," not Satanism.	Members observe birth of Hubbard and anniversary of publication of *Dianetics*. Controversy follows the group worldwide. *Time* magazine and *Reader's Digest* have published damaging exposés. Organizations related to Scientology include Narconon, Criminon, Way to Happiness Foundation, WISE, Hubbard College of Administration, Applied Scholastics.

Christianity, Cults, and Religions • 477

Islam

Founder

Founded in Mecca, Arabia by Muhammad (AD 570–632), considered the greatest man who ever lived and the last of more than 124,000 messengers sent by Allah (God). Main types: Sunni ("people of the tradition"), Shi'a ("party of Ali"), Sufi (mystics).

Writings

The Holy Qur'an (Koran), revealed to Muhammad by the angel Gabriel. Essential commentaries are found in the *Sunnah* ("tradition"), composed of *Hadith* ("narrative") and *Sirah* ("journey"). The Qur'an affirms the biblical Torah, Psalms, and Gospels, but Jews and Christians have corrupted the original texts.

God

Allah is One and absolutely unique. He cannot be known. The greatest sin in Islam is *shirk*, or associating anything with Allah. Human qualities like fatherhood cannot be attributed to Allah. Many Muslims think that Christians believe in three gods and are therefore guilty of *shirk*.

Jesus

Jesus (*Isa* in Arabic) was not God or the Son of God. His virgin birth is likened to Adam's creation. He was sinless, a worker of miracles, and one of the most respected prophets sent by Allah. He was not crucified or resurrected. He, not Muhammad, will return to play a special role before the future judgment day, perhaps turning Christians to Islam.

Holy Spirit

"Holy spirit" can refer to Allah, to the angel Gabriel, or to a spirit used by Allah to give life to man and inspire the prophets.

Salvation

Humans are basically good, but fallible and need guidance. The balance between good and bad deeds determines one's destiny in paradise or hell. Allah may tip the balances toward heaven. One should always live with the fear of Allah and judgment day.

Death

Belief in bodily resurrection. One may pray for and seek favor for the dead before judgment day. Paradise includes a garden populated with *houris*, maidens designed by Allah to provide sexual pleasure to righteous men.

Beliefs/Other

Muslims meet in mosques for prayers, sermons, counsel. Emphasis on hospitality, developing a sense of community, and maintaining honor (or avoiding shame). *Shari'a* (Islamic law) governs all aspects of life in places where it is enforced. *Jihad* ("fight") may be used to refer either to one's inner struggle to obey God or to literal warfare. Muslims who convert to Christianity or other religions face persecution and possible death.

Comparing Sunni and Shi'a Islam

Adherents
Sunni: Over 1 billion worldwide
Shi'a: Estimated 170 million, primarily in Iran, Iraq, Lebanon, Azerbaijan, Bahrain

Succession
Sunni: Muhammad's successors (called *caliphs*) should ideally be chosen by consensus/election. The first was Abu Bakr (c. AD 573–634), and over the centuries many others followed. No new caliphs since 1924.
Shi'a: Muhammad's successors (called *imams*) should be from his family and descendants (*Ahl al-Bayt*). The first of these was his cousin and son-in-law, Ali (c. AD 600–661), and thereafter all imams were bloodline descendants from Fatimah (Muhammad's daughter and Ali's wife). No new imams since AD 869.

Authoritative Writings
Sunni: The Qur'an, plus an emphasis on Hadith and other sayings attributed to companions of Muhammad such as Abu Bakr, Umar, and Aisha.
Shi'a: The Qur'an, plus an emphasis on Hadith and other sayings attributed to members of Muhammad's family and their supporters.

Main Teachings and Practices
Sunni: Five Pillars (or duties): Profession of Faith (*shahadah*); Prayers (*salat*); Almsgiving (*zakat*); Fasting during Ramadan (*sawm*); Pilgrimage to Mecca (*hajj*). Six Beliefs: in Allah; in Prophets and Messengers; in Angels; in Holy Books; in the Day of Judgment and the Resurrection; in the Decree (destiny/fate)
Shi'a: Ten Central Practices: Profession of Faith (*shahadah*); Prayers (*salat*); Almsgiving (*zakat*); One-Fifth Tax (*khums*); Fasting during Ramadan (*sawm*); Pilgrimage to Mecca (*hajj*); Religious War (*jihad*); Enjoining to Do Good (*amr-bil-ma'ruf*); Exhortation to Desist from Evil (*nahi-anil-munkar*); Loving the Ahl al-Bayt and their followers (*tawalla*); Disassociation from the Enemies of the *Ahl al-Bayt* (*tabarra*) Five Principles: Oneness (*tawhid*); Justice (*adl*); Prophethood (*nubuwwah*); Leadership (*imamah*); Day of Resurrection (*yawm al qiyyamah*)

Major Divisions
Sunni: Four "schools of law" (*Madh'hab*)—Hanafi, Maliki, Hanbali, Shafi'i
Shi'a: Three branches—majority "Twelvers" (*Jafari*), who believe in a succession of twelve infallible, divinely ordained imams; "Seveners" (*Ismaili*); and "Fivers" (*Zaidi*)

Eschatology
Sunni: Majority believe that a figure known as the *Mahdi* ("guided one"), from Muhammad's family, will appear with Jesus before the final judgment.
Shi'a: Majority believe in a series of twelve imams serving as Muhammad's spiritual and political successors. The final one, Muhammad al-Mahdi (b. AD 869), is alive but hidden (in "occultation") since AD 874; at the proper time he will appear with Jesus.

Nation of Islam

Founder

Wallace D. Fard (1877?–1934?) in Detroit in 1930, but led by Elijah Muhammad (1897–1975) since 1934. Current head is Louis Farrakhan (1933–). Headquarters in Chicago, Illinois.

Louis Farrakhan

Writings

Publicly, the Holy Qur'an is authoritative and the Bible is quoted often, but *Message to the Blackman in America*, *Our Saviour Has Arrived*, and other books by Elijah Muhammad supply its distinctive views. Current teachings are in *The Final Call* newspaper and speeches of Minister Farrakhan.

God

Officially, there is one God, Allah, as described in the Qur'an. But Elijah Muhammad's teachings are also true: God is a black man, millions of Allahs have lived and died since creation, collectively the black race is God, and Master Fard is the Supreme Allah and Savior.

Jesus

Officially, Jesus is a sinless prophet of Allah. Privately, Jesus was born from adultery between Mary and Joseph, who was already married to another woman. Jesus was not crucified, but stabbed in the heart by a police officer. He is still buried in Jerusalem. Prophecies of Jesus' return refer to Master Fard, Elijah Muhammad, or to Louis Farrakhan.

Holy Spirit

The Holy Spirit is not significant to this belief, but is generally regarded as the power of God or as the angel Gabriel who spoke to the prophet Muhammad.

Salvation

People sin, but are not born sinful; salvation is through submission to Allah and good works. Older beliefs still held include: Fard is the savior, salvation comes from knowledge of self and realizing that the white race are devils who displaced the black race.

Death

There is no consciousness or any spiritual existence after death. Heaven and hell are symbols. Statements about the resurrection refer to awakening "mentally dead" people by bringing them true teachings.

Beliefs/Other

Farrakhan's public messages coexist with earlier, esoteric doctrines. Elijah Muhammad's older views (such as polytheism, God as the black race, Master Fard as Allah incarnate, whites as devils bred to cause harm) are still distributed, but public preaching now focuses on Islamic themes (one eternal God, non-racial emphasis) with frequent use of the Bible.

478 • Christianity, Cults, and Religions

Bahá'í Faith | Judaism | Kabbalah Centre

Founder

Bahá'í Faith: Siyyid 'Alí-Muhammad, "the Báb" (1819–1850) and Mírzá Husayn-'Alí, "Bahá'u'lláh" (1817–1892). Founded 1844 in Iran. Headquarters in Haifa, Israel.

Judaism: Abraham of the Bible, about 2000 BC, and Moses in the Middle East. There are three main branches of Judaism—Orthodox, Conservative, and Reform—each with its own beliefs.

Kabbalah Centre: Shraga Feivel Gruberger (1927?–2013), now known as Philip S. Berg. Followers claim it was originally founded in 1922 by Rav Yehuda Ashlag (1885–1954) in Jerusalem. Headquarters in Los Angeles, California.

Writings

Bahá'í Faith: Writings of Bahá'u'lláh and 'Abdu'l-Bahá, including *Kitáb-i-Aqdas* ("Most Holy Book") and *Kitáb-i-Íqán* ("Book of Certitude"). The Bible, interpreted spiritually to conform to Bahá'í theology.

Judaism: The Tanakh (Old Testament), and especially the Torah (first five books of the Bible). The Talmud (explanation of the Tanakh). Teachings of each branch. Writings of sages, such as Maimonides.

Kabbalah Centre: The Zohar ("Book of Splendor"), the Centre's 23-volume translation of mystical Aramaic and Hebrew writings which first appeared in Spain in the 13th–14th centuries. Books by Philip Berg and his son, Yehuda, including *Kabbalah for the Layman*, *The Essential Zohar*, and *The 72 Names of God*.

God

Bahá'í Faith: God is an unknowable divine being who has revealed himself through nine "manifestations" (prophets), including Adam, Moses, Krishna, Buddha, Jesus, Muhammad, and Bahá'u'lláh. No Trinity.

Judaism: God is spirit. To Orthodox Jews, God is personal, all-powerful, eternal, and compassionate. To other Jews, God is impersonal, unknowable, and defined in a number of ways. No Trinity.

Kabbalah Centre: The supreme being (*Ein Sof*, "endlessness") is unknowable, infinite, and impersonal—described as both "everything" and "in everything." This Creator God is revealed through ten emanations or manifestations, called *sefirot* ("numbers"), which are illustrated with male and female aspects as ten points on the Kabbalah "Tree of Life" diagram.

Jesus

Bahá'í Faith: Jesus is one of many manifestations of God. Each manifestation supersedes the previous, giving new teachings about God. Jesus, who superseded Moses, was superseded by Muhammad, and most recently by the greatest, Bahá'u'lláh ("Glory of Allah"). Jesus is not God and did not rise from the dead. He is not the only way to God. The "Christ spirit" returned to earth in Bahá'u'lláh, who is superior to Jesus.

Judaism: Jesus is seen either as an extremist false messiah or a good but martyred Jewish rabbi (teacher). Many Jews do not consider Jesus at all. Jews (except Messianic Jews and Hebrew Christians) do not believe he was the Messiah, Son of God, or that he rose from the dead. Orthodox Jews believe the Messiah will restore the Jewish kingdom and eventually rule the earth.

Kabbalah Centre: Jesus is not God, nor is he the Jewish Messiah (who is yet to come). Some believe Jesus was a Kabbalist himself.

"Tree of Life" diagram

Holy Spirit

Bahá'í Faith: Holy Spirit is divine energy from God that empowers every manifestation. "Spirit of Truth" refers to Bahá'u'lláh.

Judaism: Some believe the Holy Spirit is another name for God's activity on earth. Others say it is God's love or power.

Kabbalah Centre: *Ru'ah HaKodesh* (the "spirit of holiness") is said to be a state of the soul that enables one to prophesy.

Salvation

Bahá'í Faith: Faith in the manifestation of God (Bahá'u'lláh). Knowing and living by Bahá'u'lláh's principles and teachings.

Lotus Temple, New Delhi, India

Judaism: Some Jews believe that prayer, repentance, and obeying the Law are necessary for salvation. Others believe that salvation is the improvement of society.

Kabbalah Centre: Man is a vessel with the spark of the Creator; he repairs God/the universe by right living and sharing so he can hold more of the Creator's light. Kabbalah enables us to understand and live in harmony with spiritual laws on which the universe operates.

Death

Bahá'í Faith: Personal immortality based on good works, with rewards for the faithful. Heaven and hell are "allegories for nearness and remoteness from God," not actual places.

Judaism: There will be a physical resurrection. The obedient will live forever with God, and the unrighteous will suffer. Some Jews do not believe in a conscious life after death.

Kabbalah Centre: Followers believe in reincarnation, not resurrection. Man is said to climb the Tree of Life back to God, and thus return to Paradise and "restore Eden."

Beliefs/Other

Bahá'í Faith: Bahá'í originated as an Islamic sect and is severely persecuted in Iran. Bahá'í teaches that all religions have the same source, principles, and aims. Stress on oneness and world unity. Regular local gatherings called "feasts," administrative meetings called "spiritual assemblies." "Universal House of Justice" in Haifa, Israel, is the ultimate governing body.

Judaism: Meeting in synagogues on the Sabbath (Sabbath is Friday evening to Saturday evening). Circumcision of males. Many holy days and festivals, including Passover, Sukkoth, Hanukkah, Rosh Hashanah, Yom Kippur, Purim. Jerusalem is considered the holy city.

Kabbalah Centre: Evil is not a moral issue, but a question of violating universal principles. Controversy over expensive merchandise, courses, and fundraising methods. Followers use the red string bracelet and other talismans to protect themselves from the "Evil Eye" and various negative spiritual influences. Extensive use of astrology and meditation.

Christianity, Cults, and Religions • 479

	Hinduism		Hare Krishna (ISKCON)		Transcendental Meditation (TM)
Founder	No one founder. Began 1800–1000 BC in India. Main types: Vaishnavism, Shaivism, and Shaktism.	Founder	A. C. Bhaktivedanta Swami Prabhupada (1896–1977) began the International Society for Krishna Consciousness in 1965 in New York. Based on 16th-century Hindu teachings. Headquarters in Mayapur, India.	Founder	Maharishi Mahesh Yogi (1918?–2008). Founded 1955–1958 in India, based on Hinduism and karma yoga. Headquarters near Vlodrop, the Netherlands. Also called World Plan Executive Council.
Writings	Many writings, including the Vedas (oldest, about 1000 BC), the Upanishads, and the *Bhagavad-Gita*.	Writings	*Back to Godhead* magazine. Prabhupada's translations of and commentaries on Hindu scriptures, especially *Bhagavad-Gita As It Is* and *Srimad-Bhagavatam*.	Writings	Hindu scriptures including the *Bhagavad-Gita*. *Meditations of Maharishi Mahesh Yogi*, *Science of Being and Art of Living*, other writings by the founder.
God	God is "The Absolute," a universal spirit. Everyone is part of God (Brahman), but most people are not aware of it. People worship manifestations of Brahman (gods and goddesses).	God	God is Lord Krishna. Krishna is a personal creator; the souls of all living things are part of him. ISKCON teaches that what Krishna does freely for his own pleasure (intoxication, sex outside of marriage) is prohibited to his devotees.	God	Each part of creation makes up "God" (Brahman). Supreme Being is not personal. All creation is divine; "all is one."
Jesus	Jesus Christ is a teacher, a guru, or an avatar (an incarnation of Vishnu). He is a son of God as are others. His death does not atone for sins and he did not rise from the dead.	Jesus	Jesus is not important to this group. He is usually thought of as an enlightened vegetarian teacher who taught meditation. He is not an incarnation of God. Some Krishna devotees consider Jesus to be Krishna. Others say he is a great avatar (teacher).	Jesus	Jesus is not uniquely God. Like all persons, Jesus had a divine essence. Unlike most, he discovered it. Christ didn't suffer and couldn't suffer for people's sins.
Holy Spirit	The Holy Spirit is not part of this belief.	Holy Spirit	The Holy Spirit is not part of this belief.	Holy Spirit	The Holy Spirit is not part of this belief.
Salvation	Release from the cycles of reincarnation. Achieved through yoga and meditation. Can take many lifetimes. Final salvation is absorption or union with Brahman, like a raindrop falling into the ocean.	Salvation	Chanting Krishna's name constantly, total devotion to Krishna, worshipping images, and obeying the rules of ISKCON throughout many reincarnated lives, releases a follower from bad karma.	Salvation	Humans have forgotten their inner divinity. Salvation consists of doing good in excess of evil in order to evolve to the highest state (final union of the self with Brahman) through reincarnation.
Death	Reincarnation into a better status (good karma) if a person has behaved well; if badly, a person can be reborn and pay for past sins (bad karma) by suffering.	Death	Those who are unenlightened continue in endless reincarnation (rebirth on earth) based on the sinful acts of a person's previous life.	Death	Reincarnation is based on karma (reaping the consequences of one's actions) until loss of self into union with Brahman. No heaven or hell.
Beliefs/Other	Many Hindus worship stone and wooden idols in temples, homes. Disciples meditate on a word, phrase, or picture; may wear orange robes and have shaved heads. Many use a mark, called a *tilak*, on the forehead to represent the spiritual "third eye." Yoga involves meditation, chanting, breathing exercises. Some gurus demand complete obedience. Foundation of New Age, TM.	Beliefs/Other	Public chanting of Hare Krishna "Maha Mantra," yoga, food offerings, soliciting donations. "Four regulative principles" require vegetarian diet, no intoxicants, no gambling, and sex for procreation only. New members are often attracted through feasts and Indian cultural programs. Followers are given new names and may cut family ties.	Beliefs/Other	Mentally recite a mantra (word associated with a Hindu god). Meditate twice a day to relax and achieve union with Brahman. Maharishi University of Management in Iowa offers advanced T.M. programs in "levitation" and "invisibility." Practices include yoga, Hindu astrology, use of crystals, and idol worship (offerings of flowers, fruit, and cloth for Maharishi's dead teacher, Guru Dev).

480 • Christianity, Cults, and Religions

	Sikhism		Buddhism		Soka Gakkai International
Founder	Guru Nanak Dev Ji (1469–1539), in what is now the Punjab in Pakistan. Nine gurus followed (1504–1708). Main place of worship is the Golden Temple in Amritsar, India.	**Founder**	Gautama Siddhartha, (563–483 BC), also known as Buddha ("Enlightened One"). Founded in modern-day Nepal and India as a reformation of Hinduism. Main types: Theravada, Mahayana, Vajrayana.	**Founder**	Tsunesaburo Makiguchi (1871–1944) and Josei Toda (1900–1958). Founded 1930 in Japan. Based on 13th-century Nichiren Buddhism. Headquarters in Tokyo, Japan.
Writings	Main scripture is the *Sri Guru Granth Sahib* ("the master book," also called *Adi Granth*), first compiled in AD 1604. It is worshiped by Sikhs, who consider it their final and perpetual guru. Other key works include the *Dasam Granth*, *Varan Bhai Gurdas*, and *Sikh Reht Maryada*.	**Writings**	The *Mahavastu* ("Great Story," a collection covering the Buddha's life story), the *Jataka Tales* (550 stories of the former lives of the Buddha), the *Tripitaka* ("Three Baskets"), and the *Tantras* (as recorded in Tibetan Buddhism).	**Writings**	The *Lotus Sutra* (a sutra is a discourse of the Buddha as recorded by his disciples). *The Major Writings of Nichiren Daishonin*, plus writings of Daisaku Ikeda.
God	One omnipresent god (referred to as *Waheguru*, "Wondrous Teacher"), who is known to the spiritually "awakened" only through meditation. Sikhism is also pantheistic, considering the universe itself part of God (leaving no clear distinction between the Creator and creation). Representing God by pictures or idols is forbidden.	**God**	The Buddha himself did not believe in the existence of God. Others speak of the Buddha as a universal enlightened consciousness or as a god.	**God**	There is no god in Soka Gakkai. Followers hold to a monistic worldview, believing that there is no separation between creator and creature and that they are protected by Buddhist, Hindu, and Shinto gods that they regard as spiritual forces.
Jesus	Jesus is not specifically part of this belief, although the *Adi Granth* specifically denies the Trinity and describes God as "beyond birth" and incarnation.	**Jesus**	Jesus Christ is not part of the historic Buddhist worldview. Buddhists in the West today generally view Jesus as an enlightened teacher, while Buddhists in Asia believe Jesus is an *avatar* or a *Bodhisattva*, but not God.	**Jesus**	Jesus Christ is not part of this belief.
Holy Spirit	The Holy Spirit is not part of this belief.	**Holy Spirit**	The Holy Spirit is not part of this belief. Buddhists do believe in spirits, and some practice deity yoga and invite spirit possession.	**Holy Spirit**	The Holy Spirit is not part of this belief.
Salvation	Bondage to the material realm and the "five evils" (ego, anger, greed, attachment, and lust) condemn the soul to 8.4 million reincarnations. Those who successfully overcome these evils through proper behavior and devotion will be released from karma and the cycle of rebirth (*samsara*).	**Salvation**	The goal of life is *nirvana*, to eliminate all desires or cravings, and in this way escape suffering. The Eightfold Path is a system to free Buddhists from desiring anything and eventually achieve nonexistence.	**Salvation**	Enlightenment, prosperity, and healing come from chanting *nam-myoho-renge-kyo*, a mantra (phrase) expressing devotion to the law of karma. Fulfilling worldly desires brings enlightenment, which can be achieved in one lifetime.
Death	Upon death, those who escape *samsara* will be absorbed into God and lose their individuality, like a raindrop falling into the ocean. The *Adi Granth* both affirms and denies existence of a literal heaven and hell.	**Death**	Reincarnation. People do not have their own individual souls or spirits, but one's desires and feelings may be reincarnated into another person.	**Death**	Repeated reincarnation until one awakens to one's Buddha nature, then enters nirvana (escaping the cycle of rebirth). Heaven and hell are two of ten states of existence. After death, one enters a suspended state called *Ku*.
Beliefs/Other	Baptized (*Khalsa*) Sikhs are known by their use of the "five K's": the *kirpan* (a small ceremonial sword), *kes* (uncut hair), *kanga* (a small wooden comb), *kachera* (knee-length shorts), and *kara* (steel bracelet). Adult males wear a turban and include "Singh" in their names. Emphasis on full equality of men and women. Meeting places called *gurdwaras*.	**Beliefs/Other**	Eightfold Path recommends right knowledge, intentions, speech, conduct, livelihood, right effort, mindfulness, and meditation. Some Buddhist groups talk about an "eternal Buddha" (life-force). Through the "Doctrine of Assimilation" the belief systems of other religions are blended into their form of Buddhism.	**Beliefs/Other**	Worship of a scroll called the *Gohonzon* by chanting *nam-myoho-renge-kyo* (roughly translated, "hail to the mystic law of cause and effect"). *Shakubuku* (literally, "the tearing and crushing of other faiths") is their form of proselytizing, which they believe helps them change their karma. Soka University is their main educational institution in the United States.

Denominations Comparison

	Catholic Church	**Orthodox Churches**
Founder and Date	Catholics consider Jesus' disciple Peter (died c. AD 66) the first pope; Gregory the Great (pope, AD 540–604) was a key figure in the pope's office. At that time, the pope came to be viewed as ruling over the whole church.	AD 330: Emperor Constantine renamed the city of Byzantium "Constantinople," which became the city of the leading patriarch in the "Great Schism" of 1054.
Adherents	1.2 billion worldwide 62 million USA	225–300 million worldwide 1 million USA
Scripture	The Scriptures teach without error the truth needed for our salvation. Scripture must be interpreted within the Tradition of the Church. The canon includes 46 books for the Old Testament including deuterocanonical books (the Apocrypha) and 27 books for the New Testament.	The Scriptures are without error in matters of faith only. Scripture is to be interpreted by Sacred Tradition, especially the seven Ecumenical Councils which met from AD 325–787. The canon includes 49 Old Testament books (the Catholic Bible plus three more) and the 27 New Testament books.
God	The one Creator and Lord of all, existing eternally as the Trinity (Father, Son, and Holy Spirit).	The one Creator and Lord of all, existing eternally as the Trinity (Father, Son, and Holy Spirit).
Jesus	The eternal Son incarnate, fully God and fully man, conceived and born of the Virgin Mary, died on the cross for our sins, rose bodily from the grave, ascended into heaven, and will come again in glory to judge us all.	The eternal Son incarnate, fully God and fully man, conceived and born of the Virgin Mary, died on the cross for our sins, rose bodily from the grave, ascended into heaven, and will come again in glory to judge us all.
Salvation	Christ died as a substitutionary sacrifice for our sins; God by his grace infuses a supernatural gift of faith in Christ in those who are baptized, which is maintained by doing works of love and receiving Penance and the Eucharist.	In Christ, God became human so that human beings might be deified (*theosis*), that is, have the energy of God's life in them. Through baptism and participation in the church, God's people receive the benefits of Christ's redeeming work as they persevere.
Afterlife	The souls of the faithful go to heaven either immediately or, if imperfectly purified in this life, after purgatory. The souls of the wicked at death are immediately consigned to eternal punishment in hell.	At death, the souls of the faithful are purified as needed (a process of growth, not punishment), then get a foretaste of eternal blessing in heaven. The souls of the wicked get a foretaste of eternal torment in hell.
The Church	The church is the Mystical Body of Christ, established by Christ with the bishop of Rome (the pope), who may at times pronounce dogma (doctrine required of all members) infallibly, as its earthly head. It is united (*one*) in a sacred (*holy*) worldwide (*catholic*) community through the succession of bishops whose ordination goes back to the apostles (*apostolic*); Christians not in communion with the Catholic Church are called "separated brethren."	The church is the Body of Christ in unbroken historical connection to the apostles, changelessly maintaining the faith of the undivided church as expressed in the creeds. It is one, holy, catholic, and apostolic, with churches organized nationally (Armenian, Greek, Russian, and so forth) with its bishops under the leadership of patriarchs (the pope being recognized as one of several), of which that of Constantinople has primacy of honor.
Sacraments	Baptism removes original sin (usually in infants). In the Eucharist, the substances (but not the properties) of bread and wine are changed into Jesus' body and blood (transubstantiation).	Baptism initiates God's life in the one baptized (usually infants). In the Eucharist, bread and wine are changed into Jesus' body and blood (a Mystery to be left unexplained).
Other Beliefs and Practices	Mary was conceived by her mother immaculately (free of original sin), remained a virgin perpetually, and was assumed bodily into heaven. She is the Mother of the Church and is considered an object of devotion and veneration (a show of honor that stops short of worship).	Mary conceived Jesus virginally. She remained a virgin perpetually, and (in tradition, not dogma) was assumed bodily into heaven. Icons (images of Christ, Mary, or the saints) are objects of veneration through which God is to be worshiped.
Divisions and Trends	About one-fourth of Catholics are doctrinally conservative. Many priests and members tend to accept liberal, pluralist beliefs contrary to church teaching.	A significant proportion are doctrinally conservative. Most Orthodox bodies are members of the World Council of Churches, whose liberal leanings have long caused concern.

Denominations Comparison

	Lutheran Churches	**Anglican Churches**
Founder and Date	1517: Martin Luther's "95 Theses" (challenges to Catholic teaching) usually mark the beginning of the Protestant Reformation. 1530: The Augsburg Confession is the first formal Lutheran statement of faith.	1534: King Henry VIII was declared head of the Church of England. 1549: Thomas Cranmer produced the first Book of Common Prayer.
Adherents	80 million worldwide 6.5 million USA	80 million worldwide 2 million USA
Scripture	Scripture alone is the authoritative witness to the gospel (some parts more directly or fully than others). Conservatives view Scripture as inerrant. The standard Protestant canon of 39 Old Testament books and 27 New Testament books is accepted.	Scripture contains the truth that is necessary for salvation and is the primary norm for faith, but must be interpreted in light of tradition and reason. The canon includes 39 Old Testament books and 27 New Testament books (the Apocrypha is respected but not viewed as Scripture).
God	The one Creator and Lord of all, existing eternally as the Trinity (Father, Son, and Holy Spirit).	The one Creator and Lord of all, existing eternally as the Trinity (Father, Son, and Holy Spirit).
Jesus	The eternal Son incarnate, fully God and fully man, conceived and born of the Virgin Mary, died on the cross for our sins, rose bodily from the grave, ascended into heaven, and will come again in glory to judge us all.	The eternal Son incarnate, fully God and fully man, conceived and born of the Virgin Mary, died on the cross for our sins, rose bodily from the grave, ascended into heaven, and will come again in glory to judge us all.
Salvation	We are saved by grace alone when God imputes to us his gift of righteousness through faith alone (*sola fide*) in Christ, who died for our sins. Good works are the inevitable result of true faith, but in no way the basis of our right standing before God.	Christ suffered and died as an offering for sin, freeing us from sin and reconciling us to God; we share in Christ's victory when in baptism we become living members of the church, believing in him and keeping his commandments.
Afterlife	The souls of believers upon dying go immediately to be with Christ, and at Christ's return, their bodies are raised to immortal, eternal life. The souls of the wicked begin suffering immediately in hell.	The souls of the faithful are purified as needed to enjoy full communion with God, and at Christ's return they are raised to the fullness of eternal life in heaven. Those who reject God face eternal death.
The Church	The church is the congregation of believers (though mixed with the lost) in which the gospel is taught and the sacraments rightly administered. All believers are "priests" in that they have direct access to God. All ministers are pastors; some serve as bishops. Historically, apostolic succession has been rejected.	The church is the Body of Christ, whose unity is based on the "apostolic succession" of bishops going back to the apostles, of whom the bishop of Rome is one of many. It is one, holy, catholic, and apostolic. The Anglican communion is a part of the church, whose unity worldwide is represented by the archbishop of Canterbury. The church in the USA is known as the Episcopal Church.
Sacraments	Baptism is necessary for salvation; in it both adults and infants are given God's grace. The Lord's Supper remains truly bread and wine but also becomes truly Jesus' body and blood (consubstantiation).	The sacraments are "outward and visible signs of an inward and spiritual grace." Infants and converts are made part of the church in baptism. Christ's body and blood are really present in Communion.
Other Beliefs and Practices	The church's liturgy is similar to the Episcopal. Conservative Lutherans generally affirm that God chooses who will be saved before they believe. In 2009 the ELCA opened the ministry to gay and lesbian pastors in committed relationships.	Members are free to accept or reject the Catholic doctrines of Mary. The Book of Common Prayer is the norm for liturgy. Priests may marry. In 1976 the Episcopal Church approved the ordination of women. In 2009 the Episcopal Church approved the ordination of gay bishops and allowed bishops to bless same-sex unions.
Divisions and Trends	The Evangelical Lutheran Church in America (ELCA) is the mainline church. The Lutheran Church—Missouri Synod is doctrinally conservative.	In the USA, most belong to the Episcopal Church. The 39 Articles (1571) are the doctrinal basis for conservative splinter groups, such as the Reformed Episcopal Church and the Anglican Church in North America.

Denominations Comparison • 483

	Presbyterian Churches	**Methodist Churches**
Founder and Date	1536: John Calvin writes *Institutes of the Christian Religion*. 1643–1649: Westminster Standards define Presbyterian doctrine. 1789: Presbyterian Church (USA) first organized (see below).	1738: Conversion of John and Charles Wesley, already devout Anglican ministers, sparks Great Awakening. 1784: USA Methodists form separate church body.
Adherents	40–50 million worldwide 2 million USA	61 million worldwide 11 million USA
Scripture	Historic view: Scripture is inspired and infallible, the sole, final rule of faith. PCUSA: Scripture is "the witness without parallel" to Christ, but in merely human words reflecting beliefs of the time. The standard Protestant canon is accepted.	Historic view: Scripture is inspired and infallible, the sole, final rule of faith. United Methodist Church: Scripture is "the primary source and criterion for Christian doctrine," but (for most) not infallible. The standard Protestant canon is accepted.
God	The one Creator and Lord of all, existing eternally as the Trinity (Father, Son, and Holy Spirit).	The one Creator and Lord of all, existing eternally as the Trinity (Father, Son, and Holy Spirit).
Jesus	The eternal Son incarnate, fully God and fully man, conceived and born of the Virgin Mary, died on the cross for our sins, rose bodily from the grave, ascended into heaven, and will come again in glory to judge us all.	The eternal Son incarnate, fully God and fully man, conceived and born of the Virgin Mary, died on the cross for our sins, rose bodily from the grave, ascended into heaven, and will come again in glory to judge us all.
Salvation	We are saved by grace alone when God imputes to us his gift of righteousness through faith alone (*sola fide*) in Christ, who died for our sins. Good works are the inevitable result of true faith, but in no way the basis of our right standing before God.	We are saved by grace alone when God regenerates and forgives us through faith in Christ, who died for our sins. Good works are the necessary result of true faith, but do not obtain forgiveness or salvation.
Afterlife	The souls of believers upon dying go immediately to be with Christ. At Christ's return, their bodies are raised to immortal, eternal life. The souls of the wicked begin suffering immediately in hell.	The souls of believers upon dying go immediately to be with Christ; and, at Christ's return, their bodies are raised to immortal, eternal life. The wicked will suffer eternal punishment in hell.
The Church	The church is the body of Christ, including all whom God has chosen as his people, represented by the visible church, composed of churches that vary in purity and corruption. Christ alone is the head of the church. Congregations choose elders to govern them. Regional groups of elders (presbyteries) meet in denomination-wide General Assemblies.	The church is the body of Christ, represented by visible church institutions. Bishops oversee regions and appoint pastors. In the United Methodist Church, clergy and laity meet together in a national "General Conference" every four years. All pastors are itinerant, meaning they move from one church to the next as directed by the bishop (on average once every four years).
Sacraments	Baptism is not necessary for salvation but is a sign of the new covenant of grace, for adults and infants. Jesus' body and blood are spiritually present to believers in the Lord's Supper.	Baptism is a sign of regeneration and of the new covenant and is for adults and children. Jesus is really present, and his body and blood are spiritually present, to believers in the Lord's Supper.
Other Beliefs and Practices	Conservatives affirm the "five points of Calvinism": humans are so sinful that they cannot initiate return to God; God chooses who will be saved; Christ died specifically to save those whom God chose; God infallibly draws to Christ those whom he chooses; they will never fall away.	"Entire sanctification" is a work of the Spirit subsequent to regeneration by which fully consecrated believers are purified of all sin and fit for service—a state maintained by faith and obedience. Methodists are Arminian, i.e., they disagree with all five points of Calvinism.
Divisions and Trends	The Presbyterian Church (USA), or PCUSA, is the mainline church. The Presbyterian Church in America (PCA) is the largest doctrinally conservative church body.	United Methodist Church (7.7 million) and the African Methodist Episcopal church bodies (2.5 million) are mainline churches. The Free Methodists are a small conservative body.

John Calvin

John Wesley

Denominations Comparison

	Anabaptist Churches	Congregational Churches
Founder and Date	1525: Protestants in Zurich begin believer's baptism. 1537: Menno Simons begins leading Mennonite movement. 1682: A Quaker, William Penn, founds Pennsylvania.	1607: Members of a house church in England, illegal at that time, who were forced into exile. 1620: Congregationalists called Pilgrims sail on Mayflower to Plymouth (now in Massachusetts).
Adherents	2 million worldwide 1 million USA	2.5 million worldwide 1.1 million USA
Scripture	Most view Scripture as the inspired means for knowing and following Jesus, but not as infallible. Jesus is the living Word. Scripture is the written Word that points to him. The standard Protestant canon is accepted. How believers live is emphasized over having correct doctrine.	Most view Scripture as "the authoritative witness to the Word of God" that was living in Jesus, rather than viewing Scripture as the unerring Word of God. (UCC, see below.) The Bible and creeds are seen as "testimonies of faith, not tests of faith." The standard Protestant canon is accepted.
God	The one Creator and Lord of all, revealed in Jesus through the Holy Spirit. Most affirm the Trinity in some way.	The Eternal Spirit who calls the worlds into being and is made known in the man Jesus.
Jesus	The Savior of the world, a man in whom God's love and will are revealed by his life of service and his suffering and death. His deity, virgin birth, and resurrection are traditionally affirmed.	The crucified and risen Savior and Lord, in whom we are reconciled to God. (His deity and virgin birth are widely ignored or rejected except in the conservative church bodies.)
Salvation	Salvation is a personal experience in which, through faith in Jesus, we become at peace with God, moving us to follow Jesus' example as his disciples by living as peacemakers in the world.	God promises forgiveness and grace to save "from sin and aimlessness" all who trust him, who accept his call to serve the whole human family.
Afterlife	No official view of what happens immediately after death. At Christ's return God's people will be raised to eternal life and the unrepentant will be forever separated from God (the traditional view).	Those who trust in God and live as Jesus' disciples are promised eternal life in God's kingdom. No position is taken on the future of the wicked (most reject the idea of eternal punishment).
The Church	The church is the body of Christ, the assembly and society of Christ's disciples who follow him in the power of the Spirit. It is to be marked by holiness, love, service, a simple lifestyle, and peacemaking. No one system of church government is recognized; leadership is to be characterized by humble service and is primarily but not exclusively local.	The church is the people of God living as Jesus' disciples by serving humanity as agents of God's reconciling love. Each local church is self-governing and chooses its own ministers. The United Church of Christ is not part of the "Churches of Christ" but was formed in 1957 as the union of the Congregational Christian Churches and the Evangelical and Reformed Church, a liberal Protestant body.
Sacraments	Baptism is for believers only, a sign of commitment to follow Jesus. The Lord's Supper is a memorial of his death. Most Quakers view sacraments as spiritual only, not external rites.	Congregations may practice infant baptism or believer's baptism or both. Sacraments are symbols of spiritual realities.
Other Beliefs and Practices	Anabaptists and similar bodies are "peace churches," teaching nonresistance and pacifism (the view that all participation in war is wrong). Doctrine is deemphasized, and liberal views with social emphasis prevail in some church bodies, including most Quaker churches.	The United Church of Christ (UCC) is one of the most theologically liberal denominations in the USA. Individual ministers and churches vary widely in belief. The United Church of Christ ordains openly homosexual men and women to ministry.
Divisions and Trends	The Mennonite Church and Church of the Brethren are the largest bodies; the Amish (1693) are a variety of Mennonites. Quakers (Friends) originated separately but share much in common with Anabaptists.	United Church of Christ (1 million) is staunchly liberal. The National Association of Congregational Christian Churches (70,000) is a mainline body. The Conservative Congregational Christian Conference (42,000) is evangelical.

Denominations Comparison

	Baptist Churches	**Churches of Christ**
Founder and Date	1612: John Smythe and other English Puritans form the first Baptist church. 1639: The first Baptist church in America established in Providence, Rhode Island.	1801: Barton Stone holds his Cane Ridge Revival in Kentucky. 1832: Stone's Christians unite with Thomas and Alexander Campbell's Disciples of Christ. They have different beliefs in some areas.
Adherents	100 million worldwide 32 million USA	5–6 million worldwide 3.5 million USA
Scripture	Scripture is inspired and without error, the sole, final, totally trustworthy rule of faith. The standard Protestant canon is accepted. (Mainline churches vary in the extent to which they continue to view Scripture as without error.)	"Where the Scriptures speak, we speak; where the Scriptures are silent, we are silent." Churches of Christ view Scripture as the inerrant word of God; Disciples of Christ generally view Scripture as witness to Christ but fallible. The standard Protestant canon is accepted.
God	The one Creator and Lord of all, existing eternally as the Trinity (Father, Son, and Holy Spirit).	The one Creator and Lord of all. The creeds are rejected, but most conservatives accept the idea of the Trinity.
Jesus	The eternal Son incarnate, fully God and fully human, conceived and born of the Virgin Mary, died on the cross for our sins, rose bodily from the grave, ascended into heaven, and will come again in glory to judge us all.	The Son of God, fully God and fully human, conceived and born of the Virgin Mary, died on the cross for our sins, rose bodily from the grave, ascended into heaven, and will come again in glory to judge us all.
Salvation	We are saved by grace alone when God imputes to us his gift of righteousness through faith alone (*sola fide*) in Christ, who died for our sins. Good works are the inevitable result of true faith, but in no way the basis of our right standing before God.	Churches of Christ: A person must hear the gospel, believe in Christ, repent, confess Christ, be baptized, and persevere in holiness to be saved. Disciples of Christ: God saves human beings (possibly all) by his grace, to which we respond in faith.
Afterlife	The souls of believers upon dying go immediately to be with Christ; and, at Christ's return, their bodies are raised to immortal, eternal life. The wicked will suffer eternal punishment in hell.	Churches of Christ: Believers immediately go to be with Christ and at his return are raised to immortality; the wicked will suffer eternally in hell. Disciples: Most believe in personal immortality but not hell.
The Church	The church (universal) is the body of Christ, which consists of the redeemed throughout history. The term "church" usually refers to local congregations, each of which is autonomous, whose members are to be baptized believers and whose officers are pastors and deacons. Churches may form associations or conventions for cooperative purposes, especially missions and education.	Churches of Christ: The church is the assembly of those who have responded rightly to the gospel; it must be called only by the name of Christ. Only such churches are part of the restoration of true Christianity. Each local church is autonomous and calls its own pastors. Disciples of Christ have a similar form of church government but are ecumenical, and thus do not claim to be the sole restoration of true Christianity.
Sacraments	Baptism is immersion of believers only as a symbol of their faith in Christ. The Lord's Supper is a symbolic memorial of Christ's death and anticipation of his return.	Baptism is immersion of believers only, as the initial act of obedience to the gospel. Many Churches of Christ recognize baptism in their own churches only as valid. The Lord's Supper is a symbolic memorial.
Other Beliefs and Practices	Most Baptist bodies emphasize evangelism and missions. Church and state are to be separate. Some Baptist denominations, such as Free-will Baptists, are Arminian. Others, such as the Southern Baptist Convention, include both Calvinists and non-Calvinists.	Many but not all Churches of Christ forbid the use of instrumental music in worship. International Churches of Christ teaches that its members alone are saved and is widely reported to strongly influence its members.
Divisions and Trends	Southern Baptist (15.7 million), a conservative body, are the largest Protestant denomination in the USA. American Baptists (1.3 million) and the National Baptists (8.5 million) are mainline churches.	Churches of Christ (2 million) are conservative, some militantly and others not. Christian Church (Disciples of Christ) (650,000) is the mainline church body.

Denominations Comparison

Pentecostal Churches

Founder and Date	1901: Charles Fox Parham's Kansas Bethel Bible College students speak in tongues. 1906: The Azusa Street revival (led by William J. Seymour in Los Angeles) launches Pentecostal movement. 1914: Assemblies of God organize.
Adherents	250–500 million worldwide 13.6 million USA (estimates vary)
Scripture	Scripture is inspired and without error, the final, totally trustworthy rule of faith. The standard Protestant canon is accepted. Some church bodies view certain leaders as prophets with authoritative messages that are to be confirmed from Scripture.
God	The one Creator and Lord of all, existing eternally as the Trinity (Father, Son, and Holy Spirit).
Jesus	The eternal Son incarnate, fully God and fully human, conceived and born of the Virgin Mary, died on the cross for our sins, rose bodily from the grave, ascended into heaven, and will come again in glory to judge us all.
Salvation	We are saved by God's grace, by Christ's death for our sins, through repentance and faith in Christ alone, resulting in our being born again to new life in the Spirit, as evidenced by a life of holiness.
Afterlife	The souls of believers upon dying go immediately to be with Christ, and at Christ's return their bodies are raised to immortal, eternal life. The wicked will suffer eternal punishment in hell.
The Church	The church is the body of Christ, in which the Holy Spirit dwells, which meets to worship God, and which is the agency for bringing the gospel of salvation to the whole world. Most church bodies practice a form of church government similar to Baptists.
Sacraments	Baptism is immersion of believers only, as a symbol of their faith in Christ. The Lord's Supper is a symbolic memorial of Christ's death and anticipation of his return.
Other Beliefs and Practices	Pentecostals in the strict sense view speaking in tongues as the initial evidence of baptism in the Holy Spirit (a second work of grace akin to entire sanctification in Methodism). Charismatics accept tongues but don't view it as the only initial evidence of baptism in the Holy Spirit.
Divisions and Trends	Assemblies of God (3 million USA, historically white) and Church of God in Christ (6.5 million USA, historically black) are the largest church bodies. "Oneness" churches reject the Trinity.

Other Significant Church Bodies

There are many other Christian denominations that are not mentioned here. The following are some of the better known or more influential of these denominations.

Seventh-day Adventists
About 17.5 million worldwide; 1 million in the USA. Founded in 1863. Early leader Ellen G. White is considered a prophet. *The Clear Word* paraphrase is the favored Bible version.

Calvary Chapel
Roughly 500,000, mostly in the USA. Started by Chuck Smith in California as an independent charismatic church oriented to youth. Staunchly evangelical.

Christian and Missionary Alliance
About 430,000 in the USA; 6 million worldwide. Founded by A. B. Simpson, a faith-healing evangelist of the late nineteenth century, it is an evangelical denomination in the Holiness tradition, emphasizing personal piety and evangelism.

Church of God (Cleveland, TN)
About 1 million in the USA; 7 million members worldwide and growing rapidly. The largest of the Pentecostal "Church of God" bodies.

Church of the Nazarene
Roughly 650,000 in the USA; 2.2 million worldwide. A Holiness church body founded in Texas in 1908.

Evangelical Covenant Church (100,000 USA)
Evangelical Free Church of America (350,000)
Two evangelical denominations in the USA with origins in the Free-Church tradition (which broke with the national Lutheran church bodies) of Scandinavia.

International Church of the Foursquare Gospel
Over 350,000 in the USA; about 4–8 million worldwide. A Pentecostal church body, founded by Aimee Semple McPherson, one of America's most well-known women evangelists, and emphasizing physical as well as spiritual healing.

Salvation Army
About 450,000 in the USA. A Holiness church founded in 1878 by William Booth, a former Methodist preacher, and his wife Catherine Booth. It is best known for its ministries to the poor.

Vineyard Ministries International
Perhaps 190,000 in the USA (over 1,500 churches worldwide). Charismatic church body that started in 1974 with a single church; in 1982 a Calvary Chapel headed by John Wimber, whose ministry focused on praying for signs and wonders, became a Vineyard, after which Vineyard Ministries International (1983) began growing quickly throughout the world.

Family Tree of Denominations

1054 — The Undivided Church / Great Schism occurs between East (Orthodox) and West (Catholic)

- Orthodox Church → **Orthodox**
- Catholic Church → **Catholics**
  - 1534 → Anglican Church (Episcopal) → **Anglicans**
    - 1738 → Methodists → **Methodists**
      - (Other Holiness Churches)
      - 1738 Methodist
      - 1814 African Methodist Episcopal (AME)
      - 1890 Plymouth Brethren
      - 1887 Christian and Missionary Alliances
      - 1908 Church of the Nazarene
      - 1901 → **Pentecostals**
        - 1886 Church of God (TN)
        - 1907 Pentecostal Assemblies
        - 1914 Assemblies of God
        - 1927 Foursquare Gospel
        - **Charismatic**
        - 1965 Calvary Chapel
        - 1983 Vineyard Ministries

- 1517 →
  - 1536 → Calvinists (Reformed)
    - c. 1607 → Baptists
      - 1801 → **Churches of Christ**
      - 1844 → **Adventists**
      - Baptists → **Baptists**
        - 1845 Southern Baptist
        - 1915 National Baptist
        - 1924 American Baptist and others
      - Congregationalists → **Congregationalists**
      - 1885 Evangelical Covenant → **Presbyterians**
  - 1525 → Lutheran Church
    - 1950 Evangelical Free → **Lutherans**
    - 1537 Mennonite (USA 1725), 1530 Hutterite, 1693 Amish → Anabaptists → **Anabaptists**

Due to space limitations, this chart shows only a few major groups and offshoots.

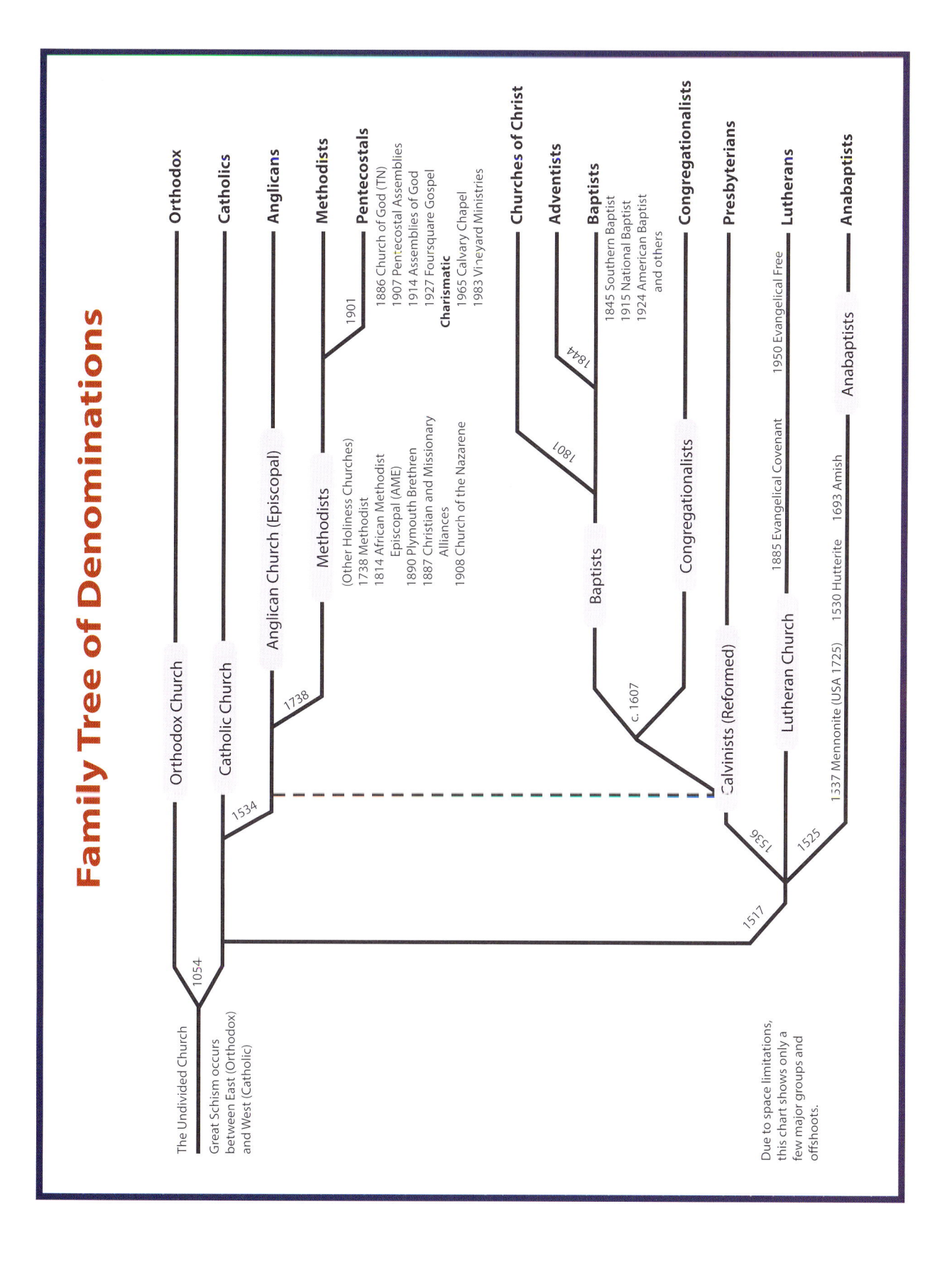

Islam and Christianity

Religious History

Muslims Believe

Islam, the Original Religion
Muslims believe that Islam (meaning "submission" to Allah) is the original religion since the creation of Adam, the first prophet. Since the beginning of time, all people who submit to Allah are called Muslims. Over the centuries, Allah appointed thousands of prophets to warn and guide mankind. Prominent among them were *Ibrahim* (Abraham), *Musa* (Moses), *Dawud* (David), and *Isa Al Masih* (Jesus the Messiah).

Muhammad, the Final Prophet
Mankind habitually strayed from the way of Allah revealed through the prophets. About AD 610 in Arabia, Allah sent the last prophet, Muhammad, who united the Arab tribes and turned them from idolatry to Islam.

The Spread of Islam
After the death of Muhammad in AD 632, Sunni Islam rapidly spread from Arabia under the leadership of the first four "rightly guided" rulers (*caliphs*) who were close companions of Muhammad. Shia Islam began to rapidly spread through the teachings of "infallible" Imams from the bloodline of Muhammad. To Muslims, the military and economic expansion of Islam liberated people suffering under the corrupt Byzantine and Persian Empires.

Christians Believe

Adam and Jesus
Christians also trace their religious history back to Adam, who brought the curse of sin upon all mankind (Gen. 1–3). In the Bible, Jesus is known as the second Adam, who came to remove this curse of sin (Rom. 5).

Abraham and Jesus
God's plan unfolded carefully over history. Abraham (*Ibrahim* in Arabic) was promised the blessing to carry out God's eternal purposes. He was blessed so he could be a blessing to all the families of the earth (Gen. 12:1–3; Gal. 3). Jesus is the promised seed of Eve who would crush the head of Satan (*Shaytan* in Arabic; Gen. 3:15) and bring the blessing of the "Good News" (*Injil* in Arabic).

The Victory of Jesus
A great war has been raging throughout the Creation, a struggle in which Satan has twisted all good things—even religion—into weapons to discredit God. The decisive battle of this war was won on the cross when Jesus destroyed Satan's power and overcame the curse of sin. By rising from the dead, Jesus conquered death, a consequence of the curse, and thereby offers the blessing of eternal life to mankind.

Misunderstandings

The Misunderstandings
Religious history between Christians and Muslims is covered with blood and war, much like all of human history. God's name has been used by both sides to justify murder and mayhem. Several key events in history continue to affect the perceptions of Christians and Muslims. These events include the Islamic expansion (7th–8th centuries), the Crusades (11th–13th centuries), the establishment of the state of Israel in 1948, the attack on the World Trade Center, the Gulf Wars of 1991 and 2003, and many other events.

Correcting the Misunderstandings
Historians have pointed out that these "holy wars" of history were more about economics than faith. Yet economic struggle cannot explain the intense hatred, cruelty and malicious evil of a Crusader, Nazi, or suicide bomber. Behind these horrors is a deeper spiritual war and a vindictive enemy, namely Satan. Christians and Muslims should not lose sight of Satan, the "enemy of souls." By recognizing the common enemy, Christians can create a context in which they can build relationships with Muslims.

Who is God?

Muslims Believe

Allah Is One.
The absolute oneness of Allah is primary to Muslims. The greatest sin is to associate any partner with him. This sin is called *shirk*. Muhammad's message advocating one God was courageous because idolatry was the established religion of Arabia. Muhammad challenged this system and finally prevailed with the message of monotheism. Islam is rooted in this commitment to the belief in one God.

Allah Cannot Be Compared.
Allah is transcendent and cannot be compared to humans or any other created thing. Allah's character and attributes are revealed through his 99 Arabic names, the two most common being "The Merciful" and "The Compassionate." Allah is never described in Islam by using human family terms such as "father" or "son." In the Quran he reveals his will for mankind to obey, not his person for mankind to relate with and know.

Allah's Ultimate Attribute: His Will.
Allah creates and sustains all life, spiritual and material. His will is absolute and cannot be questioned by his creation. He is our final judge without a mediator. The best chance on Judgment Day is for those who live lives of righteousness and submission to Allah's will—*Insha Allah* (God willing).

Christians Believe

God: A Unity, Not a Unit.
The Bible teaches that God is one, but he is a complex unity, not just a simple unit. He is completely unique, a personal God who existed in relationship from eternity.

God the Father, God the Son, God the Holy Spirit
Scripture reveals God as the ultimate Father, in name, character, and person, but always as the Creator, never with sexual references. God also reveals himself as the Eternal Word, who became flesh when the Holy Spirit overshadowed the Virgin Mary and conceived Jesus, the Messiah, who is also called the Son of God in the Bible. In his teaching, Jesus further reveals God the Holy Spirit, who was sent by the Father and himself. The Bible presents a mystery of three persons revealed as one God. Although the word "Trinity" is not in the Bible, the term captures Bible truths about God. The Father, the Son, and the Holy Spirit are God, not just three parts of God or three names for the same person. God reveals himself as a tri-unity.

God's Ultimate Attribute: His Love.
The Bible says, "God is Love." This love existed from eternity as the Father loved the Son even before the foundation of the world. God's love is expressed through creation. God does not simply choose to love; his love chooses to act. "God so loved the world that he gave his one and only Son" (John 3:16).

Misunderstandings

The Misunderstandings
Most Muslims consider Christians to be polytheists (people who believe in many gods) because of the Trinity. A popular misunderstanding of the Trinity is that Christians believe that a Father God had sex with a Mother God (Mary) to produce their "Son of God." No Christian believes this. Educated Muslims understand this false Trinity is not what Christians believe, but they still do not understand how the math can show God's unity. To them it is simple: 1+1+1=3; Father + Son + Holy Spirit = Three Gods. This is not what Christians believe.

Correcting Misunderstandings.
Rather than use an analogy of adding units (1+1+1=3), the Trinity has been explained as multiplied wholeness (1x1x1=1). The Bible says Jesus is the eternal "Word of God" revealed in flesh through the virgin birth. The Quran sets apart Jesus as "His (God's) Word" and "a Spirit from Him (God)" and mentions his virgin birth and miracles. Muslims also believe in the second coming of Jesus, because Jesus is called the "Sign of the Hour" in the Quran. Muslims like to point out how the Quran honors Jesus. Yet such positive references to Jesus in the Quran are few compared to the complete story of Jesus preserved by God in the New Testament.

Islam and Christianity

Holy Scriptures

Muslims Believe

The Only Trustworthy Scripture
According to Muslims, there is only one trustworthy Holy Scripture, the Quran ("a text to recite"). Many prophets before Muhammad were also given Allah's Word, among them: *Musa* (Moses) given the *Taurat* (Torah), *Dawud* (David) given the *Zabur* (Psalms), and *Isa* (Jesus) given the *Injil* (Gospel). However, Muslims are taught that all these writings were corrupted. Allah appointed Muhammad to receive the Quran in order to correct this corruption.

How Muslims Got the Quran
In AD 610, Allah sent the archangel Gabriel (*Jibrail* in Arabic) to Muhammad in Mecca, Saudi Arabia. Over the next 22 years, Allah "sent down" revelations to Gabriel who dictated them to Muhammad with the command to recite it to others. Shortly after Muhammad's death in AD 632, his followers gathered the texts of different lengths into 114 chapters (*Sura* in Arabic). The third caliph, Uthman, had scholars compile an official Quran, in written form, and had all other variant texts burned.

The Quran Today
The Quran is considered divine in its original Arabic form, and Muslims memorize and recite it only in this pure language.

Christians Believe

How Christians Got the Bible
Followers of Jesus believe the Bible is the authoritative, inspired word of God, composed of 66 different books, transmitted through at least 40 prophets, apostles, and holy men. The first 39 books, written before the coming of Christ, are called the Old Testament. The Old Testament was written over many centuries by various authors in diverse cultures using the Hebrew and Aramaic languages. The remaining 27 books after Christ are called the New Testament. They were written in Greek, the dominant language of the 1st century. The New Testament contains collections of eyewitness reports of the life and teachings of Jesus, followed by a history of his disciples over the next 50 years, including letters from his apostles and a vision of the end times called the "Revelation."

Inspiration
The Christian view of inspiration is that God "breathed" his Word through many people (mostly inspiring, rarely dictating). Therefore the Bible reflects cultures as diverse as Abraham's nomadic lifestyle to the royal court of King David. The result is a book of beautiful human diversity interwoven with divine unity.

Misunderstandings

The Misunderstandings
Muslims feel sorry that Christians follow a corrupted book and most Muslims avoid the Bible. Even among Western-educated Muslims, the great diversity of Bible versions and translations adds to their belief that the Bible is corrupted.

Correcting the Misunderstandings
Muhammad did not question the accuracy of the Bible; he criticized contemporary Jews and Christians for misinterpreting or not obeying their existing Scriptures. The accusation that the text of the Bible had been corrupted came centuries after Muhammad, at a time when Muslim scholars realized there were contradictions between the Quran and the Bible. Yet the Quran points to the Bible as truth to obey many times. The text of the Bible is better preserved than the writings of any ancient author. Furthermore, the discovery of the Dead Sea Scrolls confirmed the reliability of the Bible.

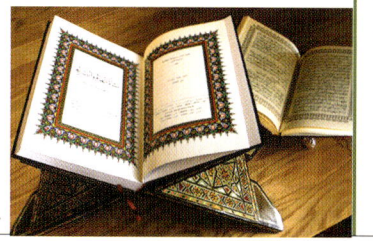

Prophets

Muslims Believe

Muhammad, the Seal of the Prophets
To Muslims, the Prophet Muhammad, called the "seal of the prophets," is the last of over 124,000 prophets going back to Adam. His name means "praised one," and he is commended by Allah in the Quran.

Muhammad, the Reformer
Mecca was a center of idol worship in AD 610 when Muhammad first challenged the people to forsake idolatry and embrace Islam. Most Meccans rejected his message and many began to persecute the early Muslims, causing them to flee to the town of Medina in AD 622. (This flight is known as the *hijara* and marked the first year on the Islamic calendar.) Medina was more receptive to Muhammad, and from this city, through battles and diplomacy, Islam was spread to the entire Arabian Peninsula within only a few years after Muhammad's death in AD 632.

Muhammad, the Perfect Example to Follow
Muslims try to follow Muhammad's example known as his *sunna* ("trodden path" or "customs") in every detail possible. Everything is prescribed, from ritual washings before prayer to hygienic practices in the bathroom. Such detailed behavior is known through large collections of *hadith*, accounts of Muhammad's life, words, and behavior passed on by his early followers.

Christians Believe

Old Testament Prophecy
New Testament writers proclaimed Jesus as the fulfillment of the Law of Moses (*Taurat*) and the predictions of Old Testament prophets. These prophets are quoted in the New Testament. For instance, Matthew quotes various prophecies concerning Jesus' birth in Bethlehem (Mic. 5:2), his mother being a virgin (Isa. 7:14), and even the killing of baby boys by King Herod (Jer. 31:15). The prophets also detail the suffering, death, and resurrection of Jesus (Isa. 53; Ps. 16:8–11). The Bible points out that God carefully planned and carried out the details of the coming of Jesus in history (Luke 24:27; Acts 3:18).

Christ's Warning about False Teachers
The Bible contains numerous warnings about false teachers and prophets. Jesus predicts the end times will be full of these (Matt. 24:11). Therefore, every teaching must be judged against the truth already revealed in the Bible. Jesus also promised that the Holy Spirit ("the Spirit of Truth") would guide truth seekers into all truth (John 14–16).

Muhammad and the archangel Gabriel

Misunderstandings

The Misunderstandings
In conversation with Muslims, do not attack Muhammad. Since so much is determined by imitating their prophet, to insult Muhammad is to attack their entire life and culture.

Correcting the Misunderstandings
It is wise to find common ground and agree that Muhammad has much in common with Old Testament prophets. Like David and Solomon, he was a political and military leader with multiple wives. Like Moses and Joshua, he united tribes and led them in battle. Like Elijah and many other prophets, he destroyed idols and confronted the corrupt political and economic powers of his day.

Just as Old Testament prophets looked forward to the coming Messiah, Muhammad looked back with respect and admiration to Jesus as the Messiah. The Quran calls *Isa Al Masih* (Jesus) "His (God's) Word" and "a Spirit from Him (God)" (Surah 4:171). It affirms Jesus' virgin birth and special role in the end times, though not in the biblical sense.

Followers of Jesus do not have to insult or embrace Muhammad in order to exalt the Messiah. It is important to lift up Jesus, not tear down Muhammad.

Practices and Rituals

Muslims Believe

The Five Pillars
The ritual practices of Islam are the pillars of their religious system. Although beliefs are important, the substance of their religion is the accomplishment of these five pillars.
- Confessing the Faith (*Shahada*)
- Prayer (*Salat*)
- Fasting (*Sawm*)
- Giving of Alms (*Zakat*)
- Pilgrimage to Mecca (*Hajj*)

The Muslim's objective is to follow Muhammad's pattern (his exact words, motions, and timing) found in the sunna as they accomplish the pillars.

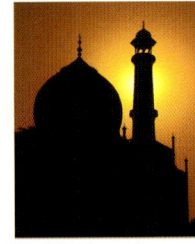

Jihad
Some Muslims also consider "struggle (*Jihad*) in Allah's way" central to their faith. This struggle could be internal (a struggle in the soul to do the right thing) or external (self-defense against attackers of Islam or Muslims). The interpretation of jihad can determine the difference between moderate and radical Muslims.

Judgment Day
Their belief in the nature of the final Judgment Day motivates Muslims to faithfully accomplish these pillars. In the Quran, these practices are of great importance.

Christians Believe

The Gift of Salvation
The Bible teaches that salvation is a gift from God through faith in Jesus Christ (*Isa Al Masih*) and there are no rituals or practices that anyone can do in order to get right with God (Eph. 2:8–9).

Jesus' Seven Commands
Even though no one can be saved by good works, followers of Jesus serve him, imitate him, and do what he commanded because they are filled with the Holy Spirit. Jesus said, "If you love me, keep my commands" (John 14:15) and that this "burden is light" (Matt. 11:30). He gave seven specific commands:
- Repent and Believe (a turn of heart)
- Love God and Others (greatest command)
- Pray (as a lifestyle, from the heart)
- Celebrate the Lord's Supper (remember Jesus)
- Be Baptized (with water)
- Give (with a joyful heart)
- Make Disciples (among all peoples)

Making disciples involves worship, fellowship, fasting, studying Scripture, and sharing the good news. Jesus said that his disciples would be recognized by their love for one another (John 13:35).

Misunderstandings

The Misunderstandings
A Muslim can be confused by Christian symbols and rituals, such as the cross (considered a military symbol to Muslims) and the Lord's Supper when using wine (alcohol is prohibited in Islam). Christians are confused by some of the Muslim rituals as well.

Correcting the Misunderstandings
If Christians and Muslims can communicate and completely understand the meaning behind these symbols and rituals, meaningful relationships can be built and truth-sharing can take place.

Following the Sermon on the Mount (Matt. 5–7) is perhaps the best way for Christians to imitate Jesus and share with Muslims. The Sermon on the Mount challenges all followers of Jesus to live a righteous lifestyle of humility and love.

Muslims need grace-motivated Christian friends who follow the disciplines of Jesus. Jesus calls his followers to pray as a lifestyle, frequently and effectively. By confronting evil and bringing healing, believers can introduce Christ to their Muslim friends.

Salvation and Paradise

Muslims Believe

Reward and Penalty
The Quran says, "For those who reject Allah, there is a terrible penalty: but for those who believe and work righteous deeds, there is forgiveness and a magnificent reward" (Surah 35:7). This great reward is *janna*, a garden paradise, an eternal place of sensual and spiritual pleasures.

No Savior, but Mercy Is Possible
In Islam, there is no savior. That is not to say salvation is impossible, for Allah is merciful and compassionate. He can always forgive—for Allah's will is supreme—but he is primarily the judge. There are many descriptive warnings about hellfire and punishment in the Quran.

Judgment Day: A Motivation to Righteous Deeds
All people should fear Judgment Day, in which each person's deeds will be weighed on a scale. "Recording angels" keep a list of every deed, both good and bad. Islamic teachers assign credits to deeds related to the pillars of Islam. It is unthinkable for many Muslims to abandon their accumulation of credits and trust a Savior.

Guarantee of Paradise?
Islamist terrorists interpret the Quran to suggest that paradise is guaranteed for jihad martyrs. Most Muslim scholars and leaders reject the terrorists' definitions of jihad and martyrdom.

Christians Believe

Judgment Day
Christians believe that after death, all people await the final Judgment when both believers and unbelievers will be resurrected. All will be judged according to the deeds they have done, but believers will be saved because God removed the record that contained the charges against them. He destroyed it by nailing it to the cross of Jesus (Col. 2:14). This would remove the list of bad deeds kept by any Muslim's "recording angel."

The Gift of Salvation
Even if one's list of good deeds outweighs their list of bad deeds, this would not make them acceptable to God. The Bible says this would only cause boasting and pride, as though someone could impress God by his or her good deeds (Eph. 2:8–10). Instead, God has credited us with the righteousness of Christ, so salvation is a gift, not earned by anyone, not even martyrs, but bought with a great price (Jesus' blood).

A Renewed Relationship with God
In addition to this great gift, God the Father adopts those he saves into his family so they may live with Jesus in heaven. To be saved involves being "born again" into a new relationship with God (John 3:5).

Misunderstandings

The Misunderstandings
Thinking about Allah as Father is unacceptable for all Muslims (Surah 112:3). Any negative view of the earthly father role will twist one's view of God. In Western cultures, parenting trends err toward permissiveness (more love than discipline). In the East, fathers tend to be negligent or authoritarian (more discipline than love). God is a Father, who shows both love and discipline. He wants loving followers, not slaves or spoiled children.

Correcting the Misunderstandings
This view of fatherhood makes it easier to relate to God as Father and to come to him as a humble child, ready to be loved and disciplined. Jesus said one must enter God's kingdom as a little child.

The final book of the Bible describes the future scene of a huge family gathering with many from every tribe, tongue, people, and ethnic group gathered around the throne of God (Rev. 5). Boasting of good deeds would be unthinkable, because Jesus, the Lamb of God, sits upon the throne. Everyone in this great crowd honors Jesus as their substitute sacrifice, just as God pictured beforehand when he provided a ram to die in place of Abraham's son (Gen. 22).

Islam and Christianity

Role of Women

Muslims Believe

The Perspective of Muslim Women
Muslim women generally consider themselves protected and satisfied within their culture. Their fulfilling social life is usually gender-separated and happens primarily within extended families and some close neighbors.

The Protection of Muslim Women
Women are valued in the Quran. Muhammad brought an end to the practice of female infanticide, widely practiced before his time, and he gave women the right to inherit. The honor of women is a major concern in Muslim societies. The reputation of the family is linked with the women. Islam helps maintain roles and expectations that predate Muhammad. The modest dress code is intended to protect women when outside the home. Muslim women do not need to wear a veil or loose clothes at home or when only women are present.

Polygamy
Since marriage and child bearing are highly valued in Islamic society, polygamy is allowed and yet controlled. Islam limits a man to four wives and requires equal treatment for each.

Christians Believe

The Perspective of Christian Women
Christians believe that the Bible teaches that both man and woman were created in God's image, had a direct relationship with God, and shared jointly the responsibilities of bringing up children and ruling over the created order (Gen. 1:26–28). Christian husbands and wives are to mutually submit to one another. Women are to respect their husbands; husbands are to sacrificially and selflessly love their wives, just as Jesus Christ loves his church (Eph. 5:21–25).

The Protection of Christian Women
Christian women are to dress modestly (1 Tim. 2:9), and all followers of Jesus are to flee from sexual immorality (1 Cor. 6:18).

Not Conforming to the World
Followers of Jesus believe that they must be transformed by renewing their minds and avoid conforming to the patterns of the secular world (Rom. 12:2). Problems arise when Christians adapt to the Western secular culture more than to the Bible. When this happens there is a decline in morality which leads to an increase in sexual immorality, drunkenness, deceit, selfishness, rage, and other sins.

Misunderstandings

The Misunderstandings
Western values conflict with Muslims regarding women perhaps more than any other category. There are several problems in Muslim societies in regard to women. However, secularism and women's liberation have brought the "Christian" West several problems as well.

Correcting the Misunderstandings
Christians, often focused on the plight of Muslim women, fail to see that many Western "solutions" are more to be feared than the problems they address. Many Muslim women prefer their lifestyle to lonely singleness, sexual exploitation, and the desire for money that makes home and family unimportant.

Societies long dominated by Islam have problems which need to be addressed, but before Christians can address these issues they must deal with their own cultural problems. As Jesus said, "You hypocrite, first take the plank out of your own eye, and then you will see clearly to remove the speck from your brother's eye" (Matt. 7:5).

Religion and Culture

Muslims Believe

The Muslim Holistic Worldview
Muslims understand religion as a whole and integrated way of life. Secular, Christian-influenced cultures can confuse and even anger Muslims who see things through their holistic worldview. They often view "Hollywood sexuality" as "Christian," or a military action as a "Crusade." To them, the cross is a military symbol.

The Islamic Community
In Islam, brotherhood and consensus is emphasized, and individualism is avoided. The "community of the faithful" is responsible to enforce the moral code. This can explain how a lone Muslim, outside a community support structure, does not feel as guilty when breaking the code. However, bringing shame on his family or community would be a great sin.

Avoiding shame and protecting honor are primary motivations of most Muslims. Shame and honor are community-related, as contrasted to an individual sense of guilt.

Radical Muslims, known as Islamists or Jihadists, use this sense of community honor and shame to recruit and motivate their followers.

Christians Believe

The Western Worldview
Followers of Jesus believe that they are to impact culture for Christ by going into all parts of the world to bring the message of Jesus to the people that live there (Matt. 28:19–20). In the West, a division exists between culture and religion. Religion is separated from government, and some people object to any influence of religion on state institutions and symbols.

Community in the West
Followers of Jesus do influence Western culture and institutions, but they seem to be a shrinking influence. Western culture affirms individualism and some people avoid community responsibility. Tolerance of sin and unbiblical practices continue to dilute the true Christian message; evolutionism and atheism also continue to influence the increasingly secular West. Only a minority of those in the West consider themselves followers of Jesus Christ. Most simply consider themselves Christian by name only, and do not follow the teaching of the Bible, of which they are largely ignorant. Generally, Western culture does not have a sense of the "community of the faithful."

Misunderstandings

The Misunderstandings
Time magazine ran a cover article asking the question, "Should Christians Convert Muslims?" The artwork featured a militant-looking clenched fist holding a metal cross, reminiscent of a Crusader's sword. This imagery correctly symbolizes some typical Muslim misunderstandings, especially when viewed with the cigarette advertisement on the back cover. The advertisement features a sensual goddess-like model with men fawning at her feet. These pictures display some fears of Muslims: to be dominated militarily and corrupted morally by "Christianity."

Correcting the Misunderstandings
The challenge is to present a correct view of the cross. The movie, "The Passion of the Christ," has been seen by Muslims all over the world. They have seen the cross as a symbol of suffering, not as a military or political icon. Followers of Jesus, through their words and actions, are called to show Muslims that God loves all people so much that Jesus died on the cross for their sins. (Islam denies Jesus' death; claims that he was lifted up to heaven and a substitute died instead of him.) Jesus also defeated Satan and death by rising from the grave. He made it possible for all of God's children to live with him forever. This "good news" should be attractive to Muslims.

The Do's and Don'ts of Reaching Out to Muslims

Do make it clear you are a follower of Christ, by your loving words and righteous lifestyle.

Don't assume your Muslim friend understands your meaning of "Christian."

Do take time to build a relationship. Practice hospitality.

Don't be surprised if you are rejected at first. It is best to offer Muslim friends store-bought sweets and to avoid anything with pork or alcohol.

Do approach your encounters as a learner. Ask questions.

Don't take notes and treat Muslim friends like an academic project.

Do correct their misunderstandings of your beliefs.

Don't argue. If they want to debate with a Christian, refer them to the website www.debate.org.uk/.

Do talk about Jesus. Use his title, *Isa Al Masih*.

Don't insult the prophet Muhammad.

Do pray out loud with your Muslim friends. Ask if you can pray for their practical needs, healing, and worries. Look for opportunities and pray in Jesus' name.

Don't start your prayer with "Our Father…" because Muslims have a misunderstanding about the fatherhood of God (as sexual). Wait until you correct this misunderstanding before using "Father" or "Abba." At first address your prayer to "Almighty God" or "Lord God."

Do use your right hand in giving and receiving gifts.

Don't use your left hand for eating food (especially when learning to eat with your hands). The left hand is used for toilet cleaning; the right hand for eating.

Do treat your Bible with respect. Store it high on a shelf. Some wrap it in a beautiful cloth.

Don't put your Bible on the floor or in the bathroom as reading material. Many Muslims are superstitious about the bathroom.

Do be gender-sensitive: interact man to man, woman to woman.

Don't allow any compromising situation, even just to protect from a possible rumor. An Arab proverb says, "A man and woman alone together are three with the devil."

Do observe body language. Take your shoes off when entering a home or place of prayer (especially if you see shoes at the threshold).

Don't sit so that the sole of your foot or shoe is facing someone. Women, don't look men directly in the eye, or at least quickly avert your glance.

Do practice modesty, even among Westernized Muslims. For women this is very important since family honor is tied to their behavior and reputation.

Don't assume Muslims think the same as you, even if they dress the same.

Glossary of Islamic and Arabic Terms

Allah—The proper pre-Islamic Arabic name for God, used even today by Arabic-speaking Christians as well as by Muslims. Scholars think the word "Allah" is originally a compound of *al-ilah* ("the god"). Although all Muslims use the Arabic name "Allah," only 20% are native Arabic speakers.

Arkan-ad-din—The Five Pillars of religion are referred to by their Arabic names by all Muslims, regardless of their native language.

- **Shahada** (confessing the faith) is a public statement said in Arabic which means, "There is no God but Allah and Muhammad is His Messenger."
- **Salat** (prayer) is a set ritual to be done five specific times every day (sometimes combined in three sessions).
- **Sawm** (fasting) is an annual community event for all Muslims (except children, pregnant women, and travelers). The fast lasts the entire lunar month known as Ramadan.
- **Zakat** (giving of alms) is obligatory giving of 2.5% of a Muslim's wealth.
- **Hajj** (pilgrimage to Mecca) is to be carried out at least once in a lifetime, providing a Muslim can afford it.

Baraka—Literally means "blessing," a term that communicates well to Muslims. It is a central biblical theme first introduced by God to Abraham in Genesis 12:1–3, and extended to all believers of all nations (Gal. 3:6–9).

Bismillah (Bis-mi-LAH)—"In the name of Allah." An invocation frequently used by Muslims.

Hadith (Hah-DEETH)—Thousands of reports of sayings or behaviors of Muhammad which set a precedent for Muslim practice and becomes the basis of Sharia law.

Ibrahim (E-brah-HEEM)—"Abraham"

Injil (In-JEEL)—Refers to the "book given to Jesus" and comes from the Greek word *evangelion*, meaning "good news." Muslims do not believe that there is an Injil remaining on the earth that has not been corrupted. Christians often refer to the Gospels or a single Gospel as "the Injil" when conversing with Muslims.

Insha Allah (In-SHA-al-lah)—"God willing." This common phrase is often tagged onto a sentence expressing hope or intention, and sometimes resignation to destiny. It is an expression of Allah's ultimate attribute: his absolute will.

Isa Al Masih (EE-saw-all-Mah-SEE)—"Jesus the Mes-si-ah." The word "Ma-sih" is similar to the Hebrew word. "Isa" for "Jesus" is an obscure version of the Arab Christians' *Yasu* (from Hebrew *Yeshua*).

Muslim—An Arabic term derived from the same root as the word for peace (*salam*). Note that the trilateral root _S_L_M_ is shared by all these related terms: **S**A**LM**, I**SLM**, MU**SLM**. The root and its derivatives are very similar to the Hebrew word *shalom*, which means peace.

Salaam Alaykum (Sa-LAAM Ah-LAY-kum)—"Peace be upon you." It is virtually identical to the Aramaic phrase Jesus spoke when appearing to the disciples after his resurrection (Luke 24:36; John 20:19).

Sharia (Sha-REE-ah)—"Path to water." Islamic religious and civil law which is based upon the Sunna, Quran, and Hadith. Sharia is a guide to everyday life and salvation.

Shaytan (Satan) (Shay-TAAN)—An evil *Jinn* (fire-born spirits in Arabic folklore), not a rebellious angel. The Quran uses this term to refer to mischievous behavior (like devilish).

Shiite or Shia (SHE-ite or SHE-ah)—"The party of Ali" (10% worldwide) that believes that the proper successor to Muhammad should be his blood relative, beginning with Ali. The Sunni-Shia split happened shortly after Muhammad's death in a violent dispute about who should lead the Muslim community.

Shirk (SHIRK)—"Associating." Idolatry or blasphemy. Making others equal to God, an unpardonable sin, like disbelief (*qufr*).

Sufi (SOO-fee)—Muslim mystics, who can be either Sunni or Shia, range from storytellers seeking to love Allah and his wisdom to those inducing trances through chanting the names of Allah or dancing (as seen in "whirling dervishes").

Sunna (SOO-nah)—"Trodden path" of Muhammad and his close companions. The Sunna (Muhammad's examples) becomes the basis of Sharia law.

Sunni (SOO-nee)—"One on the path;" how the majority of Muslims (90% worldwide) identify themselves as contrasted to Shiite.

Taurat of Musa (Tor-AT MOO-sah)—"Torah of Moses," the book given to Moses. The first five books of the Bible.

Tawheed (Toe-HEED)—"Oneness." A term used to refer to the absolute oneness of Allah.

Zabur of Dawud (Zah-BOOR DAU-ood)—"Psalms of David," the book given to David, the Psalms.

worldviews comparison

what is a worldview?

A worldview is simply a view of the world. Everyone has one. A worldview is the set of beliefs we hold about the big questions of life.

Here's how some experts describe a worldview:

> A worldview is a set of presuppositions (assumptions which may be true, partially true, or entirely false) which we hold (consciously or subconsciously, consistently or inconsistently) about the basic makeup of our world.
> —James W. Sire, *The Universe Next Door: A Basic Worldview Catalog*

> A worldview is a map of reality. It is the framework of beliefs, values, and images within which a person makes decisions and conducts the business of living.
> —Leland Ryken, *Culture in Christian Perspective*

> ...every person carries within his head a mental model of the world – a subjective representation of reality.
> —Alvin Toffler, *Future Shock*

why is your worldview important?

Whether you know it or not, your worldview influences the decisions you make in life: Whether you go to church or go surfing instead; whether you pursue earthly wealth or spiritual gain; whether you live in fear or hope.

Some beliefs you might hold strongly, while other beliefs you probably don't think about often. Your worldview changes as your beliefs change. If you change the strong core beliefs in your worldview, then your life will change drastically.

Your worldview may or may not be true, just like beliefs. A worldview can be true about some things and not true about other things. Beliefs in a worldview are true if they match up with what really is.

what are the big questions of life?

what is real?
Is the world I experience real or is it just a figment of my imagination? Are miracles real or are they just natural occurrences we don't understand? Can I even *know* what's real?

is there a God?
Is there just one God or many gods? Is God close to us or distant? Is there even a God out there?

where did we come from?
Did God create human beings or did we just by chance evolve from lower life forms? Do we have past lives we can't remember? What does it even mean to be human?

how should we live?
What can we do to get to know God? What does God want from us? How can we know what's right and wrong? Do our lives have purpose?

where are we going?
What happens when we die? Is there an afterlife in Heaven or are we reincarnated in other living beings? Or is death the end?

Worldviews Comparison

digging deeper:
what is required of a worldview?

a worldview should be coherent.
In other words, it needs to make logical sense. Take, for instance, a worldview that claims the only truth we can know is that there is no truth we can know. This belief is self-contradictory.

a worldview should be consistent.
If someone believes there is no such thing as right and wrong, then it's inconsistent to say any action—like murder or racism—is wrong, because in this worldview nothing can be right or wrong.

a worldview should be comprehensive.
If a worldview leaves the big questions of life unanswered it leaves us unsatisfied and directionless. For example, a worldview that says God is so distant from us that we can't know anything about him leaves us separated from our Creator and clueless about what God might want from us. If a worldview—Christian or otherwise—doesn't answer some of life's most important questions, then it is not much of a worldview.

digging deeper:
why is a Biblical worldview important?

interpretation: it gives us glasses through which we can see meaning to life.
Just as an unfocused camera provides a blurry image, our view of the world remains blurry without some glasses that correct it. All of us see the world through some kind of glasses; our understanding of the world depends on the glasses we use. A biblical Christian worldview gives us a lens through which we can see and interpret life.

stabilization: it gives us an anchor to which we can hold, a mooring in life.
A ship navigates in the vast ocean by plotting its position relative to the fixed position of the stars. Any sailor will tell you that it is hard to determine the position of the stars if the sea is rough. And, of course, the entire process would be worthless if the stars themselves were not fixed in the sky. In spiritual and intellectual matters, a worldview gives a person a stable deck from which he can plot his position in the universe.

proclamation: it gives us a platform from which we can speak a message of life.
In a world of chaos and confusion, a coherent worldview also gives a person a clarity and focus that attracts attention; it gives the Christian a platform from which to speak to the world.

Bibliography

Blamires, Harry, *The Christian Mind: How Should A Christian Think?* Ann Arbor: Servant Books, 1978.

Moreland, J.P., *Love Your God With All Your Mind*, NavPress Publishing Group, 1997.

Orr, James, *The Christian View of God and the World*, 5th ed. Edinburgh: Andrew Elliot, 1897.

Schaeffer, Francis, *The God Who Is There*, Downers Grove, Ill.:InterVarsity Press, 1968.

Sire, James W., *Habits of the Mind*, Downers Grove, Ill.: InterVarsity Press, 2000.

Sire, James W., *The Universe Next Door*, Downers Grove, Ill.: InterVarsity Press, 2004.

seven major worldviews

atheism

main idea: God does not exist. Literally, no (a)-God (*theos*).
examples: Naturalism, Secular Humanism, Marxism, Confucianism

Atheism asserts that there is no God. Man is material, mortal, continues to evolve, and ceases to exist upon death. History is cyclical and meaningless. Atheism allows for the existence of evil, but says it can be defeated as man evolves. True atheism is rare, as it requires a level of certainty that most people are unwilling to make. In agnosticism, a milder form of atheism, God may exist, but is of no practical value.

in the beginning
Atheism holds that space, time, matter, and energy (the universe) exploded into existence from nothing at the time of the Big Bang. There is no God, only the natural world. The spiritual does not exist (or is at best irrelevant); only this material existence is real.

what now?
Humans evolved through a natural process. Though we may be the most complex life-form, we are on our own, not only to do good or evil, but also to make the rules as we wish to define them.

end of all things
Eventually the universe will come to an end, either by burning itself out in a heat death or by contraction over billions of years in what is known as the Big Crunch, where all will again become nothing in a giant black hole. Humans when they die will also cease to exist since there is no spiritual world or afterlife.

pantheism

main idea: All is God. Literally all (*pan*)-God (*theos*).
examples: Hinduism, Buddhism, New Age Movement, Taoism

Pantheism says there is a God that is infinite, but impersonal. "Everything is God." Humans are God, as is everything else. History is cyclical, illusory, and meaningless.

in the beginning
Pantheism holds that the universe began in eternity past as a dream or emanation from God. Since the cosmos radiates out from God like a thought, it is in its essence God. But because it is but a thought or dream, the universe is not truly real, but an illusion. Matter is an illusion, only which it points to in itself (God) is real.

what now?
Humans are lost in illusion of the material world which seems so real. Only when we find God within and "realize" our godhood, will we see the true nature of all and attain fulfillment.

end of all things
The universe will eventually be reabsorbed into God or simply continue on forever in its present state. The goal of humans should be to attain their own absorption into God, realize their godhood and cease being themselves.

pan-en-theism

main idea: All (*pan*)-in (*en*)-God (*theos*). All reality is in God. God is the soul or spirit of the cosmos. The universe is God's body. God is also in process. As the Creation grows and evolves, so does God.
examples: Process Theology, Greek philosophy. Philosophers who held this view: Diogenes, Alfred North Whitehead

Pan-En-Theism does not assert that everything is God, but that everything is in God. Humans are a part of God. Evil exists, but it cannot be defeated. It must be accepted.

in the beginning
The universe and God have been evolving from eternity. Though the physical cosmos is finite and may have a beginning in time, God as the soul of the universe is infinite and eternal, constantly actualizing potential, growing and evolving.

what now?
Humans evolved and continue to grow as the spirit of the cosmos continues to unfold the history of this planet and the universe as a whole. While evil is an unavoidable reality, it may be overcome as part of this evolving growth process.

end of all things
As far as may be known, the universe and humans will continue to grow in knowledge and evolve in time under the guidance of the spirit that is in all and with all. The actual death or destruction of anyone or anything does not mean its end, since it will continue ever in the mind of God to be remembered. Some kind of eternal life is therefore a likely conclusion.

deism

main idea: God exists, but is not involved with his creation. From the word *deus* (god).
examples: Deism was a popular worldview of the Enlightenment

Deism acknowledges the existence of one true God, but does not recognize his personal ongoing involvement in the universe. For the deist, God is the "cosmic watchmaker" who set the universe in motion, but does not afterwards intervene. Evil exists, but God gave humanity the capacity to defeat it eventually. The purpose of history is the elimination of evil.

in the beginning
God the Creator made his universe, establishing the many laws and forces that govern its natural operation. Because he crafted his cosmos to be self sufficient, his continued input is not necessary. He does not involve himself with creation in any way.

what now?
Human beings are the highest order of created beings on this planet and have been left here with free hand to do good or ill. In light of the wonders of creation, the honor we should do God is to explore, understand and marvel at his work, including the remarkable human species itself. This proper understanding and enjoyment of creation is true worship and true ethics.

end of all things
There may be some type of consummation of the created order, but the universe could just as well go on forever. As far as an afterlife of rewards and punishment, justice may require it and the aspiration of mankind may point to it, but it is not strictly necessary to the core of the philosophic system.

finite god-ism

main idea: Finite (limited) God. God exists but is limited by something else besides his own nature. That something else could be a god (as in dualism), matter and energy (Plato), or some external law or principle (Openness Theology).
examples: Dualism, Openness Theology (a form of extreme Arminianism), much of contemporary pop religion

Finite God-Ism acknowledges that there is one God, but he is finite. His power is vast, and he created the universe, including man. But man is a moral free agent, and can do as he chooses. Therefore, history is what man makes it, not as God wills it. Indeed, God cannot even know what the future will hold. He is ignorant of the future.

in the beginning
God may well have made the universe, but it probably wasn't out of nothing. In other words, something else has existed from eternity. It might be space-time, it might be matter and energy. It might be another power (force of evil or free will). Human beings are God's work or end result, but they also partake of this other eternal something.

what now?
Human beings are caught in the struggle between good and evil. Through their own choice, humans may support one or the other. God, who is on the side of the good, calls mankind to align with him in the struggle to defeat evil.

end of all things
God will triumph in the end when the forces of good outweigh evil. When the forces of evil are finally destroyed, God will make the universe and humankind anew and perfect.

polytheism

main idea: There are many gods and spiritual powers. Literally, many (*poly*)-gods (*theos*).
examples: Ancient pagan religions (Greco-Roman, Egyptian, Norse), folk religions, Voodoo, Santeria, some types of Animism, Mormonism, Wicca

Polytheism says there are many gods and that man is god-like, with an immortal spirit. Evil exists, but it may be defeated. History is linear, but its purpose, while likely meaningful, is unknowable. Hinduism is an example of a polytheistic worldview.

in the beginning
Polytheistic systems often have a variety of ways to describe the origin of the universe, but the origin usually comes down to one or two pre-existing "gods." It may be the void or the sky and the earth that come before all else, and one of the difficulties for polytheistic systems is an adequate explanation for all that is. In most classic scenarios, the gods all came from a former group of gods. The current spiritual powers gave rise to humankind and thus man owes his allegiance to these reigning deities.

what now?
Humanity owes worship and allegiance to the gods. While reverence should be paid to all the deities in their places, practically speaking, only a few or one will actually be worshiped in particular. These particular gods offer their favor and protection in exchange for devotion.

end of all things
The present reign of the gods will someday end, bringing with it the end of the world as we know it. Judgment on human beings is the responsibility of the gods. When humans die, they may be immortalized if they have sufficiently pleased the divine powers. Most people, however, will go to the place of the dead where peace or punishment shall be meted out according to their life works.

monotheism

main idea: There is only one true God. Literally, One (*mono*)-God (*theos*).
examples: Christianity, Islam, Judaism

Monotheism asserts that there is one God, who is infinite. He is also both immanent (with humans), and transcendent (beyond humans). Evil exists, but God himself will defeat it, not humankind. History is linear and points toward a consummation in the creation of the Kingdom of God. The purpose of history is to bring glory to God and to unfold this purpose.

in the beginning
God created all that is, including the elements as well as space and time. He did not bring these things together out of "stuff" that already existed, but made the universe out of nothing. Human beings were specially created by God as his signature creation, as the creatures that best reflect him.

what now?
Humans have rebelled against God and broken themselves as a result. Mankind owes God worship and allegiance, but without his help they cannot overcome evil. Mankind must seek God and be found by him in order to be made whole.

end of all things
The universe will one day have an end in the final judgment of God. At that time God will judge human beings based on their works, whether they are good or evil. The good shall enter Paradise, while the evil will be destroyed. God will then make all things, including the cosmos, new.

modern, secular challenges to a Christian worldview

The following arguments are often used as attempts to refute the main ideas of a Christian worldview:

contingency Modernist reject miracles, and thereby the possibility of a transcendent and omnipotent God, by saying that all miracles can be explained by natural causes. Miracles that cannot yet currently be explained will one day be explained.

examples: Scientism, Antisupernaturalism
"So-called 'miracles' are merely rare natural occurrences that science will someday explain."

autonomy The advance of science suggests that the powers of God could one day be ours. A theistic or Christian worldview is not necessary to explain man's longing for God. That longing for God is really a longing to be God. And that longing is not evil or a sin. It is an evolutionary development, and it is pushing us toward ever greater progress.

examples: Existentialism, Secular Humanism, Darwinism
"The more humans evolve the less we 'need' God. We should put our faith, not in God, but in ourselves."

relativity There are no moral absolutes, but there are socially derived mores that are developed by man to fit the social context. Morals and ethics are possible, even desirable, but only insofar as they advance the progress of man, the definition of which is constantly evolving as man himself is evolving. Relativism doesn't try to provide answers to the big questions of life. Instead, relativism denies that we can even know what the answers are. Rather, we just construct whatever answers we think will work for us because all answers are equally true.

examples: Postmodernism, Skepticism, Agnosticism
"What is true for me may not be true for you. No one can know what's really true about the world. Therefore, all truth claims must be equally valid."

temporality Reality is limited to time and space. The idea of man's immortality, or God's existence outside of time, is therefore nonsensical or absurd.

example: Naturalism
"Everything we experience exists in time and space. So things, such as God and human souls, can't exist because they aren't in time and space."

what is a Christian worldview?

Christianity's answers to the big questions of life are far more hopeful, meaningful, and robust than those of other worldviews. Here's how Christianity answers the big questions:

what is real?

God is real. And the world he created is real. We can know both the world around us and God himself because God has built into us the capacity to do so and He takes an active role in communicating with us. He speaks to us through general revelation (the natural world) and special revelation (the Bible and Holy Spirit). (Gen. 1:26-27; Ps. 19; Isa. 45:18-19; 55:6-11; John 1:1-4, 9, 14, 18; 7:16-17; 14:6; Acts 14:14-17; 17:22-31; Rom. 1:16-32; 3:21-31; 2 Tim. 3:10-4:4)

No one wants to believe a lie. We want to know what's true and real. Unlike relativism, which denies knowledge, in Christianity God reveals truth to us. God has not left us alone with no way to figure out what's real.

is there a God?

Yes. God is transcendent, yet personal. He is all powerful, all knowing, everywhere present, and entirely good. God exists as three "persons" yet one God (Trinity). (Exod. 3:13-14; Isa. 40:21-31; 45:18-19)

In Polytheism, humans have to live in fear, trying to escape the anger of the gods and attempting to appease them through rituals and sacrifices. In Finite Godism, God is not in control. He doesn't even know what will happen in the future. However, in Christianity we can take comfort in the knowledge that there is one God who is entirely good and supremely powerful, so He will work out everything in our lives according to his good plan.

where did we come from?

God created the world out of nothing (*ex-nihilo*). He designed us and the world in which we live. Human beings are specially created in the image of God, possessing creativity, personality, intellect, emotion and will. (Gen. 1-2, Ps. 8; 139; Rom. 1-8; I Cor. 11:7-12; James 3:8-9) And we are also creatures who can do right or do wrong. Originally, human beings were created good, but disobeyed God and so the image of God became defaced. We now live in a world where evil exists—where we are in desperate need of a savior. (Gen. 1-3; Rom. 8; Gen. 3; Ps. 51:5; Isa. 52:13-53:12; 64:6; Jer. 17:9; Hab. 1:13; John 3:1-36; Rom. 1-8; Eph. 2:1-10; Titus 3:3-8)

In Pantheism, on the other hand, our identity and our selves are illusions we must escape. Our individuality and uniqueness are negative things.

And in Atheism, humans are merely highly advanced animals, just here by chance. But in Christianity, we are God's special creation, designed in his image for a purpose. We can rejoice in being created as unique individuals by God.

how should we live?

We are fallen human beings who sin, but we are not so ruined as to be incapable of restoration. God sent his Son, Jesus Christ, to earth to be crucified on the cross so we could be saved from the penalty of our sins.

In this way, God redeemed humanity and began the process of restoring people to goodness. But people can choose to reject that redemption or can believe in God's work through his Son and be saved. (Gen. 2:15-16; Isa. 45:18-19; Matt. 5:17-48; Mark 12:28-34; Rom. 1:18-32; 2:1-16; 8:1-4; 13:1-14; I Tim. 1:8-11)

This is drastically different from other worldviews like Deism and Panentheism. In Deism, God has abandoned us. We are left separated from our Creator. In Panentheism, we have no savior who redeems us through His own work and sacrifice. Instead, we and God are simply evolving over time. But in Christianity, God cares so much for us that He pursues us, calling us to be in a personal relationship with Him. He is the one who does the work to bring us back to Himself.

where are we going?

After Jesus Christ allowed himself to be crucified on the cross, God resurrected him from the dead. In this way, God showed us that physical death is not the end of our lives either. For each person death is either the gate to life with God and his people or the gate to separation from all that is good. That's why it's so important to believe in the truth that God has revealed to us. Human history is a meaningful series of events leading to the fulfillment of God's ultimate purposes. (John 3:16-21; 5:24; 8:21-24; 11:25-26; 14:1-3; Rom 2:1-16; I Thess. 4:13-18; 2 Thess. 1:3-10; Heb. 2:14-18; 9:27-28; Rev. 20:11-16; Isa. 40-48; Acts 6:8-7:60; 10:42; 17:22-31; Rom. 9-11; I Cor. 15:1-58; II Tim. 4:1; Rev. 20-22)

In Atheism and Pantheism, our lives as individual persons cease to exist when our bodies stop working. In other worldviews we have no assurance of an afterlife with God, or our souls are at the mercy of unpredictable, finite gods. Unlike these worldviews, Christianity offers hope that our lives and decisions here on earth have meaning beyond the grave. Our good God will resurrect all of us who have put our trust in him to spend eternity with him.

Author:

Alex McFarland, M.A., is the president of Southern Evangelical Seminary, has written several books on apologetics, and has spoken internationally.

Worldviews Comparison

Worldview	Is There a God?	What Is Real?	Where Did What's Real Come From?	What Is a Human Being?	Are Humans Basically Good or Evil? How Bad is the Flaw?	Is it Possible to Know Anything at All?
Atheism	There is no God	Physical matter and energy are the only reality	Unknown	Humans are a product of evolution	People can be either good or bad; humans may be flawed but can be corrected	Yes, but only by the senses and logical deduction
Pantheism	God is all	God is real, but the world is an illusion	Only God is real	The human core is the same essence as God	Humans are good internally but may be caught in outward illusion; the flaw is also illusion	Only the recognition of godhood is real, all else is illusion
Pan-En-Theism	God is in all	God is real and generates reality	God	Part of God	Humans are both; flaw is part of the growth process	Yes, by the experience of becoming/growing
Deism	God is a distant Creator	God is the maker of the real	God	Most complex creature of God's making	People can be either good or bad—they contain all that is necessary for choosing; no flaw exists	Yes, by the senses and logical deduction
Finite God-ism	There is a God, but He is limited	God and something else eternal are real	God and something else	Produced by God (possible for humans to be either created or theistically evolved)	Can be either; no flaw exists	Yes, by reason and supernatural revelation
Polytheism	There are many Gods	Gods and the cosmos are real	Various theories (myths) about origins	Creation of the gods	Can be either; no flaw exists	Yes, by reason and supernatural revelation
Monotheism	There is only one God	God is the maker of the real	God who created out of nothing	Created by God as His signature masterpiece	Originally good, but now bent; the flaw is serious but can be overcome with God's help	The worship of God is the beginning of all knowledge
Biblical Christianity	There is only one Triune God	God is the maker of the real	God who created out of nothing	Created by God as His signature masterpiece	Originally good, but now bent; the flaw is fatal, and only God can fix it	The worship of God is the beginning of all knowledge

Worldviews Comparison

Worldview	How Do We Know What Is Right and Wrong?	What is Truth?	What Is Evil?	Where Do Laws Come From?	What Happens to a Person at Death?	Can Miracles Happen?	What is the Meaning of Human History?	How Do We Get to Know God?
Atheism	By experience and reason	Truth is the ultimate explanation	Evil is that which is destructive	Humans make laws	Ceases to exist	No	There is no ultimate meaning	There is no God to know
Pantheism	Right and wrong are an illusion	Truth is an illusion	Evil is an illusion	Laws are a part of this world of illusion	Reincarnation or absorption into God	Yes, but they are illusory	History and its meaning are both illusion	Look within; God is in person
Pan-En-Theism	By growth and becoming	Truth is that which God realizes, or makes real, through growth	Evil is simply mistakes to be overcome	Laws evolve out of the ever-growing mind of God	There may be some afterlife	No	History is part of the unfolding of God	By knowing the evolving spirit of the cosmos
Deism	By experience and reason	Truth is the mind of God	Evil is that which is irrational	Laws reflect God's mind and are built into Creation	There may be some afterlife	No	History is the self-created story of humankind	By examining God's Creation
Finite God-ism	By reason and supernatural revelation	Truth is that by which God operates	Evil is God's enemy	Laws are made by God	Some kind of afterlife of reward or punishment	Yes in theory, but most systems say not in practice	History is the struggle between good and evil	By allying ourselves to God and God's cause
Polytheism	By reason and supernatural revelation	Truth is ultimate reality	Evil is disharmony, imbalance	Laws are the decisions of the gods	Soul goes to place of the dead, may be immortalized	Yes	History is entertainment for the gods	By reverencing each deity's worship system
Monotheism	By God's acting on the reason, and supernatural revelation	God is the basis for all truth	What God is not and does not do	Laws are built into Creation and God reveals them	Judgment and either heaven or hell	Yes	History is the drama God has created for His glory and for human good	By worshiping and following God only
Biblical Christianity	By God's acting on the reason, and supernatural revelation	God is the basis for all truth	What God is not and does not do	Laws are built into Creation and God reveals them	Judgment and either heaven or hell	Yes	History is the drama God has created for His glory and for human good	Only through relationship with Christ that involves believing and following Him

Index

A

Aaron, 22, 76, 81, 84, 123, 146, 164, 166
Abdon, 91
Abel, 22, 203
Abinadab, 90
Abomination of Desolation, 283
Abraham, 7, 22, 53, 73, 79, 121, 129–30, 137, 145–47, 149, 154, 159–64, 191, 203, 243, 252, 257, 259, 295, 311, 356, 421, 439, 478, 488
Absalom, 176, 184
Achaia, 264, 298–300
Adam, 22, 57, 112, 142–43, 396, 488
Adonai, 52–53, 60
adoption into God's family, 59, 64, 369
Adriatic Sea, 298–300
adultery, 126, 133, 136, 140–41, 175, 258, 317
Adventist Movement, 453
Adventists. *See* Seventh-day Adventists
Aelfric, 33
Afikomen, 93, 98, 100–103
African Methodist Episcopal Church, 483
African Methodist Episcopal Zion Church, 453
agnosticism, 496, 498
Ahab (king), 106, 134
Ahasuerus. *See* Xerxes I (king)
Ai, 25, 90
Albania, 442
Aldhelm of Sherborne, 33
Aldred, 33
Alexander the Great, 117, 180
Alexandria, 32, 50–51, 442
Alexandrian text-type, 50–51
Alfred the Great, 33
Allen, Richard, 453
altar, bronze, 84–89, 110–12, 426
altar defiled, 94, 117
altar of incense, 84–88, 111–12
altar to Baal, 133–34
altar to unknown god, 264
altars, commemorative, 53, 71, 79
Amalek, 167, 288–91

Amalekites, 25, 53, 179, 182
amillennialism/amillennialists, 274, 279, 284, 440–41
Amish, 462, 484
Ammon/Ammonites, 91
Amos, 12, 76–77, 105
Amphipolis, 264
Anabaptist Churches/Anabaptists, 428, 450, 457–59, 484
Ananias, 23, 141, 226, 262, 379
Andrew (apostle), 23, 223
angel, death, 22
angel of the Lord, 121, 132, 222
Anglican Churches, 428, 434, 436, 450, 452, 458, 462, 482–83. *See also* Church of England
Anna, 78, 113, 388
anoint/anointed, 58, 133, 143, 150, 153, 171–72, 177, 202, 218, 255, 312–13, 317
Antichrist, 277–79, 283–84, 439
Antioch in Syria (Syrian Antioch), 226, 262–64, 442
Antioch of Pisidia (Pisidian Antioch), 263
Antiochus III (Syria), 273
Antiochus IV (Epiphanes), 94, 117
Antipatris, 265
Apocrypha, 32, 34, 45, 50, 94, 481–82
Apollinarianism, 413, 444, 418
Apollonia, 264
Apollos, 23, 261
apostles, 56, 148, 259, 360, 378–79, 411, 413, 421–22, 432, 455, 464, 481–82. *See also* disciples, the twelve
Apostles' Creed, 410–11, 422, 442
Appii Forum, 265
Aquila, 226, 261, 263–64, 442
Aquinas, Thomas, 448
Arabia/Arabian Peninsula, 444–45, 454, 477, 488–89
Aram, 91
Aramaic, 30, 32, 36, 43, 219, 468, 473, 478, 489
Arius/Arianism, 413, 415–18, 421–22, 443–44, 471
ark, Noah's, 70–71, 144, 295
ark of the covenant, 22, 76, 81, 84, 87, 90, 110, 112, 133, 137, 174

Armageddon, 282–83
Armenia, 224, 442–43
Arminianism, 451, 460–61, 497
Arminius, Jacobus, 460
armor of God, 268
Artaxerxes (king), 26, 116
Asher (son of Jacob), 161
Asher (tribe), 72, 78
Ashurbanipal (king), 293
Ashurnasirpal II (king), 292
Asia Minor, 16, 223–24, 262, 273, 275, 442
Assos, 264
Assyria/Assyrian Empire, 109, 181, 292–93 (maps)
Athaliah (queen), 107
Athanasian Creed, 415, 423
Athanasius, 443, 446, 470
atheism, 491, 496, 500–501
Athens, 116, 185, 264
Atonement, Day of, 7, 76, 84, 94, 112, 429
atonement for sin, 94–95, 397, 429, 453, 461
Attalia, 263
attributes of God, 400–407
Augsburg Confession, 450, 458, 482
Augustine of Hippo/St., 32, 218, 235, 412, 440, 444, 456–57
Augustus (emperor), 118
autonomy argument, 498
Azusa Street Revival, 454, 486

B

Babylon/Babylonian Empire, 9, 11, 22–23, 73, 90, 105, 109, 115–16, 134, 153, 180–81, 185, 189, 294 (map), 295
Babylon, judgment against, 278, 281–83
Bahá'í (faith), 478
Bahrain, 443, 477
Balaam, 22
Ball, John, 455
baptism, 130, 144, 164, 424–30
Baptist Churches/Baptists, 435–36, 451–53, 462, 485
Baptist Missionary Society, 452
Barak, 77, 91, 125

Barnabas, 23, 27, 76, 226, 262–63, 379, 419, 442
Barth, Karl, 454
Bartholomew (apostle), 24, 223–24
Basil, bishop of Caesarea, 443
Bates, Joseph, 474
Bathsheba, 22, 124, 126, 133, 140–41, 175
beasts, Daniel's vision of, 115–20
beasts in Revelation, 278, 281–84
Beatitudes (NT), 148, 169, 354–60
beatitudes (OT), 356
Becket, Thomas, 447
Bede, 33
Beersheba, 75
Belshazzar, 22, 115
Benedict (monk), 22
Benjamin (son of Jacob), 23, 75, 79, 131, 159, 161
Benjamin (tribe), 72, 79
Berea, 264
Bernard of Clairvaux, 447
Beth Shemesh, 90
Bethany, 24, 213, 216, 218, 224, 241, 254
Bethel, 79, 90, 131
Bethesda, pool of, 215
Bethlehem, 24, 54, 76, 118, 127, 133, 148, 169, 187–88, 191, 243, 442, 444, 489
Bethsaida, 214, 222–23
Bible, history of the, 30–35
Bible overview, 6–17
Bible study, 199, 236, 303, 383–86, 392–93
Bible timeline, 18–21
Bible translations, 43–51
bishops, 415, 446, 481–83
Bishops Bible, 34, 450–51, 460
Black Death. *See* bubonic plague
blasphemy, 22, 138, 262, 346–47
blasphemy of the Holy Spirit, 68, 138
blindness, spiritual, 367
Boaz, 22, 127, 187–93
body of Christ (church universal), 62, 375, 377, 379–80, 431, 481–86
body of Christ (Lord's supper), 432, 437
Bonhoeffer, Dietrich, 454
Boniface (missionary), 445

Boniface VIII (pope), 455
Book of Common Prayer, 450, 459, 482
Booth, William and Catherine, 453, 486
bread of life, 53–54, 61, 86, 93, 98, 112, 203, 215, 370, 438
bread of the presence. *See* showbread, table of
breastplate, 72–73, 76, 84, 88
breastplate of righteousness, 268
bubonic plague, 448
Buddha, 412, 478. *See also* Buddhism
Buddhism, 480, 496
Bulgaria, 442
bull (papal declaration), 455–57
bull (symbol), 212
Bunyan, John, 451
Byzantine Empire, 446, 448, 488

C

Caedmon, 33, 445
Caesarea, 23, 264–65, 443
Caesarea Philippi. *See* Philippi
Caiaphas, 23, 104, 242
Cain, 22, 139
Caleb, 22, 76, 132, 149, 166
Calvin, John, 34, 434, 440, 456, 458–59, 460, 462, 483
Calvinism, 450–51, 458, 460–62, 483
Campbell, Alexander and Thomas, 453, 485
Cana, 224–25, 253, 463
Canaan/Canaanites, 81, 130–32, 148–49, 151, 154, 160, 259, 295
Cane Ridge Revival, 485
Canon (Scripture), 32, 50, 443, 463, 466, 481–86
Capernaum, 216, 222–24
Carey, William and Dorothy, 452
Carmichael, Amy, 454
Catherine of Sienna, 448
Catholic Church/Catholicism, 436, 447, 450–51, 455, 458–61, 481
catholic (universal) church, 411, 422
Chalcedonian Creed, 410, 417, 423
Charlemagne (emperor), 445–46
cherubim, 111–12
China, 185, 445–48, 450–53

Christ foreshadowed in Old Testament, 142–53
Christian Science, 418, 453, 475
Christianity, expansion of, 300 (map)
Christianity, timeline of, 442–54
Christians, world of first, 298–99 (maps)
Chrysostom, John, 443
Church of England, 34, 450–53, 458–60, 462, 482. *See also* Anglican Churches
circumcision, 130, 425–26, 428, 478
citizenship, Roman, 372
Claromontanus, Codex, 470
Clauda, 265
Claudius (emperor), 261
Clement (third bishop of Rome), 420, 442
Clement VII (pope), 448
Clement XI (pope), 452
Clement XII (pope), 452
Clement of Alexandria, 443
Cnidus, 265
Codex Alexandrinus, 34, 50–51, 451
Codex Claromontanus, 470
Codex Sinaiticus, 34, 50–51
Codex Vaticanus, 34, 50–51
Colosseum, 442
Columba, 444
Communion (sacrament), 103, 320, 432, 434–37, 457, 459, 473–74, 482. *See also* Eucharist; Lord's Supper
Concordat of Worms, 447
confession of sin, 87, 333, 371, 387, 436
Confucius/Confucianism, 185, 452, 496
Congregational Churches/Congregationalists, 484
Constantine (emperor), 32, 50, 415, 443, 481
Constantinople, 443, 446–50, 481
consubstantiation, 434–35, 482
contingency argument, 498
Copernicus, Nicolaus, 451
Coptic, 32, 443, 451
Corinth, 23, 261, 264, 432
Cornelius, 23, 388, 442
Cos, 264

Council of Chalcedon, 417, 444, 452
Council of Constance, 449, 456
Council of Constantinople (381), 416, 443
Council of Constantinople (553), 416, 444
Council of Ephesus, 444
Council of Florence, 449
Council of Nicaea, 415–16, 443
Council of Nicaea II, 445
Council of Trent, 450, 459
Counter-Reformation, 450, 458–59
courage, Bible promises for, 304, 361–66
Covenant, Abrahamic, 18, 53, 79, 161, 295
Covenant, Adamic, 18
Covenant, Davidic, 18, 175, 196
Covenant, Mosaic, 18, 165, 357
Covenant, New, 21, 32, 58, 93, 99, 135, 165, 177, 433, 483
Covenant, Noahic, 18
Covenant, Old. *See* Covenant, Mosaic
Coverdale Bible, 34, 45
covet/coveted, 136, 141, 324
creation, new, 100, 104, 138, 143, 149, 193, 279, 311, 343, 373, 411
creeds, 408–11, 413, 415–17, 422, 481, 484–85
Crete, 265
Croatia, 442
crucifixion, Jesus', 93, 249–50, 255
Crusades (evangelistic), 374, 454
Crusades (historic), 447–48, 488
crusades (modern), 374, 454
cults, 392, 418, 474–80
Cush/Cushites, 123
Cyprus, 263, 447
Cyrus (king), 22, 115–16, 180–81, 273

D

Damascus, 262
Damien, Fr., 453
Dan (city), 77
Dan (son of Jacob), 161
Dan (tribe), 72, 77
Daniel, 11, 22–23, 105, 115, 119, 129, 134, 137, 181, 295, 388
Daniel, vision of, 114–120

Darby, John Nelson, 439, 453
Darius the Mede, 116, 134
Darwin, Charles, 453
Darwinism, 498
David (king), 10, 22, 54, 73, 76–79, 90, 106, 111, 122, 124, 126–27, 129, 133, 139–41, 150–51, 153, 160, 171–78, 193–94, 196–97, 203, 250, 313, 317, 336, 388–89, 489
Day of Atonement, 76, 84, 94–95, 112, 429, 478
Dead Sea Scrolls, 30, 35–42, 50, 306, 429, 454, 489
Deborah, 22, 78–79, 91, 125, 185, 283
Deborah, Song of, 77
deism, 496, 499–501
deity of Christ, 52, 67, 395, 397, 419, 422, 453–54, 474, 484
demons, 223–25, 249, 255
devil, 113, 225, 243, 312, 353. *See also* Satan
Didache, 420, 438, 442
Diocletian (emperor), 443
discernment (spiritual gift), 383–85, 392
disciples, the twelve, 36, 221–26, 379
disciplines, spiritual, 199, 383–93, 452
dispensational premillennialism/ premillennialists, 274, 284, 439, 441
dispensationalism, 453–54
divorce, 140, 260
docetism, 412, 417–18, 442
doctrines, essential, of Christianity, 395–99
Dominicans, 449
Domitian (emperor), 283, 442
Donatist schism, 443
Dorcas, 261
doxology, 195
dreams (OT), 115, 131, 134, 147, 155, 157–58, 160
dualism, 497

E

Easter, 93, 219, 442

Easter controversy, 442
Ebionites/Ebionitism, 412, 467
Eddy, Mary Baker, 475
Edict of Milan, 415, 443
Edict of Nantes, 450–51, 460–61
Edom/Edomites, 22
Edwards, Jonathan, 452
Egypt, 7, 32, 35, 73, 75, 79, 81, 92, 97–98, 100, 103, 116–17, 123–24, 130–32, 135–36, 147–48, 155–56, 158–64, 168–70, 185, 208–209, 295, 372, 437, 442–46, 448, 450, 452, 464–65
Ehud, 91
Eli, 22, 150
Elijah, 22, 53, 102, 105, 129, 134, 137, 152, 391
Elijah, cup of, 102
Elisha, 22, 105, 134, 152
Elizabeth (wife of Zechariah), 23, 252
Elizabeth I (queen), 34, 450, 460, 462
Elon, 91
end times, views of the, 439–41
Enoch, 22
Ephesus, 264, 273
Ephraim (son of Joseph), 79, 161, 295
Ephraim (tribe), 73, 79
Episcopal Church. *See* Anglican Churches
Erasmus, 33, 51, 450, 456–58
Esarhaddon (king), 293
Esau, 22, 131, 155, 182, 317
Essenes, 40
Esther, 9, 22, 93–95, 128, 179–86
eternal life, 57, 86, 112, 142, 144, 149, 249, 305–307, 358–59, 370, 372, 374, 397, 399, 426, 431, 473, 482–86, 496
Ethiopia, 443–44, 450, 452–53
Eucharist, 432, 434–35, 438, 459, 481. *See also* Communion; Lord's Supper
Euphrates River, 276, 295
Eusebius, 32, 218, 414, 440, 443, 470
Eutychianism, 417, 444
Evangelism (spiritual discipline), 383–85, 393
evangelism plans, 374
Eve, 22, 143

exile, the, 8–9, 11, 73, 76, 109, 115, 134, 181, 184–85, 195
existentialism, 498
exodus, the, 7, 32, 55, 73, 80–81, 88, 97–98, 123–24, 132, 135, 142, 148, 163–68, 170, 175, 295
Ezekiel, 11, 22, 53, 76, 105
Ezra, 9, 22, 32, 76, 116, 185, 194, 388

F

Fair Havens, 265
false teachers, 408, 422, 489
famine, 73, 75, 79, 127, 130–31, 147, 158–59, 162, 187, 262, 442
Farrakhan, Louis, 477
fasting, 182, 383–85, 388, 392–93
fear of the Lord, 197, 204–206
Feast of Booths. See Sukkot
Feast of Dedication. See Hanukkah
Feast of Lights. See Hanukkah
Feast of Lots. See Purim
Feast of Tabernacles. See Sukkot
Feast of Trumpets. See Rosh HaShanah
Feast of Unleavened Bread. See Hag HaMatzot
Feast of Weeks (Shavout). See Pentecost
feasts of the Bible, 92–96
finite God-ism, 497, 499, 500–501
firstborn, 55, 92, 101, 373, 421
Firstfruits (Reishit), 92–93
flood, the, 70–71, 130, 139, 144
forgiveness, Bible teaching about, 68, 135, 160, 171, 175, 194, 229, 249, 258, 302–303, 308, 313–321, 335, 346, 352, 358, 365, 370, 404, 407, 425, 433, 437, 473
Fox, George, 451, 461–62
France, 442
Francis of Assisi, 448
Franciscans, 448–49
Freemasonry, 452
fruit of the Spirit, 67, 270–71, 383

G

Gabriel (angel), 24, 253, 477
Gad (son of Jacob), 77, 161
Gad/Gadites (tribe), 72, 77

Galatia, 264
Galilee, 77–78, 215, 221, 224, 256, 354, 447
Galileo, 451
garden of Eden, 112, 143, 295, 345
Gaza, 76
Gedaliah, 115
Gehenna. See hell
Geneva Bible, 34, 50, 450, 460
Genghis Khan, 448
Gentiles, 95, 124, 222, 262–64, 369, 442
Gethsemane, Garden of, 222, 336
Gideon, 22, 53, 77, 91, 129, 133, 137, 185, 283
gifts, spiritual, 305, 375–82, 392
Gilead, 91
Gnostic gospels, 413, 463
Gnosticism (beliefs/writings), 255, 340, 413–14, 418, 442, 467–69
God, attributes of, 400–407
God, names of, 52–53, 61
Golan Heights, 79
golden calf, 81, 132, 137, 164, 200
Goliath, 133, 151, 172–73
gospel, explaining the, 367–74
gospels, so-called lost, 463–71
Gospels, the four, 212–16, 218–19
grace, God's, 58, 65, 142, 153, 171, 184, 234, 257, 305, 313, 336, 340, 343, 370, 373, 383, 385, 397, 404, 425, 433–35, 461, 473
Graham, Billy, 374, 454
Great Awakening, 452, 483
Great Awakening, Second, 452
Great Bible, 34, 459
Great Commission, 223, 225, 442, 452
Greece, 117, 179, 185, 263–64, 442
Greek New Testament, 50
Gregory the Great (Pope Gregory I), 444, 481
Guardian-Redeemer, 191
Gutenberg Bible, 30, 33, 449
Gutenberg, Johann, 33, 449, 456

H

Habakkuk, 12, 105, 137, 391
Hag HaMatzot, 92–93

Hagar, 22, 53, 121, 130, 227, 295
Haggadah, 97–100
Haggai, 12, 105
Hallel, 93, 99, 101–102
Haman, 94–95, 128, 179–80, 182–85
Hannah, 22, 150
Hanukkah, 94–95, 117, 215, 478
Haran, 131, 155
Hare Krishna, 479
Hasmonean Dynasty, 117
heaven, 88, 93, 98, 103, 112, 131, 134, 152, 164, 223, 225, 229 31, 233, 259, 262, 281–82, 303, 305, 307, 311, 339–45, 349, 354, 357–59, 367, 372, 395, 398, 411, 416, 433–35, 442, 473, 481–83, 485–86, 490, 501
heaven, new, 186, 282, 311, 339–40, 345, 356, 373, 433
Heaven's Gate, 418
Hebrew Bible, 12, 30, 32, 35–36, 39, 50
Hebron, 76, 131, 174
hell, 95, 147, 233, 344, 374, 398, 411, 473, 481–83, 485–86, 501
Henry VIII (king), 34, 450, 457–59, 462, 482
heresy, 409–10, 412–14
Herod Agrippa I, 222, 442
Herod Agrippa II, 265
Herod Antipas, 23
Herod the Great (king), 24, 118
Herod's Temple, 97–98, 101, 118, 215, 237–39, 442
Hezekiah (king), 22, 78, 107
Hierapolis, 223
high priest, 22–23, 41, 56, 72–73, 76, 81, 84, 87–88, 94–95, 112, 138, 150, 153, 163–64, 429
High Priest (Jesus), 56, 88, 95, 146, 153, 201, 399
Hinduism, 479–80, 496–97
historic premillennialism/premillennialists, 274, 284, 439, 441
Hittites, 306
Holy Land, 288–91 (maps), 447
Holy of Holies. See Most Holy Place
Holy Roman Empire, 446, 451, 455, 461

Holy Spirit, 62–68
Holy Spirit, gifts of the, 62. *See also* spiritual gifts
Holy Spirit, names of the, 62–67
hope, Bible promises for, 304, 361–66
Hosea, 12, 22, 105, 137
Hubbard, L. Ron, 476
Hus, Jan (John), 449, 455–56
Hutter, Jacob/ Hutterites, 458
hymns, 10, 93, 99, 102, 196, 199, 201, 452. *See also* singing

I

Ibzan, 91
Iconium, 263
iconoclasm, 445
idolatry/idols, 76, 109, 137, 164, 168, 271–72, 277, 324, 361, 373, 445
Ignatius of Antioch, 420, 442, 466
Ignatius of Loyola, 450, 458
image of God, 139, 309, 499
Immanuel (Emmanuel), 52–53, 55, 95, 198
India, 224, 442, 447, 452, 454, 479–80
Innocent III (pope), 448
inquisition, 448–49, 456
inspiration of Scripture, 30, 380, 399, 489
Iran, 94, 180, 442–43, 447–48, 477–78
Iraq, 115, 295, 442, 448, 477
Irenaeus, 409, 414, 420–21, 439, 442, 465, 469
Isaac, 7, 22, 52–53, 121, 130, 145, 155, 161, 203, 295, 421
Isaiah, 11, 22, 53, 76–78, 93, 95, 105, 137–38, 181, 215, 227
Isaiah Scroll, the, 35, 39
Ishmael, 22, 121, 130, 161, 295
Islam, 445–48, 450, 477, 488–93, 497
Israel (Jacob). *See* Jacob
Israel (northern kingdom), 76, 79, 106, 173–74, 260
Issachar (son of Jacob), 161
Issachar (tribe), 72, 78, 91
Italy, 265, 442, 444–46, 449, 456, 459

J

Jabesh (Jabesh-gilead), 171
Jabin (king), 91
Jacob (Israel), 7, 22, 53, 73–79, 81, 129, 131, 154–55, 159–62, 203, 243, 295, 317
Jael, 125, 185
Jair, 91
Jairus, 256
James (apostle; son of Alphaeus), 224–25
James (apostle; son of Zebedee), 24, 32, 148, 169, 221–22, 225, 442
James (brother of Jesus), 16, 24, 32, 138, 213, 225–26, 392
Jehovah's Witnesses, 418, 453, 474
Jehu, 106–107
Jephthah, 91
Jeremiah, 11, 22, 79, 90, 105
Jericho, 81, 90, 124, 141, 235
Jeroboam I (king), 77, 79, 106
Jeroboam II (king), 106
Jerome, 32, 444
Jerusalem, 22–23, 37, 73, 76–79, 90, 92–93, 113, 115–19, 133, 137, 145–46, 153, 174–76, 180–81, 185, 197, 215, 221, 244, 247, 262–65, 283, 373–74, 400, 408, 442, 445, 447–48, 478
Jerusalem Council, 442, 263
Jerusalem, New, 53, 279, 345, 373
Jesse, 61, 122, 172
Jesuits, 449–50, 452, 458–59
Jesus, crucifixion, resurrection, and ascension of, 68, 93, 213, 216, 242, 246–47, 249–50, 395, 398–99
Jesus foreshadowed in the Old Testament, 142–53
Jesus, genealogy of, 220
Jesus, how to follow, 302–313
Jesus, life and ministry of, 166, 212–17, 227–34, 240–41, 245, 296–97 (maps)
Jesus, names of, 54–61, 248
Jewish Revolt, 38, 117, 442
Jezebel (queen), 134
Jezreel/Jezreel Valley, 78
jihad, 477, 490
Joan of Arc, 449, 456

Job, 10, 22, 188, 192, 210
Joel, 12, 105
John (apostle), 13, 16, 24, 32, 141, 148, 169, 193, 212, 214–15, 218–19, 221, 223, 250, 442, 464–66
John Mark (apostle). *See* Mark (apostle)
John Paul II (pope), 454
John the Baptist, 41, 76, 87, 102, 134, 151, 177, 219, 221, 224, 231, 252, 429–30
Jonah, 12, 23, 95, 105, 295
Jonathan, 23, 133, 151, 173–74, 177
Joppa, 77, 261
Jordan River, 22, 75, 77, 79, 81, 90, 93, 132, 149, 260, 335
Joseph (father of Jesus), 24, 150, 243, 253
Joseph (son of Jacob), 23, 73, 75, 79, 81, 97, 129, 131, 147, 154–62, 295, 317
Joseph (tribe), 72–73, 79
Joseph of Arimathea, 226, 250
Josephus, 32
Joshua, 8, 23, 53, 73, 76, 79, 81, 124–25, 129, 132, 141, 148–49, 153, 166, 168, 295, 386
Joshua (high priest), 153
Josiah (king), 23, 90, 107, 283
Judah (son of Jacob), 76, 79, 122, 155–56, 159–61, 225, 386
Judah (southern kingdom), 75–76, 107, 115–16, 134, 151, 173, 177, 181, 185, 293
Judah (tribe), 57, 72–73, 76, 127, 133, 243
Judaism, 40–41, 97, 262, 408, 412, 478, 497
Judas (Jude, brother of Jesus), 16, 225–26
Judas Iscariot (apostle), 24, 98, 213, 221, 225, 463
Judea, 13, 118, 215, 221, 225, 249, 262, 265, 442
judges of Israel, 91
Julian of Norwich, 448
Julius Caesar, 118
Justin Martyr, 218, 414, 420, 439, 442

K

Kabbalah Centre, 478
Kant, Immanuel, 452
Kempis, Thomas à, 449
King James Version (Bible), 33–34, 39, 43, 451, 460
King, Jr., Martin Luther, 454
kingdom, divided (Israel and Judah), 8, 106–7, 291 (map)
kingdom of God, 93, 134, 152, 193–94, 227, 229–33, 322, 349, 354–56, 372–73, 430, 459, 497
kingdom of heaven, 103, 222, 229–31, 259, 354, 357–59, 372
kingdom, united, 8, 106, 290 (map)
kings (divided kingdom), 106–9
kings (united kingdom), 106, 108
Knox, John, 456, 460, 462
Korah's Rebellion, 166
Koran. See Qur'an/Quran
Korea, 450, 453–54, 475
Kublai Khan, 448

L

Lamb of God, 57, 98, 112, 132, 145, 437, 490
lampstand, 84, 86–87, 137. See also menorah
Laodicea, 273
Last Supper, 104, 147, 215, 222–25
Lateran Councils, 445, 447–48, 450, 456
Latter-day Saints. See Mormon/Mormonism
Lavigerie, Charles, 453
Law of God. See Ten Commandments
Law of Moses, 23, 260, 489. See also Torah
Lazarus, 24, 226, 254, 370
Leah, 23, 75–76, 78, 131, 155, 161, 193
Lebanon, 264–65, 452, 477
Leif Ericson, 446
lengths, ancient and modern, 28 (chart)
Levi (apostle). See Matthew (apostle)
Levi (son of Jacob), 75–76, 139, 161
Levi (tribe), 72–73, 76, 295
Lewis, C. S., 249, 454
Libya, 116, 442

Livingstone, David, 453
Lord's Prayer, 303, 314, 333, 335, 346–53, 387
Lord's Supper, 93, 98–100, 320, 431–38, 457, 459, 473, 482–86, 490. See also Communion; Eucharist
love, Bible chapter on, 269
Luke (apostle), 13, 24, 32, 212, 218–20, 226, 235, 252, 263–65, 313, 442, 465–66, 468
Luther, Martin, 33, 434–35, 440, 450, 455–59, 462
Lutheran Churches/Lutheranism, 434–35, 450, 457–60, 482, 486
Lydia (area of Asia Minor), 116
Lydia (businesswoman), 24, 261, 263, 273
Lystra, 263

M

Maccabean Revolt, 94, 117
Maccabeus, Judas, 117
Macedonia, 117, 224, 263–65
Macedonianism, 413, 418
Magdala, 255
Malachi, 12, 105, 134, 140
Malta, 265
Manasseh (king), 107
Manasseh (son of Joseph), 16, 73, 79, 158, 161, 295
Manasseh (tribe), 73, 78, 133
Manicheanism, 412
manna, 90, 93, 148, 164
Marcion/Marcionism, 412–13, 442
Mark (apostle), 13, 24, 32, 212, 218–19, 222, 226, 442, 259, 262–63, 442, 464–66
mark of the beast, 281, 284
marriage, what the Bible says about, 140, 190–91, 201, 436
Marsilus of Padua, 448, 455
Martha, 24, 254, 336
Marxism, 496
Mary (mother of Jesus), 24, 124, 150, 223, 252–53, 396, 444, 453, 473, 481–83, 485–86
Mary (sister of Martha), 24, 225–26, 254, 336

Mary Magdalene, 24, 219, 226, 255
Mary Tudor (queen), 34, 450, 460
Masoretic Text, 39–40, 50
Matthew (apostle), 13, 24, 32, 212, 218–20, 224, 235, 259, 346, 354, 442, 465–66, 468
Matthew's Bible, 34, 450, 459
Matthias, 225–26
matzah (matzo), 93, 98–101, 103. See also unleavened bread
measures, ancient and modern dry, 29 (chart)
measures, ancient and modern liquid, 28 (chart)
Mecca, 445, 477, 489
Media/Median Kingdom, 116, 294
Medina, 445
Medo-Persia, 109, 116
Megiddo, 283
Melanchthon, Philipp, 458, 462
Melchizedek, 23, 53, 146
Mennonites, 450, 457, 484
menorah, 95. See also lampstand
mercy seat, 84, 87, 112
Mesopotamia, 116, 130, 185, 208–209, 295
Messiah, 11, 13, 41, 58, 65, 78, 93, 95, 102, 133–34, 153, 160, 165, 175, 177, 193–94, 196, 201, 203, 212, 252, 260, 262, 313, 354–55, 359, 408, 411, 430, 473, 478, 488–89
Methodist Churches/Methodists, 452–53, 462, 483
Methuselah, 23
Micah, 12, 76, 105
Michelangelo, 450
Midian, 132, 167
Miletus, 264–65
millennium, 279, 282, 284, 439–41
miracles of Jesus, 214, 249–50, 256, 306, 354, 438, 442, 463
Miriam, 23, 76, 81, 123, 148, 162, 169
Moab, 91, 124, 127, 187–88, 190
Modalism, 412, 418
Monarchianism, 412, 418
money, ancient and modern values, 29 (chart)
money, Bible teaching about, 137, 140–41, 207, 209, 233, 305, 314, 322–30, 372

Monophysitism. *See* Eutychianism
monotheism, 497, 500–501
Montanus/Montanism, 412, 442
Moody, Dwight L., 453
Moon, Sun Myung, 475
Moravian Brethren/Moravians, 452, 458, 462
Mordecai, 23, 79, 94–95, 128, 179–85
Mormon/Mormonism, 474, 497
Moses, 7, 10, 23, 32, 53, 58, 75–76, 81, 88, 90, 92, 97, 104, 123–24, 129, 132, 135, 137, 139, 148–50, 162–70, 194, 200, 203, 295, 335, 356–57, 386, 388–89, 391, 478
Most Holy Place, 76, 84, 86–87, 90, 95, 112
Mother Teresa, 454
Mount Ararat, 144, 295
Mount Carmel, 134
Mount Ebal, 90
Mount Horeb. *See* Mount Sinai
Mount Moriah, 145
Mount Nebo, 75, 81, 132, 168, 295
Mount of Olives, 93
Mount Sinai, 7, 81, 90, 134–35, 138, 163, 165–67, 357
Mount Tabor, 125
Muhammad, 445, 477–78. *See also* Islam
Munster Rebellion, 450, 459
Muratori Fragment, 465–66, 470
Myra, 265

N

Naaman, 23, 152
Nahum, 12, 105
Nain, 152
Naomi, 23, 127, 187–93
Naphtali (son of Jacob), 77, 161
Naphtali (tribe), 72, 77–78
Nathan, 126, 140, 175
Nathanael (apostle). *See* Bartholomew (apostle)
Nation of Islam, 477
naturalism, 496
Nazareth, 78, 139, 250, 253
Neapolis, 263
Nebuchadnezzar II (king), 19, 23, 40, 90, 109, 115–16, 134, 181, 120

Nehemiah, 9, 23, 116, 185, 388
Nero (emperor), 118, 222, 265, 283, 442
Nestorius/Nestorianism, 413, 417–18, 444
New Age, 476, 496
Newton, John, 452
Nicaea, Councils of, 413, 415–16, 443, 445
Nicene Creed, 415–17, 422, 443
Nicodemus, 24, 215
Nicopolis, 265
Nile River, 162–63
Nineveh, 115, 295, 388
Noah, 23, 70–71, 129–30, 139, 144

O

Obadiah, 12, 105
Obed-Edom, 90
Octavian. *See* Augustus (emperor)
Oldcastle, Jon, 455
Oman, 444
1,000 years (Revelation). *See* millennium
144,000 (Revelation), 73, 276, 281, 283
ordinance, 92, 426, 434, 436
Orthodox Church, Russian, 452
Orthodox Church, Syrian, 444, 447
Orthodox Churches, 436, 446, 448, 481
Othniel, 91

P

Pakistan, 445, 480
Palm Sunday, 240–41
Pamphylia, 263
pan-en-theism, 496, 499–501
pantheism, 414, 496, 499–501
Papal Inquisition, 448
Paphos, 263
Papias of Hierapolis, 219, 222, 439, 464–65
papyrus, 31–32, 36
parables of Jesus, 113, 135, 203, 227–236
Pascal, Blaise, 451, 461
Passover (Pesach), 55, 57, 81, 92–93, 97–104, 215, 240, 437, 442, 478

Passover, Christ in the, 97–104
Patara, 264
Patmos, 223
Patrick, St., 420
Paul (Saul, apostle), 14–15, 24, 32, 40, 62, 67, 79, 93, 95, 101, 103, 118, 135, 137, 139–42, 153, 186, 221, 226, 261–67, 273, 311, 313, 321, 333, 336, 341, 357, 359, 367, 372, 375, 377–80, 386–91, 408–410, 412–13, 419, 421–22, 426, 429–33, 437, 442
Paul's letters, 14, 32, 266, 354, 361, 375, 377, 386, 442, 467, 489
Paul's missionary journeys, 263–64
Peace of Augsburg, 460
Pelagianism, 413, 444
Pentateuch, 7, 195. *See also* Torah
Pentecost, 92–93, 103, 250, 442
Pentecostal churches, 428, 436, 486
Peoples Temple, 418
Pepin, 445
Perez, 122
Perga, 263
Pergamum, 117, 273
Persepolis, 180
Persia/Persian Empire, 94, 115–17, 128, 180–82, 185, 225, 273, 294 (map), 443, 447, 450, 488
Peter (apostle), 16, 24, 32, 62, 93, 130, 141, 148, 169, 219, 221–23, 250, 261, 317–18, 384, 390, 393, 417, 419, 442, 455, 464–66, 481
pharaoh, 81, 92, 97, 101, 123, 125, 131–32, 147–48, 156–58, 160, 295. *See also* Moses
Pharisees, 40, 103, 218, 262, 408
Philadelphia (Asia Minor), 273
Philemon, 24, 226
Philip (apostle), 24, 223, 425
Philip the Evangelist, 24, 223, 226
Philippi, 118, 261, 263–64, 333
Philistines, 77, 90–91, 172–74
Phoebe, 226, 261
Phoenicia, 263
Photian Schism, 446
Phrygia, 264, 273
Pietism, 452
Pilate, 24, 104, 118
Pilgrims (Separatists), 34, 460, 484

Index

pilgrims (to shrines), 447
Pilgrim's Progress, 451
Pisidia, 263
Pius VI (pope), 278
plagues, 75, 81, 92, 97–99, 101, 104, 132, 164, 278, 295, 448
Plymouth Brethren, 439, 453
Poetry, 10, 33, 197–98, 208
Polycarp, 273, 442, 465
polytheism, 497, 499–501
Pompey, 118
postmillennialism/postmillennialists, 274, 279, 284, 440–41
postmodernism, 498
Potiphar, 131, 156–57
prayer (spiritual discipline), 383–85, 387
prayer, Bible teaching about, 25–27, 68, 112, 123, 134, 148, 150, 182–83, 195, 199, 221, 232, 253–54, 303–304, 321, 331–38, 368, 371, 387, 389, 392–93, 430, 433. *See also* Lord's Prayer
prayers in the Bible, 25–27
premillennialism, 279, 284, 454
premillennialism/ premillennialists, dispensational, 274, 284, 439, 441
premillennialism/premillennialists, historic, 274, 284, 439, 441
Presbyterian Churches, 452, 454, 462, 483
presence of God, 339, 341, 348, 358
priest, high, 56, 73, 76, 81, 84, 87–88, 90, 94–95, 112, 138, 140, 146, 150, 153, 163–64, 201, 399, 429
priesthood of all believers, 87, 450, 458
Priscilla, 24, 226, 261, 263–64, 442
Promised Land, 7–8, 73, 75–77, 79, 81, 92–93, 121, 123–25, 132, 141, 148–49, 161, 165–66, 168–69, 180, 295, 335
promises, God's, 52, 86–87, 119, 121, 124, 130–31, 139–41, 154–55, 160–61, 163, 166, 177, 191, 201, 204, 252, 274, 302–303, 305, 307, 325, 340, 350, 354, 359, 361–67, 370–74, 407–408, 416, 425–26, 438–39, 473, 488–89

prophecies fulfilled by Jesus, 57, 93, 243–49, 262
prophets, biblical, 9, 11–12, 22–23, 30, 32, 58, 76, 93, 102, 105, 108–109, 123, 125–26, 133–34, 137–38, 140, 148, 150, 152, 162, 166, 169, 171–72, 175, 181, 191–92, 203, 226, 231, 235, 252–53, 260, 264, 356, 359, 377–78, 391, 466, 489
prophets, false, 22, 371, 489
Protestant/Protestantism, 450–51, 455, 458–59, 461. *See also* Reformation
proverbs, 10, 139, 190, 204–210, 328
psalms, 10, 93, 140, 151, 175, 194–203, 356-59, 386
Ptolemais, 264
Ptolemies, 117
Purgatory, 481
Purim, 94–95, 128, 183–85, 478
Puritans, 451, 460–62, 485
Puteoli, 265

Q

Qatar, 443
Quakers, 436, 451, 461–62, 484
Qumran, 35–42, 429
Qur'an/Quran, 445, 477, 488–91, 493

R

Rachel, 23, 73, 79, 131, 147, 155, 161, 193, 203
Rahab, 23, 124, 141
rapture, 439, 441
Rebekah, 23
Red Sea, 81, 123, 125, 132, 148, 163–64, 169
Reformation, 277, 426, 428, 434, 450, 455–62, 482
Reformed Churches, 428, 434–36, 450–51, 459–60, 462, 484
Rehoboam (king), 107
reincarnation, 475–76, 478–80, 501
Reishit. *See* Firstfruits
relativity/relativism, 498
Rephidim, 53
Restoration Movement, 453
Reuben (son of Jacob), 75, 155, 159, 161

Reuben (tribe), 72, 75
Revelation, book of, 272–84
Rhegium, 265
Rheims-Douay Bible, 34, 450, 460
Rhodes, 264
Ricci, Matteo, 451
righteousness, concept of, 357
Roman Empire, 13, 33, 118, 253, 262, 273, 276, 372, 408, 414–15, 422, 426, 442–44, 465, 473
Rome, 116, 118, 139, 222, 261, 265, 273, 278, 283, 431, 442, 444–46, 448–49, 452–53, 457, 459
Rosh HaShanah, 94–95, 478
Russell, Charles Taze, 474
Russia, 446
Ruth, 8, 23, 92, 124, 127, 187–93

S

Sabbath, 86, 93, 136, 138, 257, 478
sacraments, 434, 436, 457–58, 481–86. *See also* ordinance
sacrifice (Jesus), 52, 55, 57, 86–89, 93, 95, 99, 101, 103–104, 112, 135, 144–45, 150, 203, 371–73, 481–86, 490
sacrifice (OT), 7, 52, 55, 86–87, 89, 94–95, 97–98, 101, 104, 111–13, 130, 134–35, 144–45, 150, 253
Saladin, 447
Salamis, 263
Salvation Army, 453, 486
salvation from sin, 53, 56, 59, 68, 73, 99, 130, 132, 144, 147, 149, 164, 184, 215, 230–31, 233, 268, 279, 302–308, 311, 313, 363, 367–74, 383, 395, 397–99, 405, 413, 416–18, 420–23, 425, 428, 431, 434, 453, 454, 473, 481–86, 490
Samaria/Samaritans, 13, 137, 181, 221, 260, 263
Samos, 264
Samothrace, 263
Samson, 23, 77, 91
Samuel, 8, 23, 79, 90, 105, 133, 150, 171–72, 174
Sarah, 23, 121, 130, 145, 227, 252, 295
Sardis, 273

Sargon II (king), 181, 293
Satan, 153, 340, 353, 399, 488, 491. See also devil
Saudi Arabia, 444, 454
Saul (apostle). See Paul
Saul (king), 23, 73, 77, 79, 90, 106, 133, 141, 150–51, 171–75, 177, 179, 182, 283
Savonarola, 449, 456
schism, Donatist, 443
Schism, Great (1054), 447, 454, 481
Schism, Great Papal (1378), 448–49
schism, Photian, 446
Schweitzer, Albert, 454
Scientology, 454, 476
seals of Revelation, 275–76, 281
second coming, 102, 232–33, 274, 279, 354, 395, 399, 411, 439–41
Second Temple. See Herod's Temple
secular humanism, 496, 498
Seder, 92–93, 97–104
Seleucia, 263
Seleucids/Seleucid Empire, 94, 117
Sennacherib (king), 293
Separatists. See Pilgrims
Septuagint, 32, 39–40, 50, 117, 194
Sermon on the Mount, 41, 137–38, 229, 354, 356–57, 490
service (spiritual discipline), 383–85, 390
seven churches of Revelation, 16, 272–75, 284
Seventh-day Adventists, 453, 474, 486
Shalmaneser III (king), 292
Shalmaneser V (king), 293
Shamgar, 91
Shavuot (Feast of Weeks). See Pentecost
Shechem, 75–76
shekinah, 84, 165
Shema, 410
Shepherd, God as, 52–53, 59, 61, 199–200, 202–203, 235–36, 367
Shi'a Islam (Shiite), 477, 493
Shiloh, 90
showbread, table of, 84, 86–87, 112, 151
Sicily, 265, 446–47
Siddhartha, Gautama. See Buddha

Sidon, 265
Sikhism, 480
Silas, 24, 226, 263–64, 379
Siloam, pool of, 95, 215
Simeon (NT), 113, 150
Simeon (son of Jacob), 75, 139, 159, 161
Simeon (tribe), 72, 75–76
Simon Peter (apostle). See Peter (apostle)
Simon the Zealot (apostle), 225
Simons, Menno, 450, 456, 459, 462, 484
Sinai, 73, 164, 166–68, 182, 295
singing, 199, 343, 389. See also hymns
666 (Revelation), 277, 281, 283
Skepticism, 498
Smith, Joseph, Jr., 453, 474
Smyrna, 273
Soka Gakkai International, 480
solitude, 385, 391
Solomon (king), 10, 23, 73, 88, 90, 106, 111–12, 126, 133, 137, 151, 175–77, 194, 204, 336, 489
Solomon's Temple, 40, 73, 88, 90, 94–95, 110–13, 115–17, 119, 133, 137, 153, 175, 180–81, 194, 197, 201, 336, 442
sovereignty of God, 184, 335, 346, 349–50
Sparta, 116, 185
Spener, Philipp Jakob, 452
spies (twelve), 132, 149, 166
spiritual disciplines, 199, 383–93, 452
spiritual gifts, 305, 375–82, 392
Spurgeon, Charles, 453
Stephen, 24, 226, 262, 317, 442
Stephen II (pope), 445
Sudan, 442, 444
Sufi, 477, 493
Sukkot, 94–95, 478
Sumer, 295
Sunday, Billy, 454
Sunni Islam, 477, 493
Susa, 94, 180
Swiss Brethren, 462
Synod of Carthage, 32
Synod of Dort (Dordt), 451, 460

Synod of Whitby, 445
Syracuse, 265
Syria, 32, 79, 117, 263–64, 445

T

tabernacle, 76, 81–90, 132, 137, 142, 150, 164–65
Tabitha. See Dorcas
Tamar, 76, 122, 124, 155–56, 161, 176, 193
Taoism, 496
Tarsus, 262
Taylor, Hudson, 453
teachers, false, 408, 422, 489
Tel Aviv, 77
temple. See Herod's Temple; Solomon's Temple; tabernacle
temple (heavenly), 275, 277
temporality argument, 498
Ten Commandments, 92, 112, 135–41, 165
Tertullian, 414, 420, 425, 442
"textus receptus" ("received text"), 33, 50, 450, 456
Thaddaeus (apostle), 225, 442
Thessalonica, 264
39 Articles, The, 450, 458, 482
Thomas (apostle), 24, 224, 304, 419, 442
Three Taverns, 265
throne of God, 110, 275, 490
Thyatira, 273
Tiberius (emperor), 118, 273
Tiglath-Pileser III (king), 293
Tigris River, 295
timeline of Christianity, 442–54
timeline of the Bible, 18–21
timeline of the reformation, 455–62
Timothy, 24, 226, 261, 263–64, 386
tithe/tithing, 23, 140, 326
Titus (emperor), 118, 442
Titus (pastor), 24, 226, 442
Tola, 91
tongues (speaking in and/or interpreting), 62, 153, 379–80, 428, 454, 486
Torah, 7, 81, 92–93, 195, 478. See also Law of Moses
Tower of Babel, 295

Trajan (emperor), 118
Transcendental Meditation, 479
Transfiguration, 222–23
transubstantiation, 434–36, 448, 455, 481
tribes (Israel's twelve), 72–79, 86, 88, 125, 148, 161, 173–74, 221, 295, 439, 489
tribulation, 275–76, 279, 283–84, 439–41
Trinity, 53, 62–63, 67, 397, 402, 404, 409, 414–423, 443, 473, 481–86, 488, 498
Troas, 263–65
trumpets (Revelation), 276, 281
Turkey, 16, 223, 261–65, 295, 415, 417, 442, 447, 460, 465
Twelve, the. *See* disciples, the twelve
Tyndale, William, 33, 450, 456–59
typology, 142–43
Tyre, 264

U

Ugaritic language, 35
Unification Church, 475
Unity School of Christianity, 475
unleavened bread, 97, 103, 432. *See also* matzah (matzo)
upper room, 93, 222–23
Ur, 295
Urban II (pope), 447
Urban VI (pope), 448
Uriah, 126, 133, 141, 175
Uzzah, 90
Uzziah (king), 107

V

Vashti (queen), 179–81, 183
Vatican Council, First, 453
Vatican Council, Second, 454
Vespasian (emperor), 118, 276
virgin birth, 395–96, 416, 453, 484, 488–89
vision, Catherine of Sienna's, 448
vision, Constantine's, 443
vision, John's, 274–85; 439–41
vision, Paul's, 263
visions, Daniel's, 114–20, 134
visions, Joan of Arc's, 449, 456

Vladimir of Kiev (prince), 446
Vulgate, 32–34, 39, 50–51, 444, 449–50, 456, 460

W

Waldensians, 447–48, 451, 461
Watts, Isaac, 452
weights, ancient and modern, 28 (chart)
weights and measures, ancient and modern, 28–29 (chart)
Wesley, John and Charles, 452, 462, 483
West Bank, 36, 79
Westminster Confession, 451, 461
White, James and Ellen G., 474, 486
Whitefield, George, 452
Wicca, 476, 497
Wilberforce, William, 453
wilderness of Sinai, 167
wilderness wanderings, 73, 124, 168
William of Ockham, 455
witnesses, two (Revelation), 284
woman accused of adultery, 258
woman bent over, 257
woman, Canaanite, 259
woman, Samaritan, 260
woman subject to bleeding, 256
World Council of Churches, 454, 481
worship (spiritual discipline), 343, 383–85, 389
Wycliffe Bible, 31, 33, 448, 455
Wycliffe, John, 33, 448, 455–56

X

Xavier, Francis, 450, 459
Xerxes I (king), 116, 128, 179–85

Y

Yemen, 444
Yom HaTeruah. *See* Rosh HaShanah
Yom Kippur. *See* Day of Atonement

Z

Zacchaeus, 24
Zarephath, widow of, 192
Zebulun (son of Jacob), 78, 161
Zebulun (tribe), 72, 78

Zechariah (king), 106
Zechariah (priest), 24, 87, 150, 252
Zechariah (prophet), 12, 105
Zephaniah, 12, 76, 105, 356
Zerubbabel, 23, 76, 153
Zion, 175
Zwingli, Ulrich, 434, 450, 456–58, 462

MORE FROM ROSE PUBLISHING

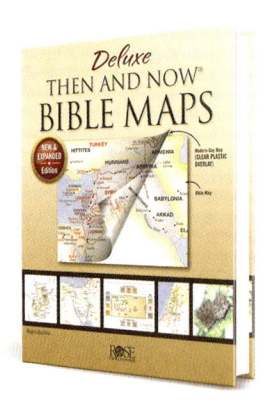

Deluxe Then & Now® Bible Maps
Then & Now® maps show where Bible places are today. Available in paperback or spiral-bound hardcover with clear plastic overlays.
ISBN 9781628628593 and 9781628628623

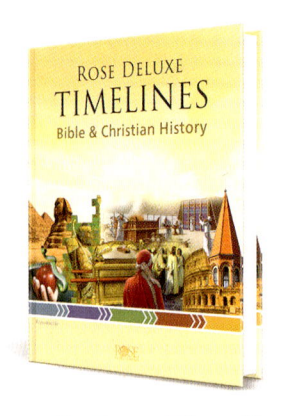

Rose Deluxe Timelines: Bible & Christian History
Spiral-bound hardcover with foldout timelines up to 32 inches.
ISBN 9781496481979

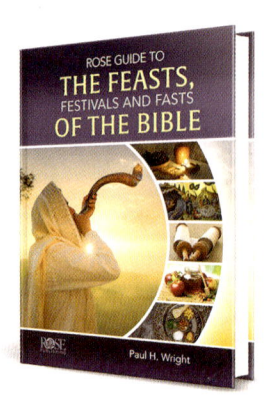

Rose Guide to the Feasts, Festivals and Fasts of the Bible
Written by five leading experts from Jewish and Christian backgrounds. Hardcover with pictures and charts.
ISBN 9781649380210

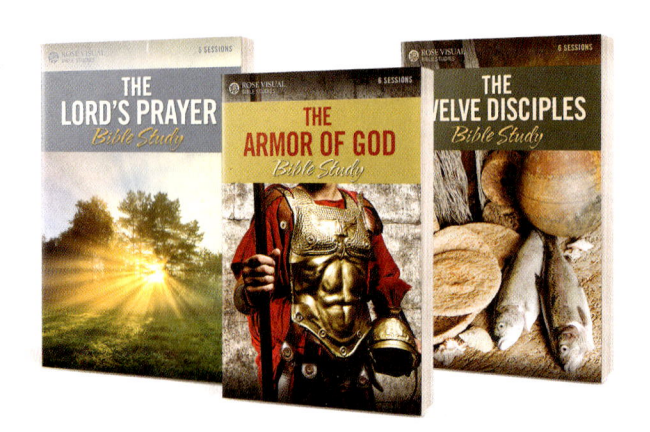

Rose Visual Bible Studies are six-week inductive Bible study guides in an easy-to-use format, with charts, diagrams, and photos to enhance learning. Perfect for small groups! Studies include: Armor of God, Twelve Disciples, Fruit of the Spirit, Life of Paul, The Lord's Prayer, Psalms, Proverbs, Women of the Bible, and more.

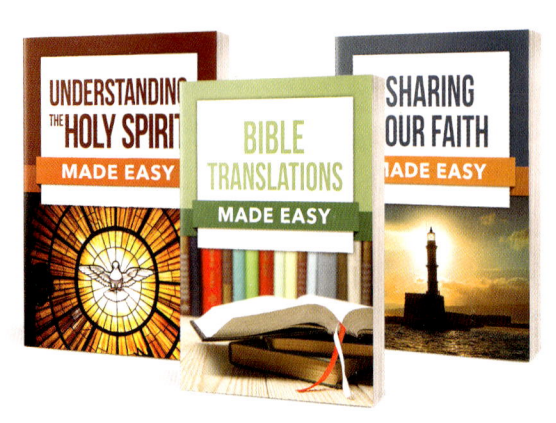

Made Easy books are pocket-sized books that help you quickly find answers to important questions, with clear explanations and key facts about the Bible and Christian beliefs. Topics include: Book of Revelation, Sharing Your Faith, The Holy Spirit, Bible Translations, How We Got the Bible, Knowing God's Will, Bible Chronology, and more.

www.hendricksonrose.com